The Holgate Miscellany

An Edition of
Pierpont Morgan Library Manuscript, MA 1057

MEDIEVAL AND RENAISSANCE
TEXTS AND STUDIES

VOLUME 438

RENAISSANCE ENGLISH TEXT SOCIETY
SEVENTH SERIES

VOLUME XXXV (FOR 2010)

THE HOLGATE MISCELLANY

An Edition of
Pierpont Morgan Library Manuscript, MA 1057

Edited by

Michael Denbo

ARIZONA CENTER FOR MEDIEVAL
ACMRS
AND RENAISSANCE STUDIES

in conjunction with
Renaissance English Text Society
Tempe, Arizona
2012

Published by ACMRS (Arizona Center for Medieval and Renaissance Studies)
Tempe, Arizona

Library of Congress Cataloging-in-Publication Data

The Holgate miscellany : an edition of Pierpont Morgan Library Manuscript, MA 1057 / edited by
Michael Denbo.
    p. cm. -- (Medieval and Renaissance texts and studies ; v. 438)
  Includes bibliographical references and index.
  ISBN 978-0-86698-486-7 (alk. paper)
1. Holgate miscellany. 2. English literature--Early modern, 1500-1700--Manuscripts. 3. Holgate,
William, 1590-ca. 1634. 4. Commonplace-books--Manuscripts. I. Pierpont Morgan Library.
  PR1127.H65 2012
  820.8'004--dc23
                                                                        2012013444

∞
This book is made to last. It is set in Adobe Caslon Pro,
smyth-sewn and printed on acid-free paper to library specifications.
Printed in the United States of America.

TABLE OF CONTENTS

Frequently Cited Sources
and Abbreviations

Ault	Norman Ault, ed. *Seventeenth Century Lyrics: From the Original Texts*. London: Longmans, Green and Co., 1928.
Baker	Herschel Baker, ed. *The Later Renaissance in England: Nondramatic Verse and Prose, 1600–1660*. Boston: Houghton Mifflin Company, 1975.
Bald	R. C. Bald, *John Donne, A Life*. New York and Oxford: Oxford Univ. Press, 1970.
Beal	Peter Beal. *Index of English Literary Manuscripts*. Vol. 1, pts. 1, 2. London and New York: Mansell Publishing Company, 1980.
B&TR	J. A. W. Bennett and H. R. Trevor-Roper, eds. *The Poems of Richard Corbett*. Oxford: Clarendon Press, 1955.
CEP	Richard Corbett. *Certain Elegant Poems*. London, 1647.
Chamberlain	*Letters of John Chamberlain*, 2 vols, ed. Norman Egbert McClure. Philadelphia: American Philosophical Society, 1939.
Crum	Margaret Crum. *First-Line Index of English Poetry 1500–1800 in Manuscripts of the Bodleian Library Oxford*. Index Committee of the Modern Language Association of America, 1969.
DNB	*Dictionary of National Biography* (see *ODNB* below)
Dobell	Bertram Dobell. *The Poetical Works of William Strode (1600–1645)*. London: Bertram Dobell, 1907.
Doughtie	Edward Doughtie, ed. *Lyrics from English Airs, 1596–1622*. Cambridge: Harvard Univ. Press, 1970.
Dunlap	Rhodes Dunlap. *The Poems of Thomas Carew with His Masque Coelum Britannicum*. Oxford: Clarendon Press, 1949.
Dyce(W)	Alexander Dyce, ed. *The Poems of Sir Henry Wotton*. London, 1843.
Dyce(BF)	Alexander Dyce, ed. *The Works of Beaumont and Fletcher*. London, 1843–46. 11 vols.
Forey	M. A. Forey. "A Critical Edition of the Poetical Works of William Strode, excluding *The Floating Island*." B. Litt. Thesis, St. Hilda's College, Oxford, 1966.
Gardner, 1965	Helen Gardner, ed. *John Donne: The Elegies and the Songs and Sonnets*. Oxford: Clarendon Press, 1965.

Gardner, 1978   Helen Gardner, ed. *John Donne: The Divine Poems*. Oxford: Clarendon Press, 1952; 2nd ed., 1978.

Grierson   Sir Herbert J. C. Grierson, ed. *The Poems of John Donne*. 2 vols. Oxford: Oxford Univ. Press, 1912.

Grosart   Rev. Alexander B. Grossart, ed. *The Complete Poems of John Donne*. London: Robson and Sons, 1872–1873.

Hebel   J. William Hebel and Hoyt H. Hudson, eds. *Poetry of the English Renaissance, 1509–1660*. New York: Appleton-Century Crofts, Inc., 1929.

H&S   C. H. Percy Herford and Evelyn Simpson, eds. *Ben Jonson*, 11 vols. Oxford: Clarendon Press, 1925–51.

HolM   The Holgate Miscellany. The Pierpont Morgan Library, MA 1057. New York, NY.

Latham   Agnes M. C. Latham, ed. *The Poems of Sir Walter Ralegh*. Cambridge: Harvard Univ. Press, 1962.

Marotti   Arthur F. Marotti. *Manuscript, Print, and The English Renaissance Lyric*. Ithaca and London: Cornell Univ. Press, 1995.

May   Steven W. May and William A. Ringler, Jr. *Elizabethan Poetry: A Bibliography and First-Line Index of English Verse, 1559–1603*. 3 vols. New York: Thoemmes Continuum, 2004.

Milgate   W. Milgate, ed. *John Donne: The Satires, Epigrams and Verse Letters*. Oxford: Clarendon Press, 1967.

OCD   *The Oxford Classical Dictionary*. Ed. N. G. L. Hammond and H. H. Scullard. Oxford: Clarendon Press, 1970.

ODNB   *Oxford Dictionary of National Biography*, http://www.oxforddnb.com/ (ac-cessed May 16, 2012).

P&R   *Poems written by the Right Honorable William earl of Pembroke, lord steward of his Majesties houshold. Wherof many of which are answered by way of repartee, by Sr Benjamin Ruddier, knight. With several distinct poems, written by them occasionally, and apart*. London, 1660. [Commonly known as *Poems of Pembroke and Ruddier*]

Poems   John Donne, *Poems*. London, 1633.

Redding   David Coleman Redding. "Robert Bishop's Commonplace Book: An Edition of a Seventeenth-Century Miscellany" [Rosenbach MS 1083/16]. Diss. Univ. of Pennsylvania, 1960.

Ringler   William A. Ringler, Jr. "The 1640 and 1653 *Poems: By Francis Beaumnt, Gent.* and Canon of Beaumont's Nondramatic Verse," *Studies in Bibliography* 40 (1987): 120–40.

Rudick   Rudick, Michael, ed. *The Poems of Sir Walter Ralegh: A Historical Edition*. Tempe, Arizona: Arizona Center for Medieval and Renaissance Studies *in conjunction with* the Renaissance English Text Society, 1999.

Saintsbury   George Saintsbury, ed. *Minor Poets of the Caroline Period*. 3 vols. Oxford: Clarendon Press, 1921.

Sanderson   James Lee Sanderson. "An Edition of an Early Seventeenth-Century Manuscript Collection of Poems (Rosenbach MS 186)." Diss. Univ. of Pennsylvania, 1960.

Shawcross	John T. Shawcross, ed. *The Complete Poetry of John Donne*. Garden City, N. Y.: Doubleday & Co., 1967.
Smith	*John Donne. The Complete English Poems*. Ed. A. J. Smith. London: Penguin Classics, 1986.
STC	Donald Wing, comp., *Short Title Catalogue of Books Printed in England, Scotland, & Ireland and of English Books Printed Abroad, 1475–1640*. 2nd ed. New York: Modern Language Association, 1972.
Sullivan	Ernest W. Sullivan, ed. *The First and Second Dalhousie Manuscripts: Poems and Prose by John Donne and Others*. Columbia: Univ. of Missouri Press, 1988.
Thompson	Howard H. Thompson. "An Edition of Two Seventeenth-Century Manuscript Poetical Miscellanies" [Rosenbach MSS 188, 191]. Diss. Univ. of Pennsylvania, 1959.
Tofte	Robert Tofte. *The Blazon of Iealousie*. London: 1615.
Variorum	*The Variorum Edition of the Poetry of John Donne*. Gen. ed. Gary Stringer, Bloomington: Indiana Univ. Press, 1995–2005.
Waller	Gary Waller. *The Sidney Family Romance*. Detroit: Wayne State University Press, 1993.
Yale	*First-Line Index of English Poetry 1500–1800 in Manuscript of the James M. and Marie-Louise Osborn Collection in the Beinecke Rare Book and Manuscript Library of Yale University*. Ed. Stephen Parks, Marc Greitens, and Carolyn Nelson. New Haven: Beinecke Rare Book and Manuscript Library, Yale Univ., 2005.

INTRODUCTION

THE TEXT

The Holgate Miscellany is a quarto comprising 165 leaves, gathered in fours with no separates. It is manuscript number MA 1057 in the Rare Book Collection of the Pierpont Morgan Library, New York City. Although several of its leaves contain writings by later owners of the manuscript, this edition presents only materials transcribed in the first half of the seventeenth century, probably by William Holgate (1590–post 1634), the author of six of its poems. Of the 184 entries made by Holgate, all but four are poems (or excerpts of poems), though it should be noted that stubs in the manuscript suggest that he wrote additional materials on leaves that were later torn out of the compilation.[1] However, despite this damage, the manuscript remains in very good condition. It has its original limp vellum binding sewn on four alum-tawed thongs. The ends of the thongs are laced through the cover at the joints. The binding never had headbands. The gatherings are sewn with linen thread, two gatherings with one thread. It is a small book, measuring 19 x 14 cms. In surface area, it is less than three-quarters of the page you are now holding. Its watermark is a pot, described by Heawood as having been found in "England 1619, Townshend Papers, MS Rough Copy."[2]

The Holgate manuscript is a miscellany comprised mostly of verse, but includes some prose passages.[3] Its italic handwriting is generally neat and legible; the spelling, though predictably irregular, is still easy for a modern reader. A reader's first impression is that this is a readable book. The writing and presentation are less meticulous or exact than that of some manuscripts with similar contents, such as the Tobias Alston manuscript at Yale (Osborn b 197) but more formal than many which were handbooks, i.e., books that traveled in a pocket or purse.[4] Also, it is *not* the work of one poet,

---

[1] The Holgate also includes an index written by John Wale, an eighteenth-century owner of the miscellany. In it, Wale identifies several poems written on the missing pages (for details, see the commentary notes to HolM 8b.).

[2] E. Heawood, *Watermarks Mainly of the 17th and 18th Centuries*, Monumenta Chartæ Papyraceæ, Vol. 1 (Hilversum, Holland: The Paper Publications Society, 1950), no. 3579.

[3] Although is it common to use the terms "commonplace book" and "miscellany" interchangeably, I follow Peter Beal, *A Dictionary of English Manuscript Terminology, 1450–2000* (Oxford: Oxford Univ. Press, 2008), 429–30.

[4] For a discussion of this and other similar texts, see my essay "Common Place, Common Space: Three Seventeenth-Century Verse Miscellanies as Examples of Material Culture," in *New Ways of Looking at Old Texts, IV*, ed. Michael Denbo (Tempe, Arizona: Arizona Center for Medieval and Renaissance Studies *in conjunction with* Renaissance English Text Society, 2008), 131–39.

like Egerton MS 3165 by Gorges, but instead it is an eclectic text, given over, if anything, to current public events, for many of the occasional poems concern the politics of the day. Most importantly, the compiler apparently wanted it to be usable, not so much by other people, but by himself. That more than anything else is the sense we have of this manuscript: it is a personal document recording the tastes and impressions of one man in a verse miscellany.

The original compiler did not paginate the volume.[5] Indeed, the book itself was created in sections. The first 147 pages are all poetry. Then, after six blank pages, there is a prose letter (pp. 153–57) followed by another twelve pages left blank. This is followed by a section dominated by poetry but with some prose (pp. 170–216), and then again there is another large section left unused by the original compiler. The end of the book is all prose (pp. 303–6, pp. 309–28), followed by another short section left blank (pp. 329–33). There are no catchwords. The writing is economical as to space, i.e., most of the pages are fully used; this is especially true of the prose, where the scribe appears to have written as many words as possible on each page. For the most part, the lines are not ruled, but in general the poems are set off by grids[6]: horizontal lines neatly drawn below titles or between poems, especially when there is more than one poem on a page. Vertical lines are drawn to create margins, generally about one inch from the left edge of the page. On occasion, the scribe did write either corrections or personal notations in the margin, but he also used the margins to create emphasis, i.e., pen flourishes or manicules to draw attention to a particular line. Pen flourishes are often found at the end of poems; final couplets are frequently offset, either spatially or by drawing a large parenthesis to clarify the end of the poem. The poetic stanzas are clearly differentiated, either through space between them or individual horizontal lines. There are no musical notations whatsoever; however, on occasion, Holgate does describe a particular lyric as a song.

PROVENANCE

But how do we know this document belonged to one William Holgate of Saffron Walden, Essex in the early seventeenth century, and who exactly was he? With the exception of the miscellany and a few surviving public records that mention him, we can assume that he was not well-known beyond his own family or friends. It appears that he was of the middle class, but, the truth be known, there is nothing except what we find in the manuscript that will tell us very much about him. Ultimately, he is an enigmatic figure, one whose personality survives only on the pages of his miscellany.

Fortunately, many questions about his identity have been posed by genealogists, and the record of that inquiry is found in a bound, unpublished volume entitled "History of the Holgate Family as collected by E. H. Dring," 1926–27 (Morgan Library C529.2 H73). Dring was managing director of Barnard Quaritch, Ltd., London, the company that sold the miscellany to the Morgan Library. Dring's search was structured around one specific question: Was William Holgate the "Mr. W. H." of Shakespeare's *Sonnets*? Dring hired Holworthy & Shilton, Archivists and Genealogists, to trace the pedigree of William Holgate, not only because of the poems subscribed by "W. H.," but because a note on the cover of the volume asserts that it was compiled by a member of the Holgate family. There was a well-known ancestor, Robert Holgate, Archbishop of York and Lord President of the North (d. 1556). Among his descendants was a William Holgate, gentleman, of Clavering, county Essex, who, as identified by Dring, had four children, a second William Holgate (1558–1630) of Saffron

---

[5] This edition includes pagination added by John Wale, an eighteenth-century owner of the miscellany. I describe this below with the provenance.

[6] All nonverbal notations are indicated in the text.

Walden, county Essex, the father of the presumptive compiler of the Holgate Miscellany; Mark Holgate (1582–1605), a recusant; and two more children, John and Mary. Mark Holgate also had a son named William, but Dring, without explanation, dismisses this William Holgate as never owning the miscellany. I suspect Dring was correct in that assumption: the book's provenance (discussed below) can be traced through the family of William Holgate of Saffron Walden, and not the family of his younger brother Mark.

William Holgate, the compiler's father, married Lettice [Laetitia] Bawcock (1562–1629). Apparently, he was quite enterprising: he owned two local inns, The Rose & Crown and The Angel. He also had tenants on several lands in and around Saffron Walden, Essex. By coincidence, Garbriel Harvey, Spenser's famous friend and probable tutor, was a neighbor. William and Lettice had five children: the eldest, William (b. 1590), Luke (dates unknown, but who may have died in infancy), Edmond (d. 1625), Jane, and John (d. 1673). The key document in this history is the Visitation of Essex, recorded in *Berry's Essex Pedigrees*.[7] The visitation is dated 1634, the last reliable date we have to help identify which William Holgate was the compiler of this miscellany. The person interviewed for the visitation was William Holgate's younger brother John, described in *Berry's* as "of Walden and of the Mid. Temple, gent. 1626, 6th and youngest but 2nd surviving son 1634; died 5 May 1673."[8] We know that William was born in 1590 and, from John's testimony, that he was alive in 1634, but that's all we know. William was not mentioned in his father's will nor has his own will been traced. And, to complicate the story, he himself had a son, William Holgate (1619–1646), but the name of his wife is pointedly omitted from the visitation. The visitation mentions the son but not the wife.

William Holgate (b. 1590) is the only possible candidate among those I have identified of that name who might have compiled this miscellany. As noted above, the watermark demonstrates that the paper was in use in 1619. If that was the year Holgate began to transcribe his manuscript, he would have been twenty-nine years old. His son was born in 1619, again the date of the watermark, but the son probably died in the Civil War in 1646, three years before 1649, the date of **HolM 182**, "An Epitaph vpon Iames Duke of Hamilton," the latest datable poem in the seventeenth-century portion of the manuscript.[9] Also, for the same reason, Holgate's father could not have compiled this miscellany because he died in 1630, long before the death of Hamilton. Holgate's wife, however, is something of an enigma, but curiously also fits with the odd circumstances of the miscellany. The *Miscellanea Genealogica et Heraldica*, under the heading "Entries in the registers of Saffron Walden, Essex, relating to the Holgate family," records the marriage "1612 Nov. 16 William Howlgate [sic] & Margaret Toppin."[10] If this William Howlgate is the compiler of this miscellany, he would have been twenty-two years of age at that time. A second interesting entry is found in *Allegations for Marriage Licenses Issued by the Bishop of London, 1611–1828* for August 5, 1641,[11]

> Robert Howard, gen., of St. Lawrence in Ipswich, Bach., 30 &
> Catherine Holgate, Spinster, dau. Of William Holgate; consent of

---

[7] *Berry's Essex Pedigrees*, in *Miscellaneous Essex Pedigrees from Harleian MS 1541 and Other Harleian MSS*, Pt. 2 (Harleian Society, 1869), Vol. 11 (1869), 666–68.

[8] Ibid., 666.

[9] There is a poem in the son's honor, on the memory of Mr. W. Holgate in Bodleian MS Rawl. Poet. 62, f. 12.

[10] Joseph Jackson Howard, ed., *Miscellanea Genealogica et Heraldica*, 2nd ser. (London: Mitchell and Hughes, 1894), 5: 161.

[11] George J. Armytrage, ed., *Allegations for Marriage Licenses Issued by the Bishop of London, 1611–1828*, Vol. 2 (London: Publications of the Harleian Society, 1887), vol. 26.

her mother [from whom her father lives apart] Margery Holgate,
who hath her care & disposal; at St. Sepulchre's. (vol. 26)

Unfortunately, the register for St. Sepulchre's was destroyed in the Great Fire of 1666, but the Margaret Toppin mentioned in the *Genealogica* and the Margery Holgate mentioned in the *Allegations* at least could be one and the same.[12] Of course, the visitation describes only a son born to William and Margaret, but perhaps when the couple separated the son remained with his father and the daughter went with her mother: at least the omissions in the story tend to support this very 'open' narrative. Also interesting is what we find in the manuscript. Again, the watermark of the paper is 1619, and the poems attributed to W: H: are close to that date, but there is also the date of 1649, the year of Hamilton's death. It is of course possible that the collection itself was not created until the mid-seventeenth century, and all its contents were the work of someone transcribing what by then were very old poems into this miscellany. But that would not account for the date of the paper, and I do not believe that a manuscript such as the Holgate, with paper that existed as early as 1619, would not have been used for at least thirty years. And, of course, minor or lesser known figures like William Holgate are very hard to trace.

There is one other possibility for William Holgate and his enigmatic marriage. There is a record of a William Holgate marrying a Saraie Hart at Clavering, Essex, on 21 September 1607. Unfortunately, no other information on Saraie Hart seems to have survived. If this is the same William Holgate who was born in 1590, then at the time of this marriage he would have been only seventeen years old, a possibility, but less likely than the 1612 date of the previously described marriage. And it is surely possible that he was married twice, and that somehow this piece of information is what is behind his brother's not mentioning the wife of William Holgate during the visitation. Had Saraie died, that would not have been information to be omitted from the visitation. Regardless, the problem remains unsolved. Clearly, Holgate was a common Essex name, and I suspect we will never with complete assurance establish the exact lineage of this anthology's compiler short of identifying its scribe's handwriting.

What is clear, however, is the provenance of the book, and that too leads us back to William Holgate, born in 1590, eldest son of William and Lettice Holgate of Saffron Walden. The book's front cover reads: "This Book was the Collection of one of the Holgate family. The Additions collected by I Wale." Then below, in the midsection of the cover: "The above Memorandum is in the hand-writing of Mr. John Wale of Colne Priory (Died 1761) The additions alluded to are from page 217 to the Item ab^t Verona in Italy. Also from p. 160. to 169. & 147 to 152[.]" And finally, in the lower third of the cover: "This M.S. Was given about 23 years ago to Chas: H. Probert by his Uncle H. H. Cawardine of Colne Priory. Transferred by C. H. P. to J. C. Dec. 11, 1871. Found amonst old Deeds by WGCP."[13] The "Additions collected by I Wale" as they are described on the cover are left

---

[12] Many seventeenth-century records were lost in the Great Fire of 1666, including those from St. Sepulchre.

[13] Chas: H. Probert sold the book to Bernard Quaritch Ltd., the company that later sold the manuscript to the Morgan Library. Probert ancestry connects to the Holgate family, not through William, the compiler, but through his brother John, who married Anne Plomer of Walden. They had one child, a son, named William Holgate, who married Hester Quarles, a descendant of Francis Quarles, an early seventeenth-century poet whose work is also found in the this miscellany, **HolM 56**. They too had a son, named, of course, William Holgate (1670–1717), who married Mary Baldwin (dates unknown). They had one son, John (b. 1693), who married Anne Wale, eldest surviving daughter of John Wale, heir to her brother Charles Wale of Colne Priory, Essex (see cover note). It is interesting to note that John Wale must have received the miscellany from his daughter, not his own parents. John and Anne Wale Holgate had a son, Charles William Holgate, who had one

out of this edition as is any other extraneous writing found in the text. My concern here is only for the work of William Holgate. John Wale did own the miscellany in the early eighteenth century and did write in it, but despite appearances to the contrary, all his additions were taken from printed books. I doubt that even eighteenth-century scholars would find them interesting. Other owners have added some material to the collection, but again, this edition omits their insertions. Most recently, however, modern scholars have added information about particular poems and lines of poetry in the margins of the text, but these were all done in pencil and are not permanent additions to the Holgate. Again, I leave them out from the text, but they are cited in the textual notes found at the bottom of the relevant pages.

ORGANIZATION AND CONTENTS

A more specific description of the Holgate manuscript's contents and organization will reveal the compiler's intentions when he created this volume. Not only is the Holgate manuscript organized by poetry and prose, the text is also divided into themes and genres. For example, the collection begins with short (often satiric) epigrams, then adds a few longer poems, after which we find a section of poems written apparently by the owner/transcriber of the manuscript, all funeral elegies. After the poems attributed to W. H., there is one very long poem, "Iter Boreale" (**HolM 25**) by Richard Corbett. The poem is over five hundred lines, and we may speculate that the amount of work and time required to transcribe this poem demonstrates Holgate's dedication to the manuscript. The section of lyric poems that follows includes Shakespeare's Sonnet 106, here entitled "On his Mistris Beauty" (anonymous, **HolM 85**), and several of Donne's great lyrics, including "Dr. D: at his goinge into Bohemia: A Himne to Christ" (**HolM 86**) and one headed simply "Dr. D: Goe and catch a Falling Starr." Following this predominately lyric section is a group of poems commemorating Henry, Prince of Wales (**HolM 101–6**), who died in 1612. Historical events play an important part in the manuscript: often we see poems with clear historic reference, including a few from the Elizabethan period. Later, in the final section of the manuscript, there is a group of religious poems, several by William Strode (also very popular in seventeenth-century manuscript collections) and two poems by Henry King, one a shortened version of his famous "Exequy" (**HolM 163**).

The political poems are scattered throughout the manuscript, including a scathing satire on the condition of the troops during the Siege of Frankenthal (1621–1623) **HolM 107** (discussed below), and a poem unique to this manuscript, "A Spanish Iournall: 1623" (**HolM 146**), apparently written by an anonymous crew member of one of the ships intended to return home with Prince Charles and the Spanish Infanta, had that match been completed successfully. What *isn't* here is also noteworthy. Although seventeenth-century manuscripts often include many humorous epigrams, the Holgate includes only a few. Moreover, many of the poems are quite long, leading one to suspect that Holgate, most frequently, read privately to himself. The meditative poems, especially those by Donne and Holgate himself, would also support the probability that Holgate read privately.

Holgate has six, and probably seven, of his own poems in the miscellany, all funeral elegies. The six are ascribed "W. H." Of these, four concern Reverend William Ashboold or his family (**HolM 19, HolM 22, HolM 23,** and **HolM 24**). There is also an elegy for a Mr. Richard Lucey, probably

---

daughter, Anne, 1752–1817. She, in turn, married Thomas Carwardine (again, see cover), whose eldest daughter married Thomas Probert of Newport House and Earls Colne. I do not know who J. C. is, but WGCP is William Geoffrey Carwardine Probert, the man who, according to the cover found the manuscript mongst old Deeds. All of this is neatly described in the unpublished Dring history maintained by the Morgan Library.

one of his teachers (**HolM 27**), and a Latin epigram for Anthony Maxey entitled "In obitum Magistri Maxia." (**HolM 22**). Reverend Ashboold was the minister of two neighboring churches in Cornhill, London, St. Peter's and St. Michael's, both of which still exist and can be visited today. Unfortunately, there is no mention of a William Holgate or Anthony Maxey in the register of either church, and there is no positive identification of a Richard Lucey anywhere (see **HolM 27** notes). The seventh poem, "A funerall elegie on Dr. Ashboold" (**HolM 10**), is actually the first of the grouping. Although it is not ascribed to the initials "W. H.", its similar contents and style have led the editor to believe that it was written by William Holgate. There are no other known surving poems dedicated to William Ashboold or members of his family except those found in this manuscript.

The poet of "A funerall elegie on Dr. Ashboold," probably W. H., shows himself to be a quiet and introspective man, well-versed in the poetic conventions of the day. It begins:

> Did I in quiet night earst while of flowres,
> of Gardens dreame for some few silent houres.   *(1–2)*

And continues:

> As I went forth into some sullen woods
> Or priuate shadowes or by siluer floods,
> Did any Herald of ill newes mee breake
> from meditation with Prophetiqu*e* beake?   *(7–10)*

And then the poet writes something quite surprising, a personal reference detailing how he came to learn of Dr. Ashboold's death.

> The Letter was afraid to shew its fate
> Least I should drown'd it with my teares for that
> And though on August 30th it was sent
> To Oxfoord soe much tyme it loytringe spent
> As that Septembers 6 and 20th Sunn
> Gaue mee first knowlidge his last Day was done: *(27–32)*

The personal reference to the date he learned of Ashboold's death is very unusual in early modern poetry. Indeed, the reference accentuates the reality of his loss. According to church records, Ashboold was buried at St. Peter's Church, Cornhill, 29 August 1622, so Holgate's information is correct. Moreover, since he more than likely integrated his own poetry into a manuscript that included poems in wide public circulation, either he was trying to see himself as a poet in the public domain or he saw his own poetry as part of a larger poetic community.

In addition to the poems discussed above, the Holgate manuscript comprises a large and varied selection of late-sixteenth and early-seventeenth century English lyric poetry. Many of the entries are anonymous or attributed by initials, a common practice for this and other miscellanies. For example, Shakespeare's Sonnet 106 is unascribed, as are several of the Donne poems, others of which are subscribed I. D. or Dr. D. Several of the poems remain anonymous even after considerable effort to identify them. Easiest to identify are the canonical poets, well represented in the Holgate. They include Sir Walter Ralegh, Ben Jonson, Thomas Carew, Francis Beaumont, Henry King, and William Herbert. There are also two poems by James I. Others poets included—less known to modern readers but surely better known in their own day—are John Davies, Benjamin Rudyerd, Henry Wotton, Hugh Holland, Dudley North, George Morley, Henry Constable, Robert Ayton, Christopher Brooke, William Strode, and Richard Corbett, the last two being among the most commonly transcribed poets of the early seventeenth century. In all, fifty poems are anonymous, and while five others are attributed with a name or initials, I have not been able to identify their authors with any degree of certainty. They are Dr. Thoris, An Italian (**HolM 101**), G. H. or I. H. (**HolM 16**), Z. T. (**HolM 18**), Sr H. N. (**HolM 124**), and T. G. (**HolM 153**).[14] Fifty poems have never been printed, and another thirteen were printed only after the seventeenth century. Of these, thirty poems are apparently unique to this manuscript. For readers looking to explore some *new* seventeenth-century poetry, the manuscript is a treasure trove. However, it should be noted that there are many manuscript collections with large numbers of anonymous as well as apparently unique verse. In this respect, the Holgate is typical.

As noted above, the Holgate Miscellany is an eclectic text with a wide variety of early modern poetry. But equally eclectic are the sources Holgate used to create his text. Although it is generally impossible to identify source texts in a manuscript as complex as this one, in certain instances we are able to say with relative certainty where he found some of the poems. The identification of a copy-text is very important to this edition. Not only does it tell us about the transcriber's reading practices for a particular subject matter, it also lets us see how he regarded his sources and whether or not he felt that he could adapt a particular verse to his own tastes. For example, collation demonstrates that Holgate started his book by copying from a printed text, Robert Tofte's translation of Benedetto Varchi's *The blazon of iealousie*, first published in English in 1615. Although it is possible his actual base text was a manuscript that had earlier been transcribed from Tofte's *Iealousie*, the accuracy of the transcription and the similarity of the minutest details suggest that Holgate copied from the printed book as his first model. This theory also relates to the organization of the entire manuscript, which seems more typical of a print miscellany rather than simply a group of poems that were transcribed sequentially. Holgate clearly copied texts from both printed and manuscript sources into his miscellany.

A second source of poems typical of early seventeenth-century transcription practices was other manuscripts, particularly those supplied by friends or groups of friends who exchanged poems as part of the normal practices of social interaction. This is a particularly subtle area of manuscript circulation because the poems, especially the political poems, trace a network by which a poem in manuscript could wend its way through the culture without ever having emerged as a complete public document, as it would have had it been published in print. What emerges here is context: ideas as poems circulate, allowing individual compilers of poetry the opportunity to create their own quasi-public record concerning events of the day. From this perspective, poems had different meanings for different people; therefore, to evaluate how a poem was understood by certain readers in the early seventeenth century, we have to see which poems surround it in various verse miscellanies.

The Holgate manuscript is a unique verse miscellany because several of its poems represent what James Knowles has described as evidence of public political culture wider than the court in the Jacobean and Caroline periods.[15] Knowles's focus is on masques and libels, which, paradoxical though they seem, in manuscript culture together become satires about political power, particularly, in the case of the Holgate, about James and his favorite, Buckingham.[16] Masques, of course, are forms

---

[14] For discussion and possible attributions, see explanatory notes for each poem.

[15] James Knowles, "Songs of a baser alloy: Jonson's *Gypsies Metamorphosed* and the Circulation of Manuscript Libels," *Huntington Library Quarterly* 69.1 (2006): 153.

[16] Other works in this emergent area of study are Alastair Bellany, *The Politics of Court Scandal in Early Modern England* (Cambridge: Cambridge Univ. Press, 2002; and Andrew McCrae, *Literature, Satire, and the*

of excess, the rich at play if you will, the participants making fun of themselves with a self-congratulatory nod toward power and wealth. But for those who despised Buckingham and the excess that he represented, Jonson's masque was an object of derision, easily converted into a libel. The Holgate manuscript represents this paradox because it is one of only two surviving manuscripts that includes (in sequential order) the Patrico's Song from Jonson's *The Gypsies Metamorphosed* (**HolM 66**) and the satirical libel of the same masque (**HolM 65**), untitled here but identified by its first line, "from such a face whose excellence."[17] Knowles also points out that many of the poems attacking Buckingham and James can be associated with manuscripts connected with Sir Edward Conway.[18] This point is confirmed by the Holgate manuscript, not simply because of its two versions of the Patrico's Song, but because of the many similarities it shares with British Library Add. MS 23229, a composite manuscript found among the Conway Papers. A composite manuscript is usually not the work of a single compiler: it is made up of parts of several manuscripts bound together into one codex. More than likely this was done because none of the original miscellanies that make up MS 23229 was complete when found. Peter Beal describes this complex document as follows:

> Folio, 170 leaves (of various sizes); composite volume of MSS,
> including, on independent leaves or small gatherings, eleven poems
> by Donne, in various hands; three of these poems (ff. 10–14ᵛ, 55,
> 76–7) in the hand of Sir Henry Goodyer (1571–1627); ff. 95–8 in
> the same hand as Leconfield MS. . . and constituting part of what
> was probably a 4° MS 'book' of Donne's satires; f. 132ʳ⁻ᵛ consti
> tuting a set of six verse epistles by Donne, the text related to West
> moreland MS . . . ; from the 'Conway Papers' belonging chiefly to Sir
> Edward Conway, Baron Conway of Ragley, later Viscount Killultagh
> and Viscount Conway of Conway Castle (1564–1631), and to his son,
> Edward, second Viscount Conway (1594–1655); early 17ᵗʰ century.[19]

The sections of BL Add. MS 23229 that are most relevant to the Holgate are not described specifically by Beal. Found at ff. 51–66ᵛ are two similar but different hands that I designate hand A on ff. 51–54ᵛ and hand B on ff. 62–64ᵛ.[20] Unfortunately, neither hand has been identified, but texts in both hands A and B show a close resemblance to the same texts that we see in the Holgate manuscript. The poems occur in the following order: **HolM 40** (A), **57** (B), **58** (B), **59** (B), **60** (B), **63** (A), **64** (A), **67** (B), **107** (B), **110** (A), **120** (A), **121** (A), **123** (A), and **130** (A).[21] Collation reveals that most of these poems are virtually identical in the Holgate and BL Add. MS 23229 and often appear in a similar

---

Early Stuart State (Cambridge: Cambridge Univ. Press, 2004). Bellany writes about the murder of Sir Thomas Overbury (**HolM 170**); McCrae's focus is on what he calls the unauthorized texts of early Stuart England, many examples of which are found in the Holgate.

   [17]   The other manuscript is University of Nottingham, Portland MS. PwV 37, where the poems are in reverse order.

   [18]   Knowles, 155–56.

   [19]   Peter Beal, comp. *Index of Literary Manuscripts, Vol. 1, part 2* (London and New York: Mansell Publishing Ltd., 1980–87), pp. 254–55.

   [20]   Two other Holgate poems are found in BL Add. MS 23229 ff. 65–66. They are **HolM 64** and **HolM 96**. However, these pages are damaged. They have a different handwriting, also unidentified.

   [21]   From the perspective of BL Add. Ms. 23229, the order is as follows. For hand B: f. 62ʳ (conclusion of **HolM 107**), f. 62ᵛ (**HolM 57**), f. 62ᵛ (**HolM 60**), f. 63 (**HolM 58**), f. 63v–64r (**HolM 59**), and f. 64ᵛ (**HolM 67**). The sequence of the hand A poems of BL Add. MS 23229 is more varied when compared to the Holgate. They

sequential order. This, by itself, is noteworthy, for although similar groupings may be found in collections of, say, Donne poems, a similar order of poems as diverse as these is unusual. Moreover, *State Papers Domestic* (Jacobus I, cliii, 113) include two poems in what appears to be hand B that are also in the Holgate, **HolM 73** and **HolM 134**, both of which are very similar to the texts in the official papers.[22] Therefore, it is at least possible that Holgate knew the transcribers of BL Add. MS 23229 (A) and (B), or, like them, that he actually worked with or for Viscount Conway. Another poem lends credence to this notion, **HolM 146**, "A Spanish Iournall: 1623: The Way" (anonymous), a first-person narrative poem written by someone on one of the ships sent by James to retrieve Charles and his anticipated bride, the Spanish Infanta. The poem includes a great deal of first-hand information about the voyage, all of which is confirmed by several documents found in the State Papers.[23] Most interesting for this study, however, is that "A Spanish Iournall:" is apparently unique to the Holgate manuscript. However, there is no direct evidence connecting the Holgate manuscript to Viscount Conway or the so-called Spanish Match except the similarity of the two manuscripts.

A second area of comparison between texts relevant to this study concerns how the texts are actually presented as physical objects, that is, how the poems appear on the page. In general — but more obviously in manuscript — the interpretation of any particular text is affected by how the text is recreated on a specific page. This can be seen most clearly in a poem entitled "On the Money Newes so generally Currant in Frankenthal about Iune: 1621" (anonymous), again, apparently surviving in only two manuscripts, the Holgate (**HolM 107**) and BL Add. Ms 23229 (hand B), which includes only the last page of the text. The poem is a biting satire about the siege of Frankenthal, written from a soldier's point of view, which, at its conclusion includes a mock signature of James as if he himself had written the poem. The two transcriptions are quite similar, showing only one substantive difference, and the script in the two manuscripts is also noticeably similar.[24] Both have a large, official-looking, mock signature, "Iacobus Dei gratia," and both have identically placed marginalia in the lower left-hand corner of the page. Both transcribers allowed space for the marginalia, but Holgate is slightly different in that he drew a vertical line about one inch from the gutter. The handwritings are similarly neat, a small italic familiar in the Holgate when the scribe needed to preserve space.

Both of these transcriptions are scribal performances: they pretend to be verse epistles written by James to the troops at Frankenthal. As we read the poem, we cannot but imagine the grime and dirt of war as compared to the far removed places of political power emblemized by James's dramatic signature. The poem also demonstrates a difference between print and manuscript as media for literary texts. It is generally believed that print and manuscript are simply two ways in which to transmit a text; this is derived from the notion that a text is only something to read, but in this case the poem would lose most of its impact if it appeared in print because it would then not be an imitation of a document signed personally by James.[25]

---

are f. 51 (**HolM 110**), f. 52^r (**HolM 120** and **HolM 121,** companion poems), f. 52^v (**HolM 123**), f. 53^r (**HolM 63**), f. 53^v (**HolM 130**), and f. 54 (**HolM 40**).

[22]   There are no substantive differences: two accidentals in **HolM 73** and one accidental in **HolM 134**.

[23]   See the Commentary for specific information about dates and ports of call. The poem ends abruptly, perhaps indicating the moment when it was learned that the Infanta had rejected Charles's offer.

[24]   Photos of the final page of both originals can be seen in my essay, "Editing a Renaissance Commonplace Book,' in *New Ways of Looking at Old Texts, III*, ed. Speed W. Hill, (Tempe, Arizona: Arizona Center for Medieval and Renaissance Studies *in conjunction with* Renaissance English Text Society, 2004), 70–71.

[25]   For a discussion of presence as an aspect of manuscript publication, see Harold Love, *Scribal Publication in Seventeenth-Century England* (Oxford: Clarendon Press, 1993), 141–48.

As a document of study, the Holgate, like many other miscellanies that are not focused on one principal writer, has not received the scholarly attention it deserves.[26] For the poems by John Donne, collations to the Holgate can be found in John T. Shawcross, *The Complete Poetry of John Donne* and, of course, *The Donne Variorum* (in progress). In "An Elegy by John Donne," E. K. Chambers argued that the poem "when myne heart was mine owne, and not by vows" (**HolM 90**) is by Donne.[27] However, the elegy has not been accepted as part of the Donne canon. The Holgate is also mentioned in scholarly editions of Shakespeare's *Sonnets* (see **HolM 85** notes). But perhaps the most helpful analysis of the Holgate is Margaret Forey's unpublished thesis, "The Poetical Works of William Strode, excluding The Floating Island." Ms. Forey's detailed and complex work demonstrates the type of analysis that will be needed if scholars are to unravel the complexities of seventeenth-century manuscript transmission.[28] Other than a few isolated references to specific poems in other books and articles, and with the very important exception of James Knowles's article discussed above, the Holgate is unexplored territory.

THE EDITION

This edition of the Holgate Miscellany is a diplomatic transcription of its contents, page-by-page, line-by-line as in the manuscript itself. Original spelling is maintained. Special uses of diacritical marks and accents are noted in the text and, when necessary, explained in the textual notes found on each page. Hyphens are recreated but modernized. Also, following the common practice, Holgate frequently used a tilde through the descender of a *p* for words that begin with *pre* or *per*. This is a standard abbreviation. In that case, I transcribe the prefix in italics and explain the word in the notes. Superscribed letters are recreated without comment. At times it was very difficult to ascertain if Holgate meant an initial letter to be majuscule or minuscule. In general, I compared an instance to other surrounding letters to make that decision, but there is no way to know for sure what he intended. The difference between long and short *s* is ignored. Words or passages that Holgate later corrected are transcribed, when possible, with angle brackets. Overwrites are described in the textual notes.

Consecutive pagination of this edition is provided in the outer top margin of each page. The pagination in the inner top margin and highlighted in a gray box follows Wale's eighteenth-century insertions, the only pagination or foliation found in the codex itself. Readers should note that some pages have been removed from the miscellany and that many pages were left blank by William Holgate. Unfortunately, those blank pages were written on (mainly by John Wale), creating non-consecutive pagination in this edition. Note, for example, that the edition skips pages 148 through 169. These omissions are explained in the textual notes. Everything written by William Holgate is included.

For each poem I identify in the Commentary, where possible, the poet as recorded by Holgate and, where differences occur, the poet who has been revealed as author by modern scholarship. I also list the first printing and the surviving manuscripts for each poem. For the well-known poems, much more information is readily available to most scholars, and in those circumstances I direct the reader

---

[26]   Obvious exceptions are the three dissertations from the University of Pennsylvania. They are James Lee Sanderson, "An Edition of an Early Seventeenth-Century Manuscript Collection of Poems" (Rosenbach MS 186), 1960; David Coleman Redding, "Robert Bishop's Commonplace Book: An Edition of a Seventeenth-Century Miscellany," 1960; Howard H. Thompson, "An Edition of Two Seventeenth-Century Manuscript Poetical Miscellanies," 1959.

[27]   E. K. Chambers, "An Elegy by John Donne," *Review of English Studies* 7 (1931): 19–21.

[28]   See especially **HolM 154** notes, **Holm 165** notes, and **HolM 174** notes.

to those other sources. Collations are highly selective, primarily designed to show the reader similar texts (either manuscript or print) that tend to situate the entire manuscript rather than demonstrate a textual history of a particular poem. Again, for poems that have been the subject of modern critical editions, I direct the reader to more thorough collations available in those works. These include, of course, John T. Shawcross's edition of Donne's poems and the Donne *Variorum*. Where relevant, collations to those texts are supplied. Abbreviations for commonly mentioned texts are found in the list of Frequently Cited Sources. Citations that concern individual works are found in the notes for each particular poem.

PAGINATION

The reader will note that each transcribed page of this edition has two separate page numbers. The numbers with the shaded background — always found in the gutter — are the numbers as they presently appear in the actual manuscript. The second set of page numbers, which include the name *Holgate Miscellany*, are the page numbers of the RETS edition. They are always found on the outside top margin opposite the manuscript numbers.

However, the page numbers now found in the manuscript were not part of the original manuscript. John Wale, a descendant of the Holgate family, added them during the eighteenth century. Unfortunately — and at a still later date — some leaves of the manuscript were removed, and as a result there are missing pages (and numbers) in the Wale pagination. For further information, see Introduction, p. xx.

Acknowledgments

There are of course many people who have helped me with an edition as complex as this, and I surely hope that I do not omit anyone. I am and always will be grateful to W. Speed Hill, my dissertation supervisor, who has been instrumental both in my education and my professional career. Unfortunately, Speed did not live to see this edition. He passed away just at the time I was preparing my final submission to the RETS editorial panel. I am sure he would have been pleased to see this project come to fruition. Speed was unique in many ways, and I am most privileged to have worked with him. Other teachers from the CUNY Graduate Center were also extremely helpful. Special thanks go to Professors Martin Elsky and Patrick Cullen, both of whom served on my dissertation committee.

I must also acknowledge the kind assistance of the entire staff of the Morgan Library, especially Robert Parks, the former Robert H. Taylor Curator of Literary and Historical Manuscripts, and Declan Kiely, the present Robert H. Taylor Curator of Literary and Historical Manuscript. I would also like to thank two wonderful librarians in the reading room, Inge Dupont, Head of Reader Services, and her assistant, Vanessa Pintado. I also thank Deborah Evetts, the former Drue Heinz Book Conservator, who assisted me in describing the manuscript.

I would also be most remiss not to mention the staff of the Folger Shakespeare Library, Washington, D. C., and especially Laetitia Yeandle, former Curator of Manuscripts. Surely, no one more than she deserves credit for helping me with this project, and I deeply appreciate the time we have spent together. I am also pleased to acknowledge Lena Cowan Orlin, Executive Director of the Folger Institute, who made available the grant-in-aid that enabled me to study Renaissance paleography at the library.

I also appreciate the kind advice of Margaret Forey, who has reviewed all the poems by William Strode. She has been most helpful.

I would also like to thank Peter Beal for his kind assistance and Thomas Warren Hopper for reading and editing the Commentary notes.

And finally, to my colleagues and friends at the Renaissance English Text Society, Steven May, who headed the committee for this project, and the other committee members, Arthur Marotti, Elizabeth Hageman, and Roy Flannagan. I also thank Professor Arthur Kinney, president of RETS. All have been wonderfully patient with me, and I am pleased to acknowledge their support.

And the person to whom this edition is dedicated, Elise Denbo. It surely would not have been possible without her tireless support and wonderful editorial assistance. I am deeply grateful.

1

[1]

Of a Poett:./

When Heau'n would striue to doe the best shee can,
And put an Angells spiritt into man,
Then all her Powers shee in that worke doth spend,
When shee a Poett to the world doth send;
The difference only twixt the Godds and vs,   5
Allow'd by them is but distinguisht thus;
They giue them breath, Men by their powres are borne
That life they giue, the Poet doth adorne:
And from the world when they dissolue mans breath
They in the world do giue Man life in Death:./////

[2]

Vppon Queene Anne by K: I

Thee to inuite, the great God sent a starr.
Whose frinds and nerest kinn great Princes are,
What though they ruine the race of men, & dye
Death seemes but to refine their Maiestie
So did this Queene her Court to heauen remoue   5
And lefte off earth to bee enthron'd aboue
Then shee is gone, not dead, no good Prince dyes
But only with the day-starr shut their eyes.

[3]

A stanza on Prince Hen: by I. S:

Iewell of Nature, Ioy of Albion
To whose perfection Heauen and Earth conspire,
That, in Times fullness, Thou maist bless this Throne
(Succeedinge in the vertues of thy Syre)
As happily thou hast begun goe-on;   5
That as thy Youth, wee may thine Age admire
Actinge our hopes (which shall reuiue our hearts)
Patterne and Patron both of Armes and Arts:.

[4]

De Amore:

Love is a Feinde, a Fire, a Heauen, a Hell,
Where Pleasure, Paine, Greife, and Repentance dwell:. }

Pagination] Shaded numbers reflect the numbers in the original manuscript. Numbers adjacent to the heading *Holgate Miscellany* are the pages of the present edition. See Introduction, page xxi. **1.10** (right margin)] Holgate frequently inserted pen flourishes at the end of some poems. Similar figures are found in many manuscripts. **3.1** *Iewell*] Ornate flourish extending into left margin from descender. **3.1** (right margin)] Modern pencil notation: "Sylvester." **4.2** (right margin, below *dwell*) Pen flourish.

[5]

An Epitaph on Prince Henry:

Reader, wonder thinke it none
That I speake and am but stone
Here lies enshrin'd Celestiall Dust
And I doe keepe it but in trust
Wherefore hence-forth aske not mee   5
Whose these sacred ashes bee
For surely it is conceal'd
For if this should bee reueal'd
All the people passinge by
Would weepe them selues to teares and dye:.

[6]

On Queene Elizabeth:./

The Queene was brought from Greene-wich to White-hall
At euery stroake the oares did teares lett fall
More clunge about the Barge, fish vnder water
Wept out their eyes of pearle, and grew blinde after
I thinke the Bargemen might with easier thighs   5
Haue rowde her thither in her peoples eyes
But how so ere thus much my thoughts haue scand
Shee had gon by water had shee gone by Land:.

[7]

On Iealosie

Pale Iealousie child of insatiate Loue
Of heart sicke thoughts with Melancholy brede
A Hell tormentinge Feare, no Faith can moue
By discontent with deadly poyson fedd
With heedelesse youth and Errour vainely ledd   5
A mortall Plague a vertue drowning flood
A Hellish fire, not quenched but with blood:.

[8a]

Of Care:

Care the consuminge Canker of the minde
The discord that disorders sweete hearts tune
Tha'bortiue Bastard of a Cowards Kinde
The light foote Lackeie that runs post to Death
The busie aduocate that sells his breath   5
Denouncinge worst to him y^t is his frinde:.

6.7 *my thoughts*] *y* appears to extend to *t*, but the words are separate. This is a common practice of the Holgate scribe. In general, these extenstions are not noted in this text. **8a.5** (right margin)] The stray ink mark at the end of line is not a period. **N. B.** Folio 2 (pp. 3–4) has been removed. See Commentary to 8b. and 9.

[9]

Thers no pennance due to innocence
Thus selfe cast all yea this white linnen hence,
To enter into these bands is to bee free
Then where my hand is sett my seale should bee
To teach thee I am naked first, why then (5)
What needes thou haue more coueringe then a man:. ⟨❧⟩

[10]

A funerall Elegie on Dr Ashboold:.

Did I in quiet night earst while of flowres,
Or Gardens dreame for some few silent houres.
Was I disturb'd by some new watchfull care
Not sufferinge mee nights common guift to share;
Did an allarum beate or passinge Bell
Toole on my eare drume or ringe some friends knell?
As I went forth into some sullen woods
Or priuate shadowes or by siluer floods,
Did any Herald of ill newes mee breake
<With> ↓from↑ meditation with Prophetique beake? 10
Did Crowes or Screech-Owles strike my hearkinge ea‿^rse
With balefull Omens, and bringe in true feares
To my amazed soule, remember I
One ceremonie of bad Augurie.
Did there distill, from my fore-tellinge nose
Three blushinge dropps guiltie of future woes
These I not know of or my memorie
Or Phansie or all signes were slipperie
Perchaunce I doe not hould them fast, y^t Man
May bee iudgd slipperie by them: Well I can 20
Remember things haue fallen out to trewe
Yet can Diuination reade a new
(If any weare) but pale the paper lookt
In whose black mourninge, these sadd woords were book't
Religious, Learned, Auncient Ashboold hee
Hath obeyd Death in Body certainely
The Letter was afraid to shew its fate
Least I should drown'd it with my teares for that
And though on August 30th it was sent
To Oxfoord soe much tyme it loytringe spent 30
As that Septembers 6 and 20th Sunn
Gaue mee first knowlidge his last Day was done:

9.4 (right margin)] Modern pencil notation: *J. Donne.*

O dogginge Death stearne Seiargant to this Earth
Of ours, that rests in our Dawninge birth
Sometimes before bringst vs dead from our wombe
(False Harbinger) vnto our gestlesse Tombe!
Some times when Nature gins to glorie in vs
And from her temptinge art begins to winn vs
Some times in our full man wee are Eclipst
Our soules in Heauen, our Co^{r}ps in graue betwixt   40
The hidinge earth, and our frame wants the light
Of Reason borrowd from the soule, whose might
Ruld all our Masse: Some times when our gray heads
Looke liker Heauens then those dull downeward Beds
Heads worthie of adoration but of thee
That suruiust Adam and his Progenie
And wilt liue with vs still stealinge (false frinde)
Our soules out of our lips till the worlds end
In whose Catastrophe (though cunningly
Thou attest it) weel see this Tragedie   50
Æternall life shall thee (vaine nothinge) banish
Out of all mankinde, thou shalt wholy vanish
Except in Hell where dyinge some shall bee
And ner'e dye makeinge Tantalus of thee
That faine wouldst kill and they assoone expire
But they shall want thee, Thou want thy desire
Hee whoe in childhood was as good as Younge
And grewe as learned as the best amonge
His Riualls, as iust to the Deities,
As learned and as happy as all these.   60
Hee who in Cambridge leaueinge homely witt
Deuourd Philosophie or dallied it
With Retoricke or Logicke Sphinks of arts
Interpreted it in most mysterious parts.
Or for the Tongues ransackt the Tresuries
Of the worlds youth, and age whose Ianus eyes
Red in them what hath bin what is what shall
Succeede by consequence Propheticall
And in all these excellinge did assume
Degrees of Art as well as Peace full Rome   70
Yet hee rests not in this perfection,
A further good's in his election.

---

40 Corps] *r* superscribed directly above *p*; a vertical line below the *r* dissects the word.   **49 Catastrophe**] C overwrites *c*.

From whome all humane learning's Ocean flowes,
Mounted vp to Diuinitie hee goes;
Nor is hee for the Theorie alone
But for the Practike, There fore hee is gone
To sow Gods seede in open furrowes, and
Now liues in Can'aan or a blessed Land
Nor is hee alien to Prophetts here
Euen with the best mee hee is welom'd, & best cheere.   80
Religious Gryndalls Holy stuard, hee
Is made most gracious in his amitie
And still deseruinge, in his better trade
Still gayninge, Hee at last is Dr made
And hath committed to his care the soules
Of two well-nourisht flocks wch hee infoulds
In armes of equall Loue, spendinge long dayes
And parts of tedious Nights in hidden wayes
That thence hee may discouer to their veiwe
The true high-way to Heauen, yt hee may shew   90
Pure Lamps to them, hee oft drinkes in ye smoake
Of burnt-out Candles, that they may not choake.
Hee chewes their meate first, where there many are
That care not what they giue, or what they share
So they can drowne ye Quick sands of an houre
With a mad torrent, or wordy showre
Or may bee not so much, some Homilie
Reade in a Homely tone, ort'h Liturgie
Will serue the turne, wheras our Dr Dead
Staru'd Nature that his people might bee fedd.   100
Now his weake hand takes downe a Massie father
Ierome perchaunce, determininge that rather
Then hee would giue them raw drest <meate> foode
Would haue yt from him, wch was as strong as old.
Him hee consults vppon the Text hee meanes
To handle, then from many Saints hee gleanes
The best from Austins Eloquence hee beares
A dew of honey to their hyuinge eares.
From Barnards Garden hee brings such a flower
As smells fresh after hee hath spent his hower   110
From Goulden Chrisostome hee brings such oare
As Nature cannot shew, nor the world more
Besides it selfe and whiles hee speakes to some
God-fearinge Swearers, hee proues Chrysostome
Both their cares are the same, his Labour more

---

80 best mee] Line correction notated by ampersand, then *best cheere*. **80 Welom'd**] Top half of *l* not formed.

Besides his owne writts, others turninge or'e.
May bee a Thorny Question growes amonge
The lillies of the word, his well spoke tongue
So punctually defines the place, and shape
That all the danger wee may safely scape   120
For which that all men might bee vnderstanders
Hee trauaild had before Scholemens Meanders
Thus did hee waste his strength and God did giue
Late old age to him that deseru'de to liue.
Hee gave him comforts which not common were
A Wife, a Daughter, and an Age gott Heire.
Hee gave him children whose pale ashes tell
Suruiuers they dy'de cause they liu'd so well:
And hee good Father liuinge had preferred
One Common house wher hee'ld bee all inter'd.   130
Saue famous memory of him
When wee should want him, would become our bliss
Neere to the Communion Table Hee will bee
Reposd till th' Iudgment, and his progenie
As if bith' place bearinge Christ' figuringe bred
And bloud betokeninge wine, with which hee fedd
Beleeuinge soules, Since hee that faith embrast,
Aliue, his cheifest ioy were to bee plas'te.
Hether before descended of his line
Two hopefull in the Budd, Two in the prime   140
Hee followd after; Now I see that God
Of number loues aboue the rest the Odd
And if hee fauour so disparitie
May hee loue and bless the suruiuinge three:.
But now mee thinkes I see the Coarse vp-borne
And all the Relict of great Ashboold mourne,
Then giue mee leaue to speake a word or two
Perchaunce Consolatorie vnto you
It shall not bee in praisinge his long line
Although in that hee Oriently doth shine   150
Nor yet in limminge out his vertues which
Out-bound all woords, their beauty is so rich
Nor the Nobility which hee by them
Addeth vnto his farr extended stem.
Only consider well whome you doe mourne
And to what end, laste whether hee is borne
The wife may say that shee a husband weepes
Vnmacht in earth, and therefore heauen him keepes
The Children may say, they a Mother haue

would they might haue their ffather from his graue.   160
The Kinsfolkes may complaine that they doe want
A friend, whose like is verie scant.
The parishes may groane for his late breach
They haue lost him whose life did euer preach
Nor was his tongue for doctrine silen'st \<euer\> er'e
Except by Ages weakenes es it were.
In which tyme hee so tendered their good
Their Diett was fatt and continuall foode.
It is appointed that all men must dye
Although in most certaine vncertainety   170
And they that doe departe this life wher in
They had before parted from hydeous sinne
Shall to heauen instantly although the Mould
That gaue Man flesh do it againe infold.
The Soule a perfect substance is disioynd
From 'th prisoning body, and in heauen assignd
For it contemplates on the all-glorious God
By a good Conscience Comforted, no rodd
With secrett lashes strippeth it: there all
Reioyce i'th vision Beatificall.   180
Though wee liue here t'is not our Latter Inn
For here the Auncient Patriarkes haue beene
And haue lefte woord, if wee'l bee thither ledd
Whether thei'r gon, wee must their foote steeps tread
Therefore some slowly, Some with hasty feete
Iourney to heauen, and at last all meete
Soe when a Period to the world is put
And thy fore-lockes decrepid tyme off cutt.
(which shall bee performd at the Latter day)
Bodies shall recollect them from the clay   190
And Member ioyne to members, y^e same Soule
The selfe same flesh in forme, it did controule
And those whose eares haue hearkned to the voyce
Of God in earth, shall now bee of his choice.
First you haue lost a man, A man of God,
And a good Man, who\<se\> in his præcepts trodd.
A Husband and a Father, this Relation
Is quite destroyed by his Late priuation.
As man to dye into the world hee came,
As man of God, hee came to teach the same   200
As a good Man it was his cheife desire
Then greiue not for him, but to him aspire.

166 *es*] plural ending of *weaknesses*; space as indicated.

(And you Henries sad Mother! that you may
See him a Man, and Man of God I pray.
I doe not doubt a Good Man hee will bee
Whome Ashboold fatherd: His minoritee
Is woundrous promisinge, nay Practique: I
Haue wrote these lines for Loue of him, so nigh
Would I had beene, or happie, that I might
Haue writt his Guiftes and goodness? but that flight   210
Is for a nother winge; An Angells sure
It   mes must that worthy taske indure
I will conclude, and giue you Ashboolds Due
Hee cannot dye, whose vertues liue in you:.
        Finis

---

[11]

Vincent Corbett farther knowne
By poynters name then by his owne
Here lies ingaged till the day
Of raisinge bones, and quickninge clay
  Nor wonder reader that hee hath
Two surnames in his Epitaph
For this one did comprehend
All that two families could lend.
  And if to know more Arts then any
Could multiplie one into many   10
Here a Colonie lies then
Both of Qualeties and men
  Yeares hee liud well nigh fowre score
But count his vertues hee liu'd more
And number him by doeinge good
Hee liu'd their age before the flood
  Should wee vndertake his storie
Truth would seeme fain'd, and plainenes glorie
Beside this Tablett were to small
Add to the pillars and the wall.   20
  Yet of this volume much is found
Written in many a fertile ground
Where the Printer thee affordes
Earth for Paper, Trees for wordes.

10.203 (open parenthesis)] As indicated. **10.212 mes**] See notes to this poem.

Hee was Natures factor heere
And Leiger lay for euery sheere
To supply the ingenious wants
Of some sprung fruites and forraine plants.
 Simple hee was and wise with all
His purse nor base nor prodigall   30
Poorer in substance then in frindes
Future and publike were his ends.
 His Conscience like his Diet, such
As neither tooke nor lefte too much
So that made lawes were vseless growne
To him hee needed but his owne.
 Did hee his Neighbours bid like those.
That feast them only to inclose
And with their rostmeate racke their rents
And cousen them with their fedd consents?   40
 No; the free meetings at his boord
Did but one litterall sence afforde
No close or Aker vnderstoode
But only Loue or neighbour-hood
 His almes were such as Paule defines
Not causes to bee say'd but signes
Which almes by faith, hope, Loue, layd downe
Layd vp, what now hee weares, a Crowne.
 Besides his fame his goods his life
Hee lefte a greeu'd sonne and a wife   50
Strange sorrow scarce to bee beleeued
When the sonne and heire is greiued:
   Reade then and mourne what ere thou art
   That dost hope to haue a parte
   In honest Epitaphes, least beinge dead
   Thy life be written and not reade : R: C:

[12]

Deare Vincent Corbett who so longe
 Had wrestled with diseases stronge
That though they did possess ech limm
 Yet hee broke them ere they broke <t>him
With the iust cannon of his life
 A life which knew nor noise nor strife
But was by sweetning so his will
 All order and disposure still
His minde as pure and neately kept
 As were his Nurceries, and swept   10

11.41 *No;*] Vertical line above semicolon, possibly first intended as an exclamation mark. **11.56** (below initials)]
Modern notation: *Corbet*. **12.4 *they*]** *y* overwrites *e*; ***him*]** *i* overwrites *e*. Holgate first wrote *them*.

So of malice and offence
  There neuer came ill odure thence
And add his actions vnto these
  They were as spatious as his trees
Tis true hee could not reprehend
  His very manners taught to amend
They were so euen graue and holye
  No stubborneness so stiffe, nor folly
To licence euer was so light
  As once to trespass in his sight   20
His looke would so correct it when
  Hee chid the vice, yet not the men.
Much from him profess I wonn
  And more and more I should haue donn
But that I vnderstoode him scant
  Now I conceiue him by his want,
And pray who shall my sorrowes reade
  That they for mee their teares will shead
For truly since hee lefte to bee
  I feele I'm rather dead then hee: ✸   30

    ~ ~ ~ ~ ~ B: I: ~ ~ ~ ~ ~ ~ ~ ~ }
    I hope my pietie to which could
    It vent it selfe, but as it would
    Would say as much as both haue donn
    Before mee here the frend and sonn
    For I both lost a frende and father
    Of him whose bones this graue doth gather : ✸

Reader whose life and name did ere become
    An honest Epitaph deserues a Tombe
   Nor wants his beere through penurie or sloth   }
    Hee that builds one, so't bee yᵉ first, makes both:. }

[13]

K: I   his Invectiue against weomen:.

You Weomen that doe London loue so well
whome scarce a Proclamation can expell
And to bee kept in fashion fine and gay
Care not what fines your honest husbands pay
Who dreame on nought but vizards masques & toyes
And thinke the Cuntrye contributes no ioyes
Bee not deceiu'd the Cuntry's not so bare
But if you tradinge lacke ther's ware for ware
Or if you Musike Loue know euery springe
Both Cuckoo there and Nighting-gale doe singe.   10
Your compleate Gallant, and your proper man
Are not confind to Fleet-Streete nor the Strond
But you haue nobler Knights, then do not doe
Such ill, nor any thinge that long's ther too
Cæsar would haue <ha?> an honest woman bee
Not only chast, but from suspition free
Which you that soiourne heere can hardly shunn
You must so many temptinge hazards runn
For sa<m>↑u↓e some few here that are full of grace
The world hath not a more debosher place   20
Your owne propensnese ill enough contriues
With out the excess of Towne prerogatiues
Ther fore depart in peace and looke not backe
Remember Lotts wife ere you suffer wracke
Of fame and fortune which you may redeeme
And in the Cuntry liue in good esteeme.
Ladyes of honour grace the Court I graunt
But t'is no place for vulgar dames to haunt
The Cuntry is your orbe and proper sphære
Thence your reuenues rise, bestow them there   30
Conuerte your Coach-horse to the thriftie Plowe
Take knowlidge of your sheepe, yoʳ Corne your Cowe
And thinke it no disparagement, or taxe
T'actuainte your fingers with the wheele or flaxe
Where of examples are not farr to seeke
Where noble Princesses haue done the like
Your Husbands will as kindely you imbrace
Without your iewells or your painted face
And there your children you may educate
As well as those which French and Spanish prate   40
Visite the sicke and needy, and for Playes   & :

13.19 *saue*] After *a*, *m* blotted out; *u* superscripted.

Play the good huswiues, waste not goulden dayes
In wanon pleasures which do ruinate
In sensibly both honour wealth and state
Do't of your selues shortly the Spanish Dames
Frugality will teach you to your shames
And then no thankes, for so it comes in fashion
You will bee seruile Apes to any Nation
And you good men, t'is tyme you gett you hence
Least honest Adam pay for Eues offence:.

---

[14]

Anthonie Weastdons Anagram

Note he was and is not :. /

Note what is worth your notice: (or a man
Hee was and is not: If you would it scañe:
Rouze vp your memorie, call to minde that hee
Was lately liuinge: now dead all may see.
Louinge as long as liuinge, lik't by all   5
Who like Antæas riseth by his fall
What Art and Nature to them selues assumed
Both enemies, deaths Harbingers wel-nigh consumed.
But looke how gratious hee liu'd mong vs heere
In Heauen hee much more glorious shall appeare:.

---

[15]

In obitu͞ – Annæ Reginæ

I tristis Libitina veste pullâ
I per Cæsaris atrim superbum
Mandatoque silentio dolorem
Luctus, et Lacrymas sonosque tristes
Manda. Mox fuge mæsta per Suburrâ: 5
Dic, væ ciuibus, atque triste signum
Mortis concute funebrē cupressum:
Et si quis tacite rogabit vnde hæc?
Dic, sed cum Lacrymis, perempta morte
Ana est: tunc sileas: dolebit Orbis:

15.5 mæsta] Ligature imperfectly formed. It resembles a double *ee*.

[16]

A Funerall Elegie vppon the Death of M^r
Iohn Ryce M^r of Arts and Squire Beadle : } :

Crush forth your selues you Cloudes, & spend your powres
Aprill bee free, and weepe thy larger showers:
Thou greiu'st too Thriftily: those drops of thine
Are but Distill-ments from thy vnforst eyne.
Weepe and weepe strongly: that the iealous feares
Of men may make them weepe to see thy teares
So many, that the'nsuinge May may curse
His Harbinger, when hee shall see disburse
The whole allowance that the Tymes before
And Spring haue giuen; Yet run on Winters score;   10
Nor shall these Flouds kindely Embrace the earth
But rudely rauish, that th' u^nlawfull birth
May become ill blest weedes not Flowers; vnles
The Earth (as a signe of her last happiness)
Would weare disgrace in highway Primrose-sets
Or a pale Feare in opall Violetts.
For why should Nature our most beautious Queene
(who is no older then the Earth hath beene)
Haue so misshapen ofsprings, so few good
Flowers, and but now and then a hope full Bud;   20
When shee, that neither can pleade Youth nor Any
Aduantage, hath so often good so many?
And of these few none, Dead, can or appeare
Freshly reuiu'd vppon a second yeare.
But looke how fast how many of these dye,
So oft, so Many wants her Treasury.
One hast thou lost (and yet y^t one is more
Then might bee spard out of thy little store)
A man, an Honest man; at whose Deaths story
All those will weepe, or at the least bee sorry   30
Who either can suspect or testifie,
How great a loss it is when good men dye,
Since in this Age, tis to bee vnderstoode
Men are no more then positiuely good,
For Niggard Death hath so small Haruest lent vs
That now euen Vertues Gleamings must content vs
Yet for all this wee may perceiue at length _____
                       verte: &

---

11 *Flouds*] Majuscule *F* converted from miniscule *f*.

Death is more Enuy to the Good then Strength.
For though shee tooke him hence, shee could not take
His good name too, nor could her Malice make   40
Good men forgett him; or could strike so deepe
That with his body (too) his Soule might sleepe.
But that in a Triumphant state is gone
To claime a seate neere the Almighties Throne,

Hee died   <u>Scare had the way</u> of life displai'd his path
on Ester ⎫   To that full Maiestye that now hee hath.
Wensday: ⎭   And had bought stately Mansions and Trim
For wearie Trauellours that pass by him,
But the third night after that happy day
Hee mounted, marshallinge himselfe, This way.   50
Nor light hee out by chaunce (so Death were cheape)

He had a   Nor rashly Rañt, nor reacht hee at a Leap:
Consumptiō ⎫   Eight weary Yeeres hee soberly intended
of 8 yeeres ⎭   To goe this long-breathd iourney, Now t'is ended
Then (what to wearie Passengers is best)
Wee will no more with plaints disturbe his rest.
Sleepe, Sleepe: Good man, and take thy Rest vppo'nt
GH   Sleep, Sleep; Thou hast had a Long iourney on't:. ⊛ 🌀 🌀

[17]

In obitum Dmj Iohanis Ryce in Artibus Magistrj
et Bedellj Superioris: Carmen Funebre:./

Qualis, dum Scythica languescit rupe Prometheus,
    Vultur ad æternas itque reditque lapes;
Hunc talis depasta lues; talisque solebat
    Languere; et nondum mortuus, vmbra fuit.
Pallidulum corpus nudatos prodidit artus
    Iam-pridem nullo sanguine vena fluit
Ossa cutis retegit, macies dominatur in ore;
    Et iam verniculis desijt esse cibus,
Sæpe morj voluit, sed Mors vicina refugit
Quam miserum est, miserum non potuisse morj?   10
Sed scio iam votis quinam Deus obstitit æquis
    Noluit officium perdere Mercurius: <u>G: Morley</u>

[18]

In obitum Mrj Ryce Bedellj Superioris circiter dies
Paschales morientis   Car: Funebre: 🌀

16.58 left margin **GH**] (See commentary notes); *Long*] L overwrites *l*.

En charus Christo Simeon, en noster amicus,
Ille suum Dominum vidit; et ille suum
Discrimen tamen hoc; hic primo in limine Christum
Vt puerum et regem viderat, obstupuit
Ille semel natum aspexit, semel ille renatum
Vt*que* resurgentem viderat occubuit:.

Fuge pij mores et tanto munere digni,
Fuge fides Paulo digna, negato Petro.
Per mortem Dominum sequeris, per funera Christum
Et pariter Christj testis es, at*que* Comes.   10
Nos ipsos sequimur morientes; tu*que* priorem
Quem*que* sequaris, habes, quem*que* imitare Deum : Z: T:.

[19]

{ Vppon M^ris Gardner daughter to the right wor^ell D^r }
{ Ashboold D^r of Diuinity: Lacrymæ consolatoriæ: }

In Eden Grandsire Adam first was plast
To till and prune it with laborious hand,
But now it is so totally defas't,
As but by gues wee know not wher't did stand;
Hee was the first of men, and Gardi'ners, and
The first that Morgaigd his replenisht lande,
Thus wee in him haue lost that vnmacht life
Wee should haue ledd within those sacred bounds
And now wee know no Eden but a wife,
Whose vertues shine like vertues in the roundes.   10
So shind shee (Gardner) whome our teares bedew
And soe sang all, but Spight, her lif that knew.
Shee was an Eden, a Thessalian feilde
Of euer teeminge pleasures: and gain'st dyinge
This Tempe that it may selfe-like fruit yeeld
G: Must haue a: gardner, Hee a timely knowinge
And soe hee had such his felicityes
Hee turnd his garden to a Paradise
With wings of Zeale and feete of preparation
Shee posted Heauenward where shee takes vp Inn   20
Vntill the worlds end, when the seperation
Of Soule and body shall cease with all sinn
St Peters Church   Her Soule to Christ y^t loud it shee preferd,
in London: In <u>Peters Rock</u> her body is interd:.   W:H:

19.16 (margin) **G:**] Probably indicates that *gardner* should be capitalized.

[20]

Lydfoorde Law in Deuon-sheere:.

I oft haue heard of Lydford-Law
How in the Morne they hang & draw
   And sitt in iudgment after;
At first I wondred at it much
But now I finde their reason such
   That it deserues no laughter:

They haue a Castell on an Hill
I tooke it for an old winde-Mill
   The vanes blowne off with weather:
To lye there in one night is guest   10
Twere better to bee ston'd or prest
   Or hang'd, now chuse you whether:

Tenne men less rome with in this Caue
Then fiue mice in a Lanthorne haue
   The Keepers they are sly-ones:
If any could deuise by Art
To gett it vp into a Cart
   Twere fitt to carry Lyons:

When I beheld it Lord thought I
What Iustice and what Clemencie   20
   Hath Lydfoord whe I spy all:
I know none there would gladly stay
But rather hang out of the way
   Then tarry for a triall:./

The Prince an hundred Pounds hath sent
To mend the Leads and Plantchinge rent
   With in this liuinge Tombe.
Some forty fiue pounds more had payd
The debts of all that shall bee layd
   There till the day of doome: 30

One lies there for a peck of Salt
Another for three pecks of malt,
   Two surties for a Noble;
If this bee true, or else false newes
You may goe aske of Mr Cruse
   Iohn Vaughan or Iohn Doble:.

Neere to the men y^t lye in lurch
There is a bridge, there is a Church
   Seuen Ashes, and one Oake:
Three houses standinge, and Ten downe   40
   They say the Parson hath a gowne
But I saw nere a Cloake:.

Whereby you may consider well
That plaine simplicitie doth dwell
   At Lidfoord with out brauerie:
And in the Towne both young & old
Doe loue the naked Truth, & hold
   No Cloake to hide their knauerie:

The people all with in this clime
Are frozen vp all winter time   50
   Besure I doe not faine.
And when the Summer is beguñe
They lye like silkewormes in the Suñe
   And come to life againe:.

One tould mee in Kinge Cæsars time
The towne was built of stone & lime
   But sure the walls were clay;
For they are fallen for ought I see
And since the houses loose gott free
   The towne is run a way:.   60

O Cesar if thou there didst raigne
While one house stands come there againe
   Come quickly whiles there is one:
If thou but stay a little fitt,
But fiue yeere more y^u maist committ
   The whole Towne into Prison

To see it thus much greiu'd was I
The Prouerbe saies Sorrow is dry,
   So was I at this matter:
When by good luck I know not how   70
There thither came a strange strayd cow
   And wee had Milke and water:.

To nine good stomakes with our whigg
At last wee gott a tithinge Pigg
   This dyett was our boundes:
And it was iust, as (if twere knowne)
A pound of Butter had biñ throwne
   A mongst a pack of houndes:.

One glass of Drinke I gott by chaunce
Twas clarett when it was in France   80
   But now from it nought wider:
I thinke a man might make as good
With greene Crabbs boild wth Brasill wood
   And halfe a pinte of Sider:.

I kist the Mayres hand of ye Towne
Who though hee weare no scarlett gowne
Honours the Rose and Thistle
A peece of Corall to the Mace
Which there I saw to serue ye place
Would make a good childes whistle   90

At six a clocke I came a way
And prayd for those y^t were to stay
Within a place so arrant:
Wilde and ope to windes that rore
By Gods Grace Ile come there no more
Vnless by some Tynn-arrant:.

[21]

Vppon M^ris Thaire daughter to the right wor^ell
    Dr Ashboolde, here to-fore ye wife of Mr Weston   } : ✹

Heere lies inclos'd with in her quiet vrne
The Subiect of perfection and desarte
For virtuous life, who though to dust shee turne
Tis not a resolution but in parte:
Admitt her body moulder into day,
It shall turne sollid at the latter day
Thrice was shee married, and so happily;
That if all weomen had her fortune, sure
The Church would straight approue of trigamie
Though but the vertuous could put in vre: 10
Successiue happiness so blest her Bed
That shee enioyd a husband beinge dead,
For though to Celebrate the Nuptiall rites
Shee went but twice to Church: yet thrice espous'd
Her pietie confirmes her: Now blacke Night
Hath ceas'd vppon Her in Earths prison hous'd
Sett west, and liuinge Thayre were Hers thow list
Blinde Ignorance in Death shee married Christ:.
                      W: H/:.

[22]

In obitum Magistrj Max, ^i a'<?> quondam Ædis X^tj
    Alumnj Qui in Comitijs Hospes fato concessit: : }

Æde tuâ moritur Maxeius X^te, perennis
Vita vbi solo foret, Mors ibi sæua ferit:
Num tua dignaret iam tandem fracta potestas
Et vitæ, Mors Trux placet esse Deus?
Haud quanquam; Mors ista breuis mutatio <est> vitæ est,   5
  Is viuit cui in te Fata dedere morj:.
                  /W: H

21.6 *sollid*] *i* overwrites *e*. **22. 2** *ferit*] *i* overwrites *e*. **22.3** *dignaret*] *a* overwrites *e*.

[23]

Vppon Mistris Gardners Death & who dyed in Child-birth
of her first child:./

Where shall I fix a Senith to my Verse,
About to singe and weepe a glorious Hearse?
Where shall I know a Nidar? these extreames
Are too angust for my most August Theames.
Were I ca^tcht vpp to the starr-Chamber of heauen
And did descend thence through the wandringe seauen
Serchinge their concaues and abstractinge thence
Perfects Idæas beautie<s>, could to sence
Obiect, or tooke the pleasingst names a way
That might adorne the females late decay.   10
All heauens starr-written Index could not giue
Woords of sufficient Emphasis to liue
To her, whome but because I thinke vppon
I dare renounce the dry drawne Helicon.
When shee was borne to bless this beginge earth
Noe triforme Dietie maturd her birth
Nor tooke shee hurtfull influence from any
Wretch-rulinge Planetts, whose effects are many
But either was of the first substance made
Or by the Alphabet of Gods thus raide   20
In splendor like them selues: Yett is shee dead;
No: leauinge sublunary Leapers f_∧^ledd
Vnto her selfe-like continent of Heauen
Woofully sure wee are, wee are bereauen
Of moore then if the Indies were contracted
To make a face of Gould, that ye refracted
Splendor of Phæbus might enuye, or if
(Yett of Her that's a wantinge Hierogliph)
Pearles ioynd, or Dyamonds to make an eye
Centredd with Pollisht Iett, or if the Skie   30
Vnto those mixtures sent her Crysolites
So that Ioues winged Herauld to those lights
Opposinge his bould eyes, quite daz'led by Her,
Might conflict with the all-illuminer.
ffor stronger moisture, or dye in dispaire
Out coun'tnan'ct by a Sainte whose leaste was faire:
Such luster was in Her resultant <eye> soe
That Ioue from Venus her could neuer knowe

25 *if*] *i* overwrites unreadable letter.

Nature turnd Banckrupt since shee put to vse
All her rich portion to that face; The iuice   40
Of pretiouse Earth shee counteth all her store
Now, Iudginge Her-selfe worse then ere before
The reason is, Her worke might beere Her Mate,
Now alls vnworthy, or inanimate.
Shee, shee it was whose lookes could giue a life
To soules now only lip-lockt, by the knife
of Attropos disseuerd, to expire,
And there fore Parce in reuengefull ire,
(As the effect is non-plust by the cause)
Fassen on Her their Adamantine lawes,   50
And tooke Her hence; Yet is shee not with Them,
Ioue hath a care of his Ethereall stem,
Who iudicateth not his ofspring by
Dissheueld Cometts, Meteors in the skie,
But when the Brow of Heauen is smooth & cleere
As burnish Iasper, Venus in her spere,
Or like it selfe by suffr'ed tolerations
At truce with all the windes and exhalations,
So went shee vp to Ioue, as pure as are
Pure acts intelligences, who had care   60
Of her aliue, not that they did preserue her
(For that did God alone) but to obserue Her.
Nature is growne soe needy since of things
Qualefide rarely, that who Iana sings,
Must tract in similies Celestiall
Diuine comparisons must Her inrole.
As the rounde armes of the first mouinge Sphære
Imbracinge all the rest, all which to teare
Aiust sett day aspects, which done, yet shall
No violence hurt the Emperiall;   70
So fares it with Her compound: yt same powre
Cald vegetable, mou'd first in her bower
Of pory skin, with sensitiue, and all
Other perfection the Soule rationall
Destroide when it departed; now what is
Remaininge scornes vnder-moone similies.
Here coulde I call Her vnderstandinge Hearte
The Christall Heauen or the first mouinge parte,
Her will which did attend still to its Notions
The vnder-Orbes which thence drew all their motions: 80

Her vertues, or her Mercy such a seauen,
But not so wandringe as there bee in Heauen,
And as those worke on suffringe creatures partes,
So did Her influence on Affected <he>Arts:
Her zeale may bee as Elementall fier,
Her prair'es an aire as willinge to aspire
As water, so may bee her liquid weepings
Wastinge Her cheekes, as that by vaine like creepings
The drinkinge Bauches, Her body Notifies
Earth Motionles (like that) in graue it lies.   90
These haue some Symphasie; Her soule for aye
Like the heauen of Heauens faire-selfe, shall ner'e decay.
Reioyce then kindred to this Saintes, whome
God hath endude there with a peace full rome.
And in full praises bee your tongue neere mute,
Since that shee dyde to God, in yeeldinge fruite,
Haue not you seene an aged straight tree flourish
And both bring forth, i'ts ofspringes and them nourish
By an vnfrindly winde layd prostrate on
Tha' mazed Earth: although this trunke be gon,   100
And nere shall waue i'ts apple garnisht head
The roote may send a nother from i'tts bed.
Whose tender body when the winde it moues,
May as (of place) bee Heire too, of your loues:
And by time strengthned, iossell with the winde
And chide it with her leaues, cause twas vnkinde
To i'tts fore grower: I but you may say,
The age o'th tree was weary now to pay
A youth full tribute, and vnable too
As it had done, So was not shee   110
Water in vaine with teares to growe, vnable
Though likely with her seede to'ingirte your Table
This is most true: But yet you must bee toulde
Her likely fertileness made Her seeme ould:
And there fore shee is fall'n, yet not in vaine
Your hopes they must ingrafte a childe againe,
And may hee liue as longe, as shee was goode,
And bee as neere her goodness, as Her bloude,
T'is irreligion to mone that priuation
Which is a Ruine and a Renouation.   120
Shee well deserude an Elegie, tis true
And Paper mournes for Her in this sad Hew:
Yett ere her body visitt should itts vrne
Versles, my Muse had vow'd Sanguine to turne

84 *Arts*] Majuscule *A* overwrites minuscule *a*. **122 *Hew*]** *e* overwrites *a*; *w* overwrites unreadable letter.

Meaning thus much Her Hearte should bleede a line
Or two, in tribute at so loud a shrine.
Leaue this sad duty? as I spare your eares
Forbid your eies to versifie in teares.
Her iusts perform'd tell you what you should doe,
As they haue hid their mourninge soe doe You   130
And though this may bee calld the workinge day
Of your all-emptinge eyes, in Heau'n it may
Bee writt the triumphe (in the sacred Roule)
Or Holyday, or Birth-day of a soule:. ✾   W : H :.

[24]

✾ ⎰Both Sisters, and both dead, Both in one Graue,   ⎱ ✾
   ⎱ Both virtuouse, Both deplord, Bothe one verse haue:. ⎰

Gods why are You incen'st? what enuye thus
Whetts on Your vengance, not to threaten vs;
But act vnpartially your dread designes
Which cannot bee differd for Indias mines
Much less abortiue proue? what ist your wills
To send the world such happiness as fills
Earch heart with ioye, and then to breake itt off
By suddaine depriuation, or to scoff
Our feruent prayers, snatchinge from o^r sphere
Those glories which wee wish still fixed there: 10
O powers refraine delusions? No, for why
Of brighter starres, You cannot rob our skie
Had you then broke the fabricke of the world
Or with your latest flames the heauens courl'd,
Wee should not haue suruiu'd our deplor'd loss,
Inueigh against those Dieties that Cross
Our happiness, or wish our ruines howre,
Out daringe in our greifes your cruell power
Gods like your selues in Tempels pla'st hard stone
Or stupid Mettalls? was all pitty flowne?   20
Let mee expostulate, what causes mou'd
You to depriue vs of a paire that prou'd
Saintlike on Earth, and could not betterd bee
Were they in Heauen but in fælicitye?
Tis true, they did contemplate nothinge less
Then that the lyinge world calls happiness;
But must they therefore leaue vs? must wee want
Pious examples when they are soe scant?
Must Bankrupt Natures woorke bee made as breefe
As exquisite? Must Death that common Theefe   30
Steale such rich soules vnpunisht and in graue
Include their bodyes? Must hee guilty saue
His skeliton, when murder is committed
The murdred dungiond, And his fact acquited?
Confusd inuersion? then lett all run back
Lett all things bee their contraries, so racke

Vertue that it turne vice, Sinister fates
Lett it bee ruine that first animates.
But why are our desires refracted thus?
What are your God-heads growne less tyrannous?   40
You should haue beene thus mercifull before
You robd our tresurie, supprizd our store.
No I conceiue by suddaine inspiration
All your proceedings, for our renovation
You tooke them hence, and since wee were so <b?dd> dead
In hastinge heauenward, They the iourney ledd,
That (if not for Loue of the God-borne stem)
Wee should pursue heauen yet for Loue of them.
All happy soules you feele no greife at all,
Since you haue that sight beatificall.   50
The younger of you trod the first that way
The elders zeale deny'd her longer stay.
The Younger when dame Natures pay day grew
Neer-hand for her first fruites payd herselfe new
Vnto the world, and made a riddle thus
Shee could bee absent and yett bee with vs.
Shee gaue and lost life both at once, for why
Shee brought an heire forth to her piety;
As if in spight of fate Shee would suruiue,
And leaue her vertues in her seede aliue,   60
Or as if shee was neuer borne to bee
Barren, but euen in death a fruitfull tree.
The elder hasted after (wee may see
Euen in their ruines Consanguinitye)
The elder hasted after and both raigne
Inthrownd in heauen vntill they come againe.
Earth in one concaue keepes her quintisses,
Their purer bodies Arkes of innocens,
Thus are they new-yeeres guiftes send to Gods hand,
Swifte footed Pilgrimes to the holy Lande.   70
Then mourne not Father, Mother, Husband nor
Sister and Brother which this breach repaire
Nor kinsfolkes, wipe your eyes and smile vppon
These Babes that know not Yett what Gemms are gone,
With God their Soules, in Earth their bodyes lye
Their Vertues in their stock and Memorie:.   W: H:

---

45 <b?dd>] Unreadable letter is probably an *a*. **67** *quintisses*] What appears to be a tilde is superscribed above *es*. **74** *Babes*] Majuscule *B* overwrites minuscule *b*.

25

[25]

𝔇ʳ 𝕮𝖔𝖗𝖇𝖊𝖙𝖘   𝕴𝖙𝖊𝖗 𝕭𝖔𝖗𝖊𝖆𝖑𝖊 ☙

Fowre Clerkes of Oxford, Docters two, and two
That would bee Docters, haueinge less to doe:
With Austin, then with Galen in vacation
Changd studdies and turnd Bookes to recreation
And on the tenth of August northward bent
A iourney not so soone conceiuide as spent.
The first halfe-day they rode, they light vppon
A noble Clergy-host <u>Kitt Middleton</u>
Who numbringe out good dishes with good tales
The maior parte of cheere wai'd downe yᵉ scales   10
And though the countenance make yᵉ feast (say bookes)
Wee nere found better welcome with worse lookes.
Here wee payd Thankes and parted, and at night
Had entertainement all in on mans right
<u>At Flower a village</u>: wher our Tennant shee
Sharpe as a winter mor'ne, feirce yet free,
With a leane visage like a curued face
On a court-cubbord, offerd vp the <grace> place
Shee pleas'd vs well, but yet her husband better,
A <u>harty fellow</u>, and a good Bone setter.   20
Now whether it were prouidence or Lucke
Whether the keeper's or the stealers Bucke
There wee had venison such as Virgill slew
When hee would feast Æneas and his crew.
Here wee consumd aday and the third morne
To <u>Daintry</u> with a land winde wee were borne.
It was the Markett and the Lecture day
For Lecturers sell sermons, as the Lay
Doe sheepe and Oxen, haue their seasons iust
For both their marketts, there wee dranke-downe dust.   30
In the interim comes a <u>most officious drudge</u>
His face and Gowne drawne out with yᵉ same budge,
His pendant-pouch which was both large and wide
Look't like a Letters Patent's by his side
Hee was as awfull as if hee had binn sent
From Moses with the eleuenth Commaundement.
And one of vs hee sought, a sonne of Flower
Hee must bid stand, and challenge for an houre.
The Doctors both were quitted of their feare
The one was hoarse, the other was not theare   40
Wherefore him of the two hee seased, best

Ashton vppon the wall: Mʳ Middleton ⊛

Flower in North-hampton Sheere Dʳ Hut: benefice

Ned:Hale: ⊛

Daintry ⊛

The seargant:.

(**Title**)] Scripted in black letter. **25 *aday***] Written as one word.

	Able to answere him of all the rest,
	Because hee needes but ruminate that ore
	Which hee had chewd the Sabboth day before
	And though hee were resolud to doe him right
The Minister:.	For Mr <u>Baylyes</u> sake and Mr Wright
	Yet hee dessembled: that the Mace did err
	That hee nor Deacon was nor Minister
	No? quoth the Sergant, sure then by Relation
	You haue a Licence Sir or Toleration. 50
	And if you haue no Orders, tis the better
Puritan Ministers	So you haue <u>Dodds</u> precepts or <u>Cleuers</u> Letter.
of Banbury: ✸	Thus lookeinge on his Mace and vrginge still
	Twas Mr Wrights and Mr Baylyes will
	That hee should mount, At last hee condescended
	To stopp the gapp; and soe the treaty ended.
	The Sermon pleas'd, and when wee were to dine
	Wee all had prechers wages, Thankes and wine.
Lutterworth in	Our next dayes stage was <u>Lutterworth</u>, a Towne
<u>Leister-sheere</u> ✸	Not willinge to bee noted or sett downe 60
	By any trauellar; for when wee had binn
	Through at both ends, wee could not finde an Inn
	Yet for the Church sake turne and light wee must
Who was buried	Hopeinge to finde one dram of <u>Wickliffs</u> dust
in ye Parish ch-	But wee found none. for vnderneathe the Pole
urch: ✸	No more rests of his body then his soule.
	Abused Martyr how hast thou bin torne
	By two wild factions? first the Papists burne
	Thy bones for hate; the Puritans in zeale
	They sell thy Marble and thy Brass they steale 70
Parson Heathcote	A <u>Parson</u> mett vs there, who had good store
✸	Of liuinge some say, but of manners more.
	In whose straight cheerefull age aman might see
	Well gouernd Fortune, bounty wise and free
	Hee was our guide to Leister saue one Mile
	There was his dwellinge where wee stayd a while
	And dranke stale beere, I thinke was neuer new
	Which the Dun wench y^t brought vs did brew.
Leister: ✸	And now wee are at <u>Leister</u>: where I shall
	Leap ore six steeples (and an hospitall) 80
	Twice-told, those great-land-markes I did referr
	To Camdens eie Englands Corographer,
The Almes house ✸	Let mee obserue that <u>Almesmans</u> herauldry
	Who beinge ask't what Henry that should bee

---

58 prechers] First *e* overwrites *a*. **74 Fortune**] Uppercase F overwrites lowercase *f.*

That was their founder Duke of Lancaster
Answer'd t'was Iohn of Gaunt I assure you Sir
And so confounded all the Walls that say'd
Henry of Grismound this foundation lay'd
The next thinge to bee noted was our cheere
Enlarg'd with seuen and Sixpence bread & beere   90

Tapstors: ✳ But ô you wretches <u>Tapsters</u> as you are
Who reckon by our number not your ware
And sett false figures for all companies
Abusinge innocent meales with oaths & lyes,
Forbeare your Cousnaige to diuines that come
Least they bee thought to drinke all that you some
Spare not the Layitie in your reckning thus
But shure your thefte is scandalous to vs.
A way my Muse from this base subiect know

Rich:the 3ᵈ lies Thy Pegasus nere strucke his foote soe lowe.   100
buried there } ✳ Is not the <u>vsurpinge Richard</u> buried there
That Kinge of hate, and therfore slaue of feare
Drag'd from thy fatall feild Bosworth, wher hee
Lost life, and what hee liu'd for Cruelty?
Search finde his name but there is none O Kings
Remember whence your power and vastness springs
If not as Richard now, so shall you bee
Who hath no Tombe but scorne and memorie.

Cardinall Wolsey And though from his owne store <u>Woolsey</u> might saue
buried there: } A Pallace or a College for his graue,   110
Yet there hee lyes interrd, as if all
Of him to bee rememberd were his fall:
Nothinge but earth to earth, no pompous waight
Vppon him, but a pibble or a quaite.

Schollers of Wol- If thou art thus neglected, what shall wee
seyes foundation} Hope after Death who are <u>but shreads of thee</u>?
in Oxon– ✳ Hold? William calls to horse, <u>William</u> is hee
Who though hee neuer saw three score and three

Dᵣ Huttons Man Ore reckons vs in age, as hee before
<u>William:</u> } ✳ In drinke, and will baite nothinge of fowre score,   120
And hee commaunds as if the warrant came

Nothingam From the great Earle himselfe to <u>Notingham</u>
There wee crost Trent, and on the other side
Praide for Sᵗ Andrewes, and vphill wee ride
Where wee obserude the cuninge men like moles

The houses in the Dwell not in houses but are earth't <u>in holes</u>
<u>Rocks:</u> ✳ } So did they not build vpward, but digg through
As Hermites Caues, or Connies doe their Burrough

Great vnderminers sure as any wheare,
Tis thought the Powder Traytors practis'd there.   *130*
Would you not thinke the men stood on their heads?
When gardens couer houses there like leads:
And on the chimnyes Top the Mayd may know
Whether her pottage boyle or not belowe?
There cast in herbs, or salt, or bread her meate
Contented rather with the smoake then heate.
This was the Rockey-parish. Higher stood
Churches and howses, buildings stone and wood,

The Crosses in   Crosses not yet demolisht, and our Lady
Notingham ⊛ }   With her armes on imbracinge her whole Baby   *140*
                                       Where let vs note though tthose bee northerne parts
                                       The Cross finds in them more then southerne hearts.

The Castle ruined}   The Castle next. But what shall wee report
                                       Of that which is a ruine was a fort?
Guy & Colebrand ⊛   The Gates two statues keepe which Gyants are
                                       To whome it seemes committed is the care
                                       Of the whole dounefall. if it bee your fault

When K: Dauid K   If you are guilty, let Kinge Dauids vault
of Scots had bin }   Or Mortimers darke hole containe you both
kept prisoner   A iust reward, for soe profane a sloth;   *150*
                                       And if here after tidings shall bee brought
                                       Or any place or Office to bee bought
                                       And the lefte Lead, or vnbeggd Tymber yet
                                       Shall pass by your consent to purchase it
                                       May your deformed bul‸↑c↓kes endure the edge
                                       Of Axes, feele the beetle and the Wedge
                                       May all the Ballads bee cald in and dye
                                       Which sing the warrs of Colebrand and Sir Guy
                                       O you that doe Guild-haule and Holmeby keepe
                                       So carefully when both the founders sleepe   *160*
                                       You are good Gyants and pertake no shame
                                       With these two worthlesse Trunkes of Notingham
                                       Looke to your seuerall charges wee mst goe

The Bulhead   Though greiu'd at heart to leave a Castle soe:./
in Notingham } ⊛   The Bulhead is the word, and wee must eate
                                       No sorrow can descend so deepe as meate
                                       So to the Inn we come wher our best cheere
                                       Was that his Grace of Yorke had lodged there
                                       Hee was obiected to vs, when wee call
                                       Or dislike ought, my Lords Grace answeres all   *170*
                                       Hee was contented with this bed, this diett

---

159 haule] Lowercase *e* overwrites lowercase *d*; top portion of original letter deleted.

	That keepes our discontented stomakes quiett.	
The Inkeeper ⊛	The Inkeeper was old fourescore almost	
	Indeede an Emblem rather then an Host,	
	In whome wee reade how God and tyme decree	
	To honour thriuing Ostlers, such as hee	
	For in the Stable first hee did beginn	
	Now, see; hee is sole Lord of all the Inn	
	Marke the increase of straw and hay, and how	
	By thrift, a bottle may become a mow;	180
	Marke him all you that haue the goulden itch	
	All, whome God hath condemned to bee rich	
His daughter yᵗ	Farewell glad father of thy daughter <u>Maris</u>	
<u>yeare Mayris</u> } ⊛	Thou Ostler Phænix, thy example rare is:./	
	Wee are for New<m>↑w↓arke after this sad talke	
	And thither is no iourney but a walke	
The way betwixt	Nature is wanton there, and the highway	
Noting: et New-}	Seemde to bee priuate, though it open lay	
warke<?> ⊛	As if some swellinge Lawyer for his health,	
	Or frantike vsurer to tame his wealth	190
Trent: ⊛	Had chosen out Ten miles by Trent, to try	
	Two great effects, of art, and industry.	
	The ground wee trodd was Meadow, fertile Land	
	New trimd and leuell'd by the Mowers h<e>and.	
	Aboue it grew a Rock, rude, steepe, and high,	
	Which claimd a kinde of reuerence from the eye	
	Betwixt them both there slides a liuely streame,	
	Not lowd, but swifte. Meander was a Theame	
	Crooked and roughe. But had those Poets seene	
	Straight euen Trent, it had immortall beene,	200
	This side, the open plaine admits the Sun	
	To halfe the riuer: there did siluer runn;	
	The other halfe ran clowdes wher the curld wood	
	With his exalted head threat'ned the flood,	
	Here could I wish vs euer passinge by	
	And neuer past; now Newwarke is to nigh,	
	And as a Chrismas seemes a day but short	
	Deludinge tyme with reuells and good sport,	
	So did the beautious mixture vs beguile	
<u>Dͬ Iucks</u> ⊛ }	And the whole twelue beinge trauail'd were a mile	210
	Now as the way was sweet, so was the end,	
	Our passage easie, and our prize a friend;	
	Whome there wee did enioy, and for whose sake	
	As for a purer kinde of Coine, men make	
	Vs liberall welcome, with such harmony	
	As all the Towne had binn his familie	
	Mine Host at the next Inn did not repine	

180 *By*] *B* overwrites *A*.   **195 *steepe,***] (comma below *and*).   **210** (margin) ***Iucks***] *c* overwrites unreadable letter, signalled above word with wave-like line.   **217 *at***] *f* corrected to *t*.

That wee preferd the heart and past his signe
And when we lay, the Host and Hostise faine
Would shew our Loue was aimd att, not their gaine;   220
The very beggers were so ingenious,
They rather pray for him, the begg of vs,
And so the D^rs frinds be pleasd to stay
The Puritanes will lett the Organs play
Would they pull downe the Gallery builded new

⊛ higher then   With the Church-Wardens seate & <u>Burleighs pew</u>
<u>the Pulpit</u> } ⊛   Newmarke for light and beauty might compare
equall with y^e   With any Church, but what Cathedrall are:
<u>Rood loft:.</u> }   To this belongs a <u>Vicar</u> who succeded
Mr Mason:.   The friend I mentioned. such a one there needed   230
A man whose tongue and life is eloquent
Able to charme those mutenous heads of Trent,
And vrge y^e <u>Canon</u> home, when they conspire
Against the Cross, and bells with sword and fier;

Newmarke   There stood <u>a Castle too</u>, they shew vs here
  Castle— ⊛   The Rome where the Kinge slept, the windowe where
Hee talkt with such a Lord, how long hee stayd
In his discourse, and all but what hee sayd.
    From hence without a perspectiue wee see
<u>Beuer</u> and <u>Lyncolne</u>, where wee faine would bee   240
But that our purse, and horses both were bound
Within the circuit of a narrower grounde
Our purpose is all homeward, and twas time
At partinge to haue witt, aswell as rime
Full three a clocke, and twenty miles to ride
Will aske a speedy horse, and a sure guide.

Our way to   Wee wanted both: and <u>Loughborough</u> may glory
<u>Loughborow</u> } ⊛   Errour hath made it famous in our story.
    Twas night and the swifte Horses of the Sun,
Two houres before our iades, their race had runn.   250
No pilots, <u>Moone</u>, nor any such kinde starr
As gouernde those wise men that came from farr
To holy Bethlem. such lights had they binn
They would haue soone conuayd vs to an Inn,
But all were wandringe starrs, and wee as they
Were taught no course, but to ride on and stray,
When (O the fate of darkeness who hath tryd it)

Our error in   <u>Here our hole fleete is scatterd and diuided,</u>
ye night : }   And now wee labour more to meete, then erst
Wee did to lodge, the last cry drownes the first,   260

---

222 *the*] Modern pencil notation, not transcribed: *y* added to make the word *they*. 257 (**O**] Parenthesis used to overwrite initial *s*. Holgate first wrote word starting with *s*. 259 *then*] *e* overwrites unreadable letter.

Our voices are all spent, and they that follow
Can now no longer tracke vs by the hollow.
They curse the foremost; wee the hindmost, both
Accusinge with like patience haste and sloth;
At laste vppon a little Towne wee fall
Where some call drinke, and some a Candle call
Vnhappy wee! Such straglers as wee are
Admire a Candle oftner then a starr.
Wee care not for those glorious Lampes a loofe
Giue vs a tallowe-light, and a dry roofe.   270
And now wee haue a guide wee cease to chafe,
Now haue wee time to pray the rest bee safe,
Our guide before cryes come, and wee the while
Ride blindfolde, and take bridges for a stile,
Till at the last, wee ouercome the darke
And spight of night and error hit our marke.
Some halfe howre after enters the whole taile
As if they were committed to the iayle,

Whom they had
hired to direct } ⊛   The Cunstable that tooke them thus diuided
them—   Made them seeme apprehended, and not guided.   280
                        Where when wee had our fortunes both detested
                        Compassion made vs frinds, and so wee rested
                        Twas quickly morninge though by our short stay
                        Wee could not feele that wee had less to pay
                        All trauellers this heauy iudgment heare

Our hostiss at
Loughborow } ⊛   A handsome Hostise makes the reckninge drare.
                        Her smiles, her words, your purses must requite them,
                        And euery welcome from her, adds an <Æ>Item.
                          Glad to bee gon from thence at any rate
                        For Bosworth wee are first, behold the state   290
                        Of mortall men. Foule Error is a Mother,
                        And pregnant once doth soone brings forth a nother.
                        Wee who last night did learne to loose our way,
                        Are perfitt since, and farther out next day,

Lester fforrest: ⊛   And in a Forrest haueinge trauaild sore
                        Like wandringe Beuis, ere hee found the Bore:
                        Or as some Loue sicke Lady oft hath donn
                        Ere shee was rescu'd by the Knight O' the Sun
                        So are wee lost, and meete no comfort then

Goinge and cominge| But Carts and horses, wiser then the Men,   300
to and from the }   Which is the way? they neither speake, nor point,
 Cole pitt: }   Their tongues and fingers both are out of ioynt;
                        Such Monsters by Cole-kerton bankes there sitt<?>
                        After their resurrection from the pitt:.

Whilst in this Mill wee labour and turne round

William:./ 　　　　　As in a Coniurours circle, <u>William</u> found
A meanes for our deliuerance, turne your clokes,
Quoth hee, for Puck is busie in these okes,
If euer wee at Bosworth will be found
Then turne your clokes for this is fairy-ground,　　　　310
But ere this witch-craft was perfomd we <found> mett

The keeper of 　　　　A <u>very man</u> who had no clouen feete.
Groasby Barke } 　　Though William still of little faith doth doubt
Tis Robin, ore some spirit that walkes aboute.
Strike him quoth hee, and it will turne to aire
Crosse your selues thrice and strike it, strike y^t dare.
Thought I, for sure this Massie forrester
In strokes will proue the better Coniurer,
But twas a gentle Keeper one that knew
Humanity and manners where they grew,　　　　320
And rode a longe so farr till hee could say
See younder Bosworth stands, and this the way.
　And now when wee had swet twixt Sun and suñ
And eight miles longe to thirty broade had spunn
Wee learne the iust proportion from hence
Of the Diameter and Circumference.
　That night yet made a mends, our meate our sheetes
Were farr aboue the promise of those streetes.
Those houses that were til'de with straw and moss
Profest but weake repaire for that dayes loss　　　　330
Of patience. Yet this out side let's vs know
The worthiest things make not the greatest show.
The shott was easie (and what concearnes vs more)
The way was soe, myne host doth ride before
Mine Host was full of Ale and Historie.
And on the morrow when hee brought vs nigh

Bosworth feild: ✣ 　Where the <u>two Rroses ioynd</u> you would suppose
Chaucer nere wrote the Romant of the Rose.
Heare him! See you yo'n wood! ther Richard lay
With his hole armie, looke the other way　　　　340
And loe where Richmound in a bed of grass
Encampt him selfe e're night and all his force.
Vppon this Hill they mett; why, hee could tell
The inch wher Richmound stood, where Richard fell.
Besides, what of his knowlidge hee can say
Hee had authentike notice from the play
Which I might guess by mustringe vp the Ghosts
And pollicies not incident to Hosts,
But cheifly by that one perspicuous thinge &:/ 🜍

Where hee mistooke a Player for a King   350
For when hee would haue say'd King Richard died
And cald a horse, a horse hee Burbidge crye'd
How ere his talke, his company pleasd vs well
His mare went truer then his Cro<?>nacle
And euen for conscience sake vnspurd, vn beaten

Neweaten: ✲   Brought vs six miles, and turnd tayle at <u>Neweaten</u>
    From thence to <u>Couentrie</u> where wee scarce dine

Couentrie: Only our stomakes warmd with zeale and wine
And then from thence, as if wee were predestind forth

Killingworth ✲   Like Lot from Zodam fly to <u>Killingworth</u>.   360
The Keeper of the Castle was from home
So that halfe day wee lost, yet when wee come
An Host receiud vs there, wee'l nere deny him
My Lord of Leisters Man, the Parson by him;
Who had no other proofe to testifie,
He serud that earle, but age and bauderye;
   A way for shame, why should fowre miles diuide
Warwike and vs? they that haue horses ride.
A short myle from the towne an humble shrine
At foote of <u>an high Rock</u> consists, In signe   370
Of Guy and his de<u>uotions</u>, who there stands
Ougly and huge; more then a man on's hands.
His Helmett steele, his gorgett <u>ma</u>le, his sheild
Brass, made the Chappell fearefull as a feild.
And let this answere all the Popes complaints,
Wee sett vp Gyants, though wee pull downe Saints.
Beyond this in the roade-way as wee went

Guys Cliff:./ ✲   <u>A pillar stands</u>, where this Colossus lent.
Where hee would sigh, and Loue, and for hearts ease
Oft time write verses. (some say) such as these. <)>.   380
No other hinderance now but wee may pass
Cleare to our Inn. O <u>there an Hostis</u> was

Whose ribs are   To whome the Castle and the <u>Dunn Cow</u> are
in ye Castle :} ✲   Sights after dinner, shee is morninge ware.
Her whole behauiour borrowde was & mixt
Halfe-foole, halfe-Puppett and her pace betwixt
Meas<u>ure and</u> Iigg. her curtsey was an honor
Her gate as if her neighbour had out gone her.
Shee was bardd vp in whale bone bones, wch leese
None of the whales length for they reach her knees.   390
Off with her head, and then shee hath a middle
As her wast stands, shee lookes like the new fiddle
The fauorite-Theorbo, truth to tell yee
Whose necke and throte are deeper then then the belly: &

---

352 and 367] Modern pencil notations, right margin, not transcribed: *X*. **366 *bauderye*]** *y* overwrites *i*.

Haue you seene Monkeys chain'd about the loynes?
Or pottle potts with rings ? iust so shee ioynes
Herselfe to geather a dressinge shee doth loue
In a small print below, and text aboue.
What though her name be King? yet tis no treason
Nor breach of Statute, to inquire the reason   *400*
Of her brancht Ruff, a Cubett euery poke
I seeme to wound her, but shee strooke the stroke
At our departure: and our worshipps there
Paid for our titles deepe as any wheare
Though Beedles and Professors, both haue done,
Yet euery Inn claimes augmentation.

Warwike Castle: } ⊛ Please you walke out and see <u>the Castle? come</u>
The owner saith, it is a Schollers home.
A place of strength and health, in the same Fort
You would conceiue a Castle and a Courte.   *410*
The Orchards, Gardens, Riuer, and the aire
Doe with the trenches, rampeeres walls compare
It seemes nor Art, nor force can intercept it
As if a Louer built, a Souldier kept it
Vp to the Towre though it be steepe and high
Wee doe not climbe but walke, and though the eye
Seeme to bee weary yet our feete are still
In the same posture cousend vp the Hill.
And thus the workemans Art deceiues our sence

Sᵣ Francis Grivell: } Makeinge those rounds of Pleasure, a defence;   *420*
As wee descend the <u>Lord of all this fame</u>
The honorable Chauncellor towards vs came
Aboue the Hill there blew a gentle breath
Yet now wee feele a sweeter gale beneath
The praise and welcome of this Knight did make
The seate more elegant; euery woord hee spake
Was wine and Musicke, which hee did expose
To vs, if all our art could censure those.
   With him there was a Prelate by his place

Archdeacon Burton } ⊛ <u>Arch-deacon</u> to the Bishop by his face   *430*
A greater man, for that did counterfett
Lord Abbot of some couent standinge yett.
A corpulent relique, marie and t'is sinn
Some puritan getts not that face calld in
Amongst leane Breathren it may scandall bring
Who seeke for paritye in euery thinge.
For vs let him enioy yᵗ wᶜʰ God sends
Plenty of flesh, of liuinge, and of frinds.

Our returne to Flower ⊛ }   Imagine now vs ambling downe the streete
Circlinge in Flowre, and makeinge both ends meete.   *440*

---

421 (left margin) *Grivell*] *i* overwrites *e.*

Where wee far'd well fowre dayes and did complaine,
Like haruest folkes of wether and the raine;
And on the feast of Bartholomew wee trie
What Reuells that S^t keepes at <u>Banburie</u>.
I'th name of God Amen. first to begin

Ban:
At the signe of y^e
  Alter-stone ⊛

The Alter was translated to an Inn
Wee lodged in a <u>Chappell by the signe</u>
But in a Bankroote Tauerne by our wine.
Besides, Our horses vsage made vs thinke

Which serue for
troughs ⊛ **}**

Twas still a Church, for they in <u>Coffins drinke</u>.   450
As if twere congruous that those auncients ly
Close by those Alters in whose faith they dye;
Now you beleeue the Church hath good varietye
Of monuments when Inns haue such satietie;
But nothinge less, there's no inscription there

Ban: Church:

But the Church wardens names of the last yeere,
Insteede of Saints in windowes and in walls
Here buketts hange, and there a Cobwebb falls.
Would you not sweare they Loue Antiquitie
Who rush the Quire for perpetuitye?   460
Whilst all the other pauement and the flower
Are supplicant to the suruayers power.
Of the high-wayes, that hee would grauell keepe
For else in winter sure that will bee deepe.

The Lecturer ⊛

If not for God, for M^r <u>Wheatly's</u> sake
Leuell the walkes, what if these pitfalls make
Him spraine a lecture, or misplace a ioynt.
In his longe prayer or his fi<u>ue</u>tinth poynt.
Thinke you the Dawes or Stares can sett him right?
Surely this sinn vppon your heads <u>will</u> light.   <u>must</u>   470
And say beloued what vnchristian charme
Is this ? you haue not lefte a legg nor arme
Of an Apostle; think you, were they whole
That they would rise at last, assume a soule?
If not tis plaine, all the Idolatrie
Lyes in your folly, not Imagene.
Tis well the pinacles are fallen in twaine
For now the Deuill should hee tempt againe,
Hath no aduantage of a place so high.
Fooles, hee can dash you from your Gallerie   480
Where all your medlie meete, and doe-compare
Not what you learne, but who is longest there.
The Puritane, the Anabaptist, Brownist
Like a grandsallet: Tinkers what a Towne i'st?

The Crosses at Ban:

The <u>Crosses alsoe</u> like old stumpes of trees
Or stooles for horsemen that haue feeble knees
Carrie no heads aboue ground, they which tell. & ⸙

469 *or*] *o overwrites* a.

That Crist hath nere descended into Hell
But to the Graue; his picture buried haue
In a farr deeper dungion then a graue   *490*
That is descended to endure what paines
The Deuill can thinke, or such disciples braines
No more my greife in such prophane abuses
Good whipps make better verses then the Muses.
A way and looke not backe a way whilst yet
The Church is standing. whilst the benefitt
Of seeinge it remaines. Ere long you shall
Haue that rac't downe, and cald Apocriphall
And in some Barne here cited many an Author
Kate Stubbs, Anne Askew, or the Ladies daughter.   *500*
Which shall bee vrg'd for Fathers. stopp disdaine
When Oxfoord once appeares. Satyre refraine
    Neighbour how hath our anger thus out gon' vs
Is not St Giles-es this? and that St. Iohns?
Wee are returnd, but iust with so much ore
As Rawleigh from his voayge, and no more:.

---

[26]

On the death of S^r: W: R:.
Great heart, who taught thee so to dye?
    Death yeeldinge thee the victorye?
    When tookst thou leaue of life? If there,
        How couldst thou bee soe free from feare?
But sure thou didst, and quit the state
        Of flesh and blood before that fate
    Else what a miracle is wrought?
    I saw in euery standerby. <P>
    Pale Death, life only in thy eye:
    The Legacie thou gaust vs then   *10*
        Wee'le sue for when thou diest agen.
    Farewell, Truth shall this glory say
        Wee died, thou only liu'dst that day:./

26.1 (Left margin)] Modern pencil notation: *Ralegh.*

[27]

An Elegie vppon the worshipfull his deceased }
   Scholmaster Mr Richard Lucey : }

Stop the first Mouer pure intelligence
Of yeeres, Months, weekes, dayes make no pretence
Stand like the sluggish earth Inferiour Rounds
Forgett your Easterne and your Westerne bounds
Vp Night from Hell and wage the worlds last warrs
Pull downe the Sunn extinguish all the starrs
Contract the rarer Elementall fier
And hurle it to the Sea nere to expire
And both to Chaos: fire, aire, water, earth
Bee as you were before Your God wrought birth   10
A iumbled mass of things, that seemd not soe
A some thinge-nothinge what I doe not know
Or if this may not bee performd, Oh turne
Mee Ioue to Dust to couer the Lou'd vrne
Of my dead Master grant this benefitt
T'was my first matter change mee into it
It shall bee soe, seale vp these twins of light
My all enuyinge eyes saue Death, wisht night
And then thy Cyclop fabricated armes
Strike mee to earth. Ioue sound thy hot'st allar'ms   20
Of Thunder, know I nought at all feare thee
But that thou wilt not condescend to mee.
Sisters why doe you thus prolong my thred
Cutt all at once no numen dare forbid
Vulcan make Kniues may cut ye Center through
Beginninge at the surface, and vnto
The fatall Female Trinitie commend them
Or so I dye I care not though thou lend them
For I must hasten soone an airie poste
To ouertake dead Lucies reuerend ghoste.   30
Mee thinkes I see the blest Elisian feilds
And all the semor shade him reuerence yeelde
See how the Christall streames couch in their bankes
To see his locks surpass theirs yet with thankes
They swell againe as knowinge that the Godds
Haue put betweene them such perspicuous odds
And now they runaway disparingly
Weepinge cause they must want his company
Thither I'le hasten for mee thinkes hee stayes
To bee conductor to mee in those waies   40
Which hee pursues, I come, I come great shade
Now I am almost of thy substance made : /verte &:

Charon saist I'm no Ghoste whose funerall rites
Are finisht, why? goe thither none but sprites
Come bury mee aliue then some kinde hande
Gape any Earth I haue my length in Land
But O I heare him speake, O blessed breath
Dost thou instruct mee as in life in De<?>ath?
Must I not bee ore hasty with the fates?
Doe they ore'looke forth best our mortall states.   50
Thankes snow-white-head pardon You Gods supreame
I now retracte enlightend by the beame
Of tryinge knowlidge a more easie meane
Shall bringe mee to him, then those passions cleane
Hath now forsaken mee, Im'e turnd all Doue
Want only place in the Elizion Groue
Where when I come Ioue graunt I may but rest
Ons hand sometimes or on his Laureat crest
Blest was thou London when thy walls within them
Had such a Father as hee was to win them   60
That were degenerate from faire vertues stocke
And at so rare a Dietie did mocke.
Blest was the Man, the Doctrine that hee taught
And all the hearers who his meaning soughte.
Yett is hee dead, Noe hee liues in the mindes
Of all, and in Heauens Penetrall assign'd
To bee his quiett recess from the world
Tennis-ball-like in the airy concaue hurlde.
O how Propheticke was his name in this
Fortune or Fate imposd it not a miss   70
Hee did descend from Lucies auncient line
And now in Heauen shall neuer leaue to shine
Ancient say'd I? nay ancientest et I may
Of all good things as ancient as the day
New-struck from Chaos & vnprisninge Night
The first thinge God calls good of all was light
And truly was hee light whose opening speech
A thousand thousand in his dayes did teach
The labourd wisdome of humanitye
Subordinate to high Diuinety.   80
Wherefore for iust deserte abeene hee might
Our Pospherous our Sone our Euen light.
For puritye of life hee nere did varie
Otherwise then a Lampe of the Sanctuarie
A mutuall Loue as life hee prosecuted

43 Ghoste] the e is imperfectly formed.

Or heauen, vnto his meanes his almes hee suted.
So that I dare behould to say thus much
Hee gaue more almes the Auarice could grutch
But leaue wee him within his quiett vrne
Where nought molests him, and this last returne   90
Though Lucie in the darke earths bowells lye
Yet Lucie shines aboue the spangled skies :   W: H:

[28]

An Elegie on the Lady

Deere losse to tell the world I greiue were true
  But that were to bewaile my selfe not you:
That were to cry out helpe for my affaires
  For which not Publike thought nor priuate cares,
Noe when thy Fate I publish amongst men
  I should haue power to write with ye states pen
I should in naminge thee force publike teares
  And make mens eies pay ransome for their eares:
First thy whole life was a short feast of witt
  And Death the attendant which did waite on it.   10
To both Mankinde doth owe devotion ample
  To that their first, to this their last example.
And though it were Pride enough (with them whose fame
  And vertue nothinge but an empty Name)
That thou wert highly borne, which no man doubts
  And soe might's swathe <u>base deeds in noble Clouts</u>.
Yet thou thy selfe in tytles didst not shroude,
  And beeinge Noble, wast not ffoole nor Prowde.
And now when Youth was ripe, when now ye sute
  Of all the longinge Court was for thy frute   20
How wisely didst thou chouse fowre blessed eies
  The Kinge and thine had taught thee to be wise:
Did not the best of men the Virgin giue
  Into his hand by which himselfe did liue
Nor didst thou 2 yeeres after talke of force
  O Lady-like make suite for a deuorce;
Who when your owne wild lust was falsely spent
  Cry out my Lord my L^d: is impotent
Nor hast thou in his Nuptiall armes enioyde
  Barren embraces but werst girld and boy'd.   30
Twice pretty-ons thrice worthier were their worth
  Might shee but bringe them vp that brought them forth:

Shee would haue taught you by a thousand streames
  Her blood runs in your manners not your vaines
That glorie is a lye state a great sport
  And Cuntrie sicknesse aboue health at Court,
O what a want of her loose Gallants haue
  Since shee hath chanell her window for a graue.
From whence shee wont to dart out witt soe fast,
  And stick them in their Coaches as they past,   40
Who now shall make well colourd vice looke pale,
  Or a colour'd Meteor with her eies exhale
Or talke him into nothinge, who now shall dare
  Tell barren braines they dwell in fertile hayre?
Who now shall keepe old Countesses in awe,
  And by tart similies repentance drawe
From those, whom Prechers had giuen ore? euen such
  Whome Sermons could not reach her arrowes touch.
Here after fooles shall prosper with applause
  And wise men sinke and no man aske the cause.   50
Hee of fowre score 3 night-caps and 2 haires
  Shall marrie her of Twenty and gett heires
Which shall bee thought his owne, & none shall say
  But ti's a wondrousse blessinge, and hee may
Now (which is more you pittie) many a Knight
  Who can doe more then quarell lesse then fight
Shall chouse his weapon, ground, drawe, second thither
  Put vp his sword, and not belaught at neither.
O thou deform'ed, vnwomanly disease
  That plowst vp flesh and blood and y^u sowest pease   60
And brau'st such prints on beauty if thou come
  As clouted shoes doe on a floore of loome,
Thou that of faces honicombes dust make
  And of 2 brests 2 collanders; forsake
Thy deadly trade, thou now art rich giue ore
  And let our curses call thee forth no more,
Or if thou needes wilt magnifie thy power
  Goe where thou art inuoked euery houre
they name   Amongst the gamsters where thy name the tricke
thee thick }   At the last maine, or last pockey nicke :. /   70

---

52 **heires**] e overwrites a. 53 **none**] o overwrites an unreadable letter.

Gett thee a lodginge neere thy Clyen'd Dice
  There thou shalt practice oñ, more then one vice.
Ther's where with all to entertaine the Poxe,
  Ther's more then reason, thers rime to ye Boxe.
Thou who hast such superfluous store of game
  Why struckst thou one whose ruin is thy shame.
O thou hast murtherd, where thou shouldst haue kist
  And wher thy shott was needfull thou hast mist
Thou shouldst haue chosen out some homely face
  Wher thy ill fauourd kindenesse might add grace.   80
That men might say how beautious once was shee
  O what a peece ere shee was seizd by thee
Thou shouldst haue wrought on some such Ladyes mould
  That nere did Loue her Lord nor neuer could
Vntill shee were deform'd, thy Tyranny
  Were thou with in the rules of Charitie.
But vppon one whose beauty was aboue
  All sort of Art, whose Loue was more then Loue
On her to fixe this vgly Countefeite
  Was te Erect a Pyramis of Iet   90
And put out fier, to didge a turfe from Hell
  And place it where a blessed soule should dwell,
A soule which in the bodye would not stay
  When twas no more a bodye nor good clay
But a huge vlcer, O thou heauenly race
  Thou soule y^t shunst the infection of thy case
Thy house thy Prison, pure soule spotless faire
  Rest where no heate, nor could, nor compound aire
Rest in that Cuntrie, and enioye that ease,
  Which thy fraile flesh denyde, & her disease:.   100

[29]

Goe Soule the bodies guest	Tell Age it daily wasteth
Vppon a thankelesse arrante	Tell honour how it alters
Feare not to touch the best	Tell beauty how it blasteth
The Truth shall bee thy warrant	Tell fauour how it faulters 40
Goe since thou needs must dye	And if they dare reply
And giue them all the lye.	Feare not to say they lye:

Say to the Court it glowes,	Tell Phisicke of her bouldnesse,
And shines like rotten wood	Tell skill it is pᵣuention
Say to the Church it shows	Tell Charitye of coldnesse
W‸ʰat's good, but doth no good 10	Tell Law it is contention
If Court or Church reply	And if they make reply
Then giue them both the lye:	Then answere them they lye:

Tell Potentates they Lyne	Tell Fortune of her blindnesse,
Aidinge but others actions	Tell Nature of decay 50
Not lou'd except they giue	Tell frindship of vnkindenesse,
Not strong but by their factions	Tell Iustice of delay
If Potentates reply	And if they dare reply
Giue Potentates the lye:	Then giue them all the lye:.

Tell men of high condition	Tell Arts they haue no soundness
That rule affaires of state 20	But varie by esteeminge
Their purpose is Ambition	Tell Schooles they want profoundness
Their practise only hate	And stand too much on seeminge
And if they once reply	If Arts and Schooles reply
Then giue them all the lye.	Giue Arts & Schooles yᵉ lye: 60

Tell those yᵗ braue it most,	Tell Faith i'ts fled yᵉ Citie
They begge for more by spendinge	Tell how yᵉ Cuntrie erreth
Who in their greatest cost	Tell manhood shakes for pittye
Speake nothinge but com̃endinge	Tell vertue lest pᵣferreth
And if they make reply	And if they dare replye
Then bouldly say they lye: 30	Spare not to say they lye:

Tell Zeale it wants Deuotion	Soe when thou hast (as I
Tell Loue it is but Lust	Commaunde thee) done blabbinge
Tell Tyme it is but Motion	Although to giue the Lye
Tell flesh it is but Dust	Deserues no less then sta<u>binge</u> 70
And bid them not reply	Yet stabb at thee yᵗ will
For thou must giue yᵉ Lye:	Noe stab yᵉ soule can kill:.

Finis:.

---

10 What's] *h* is superscripted above *a*; caret is between *w* and *a*. **57 profoundness**] Tilde through *p* abbreviates *ro*. **63/64 Tell/Tell**] Modern pencil notation: Commas are added after both words; they are not transcribed. **68 Commaunde**] Modern pencil notation: final *d* added in manuscript, but is not transcribed. (Below left column)]: Modern pencil notation: *Sylvester* (see notes).

43

[30]

A Paradox in praise of a painted fface:./

Not kisse? By Loue I must and͢ ↑make↓ impession
As long as Cupid dares to hould his session
Vppon my flush of blood, our kisses shall
Oute minuite Tyme, and with out number fall
Doe not I know these bales of blushinge redde
That on thy<t> cheekes thus amorously are spreed
Thy snowey necke those veines vppon thy browe
That with their Azure crinkelinge sweetely bowe
Are artfull borrow'd, and no more thine owne
Then chaines that on St Georges day are showne   10
Are proper to their wearers; yet for this
I Idoll thee, and begge a curteous kisse.
Giue mee a face thas is as full of lyes
As Gypsies or your runinge Lotteries
The <fucos> &↑[?]↓ paint that on thy face
Thy cuninge hand doth lay to add more grace
Deceiue mee with such pleasinge fraude, that I
Finde in thy Art what can in Nature lye.
Much like a Painter that vppon some wall
On which the cadent Sunbeames ought do fall   20
Paints with such art a guilded Butterfly
That silly maydens with slow mou'd fingers trye
To catch it, and then blush at their mistake
Yet of this painted fly, most reck'ninge make
Such is our state, since which wee looke vppon
Is nought but colour and proportion
Giue mee a face: ——
As Gypsies & ——
That is more falce and more sophisticate
Then are Saints reliques, or a man of state   30
Yet such beinge glazed by the slight of Arte
Gaines admiration; wins many a harte
Put case there bee a difference in the mould
Yet may thy Venus bee more choise and boulde
A deerer treasure often tymes wee see
Rich Candean wines in wooden bowles to bee.
The odoriferous Ciuett doth not lye
Within the Muscatts nose, or eare, or eye.

1 make] Ink of the superscription is lighter; it was probably added at a later time. **6 thy**] *y* overwrites *a*; *t* deleted. Holgate first wrote *that*. **15 &**] Unreadable word is superscribed above ampersand; vertical line appears as indicated.

But in a b$_\wedge$^{a}ser place, for prudent Nature
In drawing vp of various formes and stature   40
Giues from the curious shop of her large tresure
To faire parts comlinesse, to baser pleasure.
The fairest flower which on the spring doth growe
Is not soe much for vse as for the showe;
As Lillies Hyacinth the gorgeous birth
Of all pyde flowers they dyaper the earth
Please more with their discoloured purple traine
Then holsome potherbs which for vse remaine.
Should I a goulden speckled Serpent kisse
Because the colour which hee weares is his.   50
A perfum'd Cordouant who will not weare
Because its sent is borrowd other where,
The clothes and vestments which grace vs all
Are not our owne but aduentitiall:.
Tyme ryfles natures beauty, but sly arte,
repaires by cuninge that decayinge parte
Fills here a wrinklinge and there purles <?> a vayne
And with a cuninge hand runs ore againe
The breaches dinted in by the Arme of Tyme
To make deformitye to bee more crime.   60
As when great men are grypt by sickness hand
Industrious Physicke pregnantly doth stand
To patch vp fowle diseases & doth striue
To keepe their totteringe carcases aliue.
Beauty a Candle is with euery puffe
Blowne out, and leaues nought but a stinkinge snuffe
To fill our nostrells with, this bouldly thinke
The purest candle giues the greatest stinke:.
As your pure foode and cleanest nutriment,
Yeelds the most hott, and most strong excrement.   70
Why hange wee then on things so apt to varye,
So fleetinge, brittle, and so tempararie,
That Agues, Cough's, the tooth-ake or Caterr
Slight touches of diseases spoyle and marre.
But when old age their beauty hath in chace
And plows vp furrows in their once smoothe face.

39 baser] *a* superscripted between *b* and *s*; the caret is subscripted.

Then they become forsaken and doe showe
Like stately Abbies ruin'd long agoe.
Loue graunt mee then a reparable face
Which, whilst their colours are can want no grace.   80
Pigmalions painted statue I could Loue
If it were warme, safte, and could but moue:./

---

[31]

<u>Radneys verses before hee kild himselfe</u> //
What shall I doe that am vndone?
  Wher shall I fly my selfe to shun?
Ay mee my selfe myselfe must kill
  And yet I dye against my will.

In starry Letters I behould
  My Death is in the heauens enrould
There finde I writ in skies aboue
  That I poore I must dye for Loue

Twas not my Loue deseru'd to dye,
  O no, I was vnworthy I.   10
I for her Loue should not haue dyde
  But that I had no worth beside.

Ay mee, that Loue such woe procures,
  For with out her no life endures.
I for her vertues doe her serue,
  Doth such a Loue a death deserue?

---

[32]

    Of Man:.
What is our Life? a play of passion,
  Our mirth the Musicke of diuision.
Our Mothers wombes the tyringe houses bee
  Where wee are drest for Tyms short Comedie
The Earth the Stage, Heauen the spectator is   5
  Who still doth note who ere doth act amiss
Our graues that hide vs from the whitling sunne
  Are but drawne Curtaines when the play is done:

[33]

On Samburne the Shreife of Oxfoord: A: Dī:: 1609

Fye Schollers, fye, haue you such thirsty soules
  To swill, quaffe, and carrowse in Samburnes bowles
Tell mee madd youngsters, what doe you beleeue
  It cost good Samburne nothinge to bee Shreife
To maintaine soe many capps, so many feathers
  To spend soe many beeues, soe many weathers.
Againe, is Mault soe cheape this pinchinge yeere
  That you should make such hauocke of his beere,
I feare you are soe many that you make
  Many o'fs men turn Tapsters for your sakes.   10
And that when hee euen at the bench doth sitt
  You slice his meate from off his borrowed spitt
You keepe such hurley burley that it passes
  Ingurgitateinge some whole halfe glasses.
And some of you are growne so fine
  Or else soe sawcye, that you call for wyne
As if the Shreife had put such men in trust
  As durst to draw more wyne then needs they must:
In fayth, infaith, it is not well my Masters
  Nor fitt that you should bee the Shreifs wyne tasters.   20
It is enough beinge such gurmundizers
  To make the Shreifs hence forth turne very misers.
Or to remoue the Syze for Oxfoords great disgrace
  To Henly on the Thames, or some such place.
Hee neuer had complain'ed, had it but only beene,
  A pretty ferkin, or some small Kilderken;
But when a Barrell daily is drunke oute,
  My Masters then t'is tyme to looke about.
Is this incredible I tell you noe.
  My Lord high Chauncellor is in-formed soe   30
And oh, would not all the bread in towne,
  Be enough to draw yᵉ Shreife his liquour downe.
But hee in hampers must from home it bringe
  O most prodigious, o most monstrous thinge.
Tell mee, vppon so many home-made loues of bredd
  How long might hee, and his two men haue fedd
Hee did not doubt but the poore should haue bin fedde,
  With some sweete morsells, of his broken bredd :/

---

23 *disgrace*] *s* overwrites an unreadable letter.

But when that they (poore soules) for bredd did call
  Answere was made, the Schollers eate vp all.   40
And when of broken beere, they crau'd a suppe
  Answere was made, the Schollers drunke all vpp.
Now Oxfoord Shreife is growne at last soe wise
    To repriue his beere vntill the next Assyse:
It was not strong, it was not very headdy
    The Crowners quest had found it dedd already.
But yet I know not how they change the name
    Cut did the deed, but long tayle beares the blame:}:

[34]

On a Sigh

Goe thou gentle whistlinge winde
  Beare this sigh, and if thou finde
Wher my cruell fier doth rest
  Cast it in her snowey brest
The sweete kisses though shalt gaine
  Will reward thee for thy payne
Tast her lipps and thē confesse
  If Arabia doth possesse
Or the Hibla honied hill
  Sweet like those that thence distill   10
Haueinge gott so rich a fee
  Doe a nother boone for mee;
Thou canst with thy powrefull blast
  Heate a pace and coole as fast
Then for pittie either stirr
  Vp thy fier, or Loue in her
That alike both flames may shine
  Or shee quite extinguish mine :./

[35]

/D. C: to yᵉ M: B:/   1622:.
When I can pay my Parents, or my Kinge;
  For Life, or Peace, or any deerer thinge;
Then (Deerest Lord) expect my debt to you,
  Shall bee as truly payd as it is due:
But as no other price or recompence   5
  Serues them but Loue, and my obedience;
So nothinge serues my Lord, but whats aboue
  All reach of hand, t'is vertue, and my Loue:.

[36]

M^r: B. H: verses to the Q: A: as shee past by Oxfoord

I did vnto Apollo goe	While they thus wrangled St Ebbs stood
T'intreate him that my Muse might flow	Behind, yet thought her selfe as good
O no (quoth hee) tis well fore seene,	But beinge impotent and poore
Youle giue the verses to the Queene	Shee spake little, but thought ye more 40
When I confess too much I aske	And haueinge on but bad apparrell
Apollos less then such a taske.	Shee backd St Aldate in ye quarrell

This answere to my Muse did bringe	And to St Thomas shee did send
Small hope shee ere shold raise her winge	As thinkinge him her neighboring frind
Yet need and chance did make her try	Whose dwellinge is out in ye west
A more auspicious Diety 10	But hee cryd still t'is but a iest
And callinge on great Brittans Anne	And though ye Messenger sayd noe
Loe straight way thus my Muse began:.	Yet hee would beleeue t'was soe

When Oxfoord Cittie had heard say	Indeede the cause was this I thinke
Our gratious Queene would pass y^t way.	His waters did begin to sinke 50
To woodstoke Towne to meete ye King	Or other wise as all men know't
Whose safe returne great ioy did bring	Hee quickly might haue com by Boat
A dreadfull quarrellinge befell	And thus by his distrust wee see
A mong the Saints y^t there did dwell	Hee lost ye strife & victorye

The cause was this Who should take place	St Marten then on tiptoe stood,
And for them all salute her grace 20	And sayd hee would first loose his blod
One pleaded worth, another Age	Before that hee in highest place .
Till they fell all into a rage	Would suffer such a low disgrace
And this they stroue with much a doe	Besides hee was ye Cities heart
The Saints haue their Ambition too.	And all must now speake from y^t part: 60

Because shee came in by ye South	But then St Michaell did reply
St Friswid sayd shee'd bee y^er mouth	And his weake reason straight deny
And since shee had a gallant gate	For by that reason (All saints) might
There shee would speake in ample state	Pretend sayd hee a nearer right
Nay (quoth St Aldate) I deny	But if a woman ought to speake
A woman leaue, & I stand-by: 30	All to St Maries right was weake

Peace quoth St Friswid don't you grudg	Sad Maudlin was a bout to speake
I hould a man no womans Iudg	But her discourse St Iohns did breake
A womans tongue must needs doe well	And Michaell then againe began
B'ing y^t their in they most excell.	And vowd hee should not bee ye man 70
Fy (quoth St Aldate) how shee prates	For t'was vnfill her grace should stay
Why I can likewise show Broad-gates	Before his gate in such fowle way.

1-6 (left margin, not transcribed)] Modern note: *Barton Holyday Ma Oxon 1615.*

Sᵗ Giles likewise would faine haue come
But yᵗ hee then lay lame at home
Yet in this hope did rest content
The Queene would see him as shee went
For thus hee sayd you now shall see
I beinge lame shee'l come to mee

But Maudlin here went on againe,
And now began to pleade amaine.   80
Full loath shee was after much toyle
To loose her cause & take yᵉ foyle
Shee sayd shee ought first to bee plac'd
Shee beinge wᵗʰ two Tempels grac'd

Why quoth Sᵗ Peter if yᵗ stand
The question's ended out of hand
For both in East & West all see
Two auncient Temples rear'd to mee
With yoʳ two shrines I'me well acquainted
But by yoʳ leaue yᵉˢ are not Sainted.   90

But when Sᵗ Peter was so hott
And had almost yᵉ honor gott
Sᵗ Marye sayd nay thinke not soe
To worth then number more wee owe
And thinke not then yᵗ I will loose
What you should let mee leaue or choose.

At this iust Truth they all did faint
And yeelded to this greatest Saint
Only St: Friswid shee pretended
A stronger right & thus defended,   100
To mee belongs a double due
Mine is mine owne & Christ-Church too.

Besides sayd shee my cost did reare
That Temple wᶜʰ my name doth beare
When you for yours may others thanke
And this strooke Ev'n Sᵗ Marye blanke
Wherfore Sᵗ Friswid had the honour
And all the Sᵗˢ did waite vppon her.

There is a nother Sᵗ doth dwell
With out a name by Holy-well   110
Who for his office coming after
The Sᵗˢ fell all into a laughter
And plainely sayd such prid to quell
It was not Sᵗ, but Holy-well

And after this came good Sᵗ Clement
A gentle Sᵗ & nothinge vehement
Who seeinge yᵗ hee came to late
Scarce greiud a iot, but went home strait
Yet sayd good Sᵗˢ don't bo'ast nor cracke
Clement may see yᵉ Q: come backe.   120

But now Oh heare a Vilde intent
Of wicked cuninge to preuent
Eu'n all these Sᵗˢ, oh deede mor dire
Enough to moue e'un Sᵗˢ to ire.
And but yᵗ great witts are ore seene
It doubtless had effected beene

A Fryer whom men Bacon call
His studdy stands wᵗʰ out yᵉ wall
Vppon yᵉ south bridge of yᵉ Cittie
Would faine haue shewd him selfe too witty
Hee wᵗʰ a speech yᵉ Q: would greete   131
Before yᵗ shee yᵉ Sᵗˢ should meete:.

But ca‸ᵘse yᵗ his deeke knowlidge lay
In a farr different kinde of way
Hee went to raise a sweet ton'gd spiritt
By which hee would pure phrase inheritt
And in his arched Tower hee spent
Some time to finish his intent.

But see yᵉ will of heauen yᵉ while
This crafty clarke went to beguile   140
Eu'n all the Sᵗˢ, the Q: pass'd by
And so deceiu'd his subtilty
And thus yᵉ Deuill & yᵉ Fryer
Were lefte to geither full of ire.

---

89 *acquainted*] *ted* is inserted below because of space limitation). **98 *greatest*]** *s* overwrites *r, t* is added. Holgate first wrote *greater*, then *greatest*. **118 *iot*]** line drawn through *o*.

From thence her gace did pass on straight
And quickly came to Friswids gate
Who with ye Saints did there attend
With words more honest then well pend
And thus her eloquence but weake
With trembling lips began to speake   *150*

Our ioyfull bells distinctly ringe
Long liue o^r Prince, o^r Q: o^r King
Which three by Oxford now do meet
That each may other sweetly greet   *160*
And recompence one weary night
Of absence with a treble light

Haile Brittans Empress whos full glory
Exceeds the name of Fame & Story
And since so great a Prince is come
The verie walls are striken dumbe
For else their stony mouts would cry
We're crowned with a Diety

Thus from o^r heuv'n you three dispece
The vigor of yor influence
And thus doth Oxfoord as ye heart
Bestow its blood on euery part:
But while wee now enioy yor sight
Wee doe forgett yor iourney quite:

The speech here ended and all parted
    With teares they were so tender hearted   *170*
And now great Queene amongst all these
Accept a Muse that striues to please:
Or if your grace less like the Theame
Suppose 'twas but a Schollers dreame:.

[37]

To Q: A most excellent Maiestie
And is this all? will you but thus passe by?
The'rs too much state of witt in Maiestye
Absence endeede doth more inflame desire:
But can it raise in vs a greater fier?
Rest heere (Great Queene) the Muses all intreate,
Our flame is growne too wild, lessen our heate.
Yet can your p^rsence doe it? doe but try
Your preasence how-so'ere shall satisfie.
But as a rarer gemme concealed lyes
In some rich cabinet from vulgar eis   *10*
Or when 'tis seene, is not exposd for gaine
But wonder, and is straight wrapt-vp againe
Soe does appeare your luster? which gies by
Soe soone it doth a maze, and greiue the eye:

37 (left margin, title)] Modern pencil notation: *Queen Anne of Denmark.*

The Northerne people are more blest then wee
Vnder the Hyperborean Axeltree.
For though for halfe the yeere they see no day
Yet when it comes, it halfe the yeere doth stay.
Your Chariott is too swifte and will not stand
And your disdainefull steed's know no coaund   20
For if they knew but yours: yours is so milde,
Doubtlesse they would not shew themselues so wilde.
Orpheus his Musicke mou'd the horrid wood
And Rocks: Oh had wee such a power, so good
Wee would captiue your wheeles & make them runne
But equall with the Chariott of the sunne.
They should stay heere a day you are a light
And wee ordaind to dispell our night.
Yet when the greater lights of heauen doe ioyne
Only the greatest light doth seeme to shine   30
But our three lights now meetinge, helpe each other
The Queene doth helpe the King: ye Prince his Mother.
There does appeare in heauen a goodly streete
By which the Auncients sayd the Godds did meete
Ti's cal'd the milky way, and as they sayd
Of many lesser lights of Heauen is made
This is that milkey way, wee those small fiers
Which whiles you pass, doth burne wth pure desires.
  O oftner grace vs, with yo<r>ur earthly Diety
    And oftner Wee'l express our gratefull piety :   40

[38]

<u>An Elegie vppon the death of Q: A:</u>
You towringe spiritts whose Art-irradiate eyne,
Dare peirce the conclaue of the sacred Trine
Who ere the ffatall Crimtts 'gan to appeare
Durst calculate the fate of all the yeare,
Yet when this sinne-fed flame a Month had blaz'd
True Pythagorians silent stood and gazd,
Stand euer mute, Heauens Oracle hath spoke
Shees dead breake yours, our Iacobs staffe is broke
Cease Prodegies? the supreame cause is knowne
Brytans bright Anne aboue the starrs is flowne   10
T'was starlike shott (braue Comet) faire & right
Thast hitt the heart of Albion clefte her white
Giue mee the Cataracks of Septemfluous Nile
Fo're flow each Angle of this spatious Ile.
Oh for a Spring-tyde, for a flood of verse
To beare that Arke vp of our hopes her hearse
Dissolue the eternall fountaines of my head
To Brinye Oceans; the Ocean Queene is dead,
Phebe the faire from whose rayes diuine
Th'inferior <u>lights</u> deriue'd their fainter shine / <u>starrs</u>   20
Phebe is sett that Orient font of light
Sad accident in the Occident of night
Cloudes wrap me rounde, Cymerian shades appeare
Beauty is vanisht from our Hemisphere.
You hardy Danes whose steele invred hand
(You vaunt) subdu'de, but could not keepe this Land
Resigne your Trophies to this Conqueringe Dame
Whose eye (like Cæsar) sawe, and ouercame
Sweete harmelesse power our Annuall teares shall show
How thou subdu'dst all hearts, yet nere strack'st blowe   30
Great Empress, great in spiritt great in blood
And (with agrandiz'd) all thy greatnes good
What obelisque of honour shall I raise?
Vppon what Pyramide ingraue thy praise

---

3 Crimtts] The transcriber probably intended *Comets*, or a variation of that word. A dot appears between *m* and *t*, but there is no lowercase *i*. **25 Danes**] Uppercase *D* overwrites two letters: the second is an *a*, the first is unreadable.

Ile carue it on our Marble hearts, for thee
Bee all hearts turnd to one firme Niobe.
Weepe Ladyes (You are tender-hearted) weepe
I must haue hearts obdurd, fit to keepe
And hugge a passion; Teares (your teares alone)
Can soften heard hearts, or make softe ons stone.   40
T'is not my Taske, t'aduance her princely birth
Her match (wher'in shees matcht by none on earth)
Her issue Royall by which heauen linkt line
She'xtends her Armes from sea to Sea true vine
Nor dare I ransacke that rich Cabinett
Her soule; which vertues round like Ges besett
My flagginge Muse dares not approch y^t Sphere
Diuiner heraldrye must blaze her there
As shee to vsward shind bee wee content
To forme her as shee informd our continent.   50
If hospitable vertue were a praise
In these our Frenchfyde and Quelq*ue* chose dayes
I'de say shee kept a great house, kept it 'ope
Her selfe a Recluse, gaue her house large scope
Too practique haue her Oeconomiks beene
Too much a house doue for so great a Queene
In Court what euer potent faction stroue
Our Iuno still shee reconsil'd our Ioue
It was her greatest glory all her pride
To plume the deplumde, helpe ye helpless side.   60
Aske the sadd househould, who of all indeede
Haue the inmost cause to mourne without a weede.
Theyle weepe this Truth, ye grand spight wch enerud them
Had quite disrank't them, had not shee preserud them
Who neuer knew that power dispence with lawes
Who patronize <def> a truth defectiue cause
Who neuer vs'd her greatness but to saue
And (but to giue) shee had no minde to haue
Monopolies the banes of publique state
Shee prosecuted not but with her hate   70
Indeede her vertues and her faire deserts
Monopolized had her seruants hearts :. /

---

50 *forme her*] *e* clearly added to end of *forme*, then the *e* extends to the *h* of *her*. **52 *Quelque*]** *ue* is abbreviated. **58 *Our*]** *O* overwrites an uppercase *I*. **58 *reconsil'd*]** *s* overwrites *c*.

Soe free from passions and affections thrall
Soe gratious of access, so sweete to all
Soe milde in her dispatches, that they say
Shee neuer sent a Sutor sad a-way;
For Chastitie the Turtle viduate
Was nere more constant to her absent mate
A flame <u>enyud</u> about her heart was found
Soe knew shee how to want how to abound   80
Her Zeale to Heauen shee thus exemplifide
Her Chamber Chappell-like was Templifide
But shee is dead! Dye then Pathetique Muse
No; heare the life of Passion but renewes,
Court, Citie, Cuntrie, Knights & Dames shall weepe
By vollies; yet my Passion Muse must sleepe
None but a Lullabie of Princes grones
Shall singe a requiem to my Cygnean tones
You loftie Cedars on whose tops sublime
Sitts Maiestie and primes her plumes decline   90
Drop and bedewe this Thunder-shiuer'd Palme
With sacred teares her royall corpes embalme.
Weepe Charle-Maine Eliza let thy Rheine
With fileall teares inplunge thy Palatine
Heroicke Denmarke mourne, thy Sisters dead,
(Curst bee those Sisters that haue clipt her threade.)
France thou a Sister and a Queene hast lost
Bleede teares? that title, teares of blood haue cost
Howle thine owne loss, and ours Impious Spaine
Thy vast succrescent hopes in her lye slaine.   100
But oh my Soueraigne? an Eternall Tide
Of yeerely dewe alonge your cheekes must glide
The passions which your Passions shall aduance
Must draw all Brytane, Denmarke Spaine & Fraunce.
See how they drill, how euery Riuerlinge
Payes his sad tribute to the Ocean Kinge
Soe my braue bird in royall streames indude
Full gorg'de with Princely Passions, now be'mewde
Sleepe wayward Muse, and Princes cleare your eies
Shee is but changd; your Cinthia neuer dyes :. /

83 (exclamation mark)] Lower portion is a comma.

[39]

Verses made on Sʳ ff: B: when hee was
Lord Chancellor :

When you awake dull Bryttans and behould
What treasure you haue cast into this mould
Your Ignorance in pruninge of a State
You shall confess, and that your rashness hate.
For in a senseless furye you haue slaine
A man as farr beyound the spungie braine
Of Common knowlidge, as is heauen from Hell
And yet you tryumph thinke you haue done well.
O that yᵉ Monster-multitude should sitt
In seate of Iustice, Reason, Conscience witt   10
Nay in a Throne, a Spheare aboue th<u>em all</u>
For t'is a supreame power that can call
All these to barr, and with a frowning brow
Make Senators nay mighty Consulls bow
Bold Plebeans, the day will come I know,
When such a Cato, such a Cicero
Shall more worth, then the first borne bee,
Of all your Ancestors <u>and</u> posteritye.   or
But he'es not dead youle say, O but the soule,
Once checkt once contrould, that vsd' to controule   20
Coucheth her downy wings, and scornes to flye
At any game saue faire eternitye
Each spirit is retired to a roome
And made his liuinge body but a Tombe
On which such Epitaphs may well bee reade
As would the gazer strike with sorrow dead<e>.
O that I could but giue his worth a name
That if not you your sons might blush for shame.
Who in Arethmiticke hath greatest skill
His good parts cannot number, yet his ill   30
Cannot bee cald a number, since tis knowne
Hee had but few, that could bee cald his owne.
And those in other men euen in those times
Are often prais'd, and vertues cald, not crimes./

30 *His*] *s* overwrites an unreadable letter.   **32** *bee*] the second *e* overwrites an unreadable letter.

But as in purest things the smallest spott
Is sooner found then either staine or blott
In baser stuff, euen so his chaunce was such
To haue of faults to few, and worth too much
So by the brightness of his owne cleare light
The moates hee had lay open to each sight   40
If you would haue a man in all parts good
You must not haue him made of flesh & blood,
An Act of Parlament you first must settle
To force Dame N'ature worke on better mettle
Some faults hee had, noe more then serue to proue
Hee drew his life from Adam, not from Ioue
And these small faults in Nature fost offence
Like Moones in Armorie, made difference
Twixt him and Angells, beinge sure no other
Then markes to know him from their younger brother.   50
Such spotts remou'd (not to prophane) hee then
Might well bee cald a Demye-god, mongst men
A Diamond flawd, Saphyres or Rubyes staynd
But vnderwalue'd are not quite disdain'd.
Which by a foyle recouerd they then become
As worthy of esteeme, yeild no lesse some.
The Gardner findinge once a canker growne
~Vppon a tree that hee hath fruitfull knowne
~Rootes it not vp, but with a carefull hand
~Opens the roote, remoues the clay, or sand   60
~That causd this Cankor, or with cuninge Art
~Pares off some rine but coms not neere the heart.
~Only such trees the Axes edge endure
~As nere bare fruite, or else are past all cure.
~The prudent husband-man thrusts not his sheare
~Into the corne because some weeds are there.
~But takes his hooke, and gently as hee may,
~Walkes through the feild, and cutts the weeds away.
~A house of many romes one may commaund
~But yet it still requires many a hand   70
~To keepe it cleane, and if some filth bee found
~Crept in by negligence, i'st cast to the ground?

58-72 (initial line markers)] Small dash-like marks are subscripted as indicated. **65 *sheare*]** first *e* overwrites *a*.

Fie noe, but first the supreame owner come
Examines euery office, vie'ws the romes
Makes them bee cleased with some certaine paine
Commaunds they neuer bee found so againe,
The Temple else should ouer throwne haue been
Because soe many Brookers were there in
The Arke had sunke, and perisht in ye flood
Because some Beasts crept in that were not good   80
Adam had with a Thunder boult been strooke
Because from Eue the goulden Apple hee tooke.
But should the maker of mankinde doe soe
Who should write man, who should to mans state gro^w
Shall hee bee put then to the'xtremes of law
Because his Conscience had a little flaw?
Will you want Conscience cleane, because that hee
Stubled or slipt, but in a small degree.
No. first looke backe to all your owne past Acts
Then pass your Censure, punish all the facts   90
By him committed, then I'le sweare hee shall
Confess that you are vpright Chanc'lers all.
And for the time to come with all his might
Striue to out doe you all in doeinge right.
Oh would his predecessor's Ghost appeare
And tell you how his Master lefte the chaire
How euery feather that hee sate vppon
Infectious was, how that ther was no stone
Of which some contract was not made to fright
The fatherless, and widdowe from their right.   100
Noe stoole, no bench, noe rush, noe boord, on which
The poore man was not sould vnto the rich:
You would giue larger time, the roome to aire
And what you now call fowle you would thinke faire
T'is knowne hee gaind to keepe, this but to liue
Hee rob'd to purchase Lands, and this to giue.
And had this beene soe blest with his owne treasure
Hee would haue giuen much more, wth much more pleasure.
The nigh'ts great Lampe from the rich sea will take
To lend the thirsty land, and from each Lake.   110

                &

74 vie'ws] apostrophe appears over *w*. **75 cleased**] (see glossary notes).

That hath an overplus borrow a share
Not for her owne vse, but to repaire
The ruines of some parcht, and dryd 'vp hill:
So this inconstant Planet (for more ill
Enuy can't speake of him) tooke from some flood
Not for his owne vse, but for others good;
But such misfortune dog'd his honest will
That what hee tooke with wrong hee gaue as ill,
For those his bounty nurst, as some suppose
Not those hee iniurd, proud his greatest foes.   120
The foolish mothers from their wiser mates
Oft filch and steale, weaken their owne estates
To feede the humor of some wanton boy
They silly weomen hopeinge to haue ioye
Of this ranke plant when they are sapless growne
But seild or neuer hath it yet beene knowne
That pamperd youths gaue parents more releife
Then what encrea'sd their age with care & greife.
These ouersights of Nature former times
Haue rather pittied then condemd as crimes.   130
Then wher is Charitie become of late?
Is his place beg'd, her office giuen to hate?
Is there a patent giuen for her restraint?
Or Monoply gaind by false complaint?
If so, pursue the Patenters, for sure
False information did the writt procure.
The seale is Counterfeate, the refer^rers
Haue taken bribes, then first examine these
Restore faire Charitie to her place againe
Hee now that suffers will not then complaine   140
Sett her at Iustice seate, and let the poyse
By them directed bee, and not by noyse
Consider both his mul'ct and his offence
And you shall finde a mighty difference
Raze not a goodly buildinge for a toy
T'is better to repaire then to destroy
You will not bringe his ashes to the vrne
You'le doe as much, for hee himselfe will burne :. /

---

137 *referrers*] the r is superscripted as indicated, probably added after the word was written. There is no caret.

When hee but feeles his honour to retreate
Like a fowle cag'd, himselfe to death will beate,   150
And leaue the world when ther's no helpe at all
To sigh and greiue at his vntimely fall:. /
The skillfull Chirurgion Cutts not off a lie
Whilst there is hope; O deale so then with him
hee wants not fortitude, but can endure
cuttings Incissions; soe they promise cure
Nay more shew him but where the eye sore stands
and hee shall searcht and drest with his owne hands
would you Anotamize? would you desect
for your Experience? you may elect   160
out of the house wher you as Iudges sitt
diuers for Execution farr more fitt,
And if you finde a Monster ouer growne
With fowle Corruption, lett him be throwne
At Iustice feete, lett him bee sacrifizd
Let their bee new tortures, new plagues deuisde?
Such as may fright the liuinge from such crimes
And bee a president to after times.
Which long liude Records to ensuinge dayes
shall still proclaime to your eternall Prayse:.   ffinis

---

[40]

Muse gett thee to a Cell, and wont to singe
now mourne, nay now thy hands, thy heart now wring
and if perhaps thy eyes did euer weepe
now bleed and in eternall sorrow sleepe
O shee that was, and only was, is gon
and I that was but one, am lefte a lone
who saies, that I for things nere mine am sad
that was all mine which others neuer had
no sighs, no teares, no blood but mine was shed
for her that now must bless, an others bedd,   10
As fate bound mee, had fortune made mee free
none had had her but I, shee none but mee
O had not I bin swallowed vp <u>by</u> Night   :   with
before I saw the Sunn that glorious light
whose beames alone doe only comfort bringe
where I still weepe, had euer made mee singe
Now on a strange Hori^{z}son it doth rise
where all doe liue, and elce wher each thinge dyes :.   ffinis :

40.17 *Horizson*] z is superscripted as indicated. There is no caret.

[41]

Is shee not wondrous faire? O but I see
  Shee is soe much too sweet, to faire for mee,
That I forgett my flames, and a new fier,
  Hath taught mee not to Loue, but to admire
Iust like the Sunne me thinks I see her face
  Which I should gaze on still, but not embrace
For tis heauens pleasure sure shee should bee sent
  As pure to heauen againe as shee was lent
To vs, and bidds vs as wee hope for bliss
  Not to prophane her with a mortall kiss.   10
Then how could growes my Loue, and I how hott
  O, how I loue her how I loue her not.
  Soe doth my Ague Loue torment by turnes,
  Soe now it freezeth, now againe it burnes:.

[42]

Nor teares shall lessen greife, nor sighes impart
  Ease to my minde, or comfort to my heart.
The day to forced mirth I will dispose
  The night t'imbrace my woes without repose.
Nor shall the Balsome of a greiued minde
  A friend sweete councell bee for cure assignd
With him I will diuide all that I haue,
  Only my brest to greiue must bee my graue.
I shall endure more then a halfe yeere's night
  And see no day till thy eyes giue mee light.   10
If silence vnto words haue not an eye
  Vppon their winges sorrowe away will flye:

Page 60] The entire page is written in large letters. See commentary notes to HolM 42. **42.4** *without*] there is a slight space between *with* and *out*, possibly intended as two words. **42.10** *thy*] *h* overwrites an unreadable letter.

[43]

Blasted with sighes and surrounded with teares
  Hither I come to seeke the spring
And at mine eies and at mine eares
  Receiue such balme as els cures euery thinge,
But oh selfe traitor: I doe bring
  The spider Loue, which transubstantiats all
  And cannot conuert Manna into gall:
And that this place might troughly bee thought
    True Paradise: I haue the serpent brought:.

Twere holsomer for mee that Winter did   10
  Benight the glory of this place
And that a graue frost would forbidd
  These trees to laugh and mocke mee to my face.
  But I may not this disgrace
  Endure, nor leaue this garden, Loue, let mee
Some senceless part of this plot bee
Make mee a Mandrake, so I may grow heere
Or a stone fountaine weepinge out the yeere:

Hither with Cristall Vialls, Louers come
  And take my teares which are loues winde   20
And trye your Mistris teares at home
  For all are false which tast not iust like mine
  Alas hearts doe not in eyes shine.
Nor can you more iudge weomens hearts by teares
  Then by the shadowe which shee weares.
O peruerse sex, when none is true but shee
  Who's therfore true, because her truth kills mee:

[44]

Now thou hast lou'd mee one whole day,
  To morrow when thou leau'st, what wilt thou say?
Wilt thou then antidate some new made vow?
                          or say that now
Wee are not iust such persons as wee were
Or that Oaths made in reuerentiall feare
Of Loue, and his worth, any may forsweare:
Or as our true deaths, true mariages vntye.
  So Louers contracts, images of those   &:

43.11 *Benight*] e overwrites r. 43.12 *frost*] s appears more like an f. 43/44 (Left margin notes not transcribed, entire page)] Modern pencil notations: 43.2 *J. Donne*; 43.7 *can*; 43.8 *thoroughly*; 43.14 *that*; 43.17 *groan*; 43.20 *wine*; 44.3 *J.D.*

Binde but till sleepe, deat's Image, them vnloose   10
          or your owne, and to iustify
For haueinge purpos'd change, and falshood you
    Can haue no way but falshood to bee true.
Wayne Lunatike, against these scapes I could
    Dispute, and conquer if I would
        Which I abstaine to doe
For by to morrow I may thinke so too:. /

[45]

Goe, go, &:

 So, so, leaue off this last lamentinge kisse
Which sucks two soules and vapors both away
Turne thou Ghost that way, and let mee turne this
And let our soules benight our happy day
Wee ask't none leaue to Loue, nor will wee owe
 Any so cheape to death as sayinge goe:

Goe, and if that word haue quite killd thee
    Ease mee with death by biddinge mee goe too
Or if it hath, let my words worke on mee
    A iust office on a Murderer doe: 10
Except it bee to late to kill mee soe   I: D:
    Beinge double dead, goinge, & biddinge goe. /

[46]

I fixt mine eye on thine, and there
    Pittie my Picture burninge in thine eye
My Picture drown'd in a transparant teare
    When I looke lower I espye
Had'st the wicked skill
    By pictures made, and mard to kill
    How many wayes migh'ts thou performe thy will

But now I haue drunke thy sweetest teares
    And though thou powre more I'le depart
My picture vanished, vanish my feares   10
      That I can bee endamaged by thee
      Though thou retaine of mee
One Picture more, yet that will bee
      Beinge in thine owne heart from all Malice free:./

[47]

On his Mistris ⎫
Inconstancie ⎬
By S^r H: ⎫
Wotton: ⎬

O faithless world, and thy most faithles part,
        a womans heart.
The true shop of varietie wher sitts,
        nothing but fitts.
And feuers of desires, and pangs of Loue
        which toys remoue
Why was shee borne to please, or I to trust
        words writt in dust?
Suffringe her lookes to gouerne my despaire
        my paine for aire   10
And fruit of time rewarded with vntruth
        the foode of youth
Vntrue shee was, yet I beleeud her eyes
        (instructed spies.)
Till I was taught that Loue was but a schoole
        to breede a foole.
Or was it absence that did make her strange
        (base flower of change.
Or sought shee more then tryumphs of denyall
        to see a triall: 20
How far her smiles comaunded on her weaknes
        yeeld and confesse
Excuse not thy folly; nor her nature
        blush and endure.
As well thy shames as passions y^t were vaine
        and thinke thy gaine
To know that Loue lodg'd in a womans brest
        is but a guest:.

[48]

Why should not Pilgrims to thy body come
And Miracles bee wrought at thy poore tombe?
Thou like religious men while thou didst liue
And blinde obedience to thy will didst giue.
And though it cald thee from thy sleepe to play
To drinke, to whore, to fight thou didst obey
As they doe theire superiors, and not grudge
Nor euer mad'st thy feeble reason iudge.
This brought thee vnto prison, holes, to stocks
To beatings whippings, and the primatiue pox   10
So pure that no Phisitian could it doubt
To bee the slow, Sciatica, or Goute.

47.23 *Excuse*] Possible apostrophe appears before the word itself. **47** (left margin, not transcribed)] Modern notations in ink: **47.20:** *by* **47.21:** *make* **47.22:** *my* **47.24:** *no more* **47.25:** *but for cure* X; a second X in right margin.

To all the worldly persecution
That an afflicted member can put on
Thy strict obedience drew thee, yet thy minde
Apt to endure with patience would not finde
The way to prayer, but tooke the crosses sent
With resolution, and did not repent,
These were great symtomes of a Saint, but wee
Whilst some of thee leiud did heare and see   20
How many reliques thou didst leaue behinde
For holy men in after times to finde
In pispots, brothels, and thy barbers hand
Sufficient to conuent a Sauage land
Due feare that peece which came the graue vnto
  Is not enough a Miracle to doe:

[49]

Good Madam Fowler doe not trouble mee
  To write a Sonet in the praise of thee
  I dare not crosse wise nature soe to frame
  A sonnet where shee ment an Epegram
When nature made thy body, then shee thought
Of Epigrams, that I should make, and laught,
As many lims as shee did giue thee, iust
So many Epigrams I answere must,
And though thou thinkest and truly, that thou hast
Some lims about thee that are not mispla'st   10
Yet those few parts which thou beleiust are best
Are but good Epigrams again'st the rest:
And that thou mai'st perceiue thy fate to bee
Neuer to haue a Sonnet writ on thee
Thy mothers children were conceiued all
And borne in Epigrams originall
For at the gettinge of each child, thy Dam
Against her selfe conceiu'd an Epigram:

[50]

Oh doe not dye for I shall hate
  All weomen so when thou art gone
  That thee I shall not celebrate
  When I remember thou wast one

48.25 *peece*] Second *e* overwrites *a*. **49/50** Left margin, not transcribed, modern pencil notations] **49.5-7**: *Dr. Corbet or B. G.* **50.3**: *J. D.*

But yet thou canst not Dye I know
To leaue this world behinde is death
But when thou from the world would'st goe
The whole world vapo_∧^urs with thy breath.

Or when that thou the worlds soule goest
Yet stay too! t'is but thy carcase then   *10*
  The fairest weomen but thy ghost
  But corrupt wormes, the worthiest men

Wranglinge schooles wch serch what fier
Shall burne the world, but none the witt
Vnto this knowlidge to aspire
  That this her feuer might bee it:

And yet shee cannot wast by this
Nor long time beare this tormentinge wrong
For more corruption needfull is
  To fuell such a Feuer long: *20*

The burninge fitts but Meteors bee
Whose matter in thees soone is spent
Thy beautious parts all which are thee
  Are the vnchange able firmament:

Yet 'twas of my minde loosinge thee
Though yet in thee cannot perseuer
For I had rather owner bee
  Of thee one hower, then all else euer:.

[51]

D^r D: | When I dyed last, and (Deere) I dye
       As often as from thee I goe
       Though it bee _∧ ^{but} an howre a goe
       And louers howres bee full of eternity
         I can remember yet that I
       Some thinge did say and some thinge did bestow
         Though I bee dead which sent mee, I should bee
         Mine owne Executor and Legacie:

I heard mee say tell her anon
  That my selfe (that's you not I)   *10*
Did kill mee, and when I felt mee dye
  I bid mee send my heart when I was gon:
                        &   &

50.10 Left margin, not transcribed] Modern pencil notation: *It stay*. 50.13 (before **Wranglinge**)] Modern pencil notation: a circle. 50.22 *thees*] *es* overwrites a single *u*; the transcriber first wrote *thus*. 51.4 *of*] Modern pencil notation: the word is circled.

But I alas could there finde none
  When I had ript and searcht wher heart should lye
I kild m'gaine, that I who still was true
  In life, in my last will should couzen you:.

Yet I found somethinge like a heart
  But colours it and co^{r}uers had
It was not good, it was not bad
It was entire to none, and few had part   20
  As good as could bee made by Art
It seem'd; and therfore by our losses sad
I thought to send that heart in steede of mine,
  But oh no man could hould it for twas thine:.

[52]

Off on that
was betrayd   }
by a perfume: } }

Once, and but once found in thy Company
All thy suspected scapes are laydon mee
And as a theefe at barr is questiond there
By all the men that haue beene robd that yeere:
Soe am I by this traiterous meanes surprisd
By thy Hydroptique ffather Catechised
(Though hee hath oft sworne that hee would remoue
Thy beautyes beauty and hope ‸^{of} our Loue
Hope of his goods) if I with thee were seene
Yet close, and secret, as our Loues w' haue beene,   10
Though thy immortall Mother yet doth lye
Still buried in her bed, yet will not Dy,
Take this advantage to sleepe out day light
And watch thy entryes, and returnes all night
And when shee takes thy hand, and would seeme kinde
Doth search what rings, and arme letts shee can finde.
And kissinge notes the colour of thy face
And fearinge least thou art sowlne doth thee embrace
To try whether thou lounge, doth name strange meates,
And notes thy palmes, blushinge and thy sweates,   20
And politikely will to thee confesse
The sinns of her owne youthes ranke lustines.
Yet Loue did these sorceries remoue, and moue
Thee to gull thine owne Mother, for my Loue:

---

52 (left margin) **perfume**] A tilde through *p* abbreviates *er*. **52.10** (Left margin, modern pencil notation, not transcribed)] *J. D.*

Thy little brethren, which like fayrye spiritts
Oft skip into our chamber, those sweete nights
And kist and iugled on thy fathers knee
Were bribd next day to tell what they did see;
The grimme eight foote high, ironbound seruingman
That oft names God in Oathes, and only than   30
Hee that to barre the first gate, doth as wide
As the great Rhodian Colossus stride,
Which if in Hell, no other paines ther were,
Makes mee feare Hell, because hee must bee there.
Though by thy father hee were hyr'd for this
Could neuer witness, any touch or kisse.
But, oh too cõmon ill, I brought with mee
That which betrayd mee to my enemie.
A lowd Perfume, which at my entrance cryde
Euen at thy fathers nose: so wee were spyde.   40
When like a Tyrant Kinge that in his bedd
Smelt Gunpowder, the pale wretch shiuered:
Had it beene some bad smell, hee would haue thought
His owne feete or breath, that smell had wrought.
But as wee in an Ile imprisoned
Where Cattle only, and diuers doggs are bred
The pretious Vnicornes, strange, Monsters call
So thought hee good strange, y^t had none at all.
I taught my silkes their whistlinge to forbeare
Euen my opprest shooes dumbe, and speechles were   50
Only thou bitter sweete who I had layd
Next mee, mee trayterously betrayde
And vnsuspected hast vnuis<?>ibly
At once fled vnto him, and stayd with mee.
Base excrement of Earth, which dost confound
Sence from distinguishinge the sicke from sound
By thee the silly amorous sucks his death
By drawinge in a leaprous harlotts breath
By thee the greatest staine to mans estate
Falls on vs, to bee called effeminate   60
Though thou bee much loued in the Princes hall
These things that seeme exceede substantiall.
Gods when yee fum'd on Alters were pleas'd well
Because you were burnt, not that they like'd ye smell:

---

25 (Right margin, not transcribed)] Modern pencil notation: *sprights*. 47 **strange**] the word is followed by stray ink mark that resembles a comma. 51 (Right margin, not transcribed)] Modern pencil notation: *whom*.

Y'are loathsome all, beinge taken simply alone
Shall wee loue ill things ioynd and hate each one
If you were good your good would soone decay
And you are rare, that takes the good away
All my perfumes I giue most willingly
T'imbalme thy fathers course please him to dye :. /

[53]

In Obitum Ducis Leñoxiæ
Are all diseases dead, or will death say
Hee might not kill this Prince the common way?
It was e'vn'so, and time and Death conspir'd
To make his end, as was his life, admir'd;
The Commons were not summond now I see
Meerely to make Lawes but to mourne for thee:
Nor less then all the Bishopps might suffice
To waite vppon so great a Sacrifice
The Court the Altere was the waiters Peeres
The Mirhe and Frankincense great Cæsars teares.   10
A brauer offring with more pompe and state
Nor time, nor Death did euer celebrate.   &:

[54]

Epitaph
Steward by name, by office, by account,
amongst the iustest men: an heauenly writt
the day thou shouldst in earthly robes haue sitt
Did call thee vp vnto the holy mount.
Thy Robes are now transfigured white as snow   5
And shine in happie memorie here below,
The agonies of Death to thee were spard
Nothing is suddaine to a soule prepared . ////

[55]

Like to a thought slipt out of minde
    Or like good turnes done to the vnkinde
    Or like sweete Musicks sweetest close
    Or like a shew that by vs goes
    Or like a Knell that sadly ends
    Or like a Kiss that parteth friends

    Euen such is man whose scæne is done
    The Curtaines drawne and hee is gone
    The Thoughts passeth, good turnes not thought on,
    The note dyes, yᵉ shews forgotten   10
    The bell toules, frinds kiss & seauer
    And meete againe: but once dead neuer :. /

54.8 *soule*] *e* overwrites what is probably a second *l*.

[56]

Of Mans Life:
Like to the Damaske Rose you see,
Or like the Blossum on the Tree,
Or like the dainty flowre of May
Or like the Morninge to the day
Or like the Sunne or like ye shade
Or like the Gourd which Ionas had
  Euen such is man, whose threed is spunn
Drawne out, and cutt, and soe is dunn
The Rose witheres the Blossome blasteth
The flower fades the Morninge hasteth   *10*
The sunne setts the shadowe flyes,
The Gourd consumes, <u>and</u> man dyes:.   <u>So</u> /

[57]

I may forgett to eate, to Sleepe, to Drinke,
But when I doe forgett on thee, to thinke
Or haueing meanes omitt salutes to send
To thee my choicest and most valued friend
Or cease to Loue, to honour and admire
To keepe my vow, or from fast faith retire
(Then keepinge thine) which I no more did doubte
Then that poore soules in Hell would faine gett out
Know in such sinne, and silence I am nott
In Death, Loue, vows friendshippe and alls forgott,   *10*
But whiles that Nature lendeth life to mee
Or but one draine of breath I'le honour thee.
Soe rest assured, and when my hartstrings breake
Ile send a sigh that to thy soule shall speake
Such faithfull Language, such sincere intention
As neuer any mortall yett did mention.
      Till then I contemplate on thy perfection
      Trust in thy Loue, triumph in thy election

Space between poems] Poem entitled "Man's Life" written in the hand of John Wale, eighteenth-century owner of the miscellany, not transcribed. **57.17 *perfection*]** A tilde written through the *p* abbreviates *er*.

[58]

Written to a friend in the Lowe-Cuntries :
By: H: H:
When swifte report shall with her nimble winge
Bringe thee the newes of my imprisoninge
And hee that tells thee with a doutfull pause,
Guesses or sweares hee doth not know the cause,
Perhaps thoul't straight Imagine I am in
For Murder, theft, or some Veniall sinne,
For speakeinge treason (which the heauens forbid)
Or coyninge tokens as the Tinker did
But faith thou art deceiu'd, for I sweare, yett
I'me chargd with nothinge but a thing cald debt   10
Or owinge Money, and I am afraide
To owe as much more, ere this can bee payde
But that's all one: by this time thou hast sayd
Or Sworne thou'rt Sorrye faith I was betrayd
That vext mee worst, for otherwise I am
As merrie here as you at Rotterdam
And therefore bee not, Ile reserue thy sorrowe
Till I haue neede, and then of thee Ile borrowe
ffor liuing here, I tell thee I haue ends
I trie my Patience, and I trie my friends   20
And finde them both that for my durance here
The one can suffer, and the other beare : .

[59]

A Winters Entertainement at
Saxam written by : T: C:
Though frost and snowe lookes from mine eyes
That pleasure which with out dores lyes
Thy Orchards, Gardens, walkes that so
I might not all thy pleasures knowe.
Yet Saxam thou with in thy gate
Art of thy selfe so Delicate
So full of Natiue sweete^s <ness> that blesse
Thy Roofe with inward happines
As neither from nor to thy store
Winter takes ought, orr springe adds more,   10
The cold and frozen aire had starud
Much poore, vnless by thee preseru'd
Whose prayers haue made thy table blest
With plentie farre aboue the rest,
The season hardly did afforde

Course cates vnto thy Neighbours boarde
Yet thou hadst dainties, as the skey
Had only bin thy volery,
Or else the birds fearinge the snowe
Might to a nother deluge growe   *20*
The Partridge, Phesant, and the Larke
Flew to thy house as to the Arke,
The willinge Ox of himselfe came
Home to the slaughter with ye Lambe,
And euery beast did thither bringe
Himselfe to bee an offeringe.
The scaly heard more pleasure tooke
Bath'd in thy dish, then in the brooke
Water, Earth, Aire, did all conspire,
To pay their tributes to thy fire   *30*
Whose cherishinge flames themselues deuide
In euery roome where they deride,
The could, and night a broad, whilst they,
With in like Suns made endless day
These cheerefull beames send forth their light
To all that wander in the night
And seeme to becken from a loofe
The weary Pilgrim to thy roofe
Wher if refresht hee will a way
He's fairely welcome, but if stay   *40*
for more, which hee shall harty finde
Both from the Master and the hinde,
His hartie welcome each man there
Stampt on his chere full brow doth were
Hers none obserues, muchless repines
How often this man Sups, or dines
Thou hast no Porters att thy Doore
T'xamine or keepe backe the Poore
Nor bolts, nor Locks, thy Gates haue bin
Made only to Lett strangerrs in   *50*
Vntaught to shutt they doe not feare
To stand wide open all the yeare
Careless who enters, for they knowe
Thou neuer didst deserue a fooe
And as for Theeues thy bounties such
They cannot steale thou giust so much :.

---

[60]

Vppon the Queene of Bohemia ✿

You meaner beauties of the night
 That poorely satisfie our eies
 More knowne by number then by light
 Like comon people of the skies
         What are you when the <u>Moone</u> shall rise.   <u>Sunne</u>

You violetts which first appeare
 By your purple Mantles knowne
 Like proud virgins of the yeere
 As if the spring were all your owne
         What are you when the Rose is blowne.   10

You merry chanters of the wood
 that Carroll out Dame natures layes
 thinkinge your Passions vnderstood
 by weake accents: whats your praise
         When Philomel her voice shall rayse.

So when my Princess shall bee seene
 In comlines of face and minde
 by vertue first then choise a Queene
 tell mee if shee be not Designe
         the praise and glory of her kinde :.   20
                         Finis   🦂   🦂

[61]

An Epitaph on the Lady May and Natt: feild ye player:.

It is the faire and pleasaunt Month of May,
That clads the feild in all his rich a<r>ray.
Adorning him with c_∧ ^u<l>lo<?>rs better dyde,
Then any Prince can weare or any Bride,
But May is almost spent, the feild growes Dun   5
With gazing too much on his Mays hott Sun,
Yet if milde Zepherus please not his heate to allay
Poore feild must burne euen in the midst of May :.

60.4 *skies*] *i* overwrites *y*. Holgate first wrote *sky*. **60.5 *Moone, Sunn*]** Underlining is written in ink. *Sunn* corrects *Monne*, probably corrected by Holgate. **60** (left margin)] Unreadable notation in modern pencil, probably erased. **61** (below poem)] Modern pencil notation: *Natt. Field was a player in the Kings Company with Shakespeare.*

73

Holgate Miscellany 71

[62]

D^r: C: of Oxfoord beinge kept out of
   the Haule on St George his day
   { at Windsor by the Guard, }
   { wrote the verses vnto }
    the Lord Mordent :.

My Lord, I doe confess at the first newes
Of your returne towards home, I did refuse
To visitt you, for feare the Northerne winde
Had pierct into your maners, and your minde.
ffor feare you might want memorie to forgett
Some Arts of Scotland, which might hunt you yett;
But when I thought you neere, And when I harde
You were at woodstocke seene well sund and ayr'd,
That your Contagion in you now was spent,
And you were Iust, Lord Mordent as you went.   10
I then resolu'd to come, and did not doubt
To be in season, though the Buck was out,
Windsor the place, The Day was holy Roode
St George my Muse, for bee it vnderstoode,
For all St George more early in the yeere
Broke fast, and eate a bitt, yett hee Dinde here,
And though in Aprill in Red Inke it shine
Know 'twas September made him red with wine.
To this good sport rode I, as being allowed
To see the Kinge and Cry him in the Crowde   20
And at all Sollem meetings haue the grace
To thrust, and to be trod on by my place,
Where when I come, I saw the Church besett
With tumults, as had all the brethren mett
To heare some silent Teacher of that Quarter
Enueigh against the order of the Garter.
And iustly might the weake bee greu'd & wronge
Because the Garter praies in a strange tongue,
And doth retaine traditions yett of ffrance
In an old Hony Soit Qui Mal y Pense   30
When learne you Knights that Order y^t haue tane
That all beside the Buckle is Prophane,
But there was no such doctrine now at stake
No starud Precessian from the Pulpit spake
And yet the Church was full, all sorts of Men
Religions, Sexes, Ages, were there then
Whilst hee that keepes the Quire togeither Lockes
Papists, and Puritans, the Pope, and knocks

Title (Left margin, not transcribed)] Modern pencil notation: *Corbet.* **4 pierct**] *i* overwrites *e*; *e* overwrites *i*. Holgate first wrote *peirct*, then changed it to *pierct*.

Which made some wise ons, feare that loue our Nation
This mixture would begett   A Tolleration,   40
Or that Religion should vinted bee
When they sta'yd seruice, thears the Letanie
But no such hast, thy daies deuotion lies
Not in the hearts of men, but in the eies,
Hee that doth see St George, heares him aright
For hee loues not to parley, but to fight.
Amongst this Audience my Lord stood : I :
Well edefied as any that stood by:
And know how many leggs a Knight letts falle
Betwixt the Kinge, the offringe, and his stale.   50
Aske mee but of their robes, I shall relate
The colour, the fashion, and the state;
I saw the Procession with out the doore
What the poore Knights, and what the Prebends wore
All this my Neighbours, that were by mee tooke
Who diu'd but to the garment and the looke,
But I saw more, and though I haue their fate
In place and fauour, yet I want their pate
Mee thought I then did those first ages know   59
Which brought foorth Knights so Armd; and Looking so
Who ⊛ would maintaine their oth and binde their word   ⊛
Then saw I George new sainted when such Preists
Wore him not only on, but in their breasts
Oft did I wish that Day with open vow
O that my Cuntrie were in danger now
And t'was not treason: who could feare to Dye
When hee was sure his rescue is soe nie,
And here I might a iust digression make
Whilst of some 4 particular Knights I spake   70
To whom I owe my thankes, but twer not best
By praisinge 2 or 3 to accuse the rest
Nor can I sing that order, or those men
That are aboue the Masterye of my Pen
And priuate singers may not blush: those things
Whose Author Princes are whose patterns Kings
Wherfore vnburnt, I will refraine that fire
Least daringe such a Theame I should aspire
'T'include my 'Kinge, and Prince, and so rehearse
Names fitter for my Prayer, then my verse.   80
Hee that will speake of Princes, let him vse
More Grace then witt, Know Go'ds aboue thy Muse
Nor more of Councell: Harke the Trumpets sound
And the graue Organs with the Antheam drownd
The Church hath sayd Amen to all their rights
And now the Troian horse letts loose his Knights:

With these two seales An Alter, and a Word.

61] Underlined. 62] The line is written vertically as indicated.

The Tryumph moues O what could added bee
Saue your accesse to that Solemnitie
Which I expect and doubt not but to seet
When, the Kings fauour and your worth shall meete, 90
I thinke the Robes, would now become you soe
Sᵗ George himselfe would scarce his owne Knights knowe
From the Lord Mordent: pardon mee that preach
A Doctrine which King Iames can only teach
To whom I leaue you, who alone hath right
To make Knights, Lords, and then a Lord a Knight.
Imagine now the sceane lies in the Haule
for at high Noone wee are <u>Recusant</u> all
The Church is empty as their bellies were
Of the Spectators which had languisht there. 100
And now the fauoretts of the Clarke o'th Check
Who oft yaun'd and stretcht forth many a necke
Twixt Noone and Morninge, the Dull feeders, on
fresh Patience, and reasons of the Sonne.
They who had liu'd i'th Hall Seauen houres at least
As if twere An araingment not a feast
And looke so like the Hangings they stand neere
Non' could discerne which the true Pictures were
These now shall bee refresht while the bould Drum
Strikes vp his frolicke, throw the Hall they cum 110
Here might I end (my Lord) and here subscribe
Your honors to his powre. But o what Bribe
What feare, or mulckt can make my Muse refraine
When shee is vrgd, of Nature and disdaine.
Not all the Guard can hould mee I must write
Though they should sweare, and Lay how they would fight
If I proceede: Nay though their Captaine say
Hold him, or else you shall not eate to Day,
The goodly Yeomen must not scape my Penn
I'ts Diner time, and I must speake of men. 120
So to the Hall made I with Little Care
To praise the dishes, or to tast yᵉ fare
Much less t'indanger the lest tart or pie
By any waiter there: stolne, and sett by,
But to compute the value of the meate
Which was for glory; not for hunger eate.
Nor did I farr stand backe, who past before
The presence of the Priuie Chamber doore.
But wooe is mee, the Guarde those men of warr
Who but two weapons vse: Beefe, and the Barr; 130
Began to gripe mee, knowing not in truth
That I had sung Iohn Dory in my Youth.

108 *Non'*] Apostrophe could be a comma after *And*, line 7.

Or that I knew the day when I could chaunt
Cheuy, and Arthur, and the seige of Gaunt,
And though those bee the Vertues which must trie
Who is most worthy of this Curtesie
They profited mee Nothinge: for no Notes
Will moue them now, they are deafe in their new Coates;
Wherfore on mee afresh they fall and show
themselues more Actiue then before: as though   140
They had some wager layd and did contend
Who should abase mee farthest at Armes end.
One I remember with grisled beard
And better growne then then any of the heard,
Who were hee well examind and made looke
His name in his owne parish and Church booke,
Could hardly proue his Chistendome, and yett
It seemes hee had two names for there were sett
On a white Canuass dublett which hee wore
Two Capitall Letters of a name before   150
Letters belike which hee had spud or spilt
When the great Bumbard leak't or was a Tilt
This Ironside takes mee, and suddenly
Hurles mee by Iudgment of the standers by
Some Twelue foote by the square, takes mee againe
Out throws it halfe a Barr, and thus wee twaine
At this hott exercise an houre had spent
Hee the feirce Agent, I the Instrument,
My man began to rage, but I cryd pease
When hee is dry, or hungry, hee will cease,   160
Peace for the Lords sake Nicholas least hee take vs
And vse vs both as Hercules did Cacus.
And now I breath my Lord; Now haue I time
To tell the Cause and to confess the Crime
I was in black A Scholler straight they guest
In deed I Coller for it, at the least.
I spake them faire, desird to see the Haule
And gaue them Reasons for it, this was all.
By which I learne it is a maine offence
So neere the Clarke o'th Check t'vtter sence.   170
Talke of your Embleames, Masters & relate
How Esope hath it and how Alciat
The Cocke and Pearle the dunghill & the gemm
This passeth all to talke sence among them.
Much more good seruice was committed yet
Which I in such a tumult must forgett
But shall I smother that prodigious fitt
Which past in Cleane inuention and pure witt

As thus: A nimble Knaue though some thing fatt,
Strikes at my head and fairely steales my hatt.   180
Another breakes a Iest: Well winsor well,
What will insue therof I cannot tell.
When they spend witt: (serue God) yet twas not much
Although the Clamor and applaus were such
As when St Arche, or Garret doth prouoke them
And with wide Laughter, and a cheat lofe choke them,
What was the Iest; doe yee aske; I dare repeate it
And put it home before you shall intreate it.
Hee cald mee Bloxfoord Man, Confess I must
Twas bitter, and it greiud mee in a thrust,   190
That most vngratefull: word Bloxfoord to heare
Of him whose breath stunke yett of Oxfoord beere
But let it pass, for I haue now past throw
Their Holberds, and worse weapons, their teeth too,
And of a worthy officer was inuited
To Dine: who, all their rudeness hath requited
Where wee had mearth and meate, and a large borde
furnisht with all the Kitchen could afforde.
But to conclude, to wipe of from before yee
All this wich is no better then a story.   200
Had this affront bin done mee by Commaunde
Of Noble ffenton, had their Captaines hand
Directed them to this. I should beleeue
I had no cause to Iest: but much to greiue
Or had discerninge Pembrooke seene this don
And thought it well bestowd, I would haue runn
Wher no good man had dwelt, nor Learnd, should fly
Wher no disease would keepe mee company.
Where it should bee p^rferment to endure
To teach a schoole or else to serue a Cure   210
But as it stands the Persons and the Cause
Consider well: my Manners <wee> and their Lawes
T'is no affliction to mee, for euen thus
St Paule hath fought with Beasts at Ephesus
And I at winsor, Let this comfort then
Rest with all Able and deseruinge men
Hee that will please the Guarde and not prouoke
Court witts must sell his Learning; buy a cloke
Masques   ffor at all feasts and Mas^q<?>^ues the doome hath been
A man thrust out, and A gay cloke Lett in :
                                    Finis

[63]

Of the Springe:
Now that the Winters gone, the Earth hath lost
Her snowey Robes; and now no more the ffrost
Candies the grasse; nor casts an Icie Creame
Vppon the siluer lake, or Cristall streame,
But the warme Sunn thaws the benummed earth
And makes it tender; giues a second birth,
To the dedd swallow, wake in hollow tree
The drowsy Cuckoo, and the humble Bee,
Now do a Quire of chirpinge Minstrills bringe
In triumph to the worlde, the youthfull Springe   10
The vallies, hills, and woods in rich aray
Welcome the cominge of the longd for May
Now all things smile, only my Loue doth Lowre
Nor hath the scaldinge Nooneday Sun the powre,
To melt that Marble Ice which still doth houlde
Her heate Congealede, and make her pittie Colde
The Oxe which lately did for shelter fly
Into the Stall, doth now securely lye
In open feild; and Loue no more is made
By the fire side, but in the coulder shade,   20
Amintas now doth with his Phillis sleepe
Vnder a Sicamoure, and all things keepe
Time with season, only shee doth carry
Iune in her eyes; in her heart Ianuary:.
                              finis :

[64]

An Elegie on the death of the Lady Marcum:.
As vnthrifts groane in straw for their pawnd beds
As weomen weepe for their lost Mayden heads
When both are with out hope of remedie
Such an vntimely greife I haue for thee
I neuer saw thy face, nor did my harte
Vrge forth mine eyes vnto it whilst thou werte
But beinge Lifted hence that which to thee
Was deaths sad darte, prou'de Cupids shaft to mee
Who ere thought mee so foolish that the force
Of a report could make mee Loue a Coarse   10
Know hee that when with this I do compare,
The Loue I doe a liuing woman beare
I finde my selfe most happy now I knowe
Where I can finde my Mistriss, and can goe
Vnto her trimde bed, and lifte a way
Her grass greene mantle, and her sheete display

And touch her Naked, and (though enuious) would
In which shee lyes vncouerd, moyste and colde).
Striue to corrupt her. Shee will not abide,
With any Arte her blemishes to hide,   20
As many Liuing doe, and know they neede
Yett cannot they in sweetnes, her exceede
But make a stinke, with all their Arte and kill
Which the Phisitions warrant with a Bill,
Nor at her doore do heapes of Coaches stay
Footmen and Midwiues to bar vp my way
Nor neede shee any Maide, or Page to keepe
To knock mee early from my golden sleepe
With Letters that her honour all is gon
If I not right her cause, (on such a one)   30
Her heart is not so heard, to make mee pay
For euery Kiss a Supper, and a Play
<u>Nor will shee euer open her pure lipps</u> ❀
❀ To bringe a plague, a ffamine or the Sworde
Vppon the Land, though shee would keepe her worde.
Yett ere an howre bee past in some new vaine
Breake'em, and Sweare em, Ouer all againe,
Pardon that with thy blest Memorye
I mingle mine owne former miserie   40
Yet dare I not excuse the fate that brought
These crosses on mee, for then euery thought
That tended to my Loue was blacke and fowle
Now all as pure as a new baptized soule
For I protest, for all that I can see
I would not lye one night in bed with thee,
Nor am I Ielous, but could well abide
My foe to lye in quiett by her side
You wormes my Arriualls, while shee was aliue
How many thousands were there y^t did striue   50
To haue your freedome, for their sakes forbeare
Vnseemely hooles in her softe skin to weare
But if you must, as what wormes can abstane
To taste her tender body, yett refraine
With your disordered eatings to deface her
But feede your selues as you may most grace her
Fleet through her eare tipes se you worke a paire
Of hooles which as ye Moist cold ayre
Turnes into water may the dropps take
And in her eares a paire of Iewells make: 60

To vtter these enough to drowne o^r shippe . ❀

33] Underlined. 34] Written vertically as indicated, including flowers as page decorations.

That once vppon her bosome make your feast
Wher in a Crosse, graue Iesus: on her brest.
Haue you not yet enough of that white skin
The touch wher of in times past would haue beene
Enough to haue ransomde many a thousande soule
Captiud to Loue) If not then vpward rowle
Your Little bodys, wher I would you haue
This Epitaph vppon her fore head graue.
   Liuinge shee was Younge, faire and full of witt
   Dead, All her faults were in her forehead writt:.   70
                  F: B:

[65]

Seeinge

From such a face whose excellence
May captiue my Soueraignes sence
and make him Phebus like his Throne
resigne to some young Phayetone
whose skilless and vnsteady hande
may proue the ruine of a Lande
Vnless great Ioue downe from the skie
beholdinge Earths Calamitie
Strike with his hand that cannot erre
the proud vsurpinge Charioter   10
and cure (though Phæbus greiue) our woe
from such a face that can worke soe
wher so'ere thou hast a beeinge
Blesse my Soueraigne and his seeinge:

Hearinge:

From Iests Prophane, from flattringe tongues
from bawdy tales, from beastly songs
from after supper sutes that feare
A Parlament or Councells eare
from Spanish Treates that may wounde
our Cuntries <u>good</u>, the Gospell sound   peace   20
from Iobs falce friends that would intice
my Soueraigne from Heauens Paradize
from Prophett such: as Ahabbs were
whose flatteringe Sooth my Soueraignes eare
his frounes more then his makers fearinge
Bless my Soueraigne and his hearinge :.

Tastinge:

From all fruite that is forbidden
such for which Old Eue was Chidden
from the Labourers sweate and toyle
from the poore widdows meale, and oyle   30

64.70 (Below poem, center)] Modern pencil notation, not transcribed: *Beaumont.* **65.2-3** (Right margin)] Modern pencil notation, not transcribed: *B. J's version is on p. 82.*

from blood of innocents oft wrang_∧^led
from their estates and from those strangled
from the Candied poysond baytes
Of Iesuites and their deceites
Italian salletts, Romish Drugges
the Milke of Babells proud whores Dugges
from wine that can destroye the braine
and from the dangerous figg of Spaine
from all banquetts and all feastinge
Bless my Soueraingne and his tastinge: 40

Feelinge ⊛	From pricke of Conscience such a stinge

From pricke of Conscience such a stinge
as slayes the Soule, Heauens bless my Kinge
from a title as may with drawe
his minde from equitye or Lawe
from such a smooth and beardless chinn
as may prouoke or tempt to sinne:
from such a hand whose moyst palme may
my Soueraigne leade out of the way
from things polluted and vncleane
from all thats beastly and obsceane   50
from what may sett his soule a reelinge
Blesse my Soueraigne and his feelinge:

Smellinge ⊛

Where Mirrhe, and ffrankencence is throwne
On Alters built to Gods vnknowen
O Lett my Soueraigne neuer smell
such dam'd perfumes are fitt for Hell
Let not such sents his Nostrills staine
from smells that poyson may the braine
Heauens still preserue him. next I craue
thou wilt bee pleasd good God to saue   60
my Soueraigne from a Gānymeade
whose whorish breath hath power to leade
his Eccellence which way it list
O let such lipps bee neuer kist
from a breath soe farr excellinge
Bless my Soueraigne and his smellinge

Seeinge: ⊛

And now Iust God I humbly pray
that thou wilt take the filme away
which keepes my Soueraignes eies from vewinge

Hearinge: ⊛

those things y^t will bee our vndoinge   70
then let him heare good God the sounds
as well of men as of his houndes

Tastinge: ⊛

giue him a taste and timely too
of what his Subiects vndergoe

Feelinge: ⊛

giue him a feelinge of their wooes
and then no doubt his royall Nose

Smellinge: ⊛

will quickly smell those Rascalls forth
whose blacke deedes haue Eclipst his worth
they tooke and scurgde, for their offences
Heauen bless my Soueraigne and his Sences:.   ffinis

31 *wrangled*] A caret is subscripted after *g*; the *l* is superscripted above as a correction.

[66]

Seeinge: ✲	From a Gypsie in the morninge	
	Or a paire of sqint eyes turninge,	
	from the Gobblinge and the Spector	
	Or a drunkard though with Nector	
	from a woman true to no man	
	and is vgly besides Common	
	A Smocke rampant and that itches	
	to bee puttinge on the britches	
	where so ere they haue their beeinge	
	Bless my Soueraigne and his seeinge.	10

Hearinge: ✲	From a foole and serious toyes	
	from a Lawer three parts Noyse	
	from Impertinence like a Drume	
	beate at Dinner in his roome	
	from a tongue with out a file	
	heape of Phrases and no stile	
	from a fiddell out of tune	
	as the Cookow is in Iune	
	from the Candle stickes of Loughburie	
	and the Lowde pure wiues of Banburie	20
	only time and yeares out wearinge	
	Bless my Soueraigne and his hearinge.	

Smellinge	From a strowlinge Tinkers sheete	
	and a paire of Carriers feete	
	from a Lady that doth breathe	
	worse aboue then vnderneath	
	from the dyett and the knowledge	
	of the Students in Beares Colledge	
	from Tobacco with the tipe	
	of the Deuills glister-pipe	30
	or a stinke all stinkes excellinge	
	A Fishmongers Dwellinge	
	Bless my Soueraigne and his smellinge	

Tastinge ✲	From an Oyster and fryde fish	
	A Sowes Baby in a dish	
	Or any portion of a Swine	
	from badd Venson and worse wine	
	Linge, what Cooke so ere it boyle	
	though with musterd sauc'd and oul<?>e	
	or what else would keepe man fastinge	40
	Bless my Soueraigne and his tastinge:	

Feelinge ✲	Both from Birdlime and from pitch	
	from a Doxie and her itch	
	from the brissles of a hogge	
	from the Ring-worme of a dogge	
	from the Courtship of a bryer	
	from St Anthonies old fire	
	from a neild or a thorne	
	i'th bedd at e'uen or morne	

66.2–3 (Right margin)] Modern pencil notation, not transcribed: *From B. J. Masque "Gypsies Metamorphoses".*

or from any Goutes least grutchinge   50
Bless my Soueraigne and his touchinge.

    Bless him too from all offences
      in his sport as in his sences
      from a Boy to Cross his way
      from a fall or a fowle Day
Bless him O bless him Heauens and lende him longe
To bee the sacred burthen of all Songe
The acts and yeeres of all our kings to out goe
    And while hee's Mortall, wee not thinke him soe:.   ffinis

[67]

☞   {A man, and two Maides in a Boate at Sea :.
From some vnknowne, but haynous Crime
   against the Gods committed
   a young man on a time (sad time
   and young man to bee pittied)

Putt forth to Sea, when stormes constraind
   the rageinge Sea, to roare,
   in a small vessell that containd
   him only and two more.

As Master, Mate, and Sayler far'd
   this youth and with his hand   10
   ruld helme, and rudder, Sayle and Corde
   and boate both sterrd and mand

And though his barke were but three stronge
   (weake vessell strong but three)
   tall shippe from Indian voyage longe
   nere brought such prize as shee

For with two Damsells was shee lade
   the one brightness such
   the Seaman her his Idde made
   and shee him scornd as much:.   20

The other though not all so bright
   As was her Mate, yett one
   that in him plac'd her whole delight
   But hee in her tooke none.

Now to appease both Heauen and Seas
   that on the offence did frowne
   hee cast a way must one of these
   or else all three must Drowne.

Hard choice where in full sad hee stood
   and doubtfull what to doe   30
   oft lookinge on the raginge floud
   and oft vppon those twoe:

67.12 sterrd] The first *r* overwrites an *e*.

The pensiue Pilote of this boate
  thus with himselfe debates,
  should I drowne her on whom I Dote
  though shee mee fondly hates. /

I loose the richest of my fraughts
  and on despairefull shelfe
  of Sorrow, Shipwracks mine owne thoughts
  and cast away my selfe.   40

And should I her that doates on mee
  destroye though her I scorne
  my Soule for such a deede would bee
  with endless horror torne

If sacrifice of mine owne life
  might satisfie the offended
  those two should liue, and yet the strife
  and storme should soone bee ended:

But fors't to resolue, at last
  the faire, and scorn full mayd   50
  whom hee so lou'd hee tooke and cast
  Or'e boa'rd, and thus hee sayd

Whom best I Loue to Death I giue
  whom best mee Loues I haue
  for why; Shee that will saue shall liue,
  Shee sinke that will not saue :.   ffinis

---

[68]

This Night is blacke, but blacker is my soule
By sinne more blacke then Inke, then pitch moure foule,
Sweet Christ with eies of Mercie looke on mee
And with thy Spiritt lett enlightned bee,
So prostrate euen in heart to thee I fly
My Sauiour deere who for my sinns didst dye
O let thy pretious bloud much cleere my heart
And by thy death my sinfull soule conuert
The blackest night to thee is clearest day
The clearest day to mee as blacke all way   10
O Lett thy blessed light soe shine on mee
That I may Loathe) my sinnes when them I see
My God thou art, my hope wherby I liue
My sinns forgett and do thou pardon giue
That when this earthly body heere must dye
My soule may liue with thee   Eternally :   ffinis :

67.50 *scorn full*] There is a space beween *scorn* and *full*, but the transcriber may have considered this as one word.
67.52 *boa'rd*] *a* overwrites probable *o*.

[69]

The Question of a Garland

Betwixt two Sutors, satt a Lady faire
  vppon her head a Garland did shee weare
  and of the enamor'd, two, the first a lone
  a garland wore like her, the second none.

ffrom her owne head shee tooke the wreath shee wore
  and on him plac't it, that had none before
  and then (marke this) their browes were both about
  besett with Garlands, and shee satt with out.

Beholdinge then these Riualls on each side
  of her, thus plac'd and deckt in equall pride   10
  Shee from the first mans head; the wreath hee had
  tooke off (and ther with) her owne browes shee clad

And then (marke this) shee and the second weare
  in Garlands deckt and the first man Satt bare,
  Now which did shee Loue best, of him to whom
  She gaue the wreath, or him, shee tooke it from:

The Answere
In my conceite shee him would soonest haue
  from whome shee tooke; not him to whome shee gaue
  for to bestowe, many respects may moue
  But to receiue none should perswade but Loue.   20

Shee grast him much, on whom her wreath shee placte
  But him whose wreath shee wore, shee much more gracte
  for where shee giues shee there a seruant makes
  butt makes herselfe a seruant where shee takes.
     { Then where shee takes, shee honours most and where
  ⊛ { Shee doth most honour shee most Loue doth beare :. ffinis

[70]

A Meditation}
Rise O my soule with thy desires to heauen
  and with diuinest Contemplation vse
  thy time when times eternitye is giuen
  nor let vaine thoughts nomore thy thought abuse
  But downe in Darkeness lett them lye
  So liue they better, lett thy worst thoughts dye

And thou my soule inspird with holy flame
  viewe and reuiewe with most regardfull eye
  that holy Crosse whence thy Saluation came
  wheron thy Sauiour and thy sinnes did dye   10
  for in this sacred obiect is such pleasure
  that in this Christ is both my life and treasure

To thee O Iesus I direct mine eyes
  to thee my handes to thee my humble knees
  to thee my heart shall offer Sacrifice
  to thee my thoughts, my thoughts who only sees
  To thee my all, my selfe and all I giue
  To thee I die, to thee I only Liue:. /   ffinis

[71]

Mary and Loue thy Flauia for shee
hath all things wher with others beauties bee
for though her eies bee smalle her mouth is great
though her Lipps be Iuory yett her teeth are Iett
though they bee Dimm yet shee is light enough
and though her harshe haires fall her skin is rough
What though her Cheekes be yellow her haire is Red
giue her thine and shee hath a Mayden head
these things are beauties Elements where these
meete in one that one must as perfect please   10
if red and white and each good qualitye
be in thy wench, neere aske where it doth lye
In buying things perfumd, wee aske if there
bee Muske and Amber in it; but not where
though all her parts bee not i'the vsiall place
Shee hath the Anagram of a good face.
If wee might put the Letters but one way
in that Leane dearth of words what could wee say
when by the Gam-vt som Musitions make
A perfecte songe, others will vndertake   20
by the same Gam-vt chainged to equall it
things simply good can neuer bee vnfitt
shee is faire as any, if all be like her
and if none bee, then shee is singulare
All Loue is wonder if wee Iustly doe,   <?>
account her wonderfull why not Louely too
Loue built on beauty, soone as beauty dyes
Choose this face, chaing'de by no deformities
Weomen <all> are all like Angells they faire bee
like those that fell to worse: but such as shee   30
like to good Angells: nothing can Impaire
tis less greife to bee foule: then to haue beene faire
for one Nights reuells gould and silke wee chouse
but in long Iournies Cloth, and Leather vse
Beauty is barren: oft best husbands say
there is best land where there is foulest way
O what a soueraigne Plaister will shee bee
if thy past sinns haue taught thee Iealosie
Heer needs no spyes, nor Euenuckes: her Committ
safe to thy foes, yea to a Marmosit,   40
When Belgias Cities the round Cuntries drowne
that dirty fouleness guards, and armes the Towne
soe doth her face, guarde her and so for thee
which forct thy basnes absent oft must bee
shee whose face like cloudes turnes ye Day to Night
who mightier then the Sea makes Moores seeme white
whom though seuen yeeres shee in the stews had layd
A Nunerie durst receiue and thinke a Maide
And though in Child-births labour shee did lye
Mydwifes would sweare twere but a Tympanie.   50

4 (left margin, not transcribed)] Modern pencil notation: *Donne*.

Whom if shee accuse herselfe I creditt less
then w<h>iches which Impossibles confess
whom Dildoes beadstaues and her veluett glass
would bee as loth to touch as Ioseph was
One like non: and likt of non fittest were
for things in fashion euery one will weare: ffinis

[72]

Dr Corbet to the Duke of Buckingham
in Spaine :   1623 :

I'ue reade of Ilands floatinge and remou'd
in Ouids time, but neuer harde it proud
till now that fable by the Prince and you
by your transportinge England is made true
Wee are not where wee were the Day starr raignes
no colder in our Climate, then in Spaines
The selfe same breath, same aire, same heate, and burninge
Is heere, and there will bee till your returninge
Come ere the Card bee alter'd least perhaps
Your stay may make an errour in our Mapps   10
Least England shall bee found when you shall passe
a thousand Myles more southward then it was
O that you were my Lord, O that you were
Now in Black friers, or had a disguised eare
Or that you were Smyths againe, two houres to bee
In Paules on Sunday att full Sea at three
There you should heare the Legend of each Day
The perrills of your time and of your way
Your Enterprizes, accidents, vntill
You could ariue at Court and reach Madrill   20
Then you should heare how the state Grandes flout you
with their twice double diligence about you
How our enuirond Prince walkes with a Guarde
Of Spanish Peeres and his owne seruants barr'd
How not a Chapline of his owne may stay
When hee would heare a Sermon preach't or pray,
You would bee hungrie haueinge dinde to heare
vitailes   The price of vi<c>ta<?>les, and the scarcitie there
As if the Prince had ventured there his life
To make a famine not to fetch a wife.   30
Your eggs (which must bee addle too) are Deare
As English Capons, Capons as sheepe here
Noe grass for horse, or Cattell, for they say
It is not cutt nor made, grass there growes hay.
Then tis soe seetinge hott in Spanie they Sweare
You neuer heard of a rawe oyster there
Your cold meate coms in reaking, and your wine
Is all burnt Sacko, the fire was in the vine,
Itm your Pulletts are distinguist there

72.17 **Day**] A majuscule *D* overwrites a minuscule *d*. 72.28 **vitailes**] spelling corrected in left margin.

Into foure Quarters, as wee carue them heere,   40
And are a weeke a wastinge Munday noone
A winge, att Supper somethinge with a Spoone,
Tuesday a Legge, and so forth; Sunday more
The liuer and the gissard betwixt foure
As for the Mutten in the best house-holder
Tis fellony to Cheapen a whole Shoulder
Lord how our Stomakes come to vs againe
When wee conceiue what snatchinge is in Spaine
And whilst I write and doe the news repeate
Am forc't to call for breakfast in and eate   50
And doe you wonder at the Dearth the while
The floud that makes it runns in the middle Ile
Poets of Pauls; those of Duke Humpheries mess
That feede on nought but graues and Emptinesse
But harke you Noble Sᵣ: in one Crosse weeke
My Lord had lost foure thousand pound at Gleeke
And though they doe allow you little meate
They are content your losses shall bee great
False on my Denerie: falser then your fare is
Or then your Difference with Conde De Oleuares   60
Which was reported strangely for one tyde
But after six howres flowinge ebd and Dyde
If God would this great designe should bee
Perfect and round with out some Knauerie
Nor that our Prince should end his enterprise
But for soe many othes So many lyes
If for a good euent the Heauens doe please
Mens tongues should bee come rougher then the Seas
And the expence of Paper shall bee such
First written then translated out of Dutch   70
Carantoes, Dittes, Packetts, newes, more newes
Which so innocent witness doth abuse
If first the Belgicke Pismire must bee seene
Before the Spanish Lady bee our Queene
With that sucksess and such an end at last
Alls welcome, pleasant, gratefull that is past
And such an end wee pray that you should see
A type of that which Mother Zebedee
Wisht for her sonnes, the Prince and you
Att either hand of Iames yee need not say   80
Hee on the right, you on the lefte, the Kinge
Safe in the Midst you both enuironinge
There shall I tell my Lord his word and band
Are forfett till I kiss the Princes hand
Then shall I see the Duke your royall freind
Haue all your other honours, this you'le end
This you haue wrought, for this you hamerd out
Like a strong Smith, good workeman and a stout

53 **Humpheries**] initial *e* overwrites unreadable letter.

In this I haue a parte, In this I see
Some new addition smilinge vppon mee   90
Who in an humble Distance claime my share
In all your greatness what so ere you are:.

[73]

Vppon Prince Charles his cominge home
out of Spaine :   1623 :

S^r: such my fate was that I had no store
T'erect a goodly Pile before my doore
Nor were my flagons tyr'd, by being taught
Their Seu'rall stages vp and downe the vault
Vppon the great blest Day of your returne
Wher in nothinge att all was seene to mourne
Except it were the Heauens, and well they might
Fearinge our tryumph should out shine their light
The poore man trickt himselfe with wine that Day
And did not feare to make his Landlord stay,   10
The tradsman shut his shoppe, and did not care
For the retaylinge his neglected ware
For well hee knew ther landed on the shore
A prize that him and all the Isle might store.
The Inland liuer that could neuer finde
The East, from west but by a Church, nor winde
In his liues compass euer yet did knowe
But that which to his Summer fruites a foe
Was better learnt; And now hee knew by Arte
What filld your sailes, and that wine fild his heart?   20
I that haue sence of Blessings cannot show
In outward things the Ioy that I doe owe
And thankes to heauen for your safe returne
Yett haue a fire with in mee that doth burne
As bright as theirs, which neuer shall decay
Till fate assigne to mee no farther Day: ffinis: I: G:

[74]

Vppon a false report of my Ld of Kenzington
And Sr George Geringe:

I hate a lie, yet late a Lie, did runn
   Of Noble Gorings death, and Kenzington
And for that they did not vntimely dye
   I lou'd that Lie, because it proud a Lie
But had it prou'd an action of such Ruth   5
   Ta'd made mee grow in hatred of the Truth
All lyes are naught, yet giue this Lie its due
   'Tis ten times better, then i'ft had beene true:.

73.20 *filld*] *d* overwrites *g*. 73.22 (right margin, not transcribed)] *Gifford ?* **74** (entire poem)] written in small hand, see commentary notes.

[75]

<u>Noli peccare:.</u> }

Deus vidit:

Forbeare to sinne; God hath thee still in sight
Nothing is hid from his all seeing ey
Though thou putt'st on the sabells of the Night,
Hee knowes in thy greatest secrecie
    All time, all place, all endes, and all thy meanes
    Hee better sees, then thou the Sunns bright beames:.

Angeli tris-
tant<u>^r</u>

Forbeare to sinn: the Angells greiue for thee,
  When by thy sinne thou greeu'st thy louing Lord
Those Noble natures our attendaunts bee
To whom both Day and night they do afford   10
    Their dearest seruice: O vnkinde to much
    To cause their greefe: whose Loue to thee is such:.

Diabolus
<u>accusat}:</u>

Forbeare to sinn: for eu'n that Damned fend
  That moud thee first, and sooth'd thee in thy sinn,
When hee hath once attaind his Cursed end
And made thee act his <w>ill, will streight beginn
    To aggrauate thy guilt: Hell vrge thy shame
    Against thy selfe that vrgd thee to the same:.

Conscientia
<u>terret}</u>

Forbeare to sinn: for out of sinn doth breed
  A bitinge worme, that gnaws the sinner still,   20
Deuouringe <u>wolfe</u>, that on thy selfe doth feede
Black register that dost record our ill,
    And makes thy soule the booke wher thou dost wright
    Sadd thoughts by day, and fearefull dreames by Night

Mors mi-
<u>natur:}</u>

Forbeare to sinn: Death standeth at the Doore,
  Ready to enter on thy house of Earth,
One day being spent, the lesser is thy store
Of time to Come; Man dyes from his first birth,
    Who euer wrights, or speakes of any thinge
    Still ends his tale with Mortus est, hees gon   30

Iudiciũ
in <u>stat:}</u>

Forbeare to sinn: there is a Day of Doome
  There are Records, wher thy sinns are inrould
    There is a Iust and fearefull Iudge from whome
    Leyes noe appeale, who cannot bee contrould
      Whom teares, Almes, Prayrs, may to mercy moue
      But then ther is no place for Peace or Loue:.

Inferni
<u>cruciant}</u>

Forbeare to sinn: Because there is a Hell
  Where Cens-less, Ease-less, End-less torments bee
    Where Deuills, and all the Damned troopes doe dwell
    And still shall dwell, for all Eternitye,   40
      Where to remaine is greiuous past conceite
      And whence, not any hope to make retraite:

❀ { Therefore (to end as I did earst begin)
    { Let these respects make thee forbeare to sinne:

23 *wright*] Large lowercase *g* overwrites *te*; the transcriber first wrote *write*. Note spelling in line 29.

[76]

Wett eyes (yet great wth teares) why weepe you soe?
Wee weepe, because wee cannot weepe enough,
Our Seas doe ebb, and yet our sinns doe flowe
Wee are too Calme, yett Conscience is too rough,
O then weepe still, Raine teares with out controule
Eye water well distilld may clense the Soule:

O sadd Remembrance what dost thou suggest?
A thousand selfe-wrought causes of my woe
A Masse of Sinne Lyes heauy on my breast
And what a burden is a bosome foe?   10
O Conscience what a Register thou art?
When thou dost file our follies on the heart.

Afflicted Soule, what dost thou then surmise
When God presents himselfe vnto thy vew
That God who is most greate, most Iust, most wise
Who knows thy sinne, and will giue sinne its dew.
The feelinge soule that hath a taste of God,
Must needs Confess hee hath deserud the Rodd:

[77]

I lost you   Deer when I thinke vppon my first sad fall
& now the   from thy faire Eys, I needs must feele with all
gaine is   the many widdowed howres I since haue numbred
double   which in wisht hands I might haue safely slumbred
to mee}   Rockt into Endless heauenly traunces, by
            thy soule inchauntinge-graces Harmonye
            whilst I Enioyd not what I did possesse
            but like an vnthrifte of my happiness
            Did not my loss (till twas to late) Espie
            as children kill their birds, and after crye   10
            But since those Cloudes that so Eclipst thy light
            (and gaue my e'ury day so many a Night
            As my life had but a dead winter binn
            had I no better after sunshine seene)
            ar fled lett vs (thou best of mee) redeeme
            Those howres wee fondly did so disesteeme
            And since past Ioyes are but bewaild in vaine
            Come and wee'l proue them ouer all againe
            That small deuision soe will come the meetter
            To make the Musique of our bliss the sweeter: ffinis :

77.12 *e'ury*] The apostrophe is misplaced.

[78]

A Letter from D^r: C: to a friend:.

My Brother, and much more hadst thou bin mine
Hadst thou in one rich present of a line
Inclosde Sr Francis, for in all thy store
Noe guifte could cost thee less, nor binde mee more:
Hadst thou (Deer Charle) Imparted his returne
I should not with a tardy welcome burne
But had lett loose to him, my Ioye long since
which now will seeme but studdied negligence,
But I forgiue thee, two things kept thee from it
First such a freind to gaze on; next the Comett,   10
Which Comett wee descerne (though not so true
As you at Sion) as long taylde as you,
Wee know all ready how will stand the Case
Twixt Barnauell and vniuersall Grace,
Though Spaine deserue the whole starr, if the fall
Bee true, of Lerma-Duke and Cardinall,
Marrie in ffrance wee feare no bloud but wine
Less dangers in her sworde then in her vine,
And thus wee leaue our blazer Coming ouer
ffor our Portents are wise, and end at Douer,   20
And though wee vse no forward Censuringe
Nor send our Learned porcters to the Kinge
Yet euery Morninge when the Sun doth rise
There is no blacke for three houres in our eyes
But like a Puritane dreamer toward this light
All eyes turnd vpward, are all zeale and white
More it is doubtted, that this Prodigie
Will turne ten schooles to one Astronomie
And the Analesis wee Iustly feare
Since eu'ry Art doth seeke for rescue heere   30
Physitions, Lawers, Glouers on the stall
The shopkeepers Mathematicks all,
And though men reade no Gospell in these signes
Yett all professions are become Diuines
All weapons from the Badkin to the Pike
The Masons Rule, the Taylors yarde alike;
Fake altitudes; and the early fidlinge Knaues
In flutes and Ho<y> boyes make them Iacobs staues.
Burton to Gunter writes, and Burton heares
ffrom Gunter, and they exchange both tongues & eares   40
By Carriage: thus doth myred Guy complaine
His wagon in their Letters, beares Charles waine

4 (left margin, not transcribed)] Modern note: *Corbet.*

Charles waine, to which they say the tayle doth reach
And at this distance, they both heare and teach.
Now for the peace of God and man aduise
Thou who hast where with all to make vs wise
Thine owne rich studdies, and deepe Heriots minde
In which there is no dross, but all refinde
O tell vs what to trust too, Ere wee wax
All stiff and stupid with this Paradax   50
Say shall the old Philosophie bee true
Or doth hee rule a boue the Moone thinke you
Is it a Meteor forced by the Sunn
Or a first body from Creation,
Hath the same starr bin obiect of ye wonder
Of our fore fathers, shall the same come vnder
The Censure of our Nephewes, writ and send
Or else this starr a Quarrell doth portend:
                                                          ffinis

---

[79]

Excuse of Absence:
You will aske perhaps wherfore I stay
(Louing so much) so long a way
O do not thinke twas I did part,
It was my body not my hearte
for like a Compas in your Loue   5
One foote is fixt, and cannot moue
the other may follow ye blinde guide
of giddy fortune, but not slide,
be yonde your seruice; nor dare venter
to wander farr, from your Center: ffinis

---

[80]

A Ladyes Prayer to Cupid:
Since I must needs into thy Schoole returne
Bee pittifull O Loue, and do not burne
Mee with desire, of cold and frozen age
Nor lett mee follow a fond boy or Page.
But Gentle Cupid, giue mee if you can   5
Vnto my Loue whom I may call a Man
Of Person comely and of face as sweete
Let him bee sober secrett and discreete,
Well practizd in Loues schoole, lett him wth in
Weare all his bearde and none vppon his chin :.   ffinis

80.3 *frozen*] r overwrites unreadable letter.

[81]

<u>Of one braginge of his Auncestors :</u>
The world Created, God made Man
why made hee him not a Gentle-man?
because hee saw that all was good
which then had priveledge not bloud,
Since Custome, wealth authoritye
hath brought in this Idolatrie,
and falsely taught vs that wee owe
to some thing that wee doe not knowe,
much like the prayers for the dead
which for o^r selues were better sayd,   10
If wee must brage, let vs rather
Make our owne deserts our father,
Let vertue, goodnes, honestie
bee Ensignes of a ffamilie,
So shall true vertue Issue finde
Not in the bloud but in the minde: I: G: ffinis

[82]

<u>An Epitaph.</u>
Stay, view this stone, and if thou beest not such,
  Reade here a little, that thou maist know much,
  It couers first, A virgin, and then, one
  who durst bee so in Court: A vertue alone
  to fitt an Epitaph, but shee had more,
  shee might haue claim'd t'aue made the Graces fowre
  Taught Pallas, Language, Cinthea Modestie,
  As fitt to haue increast the Harmonie
  of Spheares, as light of starrs: shee was
  the sole religious house and votarie   10
  Not bound by rites but Conscience, woulds y^u all
  shee was sett boulstred, in which name I call
  Vp so much truth, as could I here persue
  Might make the fable of good weomen true: B: I.

[83]

Cease booteless teares, weepe not for him whose Death
  made way to Heauen; for her that lent him breath,
  Long liu'd hee Captiue; now at Libertie
  this world of wooes turnd to felicitie
  what, is hee gon: No, wee enioye him still
  that learned worke, (the Laurell of his quill,
  Shall liue) and blaze his fame, those only dye
  that leaue no record to posteritie
  The end, the Life, the Eueinge crownes ye Day
  his Night surpast his morning euery way,   10
  ffor Samson like, Dyinge hee vanquisht more
  then all his life time hee had done before: ffinis :

83.5–8] A verticle line is drawn in left margin that is not indicated in this edition. It is a modern pencil notation.

[84]

I wonder how my Turtle can deny
Loue; when her selfe is euen Loues Harmony:
ffor euery part of her doth so consent
as that shees faire by Act of Parliament.
Her haire being seuer'd by the Iuory combe,
falls in imbraces backe vnto their home,
which shewes the Loue they beare vnto that Globe,
to which they are an ornament and Robe.
Her forehead (tablet like) beinge smooth and faire,
Doth in her hight, shew good will to the haire,   10
and saith that shee is faire cause they are browne,
therfore in duty takes the lower roome
Her quicke and speakinge eye doth still inuite
  eye pleasinge men, to vew and praise the white
Her Nose (beinge lo˄ ᵃth to loose her part in grace)
stands as a well plac'd Gnomen in her face,
Castinge a louely shadow on each side
Of two discendinge hillocks, rarely dy'de
with Natures tincture, and beneath them two
(Like a triangle poynte) two sweet budds growe,   20
from whence distills a breath that would releiue
A famisht soule, but oh it makes mee greiue
(that in a freindly manner) they should smother
Soe great a good, by kissinge still each other
Her plum pretty dimpled chinn doth looke
Like a full pointe, or period to a Booke.
Here I would rest, but then you would demaimd
wheron this rich composure should stand
this admirable Architeckt, sustaines
A curious arch, inamiled with vaines,   30
from whence discends A pillar of white Marble
that sometimes vtters a Mellodious warble
The shoulders euen straight and comely large,
Do willingly and easily discharge
their office of supportinge; then two gemms
Twin like and like two Alabaster stemmes
in them are grafted, which shee oft doth raise
vp towards heauen, to her makers praise
These curious stalkes do end in branches seu'rall
grac'd with neate Ioynts, which studded are wᵗʰ pearle   40
Her brest like hony bladders, swolne wᵗʰ sweetnes
soft are as gellue, and as Snowe in whiteness
Her pure vnspotted belly (next in ranke)
Resembles doth a risinge fallinge banke,
Which at itts bottome hath a <risinge> ↑secret↓ springe : secret
That nere was staind by a Lustfull thinge

---

17 Castinge] Majuscule C overwrites minuscule *c*.   **27 demaimd**] As is, but from rhyme sheme and sense it should be *demand*.

And on each side, two faire Limbes for defence
(As keepers fitt for beauties excellence)
Stand and from thence, two slender twiggs take life,
Mutually mouinge with out any strife.   50
And now the founder of this goodly frame,
(Least to vs Mortalls his Arte should seeme Lame,
In his vnsearched wisdome) thought it meete,
to perfect all with two most prettie feete.
But what haue I forgott; eares had shee none?
Yes sure, But they were wantinge to my mone,
Haue I not reason I should them forgett
that neare knew mee, therfore nere in their debte,
Yet cause in shew there is a way to enter
Into rich Ioyes, Ile on their praises venter.   60
These little Dores, in fashion like two shells
of Mother of Pearle, shininge plainely tells,
that though Meander-like the passage is,
the guest shall finde an easie way to bliss,
And that same power which him thither Drewe,
shall bringe him out againe, with out a clewe.
But oh Deare Saint, lett mee but enter yett
and locke mee euer in the Cabinett
Of thy sweete memorie wher let mee dwell,
Ile thinke my prison Heauen, and freedome Hell: ffinis

[85]

On his Mistris Beauty

When in the Annalls of all wastinge Time
I see discription of the fairest wights
And beauty makeinge beautifull old mine
In praise of Ladyes dead and louely Knights
then in the Blazon of sweet beauties best
of face of hand, of lip, of eye, or brow
I see their antique pen would haue exprest
Eu'n such a beauty as you master now
Soe all their praises were but prophecies
of those our dayes, all you prefiguringe   10
And for they saw but with diuininge eyes
they had not skill enough thy worth to singe
for wee which now behould these present dayes
haue eyes to wonder, but no tongues to praise:

85.3 *mine*] Underlined in Modern pencil notation, not indicated in this edition.

[86]

D^r. D : at his goinge into Bohemia :
      A Himne to Christ : }
In what torne Ship so ere I <Goe> Embarke
that ship shall bee the Emblim of thy Arke
what Sea soeuer swallow mee, that floud
shall bee to mee an Emblim of thy bloud
though thou with cloudes of Anger <dost> doe disguise
thy face, yett through that Maske, I know those eyes
which tough they turne a way some times,
they neuer will dispise.

I sacrifice this Iland vnto thee
and all whom I loue there, and who loues mee   10
when I haue put ou'r sea, tweene them and mee
put thou thy sea betwixt my sinns and mee
as the trees sapp doth seeke the sap below
in winter, in my winter now I goe
where none but thee, the Eternall roote
of true Loue I may know./

Nor thou nor thy Religion doth Controule
the Amorousness of an Harmonious soule
but thou wouldst haue that Loue thy selfe as thou
art Iealous Lord, soe am I Iealous now   20
thou lou'st not till, from Louing more, thou free
my soule who euer giues takes liberty
O if thou carst not whom I Loue
(Alas thou lou'st not mee:.

Seale then this Bill of my deuorce to all
on whom the fainten Beames did fall,
marry those Loues which in youth scattered bee
On fame, witt, hopes, (false Mistrisses to thee,
Churches are best for Prayer, y^t haue least light
  to see God only I go out of sight   30
  and to scape stormie dayes, I choose
    An Euerlastinge Night: ffinis

Title (right margin)] Modern pencil notation, not transcribed: *Donne.*

[87]

Thou that art I; tis nothinge to bee soe
thou that art still thy selfe, by these shall knowe
parte of our passage; And as a hand or eye,
by Hilliarde drawne, is worth a Historye
by a worse Painter framde: So with out pride,
when as the same by thee are dignifide
My lines are such; tis the preheminence
of frindshippe, only to impute Excellence
England to whom wee owe, what wee are, or haue
sad that her sons should seeake a forrane graue   10
(for fate and fortunes driftes) none can oth say
Honour and miserie haue one pace, one way
forth of her pregnant entrayles sigh'de a winde
which from the Æyres middle Marble rounde, did finde,
such strange resistance, that it selfe it threw
Downe ward againe; and when that it did view
how in the porte or fleete, deere time did leese
Lyinge like prisnors, that lye, but for feese
Mildly it kist our sailes, soe fresh and sweete
(as to a stomake staru'de; whose insides meete   20
Meate Comes) it come; and swole our sailes, whilst wee
soe Ioyde as Sara, her swellinge Ioyde to see
But this was but so kinde as is our Cuntrie men
that bringe vs one dayes way and leaue vs then:
Then (like two mighty Knights which dwellinge farre
A sunder; met against a third to warre)
the South and west winde Ioynde; as they blewe,
waue like a rowlinge trench, before them threwe,
Sooner then you reade this line did the gale
like shott, not feard, till felt, our sailes assaile   30
And what at first was cald a gust, the same
hath now a stormes, A non A Tempests name;
Ionas I pittie thee and curse those men
who when the storme ragde most; did wake thee then
Sleepe is paines easiest salue and duth fulf<u>ill,
all offices of Death except to Kill
for when I wakte, I saw that I saw not
the sunn which should haue taught mee had forgott,
East, West, day, night, and I could but say
had the world lasted yet; It had bin day,   40
thousands our noyses were, yett wee mongst all
Could none by his right name but thunder Call
Lightninge was all our light, and it raind more
then if the Sunn had drunke the Sea before,
Some Coffinde in ther Cabines, lye, Equally
Greiude; that they are not dead & yet must dye.

---

15 *threw*] *h* overwrites *d*. Holgate first wrote *drew*, then added *t* at start of word.   **35 *fulfill*]** Holgate first wrote *fulfull*, then blotted out the left side of *u* and dotted right side of *u* to create the *i*.

And as sinne burned soules, from graues will creepe
at the last day, some forth their Cabines peepe
And tremblinge aske what newes, and doe heare soe
as Iealous husbands, what they would not knowe,   50
Some settinge on the Hatches, would seeme there
with hideous gazinge, to feare a way feare
then note they, the shipes sicknesse, the maste
shackte with his Ague; and they hold, and waste
with a salt dropsie clogde; and all our tacklings,
snapp<ed>inge like to high strecht treble strings,
and from our totteringe sayles, raggs drop downe soe
as from one hangde in chaines, a yeere agoe,
Euen our Ordnance plac't, for our defence
striues to breake loose, and scape a way from thence,   60
Pumping hath tyrd our men, and whats their gaine
Seas into seas throwne, they sucke in againe,
hearing hath deafte our Saylores, and if they
Know how to heare; thers none know what to say,
Compard to these stormes, death's but a Qualme
Hell some what light some, and the Barmoodoes Calme,
Darkeness Deaths elder Brother, His birth right
Claimes ore the world; and to heauen hath chased light
all things are one, and that one none can bee
since all formes vniforme, deformitie   70
Doth Couer soe that wee, Excepte God say
an other fiut, shall haue no more day
soe longe and violent, these furies bee
that though my absence sterue mee; I wish not thee:.   ffinis

[88]

{ The Crosse by Dʳ: D:. }

Since Christ embrac'd the Crosse it selfe, dare I
his Image, the Image of his Crosse denye?
would I haue profitt by the Sacrifice
and dare the chosen Alter to despise?
It boore all other sinns but is it fitt
that it should beare the sinne of scorninge it?
who from the picture would auert his eye
how would hee fly his paines, who there did dye;
from mee no Pulpit no misgrounded Lawe
nor scandall taken shall this Crosse with drawe   10
it shall not for it cannot; for the losse
of this Crosse were a nother Crosse:
Better were worse: for no affliction
Noe Crosse is so extreame as to haue none
who can blot out the Crosse with the Instrument
of God drau'd one mee in the Sacrment.

Who can deny mee powre and libertie
to stretch mine armes and mine owne Cross to bee,
Swimm and at euery stroke thou art thy Crosse
the mast and yearde make one when Seas doe toss   20
Looke downe thou spiest out Crosses in small things
Looke vp thou seest birds saisd on Crossed wings:
All the Globes frame and sphæres are nothing else
but the Meridians Crossing paralels.
Materiall Crosses then good Phisicke are
but yet spirituall are the Chimicks ware,   : h
then are you your owne Phisicke or neede none
when stilld or purgd by tribulation:
for when that Crosse vngrudged stickes
then are you to your selfe⁵ a Crucifixe   30
as perchaunce Caruers doe not faces make
but that a way which hid them, ther doe take,
Let Crosses so take what hid Christ in thee
and bee his Image or not his but hee.
Yet as of Alchimists doe Coyners proue
so may a selfe despisinge gett selfe Loue
And then as worst surfetts of best meates bee
soe is pride issued from Humilitie,
For tis no Childe but Monster: there fore Crosse
your Ioye in Crosses, else tis double loss   40
And cross thy sences else both they and thou
Must perish soone, and to destruction bowe;
for if the eye seeke good obiects, and will take
No Cross from bad, wee cannot scape a snake
so with harsh, hard, sowre, stinking Cross the rest
make them indifferent and nothing best:
But much the eye needs Crossinge that can rome
and moue to yᵉ others tho'biects must come home;
and Cross thy heart for that in Man alone
points downewards when it downe wards bends   50
and when it to forbidden height pretends
and as thy braine through bonye walles doth vent
by suturs with a Cross from present
soe when thy braines worke, ere thou vtter it
Cross and Correct Concupiscence of witt
bee Couetous of Crosses let none fall
Cross no man else and Cross thy selfe in all
then doth the Cross of Christ worke f<a>ₐʳut<h>fully : frut
with in our soules when wee loue harmelesly
that Crosses pictures much; but with more care   60
that Crosses children, which our Crosses are:

---

50 downe wards] (second use) slight space between two root words. The transcriber may have intended this as one word. **58 frutfully**] The transcriber first wrote *faithfully*. Lowercase *u* created from *i* and deleted *a*; *h* deleted.

[89]

Dᵣ: D:.

Goe and catch a fallinge starr
get with childe a Mandrake roote
tell mee where all past yeeres are
or who clefte the Deuills foote
teach mee to heare Mermaides singeing
or to keepe-off enuies stinginge
   and finde what winde
    serues an honest minde}

If thou beest borne to strainge sights
things inuisible to see   10
ride then thousand days and nights
till age snow white haires on thee
then when thou returnst will tell mee
all strainge wonders that befell thee
   And sweare that no wheare
    Liues a woman true & faire}

If thou finde one Let mee know
such a pilgrimage was sweet
yet doe not I will not goe
though at next doore wee might meete   20
though shee were true when you mett her
and lasts still you send your Letter
   Yet shee will bee
    false ere I com to two or three ffinis

[90]

Dᵣ: D:

When my<ne> heart was mine owne, and not by vows
by thee oth'd, nor by my sigh'<t>s breath'd into thee
what lookes what teares, what passions what showes
did humbly begge and steale my heart from mee
through thine eyes, mee thought I might behould
thy harte, as pictures through a <c?> Cristall glass,
thy heart seemd softe, and pure as liquid gould
thy faith seemd bright and durable as brass
But as all Princes ere they haue obtaind
free soueraignety <d?> do guild their words and deedes   10
with prettie and right when they haue gaynde
full sway dare boldy then show vitious deedes
Soe after conquest thou dost mee neglect
Could not <(> thy (once pure) heart else now forbeare
nay more abhor an amarous respect
to any other? Oh towards mee I feare
thy heart to steale, that faith to wax doth turne
which takeinge heate from euerye amarous eye
melts with their flames as I consume and burne.

With shame to haue hop't for womans Constancie,   20
yet I had thy first oaths and it was I
that taught thee first, loues language t'vnderstand
and did reueale pure Loues high Misterie
and had thy heart deliuered by thy hande
and in exchange I gaue thee such a heart
as had it beene example vnto thine
none Could haue challenged the smallest part
of it, or thy Loue, they had all bin mine
they had pure they had bin innocent
as Angells are, how often to that end   30
to clere my selfe, of any foule intent
did both in precepts, and examples bend
And must it now bee an incurious Lott
to chaffe and heate, wax for a nothers seale,
to enamell and to guild a pretious pott
and drinke in Earth my selfe; O I appeale
vnto thy soule wheather I haue not Cause
to chainge my happiest wishes to this Curse
that thou from chainging still might neuer pause
and euery chainge might bee from worse, to worse.   40
yett my heart cannot wish nor thoughts conceaue
of ill to thine nor can falshood whett
my dull minde to reuenge that I will leaue
to thee, for thine owne guilt will that begett
falshood in others would no more appeare
then Inke dropp't vppon mud or raine grass
but in thy heart framde so white and cleare
twill show like blotts in paper, scratches in glass
then for thine owne respecte and not for mine
pittie thy selfe yett beinge true and free   50
thy minde from wandering doe but yet decline
all other Loues, and I will pardon thee
But looke that I haue all; for deare lett mee
either thine only Loue: or no Loue bee:.   ffinis :

---

[91]

Groane senceless earth to heare my burdenous woes
  Weepe skies in dropps of raine to see my wronge
    burne flaminge fire thy pittie to disclose
    streames stay your coorse to heare my muringe song,
    Earth, skie, ffire, streames, your aide vnto mee Lend   5
    by happy death my wretched Life to end:.   ⊛

90.26 example] *ex* appears to overwrite two illegible letters.   **91.4 muringe**] (see commentary notes).

[92]

Dr: D:

Man is the world and Death the Otian
to which god giues the lowers parts to man
this sea inuirons all and though as yett
God hath sett markes and bounds twixt vs and yett
Yet doth it roare and gnaw, and still pretend
and breakes our banke when ere it take a freind
then our land waters (teares of passion) vent
owre waters then aboue our firmament
teares which for our soules, doth for our sinnes let fall
take all a brackish tast and funerall   10
and euen those teares which should wash sinners sinnes
Wee after Gods Noah, drownd the world again.
Nothing but man of all invenoumd things
doth worke vppon it selfe with inborne stinges
teares are false spectacles wee cannot see
through passions mists what wee are or what shee
in her this sea of Death hath made no breach
but as the tyde doth waste the slimie beach
and leaue imbrothered workes vppon the sand
so is her flesh refinde by deaths cold hand   20
as men of China after an ages stay
doe take vp purslane where they buried clay
so at this graue her Limbicke which refines
the Diamonds, Rubies, Saphires, pearles & mindes
of which this flesh, her soule shall inspire
flesh of such stuffe as God when his last fire
Annulls this world to recompence it shall
make and name, then the Elixer of this all
they say the sea when it gaines looseth two
if carnall death the younger brother doe   30
vsurpe the body, our sule which subiect is
to the Elder by sinn, is freed by this
they perish both, when they attempt the Iust
for Graues Trophies are, and both Deaths dust
soe vnabnoxious now, shee hath buried both
for none to death sinns which to sinne ar loth
Nor doe they dye which are not loath to dye
so shee hath this and that virginitie
grace was in her extreamely diligent
that kept her from sinn, yet made her repent   40
of what small spotts pure white complaines alas
how little poyson crakes a christall glasse
Shee siñd but iust enough to let vs see
that Gods word must bee true, all sinners bee
So much did zeale her Conscience rarifie
that extreame truth lackt little of a lye:

<hr>

4 (left margin, not transcribed)] Modern pencil notation: *Donne.* **4 yett**] *y* overwrites an unreadable letter. **13 invenoumd**] Space between *in* and *venoumd*, possibly intended as two words. **19 imbrothered**] Space between *im* and *brothered*, similar to line 13.

Makeinge omissions ac kes layinge the touch
of sinn on things which may bee such
As Moses Cherubins whose natures doe
surpass all speed by him ar winged too   50
So would her soule already in heauen seeme then
to climbe by teares the common staires of men
how fitt shee was for God: I am content
to speake that Death, his name hast may repent
how fitt for vs how euen and how sweete
how good in all her Tythes and how meet
to haue reformd this froward heresie
that weomen can no parts of freindshippe bee
how morrall how diuine shall not be told
lest they that heare her vertues thinke her old   60
and least thou take Deaths parte and make him glad
of such a pray and to his tryumph add: ✹   ffinis :

[93]

A Dialogue betwixt a Man and a woman:

Man:.   Bee not proud cause faire, and trime
    but let those lipps, be tasted
    those eyes will hollow proue and Dime,
    that lipp and brow bee wasted,
     and to Loue whole bee perswaded
     Sullied flowers, or beauty faded

Woman   Could Rose, or Lillie, purer bee
    cause they smell, or looke <mee> like mee
    yet pride should neuer reach my minde
    but beauty though it vsiall lye   10
    is kept from staines by beinge layd by
     So'ts better to bee chast then kinde:

Man:.   O thou art soft as is the aire
    Or the words that court the faire
    then let those flames by Louers felt
    that scorcht my heart make thine to melt

Woman   Thy words are sweet as is Deceite
    sugred as the Louer's baite
    and do whisper in mine eare
    Loue makes bargaines Sweete but Deare.   20

Man   Thou knowest not then that all the faire
    giue youth to Loue, and age to praire
Woman   Tis a Doctrine cannot bee
    sound in you, or safe in me: ✹   ffinis

92.47] *ac kes*] The space is as indicated.

[94]

To the Countess of Rutland:./

Maddame, soe my verses pleasinge bee
Soe may you laugh at them, and not at mee,
thers somethinge to you I would gladly say
but how to doe it cannot finde the way
I woulde auoyde the common trodden waies
to Ladyes vs'd; which bee, on Loue or praise,
As for the first, that little witt I haue,
is not yet growne soe neere the graue;
but that I can by that dimme fadinge light
perceiue of what and vnto whome I write,   10
let such as in a hopeless, witles rage
Can sigh a quire, and reade it to a page
Such as can make them Sonnets ere they rest
when each is but a great blott at the best
such as can backes of bookes, and windows fill
with their too furious diamound and quill
such as are well resolud, to end their dayes
with a loude laughter, blowne beyounde the Seas
Such as are mortifide, that they can liue
laught att by all the world, and yet forgiue   20
write Loue to you; I would not wittingly
bee pointed at in euery companie,
As was the little Taylor, who till death
was hott in Loue with Queene Elizabeth
And for the last In all my Id'l dayes
I neuer yet did liuing woman prayse
in verse or prose, and when I do begin
I'le picke some woman out as full of sinne
as you are full of vertue, with a soule
as blacke as yours is white, a face as fowle   30
as yours is beautifull, for it shall bee
Out of the rules of Phisiognomie
soe farr that I doe feare I must displace
the arte a little to let in her face
It shall at last fowre faces bee below
the Deuills; and her parched corpes shall show
in her loose skine, as if some sprite shee were
kept in a bagg by some great Coniurer.
Her breath shall bee so horrible and vilde
as euery worde you speake, is sweete and milde,   40
It shall bee such a one, as will not bee
couer'd with any arte or Policy
But let her take all waters, fumes, and Drinke
Shee shall make nothinge but a deerer stinke.

Shee shall haue such a foote, and such a Nose,
as will not stand in any thing but prose
If I bestow my praises vppon such
tis charitie: and I shall merit much.
My praise will come to her, like a full bowle
bestowd at most need, on A thirstie soule   50
wher if I sung your praises in my mine
I loose my Inke, my Paper and my time
add nothinge to your ouer flowinge store
and tell you nought but what you knew before
Nor do the virtuous minded (which I sweare
Maddam I thinke you are) indure to heare
their owne perfections into question brought
but stopp their eares at them; for if I thought,
you tooke a pride to haue your vertues knowne
pardon mee Maddam, I should thinke them none   60
To what a length is this strange Letter growne
In seekinge of a Subiect, yett findes none:
but if your braue thoughts (which I most respect,
aboue your glorious titles) shall accepte
these harshe disorderd lines, I shall ere longe
dress vp your vertues new, in a new songe
yet farr from all base prayes, or flattery
all though I know what ear my verses bee
they will like the most seruile flattry show
if I write truth, and make my Subiect you: ffinis: F:B:

---

[95]

Fond world in thee who putteth any trust
doth painte on waters, and writes in the dust
hee doth short pleasure and long toyle endure
his hopes are doubtfull and his paines are sure
hee feedes on promises as on the winde
and empty partes, euen from who is most kinde
his bedd is witnes of his thoughts and Care
and they with out their hosts still reconinge are,
sighs are the minutes that diuide his time
and sobbs the bells that doe make vp his chime   10
teares are the dewe that giues his cares in crease
greife his Companion whose disgusts nere cease
wishing hee liues and liuing wishing still
till death his wishes and wishes his life doe kill: ffinis:

94.51 mine] Underlined in Modern pencil notation, not transcribed. 94.51 (right margin, not transcribed)] Modern notation: *rime*, correcting *mine*. 94.54 knew] *e* overwrites *o*. 94.61 (right margin, not transcribed] Modern notation: *Beaumont.*

[96]

An Eligie on the Death of the
❀ {Countess of Rutland: } ❀

I may forgett to Eate, to Drinke to Sleepe,
Remembringe thee but when I doe to weepe,
In well weigh'd lines that men shall at thy hearse
Enuy the Sorrow that brought forth thy verse
may my dull vnderstandinge haue the might,
only to know the last was yesternight,
Rutland the faire is dead or if to heare
the name of Sydney will more force a teare
ti's shee that is so dead, and yet there bee
some men aliue, profess not poetrie   10
the states-men, and the Lawyers of our time
haue busines still but doe it not in rime.
Can shee bee dead and can there bee of those
Y^t are so dull to say their prayres in prose?
Is it three days since shee did feele deaths hand
and yet this Isle not cald the Poets land
hath this no new ones made and are the ould
at such a needfull time as this growne could
they all say they would faine, but yet they pleade
they cannot write because their Muse is deade   20
heare mee then speake; who will craue no excuse
sorrowe may make a Verse, with out a Muse,
Why didst thou dye so soone, o pardon mee
I know it was the longest life to thee,
that ere with Modestie, was cald a span
since the Almightie lefte to striue with man
man kinde is sent to sorrow and thou hast
more of the busnes that thou camst for, past
then all the aged women, that (yett quicke)
haue quite out liu'd their owne Arethmiticke   30
As soone as thou couldst apprehend a greife
there were enough to meete thee, and the cheeife
blessed of weomen kinde, Mariage was to thee
Nought but a Sacramentall miserie
hee whom thou haste If wee may trust to fame
could nothinge chainge about thee but thy name.
a name wch who that were againe to doe't
would chainge with out a thousand Ioyes to boote
in all things else thou rather leadst a life
Like a betrothed virgine then a wife   40
but yett I would haue cald thy fortune kinde
If it had only tryd thy setled minde:

---

14 Y^t] Y overwrites *to*. **14 *are*]** *ar* overwrites *be*, final *e* of *are* remains. The transcriber first wrote *bee*.

With present Crosses, and the loathed thought
of worse to come, for then it might haue wrought
thy blest remembrance to haue cast an eye
backe with delight vppon thine Infancie,
But thou hadst \<r\>ere thou knew'st ye vse of teares
sorrow layd vp against thou camst to yeares
Ear thou werte able who thou werte to tell
by a sadd warre thy noble ffather fell   50
in a dull Clime that did not vnderstand
what twas to venter him to saue a Lande
Hee lefte two children (who for vertue, witt,
beauty) were lou'de of all, thee and his writt,
Two was too few, yet Death hath from vs tooke
thee a more faultless Issue then his booke,
which now the only, Liuinge thinge wee haue
from him wele see shall neuer finde a graue
as thou hast done; Alas that it might bee
that bookes their Sexes had as well as wee   60
that wee might see this married to the worth
and many Poems like it selfe bring forth
But this vaine wish, Diuinitie Controules,
for neither vnto Angells, nor to soules
nor any thinge hee meant should euer liue,
did the wise God of nature Sexes giue,
then with this Eternall worke alone
lett vs content our selues since thou art gone,
gone like the day thou dyd'st vppon, an' wee
may call that backe as Easily as thee: 70
Who should haue lookte to this? where were you all
that doe your selues the helpes of Nature call
Phisitions, I acknowledge you were there
to sell such words as none in health would heare
Soe dy'de shee, Curst bee hee that shall defende
Your arte of hastninge Nature to an end
In this you proue that phisicke can but bee
at best an arte to cure your Pouertie,
Y'are Eu'rie one Impostures, and do giue
to sicke men potions, that your selues may liue,   80
Hee that hath surfetted and cannot eate
may haue a Medicine to procure you meate
and thers the deepest ground of all your skill
Except it bee some knowledge how to kill.
Sorrow, and madness make my verses flow
Cross to my vnderstandinge, for I know

86 Cross] Majuscule C overwrites minuscule *s*.

You can doe wonders, euery day I meete
the looser sorte of people in the streete,
from dangerous diseases curde, and why
restore you them and sufferde her to dye;   90
Why should the state allow you Colledges
pensions for Lectures, and Anothomi<s>es
if all your potions, vomets, letting bloud
can only cure the bad, and not the good,
which only you can doe, and I will show
the hidden reason why you did not know
the way to cure her, you beleeude her bloud
ran in such courses as you vnderstood
by Lectures; you beleiud her Artir<?>s
grew as those did in your Anothomies   100
forgetting that the state allowes you none,
but only whores and theeues to <u>practi</u><c>ze on   practize/
and thats the reasone, why your selues and wiues,
are noted for enioyinge soe long liues,
But noble blood treades in a stranger path
to your ill gott experience, and hath
an other way to cure, If you had seene
Penelope desected<t>, or the Queene
of Sheba, then you mought haue found a way
to haue preserued her from that fatall day   110
as' tis, y' haue made her but the sooner blest
by helping her to heaue'n, wher let her rest.
I will not hurte, the peace which shee should haue
By lookinge longer in her quiet Graue :.   ffinis   F B:

Page 109] Empty space as indicated.   **93 *potions*] First *o* overwrites *a*.   **102 *practize*] *z* overwrites *c*. It is also corrected in the margin.

[97]

To Mʳ B: I:.

Neither to follow fashion nor <?> to showe
my witt against the State, nor that I knowe
any thing now, with which I am with childe
till I haue tould, nor hopeinge to bee stilde
a good Epistler through the towne, with which
I might bee famous, nor with any y'tch
like these, wrote I this Letter but to showe
the Loue I Carrie and mee thinkes do owe
to you aboue the number, which [can] best
in something which I vse not, be exprest.   10
to write this I invoake none, but the post
of Douer, or some Carriers pist-ling ghost,
for if this equall but the stile, which men
send Cheese to towne with, and thankes downe agen,
tis all I seeke for: heere I would let slippe
(If I had ˰ ᵃⁿʸ in mee) scholler shippe,
and from all Learninge keepe these liues as deere   cleere
as Shakespeares best are, which our heires shall heare
Preachers apte to their auditors to showe
how farr sometimes a mortall man may goe   20
by the dimme light of Nature, tis to mee
an helpe to write of nothing; and as free,
As hee, whose text was, god made all that is,
I meane to speake: what do you thinke of his
state, who hath now the last that hee could make
in white and Orrenge tawny on his backe
at Windsor ? is not this miserie more
then a fallen sharers, that now keepes a doore
hath not his state almost as wretched beene
as is, that is ordainde to write the geinne   30
after the fawne, and fleere shall bee ? as sure
Some one there is allotted to endure
that Cross. there are some, I could wish to knowe
to loue, and keepe with, if they woulde not showe
their studdies to me; or I wish to see
their workes to laugh at, if they suffer mee
not to know them: And thus I would Commerse
with honest Poets that make scuruie verse
by this time you perceiue you did a misse
to leaue your wortier studies to see this,   40
which is more tedious to you, then to walke
in a Iews Church, or Bretons Cõmon talke
But know I write not these lines to the end
to please Ben: Iohnson but to please my frend: ffinis: F B:

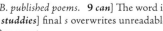

3–10 (left margin, not transcribed)] Modern pencil notation: *This is not in F. B. published poems.* **9 can**] The word is written in modern pencil. The transcriber left space in the original text. **35 studdies**] final *s* overwrites unreadable letter. **44** (under pen flourish, not transcribed)] Modern pencil notation: *F. Beaumont.*

[98]

Off Freindshippe } ✹

Friendshippe on earth wee may as easly finde
  As hee the North East passage, that is blinde
  t'is not vnlike th'imaginarie stone
  that latter'de Chymests, long haue doted on:
sofisticate affection is the best
  this age affordes; no freind abides the test:
they make a glorious showe, a little space,
  but vanish in the raine, like copper lace
or nealled in <?>↑a↓ffectction but one day
  they smoake, and stinke and vapor quite away.   10
wee miss the true materialls, choosinge friends
  On vertue wee proiect not, but Our ende
soe by degrees, when wee Imbrace so many
  wee courted are like whores, not lou'd of any
good turnes ill plact, that wee on all men heape,
  are seedes of that ingratitude wee reape
and hee that is soe sweete hee none denies
  was made of honey for the nimble flyes:
Chouse one of two Campanions of thy life
  then bee as true as thou wouldst haue thy wife   20
Though hee liue Ioyles that enioyes no freinde
  hee that hath many paies fort in the end: ffinis

Page 111] The transcriber left empty space as above. A later hand has added a twelve-line answer poem that begins with a prose question: *The Parliam^t did demand where all y^e moneys gon.* **12 ende**] final *e* overwrites *s*.

[99]

D.r: B: of teares: }
_____

Who would haue thought there could haue bin
such Ioy in teares wept for our sinne,
mine eye hath seene my heart hath proude
the most and best of earthly Ioyes
the sweete of Loue, and beinge Loude,
Maskes, feasts, and playes, and such like toyes
Yett this one teare which now doth fall
in true delighte exceeds them all.

Indeede mine eies at first let in
those guests that did those woes begin   10
therfore mine eies in teares and greife
are Iustly drownde but that those teares
should comfort bringe, tis past beleefe
O God in this thy grace appeares
thou that makes light from darkeness springe
makst Ioyes to weepe, and sadness singe.

O where am I, what may I thinke,
  Helpe, helpe, alas, my heart doth sinke
      thus lost in seas of woe
      thus laden with my sinn   20
      waues of despaire dashing
      and thereate my ouerthrow
  What heart opprest with such a weight
    Can chouse but sinke and perrish streight.

Yet as at Sea in stormes men Choose
  the shipp to saue their goods to loose
      soe in this fearefull storme
      this danger to preuent
      before all hope bee spent
      Ile choose the lesser harme   30
  My teares to seas I will conuert
  And drowne mine eyes to saue my heart.

O God my God what shall I giue
    to thee in thankes, I am and liue
    in thee, and thou dost safe preserue
    my health my fame, my goods my rent
    thou makes mee eate, whilst other sterue
    and singe whilst others do lament
    such vnto mee thy blessings are
    as though I were thy only Care.   40

But O my God thou art more kinde
    when I looke inwarde in my minde
    thou fils't my heart with humble Ioye
    with Patience meeke, and feruent Loue

41 *art*] r overwrites unreadable letter.

which

(All other Loues which doth destroy)
with faith w^hich nothing can remoue
and hope assurd of heauens Blisse
this is my state, thy grace is this: ffinis

---

[100]

A Letter from H: H of London to
    H: L: in the Cuntry :   }

Twice hath the Ivy and the pricklinge holly
proclaimde the Cittie, and the Cuntry folly
twice hast thou heard the Tabor and I twice
the Temple Musique vseringe the dice
twice haue I seene pies and plome porredge store
and carud the inside of the Brawny Bore
since I saw thee, or one selfe speakinge line
signde by thy fingers, and vnript by myne
till these, which welcome how so ere late
like to thy Loue (I hope soe) beares no date.   10
But (fond dessembler) neuer was't thy vse,
to a true friend to frame a false excuse
as thou dost now, for vollumes hadst thou pend
tha'dst fitt occasion where and when to send,
Hast thou forgott where stands the Crimson steeple
that with a tractiue scarlett draues the people
and might inuite thy Carriers horses bell
for want of others there to Ring a Knell
that could haue tould thee, or else places twenty
where wee haue drunke Cupps and tobacco plenty   20
Neither am I if I may go soe farr
as wandringe Planet though no fixed starr
that my abode should breede a vaine suspition
which might begett a needless inquisition
No : Henry no : it is your old <u>dis˜ease</u>   di-zease
that word diuided tels you if you please
tis that infectiue Lazy feauer Lurden
make the Remembrance of thy friend as burden
But goe thy wayes, be merry fatt and tipple
and hence forth halt no more before a Cripple: ffinis

---

[101]

An Elegie on Prince Henry
⊛ { by Mr Thoris: } ⊛   An Italian:

Oh shall I speake, or shall I silent bee,
or wonder, or what else will best agree,
wee stand as dead at thinges, that doe amaze
nor is it time to speake then but to gaze,
what shall I say, my minde I faine would breake
but I do breake my hearte, if I doe speake,
some say Lamentinge speeches, waken sorrow,
but these are Comforts which wee doe but borrow,
false lights that promise much and glorious seeme
As Glowormes, wch some would rich Diamonds deeme;   10
then burst heart let your blood paint out your greife
since no wordes possible can bringe releife,
or rather dye, for therein lies more pleasure
t_^hen to liue long, and so to greiue at Leasure
Alas I grow immortall in my paine
for where I end I must begin againe
better were it a man should nere begin
then such an Immortalitie to winn
but wee are tide to fate, fate not to vs
and wee must liue our taske, though wee liue thus   20
If no true comfort wee may haue; then Come
deluding Dreames, by fitts they will bringe some,
but no: for they at night do play no play
but tragedies that acted neere by day
why then forgettfullness, let vs not want
thy helpe since all helpe else, and hope is scant
But ah by this wee shall as little gett
because euen to forgett, wee may forgett,
Let vs despaire and no good more desire
since all things to afflict vs doe conspire.   30
Earth doth deny what once it must vs giue
A Graue. yet wee intombde in sorrow liue,
the Aire that others sighs to heauen beares
Letts ours lie drowned in a Sea of teares,
Water, and fire by turnes do quench and burne
least that our woes should End, and Ioyes returne
Shall I go get my selfe into a woode
put on a Pilgrims gowne and huntsmans hood,
Eccho will surely double my sad dittie
and moue the very senceless trees to pittie   40
But ah where mindes are prest with any thinge
the sollitarie shades do horror bringe :   ⧟

---

4 then] *e* overwrites probable *o*.   **14 so**] *s* overwrites *t*.   **38 huntsmans**] Space between *hunts* and *mans*, possibly two words.

Then whether shall I runn, nay whether fly
since scorned thus by Earth, by sea, by skie
Ah though I could haue comfort I will none
by Night Ile weepe, and all the day Ile moane
though Nature teach vs to beholde on high
and looke for helpe when thers no remedie
though verie weakenes hope in vs do breede
and oft makes vs euen on despaire to speede   50
Yet I must thinke that hope is banisht quite
where such faire hopes are taken from our sight
hopes that yet neuer grew on any Crowne
nor could by enuy it selfe bee puld downe,
fates   what good haue <u>fattes</u> or fortune ere brought forth
Like to this famous Princes matchless worth,
fame Came to him, not hee to her for praise
shee did not his, but hee her glory raise
Nay Maiestye from him did borrow grace
shininge both in his life, and in his face,   60
in him were statelines, and sweetnes mett
as if the one the other did begett,
what can thought apprehend, or fancie write,
what can conceite deuise, or witt indite,
yea what doth nature worke, or good ordaine,
what doth the worlds two Hemispheares containe,
that scornes to make <l> a patterne of great happ
twas all in him, as in a liuely Mapp
O Death that wouldst in one day ouerthrow
the worke that many ages cannot showe   70
thou didst stand gazinge mounted on some Hill
how in one man mights all this Iland kill
for through his sides ten thousands heartes doe bleede
that on his Loue, as on their meate did feede,
goe ffathers, and lament Childrens loss
since such a ffather, beares this, heauy Crosse,
And Mothers, neuer let your Eyes bee drye
Now that a Queene must haue a blubberd eye,
All Sisters weepe, your heaire and dressings rent
Since that soe deare a Sister doth Lament   80
Nor brethren are you free, Your eares <are>↑as↓ well
must heare the ringinge of the Dolefull Knell
O greiue a Princely brothers tender yeares
Should learne so soone to shed vntimely teares,
Let Towne and Cuntrie all their pleasures lacke
Since all the Courte thus shaded is with blacke.

---

77 And] Flourish commences lefthand ascender in the shape of a lowercase *s*. The flourish itself is in lefthand margin.

faire siluer streaming Theames, leaue your deare bed
Sith tho'nly Ioy lay by your side is dead
goe Poets fetch the Muses, from his hearse
though they bee dead, thei'le glorifie your ve\<a\>rse   90
Youle fetch more praise from his renowned graue
then all the other Lawreat Poets haue,
Weepe, singe, I care not how your Muse bee framde
soe all the worlde bee by your Muses blamde,
Curse all, and not Phisitions alone,
since all the world could not preserue that one
O world, hee that would wisely turne thy booke
would in no line of it, for saftie looke
and reade in Euery page brickle as glasse
noe words but this oft multiplide (Alas)   100
the rest though they seeme glorious and faire,
they are but Counterfeites, and smoakinge aire
O world that letts in none but on Condition
they shall not out, before they feele affliction,
And at their enteringe cry presageing soe
that all their Life, is but a world of woe: ffinis

[102]

An Epitaph on Prince Henry :
A Plant of fairest hope that euer stood
in Ida or the Callidonian wood
whose armes out stretched might haue reacht as farr
as is the Articke from yᵉ Antarticke starr
and Cyrus like his shaddows ouer spread   5
from siluer Ganges to Solls watry Bed
this plants cut downe, and if wee for his fall
Cannot lament enough, our Children shall:

[103]

An other : by H: H:
Loe where hee shineth yonder
A fixed starr in heauen
whose motion here came vnder
None of the Planetts seaue'n
If that the Moone, should tender   5
the Sunn her Loue and Marry
thy both could not engender
Soe bri\<i\>ght a starr, as Harry:

101.90 verse] Lowercase *v* overwrites *h*, then blots *a*. Holgate first wrote *hearse*.   **103.1** (right margin, not transcribed)] Modern pencil notation: *Hugh Holland*.

[104]

{ An Elegie on Prince Henry }
{ By H: Holland:. }

Hee that had tolde mee this and saide hee Dream'de
A Month agoe I should haue thought blasphe'mde
Or him in Bedlam wisht for want of reason
Or at the Towre or Tiburne for his treason
  poore Isle, y^t with thy tides dost hourely alter
Out washt with waues, and in which teares, but salter,
Wert thou so lately to thy name restorde
to haue thy breast so soone, soe deepely goar'de
thy face was with his Grandames death Confounded
in his thy hearte is broke, or hugely wounded   10
  Thy Prince (o mercy God) whose fate and meritt
Heere or in Heauen A Crowne was to inherit
 and here hee had but that our good misfortune
for his life giuers life did Heaue'n Importune
and theare hee doth, yea there hee liueth Crowned
nor is hee dead, vnless our teares him drowned
though in the Angells Crowde, perhaps hee fainted
who throng'd to see him there both Crownd and Sainted
   But as the sacringe of the King now regnant
Wee long deferde, and first prepard o^r pregnant   20
teares for the buriall of the Queene deceased
soe leaue wee now the blessed soule deceased
which (like the Kingly office) neuer dyeth
and turne to that Corpes which lowly lyeth
  O Rose, of thousand Damzells late desired
whose Crimson hue their snowy boosoms fired
the Rose of Lancaster which fairely burned
in his fresh cheekes, to that of yorke is turned
Bleede teares yee English heartes, and haue Compunction
  Your Grandfathers wept blood for their disiunction   30
   the flowre of all this age is now deflored
   in flowre of all his age, him death deuoured
Noe Catesby could do more, nor ffau^{l}x, nor Percy
Of hell the firebrands, nor haue showne less Mercy
   Tell mee you that had Hell on Earth contriud
   Or into Hell would thence haue <g> diggde and diu'de
   what feind it was; or of what feind the member
   first told you of the fatall Month Nouember
'twas not the fifth hee was a lyinge Prophet
the Sixt it was, nor Erd hee wider of it   40
Bee that a day of Iubile, and thanks giuings
But this a dismall day of groanes & greiuings
   The Court doth mourne and all with blacke is walled

2 *blasphe'mde*] An apostrophe is directly above *m*.

Nor shall in hast againe Whitᵉ Hall be called
Yeat where at Tilt and Ringe, hee vs'd his races
is desert now: his presence fild all places
   How ofte when as to westminster I trudged
About my fiue yeares suite; yet vniudged
hee cheared vp my hearte that was so heauy
to see him ride before the beautious Beauy   50
of Ladyes bright, who stood there at amazed
and with their lights the windowes double glazed
   the horse had of his loade more Pride; then feeling
Now runinge, and now boundinge, & now whealinge
the fire out of his Ample nostrells glowed
and with his mouth A long the ground hee snowed
If once hee neighed, no other trumpett needed
And like his Masters eie; or though hee speeded
thus oft I saw him for the Race pʳparinge
his Horse the windes, himselfe all Com̃ers daringe   60
   His Armor lightned and his staues did thunder
soe did the fiery steedes that flew him vnder
then broke hee staues, but now our staff is bro‸ᵃken
Soe are our hearts although our hearts were Oken
for now insteede of steedes, the beere him beareth
 no more his steede yᵉ flying Center teareth
But sadly walkes before and will no faster
  for hurting her, that must imbrace his Master
Loe with the ground, where low hee lies and leuell
  the Prince of youth, who kept yᵉ life and reuell   70
light hearts hee made, for when hee lightly bounded
no ground but shoutes vnto the Musique sounded
Nor shouldst thou bee of Earth if ought may woe yee
to him more heauy then hee was vnto thee
Art thou yett \<y\> earth for all thy mines so needy
Or by our greedines, learn'st thou to bee greedy
Wee digge thy wombe for gould, wee are so cruell
and digge it vp againe to hide our Iuell
But this which in thy boosome now is hoorded
is worth what euer vs thou hast afforded   80
 Our hopes ran on him, but his fates, ran faster
Nor less then our desire is our disaster
Ne should our teares (yᵉ less our hopes be fewer
which showre a pace and make each eye an Ewer
Each brest a Bason, thence all hopes bee washed
(No Loue extinct) whose flames there euer flashed
and shall till vs with him they burne to Cynders
And soone they would but that our weepinge hinders.

119

To bringe in Lee, this coile and lost what needeth
from euery Eye, an other Thames prcedeth.   90
which neuer should deaths Image see nor slumber
till in the south they make a second Humber
Eyes weepe out teares, teares weepe out eyes in kindenesse
for next to death, the best of things is blindeness
    When late his grandames reliques were remoud
Who would haue thought, that it would thus haue prou‸ᵉd<?>
  my life and all I had, I darst haue pawned
that vault for him would not so soone haue yawned
where him in her colde armes shee now imbraces
who liuinge warmde all breasts, and stainde all faces.   100
    Good Lord how time doth Run, wee Month can measure
But fiue betwixt our tresurer and treasure
Now all is gone: the reason may bee no‸ᵃted
why none is yet vnto the place promoted
And hee that best deserues of any other
may weepe for him, as for his fathers Mother:
Alas there is no neede, noe theefe will offer
nor yet a foole to rob an empty Coffer
One leaden Costing doth our gould inuiron
and our more leaden hearts, are lapt in Iron   110
soe dull soe h<e>arde they are, that none perceiueth
of how much good his death yᵉ Realme bereaueth
    was this hee or did I my selfe but flatter
that of my song should bee the mightie matter
this hee that should hew downe the Turkes like Cattell
And I first fight, and after singe the Battell
alas that songe must now bee turnd to sadnesse
all Mirth and Musique, are but fitts of madnesse
fye on the man that makes a Mocke of Sorrow
or that to morne; a Cloake will begg or borrow   120
<th> true greife in deede, that cannot well bee Choaked
will finde a vente, and needes not to bee Cloaked
his stoŕmes of sighs, and teares will soone bee layde
whose head with one poore riban may bee staide
giue mee a runinge head, his braine is Idle
who now vnto his teares giues not the bridle
    Where are the witts which hee him choose and Cherisht
are all braue spirites with one body perisht
the vniversities should make rehearsall
of our sadd story 'tis to vniuersall   130
    My Mother Cambridge, whom so P̲h̲e̲e̲b̲u̲s̲ loueth   : [?] yᵉ Kinge.
as hardly from thy Confines hee remoueth
are all thy Muses fled, thy witts all brained

---

111 *perceiueth*] A tilde through *p* abbreviates *er*. **112 *Realme*]** *m* and *e* overwrite unreadable letters.

Or thy sweete springs, more then thy Marshes drained
and Oxfoorde, thou that ofte didst tast his bounty
who late at woodstocke feasted all the Countye
what is the Cause that both your tongues bee tyde
are Grant and Theames and all your fountaines dried
You are the Kingdomes eyes, to you it longeth
to weepe what ere the kingdome wounds or wrongeth   140
Most sorrow through the eye ye heart perplexeth
but through ye heart, ye eyes this sorrow vexeth
for Kinge and Realme (which should I pittie rather)
haue lost: ye Kinge a Sone ye Realme a ffather
Whose guiftes (with longer Life) god graunt his Brother
in all but age, become hee such a nother
and to his memoriall name (my vow is thriftie)
O may hee fill a hundreed yeeres and fiftie
Soe may (her mothers Image and) his sister
whose pearly eyes, like both the Indies glister   150
and would to God that Death so long had taried
while hee had seene her fullie woode and married
    But O the Mother, how hath shee bedewed
 with liquid pearle, her bosom stucke and strewed
The Queene of Loue (o stay her heer) showneth
with sighs and teares, her brest both draines and drowneth
His body with those teares lett bee Embalmed
and to sweet odours those sweet sighs beecalmed
for loe the spiritt is flowne to God immortall
whose house high heauen is, and death the Portall   160
Soe wee perhaps may giue him worthy buriall
whose Tombe shall bee An other new Escuriall:.   ffinis:

---

154 *liquid*] *q* overwrites probable *k*.

[105]

On Prince Henrye :

It is not Night yett all the world is blacke
the fiats past, and yet our sunne wee lacke
I now know ioyes and greifes are measurde knowne
by our Capacities, and not their owne
The Lorde and Lowte togeither mixe their plaints\<s>
some hearts do swell, some paine, and other\<?> faints
this greife's much like a Curious Painters hand
that meetes all eyes wch way so ere they stand
who had not lay his hopes vppon his head
who must not sorrow when his hopes are dead　　　　　　　　　*10*
if euery Comõn: sorrow forceth teares
and sighs, and groanes, for his Cogisaunce beares
shall this vnthought, vnparalelled loss
this vniuersall shipwra‸^cke, greife, and Cross
carrie no other Character of woes
then such, wherin ye basest sorrow goes
though wee could not his saddest fate eschewe
yet may wee pay his memorie her due
Let then this greefe, for euer fresh remaine
and binde wee our posteritie to p‸^laine　　　　　　　　　*20*
Letts to the reuolution of this day
Of Lamentations hereby tribute pay
Let all times know our Princely Harries name
and let not age nor enuy date his fame
O Let our tongues bee liuinge Epitaphes
and let them leade our Children to the pathes
which his wise, noble pious, actions traced
where vertue keen, and he euen grac'ed
So graue a præsence, and so well composed
that grace and terror both at once disclosed　　　　　　　　　*30*
him and them selues soe to the standers by
as his Commaunds were written in his eye
and yet euen then, hee could as well obey
for to his royall ffather hee did p\<r>ay　　　　pay.
a Sonne and subiects due Obedience
O farr is it from our Experience
to see great fortunes truly moderate
and purchasers of Loue and not of hate
But I haue not so many greifes to spare
nor shall this dropsie world suck vp my care　　　　　　　　　*40*
that but to him and his vntimely fate
Could spare no sorrow from my hapless state
but not vntimely sence wee knew tis reason
that time should follow, time and seaoson, season
Hee bare ripe fruite euen in the very prime
Nature in him made haste to out run time
Dull lazie bodies pass not fast carriers
Wise men count liues by actions not by yeares:

17 *eschewe*] *s* overwrites *c*.　18 *pay*] *y* overwrites an unreadable letter.　20 *posteritie*] the second *t* is not crossed.

Wee neede admire no longer Phillips sonne
was neuer life in little beeter done   50
how did hee gouerne his well chosen traine
with out disorder or Luxurious straine
In his house peace and plentie had they bidinge
and hospitalitie acheife residinge
neuer did youth, and plentye take you Inne
where they were kept, so spotless with out sinn
nor neuer did Authoritie less harme
that oft alas doth vice not vertue arme
no venome lurked in his harmeless pleasure
they were not Masters of his time nor treasure<s>   60
nor were they Idle nor with out an end
but all to some more curious course did tend
thus did hee vse tennis Balance, and foyles
to make a well breathd body fitt for toyles
thus manag'de hee pikes, pistoletts, horse and armes
to bee preparde against his Cuntries harmes
how did hee loue that rauisher of soules
that all base muddy earthly thoughts controules
had I Prometheus bin insteed of fire
my theft had bin the songs of heauen Quire   70
yett heere his moderation kept his pace
for musique want part, though hee could grace
as well as euer yett could Carpet Knight
and could adorne a daunce to please the sight
of the most choise, a Curious Damasells eyes
yett held hee it amongst those Misteryes
that neuer are, or can bee better vsed
then when inforc't, they cannot bee refused
But runing swiminge, and such exercise
as much more Masculine hee more did prise   80
neither did these, his braue and actiue partes
hinder his minde, for though in pedint arts
hee was not lipp learnd yet his Iudgment knew
the latitude of things and how to viewe
the Courte and her inuisibilites
which seene or not seene often by the wise
No tongue can euer bee to any eares

Page 122] The whole page is underlined in Modern pencil notation.

A truer treasure of what it heares
Nor like a pettie streame that cannot beare
the least accesse, but that it straight doth reare   90
his head aboue his bankes, or else vtter
whats receiued inoto some ditch or gutter
But like the sea where no accession can
mak't visible vnto the eyes of man
wise secrecie the Ligement of frend
was his, and his euer to noble end
for by it hee read men insteed of bookes
as hee must do that into Kingdomes lookes
times past by entralls \<loo\> vsed to p\<er\>↑re↓sage
and this by humours enuyes malice, rage,   100
But run no further in this maze my Muse
hee knew vice, but no vice could ere infuse
her poyson in his well ordered minde
Religion and Conscience were combinde
and made a strong and holy warlike fence
against base crooked end, and lust of sence.
O miracle of Nature how couldst thou
keepe thy great fortunes that they did not bowe
to appetite and sensuall delighte
since they that gainst ye carnall man do fight   110
scarce trust them selues with life for feare of treason
what force had then they more then humane reason
with in the midst of all that might allure
did yet the Castle of thy minde assure
wonder of this our age, with sorrow may
thee and thy heauy loss to life display
not my dull Muse which whiles shee doth renew
the memorye knowes only what is due
But cannot pay thee, greefe hath already spent
my bodies store, but still my soule lament   120
and in a silent Doue-like dirge bomone
the ioye and beauty of the world is gone
and yet not gon, for though the world containe
Only one Phœnix, and that one is slaine
yet may our new mixt hope a nother proue
the same sunne shines of him with no less Loue
Pardon mee then sweet Prince faire blooming Youth
as you are raisde soe are You sett for truth
a degree farther then you were of late
you now with others eies must see your state   130
which though my vowes shall wish may bee aright
yet I cannot shew you a better light
Then the remembrance of your Brothers iests
whose thoughts vppon fare past Examples rests : }

Page 123] Every line is underlined in Modern pencil notation.   92 *inoto*] Slight space between first *o* and *t*. The transcriber intended *into*.   94 *visible*] *v* overwrites unreadable letter.

Hath honest Councellors as well as wise
passion in liuinge councells often lyes
the only doubt is that Examples past
in others states and mould framd & cast
are hardly fitted to these times of ours
but this feare Noble Prince neede not be yours   140
It is your selfe I set before your viewe
the print of these faire stepps are fresh and new
farr in this worlds discouerie he sailde ⊛ – <u>And neither Sirens songs nor Rocks p^{r}uayld</u>
t'm peach his course or to diuert his way
his happy voiage done he rests now in the bay
hee came home richly laden all with hartes
wonne by the prowesse of his Iust deserts
And now deere S^r your course beginneth next
take I beseech you his for mapp or text   150
and then dilate vppon it what you please
I only warne you let not sluggish ease
benum your sences, nor let hasty flight
with seeming only vpward daze your sight
man hath enough to doe wher's euer plast
and greatness is mistaken if not grac't
with Iustice goodnes, and integritye
the wisest and ye safest policie
for no law doth so deepely penetrate
into ye vaines and marrow of a state   160
All those Examples of your liues p^{r}sent
which silently drawes all men to content
and doth accord the Subiects harts to yours
louinge makeing sweet ye sharpnes of your powres.
Lastly to you great Kinge faire spreadinge Palme
that at your Entraunce all our stormes did calme
now implore you to appease your owne
theis are but hopes, you now assurance knowe
vnder whose shade, the Ilande doth possesse
all kindes of Comfort and of happines   170
but can no longer of your selfe giue way
that discontented sadnes shall betray
your peace on which your subiects peace doth liue
pardon deere S^r: If I complaine you giue
more then your owne, your Ioyes & greifes are ours
and nothing but ye dispensations yours
Should Cloudes for euer shade the blessed sunne
the Earth and all her Ofpringe were vndoñe
You are our sunn and from your glorious beames
the happiness of all you subiects streames   180
for Iustice sake, you owne and all this Land
Orecome this great Eclipse your selfe commaund
your happie fortune you could moderate
make now your glorie Compleate, beate this fate
with the like temper that the worlde may know
your happy greatness, you doe only owe
To God and vertue which do still aduance
their votaries aboue the powre of Chaunce :   ffinis ☙

Page 124] Entire page is written in a very small handwriting.

[106]

His Passion for a lost Chaine of Gould:

Not that in Couller, it was like thy haire
for Armeletts of that, thou maist let mee weare
nor that thy hands it of't I'm brast and kiste
for soe it had that good which oft I miste
Nor for that sillie ould Moral͵ᵢtie
that as these links are tide, our Loues should bee
I mourne: that I thy seauen fould Chaine haue lost
not for luckes sake, but for the bitter Cost
O, shall twelue righteous Angells, which as yet
noe leauen of vilde fodder did admitt   *10*
nor yet by my constraint; haue strid, or gon
from the first state of their Creation
Angells which heauen Commaunded to prouide
all things to mee, and bee my faithfull guide
to gaine new freindes, t'apease great enemies
to comfort my Soule, when I lye or rise
shall these twelue innocents, by thy seuere
sentence dread Iudge, my sinns great burden beare
And saue not mee, they doe not ease my paines
when in that Hell th'are burnde and tyde in chaines   *20*
were they but Crownes of ffrance I cared not
for most of them, their naturall Cuntrie rott
I thinke possesseth, they come here to vs
Soe leane, soe lame, soe ruinous
and howsoere, most ffrench Kings Christians bee
their Crownes ar Circumcisde, most Iewishly
Or weare the spanish stampes, still trauellinge
that are become as Catholike as their Kinge
those vnlike beare-whelpes, vnfield pistoletts
that more then Canon shott, Auailes or letts   *30*
which negligently lefte vnrounded; 'looke
Like manie Angled Iegaries in yᵉ booke
of some great Coniurer, which would enforce
Natur (as these do Iustice) from her Course
which as the soule quick'ns head, feet & heart
as streames like vaines run through yᵉ earth each parte
Visitt all Cuntries, and haue slyly made
Gorgeous ffrance ragged, ruinde and decaide
SCotland (which knowes no state) in one day
And mangled Seuenteene headed Belgia,   *40*
Or were it such gould, as that were with all
Almightie Chimiks from each minerall
haueinge by subtile fire a soule out pulde

---

10 admitt] d overwrites t. **25 Christians]** Circled in Modern pencil notation; a line extends toward the left margin above *Kings* and *ffrench* and stops after *most*, indicating that the line should read *most Christians ffrench Kings bee*. **32 yᵉ]** y overwrites an unreadable letter.

Are durtely and desperately gulde
I would not spett to quench that fire they were in
for they are guilty of much haynous sinn
But shall my harmeless Angells perish, shall
I loose my guarde, my ease, my foode my all,
much hope which they nourish, will bee dead:
much of my able youth, and lustie head   50
will vanish: If thou Loue mee let them alone
for thou wilt Loue mee less when they are gon
Oh bee content, that some Lou'de Squeaking Cryer
well pleasde with one leane threed bare, groate for hire
May like a Deuill roare through euery streete
and gall the finders Conscience, if hee him meet
Or lett mee Creepe to some dreade Coniurer
which with fantasticke Scheames fills full much paper
who hath diuided Heauen in tenements
And with whores, theeues, and Murderers stuffe his rents   60
soe full, that though hee pass them all in sinn
hee leaues him selfe no rome to enter in
And if when all his Arte and time is spent
hee say twill not bee found: O bee Content
receiue the Doome from him vngrudgingly
because hee is the Mouth of Desteny
thou sayst alas the goulde doth still remaine
though it bee chaingde, and put into a Chaine
Soe in those first falne Angells, resteth still
wisdome and knowledge but tis turnd to ill,   70
As these should doe good workes, and should prouid
Necessaries; but none must nurse thy pride
And they are still bad Angells, mine are none
for formes giue being, and their formes are gone
pittie the Angells yett their dignities
pass vertus, powrs, and principalities
But thou art resolute; thy will be doñe
yet with such anguish as her only sonne
the Mother in the hungrie graue doth lay
vnto the fire, the Martyrs I betray   80
Good soules, for yee giue life to euery thinge
good Angells, for good messages you bringe
Destinde you might haue bin, to such a one
As would haue Lou'de and worshipt you alone
One who would <haue> suffer hunger, Nakednesse

62 *him selfe*] Space as indicated.

Yea Death eare hee would make you numberless
But I am guilty of your sad decay
May your few fellows longer with mee stay
But O thou wretched finder, whom I hate
Soe much that I almost, pittie thy state   90
Gould beinge the heauiest mettall amongst all
may most heauy Curse vppon thee fall
ffetterd, and manacled and hangd in chaines
first maist thou bee, then chaind to hellish paines
Or being with forren gould, bribde to betray
thy Cuntrie, faile both of that, and thy pay
May the next thing thou stoopst to reach, Containe
poyson, whose nimble fume, rott thy moyst braine
Or some libell, or interdicted thinge
Kept negligently may thy ruine bringe   100
Lust bred diseases rott thee: and dwell with thee
Itchie desire, and no abilitie
May all the hurt which euer gould hath wrought
all mischeifes, which all Deuills euer thought
want after plenty, poore and gowty Age,
the plague of trauellers Loue, and Mariage
afflict thee; and at thy Liues last moment
may thy swolne sinns, to thee them selues p^rsent:
But I forgiue thee, repent then honest man
 gould is restoratiue, restore it than   110
But yet if from it thou beest loath to parte
Because tis Cordiall, would t'were at thy heart:.   ffinis :

Open space below poem] Six-line poem entered in eighteenth century by John Wale headed "Vpon Master Iohn Charles Wray. . . ." **Left margin**] Modern pencil notation: *In handwriting of John Wale of Colie Priory.*

[107]

On the Money Newes so generally Currant
in Frankendale about Iune : 1621 :

Souldier stand vp, and Liue, and do no \<more\> more,
faint at the breakinge length, of thy bold score,
that soe inuadingly, makes the walls white
within a Towne in which thou scarce canst shite
Scorninge the crombled Boorscheeke, or his leeke
more then three visible excremeents, the weeke
Butt bee curragious; There now comes coyne enough
to finde thy belly beefe, and thy backe buffe;
Thinke now on rich amendments; hope to lay by
with this months snake, thy sluffe; in which do lye   10
Armies of lice incampt, to vndermine
thy other halfe of vigor, which doth pine
in clothes more wretched, then those first which Adam
patcht vp through shame, to hide him and his Maddam;
But let this pass, for now of tidinges gladd
I meane to singe first Inuocation had
for some slight rapture, to Poets freend Apollo

Apollo Pythysass | the <u>Pythy-ass</u>, and sure hee heares mee hollow,
in doinge which, whilst I so busie am,
One y^t Homer men- | mee thinkes I feele a feirce Ethusiasme,   20
tioneth who was | that mulls my Intrailes and makes mee thus aduenture
<u>heard tenne</u> myles | and speake as freely, as If I were Stentor;
It doth appeare by inke, squirted from Brittaine
that our King Iames, who Spaniardes now doth spitt on
and meanes to cast his Scabberd, full of rust
which whilom was a sworde, euen in their teeths y^t lust
to bee his foes, I say it doth appeare
that this our Pilott will a New course steare
and minds to powre his pocketts out on warfar\<r\>e
to maintaine his bold English which now are farre   30
Dispersed in the spatious Germaine Climate
Some in rude Bohem, Some in the Palatinate,

Coullers | but since the former forsaken haue thier <u>vandall</u>
and to their Nation are become a scandall,
by sneakinge all a way, when euery man drewe
I haue no Newes for them, nor their St Adrewe
ffellowes at armes, Protectors of the Rhine

Eaden | to whose faire <u>Eden</u> you are Seraphine,
tis you to whome I singe this newes of mine }
Know then (sadd Souldiers) that, that selfe same Kinge   40
who neuer yet did eate Swines flesh or Linge,
On Information of your wants, hath sent
as much as from the Chequor could be rent,
for your releife. Huge Mountaines of bright ore   bore
Comes rowlinge towards you, which some thinke) Rawleigh\<t\> ^
a way with him, when hee returned home — a,

---

8 *buffe*] First *f* written more like an *s*, but both letters are crossed. Buste is a possible reading. **22** *Stentor*] What appears to be a tilde subscribes *e* (cf. l. 33). **27** *say*] *a* overwrites unreadable letter. **33** *vandall*] What appears to be a tilde subscribes *n* (cf. l. 22).

from the disfated conquest of St Toma,
Nor is this all, besides it is prouided,
that hence forth, our affaires bee better guided,
Hence forth the wallnut-man shall rest in quiett   50
soe shall the rascall Puddinge, (or Doggs a dyett)
which on the Markett place, was wount to acte
such greasie agonies, when Souldiers lackt
Hence forth <shall> wee shall no more bee our owne Moathes
for very hunger to goe eate our clothes
All faults shall now bee mended, and our wages
shall bee as good as twas in elder ages.
indeede his highness heares that for our labours,
and marching soe longe after pipes and tabours
for weekely pay wee take no more nor can,   60
then three pence, or <u>two Coppsticks</u>, by the man,

A Coppsticke or bald pat hath ye valewe of an English <u>shillinge</u> }

And here vppon (they say) at this his Maiestie
storm'd beyond measure, and (by my Soule) grew teastie
with doggs and men, and (with gods wounds) hee mused
wee should so longe with bald pates bee abused
Hee sweares hee doth allow the meanest Centrie
seuen shillings English, and to the Gentrie
some shillings more, and (faith) it is no euill Lawe
that yonkers should distinguist bee fro'<m> th' Quiu'la
Old Iemie stopes his Nose att this, but not his eies   70
h'es none of your Conniuers, he'll chastise
and (Nimrod-like) will hunt those foolish men,
and thinke to put vs off, <(> with 2 for ten,
The winds are turn'd, O Captaines, whether run yee
tis true the Kinge hath sents great store of Moneye,
But soft, fore ere you toucht looke that yee sweare
You'le pay the Kings allowance to a haire,
Els, by the Lyon on his breast, he vowes
hell bend his bowe att you, as well as browes
hath hee through all his Teritories, and through London   80
Causd Collections, by which some are halfe vndone
to hide a Captaines Leather-coate in gould
when his powld Souldier, for hunger die'd, or could
And had not cash inough to reach the price
of so much vnguent, as would kill his Lice?
No, no, twas meant that by such contributions,
the Souldier might confirme his resolutions
for victorie; for neuer English yet fearde harme
haueinge where with to eate, & drinke, & keepe him warme,
Then thank (O mortall God) Albions anoyuted)   90

That saist wee shall no more bee disappointed
of what is ours, and that ere wee shall want
thou' llt make thy breeches with out pleates and scant
and ere wee take more deaths, from hunger, could and vermine
thou'llt pawne (thou saist) thy Buck in
Wher art thou (Souldier) whilst I tell thee this
wher is thy voice, or face, to express thy bliss
by such great Newes ? canst thou nor smile, nor speake
and is thy Constitution growne soe weake

Powdred Cab-
bage: }

since the longe Expred date of <u>Crow</u>d, and Sallate   100
thou canst not breake the Cobwebs of thy pallet
caused by to much Iawe-rest ? or dost thou feare
thy teeth soe arm'd with setled rust, should teare,
thy tongue, like straw in Bedlam, should it but dare
to frame weake words, and send them in the ayre.
Fye, vp for shame; show (what thou oughts) a spirght
that makes the spurne the fates as well as fight,
haue I reported Newes for thy Erection,
and newes that might almost giue resurrection,
to bodyes dead? and art thou still deiected ?   110
looking as though thou wer't perboy'ld, or decected
worse then; if some feirce Limbicke had suckt out }
thy Quintisence, and vitalls, to make a doubt   }
whether thou wert an Embrion borne, or not
weake man art thou a Souldier, and dost languish
for each slight storme, of fate, doth anguish
sitt well on Mars his browe and art thou sadd
because the voyage and the men are badd,
because a Captaine that the other Day
durst not walke fleet streete, no see a play   120
and who for feare, of briers, could not come free
to Paules, that hee might dine, there wth Duke Humfrey
who to preuent his 4th dayes fasting spittall
was wount to serke th' euerlasting spittal,
and faine him pockey, to compass broth and mutton
amongst the gowtie guests of famous Sutton
Or if hee faild of that would lie in weight
for Lud-gate-baskett, when it past a straight
And with a rageinge stomack, hath beene glad
with Patience halfe naked, and halfe clad   130
on the Banke-side ta'ttend such wished floates
as might come from the wracke of Oyster boats
Because I say, that such a one doth keepe
halfe thy meanes backe, when hee thy armes doth sweepe

106 *spirght*] g overwrites probable *e*. **127** *weight*] *e* overwrites *a*.

with an Oyld feather, wilt thou bee so vnholy
to fall straight on the dint of Melancholy
and wilt thou dye if hee do͜th stop a shilling
for thy lewd absence from the Church or Drilling
Cannot a foolish Driller, that's misled
with Choller, breake his rest a thwart thy head   140
but straight thou feelst it, and laught not at yᵉ iest
that when hee sleeped not, he brake his rest.
O? Heres a Humor? on such weake groundes
to greiue, to sigh, to faint, to fall in sounds,
yea euen giue vp the Ghost some officer thats meeke
lend mee for I am bloudless, halfe a cheeke
to blush at this will any that shall fight
gainst daring Spinla, craue that hee might
Couer his Drums-head with thy skin, and think
by th'sound to make that feirce inuader shrinke   150
a way with this foule softness: Lett Heraclitus
or els some Phlegmatick vnweaned shitt house
claime title to't, but man at armes bee thou
of such a harsh composure such a brow
that if thou sawst the lightnings did intend
to burne the earths faire face, thou wouldst not send
from of thy heart one sigh, for't; but rather puffe
and helpe that fire to make the world a snuff,
thou'rt not cut out for niceness. thou art meant for one
that should triumph in the Confusion   160
and wrack of mankinde: like Tamberline to bee
An Instument of sad mortalitie
whipping all Nations: Sent to the Earth
to doe the office of a Plague or dearth.
Is this then vocation and is that trance
of heauines still on thee, for shame aduance
rise, and be brauely merrie, and from hence
of those Mortifications, haue no sence
thy Lice and hunger. Not many howres shall run
ere thou shalt haue redress, for by the Sunn   170
thers sent from England a Heidelbergian Tun
of good Iacobuses which now are in <u>Alsatia</u>
thanks to that honest fellow

Iacobus Dei gratia

Stratssburg in
Alsatia a
Towne to wᶜʰ it
was reported
the Money was
sent:.

[108]

{To his Mistris in his Death:.}

O Let mee groane one word into thine eare
and with that groane breake all my vitall springes
thou that wouldst neuer; now vouchsaffe to heare
how Leadas bird on sweete Meander sings
soe dyinge Tapers, lende their fierie flashes
and deadest cinders haue some <living>↑burning↓ Ashes   burning

Those were the lookes, y^t once maintaind my strength
those were the words y^t all my parts did cherish
And what (vnkindest) wilt thou gaine at length
if by the same, I miserable perish   10
this that ↑not↓ a frowne did in a minute starue,
that which a smile did many yeares preserue:.

[109]

Of the Sand runinge in an hower Glass
Doe but consider this small dust
        heer runing in this glass
            By Atomes mou'de
Would you beleeue y^t it your body euer was
            of one that Lou'de   5
And in his Mistriss flame playinge like a flie
        turne to Cynder by her Eie?
Yes; and in death, as life (vnblest)
        to haue it exprest
Eun Ashes of Louers finde no rest :   ffinis

[110]

Goe make thy will, and dye sad soule consumde with Care
  and to thy freinds bequeath their partes, and to thy Loue her share
  but what hast thou (Alas) for to bequeath her more
  then thy tormented Loue sicke hearte, and that shee had before
  O, no shee had it not, for shee disdainde to haue it
  And I haue none of it my selfe, for freely her I gaue it,
  then not receiued by her, yett giuen a way by mee
  what should bee come of this poore heart, or whose heart should it$_∧$ ^{bee}
  tis neither mine nor hers, nor any ons beside
  for ere since first shee prou'd vn kinde, to all y^e world it dide   10
  it dyedd but yett it liues, but liues in loathed breath
  disharted with dispairinge thoughts, and whats such life but death
  O wonder strainge to tell, that at one time should bee
  A liueless life, a liuing death, a hartless heart in mee
  And yett such wonders strainge, Can Cruell shee enforce
  turning a sumtime liuinge man into a liuing Corse
  for as a dreary Ghost voide of all liuely powres

108.11 *that/not*] Neither word deleted. 108.11 *starue*] *a* overwrites unreadable letter.

Walkes nere the less wth seeming life & Malancolly Lowres
Soe walke I (pensiue man) no substance but a shade
fall all the life my heart ere had, intombde in her is Layde,   *20*
Soe that her cruell heart, wherin my heart doth ley
serues as a Trophey of my death to tell how I did dye
for to her great disgrace, but pittie of my smart
when men but seing her doe chance to talke but of her heart
thus (pointing to her brest) shall yet by them be saide
there lyes with in a Murdered Man & y^ts y^e Murdering Mayde:

=== ffinis

[111]

That Lust is not his Aime :

O doe not tax mee with a Brutish Loue
Impute not Lust alone to my desier
No such prophane aspersions ought to moue
from you, the sacred author of my fire
I seeke your Loue, and if you that deny
All Ioyes that you and all the world can giue
My Loue sicke soule would Little satisfie
which wants your grace not foode to make it liue
It is your better parte I would enioy
Your faire affections I would call mine owne,   *10*
tis but a prostitute, and bestiall Ioy
which seekes the gross materiall ^<vse> <of a Lone> vse a lone
the towns not ours; the Market place vnwoñ
nor do I her enioye whose hearts not mine
Hearts Conquest is the worthy Ambition
Seale of our worth A rauishment diuine
Invincible to strength of human hand
vnion deuine of mutuall burninge hearts
which both subdude tryumphinge, both commandes
Soueraigne delights, which God to man Impartes   *20*
      Oh Let mee in, this true Ioy happie bee
      Or neuer may you be enioyde by mee :   }

[112]

Of playing at Tenis by S^r E: D:

When as the hand at teñis playes
and men to gaming fall
Loue is the Courte, Hope is the house
    And Fauour serues the Ball
This Ball it selfe, is due desert
    the line that measure showes
Is reason wheron Iudgment lookes
    where players winne or loose
The Iutties are deceitfull shifts
    the s^t<p>oppers Ielo^usy   10
which hath Sr Argus hundred eyes
    ther with to watch and pry
The fault wherby fifteene are lost
    is want of witt and sence
And hee that brings the Rackett in
      is double diligence
But loe the rackett is free will
    which makes the Ball rebounde
And noble beauty is the Chase
    of euery game the ground   20
Then rashnes strikes the Ball a way
    And there is ouer sight
A bandy ho: the people cries
    And soe the ball takes flight
Now at the length good likinge proues
      Content to bee their game
Thus in the Tennis Court Loue is
    A pleasure mixt with paine: ffinis :

[113]

Wronge not deere Empress of my heart
the merits of true passion
which thinketh that hee feeles no smart
that sues for no Campassion
since of my plaints, seem not to proue
the Conquest of thy beauty
It coms not from defect of Loue
but from excess of duty
For knowinge that I sue to serue
a Saint of such perfection   10
as all deuine, but none deserue
a place in her affection

112.2 (right margin, not transcribed)] Modern pencil notation: *Sir Edw. Dyer.*   **112.25** *at the*] A line appears to delete both words, but the line has bled through the leaf from the recto.   **113.11** *as*] *s* overwrites unreadable letter.

I rather chose to want releife
then venter the reuealinge
where glory recommends the greife
despaire destroyes the healinge.
Thus those desires that Clime to highe
for any Mortall Louer
when reason cannot make them dye
discretion doth them Couer   20
Yet when discreation doth bereaue
the plaintes which I should vtter
then thy discreation may perceiue
that Silence is a Sutor
Silence in Loue bewraies more woe
then wordes though nere so wittie
the begger that is dumbe you know
may challenge double pittie,
then wrong not deare heart of my heart
my true though secrett passion   30
hee smarteth most that hides his smart
and sues for no Compassion:

ffinis

[114]

This blacke Night represents my blacker woe,
This burning light, like my harte doth waste,
This mourning Inke, and paper weakest showes
of strongest passions which my Ioyes defaste
Night, Candle, Inke, and paper doe your best
To tell that Loue is cause of my vnrest:

This Night her loathed darkeness doth not see
This Candle wasts, yet dyinge feeles no paine,
This Inke and Paper greifes cheife heraulds bee
and yet themselues, doe free from greifes remaine   10
Night, Cadell, Inke, and paper, you are blest
And being senceless only breederth rest: ffinis

[115]

Art thou so fond to thinke I can bee thine
Since long agoe I was not mine to giue
A nother holdes my heart in dearest shrine
And vnto that dere choice I Constant Liue
Yet will I say I loue thee as my heart   5
But oh a worthier hath my dearest parte:.

113.27 *know*] A dot after this word appears to be a period, but it is higher than normal. It is probably a stray ink mark.   **113.30 *though*]** *o* overwrites *r*.   **114.4 *of*]** Tail of *f* in *of* is extended to make it appear that l. 5 starts with an apostrophe, *'Night.*

[116]

I labor still in vaine
 my hopes end in dispaire
 my pleasure is but paine
 rewarded still with care.
 I clothed am with cares
 my meate is nought but greefe
 my drinke is bitter teares
 Contempt is best releife
 My Chamber nought but woes
 my bed a restless heart   10
 borne vp with fained shows
 my Ioy is bitter smart
 the Mate-less Doue my guest
 my Musicke sighs and Cryes
 Complaints are all my rest
 like streames my wat<er>rie eyes
 My sleepes are watrie groanes
 through gastly shapes of woe
 My wakeinge Endless moanes
 these ills, I vnder goe   ✿   ffinis

[117]

O clearest Moone why dost thou shew thy face
 To such a wretch as hates to view the light
 but still in loathed darkeness would imbrace
 those waies blind fortune, hath to mee behight
 O that thy light, mine eyes might neuer see
 Nor Sunn, nor Starr, might neuer shine on mee.

But wherfore do I shun this light of thine
 since thy pale hew doth shew thou art not free
 from greifes that doth torment this heart of mine
 and thou my partner: Comes to comfort mee   10
 O no this thought doth still augment my Care
 the wofull weight may not with mee Compare :   ⚇   ffinis

[118]

S^r. Henry
Wotton

How happie is hee borne or taught
  that serueth not a nothers will
  whose armor is his honest thought
  and simple truth his highest skill
  whose passions not his Masters are
  whose soule is still prepard for death
  vntide vnto the world <u>with</u> care   <u>by</u>
Of Princes Loue or vulgar breath
  who hath his life from Rumor freed
  whose Conscience is his strong retreete   10
  whose state can <u>neuer</u> flatterers feede   <u>neither</u>
  nor Ruine make <u>accusers</u> greate   <u>oppressors</u>
  who Enuieth none whom Chance doth raise
NOr vice <u>who neuer</u> vnderstood   <u>hath ever</u>
  how deepest wounds are giuen with praise
  nor rules of state, but rules of good
  who vnto God doth Late and early pray
  more of his Grace, then guifts to Lend
  and entertaines the harmeless day
  with a well chosen booke or freind   20
  this man is free from seruile bands
  of hope to rise or feare to fall:

Lord   <u>free</u> of himselfe though not of lands
  and haueinge Nothing, yett hath all:. ⊛   ffinis

[119]

Sweet stay a while, why will you rise,
  the light you see, Comes from your eies,
  the Day breakes not, it is my harte
  to thinke that you and I must parte,
  O stay a while, or else I dye
  and perish in my Infancye:

Deare let mee Dye, in thy faire breast
  ffarr sweeter then the Phenix nest,
  Loue raise desire, with thy sweet Charmes
  With in this Circle of her armes,   10
  And with thy blisfull kisses, Cherish
  My Infant Ioyes, or else they Perish:.

118.14 Nor] *N* added by the transcriber. **119.2** (right margin, not transcribed)] Modern pencil notation: *J Dowlands.*
119.7–12 (left margin, not transcribed)] Modern pencil notation: *This verse is Not in his collected poems.* **119.11 And**]
A flourish is added on lefthand ascender of *A*.

[120]

Verses made by the E: of P:

If her disdaine in you least chaine cann moue
     you do not Loue
for while that hopes giue fuell to your fire
     you shall desire
Loue is not Loue, but giuen free
     And so is mine, soe yours should bee
Her heart that melts at others moane
     to mine is stone
And eies that weepe a strangers hearte to see
     Ioye to wound mee   10
Yett so much I affect each parte
     As causde by them I loue my smarte,
Thus her vnkindeness Iustly must bee gract'd
     with name of Chast.
And that shee frownes, least longing should exceed
     and rageing breed
So can her Rigor neare offend
     Except selfe Loue seeke priuate End.

[121]

{ The Answeare }

Tis Loue breedes Loue in mee, and Colde disdaine
     kills it a gaine
As water maketh fire to fret and fume
     till it consume
None can of Loue More free guifte take
     then Loue from Loue, for Loues owne sake
Ile neuer digge in quarry of a harte
     to haue no parte.
Nor rest in those faire eies, wch alwaies are
     Caniculare.   10
Whoe this wagg, would a Louer proue
     doth show his patience not his Loue
A frowne may bee sometime for phisicke good
     but not for foode
And for that rageinge humor, there is sure
     A gentle cure
Why barr you Loue of priuat End
     which neuer should to publicke tend:.   ffinis

[122]

Once Delia, on a Sunny banke her laide
 And Cupid tooke her for his Mother
     But when hee saw it was a nother
  The Boy gan blush, and straight through feare dismaide
 a way hee flew, and as hee flew, hee Cride   5
     Venus on Earth, lo now I haue espide:

---

120 (after title, not transcribed)] Modern pencil notation: *Pembroke.*   **120.16 *rageing*]** *a* is an altered *i.*   **121** (after title, not transcribed)] *by Ben Ruddier.*   **121.11 *this*]** A short line appears before this word. It resembles the top half of a virgule.

[123]

That hee would not bee beloued:.

Disdaine mee still, that I may euer Loue
  for who his Loue enioyes can Loue no more
  the warr once past, with Peace men Cowards proue
  And shipps retournd, doe rott vppon the shoare
  then though thou frowne, Ile say thou art most faire
  And still Ile Loue, though still I must despaire.

As heat's to Life, soe is desire to Loue
  <?> for these once quencht, both life and Loue are done
  Lett not my sighs, nor teares, thy vertue moue
  like basest mettell doe not melt to soone,   10
  Laugh at my woes, all though I euer mourne,
  Loue surfetts with rewards, his Nurse is scorne:.

[124]

Sʳ: H :. N :

Faire Phillis in a wofull wise
Lay downe vppon A Mirteles roote
when from the Hauen of her Eies
I saw teares fall; Nay starrs shoote,
O death of Deaths (quoth shee) O paine   5
that none, but cruell weightes, shall tell,
Damon till thou returne againe,
In horrors I will only dwell,
    Where restless my sadd howres shall bee
    Vnless I sleepe to dreame on thee:.

---

124 **Heading** (right margin, not transcribed)] Modern pencil notation: *Henry Nevill of Billingbeare.*   **124.3 Hauen**]
Majuscule *H* overwrites minuscule *s*.   **124.8 dwell**] space between *w* and *e*.

[125]

The picture of his Mistris

When mine eies, first admiringe your rare beauty
Secretly stole the picture of your face
they, fearinge they might Err, with humble dutye
through vnknowne paths, Conuaide it to that place
Wher Reason, and true Iudgment, hand in hand,
Satt and Each workmanshipp of sences scand:.

Reason would finde no reason but to Loue it,
 Soe rich of beauty was it full of grace,
 true Iudgment scande each place
 And did approue it, to bee the modell of some heauenly face   10
 And both agreed to place it in my hearte
 whence they decreed, it neuer should departe.

Then, since I was not borne to be so blest,
Your reall selfe faire Mistris to obtaine
yett must your Image dwell with in my brest
And in that secrett Closett still remaine,
where all alone retired, Ile sitt and viewe
Your Picture Mistris since I may not you: ffinis

[126]

T'is true, t'is Day, What though it bee?
O wilt thou therfore rise from mee?
why should wee rise? because tis light?
Loue, that in spighte of darkenesse brought vs hither
Should in dispighte of Light keepe vs to geither

Light hath no tongue but is all Eye
if it could speake as well as spie
this were the worst that it could say
that being well, I faine would stay
and that I loued my hart and Honor soe   10
that I would not from him that bad thee goe.

Must busnesse thee from hence remoue
O thats the worst disease of Loue
the poore, the fowle, the falce, Loue can
Admitt but not the busied man
Hee which hath business and makes loue, doth doe
 Such wrong, as when a married man doth woe:

[127]

Q ueene of beauty most Diuine
  from whose charming shrine
  humane power cannot parte
  without sacrifice of hearte
  Thetis Nimphes had little grace
  whilst your beauty was in place
  and their Influence was cold
  as sent from a watrie mould
  shall I happy call that Night
  where to gaine a pleasing sight   *10*
  pretious Libertie I lost
  and now am on Loues seas tost
  by a Tempest of desire
  mixed full of heauenly fire
  raised by that in chanting face
  of her Sex tho'nly grace
  yes most happy I it call
  though it doe my freedome thrall
  freedome none may nere Compare
  to that happy state where are   *20*
  those in thy faire seruice placed
  and that please to make them graced
  happie Martyr of Constrainte
  whose paine is for such a Sainte
  and who hath for obiect giuen
  the sweete hope of such a heauen
  faire, A strainger terme mee not
  that your Dietie would blott:.   ffinis

[128]

Thou foolish man, that louest to liue in bands
and serue and sue, yea dye, being ouer prest
tying thy soule (borne loose) with thine owne hands
to Liue in Prison in a strangers brest
    Tell mee what gett your broken sleepes? what doe
    your willing Martyrdomes amount vnto.

Sighes with out number, teares that haue no end
 a harte whose best acquaintance is dispaire
 all this and more, what can it else pretend
 but one poore sillie smile or sum such weare   10
      Like to the seruing man who bides much paine
      and Cappes, and kneeles to weare a golden chaine.

What prison can delight, though Diamonds
the wall, and doores bee all of beaten gould
Our soules that should bee Kings liuing in bonds
are subiect vnto those that doe them holde
    Its a poore price of vallor there to die
    where all our Conquest is but slauerie.

Goe then you Amorous Lads to Cupids tents
in the'nd you shall but Venus souldiers proue   20
bestow your spiritts, thoughts and best intents
to make a skirmish in a Maske of Loue
    Your honors and your selues bleede in this warre
    where lipps your swordes kisses, your Conquests are:

[129]

Sweet Lady liue and liue in pleasure
While God, while Nature, giues you leasure,
all haue a time, and time being gon
to vs againe returneth none
wee liue not while, wee thinke on death
for wee euen dye while wee haue breath
to thinke of Death; as of the thinge
which once to all an end must bringe,
is good; but not so to apply it
as good to wish, or badd to flye it.   10
Life is Gods guift, the dearest treasure
the world still hath in highest measure
not to bee bought for wealth or gould
for Crowne, nor Kingdomes, to be sould,
No wretch soe Low, no Kinge so high
but would loose all rather then dye.
sweet is life, by Natures reason
Death neuer comes but out of season
Many that wish death when they see it
for small delay, would richly fee it   20

128.20 *souldiers*] *e* overwrites unreadable letter.

The sunn falls, but returnes againe
the Moone growes new after her wane
waters to floods, then Ebes doe turne
but life, once past, doth nere returne
Then Lady take your time and liue
to life giue time, to tyme life giue
Say Death ends paine; procureth ease
say Death hath naught that may displease
Say Death no feeling hath, nor sence
and soe is fenced from offence   30
Say life, doth feeling to vs bring
and feeling is it that doth stinge
yett let the sting, sting nere soe much
Life tickles it with sweetest touch
and euen the heart that liues in paine
still couetts life, to paine againe,
Nay say that which you best may say
you reasons most assured stay
That nothinge here desires your beinge
vnto your worth, nothinge agreeinge   40
Your minde wch heauen sweetly storeth
on Earth no worldly thing adoreth,
Aboue the skies, your Climing thought
Soares still and elce doth wonder nought
heauens a house, thats fitt for you
And Angells fit Companions too
You so are pleasd beneath to Liue
As halfe youre selfe, to heauen you giue
and make the world, and heauen agree
while world, and heauen, in you wee see.   50
yett time will bee, when with out Camber
of earthy mould or worldly slumber
Eternity you shall enioye
freed from all Care, from all annoy
meane while thou you the world hate
scorne not to mend the worlds estate
and liue yet for the worlds sake
though no account of life you make
shall vertue fade, shall beauty die
which is the worlds glorious eye   60
those things the world which life do fill
and God thus grace the world will
Angellike Creatures, som must liue
which glorie to the world may giue
Then Lady since God did not daine
A life to you, thinke it not vaine: ⊛

21 *againe*] There is a small space between *a* and *gaine*. 49 *agree*] There is a space between *a* and *gree*. 66 *A*] A flourish extends from lefthand ascender.

[130]

Why do wee loue these things which wee call weomen
which are like feathers blowne with euery winde
regardinge least, those which do most esteeme them
and most deceitfull when they seeme most kinde
and all the <be> vertue that their beautie graces
It is but painted like vnto their faces.

Their greatest glory is in Rich Atire
which is extracted from some hopefull liuers
whose witts and wealth, are bent to their desire
when they regarde ye guifte more then the giuers.   10
And to encrease their hopes, of future bliss
theyle sometime stretch their Conscience for a Kiss

Some loue the windes that bringe in golden showres
And some are meerely won with Commendation
Some Loue and hate and all with in two howres
and thats a fault a mongst them most in fashion
but put them all with in a scale to geither
their worth in waight will scarce pull downe a feather

And yet I would not discommend them all
If I did know some worth to bee in any   20
tis strange that since the time of Adams fall
that God did make none good, and made soe many
And if hee did, for those Ile truly mourne
because they died before that I was borne: ffinis :

[131]

Catch mee a starr y^ts falling from the skie,
Cause an immortall creature for to die.
Stop with thy hand the current of the Seas
Pass through the Center to the Antipodes.
Cause time returne, call backe yesterday,   5
Cloth Ianuarie like the Month of May.
Weigh out an ounce of flame, blow backe ye winde,
And then finde faith in a womans minde:. ///

130.12 *sometime*] There is a slight space between *some* and *time*.   130.16 *them*] *e* overwrites an unreadable letter.
131.1-6 (right margin)] large bracket, as indicated.

[132]

There is a place where Care shall not molest,
where Discontent shall not robb hearts of ease
where Sorrow not, make warr vppon our rest
nor yet dispaire haue power to displease
where hope enuirond with faire beames shall chase
as a bright Sunn all vapors of disgrace

What a world is this, Seas full of Danger
Laide with out saftie, Ayre stand with infection
ffire tiranizinge like a Conquering strainger
all takeing harme, from harmes as by reflection   10
hurt so with hurt, and ill is chaing with ill
that Mischeife needs must all wth mischeife fill.

Why stay wee then engulft, in dangerous waues
why take wee not our oares and hoise vp saile
to gaine that Land which knowes not any graues
and wheare no feare, no sinn, no death preuailes
then in immoderate greife lett vs not rest
there is a place where Care shall not molest: ffinis :

[133]

A Song which
Childock Tich-
-borne traytor
made of him-
selfe in the
Towre ye night
before hee
sufferd.

My prime of youth is but a frost of Cares
My feast of Ioy, is but adish of paine
My crop of corne, is but afeild of T<?>ares
And all my good, is but vaine hope of Gaine
The day is fledd, & yet I saw no Sunne
And now I liue, and now my life is done.

My spring is past, & yett it hath not sprung
The fruit is deade, & yet ye leaues be greene
my youth is past, and yet I am but young
I saw ye world, & yet I was not scene   10
My thredd is cut, and yet it is not spunn
And now I liue, and now my life is done.

I sought for death and found it in my wombe
I look'd for life, and yet it was a shade
I trode ye ground, & knew it was my tombe
And now I dye, & now I am but made
The Glass is full, & yet my glasse is runne
And now I liue, & now my life is donne.///
                               ffinis

132.3 rest] *t* overwrites probable *e*.   **133.2 adish**] written as one word.   **133.3 T<?>ares**] The cancelled letter is probably an *e*.

[134]

Natura negat facit indignator versum.

.

.

.

.

.

.

. Has left his boys play, scornes to bee so base
as bow his witts to those forgotten rimes
whose often births indee'rd his former tymes
to Tapsters Ostlers, and that loyly Crewe
of Soueraigne Bacchus wittie mate Iet true
his wanto youth and verse hath made them merrie
and serues to drawedowne white Canarie Sherrie
And hee by some was then deemde borne for nought
but to imploye some ballet singers throat
These times are chaing'd: hees great and tis the guise   (10)
of rai'sd estates (though madmen) to growe wise
One pattents Power hath chaingd both minde and bloud
and made him at a clapp as great, so good,
tis blame to thinke him what hee was: his Coats
and Cassockes worth, hath kild his wilder Oates
his former toyes (beleeu't) hee now disdaines
as much as Caluin or the Puritanes
whose huckstringe rimes preuent the dearth of Spaine
in his owne gutts: who hath not what to eate
Or weare, butts witts, they're all his Cloath and meate   (20)
Some Taylor or Some Fennor dares to lye
and clapp his name to theire Sale Poetrie
Or else perhaps, twas some Satiricke Quill
that whipt and scurgd our Wood stocke sceane, who still
beare Malice in their Inke: Some such did doe it
and Coin'd a Deanery to steale Creditt to it
beleeue or this or worse, but nere suppose
heele yeeld to owne such flatteries as those
such an extortion can not but vndoe
the seruil'st minde to pay and flatter too   (30)
I'st possible' to thinke that hee should longe
Once more to bee the ground of Pigions songe

---

134 (space and dots, including line numbers)] (See notes).   **134.(5)** *wittie*] *w* overwrites *d*.

Or that hee should prouoke Court witts to singe
the second part of band stringe and the ringe
Or Letts suppose that hee (which here my braine
will not admitt) made triall of that vaine
that earst his Muse enrich'd him with: that hee
once more awak't his slumbring facultie
Yet sure hee would prouide his verse might bee
perfect and round with out all knauerie   (40)
The Sacred volume questionles should scape
the violence of a Poetick rape
that Nickname Mother Zebede could not
proceed from one engraf'te in Leuies Lotte
Since each abuse of Scriptures purer line
giues stronger proofe of th<?>' Atheist then Deuine
In breefe, his callinge, place, degrees, disclaime
this stupid act; this iniurie of fame,
nor will I ere beleeue Soe rich a spiritt
Should raise it selfe by ballads more then merritt :

Page note] Open space left unused as indicated. Two poems have been added at later date. The first is entitled "An Epitaph upon a Pigmie"; the second is headed "Aliud Epitaphium." (Left margin, not transcribed)] Modern pencil notation: *In handwriting of John Wale.*

[135]

To the Kings most Excellent Maiestie.
the humble petition of M^r. ffra‸^uncis
Phillippes Esquier : in the behalfe of his
Brother Sr Robert Phillipps : who
was a Prisoner in the Tower of   }
London : Anō Domi 1622 :   }

Most Dread Soueraigne: ⊛

If the Thrones of Heauen, and Earth, were to bee sollicited one and
the same way, I would haue learned by my often prayinge, to God
for your Maiestie how to pray to your Matie: for others. But the
Liturgies of the Church, and Courte, are Different, as in many poynts,
soe especially in this, that in ‸↑γ^e↓ one there is not so poore a sinner but
may offer his vowes ymediatelye to the Almightie, wher as the
other a right Loyall Subiect may powre out his soule in vaine
with out Ora pro nobis : now such is the obscure condition of your
humble suppliant, as I know no Saint a boue your sacred person,
to whom I can addresse my orisons, or on whose mediacõn I dare   10
repose the least assurance, lett it therfore bee lawfull in this extraordinarie occasion to pass the ordinary formes and <?>raysinge
my spiritt a boue vncerten<?>ties, fix my entire faith vppon your
Maties: supreame goodnesse, which is and euer aught to bee, esteemed
both the best tribunall, and best Sanctuarye for a good Cause, But
how so euer my Cause bee, itt would bee high presumption in mee to
stand vppon itt, I haue therfore rather chosen to cast my selfe
att your Maties: feete, from whence I would not willingly rise, but
there remaine a monument of Sorrow, and Humillitie, till I had obtained some gratious answere, to my petition. for though your   20
Maties: thoughts cannot descend soe Lowe, to conceiue how much it
imports a distressed Subiect, to bee reliued, or neglected, yett you
may bee pleased to beleiue, that wee are, as highly affected, and as
much anguished with the extremities that oppress our Little
fortunes, as Princes are with theires. I speake not out of any pride

Page 153 (commencing line 2)] Every line is underlined in Modern pencil notation.

I take in comparing smale things with great, but only to dispose yo[r] Matĩe
to a fauorable Construction of my words, if they seeme ouer chardge with
Zeale and affection; or expresse more ernestnesse then perhaps yo[r] Ma[tie]:
may thinke the busines merritts. ffor as my selfe values it, the sute I am
to make to yo[r] Ma[tie]: is no slight one. and it may safely bee graunted with   *30*
out the trouble of Referrees, for I dare assure yo[r] Mat[ie] vppon my life, it
is neither against the Lawes of your Kingdome nor will diminish
any of your Royall Treasure, either that of your Coffers, or that of
your peoples hearts. itt beinge only an acte of Clemencie or a
worde, for euen that will suffice to create in your poore distressed
suppliante a new hearte, and send him a way as full of contentment
as hee is now of greife, and Despaire: Nor is it for my selfe that I
importune your Ma[ties]: grace but for one that is farr more worthie, and
in whome all that I am, consisteth; my Deare and only Brother who
by (I know not what misfortune) hath fallen, or rather beene pusht   *40*
into your Matỹes high Displeasure, not in Darke and crooked wayes
(such as corrupt ill affected subiects vse to walke, and were wount to
breake their neckes-in) but euen in the greate Roade, which both him
selfe and all good Englishmen (which know not the priuie path of
the Courte) would haue swer[e]n had Led most safely and most directly
to your Ma[ties]: seruice; from your Ma[ties] Displeasure (then which
there needes no other inuention, to Crucifie a generous and honest
minded Subiect) hath issued, and beene deriued vppon him a
whole torrent of exemplarie punishments. wherein his reputation, his
person, Estate haue greiuously suffered. ffor haueing vppon the   *50*
last recesse of Parliament retired himselfe to his poore home in
the Cuntrie, with hope to haue breathed a while after the trouble some affaires, and still breathing nothing but your Ma[ties] seruice
he was sent for, ere hee had finished his Christmas, but a Seriant at
armes, who arested him in his owne house, with as much terror
as belonges to the apprehendinge of Treason it selfe, but thanks
bee to god his Conscience neuer started, and for his obedience,
hee well shewed itt was not in the powre of any authoritie to
surprize it, for at the instant with out asking so much as a minutes
time of Resolution, hee rendered himselfe to the officers discretion   *60*

Entire page] Every line is underlined in Modern pencil notation.

who accordingly to his direction brought him vpp a Captiue, and presented him to the Councell Table as a Delinquent, from whence hee was as
soone committed to the Tower, where hee hath beene euer since kept close
Prisner, a˄nd that with so strict a hand as his Deare beloued wife, and my
selfe haueing some time since, an vrgent and vnfeyned occation, to speake
with him about some priuate busines of his familie, and there vppon
makeinge humble sute to the Lords of your Maties: most honorable priuie
Councell, for the fauour of access wee weare (to the great discomforts)
Denied; by reason (as their Lordships weare then pleased to declare vnto vs)
that he had not then fully satisfied your Mat^ties in some pointes, which is   70
soe farr from beinge his faulte, as I dare say, it is ye greatest part of his
affliction, that hee sees himselfe debarde from the meanes of doing itt

   The Lordes Commissioners that were appointed to examine his offence, since
the first weeke of his imprisonment haueing not done him the honor to bee
with him, by which meanes not only his bodye, but the best parte of his
minde, namely his humble intentions) are kept in restraint

   May it therfore please your most Excellent Matie: now at the Length after three Months extreame durance to ordaine some such course of expedition in this Cause as may stand with your Iustice; and yet not
auert your Mercye, either of them will serue our turnes. But that   80
which is most agreeable to your inclination, will best accomplish o^r desires,
to liue still close is all one, as to bee buried aliue, and for a man that
hath any hope of Saluation, itt were better to pray for the day of
Iudgment: then to lie Languishinge in such wakeinge miserie, yett not
our, but yor Maties: will be done: ffor if in your Princelie wisdome
you shall thinke it to soone to restore him to his former Condition or to
accept of the fruites of his correction, an humble and penitent submission for his vnhappiness in offendinge your Maties: which I assure
my selfe is Longe since ripe and growne to full proportion, in so forward
an affection and soe proper for all manner of Loyall Duties, as hee   90
hath euer beene, if I say itt be not yet time, to shew Mercie but y^t
hee must still remaine with in the walls of Bondage to expiate what
hee did with in those of priuiledge, my hope is that hee which will
Die at any time for yor Maties seruice, will find patience to liue
euery where for your Maties: pleasure : Only Let mee beseech your
Matie: againe and againe not to Deny your most humble and obedient
Subiect that mittigation of the Rigor of his suffering so farr as to

Entire page] Every line is underlined in Modern pencil notation.

graunt him the Libertie of the Tower, and that hee may no Longer groane
vnder the burthen of these incommodities, which daily preiudice his health
and fortunes in a \<greater\>↑higher↓ degree (I beleeue) then your Matie: either knowes
or intends.   *101*

    I am the more bould to importune your Matie: in this pointe of fauour, because
it concernes my owne good, and preseruation, for yor Matie: shall vnderstand
that I haue no meanes to Liue your Subiect, but what proceedes from his
Brotherly Loue and bounty, soe that if I may not bee suffered to go
vnto him, and receiue order for my maintenance, I know not but our
ffather which art in Heauen, of whom I can begge my Daily bread,
hee that was my ffather vppon earth, is Longe since departed, and if I
haue not beene misinformed who was then beyond Seas
Yo^{r} Maties: anger was to him, Little better then the Messenger of Death;   *110*
Though I perswade my selfe it was rather sent in yor Maties: name
then by your warrent, for what vse could your Matie: haue of his
beinge no more, who neuer was, nor euer could bee, but your faithfull and affectionate Seruante, who in his soule addored your Royall
Person, as much as euer any Mortall Man did a Mortall God.

    And Lastlye whose heart was so bent to please yor Matie: that y^{e}
verie sound of your Displeasure was enough to breake itt. More
perfect Obedience then this, can no Subiect shew to make his Soueraignes fauour, and Disfauour equall, to Life and Death; Pardon
mee Dread Soueraigne in this action I cannot hinder my ffathers   *120*
Ghost from appearinge, for how can it possible bee at rest, as
Longe as your fatall displeasure raignes in his poore familie and
make it the house of Continuall mourninge. Remoue then if it
bee your blessed will, the Cloudes that haue so Longe hunge ouer
our heads, and Lett not the present storme that wants matter
to produce, extort a Thunderbolt, for what is Phillipps, or the
sonne of Phillippes that your Matie: should destroye them

    Wee are vnworthy of Cæsars anger, as well in regarde of o^{r}
meanes as of our innocency:

    To conclude my prayers. I most humbly beseech yor Matie: to   *130*
forgiue them, and lett not the Ignorance of the stile of Ceremonies: vsde in Courte bee imputed to the humble and well
meaning Suppliant, as a willfull want of reuerence, for there
liues not the Dominions a Subiect in whose breast, the two
Loyall qualities of Loue and feare doe more religiously meete
or who could more willingly part with his owne essence to add
the least acquisition to the greatnesse and Matie of his Souerainge.
True it is the subiect that imployed the facultye of my Loue

Entire page] Every line is underlined in Modern pencil notation.

at this present, was of such a nature as I could not denie itt the
vttermost of my affection, and hee who thinkes hee can neuer speake   140
enough may easilie speake too much, my comfort is, that neither my
brother nor my selfe can bee saide to haue failed or exceede ed in
any thing but word<e>s, but what will that auaile vs. vnless yor
Matie will pardon with out which all Crimes are equall and as
much danger Lieth in an humble petition, as in a plott of high
Treason . Bee pleased then most gratious Soueraigne, to
giue to vs backe of our questionable words, and keepe our vndoubt-
ted hearts. att least shew vs so much mercie as to Iudge vs accordinge to your owne goodnes: ffor if wee had not Libertie to
appeale thither wee should bee in danger of loosinge the happiest   150
parte of our Birth-right: and instead of beeinge your Maties subiects
become other mens slaues. ffrom your Matie therfor your faithfull Subiect craues and expectes the ioyfull worde of Grace, which
If I may bee soe happye, as to carrie my poore Brother before
hee growes any elder in miserie I shall fill many an honest heart
with praise and thankes giuinge, and for my particular, your
Maties: greatest fauour, and Liberalitie, shall not more obli‸^ege
or affect others, then this your Royall Clemencie shall mee:.
 In Memorie wherof I shall daily pray that your Maiestie
may obtaine all your desires in heauen and bee obeyed in all your   160
commaundes on Earth, that you may <see> Liue to see your holy Intentions take effecte for the good of Christendome, and soe honor
the age wee Liue in, with the merritts of your wisdome,
  ffinallie that your felicitie in this world may ouer take that
  in the next, and make you weare a parpetuall Crowne
  to Gods glory and your owne:
            Yo^r Maties: Most humble Loyall
                and English Subiect

                ffrauncis Phillippes

                1622:

139–163] Underlined in Modern pencil notation. **142 *exceede ed*] Final *e* of root word, a minuscule *e* appears to overwrite a minuscule *e*. As indicated, there is a space before the inflection.

[136]

Muld Sacke :
or
The Apologie of Hic Mulier :　　　　}
To the late declamation against her　}　　　The books name
Exprest in a short declamation.　　　}
Non est mollis e terris ad astra via <?>.　}

Muld Sacke
His gratulatorie thankefullnesse verse to Hic Mulier,
for her dedication :　　1620.

In recompence, swet heart, of thy sweet Booke,
　My picture I thee send, wheron pray looke.
　All Maides, and Bookes, not thus rewarded bee,
　Loue hath a Tongue; although no Eyes to see.
　Then fairest faire, in this sweete little frame,　　　　　　5
　My heart and selfe I prostrate to thy name.
　Vowinge my sword, my yellow Band, and ffeather,
　My smoking pipe, Scarfe, Garters, Roses either
　With my spruse Bootes, neat Hornes, and all I giue
　To thee, by whose sweet Loue, I breathe, reigne, liue :.

---

10 reigne] *e* overwrites probable *a*.　**Space below poem**] The transcriber left the bottom portion of page unused. At a later date, a poem headed *Sr Thomas Overbury, Epitaph written by himself* was added.

[137]

Mistris Turners Repentance;
Who, about the poysoning of that Ho: Knight Sir
Thomas Ouerbury, was executed the 14th day
of Nouember : 1615 : :

To stay the venome of Ill speakinge breath
Kills men aliue, and makes them liue in Death
By his il-sounding Language, this poore scrowle,
My Christian Loue, to a Repentant soule
Sends to the view of all; that all may see,
That did not see her, all the signes that bee
Soule-sauing greifes bewrayers: how her hands,
(While shee with heauy suspiration stands)
To Heauen are raised: how her eies are bent
The way of Angells; fixt, as then shee meant,   *10*
(with Egle-sight) that Glory to behould
Eye neuer saw; Eare heard, nor Tongue hath told.
How humbly-lowe, in her deuotious prayer
Shee bends her knee, escaped from the snare,
Of Hells temptation. Heare her likewise speake:
While her Repentant sorrow striues to breake
Her very heartstringes; when her tongue bewr^ayes
The many mischeifes, of those many dayes
Shee had bin slau'd to Sathan. Heere sayd shee,
Are many come, a wretched thing to see,   *20*
Take her deserued Death: may my sad end
Teach euery bad beholder, how to mend
All ill (in cogitation) fore it growes
To that foule act, our frailty ouerthrowes.
Dehorting still from those beloued sinns,
Are bosome Traytors; baites: By which Hells winnes
Increase to his blacke Kingdome. But in cheife
From those whose sad remembrance, were her greife
In that last houre of life: lust, gawdy pride,
And wanton painted pleasures, whose strong tide,   *30*
Had borne her so from goodness. And in summe
(For sinne, with her, to this account did come)
All, all is vaine; and this vaine world can showe
Nothing that's good, but what from Heauen doth flowe,
Then liftinge vp her fingers to her eye
And feelinge those faire fountaines to bee drye
From which had runne so large a flood of teares
Alas (said shee) heere little Grace appeares.

And some (I feare mee) that behould this face,
Will iudge this want of teares, my want of Grace.   40
But good, good People doe not, my heart's sore,
And I haue wept so much, I can no more.
With that, fresh teares vppon the sudden fall,
Extortinge water, from the eies of all
That stood to see, and heare her: from the deepe
of greife, shee weepes, to thinke shee could not weepe.
And through those teares, from her suspitious thought,
(Knowinge, men knew shee had much mischeife wrought)
Shee thus breaks out: When Death hath clo'sd mine eies
And that my body, colde, and sencelesse lyes,   50
My spotted Soule, will bee imagin'd straight,
To sinke to Hell, vnder my sinns sad weight.
But, Heauen hath seal'd, to my afflicted bre\<a\>st
My sinns forgiuenesse, and my soule possest
With full assurance, of that endless good
Is purchas'd only, by my Sauiours blood.
I know (said shee) that shee that with her teares,
Washt Iesus feete, and wipt them with her heires,
Was, like my Selfe a Sinner; yet her Sinne,
Did Mercy wipe (as it had neuer bin)   60
From forth the booke of Iustice, this I know,
And know that God, that did that Mercy showe
Hath showen the like to mee, for in my heart,
I feele heau'ens pleasure, dreadless of Hells smart.
Then wistly looking, on that fatall place,
Where life must leaue her, and pale Death imbrace
Her key-cold Body, as that Death to dye
Did more then Deaths grim visage, fright her eye;
From such conceit (disturbant to her minde)
Doct: That <u>man</u>, (in Death, the way of Life to finde,)   70
\<Th\> Did then direct her; with religious care,
Doth thus recall her: You must now forbeare
To place a thought, on earth, or Earthly things
And only that, Cælestiall comfort brings
Fixe heart & eye on: Now should you transend
The troublous view of this repro^achfull end;
Regardinge no disgraces. On a tree
Dyd Our Redeemer; hee that dyed for thee,
And all repentant Sinners. For the way,
It makes no matter (greatly) how wee pay   80

44 *eies*] Initial *e* overwrites an unreadable letter.

This debt of Life, so Heauen assurance geiue,
That then wee dye, a better life to liue.
Fire, water, Torture, any way: 'tis well
To goe to Heau'<e>n, eu'n by the Gates of Hell.
From these sweete woordes, her weakeness did receiue
Such heauenly comfort, shee prepares to leave
The body es burthen (and her Soule release,
From that sad Prison, to Eternall Peace)
With cheerfull freenesse. No man knows ye brest;
But this, her Language, to the life exprest;   90
In this blest manner: Let not any heere,
That notes mee pale, and quaking, thinke tis feare
To see my Deaths-man: Or to meete with Death
That now attends mee, for the minutes breath
Is yet within mee. No, 'tis no such thinge,
This little paine, nere-endinge pleasures bringe
And therefore I embrace it. This pale cheeke,
Sighes, palsy quaking faintnesse and the like,
Are the effects of greife; a harty woe,
That makes mee heart˜t-lesse: to the best I knowe.   100
As if shee thus had sayd: These Embleames are,
Of Peters sorrow; not of Cains despaire.
To that, shee adds this comfort; Lord my God
So deerely welcome to mee, is this Rod,
That (stead of harsh repininge) I giue praise
And humble thanks, that through soe many dayes
Of Soule-polutinge mischeife, 'twas thy will,
I liue to tast it. In the prime of ill,
Had sodaine sicknesse, or some other Crosse;
(When drosse was Gold, and golden vertue drosse)   110
Bereau'd my Life,'I had then most wretched bin,
And vnrepented, perisht in my sinne.
Then with a Mothers tender Loue, and care,
Shee calls to minde her children; and her Prayer
Directs to Heau'en; desiringe, thence descend
Those holy blessings, might their soules defend
'Gainst Hells suggestions; that, (as shee had done)
They neuer might, in graceless courses runne.
And (now) to make her penitence more cleare,
That Image-worship, that her breast once b<e>are   120
A heart Deuote to; Shee in death denyde,
And Rome, and Romes fowle Heresie defide.
Praies, Heau'ns best blessings, On our Royall Kinge

---

86 *leave*] *v* overwrites unreadable letter or letters. 100 *heartlesse*] Hyphens added as indicated, before and after ˜t-
111 *Life,*] A second comma appears directly above the first, creating a diacritical mark in the shape of a colon, but made of two commas.

Might still bee shewr'd; and a continuall springe,
Of Peace, content, and happy dayes remaine,
With him, with his, and all his right maintaine.
Thus shee, in life, was so extreamely nought
As if one Act, or sound Religious thought
Remaind not in her; in her end appear'd
A blest Repentant; as if heauen had clear'd   130
Her spotted Soule, and in, his secret will,
Then made all good, that was before all ill.
What God will doe, hee can: with this I rest:
'T becomes a Christian, speake, and hope the best.

ffinis : T. B.

[138]

Saint Thomas haueinge lost his Master, sought about,
But in good faith hee could not finde him out.
But when those bands of Inbeleefe were broke, that bound him,
Hee then cryd out, by Gods wounds I haue found him.   ffinis

[139]

With in this Rocke the Rock him selfe is layd,
Who both the Tombe, and the tombe maker made.
A Man hee was, there was noe such man beside
None liud so Iust, none so vniustly dyde.
A world of sinns were layd vnto his charge
To saue a world hee's willinge to discharge
and suffer all: yet not the least his spott
Great need hee dyed, and yet hee needed not.
One day hees dead the Sone of Heauen here sleepes
The second rest the ffather his Sabboth keepes   10
The Third, the quickninge spirit him reuiues,
Now haueinge vanquisht Hell, and broke deaths giues
You holy weomen may your labour saue
Vnless you'le giue your vnction to a graue.
To anoynt the Lords anoynted tis in vaine
This Trinity of dayes hee's rose againe :.

ffinis

139.1 him selfe] Space as indicated.

[140]

A one eyd boy borne of a halfe blinde Mother
Match less for beauty both saue the one to tho'ther.
Lend her thy light sweet boy and shee shall proue
The Queene of beauty, Thou the God of Loue :   ffinis

[141]

Loue, if a God thou bee'st, then euer more bee merci full & iust.
If iust, O wherefore did thy dart
wound mine alone and not my Mistris heart
If Mercifull, why then am I to paine reserud
  Who haue thy Dietye soe truly serud   5
  Whiles shee, who for thy power cares not a fly
  Laughs thee to scorne yet liues at liberty
O then If thou a God wouldst counted bee
  Heale mee like her, or else wound her like mee

[142]

Loue whats thy name, a ffrenzy?
Whence thy birth? from Heauen.
How coms it then thou liu'st on Earth,
I liue not there, No? each vsurps thy Name.
Tis true, But hence resounds the shame.   5
I liue not there, My natures pure and Iust.
But lust raignes there, and Loue's a foe to Lust.
                                ffinis

[143]

  A renouation of an Auncient Bishp: }}
    wth will: ye Conq^r: <of> out of St Pauls: }}

Walkers (who so ere you bee)
If it proue you chaunce to see
Vppon a solemne scarlett day,
The Citties Senate pass this way
Their gratefull Memorie to showe   5
Which they the reuerent ashes owe
Of Buishop <u>Norman</u>, heere in hum'd
By whom this Cittie hath assumd
Large priuilidges, they obtain^{e}d
By him, when Conqueringe William raignd
  This beeinge by Barkhams thankfull Minde renewd
  Call it the Monument of Gratitude :   }} ffinis

140.2 *Match less*] There is a space between the syllables, as indicated.   141.1 *merci full*] There is a space between the syllables, as indicated.   143 (below poem)] Written in the hand of John Wale, later owner of the miscellany, describes the subject of this poem. See commentary notes.

[144]

<table>
<tr><td>Kinge
Iames}</td><td>

Mr Martins speech to ye Kinge in ye names of ye Shreifs of London:

The common feares and difficulties wch perplex most confident Orators speak-
inge before Princes, would more confound my distrustfull spirtt, speakinge to
yor highe Matie (most mightie K: and o^r dread Sou'aigne Lord) did I not
know, y^t the message wch I bringe, is to a good Kinge allwayes gratefull.
Curiositye of witt & affected streames of Oratorie I leaue to those
wth more delight to tickle the Princes eares, then satisfie his deeper
iudgment. To mee (most gratious Soueraigne) yor Maties meanest Subiect,
vouchsafe yor milde and princely attention, whiles in the names of these
graue Cittizens, the Shreifs of London and Middlesex, I offer to your
benigne grace, that loyall and harty welcome, wch from that honorable
and auncient Cittie (the heart of this Kingdome) is brought by them.
Whose deepe and inward greife, conceiued for the losse of o^r peerelesse and
Sou'aigne Queene Elizabeth is tourned into excessiue Ioye, for the
approache of yor excellent Matie: by whome the longe and blessed peace of 45
yeeres, is made perpetuall. Greate is the acknowledgement wee owe to the
Memorye of o^r Late Princs gou'nement: Whose farr spred fame, as it
shall liue recommended to posteritye, for euer: so of her flowrishinge Raigⁿe no
other testimonye need to bee required, then y^t of yor high Matie (since none can
bee more honorable) that the like hath not binn read or heard of, in o^r dayes,
nor since the raigne of great Augustus. So that glorious and Victorious
Kings haue iust cause te enuye the glorye and vertue of a woman. But
shee is gatherd in Peace to her ffathers; a memorable instance of yor Maties diuine
observation, y^t Princs differ not in stuffe, but in vse, from Common men.
   Out of the ashes <(> of this Phænix, wert thou Kinge Iames borne for
our good, the bright starr of the North, to wch all true Adamant hearts
had long before tourned themselues: Whose fame, like a new Shunshine,
dispersed those clouds of feare, wch either o^r politique frends, o^r open enemies,
or the vnnaturall factors for the fyft Monarchye, had giuen vs some cause
to apprehend, yea o^r Nobilitye Counsellors and Commons, whose wisdomes and
fidelitie is therefore renowned, as far as this Iland is spoken of, wth a
generall Zeale posted vnto yor Maties subiection: Not more incited here vnto by
the right of yor Mat^{is}: discent, and Royall bloud drawne to this faire inheritance
from the Loynes of o^r auncient Kings; then inflamed wth the fame of yor
Princely and emene_∧ⁿt vertues: Wherewith, as wth a rich Cabinet of p^r-
cious Iuells, yor Kingly minde is furnished, if constant fame haue deliu'ed vs
a true Inuentorye of yor rare Qualities.   A Kinge whose youth
needs no excuse, and whose affections are subdued to his reason: a Kinge w^{ch}
doth not only doe Iustice (wch euen Tyrants doe somtymes) but loues Iustice
(which habit none but virtuous Princes can put on) who imitatinge the free
bounty of the Kinge of Kings, inuites all distressed people to come vnto him:
Not permittinge Gahazi to take tallents of siluer, nor chaunge of rayments.
   In some princs (my Sou'aigne Lord) it is enough y^t they bee not euill,
                                                 but from &

</td></tr>
</table>

10

20

30

40

---

15 *perpetuall*] A tilde through the *p* abbreviates *er*.

but from yor Matie: wee looke for an admirable goodnesse and particular redresse. So straunge an expectation fore runninge yor Matie
cominge, hath so inuested the minds of good men wth comfort, of bad
with feare. And see how bounteous Heauen hath assigned fowre
Kingdomes, as proper subiects, for yor Ma̅ts fower Kynglye vertues.
Scotland hath tryed yor Prudence, in reduceinge those things to order
in the Church and Common wealth, wch the tumultuous tymes of yor
Ma^{ts} infancie, had thare put out of square. Ireland shall re-   50
quire yor Iustice, wch the miseries (I dare not say the Pollicies) of
Ciuill warrs, haue there defaced. ffrance shall proue yor Fortitude,
when necessa͜^rye reason of state shall binde yor Matie to that enterprise.
  But let England bee the Schoole, wherein yor Matie will practise
yor Temperance and Moderation. For heere flattery will assay to vnder
mine or force yor Maties strongest constancie and integritye. Base
assentac̃on the bane of virtuous Pri̅ncs wch like Lazarus doggs licke euen
the Princs soares. A diuise made so familiar to this age by long vse, that
euen Pulpitts are not free from that kinde of treasone. A Treason I   60
may call it most capitall, to poysone the fountaine of wisdome and
Iustice, wherat so many Kingdoms must bee refreshed. Nor can I
bee iustly blamed, to lay open to a most skillfull Physition, o^r true greifs;
Nay it shall bee the comfort of my age to haue spoken the truth to
my Lord the Kinge: and with a heart as true to yor Matie as yor owne,
to make knowne to an vncorrupted Kinge the hopes and desires of his
best Subiects: who as if yor Matie were sent downe from Heauen to
reduce the golden age, haue now assured themselues, that this Iland by
a strange workeinge and reuoluc̃o now vnited to yor Maties: obedience, shall
neuer feare the mischeifs and misgouernements wch other Cuntryes and
other tymes haue felt.   <u>Oppression shall not bee the badge of autho-</u>   70
<u>rit</u>ye, nor insolence the marke of greatnesse. The people shall euery one
sit vnder his owne oliue tree, and annoint himselfe wth the fat thereof;
his face not grinded <u>with extorted suites</u>, nor his Marrow suckt wth
most odious Monopolies, and vnconscionable Lawyers and greedy officers
shall no longer spin out the poore mens cause in length to his vndoinge,
and the delayinge of Iustice. No more shall bribes blind the eies
of the wise, nor gould bee reputed to com̃on measure of mens worthy-
nesse; Adulterate goulde, y^t can gilde a rotten post, make Balam a
Bishop: and Isacar as worthy a iudiciall Chayer as Salomon, where hee
may wickedly sell that Iustice, wch hee corruptly bought. The money   80
changers and the sellers of doues, I meane those wch traffique the
liuings of simple and religious pastors, shall yor Matie whip out of y^e
Temple and common Wealth. For no more shall Church liuings bee
pared to the quicke, forcing ambitious Churchmen (partakers of this
sacriledge) to enter in at the windowe by Symonie & corruption
which they must afterwards repaye wth vsurie, and make vp with
pluralities. The Ports and hauens of these Kingdom^es, wch haue long
                          bin barred shall open the mouthes of their
                                                              Riuers.

---

47 *proper*] A tilde in *the* p abbreviates *ro*.   84 *partakers*] Tilde in *p* abbreviates *ar*.

riuers, and the armes of their Seas, to the gentile amitie, and iust traffique
of all Nations, washinge a way our reproche of vniuersall Pyrats, and
Sea wolues, and deriuinge by the chaunge of homebred commodities   90
with forreigne, into the veins of this Land, that wholsome bloud, and
well gott treasure which shall strengthen the synewes of yor Maties
Kingdoms.   The neglected and almost worne out Nobilitye, shall
now as bright diadems and burninge Carbuncles adorne the Kingly dyadem
     The too much contemned Clergie, shall hange as a p^rtious eareringe at
yor Princely eare, Yo^r Mat$\tilde{y}$e still listninge to their holye Councells.
     The wearied Commons, shall bee worne as a rich ringe on yor royall finger,
which yor Matie with watchfull eye will gratiously looke vppon. ffor
wee haue now a Kinge, y^t will heare with his owne eares, see with
his owne eyes, and bee euen iealous of any great trust, which beinge   100
afterwards become necessarie maye bee abused to an vnlimited Power.
     O my gratious Leige, let neuer any wrye councell divert or puddell
the faire streame of yor Naturall goodnesse: Let not wicked vsurpers
seed lewd Arts to maintaine their lewd purchase to yor Matie, called
to this Empire by the Councell of God & Men, and now beinge Kinge
of so many faithfull hearts, plaine and direct vertue is the safest Policye,
and Loue to them, who haue sworne such loyaltye to you is as a wall of
brasse. They meane to sell the Kinge to his Subiects at their owne price,
and abuse the authoritye of his Mat^ie to their priuate gaine & greatnesse
who per swade him that to shut himselfe vp from the accesse of his   110
people, is the meanes to augment his state. Let mee not seeme tedious
to yor Matie (my gratious Soueraigne) nor yet p^rsumptuos, for I councell
not, but <u>whiles</u> yor Matie hath beene perchaunce, wearied wth ye Complaints
and insinuations of particulars, for priuate respects, Let it bee Lawfull
(my Leige) free from feare or hope, to shew yor Matie the agues wch keepe
longe this great bodye, where of yor Matie the sound head.   Nor
are wee fed with hopes of redresse by imagination, as hungrye men with
a painted banquet, but by assurance of <u>certaine</u> knowledge, drawed out of
the observation of yor Matie fore past actions, and sound book now fresh in
euery mans hands, beinge (to vse yor Ma^te owne words) the viue Ideas   120
and rep^rsentacons of the minde.   Whose excellent and wholesome Rules
yor Matie will neuer transgresse, haueinge bound yor Princely sonne by such
heauy penaltyes to obserue them after you. Nor doth any wise man
Coun- }
cailes }   wish or good man desire y^t yor Matie would follow other <u>Councilles</u> or
examples then yor owne, by which yor Matie is so neerely bounde.
     To conclude therefore, what great cause haue wee to welcome to the
territories of this Cittie yor most excellent Matie. who to make vp the
glorious and happy head of this Iland haue by yor first entrance
brought vs th'addition of an other Kingdome, wch warre could
                                        neuer subdue.

---

103 vsurpers] A tilde in *p* abbreviates *er*. **110 per swade**] There is a space between *per* and *swade*. **113 perchaunce**]
A tilde in *p* abbreviates *er*. **114 insinuations**] There is a line above word, as indicated. **119 actions**] There is a line
above the word.

neuer subdue. As ^{yor} Mat^e vpright gou'ment shall make vs   *130*
partakers of that falicitie wch diuine Plato did only appre-
hend, but neuer see, whose Kinge is a Philosopher, a Philosopher beinge our Kinge; Receaue then (most gratious Sou'aigne)
that loyall welcome wch o^r Cittie sendeth out to meete yor Mãtie.
Our Cittie which for her Loyaltie obedience and faithfull readinesse in all
aciõns, yor Ma^{ts} royall progenitors, had honoured wth the title of their chamber.
  Whose faithfull Cittizens wth true and well approued hearts, humbly lay
at your royall feete their goods and liues, wch they will sacrifice for yor
Matỹes seruice, and defence; with longinge eyes desiringe to receiue
yor Maiestie wth in their walls, whom long since they haue lodged in   *140*
their hearts: Prayinge to Heauen that yor Ma^{ts} person may bee free
from practise, yor soule safe from flatterye, yor life extended
to the possibilitye of Nature; and if not ^{yor} naturall life, yet
yor royall lyne may haue one period with the world, your Princ-
ly of springe sittinge vppon the Throne of their ffathers for
euer more, And wee yor Ma^{ts} humble Seruants, humbly
surrendringe vnto yor Ma^{ts} hands y^t authoritye which wee
hould from you, wishinge from o^r hearts, that all pla<i>gues
may pursue   his   posteritie y^t ˄^{but} conspires yor Ma^{tis} danger: ffinis

---

Double line, center of page] Red ink. **N.B.** Holgate left space open as indicated. John Wale, an eighteenth-century owner of the miscellany, used it to record a short address beginning "To the Queens Most Excell^t Mai^{ty}."

[145]

If shaddowes bee a pictures excellence
And make it show more liuely to the sence
If starrs in bright day doe loose their light
And shine most glorious in the maske of night
Why should you thinke faire creature y^t you lacke
Perfection when your eies & haire bee blacke?
Or that yor beauty which so farre exceedes
The new sprung Lillies in their maiden-heads
That cherry colour of your cheekes and lipps
Should by that darkenesse darken & eclipse.   10
Nor is it fit that Nature should haue made
So faire a Suñe without a cloudy shade,
It seemes y^t Nature when shee first did fancie
Yo^r rare composure studied Nigromancie.
And when to you those guifts shee did imparte,
Shee vsed altogeither the blacke Arte,   A
Shee drewe the Magicke Circle of yor eyes,
And made those sable haires wherein shee tyes
Rebellious hearts, those blew vaines which appeare
Turnd in meander-like to either Sphære   20
Misterious figures are, and when you list
Your voyce commaundeth like an exorcist.
  O if in Magicke you haue power so farr,
  vouch safe to make mee your familiar.
Nor hath kinde nature her blacke art reuealde
In outwarde parts aboue, some bee concealde,
By ye springe head men may, And often knowe
The nature of ye streames wch runne belowe.
So yor blacke haires & eies, doe giue direction
To make mee thinke ^{ye} rest of that complexion.   30
The rest where all rest lyes ^{yt} blesseth man
That Indian mine, that straight of Ma<l>gelan,
That world diuidinge gulph, which who so venters
with swellinge sayles, and rauisht sences enters
In t' a world of blisse, pardon I pray
If my rude Muse p^{r}sume here to display
Secrets vnknowne, or hath her bound ore past
In praiseinge sweetenesse, which I neere shall taste.
Star'ud men know the'rs meate, & blind men may
Though hid from them, yett thinke there is a day.   40
A rouer in the marke his arrowe stick^{e}s
Somtimes as well as hee that shootes at prickes
And if I might direct my shafte aright
That blacke marke would I hitt, but, not the white: ffinis

      D: C: on a blacke Gentlewoman:/

4–9 (left margin, not transcribed)] Modern pencil notation: *Corbet not in poems* (see notes).   **16 Arte**] Majuscule *A* overwrites lowercase *a*, which is also corrected in the right margin.   **35 In t'**] Lower half of an *o* appears after apostrophe. The transcriber may have started to write *in to*, then emended his text to *in t'*.

[146]

The Day :.	A Spanish Iournall: 1623:. The Way :.	

<u>The Day</u> :.   A Spanish Iournall: 1623:.   <u>The Way</u> :.

Aprill: 13!
For Iacke and Tom Pan mourned sore,
Their absence did make knowne their worth
To hasten their returne therefore
The English Saint, Pan manneth forth.

On board: 22.
Saint George, a shipp as snugg, as tight
as euer to the Seas was sett
Then Non-pareil'd by any wight,
Vnlesse parhaps by Dædalus Pett: Rochester

St George his ⎫
day: 23 : ⎭
Lett loose from prison where shee lay
within the Streights of Chattham boomes,
breakes off her chayne in her owne day
as merrily to Gillingham comes   Gillingham   10

But here was drownd her first Commission,
and shee (fast bound) with out her Chayne
Lay 14 dayes, till a new mission
bad hoise sailes to the Downes a mayne.

Of Trumpets, Drums, and Musicks sound
Of shoutes and cryes there was no lacke
But braue St George still keepes her ground
vnmoud, for, the winde was slacke.   20

Maÿ : 8°
The Eight of May, when Neptunes fellowes
had fill'd their gutts with porke and pease
they pufft such winde out of their bellowes
as blew vs right into the Seas.   Maris ostium.

9°
The Ninth of Ioue, and Ponnyatt
wee passing safely ore the sands,
the foule-Sowbeacon, and the flatt,
cast anchor at the North fore land.   North for land.

Reculuers sight was this day's werke,   Reculuers.
god bless vs from such Puritan people   30
who care not for Gods holy Kirke,
yet make shew of a double steeple:

10°
Some Sea-Nimph now had angerd Æolus
who with swolne cheekes pufft so contrarye,
that hence a winde came forth so furious
Our ancors head wee durst not va˄^rye.   ˄r

11°
Fayre Thetis soone swagd Æolus flownes,
blest bee the ayre when shee gan sing
it brought St George to Bedith Downes   Downes
and sent our Capten to ye Kinge   40

Maÿ
Meane while our Masters and the rest
Salute our narrow Seas-Admirall; bold,
And were rehayld by Deputie Best
But the Admiralls selfe was in the Hold.

Maÿ 12°:13°:14°	Our Captaine gone; there fell debates,		The Way
	twixt Dele and vs, for 3 days after		
The Day:	the fight so hott, some of our mates		
	were braine-shot tween yᵉ winde & water.		
15°	But his vnlookt for quicke returne,		50
	did by good fortune part the fray,		
	for hee set saile ten houres past morne,		
	and tooke his souldiers quite a way.		
16°	The 16ᵗʰ shew'd vs Dongeynesse !	Dongeynesse	
	wee look'd for fire, yᵉ Seamans marke		
	but wee perceiued nothinge lesse,		
	twas pist out long since by a Sharke		
	Here gan the winde to blow Contrarie		
	Some foule mouth sure had made a breach;		
	which wee no sooner salud by prayer,		
	but wee past swiftly by the beach.		60
17°	Not long but wee descryd yᵉ wight		
	the Cloyster of yᵗ Southerne Earle,	Weight	
	Oh yᵗ a small shell should benight		
	the beauty of a glorious Pearle		
<18°>	From thence, of winde wee had no wante		
	(as may appeare to cuninge wizards)	Cant Lizards	
	for wee lost eueninge at the Cant		
	and found oʳ morrow at the Lizards		
18°	Now are wee Lanchd into the deepe		
	with west south west our Cape doth match;		70
	and, though wee in our turnes doe sleepe		
	yet Tenne Leagues saile wee in a watch.		
19°	Next morne the force of winde did slacke,		
	but as wee raysed our Deuotion		
	the winde grew higher in our backe		
	and wee runne head a South-west motion<?>		
	Wee constantly held on our Course<s>		
	and had next day with outen faile	Cape Ortegall	
	put in at Groyne, but yᵗ yᵉ Source		
	of Seas held vs to Ortegall:		80
	Oh Enuious Cape, ffuries to rayse		
	of sudden tempests, haile and raine,		
	to barre the Sᵗ George from the praise		
	of 3 days iourney into Spaine.		
Maÿ: 21: 22:	Fowre days the winde here kept vs play	<her>	
23: 24:	and ticktacke was their only sport,		
25:	till on the fiue and twenteth Day		
	wee gott sight of our wished port.		
	The fowre-squa'rd and six storied Tow‸ᵉr<e>		
	where Hercules kept his dearest soule,	Feroll	90
	wee past, but, for the windes did lower		
tack'd	wee tack'd a gaine, and wan Feroll:		

---

54 *Dongeyness*] *y* overwrites *r*, corrected in margin.   **58** (semicolon)] Imperfectly formed, dot to the right of what might have been intended as a comma. Similar to semicolon at line 70.   **76** <?>] Holgate deleted a question mark.

Here had wee visitts by these swinckers
the Capuchine, and Dominicke
good fellows, braue Tobacco drinkers
but that the pipes wrong end they licke

Their booke and beads do make a shewe
they might haue skill to say a Mattin
but their mute tongues gaue vs to know   Galizia :
the Deuill a word they could of Latin.   100

Maÿ: 26°

To Groyne by Barge hence are wee bound
where wee are fedd with salt and grassse
and in the hund-red payd twelue pound
our purest gould to change for brasse.

Wee singe Yorke Yorke for our money
an old but heauy songe God wott
hee rob'd our purse pincht our belly
and put vs all into the pott.

27°

On Tusday euen wee forc'd to straddle
the long eard Mule, to hast our iourney   110
but mounted each into his saddle
seemd fitter for the Spanish tourney.

Verre Mula by line, and by leasure,   3 Leagues
Poco, y, poco, soft and faire;   Petansey :
3 leagues in 5 houres right Dons measure
Petansey is our first days chaire

A faire bridge wafs vs to the towne,
late beautifide with new built housinge,
the old a drowsy Hag burnt downe
as shee in straw her selfe was low singe.   120

28°

Wee reached Perga Wensday night
St Iago giue vs good stomachs to eate,   } 2 Leagues to
for in the selfe same pott wee <u>dright</u>,   <u>dright</u>   } St Iago de
where in their cleaneness drest our meate.   Perga.

29°

On Thursday morne wee passed by
St Alberts Church, a place much blist,
with sacred streames to purifie
Dæmonkes, beleeu't who list.

At Lugo wee this day repose vs,   } 4 legues to
expectinge many great regalo's   } Lugo:.   }   130
but our hearts fell into our hoses   }
where meate, bread, wine, and all did faile vs.

All but bare walls, and they may feede
the eies of a hungrye Trauellier,
with faire round Turretts two-hundred,
and in each one a Cauellier.

The walls are made so thinke and wide
to fend ye Citie from the foe,
that Ten Carts ioyned side by side
may runne vppon them on a row.   140

Hercules did these Towne walls builde
the Church was founded by St Iames
but empty stomaks are not fild
with these old weather beaten theames

109 *straddle*] r overwrites probable *a*.   123 first **dright**] Overwrites *drink*.

Thence pass wee therefore to bee fed
to th'Hospitall a place of rest,
where each man knock'd his egg 'oth head
and so tooke lodginge in a Chest.

Oh you that will no famine feele
on Spanish ground vppon your Machio,
see that you bring your sundred heele
your bread, your cheese, and your borachio!

                  150

Wee had all this and somewhat more,
but that the Galiego-theefe
did runne a way with all our store
of wine, bread, cheese, bacon, and beefe.

Maÿ 30°

Next day yᵉ place for vs is sett
at Galiegos, where to dyne,   }4 leagues to
but all the meate that wee could gett } Galiego :
would not put out one of our eyne.

                  160

Then gan wee plaine of our distresse
Captaine Del Campe bids vs beare vp, }
for at the Hospitall of Condesse   }
all shall bee mended where wee'l <dine> supp.

But ere wee came twas Fryday night   5 legues to the Hos-
a cup of wine, a crust of bread   } pitall of Condesse.
(quoth hee) for a religious weight   }
sufficient is and soe to bedd.

Some layd their elbowes on yᵉ settle
some thrust their buttocks in the strawe
some for a pillow tooke a Kettle
and some their heads lay in yᵉ Paw.

                  170

All fellowes ! Mule, horse, oxe, sheepe, hog,
goate, Mulitieros, children, Maide,
the host, the Hostisse, and their dog,
with in one roome, by vs were layd!

Sleepe wearied limbes and take no care,
to gratulate your welcome hither
wee'll bless you with a Spanish aire,
Harke how the Musicke sounds to geither.

                  180

The hogs do grunt, yᵉ Oxen low,
the Mules de eke, the horses nea
the hens do cackle, yᵉ Cocks do crow,
the dogs doe barke, yᵉ sheepe do bea:

The Goates do ehe, yᵉ Mule moze snorts
the maydens fizzle, the children cry
the gooman grones, yᵉ goodwife farts,
who sents not this good harmony.

To strike vp yet one sweeter note
Captaine Dell Campe playes yᵉ good fellowe
putts his foule Mouth into a pott,
and like him selfe doth beastly bellowe!

                  190

---

147 *knockd*] d overwrites t.   **169 yᵉ]** y overwrites unreadable letter.   **182 *Mules*]** Uppercase M overwrites lowercase m.

In paine wee wake out all this Night
on Morrow passe Sabrero Grange,   }   Sabrero
which doth informe vs of a sight   }   Mouall :
y^t men vntrauail'd may thinke strange.

Christs very blood, and nturall flesh,
made by a Preist, kept in a glasse
there in lies yet, a Monument fresh
gainesay   for those that gai<r>↑n↓e say holy Masse   200

By this time wee are ore the Mountaines
and set Galizia at defiance,   Lyon   }
well pleased with the siluer fountaines   }
that runne a long the vale of Lyons

And trusting now to mend our fare
to Bega de Bergasse came   }   4 legues to Pego
where wee do finde a chainge of ayre   }   de Bergasse.
but still our viands are the same.

Here's heate of Day, some herbs to coule vs   210
some aqua frischa, wine will kill <us> yee
soe did Campes Captaine still befoole vs
vntill wee came to ffranca villa.

There found wee riuers, walls, and ffryers,
Nunns, Churches, a faire market place
Of Crosses store, & they no lyers
for wee were in a crossed case.

Wee call for Chambers, bread, and Drinke
some meate (good wife) loe heere are pence
but the old Hag doth vp her shoulders shrinke,
and answeres Senior, Patience: 220

Iunÿ 1°:   Well, Patience bee our food and Bed,
and therein rest wee till the morrowe !
when wee our iourney forward sped
and in these stories lost our sorrowe.

Cocouilla :   This is the Towne of y^t great Theefe
whome Hercules slew in time of old   }
Eremita   and this an Hermite, where the theefe }
of Moores three Millions hid of gold.

Yonder is seated by that meadow
where runns a riuer of water cleere } Caressedo   230
the Monestery of Carressedo   }
worth 40 thousand Crownes a yeere.

This Pomperado is Del Rey,
and these walls doe as much containe
beefe, Deere, sheepe, goate, fish, hare, Coney
foule, Partridge, Phesant, as all Spaine;

This veril<y>-ly our way did shorten
and quickly brought vs where wee dine,
to Molni seca which by fortune
afforded vs both bread, and wine.   240

---

200 gaine] Holgate first wrote *dare*: *g* overwrites *d*, *r* deleted, *n* superscripted; corrected in margin.   **220 answeres**]
Second *e* overwrites unreadable letter.

An oliue too, and eke a Cherry,
blest bee the hostisse of this bargo !
by whose regallesse wee are merry
and so ride on to well walld SFurgo
                8 Lea: to SFurgo

To seuer Lions and Castile old
a Cross there stands as I a read
by which if any Mayden bold
passe and repasse, it costs her head.
                Castilia
                recha : /

The Second of Iune I tooke no keep
of any passage more or less
saue only that I fell a sleepe
and lost my dinner at Baynesse.
              A lea: to
              Baynesse :   250

And lodg'd that night at Beneuent
where Preist and people were at a play
this was as wee were homeward bent
at ten a clocke o'th Sabboth day.

To Villa Pondo are we brought
on Tuesday where wee dine and rest,
and not Complaine, for wee are taught
that cheese and Onions are a feast.
            4 Lea: to
            Villa Pondo   260

Wee take our vent at Villa grace
and saw a faire built Monastere
of Eighty Iesuites in that place
beside two hundred Schollers there.
Villa Grace:

This townes Maior, to supply our lacke
regales vs with a pound of beefe
but before hee had turnd his backe
hee beggs a crowne for his releefe.

Thus passe wee, but wee cannot passe
the Monastery Del Espines.
which yeilds ten thousand pounds by'th Masse
a yeare, beside deere, goate, sheepe, vines.   270

Forward wee go, with as much speed
as one can driue a Spanish Mule.
and bring South Sunne to Valdo lid
to see the houses of good rule.
            Valdo lid.

The Couents of the Priests and ffryers,
the Colle^ages of the Iesuites,
the Churches and ye Monasteries,
the Inquisition, ware that bites !   280

Go on and you shall see the Markett
but where's in Gods name ye Kings case
the buildings of ye Monkes do darke it
and i'ts a shamd to shew his face.

Thence pass wee to the Arcenall
which at ye sound of one alarme
two hundred thousand souldiers tall
att all poynts fittinge well can arme
           Hiperbole
           Hispanica:

Yet on, there stands Lucuna guard
the fifte Charles house of barefoote beggers   290
who rentless keepe farr better ward
then some in silke, and gold y^t swaggers.

Here did wee pass ye riuer Guere
which to the King himselfe is thrall,
and payes 300 crownes a yeere
for his free passe to Portugall.

Iunÿ: 5°   Maxado this days worke doth end
next morne as soone as dawne giues leaue } 8 Leg: to S^t
vp, and begon, for wee intend   } Mary de Neiue }
to dyne with St Mary de Nieue

Twas Corpus Christi day I trow   301
St Mary was in her best attire,
her child beside her, but below,
the Mother still must bee the higher.

Shee sate vppon a Tissue chaire
aboue her a silke Canopie
about her stood ye people bare
all harkening to a Comedy

I hearkned too, as I did passe
there was a Fryer and a Deuill   310
the Subiect as I guessed was
which of them was ye greater euill ?

The end was this, One in his clutch
did toth<er> take, I know not whether
Deuill or ffryer, nor skills it much,
this I am sure, both went to geither.

That done, ye bagpipes play before
the whislers daunce with apish gestures
men, weomen, Preists, and ffryers store
doe follow in their holyday vestures.   320

Comes Christ his Crosse, and their new God,
they scarcely bow, or doff their hatt,
comes smiling Mary, giues a nod,
now here, now there, they fall downe flatt

And reason good twixt one and other
much difference is, Christ is their Creature,
and Mary is Gods holy Mother,
and I dare sweare it far the greater.

Wee leaue them to their sacred game
to lodge at Melferesias   } 2 Lea: to Mel: 330
and only <sh> see that towne of Fame }
Segonia, as wee onward passe.

At our returne it lodged in't
and noted though wee were full weary
the Church ye Sc^hoole, ye cloth, ye Mint,
the Kings house & ye Monastery.

---

314 *toth<er>*] er possibly not deleted; ink may have bled through paper.

But aboue all the Deuills bridge
of which to the Virgin Maryes glory
<?> out of old records wee alledge
and make a Creed of this same story.   340

Two louers did appoyntment make
their filthy Loues heere to inioy
but cominge to this riuers Lake
the boate was gon they want conuoy

The woman falls into a passion
and needs must dye of Melancholy
the Deuill takes commiseration
and bargaines to effect her folly:/

Hee'd make a bridge by foure i'th' morne
that shee might passe, and ioy her Loue.   350
soe shee for this receiud good turne
her soule to th Deuill would giue ouer.

Hands strooke, ye Spiritts to their worke fall
the stones they hew, they saw, they lay,
they raise the walls and had done all
had not St Mary stood ith way

But shee to saue a Virgins soule
(so that the Towne might bee befriended)
at very brinke did them controule
where yet shee stands least it bee ended.   360

I no man of his faith bereaue
which by Tradition hee hath suck'd
yet I tell you, what I conceiue
tis no bridge but an aquaduct.

This tale lends to the Escuriall
the like where of was neuer heard
not so much for the buriall
of three Kings who lye there interd

As for an hundred fifty ffryers
Hieronimies, who there conuert them   370
Kinge Philip hauinge his desires
in Turkish warrs, did so content them.

One hundred fifty yards t'is square
the windowes glass with clearest Christall
built vp with stones, and they all are
partly Iaspis, and partly Marble.

Dores and windowes fifteene hundred
Courtes seuenteene, stay here a while
for this may most of all bee wondred
tis in dyamiter hundred fiue mile.   380

The Chappell shall conclude the rest
with bookes and Organs all of gould
but the Ater (trust them) is the best
that euer Europe did behoulde

382 Organs] O overwrites unreadable letter.

Their fountaines, fish ponds, stillatories
their gardens walls for their repast
I here omit, with their Libraries
for to Madrid I must make hast.

No sooner entred wee the Citty
but there met vs a Spanish rable   390
who for our welcome sang this ditty
Les inglesey ale Diable.

Wee tak't not ill, 'tis their God speed you
they haue no complements but Machio
Hÿo de puto, mula Corundo,
Villaco, ladron, grand borachio:

Two days at Madrid wee remain : d̲
but how our tyme wee there did spend
is not with in this chart contain'd
because my Iournall is at end.   400

Yet you for newes of State that fish,
 and would my silence heere conuince
 Ile tell you what my heart doth wish
 I saw; th' Infanta, and my Prince!

And can informe Pan's Maiestie
that Iacke and Tom are very well.
But when the'yll come to Arcady
I leaue for good St George to tell   ffinis

---

397 *remaind : d*] First *d* is in secretarial hand that overwrites italic *ed*.   404 *saw*] *w* overwrites *g*.

[147]

By Ld Carr : Earle of Som'sett: his owne verses :

If euer woe possest a stubern heart
If punishment bee dew to bad deserte
If euer greife or Sorrow man hath croste
Lay all on mee, I haue deseru'd the moste.

Let all the world complaine vppon my name
Let all the world reporte nought but my shame
Let all the world beare these my words in mynde
That to my friend Like Iudas proued vnkinde

I that on Earth had all I could desire
I, that like Phaieton did aboue all aspire
Haue nothinge els to comfort my sad mones
But thus to tell my greife to wrathlesse stones.

Lett all my friends beare theis <t> my words in minde
Bee not like mee to your best friend vnkinde
Beare this same prouerbe allwayes in yor view
for to my greife I finde it to be trewe.

Hee that begins to Clyme & climes but slowe
Can catch small harme though hee fall nere so lowe
But hee y^t when hee clymes a mayne
Hee fales so lowe hee nere can rise againe

Thus I aduertise all before I dye.
Hee must needs fall to lowe y^t clymes to hye
I that was rich in state though meane in birth
Ame now ye meanest creature one the earth.

The world condems mee for my monstrous deed
And that which makes my heart with sorrowe bleed
Is this, that more besides poore wretched I
for this offence in this strong hold must lye.

Oh had I lyuen poorely as at first
But twas for honour that my minde did thirst
Hono^r I aym'd at and I hitt the white
first from a Page the Kinge made mee a Knight

ffrom thence I stept into a vicounts place
And beinge Earle I reaped this fowle disgrace
Then did I thinke my fate coulde neuer fall
And like a gamster then I threw at all

10

20

30

31 **aym'd**] *y* overwrites unreadable letter.

But then the Lord that doth disclose all crimes
That ere hath bin committed in these <th> tymes
Hee did disclose this plott y^t Hell inuented
The which till now my heart hath nere relented   40

Mercy O Lord I craue for my fowle sinne
A penitent soule I know much mercy wyñes
Let not thy angry browe gainst mee be bent
ffor with a feruent heart I do repent.   ffinis

[148]

Lifelesse my selfe, I keepe the life of all:
with out my helpe, all liuinge things doe die.
Small, great, poore, rich, obey vnto my call:
Feirce Lyons, fowles, whales, fishes in the Sea.
Not meat nor drinke, the hungrie I supplie:
By drinke 'ore come, I quicken new againe.
Dearer to Kings, then Crownes and Septers high
Vnto the Rich then all their wealth and gaine.
I am not nice, the poore Ile not disdaine
Poore wretches more then Kings may mee commaund   10
When I come in, all sences must refraine.
Softer then silke, more ponderous then the sand
I hurt, I helpe, I slay, I cure the same:
(Sleepe) and aduise, and pause well what I am.   ffinis

[149]

All that haue eies, now wake and weepe:
Hee whose wakeing was our sleepe,
Is falne a sleepe himselfe, & neuer
Shall wake more till wak't for euer.
Deaths iron hand hath closd those eies,
That were at once three Kingdomes spies,
Both to fore see and to preuent
Dangers, as soone as they were meant.
That head whose wakeinge braine alone
wrought all mens quiet but i'ts owne,   10
Now lies at rest . O Let him haue
The Peace hee lent vs, to his graue.
If no Naboth all his raigne
were for his fruitefull vineyard slaine,
If no Vriah lost his life
Because hee had too faire a wife
Then let no Sheme'is curses wound
His honour or prophane this ground.

149.4 *wak't*] *t* overwrites *d*;   (right margin, not transcribed)] Modern pencil notation: *1625.*

Let no black-mouth'd ranck-breathed curre
Peacefull Iames his ashes stirre   20
Princes are Gods, Ô doe not then
   Rake in their graues to proue them men.
For two and twenty yeeres long care,
For prouidinge such an heire,
That to the Peace wee had before
May adde thrice two and twenty more.
For his day trauells, & night watches
For his crazd-sleepe stolne by snatches
For two feirce Kingdomes, ioind in one
For all hee did, or meant t'haue done   30
Doe this for him, write o're his Dust
Iames the Peacefull and the Iust:.

---

[150]

On King Iames }

Hee who was our Life is dead
Hee to whom wee flew is fled
Our Lyon sleepes whom none shall rouse
But Iudai's Lyon Englands Spouse
Our Pelican is dead but wee
Haue heere his blood his Leagacie.
Our Doue is flowne but yet wee finde
Olife   An olife branch still left behinde
The Star of Iacob is falen, but see
Heer's a Charles waine, as bright as hee   10
Our Phebus setts but yet no night
Ensues wee haue his sone and light. ·
His soñe but yet no Phaeton
That will sett fire on his Throne
And instead of light enflame
Our land more then a Sea can tame.
T'is Charles that mounts into his Carr
with light of Peace and flames of warr
Charles out of his ashes springs
A nother Phænix amongst Kings.   20
Charles the first y^t euer came
To Christen England with that name
Like as his father Iames had none
To paralell his name and throne
Iames the best obiect of desire
Iames with whom our Ioyes expire.

150.8 Olife] *f* overwrites *u*, corrected in left margin.   **150.20 Another]** Space left open between *A* and *nother*.

Our Ioyes with him a death would haue
Did not Charles raise them from the graue.
<u>L</u>et   Yet let vs pay to him that's gone
Teares which hee liuinge were vnknowne   30
Let vs bedewe our Soueraignes graue
with teares that no true heart can saue
If wee haue moisture let vs shedd
Because the Ocean King is dead.
If Loue ? let ye peace wee lou'd winn
Our hearts and tongues to honour him.
Our vines and fig trees els will call
vs thankelesse and vnnaturall
His title was a Peacefull Kinge
Made true in vs but not in him   40
Hee pour'd his peace on vs but care
Insteed of Peace fell to his share
Let him enioye then what hee gaue
Aliue, now hee is in his graue
whilsts ther's a heuenly Celebration
Of his soules glorious, Coronation.
Whilst his Kingly bodies foode
for wormes borne of ye royall blood
Let no vng^{r}atefull wormes remaine
with vs that may consume his fame   50
Better it were that they should haue
Aliue, what hee hath dead, a graue
And a Curse grauen on their stone
should bee their sole inscription
whilst on his sacred Tombe wee write
This wth a sacred Conscience may endite
Heere lies Great Brittaines peace and health
That ruld two Kingdomes and himselfe :.   ffinis :

[151]

On Kinge   Is hee dead? noe, opinion argues farr wide
<u>I</u>a<u>m</u>es   Abijt non obÿt hee's but stept aside.
Crownes that are Earthly are but transitorie
Our Iames went hence to weare ye Crowne of glory.
Berefte of life hee endlesse life hath gain'd   5
Vertue still grac't him and his blisse obteyn'd
Substance for shadowes hee doth now enioye
Rich in true pleasures, free from worlds annoye.
Of all admired for his gratious parts
Xerxes though conqueringe much, nere wonn more hearts :.

[152]
Dr: C: Elegy on Bp. Rauis of London who dyed 1607

When I past Pauls & travaild in the walk
Where all our Britayne Sinners sweare and talke,
Old Harry Ruffians, Bankrupts, Soothsayers
And youth whose Courage is as old as theirs:
And there behold yᵉ body of my Lord
Trod vnder foot by vice which hee abhord;
It wounded mee, the Landlord of all times
Should let long liues & leases to their crimes:
But to his surging honors doth afford
Scarce so much sun, as to yᵉ prophets goord   10
Yet since swifte flights of vertue haue apt ends
Like breath of Angels, which a blessinge sends,
And vanished with all: whilst fowler deeds
Expect a tedious haruest of bad seeds:
I blame not fame and nature if they gaue
where they could add no more their last a graue:
And iustly do thy greiued friends forbeare

Before hee   Bub   & Alabaster boys to reare
had a Tombe }} Ore thy religious dust, but did men know
made: }} Thy life wᶜʰ such illusions cannot show: 20
              For thou hast trod amongst those happy-ones
              That trust not in their Superscriptions,
              Their hired Epitaphs and periurd stone
              which oft belyes yᵉ soule when shee is gone:
              And darst commit thy body as it lyes
              To tongues of liuinge men, not vnborne eyes:
              what profitts thee a sheete of lead, what good
              yf on thy coarse a Marble quarry stood ?
              Let those yᵗ feare their risinge purchase vaults
              And reare them statues to excuse their faults   30
              As if like birds that picke at painted grapes
              Their Iudge knew not their parsons from their shapes:
              Whilst thou assur'd through thy ayᵉry dust
              Shalt rise at first: they would not though they must:

Hattons To be   Nor need the Chanclor bost whose Pyramis
aboue the   Aboue the Host & Alter raysed is
Alter: For though thy body fill a viler roome
                Thou shalt not change deeds wᵗʰ him for his Tombe :   ffinis

2 (left margin, not transcribed)] Modern pencil notation: *Corbet.* **7 *times*]** A line is drawn after this word extending down into the *s* of l. 8, *Crimes.* **13 *fowler*]** *r* overwrites *d.*

[153]

Reuerand
A funerall Elegie, vppon the right ˄ ffather in God / <u>Reu'end</u>
Iohn King, Late Ld Bp : of London : //

I know how wittie greife is to inuent
Varietie of Mornefull Complement
Passion eu'n Death in new waies emulates
Makeinge our sorrowes diuers as our fates.
As Nature makes it common for to die
Soe common tis' one dead mens fames to lie.
But (ô thou reuerend Prelate) whose great name
Is wing'd with vertue, farre too swifte for fame.
And out flies her as farr, as here to fore
Shee out went Truth, thou, who soe late didst soare   10
To such an height in heaue'n; thy rauisht spirit
Scornes all praise in Death, as much as merit
Could in thy life time challenge, witnes the stone,
On which is caru'd thy Resurrection.
O ther's an Epitaph, which who dares take
With Confidence t'himselfe, hee's sure to make
His bodie easie passage from below,
when the eternall Trumpe begins to blow.
with which what Kingly attendants thou shalt haue
Rise cherefully with thee, who from their graue   20
Awak't heare Kinge amongst yᵉ happy nam'd.
To whom the'ternall tidings are proclam'd
Of come you blessed; They which thou didst teach
This way to life, will hope to heare thee preach
Againe in heav'n, and shall bee made rehearse
At the assembly of the vniuerse
How well thy cominge all the Saints invite
To heare thy Halle lu-iah's, whilst delight
Stands mixt with wonder to heare thee relate,
How thou thy Masters taske didst consecrate.   30
With what a solem̄e and Maiestike tone
Thou reig'ndst, and made each Pulpit bee thy Throne.
Who in thy vaine had'st none to Emulate,
All, who suruiue, dispaire to imitate.
O sure they must. I am no Poet now,
Nor will I feare, what Conscience speakes, t'avow.
Of all the Reuerend ffathers (Reuerend all,
Each in Gods message Euangelicall.)
Of all whom to enflame, whom to enspire,
Their Angell tipp's their tongues with holy fire   40
From thy blest Alter, and makes them inuoke
Hearers, with tellinge them the Lord hath spoke.

32 *reig'ndst*] *e overwrites a.*

Of all (and free from Envie bee my Pen,
As free as flattery is from buried Men).
There seem'd from God none more immediate sent,
More in Gods cause diuinely violent;
And, for his thoughts did still his tongue vntie
though that most swiftly happye, hee did soe
speake with each limbe, y^t wee heard Gods commaunds
From's heart and eyes, nay from his armes & hands.   50
Ô shall wee ere forgett how hee could make
His eies dart through a vice: hee could awake
A sinne y^t slept i'th bosome; an offence
Stood before him, as before Conscience,
Amazed still; and let none bee secure;
For though hee sleepes, his vrne will not endure
Presumption yet in vice great Prophet hee
Hath Prophets children, lefte, & from that tree
Branches of Prophets Spring: Hee had the vine,
By which hee fram'd and drest vine Palatine.   60
Thus wert thou borne for businesse, each great taske
was thine in heritance, wee'le no other aske,
But thee and yet thou'rt gone, & wth thee dide
Not only thou, but a whole age beside.
How did hee strike all hearts with sacred feare,
whilst they a new Amittai's sonne did heare.
Two twins most vndistinguisht from each other
the happye ofspringe of one fruitfull Mother,
Both rous'd our Niniue's, which as great haue beene
Though not in compasse yet Im'e sure in sinne.   70
How did Religion Zeale and vertue striue
To keepe two Ionasse's in them aliue.
Theire Loue like to their Meditations, euer went
Iust hand in hand; But now wee must lament.
Death now hath taught ye Chruch, Mother to both,
What She t'acknowledge was before soe loath.
Theire knowne a sunder now, the veiles remou'd.
Mortalitie hath don't; who, who shall now
(when Brittaines Monarche shall ordeine a vow
The sonne of Isha'is deeds to imitate,   80
And bringe the Temple to i'ts former state;
When Englands Dauid shall in Triumph ride,
To see Gods fallinge, buildinge beautified)
who then shall solemnise that blessed day,
when dust and rubbish shall bee swept a way

---

62 *in heritance*] Space left open as indicated.   **68 *fruitfull*]** *i* is blotted, overwriting unreadable letter.   **85 *swept*]** *w* overwrites an unreadable letter.

From Gods house, who shall tell Kings the roomes
which Kings should build, are Temples, and not Tombes.
Thus was his last and his best taske fulfild,
T'incite o^r Israells King, that hee should build
The walls o'th Tabernacle, whilst hee for hast,   90
Fearinge without much speede they would not last,
Hee tooke a course how hee himselfe might bee
A pillar there.   for still vnwearied hee
By toilesome paines did in a sort become
In some parts Marble, breedinge his owne Tombe
with in his bowells, <and> and what now wee moane,
Himselfe in Paules lies a foundation stone.
Where rest you blessed Ashes, peacefully rest,
And let no noise from Babell er'e molest
Thine vrne with slaunder; Though some vndertake   100
with clamors of confusion to awake
Thee from thy peace. No blessed soule can hearke
Vnto such dog'gs that stand without & barke.
Boast not proud Iezabel, such a victory
That thou, or thine adulterate vanity
could ere entice his eyes to bee or'e tane
with such a painted beauty, whose prophane
And harlot superstition hee abhor'd
For now mee thinks ye vision of y^t Lord
Commands wth iust wrath, that wee should relate   110
How (though in heau'<e>n) his soule wth zeale doth hate
And scorne those foule reports; No, Let Rome know
Hir prophesied ruins not preuented soe.
His name shall neuer add one relique more
Vnto such reuerend sin, where to adore
Or be ado'rd hee thought a Calumny,
And fame so gott to bee worst infamy.
Could his heau'n greedy thoughts obteine one houre
To visit earth againe, with what a power

Explicit T.G.
Obÿt Ep:L:
p^rdict:30 Mart
1621. qui et
tunc incidit
in plũ Diem
passionis Dominæ

Of Indignation would hee to'th world declare   120
His stedfast innocence ? how may all good men sweare
For his integrity? seeke prodigious Lyars
Mong th'vrnts of Legended and walkinge ffryars
Delusiue phantasm'es: seeke mongst Goblins those
To father lyes vppon: hee y^t best knowes
The secretts of all hearts, who tries the reines
And from whom nought is hid, he who susteines
Mans staggeringe faith, hee doth from heau'n deride
Their folly, where with good men are belide:.::   ffinis

---

96 *with in*] Space left open as indicated.   **120 G** (Margin)] G overwrites C.

[154]

On ye Death of
M^ris Marye
Prideaux }}

Weepe not because this Child hath died so younge
But weepe because your selues haue liued so longe.
Age is not fill'd by growth of time, for then
What old men liue to see ye state of Men?
Who reach the youth of grand Methusalem
Ten yeeres make vs as old as hundreds him.
Ripenesse is from our selues & then wee die
When Nature hath obtaind maturitie.
Summer and Winter fruites there bee, & all
Not at one time but beinge ripe must fall.   10
Death didd not erre, y mourners are beguild
Shee died more like a Mother then a Childe.
Weigh the composure of her prettie parts
Her grauitie in Childhood, all her Arts,
Of woman-like-behauiour, weigh her tongue
Soe wisely measured, now nor short nor long.
Add onely to her growth some inches more
Shee tooke vp now what due was at Threescore
Seauen yeares shee liu'd our ages first degree
Iourneys at first steppe ended happy bee.   20
　　Yet take her stature wth ye age of Man
　　They well are fitted, both are but a spanne.

[155]

Butler of Ch:Ch:
In <u>Oxon:</u> Iohn: }

Dauson the Butlers dead; although I thinke
Poets were ne're infusd wth single drinke
Ile spend a farthinge Muse, some watry verse
will serue the turne to cast vppon this hearse.
If any cannot weepe amongst vs heere
Take off his pott and so squease out a teare.
Weepe Ô yee Cheeses, weepe till yee bee good
Yee that are dry or in the Sunne haue stood,
In Mossie coates & rustie liu'ries mourne
Vntill like him to Ashes yee shall turne.   10
Weepe Ô barrells, let your drippings fall,
In trickling streames make wast more prodigall.
Then when our drinke is bad, y^t Iohn may floate
To Stix in Beare and lift vp Carons boate
With wholesome waues, & as our Cunduites run
with Claret at the Coronation
So lett our Chanels flow with single tiffe,
For Iohn I trust is crownd, take off your whiffe
Yee men of Rosemary, now drinke of all
Remembringe t'is the Butlers funerall   20
　　Had hee ben Master of good double beere
　　My life for his Iohn Dawson had ben here:}}
　　　　　ffinis

[156]

Epytaph's

Let no propha_∧ⁱ ne ignoble foote tread neere
This hollowed peece of Earth. Dorsett lyes heere.
A small poore relique of a noble spirit,
Free as the Ayre, and ample as his merrit,
Whose least perfection was large, & great
Enough, to make a Common man Compleat
A soule refin'd and c<?>u'ld from many menn
Who reconsiled the sword vnto the penn
vsinge both well, noe proud forgettinge Lord
But mindfull of meane names & of his word.   10
Who loued for honour, and not for end's,
And had the noblest way of makeinge friends,
By louinge first. One who knew the Court
But vnderstood it better by report
Then Practise, for nothing tooke from thence
But the Kings fauour for his recompence.
One for Religion or his Cuntryes good,
Valued not his honour, nor his blood.
Rich in the worlds opinion and mens praise
All full in all wee could desire, but dayes.   20
  Hee thus is war'nd of this & shall forbeare
  To vent a sigh for him or spend a teare.
  Let him liue long & scorn'd, vnpittied fall,
  And want a mourner at his funerall.

[157]

Heer lies his Parent's hopes, and feares,
Once all their ioyes, now all their teares.
Hee's now past sence, past feare of paine,
twe're sinne to wish him here againe
had it liued to haue b<u>ee</u>_∧ⁿ a Man,   ____beene
This inch had growne but to a spanne
and now hee takes vp y^e less roome,e
rock't from his Cradle to his Tombe.
T'' is better die a child at fower,
then liue and dye soe at foure score.   10
Vew but y^e way by which wee comee
Thou' lt say hee is blest, y^{ts} first at home. Morley.

[158]

Nature in this small volume was about,
To perfect what in woman was left out.
Yet carefull least a peece soe well begunn
Should want p^rseruatiues when shee had donner
Ere shee could finish what shee vndertooke,
Threw dust vppon it & shutt vp ye booke.   5

[159]   Browne.

As carefull Mothers to their beds doe laye
Their babes wch would to long ye wantons playe
So to p^ruent my youth ensuinge crimes,
Nature my Nurse layd mee to bed betimes.

157.2 *now*] What seems to be an apostrophe appears directly over the *w*. 157.5 *been*] *ee* overwrites unreadable letters. The word is corrected in the margin.

[160]

Within this Marble casket lyes,
A daintye Iewell of great prize,
which Nature in ye worlds disdaine,
But shew'd and put it vp againe.

[161]

Hee that's imprisond in this narrowe roome,
wert not for custome, needs nor verse nor tombe.
Nor from those cann theire memory be lent
to him who must bee his toombes Monument.
and by the vertue of his lastinge name,
must make his toombe liue long not itt his fame.
for when his gaudie monument is gone,
Children of the vnborne world shall spy ye stone
that couers him, & to theire fellowes crye,
t'is heere iust here abouts Barckley doth lye.   10
Let them with fayned titles glorifie,
theire toombes, whose sickly virtues feare to dye
And let their toombes bely them call them blest,
And charitable Marble, fayne the rest
Hee needs not when his lifes trew story's donne
the post-script of a periurd stone
Then spare his toombe y^ts needlesse & vnsafe
whose vertue must outliue his   Epitaphe.

[162]

Renowned Spenser, ly a thought more ny
To learned Chaucer, and rare Beaumont, ly
A little nearer Spencer to make roome
for Shakespere in thy threefould fourefould tombe.
To lodge all fowre in one bedd make a shift
vntill domes-day, for hardly will a fift
Betwixt this day and that by fate bee slaine
for whom your Curtaines may bee drawne againe.
If your p^rcedencie in death doe barre
A fourth to haue place in yor Sepulcre,   10
Vnder this sacred Marble of thine owne
Sleepe rare Tragædian ? Shakespeare sleepe alone
thy vnmolested Peace, vnshared caue
possesse as Lord not tennant of thy graue.
That vnto vs or others it may bee
Honour her after to bee layd by thee.   Bass. ///

[163]

Accept thou shrine of my dead saint
Insteed of Dirges this complaint
And for sweet flow ers to crowne thy hearse
Receiue a strew of weeping verse.
from thy greeu'd freind whom thou mights see
quit melted in teares for thee.
Deare Loue thy vntimely fate
My taske hath bin to meditate,
On thee, on thee, thou art the booke
the Library where on I looke   10
Though almost blind for thee (lou'ed Clay)
I languish out, not liue the Day.
Vsinge none other Exercise
but what I practise with <mine> ↑my↓ eyes
By which wett glasses I find out
how lazilie time creep's about
To him that mournes . this only this
My exercise and busines is.
Thus I compute my weary houres
With sighs dissolued into showres.   20
No wonder if my tyme goe thus
backward and most preposterous.
Thou hast benighted mee, thy sett
The eue of blacknesse doth begett
Who wast my Day though ouercast
before thou hadst thy Noonetide past.
And I remember must in teares
thou scarce hadst seene soe manie yeares
As Day tells howres, by thy cleare sunne
My Loue and fortunes first did runne   30
But thou wilt neuer more appeare
foulded with in my Hemispheere,
Since both thy light and motion
like a falne starr is fled and gone
And twixt mee and my soules deere wish
An earth now interposed is.
Which such a strange Eclipse doth make
As nere was reade in Almanacke.
I could allowd thee for a time
To darken mee and my sadd clime   40
Were it a Moneth, a yeare, or Tenn<e>,
I could thy Exile li<?>ᴧᵘe till then   liue
And at that space my mirth reioᴧʸⁿᵉ<yce>
So thou wouldst promise to retorne.
And puttinge off thy ashy shroud
Att length dispearse the sorrowes cloud

2–6 (Right margin, not transcribed)] Modern pencil notation: *By Henry King Bishop of Chichester ?* **14** <mine>] There is a caret below the deleted text to indicate correction: *my*.

But woe is mee the longest date
too narrow is to calculate
theire emptie hopes neuer shall I
bee so much blest as to discrie   50
A Glimpse of thee till that day come
Which all the Earth to Cynders doome
And a feirce feauer shall Calcine
The<?> bodie of this world like thine
My little world. that fitts of fire
Once come our bodies shall aspire
And view our selues wth clearer eyes
in liuely shapes aboue ye skies
In y^t calme Region where no night
cann hide vs from each others sight   60
Meane time thou hast her earth much good
May my harme doe thee sure it stood.

[164]

On Mris Mallett : R: C:

Haue I renounct My faith, or basely sould
Saluation, & my Loyalty for gold?
Haue I with forraigne practise vndertooke
By poyson, shott, sharpe-knife, or sharper booke
To kill my King ? haue I betrayd ye state
To fire, to fury, or some newer fate?
wch learned Murtherers ye grand destinies
The Iesuits<s> haue nursd: if of all this
I guilty am, proceed I am content
Mallet may take mee for my punishment: 10
For neuer sin was of so high a rate
But one nights hell with her might expiate.
Although ye Law with Garnet & ye rest
dealt far more mildly, hanging's but a iest,
To this immortall torture had shee been then
when torrid dayes ingend'red, when
Cruelty was witty & inuentions free
Did liue by blood & thriue by cruelty:
Shee would haue bin more horrid engines farr
Then Racks, or halters, fyre or famine are.   20
whither her witt, forme, talke or tyre I name,
stroke   Each is a stook of Tyranny & shame.
But for her breath, spectators come not nigh,
That lays about, God bless the Company.
The Man in the beares skin baited to death
would chuse the doggs farr rather then her breath. | death
One kisse of hers and 18 words alone
Puts downe the Spanish Inquisition

163.54 The] *e* overwrites *i*.

Thrice happy wee (quoth I) thinking thereon
That know no dayes of persecution   30
For were it free to kill this grisly elfe
would Martyr make in compasse of her selfe:
And were shee not p^ruented by our prayer
By this tyme shee infected had ye ayer:
And am I innocent ? & is it true
That thing which Poet Pliny neuer knew
Nor Affrick, Nyle, nor euer Hacluits eyes
descryd in all his East, West voyages;
That thing, wch Poets were a frayd to fayne
For feare her shadowe should infect their braine: 40
Should dote on mee ? as if they did contriue
The Deuill and shee should Damne a man aliue:
This spouse of Antickt and his alone   Antichrist
Shee's drest so like ye whore of Babylon:
Why doth not Welcome rather purchase her
And beare about this rare familiar:
Six market dayes, a wake & a fayre too't
will quit ye charges & ye Ale to boot:
Not Tygerlike shee fed, vpon a Man
worse then a Tyger or a Leopard can: 50
Lett mee goe pray & thinke vppon some spell
At once to bid ye Deuill & her farewell:

[165]

Vppon Mortalitie

Like to a rowlinge of an eye
  or like a starrr shot from the skie
  Or like the hand vppon a Clocke
  Or like a waue vpon a rocke
  Or like a blast or like a flame
  Or like false newes wch people frame.
  Euen such is Man of equall stay
  Whose very groweth leads to decay,
  The eye is turnd ye starr downe bendeth
  The hand doth steale ye waue descendeth   10
  The blast is spent ye flame onc fir'd
  The newes disproou'd mans life aspir'd.

Vppon Resur-   Like to the eye which sleepe doth chaine
   rection:. }   Or like the starr whose fall wee faine
                     Or like ye shade on Ahabs watch
                     Or like the raine wch gulfe doth snatch
                     Or like the winde or flame tha'ts past
                     Or smothered newes confirm'd at last.

164.36 *Pliny*] *y* overwrites *ie*. **164.37** *Nyle*] *y* overwrites *i*.

Euen so mans Life paund in the graue
waights for a risinge it must haue   20
he eye doth see the starr still blazeth   e
the shade goes back y waue escapeth
The wind is tur'nd ye flame reuiu'd,
the Newes renew'd, and man new liu'd.

[166]

Vppon Iustification
See how the Rainebowe in the skie
Seemes gaudie by ye sunns bright eye
Heare how an Ecco answere makes
feele how a board is smooth'd wth wax
smell how a gloue putts on *per*fume
tast how their sweetnesse pills assume
So by imputed Iustice: clay
Seemes faire, well spoke, smooth, sweet each way
The eye doth gaze on robes appearinge
the promisd Eccho takes our hearinge   10
To board our touch ye sent o^r smell
the pill o^r tast, Man, God as well:

[167]

I saw faire Cloris walke alone
Whe[n] fethered raine came softly downe
And Ioue decended from his Tower
To court her in a siluer showere
The wanton snow flew in her brest   5
As little birds into their nest
And ouercome wth whitenesse there,
for greife it thawd into a Teare
Thence fallinge on her garments heme
To deck her freezd into a Gemme:
                                    W: S:

[168]

On the standinge for a Beedells place:

No sooner old Bell
were at his last knell
past prompting of Proctors
giu'n ore by ye Doctors
but Death not soe speedie
as some youngsters were needie
    To shew for his place:

At first Potecarie
his panch would not tarrie
a bigg fellow and burrell   10
of the Colledge of Oriell
tooke many a large stride
for his bulke to prouide
but it was not so wide
    To compasse ye Mace

Tom Ratliffe tis sedd
in each house made head
his leggs were intire
yet a staff did require
and to purchse ye same   20
old Ionas ye lame
his pace did new frame
    without leaue of his Crutches

But Car Couentry
far brisker then hee
the surest of many one
                to bee &

to bee Lychfeilds Companion
threw the Dice with his Letters
of Noble Abetters
and would make our debtters
    The Duke and the Duches   30

Alas Robin Moore
thy strength was too poore
to take vp the wasters
to bandie with Masters
hee quicklie was coude
to his betters hee boud
and back againe croud
    like a yeoman forlorne.

Now laughs dapper Harry
that binder by St Mary   40
this youth did aspire
would you bee an Esquire
but hee silly rooke
was in no bodies booke
but his fryzeld pate shoke
    And puld in his horne

Then fresh from the tapping
came Prideaux in drapping
the case to dispute
and broach his suite   50
    But his hopes are as thinn
as the Chipps in his binn
        and his shirt bordered ore

166.5 *perfume*] Tilde through *p* abbreviates *er.* **167.2 *when*]** There is a tilde over *e.* **168.53 *shirt*]** *i* overwrites *a.*

Next Langley did reele
from yᵉ Katherine wheele
to gripe the stafe handfast
for indeed his wife canuasst
but mine hostesses second
with out his Hoast recond
No hand to them becond   60
though to wipe out a scrore

But Iohn Smyth far brauer
that Iolley mad shauer   70
with this would increase
his Patrimonie grease
which though hee would rather
Then all Tom did gather
yet with his Cake ffather
Must lye to yᵉ potte

Of Clauer they talkt
but hee suddenly stalkt
and satt downe out of hand
hee was but obscure
and therefore secure
And-wounderous sure
It was not lost

For now by strong hand
Iohn Bell hee could stand
braue Chemicall Vause
had cozend Deathes iawes   80
his health did them gale
his life killd them all
and gaue them the fall
And his Mace againe gott.   ffinis.

[169]

On the
Nightin
gale

My limes were weary, and my head opprest
with drowsines, and yet I could not rest
My bedd was such, nor downe nor feather can
Make one more soft, though Ioue againe turne swan
No feare distracted thoughts my slumbers broke
I heard no Scritch owle squeake, nor Rauen croke,
Nor yet the flea, yᵗ proud insultinge Elfe
had taken truce, and was a sleepe it selfe.
But twas Nights darlinge, and y woods best iewelle
the Nightingale yᵗ was so sweetely cruell.   10
It wood mine eares to robb mine eies of sleepe
That while shee sung of Tertus they might weepe.
And yet reioyce the Tyrant did her wronge
her cause of woe was burthen of her Songe
which while I listned too & stroue to heare
twas such I could haue wisht my selfe all eare.
Tis false yᵗ Poets faine of Orpheus, hee
could neuer moue a stone, or beast, or Tree,
To follow him; but where so ere shee flies
Shee makes a groue. Satyres & Fairyes tries   20
About her pearch to daunce their roundelaies
for shee sings ditties to them, while Pan plaies
But while shee chaunted thus, the cock for spight
Daies hoarser harold, chidd a way yᵉ Night,
Thus robd of sleepe mine eye lids nightly guest
My thought I lay content, though not at rest.   finis

169.12 Tertus] Possibly an *e* superscripted over the second *t*. (Right margin, not transcribed)] Modern pencil notation: *Tereus*. 169.17 *faine*] "fame" is a possible reading. 169.24 *a way*] There is a space between *a* and *way*.

[170]

On the Death of S^r Th: Pelham

Meerely for Death to greiue and mourne
Were to repine that Man was borne,
When weake old age doth fall asleepe,
Twere fowle Ingratitude to weepe.
Those threds alone should pull out teares
Whose sudden cracke breakes-of some yeares;
Here tis not soe; full distance here
Sunders the Cradle from the beare.
A fellow trau'ller hee hath bin
So long with time, so worne to skin,   10
That were hee not Iust now bereft,
His body first the soule had left.
Three score and tenn is Natures date,
Our Iourney when wee come in late;
Beyond that state the ouerplus,
was granted not to him but vs;
For his owne sake the Sun ne're stood
But only for the peoples good,
Ev'n soe His breath held out by Aire
which poore men vttered in their prayer.   20
And as his goods were lent to giue
Soe were his dayes y^t they might liue.
Soe Tenn yeares more to him were told
Enough to make another old:
O that Death would still doe soe
Or else on good men would bestowe
That wast of yeeres wch vnthrifts fling
Away by their distemperinge,
That some might thriue by this Decay
As well as that of Land and clay.   30
Tw'as now well done: No cause to moane
On such a seasonable stone
Where Death is but an Hoast: wee sin
Not bidding welcome to his Inne.
Sleepe, Sleepe, thy rest good man embrace
Sleepe, Sleepe, t'hast trode a weary race: ffinis

---

31 *Tw'as*] Apostrophe as indicated.

[171]

_____

To his Sister:
_____

Louinge Sister euery line
Of your kinde Letter was so fine
with the best Mettall y^t y^e graine
<Of> Or Scriueners pindust were but vaine.
The touch of gold did sure instill
Some vertue More then did the quill
Or else yor Loue did seeme to trye
which had the more Soliditie
the Gold or it; nor can I guesse
which did neede the touchstone lesse.   10
But since you write no cleanely hande
Yo^r token bidds mee vnderstande
Mine eyes haue here a remedy
whereby to reade more easily.
    I doe but ieast your Loue alone
 Is my interp^rtation;
My words I will recant and sweare
I know your hand is wondrous faire:
_____

[172]

On a blisterd }
Lippe   }

Chide not thy sproutinge lippe, nor kill
the iuycy bloome with bashfull skill
Know it is an amorous dew
That swells to court thy Corrall hue,
and what a blemish you esteeme
to other eyes a Pearle may seeme,
whose wary growth is not aboue
The thrifty size wch pearle doth loue
  Does any iudge y^t face more faire
whose tender silke a Mole doth beare,   10
Or else y^t eye a finer Nett,
whose glasse is ring'd about wth iett
Or is an Apple thought more sweete
 when hony specks & red doe meete.
Then is your lippe made fayrer by
Such sweetenesse of Deformitie.
  The Necter which men striue to shippe
 Springs like a well vppon your lippe
 O who will blame the fruitfull trees
 when too much sappe & gumm hee sees.   20
 Here Nature from his store doth sende
Onely what other partes can lende.
The bud of Loue which here doth growe
were too too sweet if pluckt belowe :

_____

171.15 (right margin, not transcribed)] Modern pencil notation: *jest*.   **172.10 *Mole*]** Majuscule *M* overwrites minuscule *m*.

[173]

On the Bible

Behold this little volume here inrold
T'is the Almighty's Present to the world
Hearken Earth, Earth each senceless thing can here
His makers thunder though it want an eare.
Gods word is Senior to his worke, nay rather
If rightly weigh'd the world may call it father
God spake <a word> twas doñe. This great foundaçon
Is the Creators Exhalation
Breathd out in speaking. The best worke of Man
Is better then his word, but if wee scanne   10
Gods word aright his worke farr short doth fall
The word is God, the worke are creatures all.
The Sundry peices of this generall Frame
Are dimmer Letters all which spell the same
Eternall wordes: but these cannot expresse
His greatnesse with such easie reᵃdinesse.
And therefore yeild. The Heauen shall pass a way
The Sunne and Moone & Starrs shall all obay
To light on generall Bonfire; but his worde
His builder vp, his all distroyinge sworde.   20
That still suruiues, noe iot of that can die
    Each tittle Measures im mortalitie
  The words owne Mother one whose brest did hang
The worlds vpholder drawne into a spanne
Shee shee was not so blest because shee bare him
As cause her selfe was new borne & did heare him
Before shee had brought forth shee herd her sonne
first speake in the Annuntiation
And then eu'n then before shee brought forth childe
  By name of Blessed shee herselfe instild   30
    Once more the Mightie word his people greete
    Thus lapt & thus swathd vpp in paper sheetes
  Read here Gods Image wᵗʰ a zealous eye
      The Legible and written Deity.

3 *senceless*] There is a space between *sence* and *less*.   7 *foundacōn*] A tilde extends over *con* to omit *i*.   13 *peices*] The *c* is written in a secretarial hand; "peires" (obs. of piers) is a possible reading.   22 *im mortalitie*] There is a space between *im* and *mortalitie*.

[174]

To a Gentle man, on a strange Cure:

Welcome a broade, o welcome from your bed
I ioy to see you thus deliuered
After fowre yeeres in <u>Trauell</u> issues forth   <u>Trauell</u>
A birth of lastinge wonder, where at Truth
Might well suspect her-selfe, a New disease
Borne t'aduance ye Surgeons of our Dayes
Aboue all others: A perfideous bone
Eaten and vndermi'nd by humors growne.
Lodg'd in that Captiue Thigh, which first of anie
Halted though furnisht with a bone too manie;   10
Noe Golgotha, noe Charnel-house, nor feild
If all were searcht could such a nother yeeld
A bone soe lockt and hugd in as a barre
That backe and forward May bee wrested farre
But not puld out at th'key-hole, neither could
The cuninge workeman come to't as hee would
Crosse vaines did guard the sore, a hollow caue
Must wade into the flesh, the Surgeons graue
Thus being dig'd, the file with harsh delay
Must grate the bones and carue those chipps away   20
     Blest bee the Midmen, whose dexteritie
Pulld out a birth like Bacchus from that thigh
 Tutors of Nature, whose well guided Art
 Cann rectifie her wants in euery part
who by preseruinge others pay the Debt
They owe to Nature, and doe rebegett
Her strength growne ruinate: I could bee glad
Such liu'd the daies, wch they to others add.
   Nor can I rightly <er>$_\wedge$ ^{tell} the happier Man
The Patient or the Surgion, doe but scanne   30
His Praise, thy ease, t'was sure an Exstasie
That kil'd Van Otto not a Lethargie.
 Striuinge to crowne his worth, hee manly tryde
His last & greatest cure then gladly di'de.
Barnard must tarrie longer, should hee fly
 After his Brother, then the world must dye
 Or liue a Cripple, Griffiths happie fate
Requires ye same hand still to Iterate
No less a Miracle. the Ioyners skill
Could neuer mend his carued pate so well   40
                    As hee hath &

---

3 *Trauell* (in text)] Majuscule *T* overwrites minuscule *i*.   7 *perfideous*] Second *e* overwrites *i*.   12 *searcht*] *a* overwrites *r*.   29 *rightly*] *y* overwrites *ie*.

As hee hath heald a Naturall: the stoute
And bostinge Paracelsus who giues out
His rules cann giue our flesh Eternity
Would faintly doubt of this Recouerie
Hee that wrought these Cures I thinke hee can
As well of scrapps make vp a perfect man
O had you seene his Marrowe droppe away
Or the others braines strart out, then would you say
Nothinge could heale this fracture or y^t bone
Saue Barnard or the Re surrection   50
   Now smile vppon this torment; pretty thing
How will yee vse it ? bury't in a ring
Like a Deaths head, or send it to the graue
In earnest of the bodie it must haue.
Or if you will you may the same conuert
Into a Die because twas fortunate.
The ring were best; t'is like a diamond borne
Out of the Rocke soe was it hewn & torne
Out of your thigh, the Gemme worth nothing is
Vntill it bee cut out, no more was this   60
 Happie are they who know what treasure t'is
To finde their health they only feele their blisse
Y^u<?> that haue felt these pangs maist well maintaine
Mans greatest pleasure is but want of paine
Inioye thy selfe for nothinge worse can come
To one soe <s?> schoold and versd in Martyrdome.   ffinis

[175]

A Register }
for a Bible }

I am the faithfull deputie
vnto your fadinge memory
A faithfull watchman to whose trust
Allotted bee 12 places iust
your index lon in search doth hold
your folded wrinkles make bookes old
But I the Scripture open plaine
And what you heard soone teach againe
The Text I keepe which I am cast on
Better some times then doth ye person   10
And what the hand of God hath writt
Behold my fingers poynt at it.

    Alias

174.48 say] The word appears added; the writing is less bold, perhaps using a different pen.   **174.50 Re surrection**] There is a space between *Re* and *surrection*.   **175.10 person**] A tilde through *p* abbreviates *er*.

[176]

I your Memory's recorder
Keepe my charge in watchfull order
And on the Margent where I stande
You neede no folde nor printed hande
I point out Scripture, Day and Night
My strings deuide ye word aright
St Peter cannot wth his Keyes
Vnlocke Heauen Gates soe soone as these
By these the Welch-men well may bring
Him'selfe to Heauen in a stringe.

5

[177]

Anagram:.
Iohn Portemane
Mother no paine.

Deare Mother I haue lately mett with one
The best Phisition and Chirurgion,
Who suddenly gaue perfect ease to mee,
Although hee tooke my body for his fee.
This was the most hee causd mee to endure
I could not speake with you before my cure.
Yet fate who would not lett mee die amonge
My friends, hath giuen my name a tongue.
Scann ouer that sad Mother once or twice
And you shall finde both comfort & aduice.
On paine of great detraction from my blisse
Weepe not for mee, who am where no paine is.

10

[178]

On the Death of young Barronet Portman
dyinge of an Impostume in his head :

Is Death so cuninge now that all her blowe
Aimes at the head, doth now her wary bow
Make surer worke, when heretofore the steele
Slew war like Heroes only in the heele?
Now find out slights. when men them selues beginn
To bee their proper Fates, by new found sinne?
Tis cowardise to make a wound so sure
No Art in killinge where no Arte can Cure
Was it for hate of Learninge that shee smote
This vpper shoppe where all ye Muses wrought.

10

178.6 *Fates*] Majuscule *F* overwrites minuscule *f*.

Learninge shall Crosse her drift, and du^ely trie
All waies and meanes of Immortalitie.
Because her head was Crush'd doth shee desire
Our equall shame? in vaine shee doth aspire
Noe, Noe, wee know where ere shee made a breach
Her poysonous sting onely the heele can reach,
The head it selfe looke on the soule of Man
Is but a lower Inch of such a spann.
Yet hath shee straind her vtmost Tyranny
And done her worst in that shee came so high,   20
Had shee reseru'd this stroke for haughtie men
For Politicke Contriuers; iustly then
The punishment were matcht wth the offence
But when Humilitie and Innocence.
Soe indiscreetely in the head are hitt
Death hath done Murther & shall die for it.
    Thinke it no fauour showne, because the braine
Is voide of sence, & then more free of paine;
Thinke it no kindnesse when soe stealingly
Hee rather seemd to iest away then die,   30
And like the Innocent the widdowes Child
Cried out my head my head & sweetly died
Thinke it was rather double Cruelty
Slaughter intended on his Name, y^t hee
Whose thoughts were nothinge tainted nothinge Vaine
Might seeme to hide corruption in the braine.
How easie might this blott bee wipt a way
If any Penn his worth could open lay;
for which, those harlott praises which wee reare
On common dust, as much to slender were   40
<u>gentle:</u>   As _____ for others. Bostinge Elegies
Must here bee dumbe; desert y^t ouer weighs
All her reward stopps, all o^r praise, least wee
Might seeme to giue a looke, to them & thee
Wherefore an humble verse & such a straine
As mine will hede the truth, cause others faine:.

[179]

If Hercules tall stature might bee guest
But by his thumbe whereby to make the rest
in due proportion: the best rule that I
would chuse to measure Venus beauty by
should bee her legg and foote, if Husband men
Measure their timber by the foote, why then
Not wee our wiues ? whether wee goe or stride
Those Natiue compasses are seldome wide
Of telling true: the round & slender foote
Is a sure Index and a secrett Note   10
Of hidden parts, & well this way may leade
Vnto the closet of a Maiden head.
Here emblemes of our youth wee roses tie
And here the garter loues Deare Mysterie:
For want of beauty here ye Peacocks pride
Letts fall her traine & fearinge to bee spide
shutts vp her painted witnesses to lett
those eyes from view wch are but counterfeit
Who lookes not if ye part bee good or euill
May meete with clouen feete & Match ye Deuill   20
For this did make the difference betweene
The more vnhollowed creatures & ye cleane
Well may you iudge her other steps are light
Her thoughts awry that doth not tread a<p>right
But then their true perfection when wee see
Those parts more absolute which hidden bee.
Nature nere lent a faire foundation
For an vnworthy frame to rest there on
Let others view the topp & limbes through out
The deeper knowledge is to know the roote   30
And readinge of the face, the weakest know
What beauty is, the learned looke below
Who looking there doe all the rest discrie
As in a poole the Moone wee vse to spie
Pardon sweet heart the pride of my desire
If but to kisse your toe it should aspire:./

---

24 aright] *a* overwrites *u*. The scribe first wrote *upright*. The probable intention was *a right*, using the deleted *p* as the space between the two words.   **25 perfection**] There is a tilde through *p* to abbreviate *er*.

[180]

A translation of the Nightingale out of Strado:

Now the declininge Sun gan downeward bend
From higher heauen, & from his locks did send
A milder flame, when neere to Tibers flow
A Lutinest allaid his carefull woe
With soundinge charmes & in a greeny seate
Of shadie Oake tooke shelter from the heate.
   A Nightingale ore heard him that did vse
To soiourne in these Nighbour groues, the Muse
That filld the place, the Syren of the woode
Poore harmelesse Syren stealinge neere shee stood   *10*
Close lurkinge in the leaues attentiuely
Recording that vnwonted Melodie
Shee cond it to her selfe and euery straine
His fingers plaide her throate returnd againe.
   The Lutinest perceiud an answere sent
From the imitatinge bird & was content
To shew her play; more fully then in hast
Hee tries his Lute, and giuinge her a tast
Or ye insuinge quarrell nimbly beates
On all his strings, as nimbly shee repeates   *20*
And wildly rangeinge or'e a thousand Keyes
Sounds a shrill warninge of her after layes.
   With rolling hand the Lutinest then <playes> plies
The trembling threeds, sometimes in scornefull wise
Hee brushes downe ye strings, & keemes them all
With one eu'n stroke, then takes them seuerall<?>
And culls them ore againe; his sparkeling ioynts
With busie discant Minsing on the points
Reach backe againe wth nimble touch, y^t donne hee stayes,
The bird replies and Art with Art repayes;   *30*
Sometimes as one vnexpert or in doubt,
How shee might weild her voice shee draweth out
Her tone at large, and doth at first prepaire
A solemne straine not weard wth winding ayre
But with an equall pitch & constant throate
Make cleare the passage for her glidinge note.

---

7 **Nightingale**] A mark similar to an apostrophe appears over the *a*.   **33 Prepaire**] Probable spelling; *ir* overwrites probable *r*.

Then Cross diuision diuersly shee playes
And loudly chaunting out her quickest layes
Poyses the sound, and with a quiv'ring voyce
Falls backe againe. Hee wondringe how so choyce   40
So various harmony could issue out
From such a little throate, doth goe about
Some harder lessons, & with wondrous art
Chaunging the strings doth vp ye treble dart
And downeward smite the base, wth painefull stroke
Hee beates, & as the Trumpet doth prouoke
Sluggards to fight, ev'n so his wanton skill
with mingled discord ioynes the hoarse & shrill.
     The bird this alsoe tunes, & whilst shee cutts
Sharpe notes with meltinge voyce & mingled putts   50
Mesures of middle sound, then suddenly
Shee thunders deepe, & iugges it inwardly
With a gentle murmer, cleere & dull shee singes
By course, as when the Martiall warninge ringes.
     Beleeu't the Minstrill blust wth angry moode
Inflamd quoth hee, Thou Chauntresse of the wood
Either from thee I'le beare the price a way
Or v_∧^anquisht breake my Lute: with out delay
In-imitable accents then hee straines
His hand<e> flies ore the stringes, in one hee chaines   60
Farr different numbers, chasinge here and there
And all the strings belabours euery where
Both flatt and sharpe hee strikes, & stately growes
To prowder straines, and backward as hee goes
Doubling deuides, and closing vp his layes
Like a full quier a shouting <u>comfort</u> playes   consort
Then pausinge stood in expectation
yf his Corriuall nowe durst answere on
But shee when practise long her throate had whett
Induring not to yeeld at once doth sett   70
Her spiritts all to worke, & all in vaine
for while shee labours to expresse againe
With Natures simple voyce such diuerse keyes
With slender pipes such loftie notes as these.

---

53 *singes*] Secretarial *e* overwrites italic *s*. **66 *comfort*]** *f* overwrites unreadable letter, probably an *s*. The word is corrected in the right margin. **68 *Corriuall*]** Second *r* overwrites *i*. **69 *when*]** *n* overwrites *r*.

Ore matcht with high \<des?ines\> designes, ore watcht wth woe
Iust at the last incounter of her foe
Shee faints, shee dies, falles on his Instrument
That conquerd her, a fittinge Monument.
    So farre eu'n little soules are driuen on
    Struck with a vertuous Emulation   ffinis

[181]

    On a ffountaine.
The Dolphines twisting each on others side
for ioy le_^^apt vp and gazing there abide,
And where as other waters fish doe bringe
Here from fishes doth the water springe,
Who thinke it _^ ^{is} more glorious to giue
Then to receiue the iuyce where by they liue
And by this milke white bason learne you may
That pure hands you should bringe, or beare away.
For which the bason wants no furniture
Each Dolphin waitinge makes his mouth an Ewre   10
    Yo^r welcome then you well may vnderstand
    When fish themselues giues water to your hand:

N. B. The open space on this page has a poem entitled "Vpon Sr Walter Raleigh," written in the hand of John Wale.

[182]

An Epitaph vpon Iames Duke of
    Hamilton:.   Año Doͫi : 1649° }}
He that three Kingdoms made one flame,
Blasted their beauty, burn't the frame,
Himselfe now here in ashes lies
A part of this great Sacrifice:
Here all of Hamilton remaines,
Saue what the other world containes.
But (Reader) it is hard to tell
Whether that World bee Heav'en, or Hell.
A Scotch man enters Hell at's birth,
And 'scapes it when hee goes to earth,   10
Assur'd no worse a Hell can come
Than that which hee inioy'd at home.
 How did the Royall Workman botch
This Duke, halfe-English, and half-Scotch!
A Scot an English Earldom fits,
 As Purple doth your Marmuzets;
Suits like Nol Cromwell with the Crowne,
 Or Bradshaw in his Scarlet-gown
Yet might hee thus disguis'd (no lesse)
 Haue slip't to Heau'<e>n in's English dresse,   20
But that he'in hope of life became
 All Scot, and quit his English Claime.
 This mystick Proteus too as well
 Might cheat the Deuill, scape his Hell,
Since to those pranks hee pleas'd to play,
 Religion euer pav'd the way;
Which he did to a Faction tie,
 Nor to reforme, but Crucifie;

---

182 *An Epitaph vpon Iames Duke of Hamilton* (complete), pp. 227–29] Poem written in larger script, underlined as indicated (see text note). **21 *he'in*]** The apostrophe appears as indicated. Although *i* has a dot, it is imperfectly formed. *he'n* is a possible reading.

'Twas he that first alarm'd the Kirk
 To this prepost'rous bloody work,   30
Vpon the Kings to place Christs Throne,
 A step and foot-stoole to his owne;
Taught Zeale a hundred tumbling tricks,
 And Scriptures twind with Politicks;
The Pulpit made a Iuglers Box,
 Set Law and Gospell in the Stocks,
As did old Buchanan and Knox,
In those dayes when (at*once) the Pox,
 And Presbiters a way did finde
 Into the World, to plague mankinde.
'Twas hee patch't vp the new Diuine,
Part Caluin, and part Cataline,
Could too transforme (without a Spell)
 Satan into a Gabriell;
Iust like those Pictures, which wee paint
On this side Fiend, on that side Saint.
 Both this, and that, and euery thing
 Hee was; for, and again'st the King:
Rather than hee his ends would misse,
 Betrayd his Master with a kisse   50
And buried in one Common-Fate
 The Glory of our Church and State
 The Crowne too leuell'd on the ground,
  And hauing cook'd all parties round,
'Faith it was time then to bee gone,
 Since hee had all his businesse done.

* The Pox
Presb: and Iesu-
itisme are of
same standing-//

---

49 than] *a* overwrites *e*.

Next, on the fatall Block expir'd,
 Hee to this Marble-Cell retir'd;
 Where all of Hamilton remaines,
 But what Eternity containes:. ////   Finis. //

(**Open space below poem**)] This space was left open in the text. John Wale, a later owner of the manuscript, transcribed a speech headed: "To the Queen's most Excellent maiesty."

[183]

Honos. alit artes: R: C:

My sonne; the vertuous inclination of thy matchless Mother, by whose tender and godly care thy infancy was gouerned,
togeather wth education vnder soe Zealous a Tutor putts
mee rather in assurance then hope, that thou art not igno-
rant of that summary band wch only is able to make thee
happye, as well in thy Death as life; I meane ye knowledge & worship of thy Creator & redeemer; Without which
all other things are vaine and miserable. Soe that thy youth
beinge indeed guided by soe sufficient a teacher I make no
doubt but hee will furnish thy Life with Diuine & morall   10
documents: Yet that I may not cast of the care that
beseemeth a Parent towards his child; or that thou shouldest
haue cause to deriue thy whole felicitie and welfare rather
from whome thou receiued'st thy birth and beinge then from
those vnto the charge of thy well liuinge is allotted. I
thinke it fitt and agreeable, to helpe thee wth such aduertise-
ments for the squaringe of this life as are rather gained by
longe experience then much readinge. To the end that thou
entringe into this exorbitant age maist bee ye better prepared to shun those courses, where vnto this world and y^e   20
want of Experience may easily draw thee. And because
I would not confound thy memorye I haue redu‸^ce‸<cted> them
into Ten Precepts And next vnto Moses his Tables if y^u
imprint them in thy memorye thou shalt reape ye benefit &
I the contentment.   And here they followe.

I   When it <?>shall please God to bringe thee to mans estate vse
great prouidence and circumspection in choyce of thy wife: for
from thence will springe all future good or euill. And yt is <a>
<st> an action like a stratagem in warre where in a Man can
erre but once. If thy estate bee good, match neere home   30
& at leisure, if weake farr of, and quickly. Enquire diligently
of her education and how her parents haue beene enclined
in their youth. Lett her <l> not bee poore how generous soeuer,
for a man can buy nothinge in ye markett for gentilitie.
Nor chuse abase or vncomly creature although wealthy,
for that will cause contempt in others, and loathinge in thy
selfe; Neither make choice of adwarfe or a foole: for of the
one thou shalt begett a race of Pigmies and ye other will bee thy
daily disgrace. And yt will irke thee to heare her talke,
for thou shalt finde to thy great greife yt there is nothinge more   40
irkesome then a shee foole. And touchinge the gouerment

---

4 (left margin, not transcribed)] Modern pencil notation: *Corbet*. **37 adwarfe**] The words are written together as
one: *a dwarfe.*

of thine house, lett thy hospitalitie bee moderate and accordinge to the measure of thine estate; rather plentifull then
sparinge but not costly; ffor I neuer knew any grow poore
by keepeinge an orderly table: But some consume themselues
by secrett vices and then hospitality beareth the blame.
But banish swinish Drunkards out of thy howse. It is a vice y^t
impaireth health, consumes much, and makes no shew. And I
neuer heard praise ascribed to a Drunkard but the well
bearinge of Drinke which is a Commendačon fitter for a   50
Brewers horse, or Drag man, then for a Gentleman or seruingman.
  See that ye spend not aboue 3 parts of the fowre of thy reue-
newes, nor aboue a 3 part of that in thine house: for the other
2 parts will doe no more then defray thine extraordinarye,
which will alwaies surmount the ordinarye by soe much, otherwise thou shalt liue like a rich begg^{a}er, in continual want.
And ye needy man can neuer liue contentedly; for euery least
infortunate estate makes him ready to mor^{t}gage or sell <all> land.
And y^t Gentleman that sells one acre of land sells an ounce of
creditt: for Gentilitie is nothinge but auncient riches; soe that   60
if the foundation shrinke the bu^{i}ldinge must needes followe after./

2 | Bringe thy child vp in learninge & obedience, yet wthout austeritie,
praise them openly, rep^{r}hend them secretly, giue them good countenance and conuenient maintenance accordinge to thine abilitie other
wise thy life will seeme their bondage: and what portion thou
shalt leaue them at thy Death, they will thanke death for, and
not thee.   I am perswaded that ye foolish cockeringe of some,
and the austere carriadge of others, cause more men & weomen
to take euill courses then their owne vicious inclinations./
Marry thy daughters least they marry themselues and suffer   70
not thy sonnes to passe ye Alp^{e}s for they shall bringe home nothinge
but pride, blasphemie and Athisme. And if by trauaile they
gett a few broken languages it will <pe> profitt them no more then
to haue one sort of meate serued in diuerse dishes. Neither by
my aduise traine them vpp to warrs: for y^t hee y^t setts his rest
to liue by that can hardly bee an honest or good Christian.
ffor euery warre is of it selfe vniust except ye cause bee iust.
Besides that is a science noe longer in request then vse, for Souldiers in Peace, are like as Chimnies in summer:

3 | Liue not in the Cuntrie with out Corne and Cattell about thee,   80
for hee y^t p^{r}sents his lands to his purse for euery expences, is like

---

67 (after *thee*, space)] As indicated. **67 perswaded**] A tilde through *p* abbreviates *er*.

him that thinketh to keepe water in fire: And what prouision
thou shalt want prepare to buy at the first hand for there
is a penny in ⁴fowre saued betweene buyinge at need and when
the season or markett serues fittest for yᵗ.

4   Bee not serued wᵗʰ kinsmen freinds or men intreated to serue
(for they will expect much and doe little) or wᵗʰ such as are
amarous (for their braines are euer intoxicated) and rather by twoe too few, then one too many. ffeed them well and
pay them wᵗʰ the most and thou maist boldly require duty and   90
seruice at their hands./

5   Lett thy kyndred & aliances bee welcome to thy table grace
them wᵗʰ thy countenance and further them in all honest
actions, ffor by this meanes thou shalt finde many aduocates to
pleade an Apologie for thee behinde thy backe. but shake off
those glow‸ᵂormes I meane parasites & hypocrites: who will feed &
fawne vppon thee, in prosperitie, they will shelter thee no more
than an arbor in winter.

6   Beware suretyeshippe for thy best freinds. Hee yᵗ payeth an
other mans debt seeketh his owne ouerthrowe. But if thou   100
canst not chuse, rather lend thy money thy selfe vpon good
bands, though thou borrow. for soe shalt thou both please thy
freind and secure thy selfe. Neither borrowe money of a
Neighbour or freind, but of a stranger, where payinge for yᵗ
thou shalt heare no more of yt: otherwise yᵘ shalt eclipse
thy creditt, loose thy freedome and yet pay as deare as to an
other. But in borrowinge bee pʳtious of thy word for hee yᵗ
hath a care to keepe his daies of paiment is Lord ouer an
other mans goods./

7   Vndertake noe suite against any ‿ᵖᵒᵒʳᵉ man wᵗʰout receiuing much   110
wronge, for thou makest him thy Competitoᵘr, and it is base conquest to triumph where there is small resistance. Neither
attempt law wᵗʰ any man before thou bee throughly resolued
that thou hast right on thy side, Then neither spare for
money nor paines for a cause or twoe soe followed will free
the from suits a greate parte of thy life after./

8   Bee sure to keepe some great man thy freinde but trouble him
not wᵗʰ euery trifelinge complaint. Often pʳsent him wᵗʰ many
yet small guifts, And if thou haue cause to bestow any gratuity,
let it bee such as may bee alwaies in his sight, otherwise in   120
this ambitious age thou shalt remaine like a hop wᵗʰout a
pole liue in obscuritie and bee made a foote stoole for euery
insultinge companion to spurne at.//

                           Towards &c//

---

82 prouision] A tilde through *p* abbreviates *ro*.   **96 parasites**] A tilde through *p* abbreviates *ar*.   **101 good**] Second *o*
resembles an *a*; final *d* not fully formed.   **116 parte**] A tilde through *p* abbreviates *ar*.

9 | Towards thy superiors bee humble generous to thy equalls, familiar
yet respectiue to thy inferio^{u}rs, shew much humilitie and some
familiaritie as to bend thy body, stretch forth thy hand, and to
vncouer thy head, wth such popular complements. The first
p^{r}pares ye way to aduancement: the second makes thee knowne
as well bred, the third gaines a man good report which once
gotten is easily kept. ffor high humilities takes such deepe   130
roote in the mindes of the multitude, as they are more easily
won by vnproffitable curtesies then curteous benefitts. Yet I
aduise thee not to affect, nor neglect populariite. To affect as
E^x: or neglect as R: Trust not any man wth thy estate, for
it is a meere folly for a man to inthrall himselfe to his freinds,
as though if occasion were offered hee should not dare to become
his enemie:/

10 | Bee not scrupulous in thy conuersa$\tilde{c}$on nor stoicall in thy iests
the one will make thee vnwelcome to all companie: the other will
breed quarrells, and gett thee hatred of thy best freinds. for   140
iests when they sauour too much of truth, leaue a bitternes in y^e
minde of those that are touched. Although I haue pointed at
all these inclusiue, yett I thinke it fitt and necessarie to leaue it
thee as a speciall caution because I haue seene many so prone
to quipp and gird y^t they will rather loose their freinds then
their iests. And if by chance their boylinge braines yeild a
scoffe they will trauell to bee deliuerd of it as a woman wth
Childe. These nimble app^{r}hensions are but ye froth of witt://

[184]

Mr Earl's Characters.　　}

A Child

Is a Man in a small letter, yet the best coppie of Adam before hee tasted
of Eue, or the Apple: And hee is happie whose small practi<s>ce in yᵉ world
cann only write a Character. Hee is Natures fresh picture newly drawne
in oyle, which time & much handlinge dimms & defaces. His soule is a
white paper vnscribled with obseruac̃ons of the world, where with att
last it becomes a blurd Note booke. Hee is purely happie because hee
knowes no ill, Nor hath made meanes by sinne to bee acquainted with
Miserie. Hee arriues not at the mischeife of being wise, nor endures
euills to come by foreseeinge them. He kisses and loues all, and when
the smart of the rod is past smiles on the beater. Nature and　　　　10
his Parents alike dandle him, and tice him on with a baite of suger
to a draught of wormewood. Hee plaies yet like a young Prentise
the first day, and is not come to his taske of Melancholie. His har-
dest labour is his tongue, as if hee were loath to vse so deceiptfull
an Organ; and hee is best companie with it, when hee can but
prattle. Wee laugh at his foolish sportts, but his game is ouer earnest, His Drum̃es, rattle, and Hobbihorse, but the Embleame and
mockinge of our businesse. His ffather hath writ him as his owne
little storie; where in hee reades those dayes of his Life that hee
cannot remember, and sights to see what innocence hee hath ouer　　20
liued. The elder hee growes hee is a strayer lower from God: &
like his first ffather much worse in his breeches. Hee is the Christians Example, and the old mans fare; the one imitates his purenes; &
the other falls into his simplicitie. Could hee putt off his bodie with
his little Coate, hee had gott eternitie without a burden, and ex-
chaung'd but one heauen for a nother: &　+　+　+　+　+　+:

A younge raw Preacher.

Is a bird not yet fledg'd that hath hopt out of his nest to bee chirpinge on a hedge, & will bee stragglinge a broade at what perill so-euer.
His backwardnesse in the Vniuersitie hath thus sett him forward; for
had hee not truanted there he had not binn soe hastie a Diuine:
His small standinge and time haue only made him a proficient in
boldnesse: out of which and his table bookes hee is furnished for a
preacher. His Collections of studdy are the Notes of Sermons, wᶜʰ
taken vp at Sᵗ Maries hee vtters in the Cuntrie, and if hee write
Brachigraphy his stocke is soe much the better. His writinge is more
then his readinge for hee reades only what hee getts without booke.　　10
Thus accomplisht hee comes downe to his friends, and his first salutac̃o
is grace and Peace out of the Pulpitt. His praier is conceipted
and no man remembers his Colledge more at large. The pace of his
Sermon is a full careere, & hee runns wildly ouer till the clocke stops him.

verte.

Title: *Earl's*] Apostrophe above *l*. **A Child: 2 *practice*]** Second c overwrites e. The word was originally *practise*.

The labour of it is cheifely in his lungs, and the only thinge hee hath
made of it himselfe is the faces. Hee takes on against the Pope
without Mercye, and hath a Iest still in Lauander against Bellermine.
His Action is all passion and his speech interiections; Hee hath an
excellent facultie in bemoninge the people, and spitts with a very
good grace. Hee will not draw his handkercheife out of his   20
due place nor blow his nose without discretion. His commenda-
coñs is that hee neuer lookes vpon booke, and indeede hee was
neuer vsd to itt. Hee preaches but once a yeere though
twice a Sunday: for the stuffe is still ye same onely ye dressinge
a little altered. Hee hath more tricks with an old Sermone
then a Taylor hath with an old cloake; to turne & peece it &
at last quite disguise itt with a new p^rface. Yf hee haue
waded farther and will shew his readinge, his Authors are
Apostells, and his schoole Diuinitie Chatechesme: His fashion &
demure habitt, getts him in with some towne p^rcision, and makes   30
him a guest on fryday night. You may know him by his narrow
veluet cape and serge facinge, and his ruffe next his haire
the shortest thinge about him. The Companie of his walke
is some zealous tradesman whom hee astonisheth with strange
points which they both vnderstand alike. His friends and
much painefullnesse may p^rferre him to thirtie pounds a yeere, &
his meanes to a chamber maide, with whom wee leaue him now in
the bands of wedlocke, & next Sunday you shall haue him againe: +

A graue deuine:

Is one that knowes the burthen of his callinge, and hath studied to
make his shoulders sufficient. for the which hee hath not bin hastie
to launch out of his port, the Vniuersitie but expected the ballast
of learninge and wind of opportunitye. Deuinitie is not the
beginninge but ye end of his studies, the which hee takes his ordinarie
staire, and makes Arts his way. Hee counts no prophanenesse to bee
polished with humane learning, or smooth his way by Ale to schoole
Diuinitie. Hee hath sounded both Religions, and anchored in the best; &
is a Protestant out of Iudgment, Noe faction, not because his Cuntrie,
but reason is on his side. The Ministrie is his choice, not refuge, &   10
yet the pulpitt is not so much his itch as feare. His discourse is
substance, not all Rhetoriqe, and he vtters more things then words.
His speech is not help't with enforced actions, but the matter acts
it selfe. Hee shoots all his meditation att one butt, and beates on
his Text not the Church Cushion, makeinge his hearers not the
Pulpitt grone. In citinge of Popish errors hee cutts them wth Argūts

---

Preacher: 25 *Sermone*] The final *e* appears added. **A graue deuine: 6 *prophanenesse*]** A tilde through *p* abbreviates
ro. **7 *Ale*]** A line is drawn through the top portion of the word. **12 *Rhetoriqe*]** The *q* is shaped like a *g*.

not cu^dgells them with barren inuectiues; and labours more to
shew the truth of his cause then his spleene. His sermone is
limited by the Method not the houre glasse, and his Deuotion goes
with him out of the pulpitt. Hee comes not vp thrice a weeke
because hee would not bee Idle, Nor talke three howres to geither
because hee would not talke nothing, but his tongue preaches at
fitt times, and his conuersacon is the euery dayes <sacrifice> exercise.
In matters of Ceremonie, hee is not Ceremonious, but thinkes hee
owes that reuerence to the Church to bow his Iudgments to it,
and makes more Conscience of a schīse than of a surplesse.
Hee esteemes the Churches Hierarchy as her glorye, and how
euer wee iarr with Rome would not haue our confusion
distinguish vs. In Symonaicall purchases hee thinks his
soule goes in the bargaine, and is loath to come by promotion
soe deare. yet his worth at length aduances him, and the
price of his owne meritt buies him a Liuinge. Hee is no base
grater of his tithes, and will not wrangle for the odd egge.
The Lawyer is the only man hee hinders by whom hee is spited
for takeinge vp quarrells. Hee is a maine pillar of ye Church
yet neither Deane nor Cannon, and his life is our Religiouns
best Apollogie. His death is his last sermone, where in the
Pulpitt of his bedd hee instructs me<?>n how to die by his
Example:. +   +   +   +   ⸗

20

30

A meere dull Physitian }

His practise is some businesse att bedds sides, his speculacon is
an vrinall. Hee is distinguisht from an Empyricke by a round
veluett capp & Doctors gowne, yet no man takes degrees more superfluously, for hee is Doctor howsoeuer: Hee is sworne to Galen &
Hypocrates as vniuersitie men to their statutes though they
neuer saw them, and his discourse is all Aphorismes, though his
readinge bee only Alexis of Peckmount, or ye regiment of health.
His learninge consists much in reckoninge vp ye hard names of
diseases, and superscriptions of Gally potts in his Apothecaries shopp.
The best cure hee hath done is vppon his owne purse, which from
a leane sicknesse hee hath made lusty and in flesh. If hee
hath bin but a by stander att some desperate recouerie, hee is
slandered with it though guiltlesse: this breeds his reputation
and that his practise for his skill is meerely opinion. Of all
Odours hee likes best the smell of vrin, & holds vespatious rule
that no grine is vnsauorie: If you send this once vnto him
you must resolue to bee sicke howsoeuer. ffor hee will neuer leaue

10

A graue deuine: 30 *promotion*] A tilde through *p* abbreviates *ro*. **A meere dully Physitian: 3–4 *superfluously*]** A
tilde through *p* abbreviates *er*. **9 *superscriptions*]** A tilde through *p* abbreviates *er*.

examininge your water till hee hath shakt it into a disease,
then followes his writt to his drugger in a strange language
which hee vnderstands though hee cannot constrew. Yf hee see   *20*
you himselfe his p^rsence is the worst visitacoñ, for if hee
cannot heale the sicknesse, hee will bee sure to helpe it. Hee
translates his Apothecaries shop into your chamber, and the
very windowes and benches must take Physicke. Hee tells
you your Maladie is great though it bee but a could or
headache, which by good endeauo‸^urs & diligence hee may bringe
to some moment. His most vnfaithfull act is that hee
leaues a man gaspinge and his p^rtence is death, and hee hath a
quarrell and must not meet, but his feare is least ye carkase
should bleed. Anatomies & other spectacles of Mortalitie   *30*
haue hardned him, and hee is no more struck with a funerall,
then with a graue maker; Noble men vse him for a direction
for their stomacke, and Ladies for wantonnesse especially beinge
a proper man. if hee bee single hee is in league with his
Shee Apothecarie, and because it is ye Physition, her husband
is the patient. if hee hath leisure to bee idle that is to studie
hee hath a smatch att Alacryme, and is sicke of the Phylosophers
stone, a disease vncurable but by an abundance of Phlebotomy
of the purse. His too many opposites are a Mountebanke And
a good woman, and hee neuer shewes his learninge so much as   *40*
in an inuective against them and their boxes. In conclusion
hee is a suckinge consumption & a brother to the worme, for
they are both ingendred of mans corruption:. +   +   +   +

{{ An Alderman }}

Hee is venerable in his gowne more in his beard, where with hee
setts not forth his owne soe much, as the face of the Citty, you
must looke on him, as on the towne gates: and not consider him as a
bodye but as a Corporačon. His emenencie aboue others hath
made him a man of worshipp, for hee neuer had bin preferd had
hee not bin worth thousands. Hee ouersees the Coṁon wealth
as his shopp, and it is an argument of his policie that hee hath
thriuen by his <craught> ↑<cru>↓ craft. Hee is a rigorous magistrate in his
word, yet his scale of Iustice is suspected, least it bee like the
ballances in his ware house. A ponderous man hee is and a sub-   *10*
stantiall for his weight is commonly extraordinary, and in his
preferment nothinge rises so much as his belly. His head is of no
                                                      great depth

313

yet well furnished, & when it is in coniunction with his brethren may bringe forth a Cittye Apothegme or some such sage
matter. Hee is one that will not hastily runne into error,
for hee treads with graue deliberation, and his iudgment con
sists much in his pace. His discourse is commonly the Annalls
of his Mayraltie and what good gouerment there was in the
dayes of his gold chaine, though his doore posts were the only
things suffered reformacon. Hee seemes sincerely religious
especially on solemne dayes for hee comes oft to Church to make
a shew. Hee is the highest starre of his profession, and an
Example to his trade what in time they may come to. Hee
makes verie much of his authoritye, but more of's Sattin dublett,
which though of good yeeres yett beares his age very well,
and lookes <sh> fresh euery Sunday. but his scarlett gowne is
a monument and lasts from generacon to generation. + + +

20

{{ A discontented Man }}}

Is one that hath fallen out with the world and will bee reuengd
on himselfe. ffortune has denied him some things & hee now takes pett and
will bee miserable in spite. The roote of his disease is a selfe humoringe
Pride, & an accustom'd tendernesse not to bee crost in his fancie, and
the occasions commonly one of those. A hard ffather, and peeuish wench, or
his ambition twharted. Hee considered not ye Nature of ye World, till
hee felt it, & all blowes fall vppon him heauie because they light not
first on his expectation. Hee has now forgone all but his Pride, & is yet
vaineglorious in ye ostentacon of his Melancholy. His composure of himselfe
is a studied carelessnesse, wth his armes a Crosse & a neglected hanging
of his head and cloake, beinge as great an enemie to a hattband as
fortune. Hee quarrells at the time & vpstarts, & sighs at the neglect of men of parts, that is such as himselfe. His life is a perpetuall
Satire still girdinge the ages vanitie, when his verie anger shewes hee
too much esteemes it. Hee is greatly displeased to see men Merry, and
wonders what they can finde to laugh att. Hee neuer drawes his owne
lipp's higher then a smile, and frownes wrinkle him before forty.
Hee at last falls into that deadly Melancholy to bee a bitter hater
of men, and is ye aptest companion of any mischeife. Hee is the
sparke that kindles ye Common wealth, and the bellowes himselfe
to blow it, and if hee turne any thinge, it is commonly one of
these; either ffryer, Traytor, or Mad-man : + + +

10

20

A discontented Man: 13 *perpetual*] A tilde through the initial *p* abbreviates *er*.

The Comõn vicars or singing men in Catherall Churches./

Are a bad societie, yet a companie of good fellowes: y^t roare deepe in ye Quire,
deeper in the Tauerne. They are the eight parts of speech that goe to the
Syntaxis of seruice, and are distinguisht by their voices much like bells,
for they make not a consorte but a peale. Their pastime or recreation is
prayers, their exercise drinkeinge, yet herein so religiously addicted
that they serue God oft's when they are drunke, their humanitie is a
legg to the recidencer, their learninge a Chapter, for they learne it
commonly before they reade it. Yet the old Hebrewe Names ar little
beholdinge vnto them, for they becall them worse then one a nother.
Though they neuer expound the scripture they handle it much: and   10
pollute the Gospell with two things: their conuersion & their thumbes.
Vppon workiedaies they behaue them selues at prayers as att their potts,
swallow them downe in an instant. Their gownes are laced commonly
with streames of Ale, the superfluities of cupps or throat aboue
measure. Their skill in melodie makes them better companions abroad,
and their Anthemes abler to singe catches. Long liue for the most
part they are not especially the base, they ouerflow their banck so
oft to drowne their organs. breefely if they escape a resting they dye
instantly in Gods seruice, and to take their death wth more patience
haue wine & cakes at their funerall. And now they keepe the Church   20
a great deale better, & helpt to fill it wth their bones as before wth
their noise:.   +   +   +   +   +   +   +   +

An Antiquary }}

Hee seemes to haue giuen time purgation for hee fetches many things out
of his maw when they are now rotten & stinking. Hee is one that hath
that vnnaturall disease of beinge enamored of old age, & wrinkels, &
loues old things as Dutch men doe cheese, the better for beinge Moldie,
and worme eaten. Hee is of our Religion because wee say tis most antient,
and yet a broken statuet would almost make him an Idolater. A great admirer
hee is of y^e wast of old monuments, & reads only those characters where time hath
eaten out the Letters. Hee will goe fortie myles to a S^{ts} well, or ruin'd Abbie; & if
there bee but a Crosse or stonefootestoole in ye way, hee will bee consideringe it so
longe till hee fo^{r}gett his Io$_\wedge$^{u}rney. His state consists much sheckells & Romane   10
Coine, & hee hath more pictures of Cesar then Iames or Elizabeth. Beggers
cosen him with mustie things which they haue rack't from dunghills, and hee
p^{r}serues their raggs for p^{r}tious reliques. Hee loues no Librarie but where are
more spiders volumes, then Authors: and lookes wth great admiration on the
Antiqe worke of Cobbwebs. Printed bookes hee contemñs as a noualtie of
this latter age, but a manuscript hee pores on euerlastingly especially if
the couer bee moath eaten & the dust make a parenthesis betweene
euery sillable. Hee will giue all the bookes in his studdie (wch are rarities)

**The Comõn vicars: 21 *helpt*] The *t* is not crossed. **An Antiquary: 6 *statuet*] The final *t* is not crossed. **10 *Romane*]
Secretarial R.

for one of the Romane bindinge or six lines of Tully in his owne hand.
His chamber is hung com̃only with strange beasts skins, & is a kind of   *20*
Charnell house of bones extraordinarily, & his discourse vppon them
if you will heare him shall last longer. His verie attire is that
which is eldest, out of fashion, & his hatt is as antient as the towre
of Babell. Hee neuer lookes vppon himselfe till hee bee gray headed,
and then hee is pleased with his owne Antiquitie. His graue doth
not fright him for hee hath bin vsed to sepulchers, and hee likes
Death the better because it gathers him to his ffathers.   +   +   +

An Atturney. }}}

His Antient begininge was a blew coate, since a Liuerie; and his hatchinge
vnder a Layer: wherein though but penfeatherd, hee hath now nested
for himselfe, and with his hoorded pence purchas't an office. Two deskes
and a Quire of paper sett him vpp, where hee now sitts in state for
all commers. Wee can call him no great Author yet hee writes much,
and with the infamie of the Court, is maintayned in his libells.
His skill is verie constant, for it keeps still the forme aforesaid:
and yet it seemes hee is much troubled in it, for hee is allwaies
complaininge yor poore Oratour. Hee hath some smack of a Scholler,
yet vses Lattin verie hardly, & least it should accuse him cutts it   *10*
offe in the mids't, and will not let it speake out. Hee is contrarie
to great men, maintaind by his followers, that is, his poor cuntry
clyents that worshipp him more then their Landlord, and bee they
neuer such churles hee lookes for their curtesie. Hee first rack's them
soundly himselfe, then deliuers them ouer to ye Layer for execution.
His lookes are very solicetous importing much hast and dispatche, &
hee is neuer without his handfull of businesse, that is of paper.
Hee talkes statutes as fiercely as if hee had mooted seauen yeeres
in the Inns of Court, when all his skill is stuck att his girdle, or
in his office windowe: strife and wranglinge haue made him rich &   *20*
hee is thankfull to his benefactors.
                                   If hee liue
in a Cuntrie village hee makes all his Neighbours good Subiects, for there
shall bee nothinge done but what their is law for. His businesse
giues him not leaue to thinke on his Conscience, and when the time or
terme of his life is goinge out for doomes day hee is secur'd, for
hee hopes hee has a tricke to reuerse Iudgment: //   +   +   +

A younger Brother }}

His elder Brother was the Esau y^t came out first and left him like
Iacob at his heeles. His ffather hath done with him as Pharoah did to
the Children of Israell, that would haue them make brick and giue thẽ
no straw: so hee taskes him to bee a Gentleman, and leaues him no meanes
to maintaine it. The Pride of his house ha^s <th> vndone him wch his eldest

w^{ch}<ith> his eldest brothers Knighthood must sustaine, & his beggerie that
knighthood. His birth and bringinge vp will not suffer him to descend
to the meanes to gett wealth, but hee stands at ye mercy of ye world,
and which is worse of his brother. Hee is some thing better then
the seruinge man, & yet they more saucy with him then hee bould   10
with their Master, who behoulds him with a countenance of steere awe,
and cheecks him oftner then his liueries. His brothers old suite &
hee are much alike in request, and cast offe nowe and then one to the
other. Nature hath furnisht him with a little more Witt vppon
compassion, for it is like to bee his best reuenew. If his anuuitie
stretch soe farr hee is sent to the Vniuersitie, and with great
heart burninge takes vppon him the Ministrie as a *profession* hee is
condemned too by his ill fortune. O thers take a more crooked path
yet the Kings high way, where at length their vizard is pluckt
ofe and they strike faire for Tyburne; But their Brothers pride   20
not Loue getts them a pardon. His last refuge is the Low Cuntries
where raggs & lice are no scandall: where hee liues a poore gentleman of a Companie, and dies with out a shirt. The only thinge whereby
hee may better his fortunes, is an art hee has to make a Gentlewoman.
     Therewith hee baites now and then some rich widdowe that is
hungrie after his blood. Hee is com̃only discontented & desperate
and the forme of his Exclamation is that churle my Brother. Hee
loues not his Cuntry for that vnnaturall custome, & would long
Kent   since haue reuoulted to ye Spaniard but for Rent onely which
hee holds in admirãcon   + // + + + // + + // +   30

A meere formall Man: }}

Is somewhat more then the shape of a man, for hee has his length, breadth
& colour. when you haue seene him wth out you haue looked through him,
& neede imploye your discouerie no farther. His reason is meerely example, and his actions not guided by his vnderstandinge, but hee sees
others doe this and hee followes them. Hee is a nagatiue for wee
cannot call him a wise man but not a foole; nor an honest man, but
not a knaue; nor a Protestant, but not a Papist. The cheife burthen
of his braine is the <ch> carriage of his bodie, & ye settinge of his face
in a good frame, wch hee *p*erformes ye better because hee is not dis-
iointed with other Meditãcons. His religion is a good quiet subiect   10
and hee praies (as hee sweares) in the phraise of ye Land. Hee is
a faire guest, & a faire inuiter & can excuse his good cheare in the
Custom'd apologie: Hee hath some facultie in the manglinge of a rabbett
and the distribution of a Morsell to a Neighbours trencher. Hee ap-
p^rhends a iest by seeinge men smile, and laughs orderly himselfe when
it comes to his turne. His discourse is the newes hee hath gathered

---

**A younger Brother: 9 *some thing*] There is a space between *some* and *thing*. **18 O *thers*] There is a space between O
and *thers*. **23 *with out*] There is a space between *with* and *out*. **24 *gentlewoman*] There is a space between *gentle* and
woman. **A meere formall Man: 9 *performes*] A tilde through *p* abbreviates *er*.

317

in his walkes, & for other matters his discretion is that hee will only
what hee can, (that is) say nothinge. His life is like one that comes
to the Minster walke to take a turne or two and soe passes. Hee
hath staied in the world to fill a number, and when hee is gone,　　20
there wants one, & there is an end. // . + // + // + +

A Church Papist }}

Is one that parts his Religion betwixt his Conscience and his purse,
and comes to Church not to serue God, but the Kinge. The face of
the Lawe makes him weare the Maske of yᵉ Gospell which hee vses
not as a meanes to saue his soule but his charges. Hee loues Poperie
well but is loath to loose by it, & though hee bee sometimes sturd
by the Bulls of Rome, yet they are farr ofe, and hee is strucke with
more terrour at the Apparitor. Once a Moneth hee pʳsents himselfe
at the Church to keepe ofe the Churchwarden, & brings in his bodye
to saue his bayle. Hee kneeles with the Congrega͡con but praies by
himselfe, and askes God forgiuenesse for comeinge thither. if hee bee　　10
forc't to stay a sermon<d> hee pulls his hatt ouer his eyes and frownes
out the houre, and when hee comes home thinks to make a mens
for his fault by abusinge the Preacher. His maine Policie is to
shift ofe yᵉ Communion for which hee is neuer vnfurnisht of a
quarrell & will bee sure to bee out of Charitie att Easter: and indeed
hee is not for hee hath a quarrell to the Sacrament. Hee would
make a badd Martire, & good traueller, for his Conscience is so
large hee can neuer wander out of it, And in Constantinople would
bee crucified with a reserua͡con. His wife is more zealous &
therefore more costly: and hee bates her in attire, what shee　　20
stands him in Religion. But wee leaue him hatchinge plotts
against the State & Expecting the Spaniard :. // + + + +

{{{ A selfe conceipted Man: }}

Is one that knowes himselfe soe well that hee does not know himselfe.
Too excellent well dones has vndone him, & hee is guiltie of it that
first commended him t madnes. Hee is now become his owne booke wᶜʰ
hee pores on continually, yet like a truant reader ships ouer the harsh
places and suruaies only that which is pleasant. In yᵉ specula͡co
of his owne good parts his eies are like a drunkards see all double,
and his fancie like an old mans spectacles makes a great letter in a
small print. Hee imagines euery place where hee comes his Theater,
and not a looke　　　　but his spectatoᵘr, conceiuinge mens thoughts
to bee verie Idle that are onely busie about him. His walke is still　　10
the fashion of a March, and like his opinion vnaccompanied, with
his eyes most fixt on his owne p[er]son, or on others wᵗʰ reflection to
　　　　　　　　himselfe. If hee haue done any

A Church Papist: 11 *his*] *s* overwrites *t*. **18** *And*] Majuscule *A* overwrites minuscule *a*.

thinge that hath past with applause, hee is alwaies actinge it alone,
and conceiues the extasie of his hearers, his discourse is all positions and
definitiue decrees with thus it must bee & thus it is, and will not
humble authoritie to proue it. His tenent is almost singular, and
as a loofe from the vulgar as hee cann from which you must not hope
to wrest him. Hee has an excellent humour for an Heretique, &
in these daies made the first Arminian. Hee p^{r}ferrs Ramus
before Aristotle. Paracelsus before Galen, And Lypsius hoppinge   20
stile before either Tullie or Quintilian. Hee much pitties the
world that has no more insight in his parts, when hee is too well
discouered, euen to his verie thought. A flaterer is a Dunce to him,
for hee can tell him nothinge but what hee knowes before: yet hee
loues him because hee is like himselfe. Men are mercifull to him
and let him alone, for if hee once bee driuen from his humor, hee is
like two inward friends fallen out, his owne bitter enemie & discontent presently make a murther. In sum̃ hee is a bladder blowne-
vpp with winde, which the least flaw crushes to nothinge: + +

{{ A Tauerne }}//

Is a degree or if you will a paire of staires aboue an Ale house, Where men
are drunke with more creditt & apologie. If ye Vintners faire wife bee
at the doore it is commonly a signe sufficient: but the absence of this is
supplyed by an Iuy bush. The roomes are all breathed like the drinkers
that haue bin washt well ouer night & are   to fastinge next morninge: not furnisht with bedds apt to bee defiled, but more necessarie
implements, stooles, Table, & a chamberpott. It is a broacher of more
newes then hogs-heads, and more iests then newes: the which are suckt vp
heere by some spungie braine, and from thence squeisd into a Comedie.
Men enter heere to make merrie but in deede to make a noise, and their   10
musique aboue is answered with the chinckinge belowe. The drawers
are the ciuellest people in it, men of good bringinge vp, & how so euer wee
esteeme of them, none can bost more iustly of their high callinge. Tis y^e
best Theater of Nature, where they are truly acted not plaide: and the
businesse as in the rest of the world, vp & downe; from the bottome of
the Celler to ye great chamber. A melancholye man would finde matter
there to worke vppon, to see heads as brittle as glasse and oftner broken.
Men come hither to quarrell, and come hither to make friends. And if
Plutarch will lend mee his smile it is like euen Telephus his sword
that both makes wounds & cures them. It is the Common consump-   20
tion of the afternoone, & the Murderer or maker a way of raynie
dayes. It is ye torrid Zone that schorches his face and Tabacco the
  Gunpowder that blowes him vp, much harme would bee done if y^e &

A Tauerne: 1 Ale house] There is a space between *Ale* and *house*.   **12 bringinge**] First *g* overwrites unreadable letter.

379

Charitable Vintner had not water to quench these flames. A house
of sinne you may call it but not a house of darkenesse, for ye candles
are neuer out: and it is like those Cuntries farr in the North
where it is as light at midnight as att midday. After a longe sittinge
itt becomes like a streete in a dashing showre, where the spouts are
flashinge about, whilst the iordans like swell'inge riuers ouerflow
their banks. To giue you the totall reckninge of it tis the busie   30
mans recreation, the Idlemans businesse, the Melancholy mans
sanctuarye, the Inns <of> a court mans intertainement, the
strangers welcome, the schollers kindnes, and the Citisens curtesie. It is the studie of sparkling witts; and a Cup of sherry
theire booke, where wee leaue them :. // : // : // : + + :

A downe right Scholler }}

Is one that hath much learning in the Oxe, vnwrought and Vntride
which time and experience fashons & refines. hee is good mettle in

Inside the ^iinside though rough & vnscourd with out and therefore hated
by the courtier, that is quite contrarie. The time hath gott a Veyne
of make <hau>inge him ridiculous, and men laugh at him by tradicõn:
and no vnluckie absurditie but is putt vpon <him> his profession, &
done like a scholler. but his fault is only this that his minde is taken vpp with his vaine appetites; & his thoughts not loaded with
any carriage besides. Hee hath not put on the quaint garbe of y^e
age, which is now become a mans totall. Hee humbles not his meditacõn   10
to the industrie of complements, nor afflict his braine with elaborate
leggs. His body is not sett vppon vice-pinns to bee turninge and
flexible for euery motion, but his scrape is homely and his nodd worse.
Hee cannot kiss his hand and cry Madam, nor talke Idle enough
to keepe her company. his smackinge of a gentlewoman is some what
too sauory, & hee mistakes her nose for her lippe. A very woodcocke
would puzzell him in caruinge & hee wants the Logick of a Capon.
Hee hath not the glibb facultie of slydinge ouer a tale, but his
words come out squemishly, and ye laughter commonly before ye iest.
Hee names the word Colledge too often and his discourse beates too   20
much vppon the vniuersitie. The perplexitie of mannerlinesse will
not let him eate, and hee is sharpe sett at an argument; When hee
should eate his meate. Hee is discarded att all games for a gamester,
but one and thirtie: & att Tables reaches no farther then doubletts.
His fingers are not long & drawne out to handle a fiddle, but his fist
is clu<?>cked with ye habit of disputinge. Hee ascends a horse
somewhat sinisterly yet not on the lefte side, and they both goe a
iogging togeither. Hee is exceedingly censured by Inns a Court men.
for that vice beinge out of fashion. Hee cannot speake to a dogg
in his owne dialect, & vnderstands greeke better then ye language of   30
a falconer   &   & :

A Downe right Scholler: 3 *inside* (text)] The initial *i* is raised. There is a possible deletion before *n*. The word is
corrected in margin. **3 with out**] There is a space between *with* and *out*.

Hee hath bin vsd to darke roome & darke clothes, and his eyes
dazzell at a sattin dᵒublett. The Hermitᵉ⁻<age> age of his studye
hath made him some what vncoth in the world, and make him
worse by staringe on him. Thus is hee sillie & ridiculous, and it
continues with him some quarter of a yeere out of yᵉ Vniuersitie,
but practise him a little in men and brush him ore with good
companie, and hee shall out ballance these glisterers, as farr as a
solid substance doth a feather, or gold gold lace. +   +   +

A too Idle reserud man: }}

Is one yᵗ is a foole with discretion, or a strange peece of policie yᵗ mana-
ges yᵉ state of himselfe. His actions are his priuie Councell where in
no man must partake; besides hee speakes vnder rule & pʳscription &
dares not shew his teeth wᵗʰ out Machiauell'. Hee conuerses with his
Neighbours & hee would in Spaine, & feares an inquisitiue man as much
as the inquisition. Hee suspects all Questions for examinacõn & allwaies
thinkes you will picke some what out of him. His brest is like a
Gentle womans closett yᵗ locks euery toye & triffle; or some bragginge
Mountebanke yᵗ makes euery stinkinge thinge a secrett. Hee deliuers
you comõn matters wᵗʰ great admiracõn of silence, & neuer speakes   10
aboue yᵉ audite of a whisper. you may assoone wrest a tooth from
him as a paper, & what soeuer hee reades is Letters. Hee dares
not talke of great men for feare of badd Comments; & hee knowes
not how his words may bee misapplyed. Aske his opinion and hee tells
you his doubt, and hee neuer heares any thinge with more astonishment then what hee knowes before. His words are like yᵉ Cardes at
Primiuisty, where six is eighteene & seauen & twentie; for they
neuer signifie what they sound. But if hee tell you hee will doe
a thinge it is as much as if hee swore hee would not. Hee is one
indeede that takes all men to bee craftier then they are, and putts   20
himselfe to a great deale of affliction to hinder their plotts & assignes,
where they meane freely. Hee hath bin longe a riddle him selfe, but
at length finds Ædipusses; for his ouer acted dissimulacon disco-
uers him, and men doe with him as with Hebrew Letters
spell him backward and reade him: // : +   +   + //.

A Sharke }}

Is one whom all other meanes haue failed & now hee liues of himselfe, hee
is some casheird fellow whome the world hath flunge offe, yet still
claspes againe, and is like one a drowninge fastens vppon any <thinge>
that is next at hand. Amongst others of his shipwracks hee has
happilie lost shame, and his want supplies him. Noe man putts his
braines to more vse then hee, for his life is a daily inuention and each
                                        meale a new stratagem:

A downe right Scholler: 33 *some what*] There is a space between *some* and *what*. **A too Idle reserud man: 3** *partake*]
A tilde through *p* abbreviates *ar*. **A Sharke: 6** *is*] *i* overwrites *a*.

Hee has an excellent memorie for his acquaintance, though
there passed but how doe you betwixt them seauen yeares a goe,
it shall suffice for an imbrace, and that for money; Hee offers
you a pottle of Sacke out of his ioy to see you, & in requitall of   10
this Curtesie you can doe no lesse then pay for it. He is fumblinge
with his purse strings as a schole-boy with his points, when hee
is goinge to bee whipt, till the Master (wearie with long stay)
forgiues him. His borrowings are like Subsidies, each man a shillinge
or two leuied as hee can well dispend: which they lend him not
with hope to bee repaid, but that hee will come no more. Hee
holds a strange tyranie ouer men, for hee is their debtor and they
feare him as a creditor. Hee is proud of any imployments
though it bee but to carrie Commendaçons, which hee will be sure to
deliuer at Eleuen of the clock, they in curtesie bid him stay, and   20
hee in manners cannot denie them. If hee finde but a good looke
to assure his welcome, he becomes there halfe a border, and
haunts the threshold soe long till hee forces good natures to y^e
necessitye of a quarrell. Publique inuitaçons hee will not
wrong with his absence, and is the best witnesse of ye Shreiffes
hospitality. Men shun him at length as they would the Infection
and hee is neuer crost in his way if there bee but a lane to escape
him. Hee hath done with ye age as his cloake to him, hunge
on so longe as hee could, and at last dropp's off:.   //   +   +

A Carrier//}}

Is his owne hackney man, for hee letts himselfe out to trauell aswell as his horses. Hee is the ordinary Embassador betwixt the
ffather & the soñe, & brings rich p^rsents to the one but returnes
seldome any thinge back againe saue paper. Hee is no illiterate
man though in shew simple, for Questionlesse hee hath much in his
budgett which hee can vtter too in fitt time & place. Hee is the
vault in Goster Church which conueies whispers at a distance,
for hee takes the sound out of y^or mouth at Yorke, and makes
bee heard so farr as London. Hee is the young students ioy and
expectaçon & the most accepted guest to whom they lend a   10
willinge hand to discharge him of his burthen. His first gree-
tinge is your friends bee well and to proue it in a peece of
Gold deliuers their blessinge. You would thinke him a churlish
blunt fellow but they finde in him many tokens of humanitie.
Hee is a great afflictor of the high wayes, and beates them out
of measure, which iniurie is sometimes reuenged by the purse ta-
kers & then thy voyage miscaries. Noe man domineeres more in his
Inn, nor calls his

A **Sharke: 8** *a goe*] There is a space between *a* and *goe*.

host vnreuerendly with more presumption, and this arrogancie
proceeds out of the strength of his horses. Hee forgetts not his
loade where hee takes his ease, for hee is drunke commonly before hee   20
goes to bedd. Hees like the prodigall child still goinge & still
returninge againe, but let him passe: // +   +   +   + //

A Constable // }}

Is vice-roy in ye streets, and no man stands more vp pon't that
hee is the Kings officer. His iurisdiction extends to ye next stocks,
where hee has Commission for the heeles only, & setts the rest of
the bodye at libertie. Hees a scarcrow to that Ale-house,
where hee drinkes not his mornings draught, and apprehends a
drunkard for not standinge in the Kings name. Beggers
feare him more then the Iustice and as much as the whip-
stocke, whom hee deliuers to the subordinate Magistrate the
Bridewell man or the Beedle. Hee is a great stickler in the
tumults of double iuggs, and venters his head by his place; which   10
is broken many times to keepe whole the peace. Hee is neuer so
much in his Maiestie as in his night watch where hee sitts in
his chaire of state, a shopp-stalle; <Hee is a verie carefull
man in his office,> and inuiron'd with a guard of hobberds examines all passengers. Hee is a very carefull man in his
office, but if hee stay vpp after midnight you shall take him
nappinge :.   +   +   +   //

A Detractor:. }}

Is one of a more cuninge and actiue enuie, where with hee knowes not foo-
lishly his owne selfe, but throwes it abroade and would haue it blister
others. Hee is commonly some weake patted fellow, & worse minded, and
endeuours not to mount to the worth of others, but to bringe downe
them with his tongue to his owne poorenesse. Hee is indeede like
the redd dragon that pursued the woman, for when hee cannot
ouer reach an other, hee opens his mouth and throwes a floud
after him to drowne him. you cannot anger him worse then to
doe well, & hee hates you more bitterly for this then if you had
cheated him of his Patrimony with your discredit. Hee is alwaies   10
slightinge att ye generall opinion, & wondring why such & such
men should bee applauded. Hee comes to Sermons not to learne
but to catch: & if there bee but one solecisme that is all hee carries
a way. Hee lookes vppon all things with a p^rpard sourenesse, and
is furnisht still with a pish before hand, or some such mustie prouerbe
that disrellishes all what soeuer. yf ye feare of the Comapny make
him second a Commendac̃on, It is like a Lawe writt with a clause
                              and exception:. /

A **Detractor: 15** *prouerbe*] A tilde through *p* abbreviates *ro*.

or to smooth his way to some greater scandall. His speech still
concludes with an oh, but, & I could wish one thing amended, &
this one thinge shall bee enough to deface all the former commendacōn. Hee will bee verie inward with a man to fish some
bad thing out of him, & make his slaunders heereafter more
authenticke, when it is said a freind reported it. Hee will
bee your Pandor to haue you on the hip for a whore master &
make you drunke to shew your reelinge. Hee passes the
more plausibly because all men haue a smatch of his humour, &
it is thought freenes which is malice. Yf hee can say nothing
of a man hee will seeme to speake riddles, as if hee could tell
strainge stories if hee would. And when hee racks his inuention
to the extremitie hee ends, but I wish him well & therefore
must hold my peace. Hee is allwaies listninge & enquiringe
ofter men & suffers not a cloake to passe by him vnexamined.
In short hee is one, that hath lost all good himselfe, and
is loath to finde it in another :. + + + //

20

30

A ploddinge Student:.}}

Is a kinde of Alchymist or persecutor of nature, that would change
the dull leade of his braine into finer mettall, which successe many
times is vnprosperous, or att least wise not quitting the cost (to witt)
of his owne oyle & candles. Hee has a strange forct appetite to
learninge & to atcheiue it brings nothinge but patience and a bodye,
His studie is not great but continuall, & consists much in the
sitting vp till after midnight in a rugg-gowne & a night capp to yᵉ
vanquishing perhaps of some six lines, yet what hee has hee has it
perfect, for hee reades it soe long to vnderstand it till hee getts it
with out booke. Hee may with much industry make a breach into
Logick, and ariue at some abilitie in an argument, but for po-
liter studies hee dares not skermish wᵗʰ them, & for poetry
accounts it impregnable. His inuention is no more then yᵉ findinge
out of his papers & his few gleamings there, his disposition of
them is iust as yᵉ booke binders a setting or glewinge of them
to-gether. Hee is a great discomforter of young students by tellinge them
what trauell it hath cost him, & <?>how oft his braine turned at Phylo-
sophy, & makes others feare studyinge as a cause of Duncerie. Hee is a man
much giuen to Apothegmes wᶜʰ serue him for witt, & seldome brings any iest forth
but what begins by some Lacedemonian or Romā Lycosthenes. Hee is like a dull Carriers horse yᵗ will goe a whole weeke to geither but neu' out of a foote pace,
and hee yᵗ setts out on Satterday shall ouertake him:/

10

21

A ploddinge Student: 1 *persecutor*] A tilde through *p* abbreviates *er*. **8** *perhaps*] A tilde through *p* abbreviates *er*. **9**
perfect] A tilde through *p* abbreviates *er*. **12** *skermish*] *e* is converted from *i*.

An old Colledge Butler }

Is none of the worst students of the house, for hee keepes the sett
houres att his booke more duly then any. His authoritie is great ouer
mens good names, which hee charges sometimes with shrew'd aspersions,
which they hardly wipe offe without payment. His box & Counters
proue him to bee a man of reckoninge, and hee is stricter in it
then a vsurer, for hee deliuers not a farthinge with out writinge.
Hee doubles the paines of Gallo belgicus, for his bookes goe out once
a quarter, & they are much in the same nature; breefe notes and
summs of affaires, & are out of request assoone. His comings in are
much like a Taylors from the shredds of bread the chippings & ye rem-   10
nant of a broken crust: exceptinge his vailes from the barrell, which
poorefolkes buy for their hoggs but drinke them selues. Hee deuides
a halfe pennie loafe with more subtilty then Keckerman, and sub-
diuides (a primo ortu) soe nicely that a stomacke of great ca-
pacitie can hardly apprehend it. Hee is a verie sober man consideringe his great temptations of drinke & strangers: and if hee
bee ouerseene it is with in his owne liberties, and none ought to take
exceptions. Hee is neuer so well pleas'd wth his place, as in the entertainement of some Gentleman stranger in his butterie, whom hee
greets with a cup of beere & a carued manchet, where in hee shewes   20
his qualitie. Hee domineeres with fresh men when they first
come to his hatch, and puzzells them with strange language
of Cues & Cees, and some broken Lattin as <u>sic probo</u> which hee hath
learn't att his binn. Hee app^rhends no punishment so great as
sconsinge, and thinks all honestie compris'd in payinge of battells.
His faculties extraordinarie are ye warning of a paire of Cards,
and tellinge out a dozen of <?> Counters, for post & peare.
And hee is a man of much Method in these businesses. Thus hee
spends his age till ye tapp of it bee runne out, and then a fresh
is sett abroach : //   +   +   +   +   +   +

A Seriant or Catchpole }}

Is one of Gods Iudgments, & which ouer rorers onely conceiue terrible.
Hee is the properest shape wherein the fancie Sathan. for hee is at
the most but an arester, a Hell & a dungeon. Hee is the creditors
hawke wherewith hee seazes vppon flying birds, & fetches them
againe in his tallons. Hee is the period of young Gentlemen, or their
full stoppe, for when they meete him they can goe no farther. His
ambush is a shopp stall or close lane, and his assault is cowardly att

---

An old Colledge Butler: 17 *with in*] There is a space between *with* and *in*. **A Seriant or Catchpole: 2 *Sathan*]** A dot
after the *n* appears to be a period, but it is probably an unintended ink mark. **4 *wherewith*]** There is a space between
where and *with*.

backe. Hee respites you in noe place but in a Tauerne where hee
sells his minutes dearer then a clockmaker. The common way to
runne from him is through him, which is often attempted and at- 10
chiued, and the clubbs out of charitye knocke him downe. Hee is
the worst guide in the world for hee leades you into miserable
blinde wayes, where you shall hardly euer finde the way out againe.
Hee is the first handsell of the young Templers rapiers, and they
are as proud of <their> ↑his↓ repulse as a hungarian of killinge a Turke.
Hee is a moueable prison, & his hands two manacles hard to bee
fild offe. Hee is an occasion of disloyall thoughts in the common
wealth, for hee makes men hate the Kings name, worse then the
Deuills.   +   +   //   //

A Plaier   }}

Is one that knowes the right vse of the World, where in hee comes to
play a parte & soe away. His life is not idle, for it is all action,
and no man needs more circumspection in his doings, for the eies of
all men are vppon him. His profession hath in it a kinde of con-
tradiction, for none is more disliked, & yet none more applauded,
and hee has this misfortune of a schollar that too much witt
makes him a foole. Hee is like our paintinge Gentleweomen
seldome in his owne face, seldome in his clothes: and hee pleases
the better because hee counterfaites, except only where hee is
disguisd with straw for gold lace. Hee does not only personate 10
on the stage but sometimes in the streets, for hee is still
mask't vnder the habitt of a Gentleman. His parts finde
him oathes and good words which hee keepes for his vse and discourse, and makes shew with them of a fashionable companion.
His comings in are tolerable yet in small money, & like Holle-
fax great vicaraige most in two pences. The waightinge
weomen Spectators are ouer the eares in loue with him, &
Ladyes send for him to act in their chamber<?>. Your Inns a
Court men were vndone but for them, hee is their cheife guest & employ-
ment, & the sole businesse yᵗ makes them after noone men. The Poet only 20
is his Tyrant, & hee is bound to make<?> his friends friend drunke at his
charges. Shroue tuseday hee feares as yᵉ baud, & Lent is more dangerous to him then the Butcher. Hee was neuer soe much discredited as
in one Act of Parliament, which giues Hostlers priuiledge before him.
for which hee abhorrs them more then a corrupt iudg. But to
giue his <u>due</u> one well furnisht actor hath enough in him for fiue
common Gentlemen, and if hee haue a good bodie for six, & for resolution
hee shall challenge any Cato, for <u>it hath bin his cheife practise to die well:</u>

dwe

A Seriant or Catchpole: 13 *againe*.] The word is written at the righthand edge of leaf. The period was inadvertently
written on the outer edge of the following leaf.   A Plaier: 1 *where in*] There is a space between *where* and *in*.   10
personate] A tilde through *p* abbreviates *er*.   26 (Margin) *dwe*] *w* is clearly written, but it is possible the transcriber
exaggerated the right hand ascender of *u*.

A Hansome Hostesse:./ }}

Is the faire Commendacōn of an Inn aboue the faire signe, or
faire lodginge, shee is the loadstone that attracts many iron
gallants & roarers, where the cleuie sometimes long, & are not
easily gott off. Her lipps are the welcome, & your intertainement her companie, which is putt in the reckoninge too & is
the dearest parcell in it: No Citizens wife is demurer then she
at the first greetinges, nor drawes in her mouth with a Chaste
symper, but you may bee more familiar with out distast, &
shee doth not startle att baudry. Shee is the Confusion of a
pottle of sacke more then would haue binn spent elsewhere,   10
and her little Iuggs are accepted to haue her kisse excuse
them. Shee may bee an honest woman, but it is not be-
leued soe in her parish, & no man is a greater infidell
in it then her husband :   +   + //   :   //   :   ♗

A Shopp keeper: }}}

His shoppe is the well stuft booke, & himselfe yᵉ little page of it
or index. Hee vtters much to all men though hee sells to few
and intreats for his owne necessities by askinge others who
they lack. No man speakes more & no more, for his words are
like his wares twenty of one sort, and hee goes ouer them
alike to all commers. Hee is an arrogant comma<?>nder of
his owne things for what soeuer hee shewes you is yᵉ best in
the towne though the worst in his shoppe. His Conscience is
a thing that would haue layd on his hands, and hee was
forct to putt it off & makes great vse of honesty to pro-   10
fesse vppon. Hee tells you lies by rote, they beinge as it
were his phrase to sell in, & yᵉ language hee spent most of
his yeeres to learne. Hee neuer speakes soe truly as when
hee sayes hee will vse you as his brother, for hee would not
sticke to cozen him & in his shopp thinke it lawfull. His
religion is much in yᵉ nature of his Customers, & indeed the
pandor of it, and by a misinterpʳted sence of Scripture
makes a game of his godlinesse. Hee is your slaue whilst
you pay him ready money, but if hee once befreind you, yᵒʳ
Tirant, & you had better deserue his hate then his trust:/   20

                                ♗

A Hansome Hostesse: 2 *lodginge*] *e* overwrites a comma.

{{ A partiall Man: }}

Is the opposite extreame to a defamer, for the one speakes
ill falsely, & ye other ill, & both slander Truth. Hee is one
that is still wayinge men in the scale of Comparisons and
putts his assertions in one ballance, & y^t swayes that his freind
alwaies shall doe best; but shall rarely heare good of his enemie. Hee considers first the man & then the thing; and
restraines all meritt to what they deserue of him. Commendaĉons
hee esteemes not the depth of worth, but ye requitall of
kindnesse: & if you aske his reason, hee shewes you his interest,
and tells you how much hee is beholdinge to that man. Hee   10
is one that ties his iudgment to the wheele of fortune, &
they determine giddily both alike. Hee p^rferrs England before other Cuntryes because hee was borne there, & Oxfoord
before other Vniuersities because hee was brought vpp there,
and the best scholler there is one of his friends in the same
Colledge. Hee is a great fauorer of great Persons, and his
Argument is still that which should bee his Antecedent. Hee
is in high place therefore virtuous. Hee is preferd therfore worthy. Neuer aske his opinion for you shall heare
his faction, & hee is indifferent in nothinge but Conscience.   20
Men esteeme him for this a zealous affectionate, but they
mistake him many times for hee doth it but to bee esteemd soe.
Of all men, hee is worst to write a Historie for hee will
praise a Seianus or a Tiberius and ₄ f^or some pettie respect of
his all posteritie shall bee cozend : //   +   +   : / / :

{{ A plaine Cuntry ffellowe: }}}

Is one that manures his ground well, but lets himselfe lie fallowe
and vntill'd, hee hath reason enough to doe his business and not
enough to bee idle or Melancholy. hee seemeth to haue the
iudgment of Nabuchadnezar, for his conuersation is a mongst
beasts, & his tales are none of the shortest, onely hee eates
not ieasts, because hee loues not salletts. His hand guides the
plow and the plow his thoughts, and his ditch and land-
markes are the very mounds of his meditacōns. Hee expos-
tulates with his oxen very vnderstandingly & speakes
                    Gee & Ree better then English: 10

A **plaine Cuntry ffellowe: 4** *a mongst*] There is as space between *a* and *mongst*.

His minde is not much distracted with Obiects, but if a good fatt Cowe come
in his way hee stands dumbe & astonisht; and though his hast bee neuer
so great, hee fixes heere halfe an howres Contemplation. His habitation
some poore thatcht roofe, distinguisht from his barne by the Loope-
holes y^t lett-out smoake, which the raine had long since washt
through, but for the double seeling of bacon, which hath hung
there from his Grandsires time, & is yet to make Rashers for
Posteritie. His dinner is his other worke, & hee sweates at it
as much as his labour. Hee is a mercilesse fastner on a peece of
beefe, & you may hope to saue ye Guards off sooner. His Religion   20
is a part of his Coppie hould, which hee takes from his Landlord
and referrs it wholy to his discretion, yet if you giue him
leaue hee is a good Christian to his power, y^t is goes to ye Church
in his best clothes, & sitts there with his neighbours, where hee is
capeable only of 2 Prayers, for Raine & faire weather:./ + +

A meere young Gentle man of ye Vniu'sitie: }}

Is one y^t comes there to weare a Gowne, & to say hereafter hee <hath> ↑has↓
biñ at ye vniuersitie. His father sent him hither because hee heard
there was ye best dauncinge & fen<s>cinge schooles; from these hath
his educa͠con, from his Tutor ye ouersight. The first element
of his knowledge is to bee shewne ye Colledges, & initiated in a
Tauerne by the way, which hereafter hee shall learne of himselfe. The 2 markes of his senioritie are, the bare veluet of
his Gowne, & his proficiency at the Tennis, where when hee can
once play a sett hee is a fresh man no more. His studdie has
commonly handsome shelues, & his bookes neat silke strings, which   10
hee shewes to his ffathers Man, & is loath to vntie or take downe
for feare of misplacinge. vppon fowle daies for recreation hee
retires thither, & lookes ouer the prettie booke his Tutor reades
to him, which is commonly som odd Historie or a peece of Euphormio, & for this hee has money giuen him to spend ye next day.
his maine loitering is in ye Library, where hee studies armes &
books of honor, till hee growes as perfect in pedegrees as ye Herauld.
Of all things hee endures not to bee mistaken for a Scholler, & hates a
blacke suite though it bee of sattin, his Companion is some stale
fellow, that has bin notorious for   to   gold hatbands   20
whom hee admires att ye first, afterward   If hee haue spiritt
or money hee may light of better company & learne some flashes of Witt, wch may
doe him good seruice in ye Cuntry here after. But hee is now gone to y^e
Inns a Court; where hee studdies to forgett what hee learnt before his acquaintance
& fashion :   ffinis

A plaine Cuntry ffellowe: 23 Church] The word is written in a secretarial hand.   A meere young Gentle man of y^e
Vniu'sitie: title (apostrophe)] The diacritical mark is written in secretarial style.   2 biñ] The tilde probably suggests
the shortening of the word. The transcriber generally wrote *been*.   17 perfect] A tilde through secretarial *p* abbreviates
er. 20–21 (spaces in text)] There are spaces left open in the text, as indicated. Perhaps the transcriber was unable to
read the copy-text.

COMMENTARY

Abbreviated references in the Commentary follow the list of "Frequently Cited Sources and Abbreviations" (p. vii) or are given a full bibliographic entry at the end of the commentary for that poem.

Abbreviations for the Commentary: Pr = Printed; f. = folio; ff. = folios; l. = line; ll. = lines; qtd. = quoted in.

• • •

1. Michael Drayton (1563–1631), "Of a Poett," 1. Pr. Robert Allot, *Englands Parnassus* or *Flowers of Our Modern Poets* (1600), 236; Robert Tofte, *The Blazon of Iealousie* (1615), 48.

The copy-text for this poem is a printed book, Tofte's *Blazon*, which contains four of the first eight poems and very likely five of the first nine in the Holgate manuscript. Collation, especially with **HolM 8a** (see below), shows that Tofte's *Blazon* was the copy-text and not Allot's *Englands Parnassus*. For discussion, see Introduction, p. xvii. This poem, like the others from Tofte, are from his sidenotes to poems of his translation of poems by Benedetto Varchi (1502?–1565).

The passage itself was first printed in Drayton's *Englands Heroicall Epistles* (1597), "Henry Howard, Earle of Surrey, to the Lady Geraldine," ll. 113–22. But collation between the text of *Englands Heroicall Epistles* and the Holgate demonstrates that the last four lines have been largely altered. In Drayton, they read: "Whom they in birth ordain to happy days / The gods commit their glory to our praise; / T'eternal life when they dissolve their breath, / We likewise share a second pow'r by death."

There is no way to know the exact date of this first entry, but the watermark shows that the paper was available for use by 1619, the same year as the death of Queen Anne, who is the subject of **HolM 2**.

> ◆ Collations: *Englands Parnassus EP* / *The Blazon of Iealousie BI*. Title: Of a Poet] om.
> *EP BI* ; 2 into man] into a man *EP BI*

• • •

2. King James (1566–1625), "'Vppon Queene Anne' by K: I.," 1. Pr. Camden's *Remaines* (1637), 398; *Wits Recreations* (1640), sig. 2B3, "On Queene Anne."

James was an occasional poet, sonneteer, and translator of the Psalms. No authorized version of this poem exists, although there is a copy in the *State Papers Domestic*, James I (14/190), f. 27, the National Archives (TNA), Kew.

HolM 2 and **HolM 13** are among James's later poems. His early poems, written before he became King of England, contain many Scotticisms, wholly absent from his later poetry (for full citation, see below: *Bodleian Quarterly Record* 2–3).

The poem commemorates the death from dropsy of James's wife, Anne of Denmark, at Hampton Court, 2 March 1619. The Queen's death had been commonly associated with a comet that appeared over England in 1618 (Gullans 49).

Holgate contains two other poems occasioned by the death of Anne, the first by Giles Fletcher, **HolM 5,** the second possibly by Robert Fletcher, **HolM 38.** The two were not related.

> **1. God sent a starr.** James wrote a second poem denying that the comet should be taken as an omen, beginning "You men of Britaine, wherefore gaze yee so" (Craigie 172–73).
> **2. Whose frinds. . . .** Literal statement associating the monarchy as "nerest kinn" to God.
> **3. ruine the race.** Based on Craigie collation (258), this is a unique reading which should read "runne the race."

✦ Manuscripts: Crum T1631, T3410, H645. Yale T1543. **Bodleian:** Ashmole 38 (p. 169); Ashmole 47 (f. 38ᵛ) Eng. poet. e. 40 (f. 139); Eng. poet. e. 97 (p. 10); Eng. poet. f. 10 (f.92); Malone 19 (pp. 5, 140); Eng. poet. e. 14 (f. 99v [rev]); Rawl. poet. 153 (f. 8ᵛ); **British Library:** Add. MS. 5830 (f. 188ᵛ); Add. MS. 15227 (f. 83); Egerton MS 923 (f. 45); MS Harley 791 (f. 61); MS Harley 6917 (f. 32); Harley 6931 (f. 59); Sloane 1489 (f. 11); Sloane 1786 (f. 93); **Corpus Christi College, Oxford:** MS 328 (f. 62); **Folger:** V.a. 97 (p. 2); V.a. 319 (f. 22); V.a. 269 (p. 55); V.a. 162 (f. 33ᵛ); W.b. 455 (p. 41); **Harvard:** MS Eng. 686 (f.16); **Rosenbach:** MS 239/27 (p. 357); MS 1083/16 (p. 96); MS 239/22 (p. 9); **Yale:** Osborn b 62 (p. 1); Osborn b 200 (p. 236); Osborn b 356, (p. 254); Osborn fb 143 (p.25).

✦ Pr. *The Athenæum,* No. 4575 (3 July 1915), 13; *Bodleian Quarterly Record* 3, 32 (1921), Supplement, 4; *The Poems of James VI of Scotland,* ed. James Craigie, 2 vols., The Scottish Text Society, 3rd ser., 26 (Edinburgh: William Blackwood and Sons, 1958), vol. 2. Also see *The English and Latin Poems of Sir Robert Ayton,* ed. Charles B. Gullans, The Scottish Text Society (Edinburgh: William Blackwood & Sons, 1963).

• • •

3. Joshua Sylvester (1563–1618), "'A stanza on Prince Hen:' by I. S," 1. Pr. *Du Bartas, His Divine Weeks and Works; His Second Weeke, David. The Fourth Day of the Second Week* (1611), 515.

This is a dedicatory poem to Prince Henry (d. 1612), James's eldest son, Prince of Wales, and heir to the thrones of England and Scotland. This poem appears in no other manuscript. Since the parentheses (ll. 4, 7) are identical in the 1611 printing, it is likely that the first print version was Holgate's copy-text. Collation between the Holgate and the first printing reveals no substantive variants.

Sylvester later published *Lachrimæ Lachrimarum,* a group of poems commemorating the 6 November 1612 death of Prince Henry, probably from typhoid. **HolM 104** and **HolM 105** are found in that volume.

• • •

4. Anon., "De Amore," 1. *Bodenham's Belvedere or the Garden of the Muses* (1600), 29; Tofte, *Blazon,* 3.

Holgate's text is virtually identical to Tofte's *Blazon,* his copy-text; the Holgate has "Feinde" (l. 1) and "Greife" (l. 2), whereas Tofte has "Fiende" and "Griefe." Tofte's copy-text is unknown, but it may have been *Bodenham's Belvedere,* which shares twenty-nine passages with *The Blazon* (Kahrl 57). In many of them Tofte alters a passage to suit his own taste (see **HolM 8 notes**).

✦ George Morrow Kahrl, "Robert Tofte's Annotation in *The Blazon of Iealousie," Harvard Studies and Notes* 18 (1935): 47–67.

5. Giles Fletcher (1588?–1623), "An Epitaph on Prince Henry," 2. Pr. Camden's *Remaines* (1614), 381; Stowe's *Survey* (1633), 518; In *Epicedium Cantabrigiense* (1612), sig. C1, "Miraris qui saxa loqui didicere, Viator," initialed G[iles]. F[letcher]. T[rinity]. C[ollege].

Epicedium Cantabrigiense is a volume of commemorative poetry on the death of Prince Henry. The poem itself is a translation of a Latin epitaph. For a group of poems commemorating Henry's death, see **HolM 101–105**. **HolM 3** was written during Henry's lifetime. Also see **HolM 160 notes.** Comparison with *Remaines* reveals that there were multiple versions of this poem, especially with ll. 5–8 (*Remaines*) omitted in the Holgate.

   ✦ Manuscripts: Crum R76. Yale R0069. **Bodleian:** MS Ashmole 38 (p. 178); MS Ashmole 47 (f. 108ᵛ); Ashmole 781 (p. 149); Don.e.6 (f. 6ᵛ); MS Eng. misc. 241 (f. 124ᵛ); MS Eng. poet. e. 14 (f. 99 [rev]); MS Rawl. poet. 117 f. 183ᵛ [rev], 268 [rev], 279 [rev]; MS Rawl. poet. 160 (f. 26ᵛ); MS Eng. misc. 241 (f. 241ᵛ); **British Library:** Add. ms. 15227 (f. 73); Add. MS 33998 (f. 85); **Corpus Christi College, Oxford:** MS 328 (f. 57ᵛ); **Folger:** V.a. 125, pt. II (f.5); V.a. 97 (p. 3); V.a. 269 (f. 86ᵛ); V.a. 103, pt. I (f. 3) (Mr. C. W.); W.b. 455 (p .37); **University of Nottingham:** Portland MS Pw V 37 (C.W.); **Yale:** Osborn b 197 (p. 205); Osborn fb 143, (p. 23).

   ✦ *Giles and Phineas Fletcher: Poetical Works*, ed. Frederick S. Boas, 2 vols. (Cambridge Univ. Press, 1908), 1:270 (Latin); H&S, 8:432–33 (English/Latin).

• • •

6. Thomas Dekker (1570?–1632), "On Queene Elizabeth," 2. Pr. Thomas Dekker, *The Wonderfull Yeare* (London, 1603), sig. B4ᵛ; William Camden, *Remaines* (London, 1614), 378; Thomas Heywood, *The Life and Death of Queene Elizabeth* (London, 1639).

Dekker is best known as a playwright, especially for *The Shoemaker's Holiday* (1600). He turned to pamphleteering in 1603 when plague forced the theatres to close. *The Wonderfull Yeare* was Dekker's first pamphlet. More than likely he is the author, but positive identification cannot be established (Wilson xi). Although the text as it appears in the Holgate is about Elizabeth, the pamphlet itself is more focused on James. "It presents a vivid account of the changing climates of feeling during the events of the past momentous year: the anxiety of the opening months as the Queen's death approached; the relief felt throughout the land when James VI of Scotland succeeded peacefully to the English throne as James I; the sense of relief interrupted when the plague descended on the capital city like some heaven-sent reminder of the loss the land had suffered in the death of the great Queen. The latter half of *The Wonderfull Yeare* presents (as the cover page advertises) 'the Picture of London Lying Sicke of the Plague'" (Cyrus Hoy, "Thomas Dekker" in *Elizabethan Dramatists*, ed. Fredson Bowers, *Dictionary of Literary Biography Comnplete Online*, vol. 62, pp. 45–70, especially 46; web).

Although the 1603 plague is itself a serious theme, *The Wonderfull Yeare* creates a satiric portrait of London in the early seventeenth century. Describing the death of Elizabeth, Dekker writes: "The report of her death (like a thunder-clap) was able to kill thousands, it tooke away hearts from millions: for hauing brought vp (euen vnder her wing) a nation that was almost begotten and borne for her name, neuer sawe the face of any Prince but her selfe, neuer vnderstoode what that strange outlandish word *Change* signified, how was it possible, but that her sicknes should throw abroad an vniuersall feare, and her death an astonishment? She was the Courtiers treasure, therefore he had cause to mourne" (Wilson 12, see below). Wilson describes this epigram as "absurdly conceited" (221). Without this context, the Holgate text does not show the comic nature of this epigram.

✦ Manuscripts: Crum T1217. Beal DkT 3–36.5. Yale T1125 ✦ **Bodleian**: Add. A. 368, f. 45ᵛ (Tho. Heywood); MS Eng. poet. E. 40, f. 124; Rawl. poet. 117, f. 163 (rev.); Rawl. poet. 153, f. 8ᵛ; MS Eng. poet. F. 27, p. 156. **Bradford Central Library**: Spencer-Stanhope MSS, Calendar No. 2795 (Bundle 10, No. 34), f. [6v]. **British Library**: Add. MS 15227, f. 2ᵛ; Add. MS 27406, f. 74ᵛ; Add. MS 30982, f. 23ᵛ; Add. MS 33998, f. 89; Add. MS 47111, ff. 11ᵛ–12; Egerton MS 923, f. 15; Egerton MS 2421, f. 45ᵛ; Egerton MS 2877, f. 16ᵛ; Sloane MS 1792, f. 1222ᵛ. **Cambridge**: MS Add. 7196, f. [1]. **Corpus Christi College**: MS 176, f. 32; MS 328, f. 49ᵛ. **Folger**: MS V.a. 97, p. 9; MS V.a. 162, f. 83; MS V.a. 262, p. 137; MS V.a. 319, f. 3; MS V.a. 322, p. 27; MS V.a. 345, p. 111. **Huntington**: HM 116, pp. 37–38; **Owned by Sir Geoffrey Keynes**: Bibliotheca Bibliographici No. 1863, f. 11. **Leeds Archives Department**: MX 237, f. 35ᵛ. **Meisei University Library, Tokyo**: Crewe MS, (formerly Monckton Milnes MS), 40. **National Library of Wales**: NLW. MS 12443A, pt. ii, p. 44. **University of Nottingham**: Portland MS Pw V 37, p. 1. **Rosenbach**: MS 239/18, p. 325. **Shakespeare Birthplace Trust Record Office**: ER 93/2, f. 190. **Yale**: Osborn b 62, p. 42, Osborn b 208, p. 57.

✦ *The Plague Pamphlets of Thomas Dekker*, ed. F. P. Wilson (Oxford: Oxford Univ. Press, 1925), xi, xxix–xxxlv, 1–61. For extended commentary, see Frederick O. Waage, *Thomas Dekker's Pamphlets, 1603–1609, and Jacobean Popular Literature* (Salzburg, Austria: *Studies in English Literature*, 1977), 1:1–187. *The Non-Dramatic Works of Thomas Dekker*, ed. Alexander B. Grosart (New York: Russell & Russell, 1963), 1:93–94.

• • •

7. Michael Drayton, "On Iealosie," 2. Pr. Michael Drayton, *Mortimeriados, The Lamentable ciuell warres of Edward the second and the Barrons* (London, 1596), ll. 113–19; Allot, *Englands Parnassus*, 144 (see note to poem 1 above); Tofte, *Blazon*, 11; Robert Burton, *The Anatomy of Melancholy* (1628), III, 3, I, 2.

The copy-text is Tofte's *Blazon*, which contains four of the first eight poems and probably five of the first nine (see Introduction, p. xvii). There are no variants between the Holgate text and Tofte's *Blazon*. The poem is correctly ascribed to Drayton in Allot's *Englands Parnassus*, again with no variants.

✦ *The Works of Michael Drayton*, 5 vols., ed. William Hebel (Oxford, 1931), 1:312.

• • •

8a. Henry Constable [?] (1562–1613), "Of Care," 2. Pr. Henry Constable, *Diana* (1598), 5th Decade, Sonnet vii, ll. 2–8. Allot, *Englands Paranssus*, 25; Tofte, *Blazon*, 10.

This poem confirms that the scribe started the miscellany with lyrics copied from Tofte's *Blazon*. Tofte's is the only six-line version of the poem, the other known texts having seven lines, with l. 5 reading "Bearing the letters which contain our end." Holgate and the *Blazon* text also agree against Allot in reading "a Cowards Kinde" rather than "a coward minde" (l. 3), "post to Death" versus "poste by death" (l. 4), and "his frinde" instead of "most his frend" (l. 6). More than likely, the poem should not belong to the Constable canon. Joan Grundy includes it among Constable's "doubtful sonnets." However, Tofte ascribes the poem to Constable. There are no variants between the Holgate text and Tofte's *Blazon*.

✦ Manuscript: Crum C91. ✦ **Bodleian:** MS Eng. poet. e. 14 (f. 14).

✦ *The Poems of Henry Constable*, ed. Joan Grundy (Liverpool: Liverpool Univ. Press, 1960), 200–1; also see George Morrow Kahrl, "Robert Tofte's Annotation in *The Blazon of Iealousie*," *Harvard Studies and Notes* 18 (1935): 47–67.

8b. Folio 2 (pp. 3–4) has been removed from the manuscript. All that remains is the top left-hand corner of the recto (p. 3) and the top right-hand corner of the verso (p. 4). The poem on page 3 begins "Will putt." The leaf itself, however, was not destroyed by Holgate. We know the leaf remained in the miscellany throughout the seventeenth century, because the index on pp. 330–33 (not included in transcription) is written in the hand of John Wale, the early eighteenth-century owner of the miscellany and a later descendant of the Holgate family (see Introduction, pp. xiv–xv).

Wale identified two poems on page 3, "of Fear" and "of Hope." However, there was another poem — at the top of page 3 — entitled "of Will." It is not listed in the Index because Wale indexed no entries after the letter "R." Line 1 begins "Will putt. . . ." Only the top portion of the first word in line 2 can be seen: it probably starts with the word "Will. . . ." Thus, the word "Will" starts lines 1 and 2. Tofte's *Blazon* contains a poem that meets that description: "Will puts in practise what the Wit deuiseth. / Will euer acts, and Wit contemplates still: / And as in Wit the power of Wisedome riseth / And other Vertues, Daughters are to will." Although the poem is unattributed in Tofte's *Blazon*, it is attributed to D. Lodge in Allot's *Englands Parnassus*, 30; in fact, it is from Sir John Davies *Nosce Teipsum* (1599), sec. xxvii, st. 2.

•••

9. John Donne (1572–1631), ["Upon his Lady] goinge to Bedd [D^r C]." Pr. *Poems* (London, 1669).

As noted above, folio 2 is missing from the manuscript. It contained at least two poems on the recto (see notes to Poem 8b) and John Donne's Elegy XIX on the verso. All that remains of the leaf are three words from the title, "goinge to Bedd" and the last word of line one, "defie." The leaf was removed sometime during or after the eighteenth century. We know this because the poem is entered in the index, which was written by John Wale. The title is reconstructed based on Wale's index, letter "L", entry no. 4. Poems were indexed by Wale by first important word, thus "Lady" not "Upon.

Nothing explains a second entry in the Wale index, letter "M," "To his M^{rs} goeing to bed - - - 41." More than likely this is an error because page 41 does not contain a poem with that title. Since there is no indication that the binding has been tampered with, it is clear that the poems as they now exist are in the order they were first transcribed.

Assuming that John Wale copied the original title correctly, the ascription to "D^r C" (Richard Corbett) is noteworthy. The only other known manuscript that ascribes this poem to Corbett is Bodleian, MS Rawl. poet. 199, p. 14.

Even without the expurgation, this is a poor text. For example, a line-by-line comparison with Grierson reveals little similarity: Holgate line 1 is Grierson line 46; Holgate l. 2 is Grierson l. 45; Holgate l. 3 is Grierson l. 31; Holgate l. 4 is Grierson l. 32; Holgate l. 5 is Grierson l. 47; Holgate l. 6 is Grierson l. 48.

Elegy XIX is one of Donne's most explicitly sexual poems. According to Marotti the elegy was suppressed by "ecclesiastical censors . . . from the collection of poems published by Marriot in 1633" (76n).

✦ Manuscripts: Crum: C543, C546. Beal: DnJ 3155–3218. Yale: C0386. ✦ ***Aberdeen University Library:*** MS 29 (pp. 173–75); ***Bodleian:*** MS Eng. poet. e. 112 (ff. 14^v–15); MS Eng. poet. f. 9 (pp. 64–66); MS Rawl. poet. 117 (ff. 222^v–21 [rev]); MS Ashmole 38 (p. 63); Don. b. 9 (ff. 57^v–58^v); MS Eng. poet. c. 50 (f. 42^v); MS Eng. poet. e. 97 (pp. 103–4); MS Eng. poet. f. 25 (f. 17); MS Eng. poet. f. 27 (pp. 116–17); MS Rawl. poet. 160 (f. 171); MS Rawl. poet. 199 (p. 14); Hopkinson MSS, Vol. 17 (ff. 19^v–20); ***British Library:*** MS Harley 4955 (ff. 95^v–96); Add. MS 18647 (f. 28); Lansdowne MS 740 (f. 85); Add. MS 25707 (f. 11); Add. MS 30982 (f. 46); Add. MS 19268 (f. 24); MS Harley 6931 (ff. 7^v–8); MS Sloane 542 (f. 11); MS Sloane 1792 (ff. 27–28); Stowe MS 961 (f. 24); MS Stowe 962 (ff. 82^v–83); ***Cambridge:*** MS Add. 5778 (f. 25);

MS Ee. 4.14 (f. 78); CL 1(p. 10); *Folger:* V.a. 103, pt. I (ff. 40ᵛ–41); V.a. 345 (pp. 80–81); V.a. 97 (pp. 68–70); V.a. 124 (ff. 24–25); V.a. 125, pt. I (f. 31); V.a. 170 (p. 89); V.a. 269 (p. 73); V.a. 319 (ff. 24ᵛ–25); *Harvard:* fMS Eng. 966.1 (f. 18); fMS Eng. 966.3 (ff. 43ᵛ–44); fMS Eng. 966.4 (f. 144); fMS 966.5 (ff. 65–66); fMS 966.6 (ff. 84–85); MS Eng. 686 (ff. 35ᵛ–36ᵛ); *Huntington Library:* EL 6893 (f. 106); HM 198, pt. 1 (pp. 43–44); *Owned by Sir Geoffrey Keynes:* Bibliotheca Bibliographici No. 1860 (f. 20ᵛ–22); Bibliotheca Bibliographici No. 1861 (f. 28); *Leeds Archives Department:* MX 237 (ff. 59ᵛ–60ᵛ); *Leicestershire Record Office:* DG.7/Lit. 2 (f. 281); *New York Public Library:* Arents Collection, Cat. No. S191 (Elegies, pp. 16–18); MS 239/27 (pp. 47–48); MS 239/22 (ff. 52ᵛ–53); *St. John's College, Cambridge:* MS S. 32 (James 423) (ff. 37ᵛ–38); *St. Paul's Cathedral:* MS 49.B.43 (?); *South African Library, Cape Town:* MS Grey 7 a 29 (pp. 48–49); *Texas Tech University:* Dalhousie I (f. 33); Dalhousie II (f. 17); *Trinity College, Cambridge:* MS R 3.12 (James 307) (pp. 63–64); *Trinity College, Dublin:* MS 877–I (ff. 56ᵛ–57ᵛ); *Victoria and Albert Museum:* Dyce Collection, Cat. No. 18 (Pressmark 25.F.17) (f. 23); *Westminster Abbey:* MS 41 (ff. 14ᵛ–15); *Yale:* Osborn b 62 (pp. 97–98); Osborn b 114 (pp. 69–71); Osborn b 148 (pp. 79–81); Osborn b 200 (208–9).

✦ Grierson, 1:119–21; Gardner (1978), 14–16; Shawcross, 57–58.

• • •

10. William Holgate [?], "A funerall Elegie on Dr Ashboold," 5–10. No known printing.

Although this elegy is unascribed, its placement and subject matter suggest that it was written by "W. H.," presumably William Holgate himself. These initials are subscribed to elegies for Dr. William Ashboold's daughters, M[ist]ris Gardner (**HolM 19, 23**), for M[ist]ris Thaire (**HolM 21**), and a fourth elegy for both of them (**HolM 24**). The women died within two years of each other. We do not know why Holgate took such an active interest in the family. Ashboold was rector of two churches in Cornhill (London), St. Peter's and St. Michael's, both of which are on the same block. He was buried at St. Peter's Church, 29 August 1622.

A textual problem is found at line 212, "It mes must that worthy taske indure." As indicated in the transcription there is a space before "mes." It is possible that a scribe could not read the copy-text and therefore left an open space in the manuscript. If the scribe was also the poet, he more than likely would have known the correct word. Therefore, it is possible that Holgate did not perform both functions.

There is no mention of Holgate in the St. Peter's Church Parish Register. Moreover, according to line 30, the poet received the news of Ashboold's death while he was at Oxford. Surviving records provide no indication that Holgate was a student at the university.

> **37. gins.** Poetic form used before infinitive (*OED*).
> **44. liker.** Poetic comparative, rare (*OED*).
> **81. Gryndalls.** Edmond Grindal (1519?–83), made Bishop of London, 1559, Archbishop of York, 1570, and Archbishop of Canterbury, 1575. (*The Oxford Dictionary of the Christian Church,* 1958).
> **86. Two well-nourisht flocks.** St. Peter's and St. Michael's.
> **107. Austins Eloquence.** Probably St. Augustine of Hippo.
> **108. hyuinge.** Hiving, to collect bees for honey.
> **109. Barnards Garden.** St. Bernard (1090–1153), a Church Father, or "Massie father," as described in the text (l. 101). "Massie," a form of "massy," full of substance (*OED*).
> **111. Chrisostome.** Note different spelling, l. 114. As an adjective, golden-mouthed, but here the name of the third-century Greek saint and Church Father.
> **212. mes.** Unclear usage. See commentary above.

11. Richard Corbett (1582–1635). Untitled, subscribed "R: C:," 11–12. Pr. *CEP*, 19–20; *Poëtica Stromata* (n. p., 1648), 14.

Corbett was an Arminian, a proponent of a theological system opposed to the Calvinistic doctrine of predestination. He attended Westminster School, Broadgates Hall, and Christ Church, Oxford. He became Dean of Christ Church (1620), Bishop of Oxford (1628), and Bishop of Norwich (1632). Corbett's principal patron was George Villiers, Duke of Buckingham, the subject of several poems in the miscellany.

This is the first of eleven poems by Corbett in the Holgate. His poems are frequently found in seventeenth-century commonplace books. A popular figure, he was known for his poems and practical jokes, as well as his important church positions. His most popular poem, "Iter Boreale," is **HolM 25**. He published none of his many poems during his lifetime. *CEP* and *Poëtica Stromata* were published posthumously by his friends.

Corbett's father, Vincent, also known as Poynter (l. 2), died 29 April 1619. He was well-known as a gardener. Ben Jonson wrote an epitaph in his honor; see **HolM 12**.

The many variants between the Holgate and the first printed version of Corbett's work, *CEP*, are typical of this manuscript.

> **2. poynters name.** It is unknown why Vincent Corbett had two names. See ll. 5–8.
> **16. flood.** Clear hyperbole, the reference is to Noah.
> **26. Leiger lay.** A general agent. Baker transcribes this "ledger-large."
> **26. sheere.** Shire.
> **39. racke their rents.** Raise their rents unfairly.
> **43. close or Aker.** Enclosure or acre.
> **45. Paul defines.** Corinthians 13.3,13 (Baker 112).

✦ Manuscripts: Beal: CoR 79–93. Yale: V0053✦ *Aberdeen University Library:* MS 29 (pp. 56–57); *British Library:* Add. MS 30982 (f. 143ᵛ–144ʳ [rev]); Harley 6931 (f. 27ᵛ–28ᵛ); MS Sloane 1792 (ff. 62–63); Add. MS 19268 (ff. 35ᵛ–36); *Owned by Sir Geoffrey Keynes:* Bibliotheca Bibliographici No. 1301 (pp. 53–51[rev]); *Folger:* V.a. 170 (pp. 222–24); V.a. 269 (pp. 44–45); *Huntington Library:* HM 116 (pp. 108–9); *Rosenbach:* MS 239/18 (pp. 4–5); *St. John's College: Cambridge:* MS S. 23 (James 416) (ff. 52–53); *Yale:* Osborn b 197 (pp. 34–36); Osborn b 200 (pp. 216–17); Osborn b 356, p. 200; Osborn fb 230.

✦ The only edition of Corbett's verse is B&TR. Mary Hobbs points out that these editors use the printed texts as copy-texts and claim that manuscripts like the Holgate all derive "from printed sources." However, Corbett's verses were not printed until 1647 and 1648, more than ten years after his death. See "Early Seventeenth-Century Verse Miscellanies and Their Value for Textual Editors," *English Manuscript Studies, 1100–1700*, ed. Peter Beal and Jeremy Griffiths, Vol. 1 (London and New York: Blackwell, 1989), 182–210; Baker, 111–14.

• • •

12. Ben Jonson (1573?–1637). Inset "B: I:" l. 31, 11–12. Pr. *The Vnder-wood* (xii) in *Works* (London, 1640); "An Epitaph on Master Vincent Corbett," H&S, 8:151–52.

This is a companion piece to the previous poem. Jonson and Richard Corbett were friends; Jonson frequently stayed in Corbett's home when he visited Christ Church (*DNB*).

The rarity of this poem in verse miscellanies is noteworthy. Typically, the poem appears with the first line, "I have my Pietie too, which could." B&TR suggest that this line refers to the Corbett poem. If so, then the Holgate transcription, which changes 'have' to 'hope' and moves the entire opening stanza to the end of the poem (l. 31), seems to personalize this tribute because it moves the name, "Vincent Corbett," to the first line. Rosenbach MS 239/18 begins with the same line as the Holgate. This manuscript with Rosenbach MS 239/18 and BL Sloane MS 1792 preserves both poems.

> **14. spatious.** "Spatious" clearly makes sense, but "specious," meaning splendid, from the Latin "speciosus," sounds more like Jonson. The *OED* notes uses of "specious" (meaning fair or beautiful) in the early seventeenth century.
>
> **22. Hee chid the vice, yet not the men.** "Parcere personis, dicere de vitiis," Martial, 10.33.10, "to spare the person, to name the vice" (Parfitt 521).
>
> **34. frend and sonn.** H&S point out that the friend is unknown (11:54). Jonson may have meant that Corbett was Vincent's son and Jonson's friend.

✦ Manuscripts: Beal: JnB 138–42. ✦ *British Library:* MS Sloane 1792 (ff. 61–62); *Folger:* V.a. 170 (pp. 224–26); V.a. 269 (p. 42); *Rosenbach:* MS 239/18 (p. 4).

✦ H&S, 8:151–52; 11:54. George Parfitt, ed., *Ben Jonson, The Complete Poems* (New Haven and London: Yale Univ. Press, 1975), 142–43, 512.

· · ·

13. James I (1566–1625), "K:I, his Invectiue against weomen," 13–14. No seventeenth-century printings.

For additional comments on James, see **HolM 2 notes.** "His Invectiue against weomen" is one of James's uncollected poems. No authorized version exists, nor is there a copy in the *State Papers Domestic.*

In response to a trend of country gentry moving to London, James issued "A Proclamation commanding all persons, Noblemen, Knights, and Gentlemen of Quality, to repayre to their Mansion houses in the Country, to attend their services, and keepe hospitality, according to the ancient and laudable custome of England." The proclamation was issued four times between 1622 and 1624 (Craigie 261–62). This poem is a companion piece to the proclamation.

> **2. Proclamation.** See note above.
>
> **5. vizards.** Masks.
>
> **12. the Strond.** The Strand, London.
>
> **15. Cæsar would have. . . .** Caesar, asked why he divorced his wife based only upon accusation, responded that even though he thought she was innocent, his wife had to be above suspicion.
>
> **20. debosher.** Comparative variant of debauch (*OED*).
>
> **24. Lotts wife.** Genesis 11–14; 19. Unidentified in the Bible by name, when she looked back at the destruction of Sodom and Gommorah, she turned into a pillar of salt.
>
> **45. Spanish dames.** Possible allusion to proposed marriage of Prince Charles and the Spanish Infanta.

✦ Manuscripts: Crum: Y398, Y–168. Yale: Y0433. ✦ *Bodleian:* MS Eng. poet. c. 50 (f. 29ᵛ); MS Eng. poet. e. 14 (f. 54); MS Eng. poet. f. 10 (f. 90); MS Malone 23 (p. 56); MS Rawl. poet. 26 (f. 63); *British Library:* Add. MS 10308 (ff. 78–79); Add. MS 25707 (f. 73); Add. MS 28640 (f. 126ᵛ); Egerton MS 923 (f. 21); *Folger:* V.a. 275 (p. 89); V.a. 276, pt. II (f. 31); V.a. 345 (p. 125); *Rosenbach:* MS 239/16 (p. 6); *Yale:* Osborn b 197 (pp. 134–35).

✦ Pr. *The Athenæum* No. 4575 (3 July 1915), 13; *Bodleian Quarterly Record*, Supplement 5 (1921), 3, 32. See also *The Poems of James I of Scotland*, ed. James Craigie, The Scottish Text Society, 3ʳᵈ ser., 26 (Edinburgh and London: William Blackwood & Sons, 1958).

14. Anon., "Anthonie Weastdons Anagram," 14. No known printing.

"Weastdons" is possibly a corruption of "Weston," first husband of M[ist]ris Thaire, subject of **HolM 21**.

• • •

15. Cor[nelious] Fairmedow, "In obitu˜Annæ Reginæ," 14. Pr. *Academiæ Oxoniensis, Funebria Sacra* (London, 1619), sig. G4.

The poet, Cor[nelius] Fairmedow, is identified in *Funebria Sacra*.

For further information on the death of Queen Anne, see **HolM 2 notes**. For biographical information, see **HolM 38 notes**. Anne died 2 March 1619.

I am grateful to William L. Mitchell, Associate Special Collections Librarian, Kenneth Spencer Research Library, University of Kansas, for his help in identifying this poem. It is catalogued in the Boys-Mizener Index at the University of Kansas.

• • •

16. Subscribed "GH," "A Funerall Elegie vppon the Death of Mr Iohn Ryce M^r of Arts and Squire Beadle," 15–16. Unprinted.

The attribution to "GH" is probably correct, but "IH" is a possibility. As a majuscule "G," it is more constrained than the scribe's typical handwriting, thus making it look more like an "I". However, the scribe generally makes his majuscule "I" with a vertical line, lacking here, thus making "G" a more likely reading. A similar "G" is found on page 17. In the margin of **HolM 19**, the scribe writes a majuscule "G," probably correcting his minuscule "g" in "Must have a: gardner."

In a modern pencil notation (found in the Holgate but not transcribed in this text) is written "John Holgate," William Holgate's younger brother. However, ascription to John Holgate is impossible. John Ryce, the University beadle, died between 1614 and 1616 (Andrew Clark, *Register of the University of Oxford* [Oxford Historical Society, 1885], 2:258). John Holgate was born in 1605; he was admitted as a pensioner to Caius College, Cambridge, in 1622/3. Clearly, he would have been too young to have written this poem.

There were two types of beadles, esquire and yeomen. Their duties were essentially processional (*OED*). A better known Latin elegy to a university beadle is Milton's *Elegia Seconda*. Merritt Y. Hughes describes the beadle of that poem, Richard Ridding, as the "official crier of the university for thirty years" (*John Milton: Complete Poems and Major Prose*, ed. Hughes [New York: Macmillan, 1957], 12, n. 1).

This is the first of three consecutive elegies written on the death of John Ryce. For commentary on the final couplet, see **HolM 170 notes**.

• • •

17. Subscribed "G: Morley" (George Morley [?] 1597–1684). "In obitum Dmĩ Iohanis Ryce in Artibus Magistrj et Bedellj Superioris: Carmen Funebre," 16. Unprinted.

This is the first of four poems in the manuscript ascribed to George Morley (see **HolM 149, 157, 169**). Since John Ryce died between 1614–1616, Morley would have been a student at Oxford when he wrote this poem. He received his B.A. from Christ Church, Oxford (1618) and M.A. (1621). Later, he became a King's scholar at Westminster School and chaplain to Robert, Earl of Caernarvon, where he remained for more than twenty years. He was given a prebendship at Christ Church, Oxford, by Charles I. He was also made rector of Hartfield, Sussex. During the Civil War, he was with Charles II in exile. In 1660, he was made Bishop of Worcester, then in 1662 translated to the see of Winchester on the death of Brian Duppa (*Athenæ Oxoniensis*).

For more information on this poem, see **HolM 16 notes**.

18. Anon., subscribed "Z.T," "In obitum M^rj Ryce Bedellj Sup[er]ioris circiter dies Paschales morientis Car: Funebre," 16–17. Unprinted.

The only known candidate for the initials "Z. T." is Zouch Townley. Very little has been written about him. He was a coterie poet who was later forced to flee England because he supposedly wrote a panegyric on John Felton, Buckingham's assassin. Buckingham was assassinated in 1628. See Andrew McRae, "The Literary Culture of Early Stuart Libeling," *Modern Philology*, 97. 3 (2000), 374. For information on John Ryce, see **HolM 16 notes**.

• • •

19. Subscribed "W:H:" (William Holgate [?]), "Vppon M[ist]^ris Gardner daughter to the right wor^ell Dr Ashboold D^r of Diuinity: Lacrymæ consolatoriæ," 17. No known printings.

William Holgate is the obvious candidate for "W. H." This is the first of two funeral elegies written by "W. H." for Mistress Gardner; the second is **HolM 23**. She was the daughter of Dr. Ashboold, rector of St. Peter's Church, Cornhill, London (see **HolM 10**). There is also a funeral elegy to her sister, Mistress Thaire, **HolM 21**. Mistress Gardner was buried at St. Peter's Church, 6 November 1621. The church register reads "Mrs Jeane Gardner wife of Mr. Robert Gardner, free of the mercers & daught[er] of Mr. Doctor Ashboold in ye chancell" (178).

> **10. roundes.** Probably the music of heavenly spheres.
> **13. Thessalian feilde.** Thessaly, an area of Northern Greece.
> **18. garden.** See note for l. 16. Here, Holgate started to write a majuscule "G," then wrote lower case "g." However, there is no deletion.

• • •

20. William Browne of Tavistock (1590?–1645?), "Lydfoord Law in Deuon-sheere," 18–19. Pr. John Philips, *Sportive Wit* (London, 1656), sig. 2B1.

Browne was well known in literary circles. His father was a Latin playwright and headmaster of Westminster School. Browne himself was educated at the Tavistock School and Exeter College, Oxford. He later attended Clifford's Inn and was admitted to the Inner Temple. He was tutor of Robert Dormer at Oxford in 1624, then tutor to the family of William Herbert, third Earl of Pembroke. Among his published verse is *Brittania's Pastorals* (1613–16)

Lansdowne MS 777 has served as the primary copy-text for later editions of this poem. Although the manuscript was never owned by Browne, it is believed to have been transcribed from an original text belonging to him. For additional information on Browne and Lansdowne 777, see **HolM 158 notes**. Collation with the Holgate reveals important variant differences, especially Lansdowne MS 777 ll. 73–78, that are missing from the Holgate.

Surviving copies of *Sportive Wit* are extremely rare. The only copy now in the United States is at the Huntington Library. It has not been used as a copy-text for any later version of this poem. Westcote [?], *View of Devonshire in 1630* (London, 1845), p. 360, describes the town of Lydford: "It hath neither fair nor market to comfort itself withal, and little fruitful land. It is only entrusted with the keeping of the prince's prisoners, for stannary causes" (qtd. Goodwin 352).

> **33. surties.** Obsolete form of surety.

✦ Collation: Lansdowne MS 777 *L*. Title: Lydfoorde Law in Deuon-shere] Lidford Iourney ; 9 with] by *L* ; 10 To] Then *L* ; 11 Twere] tis *L* ; 22 I] they *L* ; 24 a] his *L* 31 peck of Salt] seame of Malt *L* ; 32 malt] Salt *L* ; 46 And] ffor *L* ; the] that *L* ; old] Graue *L* ; 47 hold] haue *L* ; 48 Cloake] Cloakes *L* ; 59 loose] were *L* ; 63 whiles] ; while *L* ; 65 y^u] they *L* ; Holgate *om.* ll. 73–78

Sure I bellieue it then did rayne / A cow or two from Charles his Wayne / for none alyve did see / Such kynde of creatures there before / Nor shall from hence for euermore / Saue prisners Geese and Wee. *L* ; 76 it] that *L* ; 77 A] One *L* ; 81 it] that *L*

✦ Manuscripts: Crum: I–367; Beal: BrW 62–67. ✦ ***Bodleian:*** MS Rawl. Poet. 84 (f. 54 [rev]); ***British Library:*** Lansdowne MS 777 (ff. 5–7); MS Harley 3910 (ff. 1–3ᵛ); MS Harley 4931 (f. 15); ***Folger:*** MS Y.d. 24 29 (148); ***Rosenbach:*** MS 239/27 (pp. 177–79).

✦ *Original Poems never before published, by William Browne, of the Inner Temple, Gent.*, ed. Sir Egerton Brydges (Lee Priory, 1815), 9–16; William Browne, *The Whole Works*, ed. W. Carew Hazlett ([London,] 1868–69), 2:352–55; William Browne, *Works*, ed. Gordon Goodwin (1894), 2:305–9, 351–52.

• • •

21. Subscribed "W:H:" (William Holgate [?]), "Vppon Mᴿⁱˢ Thaire daughter to the right worᵉˡˡ Dʳ Ashboolde, here to-fore yᵉ wife of Mʳ Weston," 19. Unprinted.

This is a funeral elegy to Dr. Ashboold's second daughter, Mistress Bridget Thaire. The register of St. Peter's Church, Cornhill, states that there occurred on "1587, October 27 'Sonday Chrisining of Bridget Ashbold daughter of Mr.William Ashbold our parson, born the 18ᵗʰ day of this month'" (32). The register also notices her death, "January 3, 1621, 'buried Mʳˢ Bridget Tharyers wife of Mʳ Anthony Thayres free of the leathersellers & daughter of Mʳ Ashboold, p[ar]son Chancell'" (178). Bridget Thaire's brother-in-law, Mr. Gardner, was a mercer (see **HolM 19 notes**).

> **2. desarte.** Obsolete form of desert, dessert (*OED*).
> **10. in vre.** In use or practice.

• • •

22. Subscribed "W:H:" (William Holgate [?]), "In obitum Magistrj Maxia quondam Ædis Xᵗʲ Aluminj Qui in Comitijs Hospes fato concessit," 22. Unprinted.

This is the only Latin poem ascribed to William Holgate in the miscellany.

Anthony Maxey (d. 1618) was educated at Westminster School, then Trinity College, Cambridge, where he received his B.A. (1581), M.A. (1585), and D.D. (1608). He became a chaplain to James I, apparently in recognition of his eloquence and his stance against tobacco, a product James strongly opposed. In 1612, he became Dean of Windsor and registrar for the Order of the Garter (*DNB*).

Maxey was known as a simonist, one engaged in the purchase of ecclesiastical preferments. The *DNB* says, "He offered money to Sir Henry Hobart for preferment (letter in *Tanner MS cclxxiii*, 195) and two months before his death made the highest bid for the vacant see of Norwich (*Cal. State Papers, Domestic, 1611–18*, 532)."

• • •

23. Subscribed "W:H:" (William Holgate [?]), "Vppon Mistris Gardners Death & who dyed in Child-birth of her first child," 20–23. Unprinted.

This is Holgate's second poem to Mistress Gardner, daughter of Dr. Ashboold. She was buried 6 November 1621. For further information, see **HolM 19 notes**.

The poem suggests that the child survived (ll. 96–102). This is more clearly described in **HolM 24**, an elegy to Mistress Gardner and her sister, MistressThaire.

1. Senith. Variant of "zenith" (*OED*).

3. Nidar. *OED* does not list this as a variant, but clearly "nadir."

41. pretiouse. Obsolete form of "precious."

56. Iasper. A precious stone.

73. pory. Obsolete for "porous."

89. Bauches. Unclear meaning. Perhaps the Greek god Bacchus, or from the adjective "bauch," weak or without substance.

91. Symphasie. Possibly a unique usage.

94. endude. Endued. Brought in or introduced.

112. ingirte. Obsolete variant of "engirt," to encircle or surround.

124. Versles. Verseless.

. . .

24. Subscribed "W:H:" (William Holgate [?]), "Both Sisters, and both dead, Both in one Graue, / Both virtuouse, Both deplord, Bothe one verse haue," 23–24. Unprinted.

This is Holgate's elegy for both Mistress Thaire and Mistress Gardner (see notes for **HolM 19, 21, 23**).

7. Earch. Unique variant or scribal error.

. . .

25. Richard Corbett (1582–1636), "Dr: Corbets 'Iter Boreale:,'" 25–36. Pr. *CEP*, 1–17; O. Gilchrist, *The Poems of Richard Corbet* (London, 1807).

The exact date of this long poem is in dispute. Corbett's twentieth-century editors, B&TR, believe it was written ca. June 1620, when Corbett became Dean of Christ Church (xx–xxi). The poem describes a Midlands journey Corbett took with three of his Oxford friends, one of whom was Dr. Leonard Hutten, a canon and sub-dean of Christ Church. Corbett later married Hutten's daughter. The identity of the other two is unknown, but, according to the editors, they were not Barten Holyday or Brian Duppa, "for they were both abroad at the time" (119).

Mary Hobbs (see citation below), however, does not accept the 1620 date because she believes that Brian Duppa, later a Dean of Christ Church, was one of the four. Duppa is identified as a participant in British Library MS Harley 6917, a notebook transcribed by Thomas Mann, a resident member of Christ Church, and, as such, "one would expect him to be correct over their identity" (190).

Comic travel poems were popular among Oxford men. B&TR believe Horace's journey to Brundisium (*Sat.* I. v) is the earliest model.

By its sheer size, this poem seems to dominate any miscellany in which it appears. The fact that it was copied at all is clear evidence that it was enjoyed by those who understood its myriad topical references.

For further information on Richard Corbett, see **HolM 11 note**. B&TR are clearly the authorities on this poem. As indicated below, they occasionally cite the Holgate marginalia to explain references in the poem.

Comparison to *CEP* reveals an impressive list of variants.

3. Austin. Performing "austins," a university exercise, from "disputationes in Augustinesibus." Also, the Augustine friars (*OED*).

3. Galen. Medical studies. Galen was a second-century physician and very prolific writer. His *De Naturalibus Facultatibus* was printed in England in the early sixteenth century.

8. Kitt Middleton. A parish priest from Ashton upon the Wall, twenty-five miles north of Oxford.

15. Flower. A village.

23–24. Virgill . . . Æneas. *Aen.* l. 187 and following.

26. Daintry. Now Daventry.

27. Markett . . . day. Wednesday.

27. Lecture day. Church exercises, or lectures, were held once a month on Market day.

46. Mr. Baylyes . . . and Mr. Wright. B&TR conjecture that they were local lecturers.

52. Dodds precepts or Cleuers Letter. The marginalia are correct. John Dod, a Puritan preacher, wrote *Plaine and Familiar Exposition of the Ten Commandements* (1603).

64. Wickliffs dust. John Wycliff spent most of his life around Oxford.

68–69. the Papists burne Thy bones for hate. Wycliff's body was exhumed and burned in 1428.

71. Parson [Heathcote]. John Heathcote was rector of Aylestone, a town between Leicester and Lutterworth. The travelers are continuing north.

82. Camdens eie. William Camden (1551–1623), author of *Britannia* (a chorographical study of England) and *Remaines concerning Britian*. He was also Headmaster of Westminster School.

85. Duke of Lancaster. The hospital (l. 80) was founded by Henry, earl of Leicester and Lancaster (B&TR), mistakenly credited to John of Gaunt's son, Henry Bolingbroke, duke of Lancaster and later to King Henry IV.

88. Henry of Grismound. B&TR believe that Corbett meant Henry of Grosmont, i.e., Grosmont, the birthplace of the Duke of Lancaster (l. 85).

101. vsurpinge Richard. Richard III is buried at Grey Friars.

103. feild Bosworth. Site of Richard's death, 1485.

109. Woolsey. Cardinal Wolsey is buried in the Abbey of St. Mary de Pratis, Leicester.

117. William. The Holgate and Bodleian MS Wood D. (2) identify him as "Dr. Huttons Man." (B&TR 117).

122. the great Earle himselfe. Charles Lord Howard of Effingham was the Earl of Nottingham. He served as the Lord High Admiral but was replaced by Buckingham in 1619.

122–23. Notingham . . . Trent. Nottingham is on the River Trent.

124. St Andrewes. B&TR suggest that in Corbett's mind, they are getting closer to Scotland. There is no church in or near Nottingham with that name.

126. Dwell . . . in holes. The Nottinghamshire cave-dwellings, which, according to B&TR, were famous during the seventeenth century.

130. Powder Traytors. The Gunpowder Plot, 1605.

139. Crosses not yet demolisht. Cf. John Donne, "The Crosses," **HolM 88**. Wayside crosses were considered symbols of the Roman church.

143. The Castle next ["ruined" in marginalia]. No specific reference is noted. "Many of the buildings had been pulled down, and the materials sold, when the castle and park were granted to Francis, Earle of Rutland, in the sixteenth century" (B&TR 122).

145. two statues keepe ["Guy & Colebrand" in marginalia]. Leland's *Itinerary*, ed. Lucy Toulmin Smith (London: 1909), 95, describes a bridge bearing "bestes and giantes." Guy of Warwick is said to have defeated the Danish giant Colbrand, who was frequently mentioned in seventeenth-century ballads (*Bishop Percy's Folio Manuscript*, ed. Hales and Furnivall, 2:509 and following: B&TR 122).

148. Kinge Dauids vault. ". . . ther goith also downe a stair ynto the grounde, wher Davy King of Scottes, as the castellanes say, was kept a prisoner" (Leland, op. cit., qtd. in B&TR 122).

149. Mortimers darke hole. ". . . wher the kepers of the castelle say Edwarde the thirdes band cam up thorough the rok and toke the Erle Mortimer prysoner" (Leland, qtd. in B&TR 122).

159. Guild-haule and Holmeby. There are statues of Gog and Magog in the London Guildhall. There were apparently similar statues that guarded the home of Christopher Hatton (d. 1591), Holmby, a Northampton-shire mansion.

165. Bulhead. Apparently the name of the Inn.

180. mow. A stack or bundle of grain (*OED*).

183. Maris. Variant form of Mary (B&TR, 123).

210. Dr. Iucks [margin]. Probably Simon Jacks, Vicar of Newark.

218. preferd the heart. The White Hart was a Newark inn. It was next to another inn, the Saracen's Head (B&TR 123).

225–28. Would they pull downe . . . what Cathedrall are. The New Church of St. Mary Magdalene, Newark, considered a particularly beautiful English parish church. B&TR use the Holgate to gloss the Burleigh pew. It belonged to Thomas Cecil, second Lord Burghley, who owned what is described as "the impropriate Rectory, and other property near Newark" (123).

230. Mʳ Mason [margin]. Edmund Mason, a tutor to Prince Charles, vicar of Newark (1617–28).

235–36. a Castle too . . . where the Kinge slept. James I stayed in Newark on his way to Scotland, 7 April 1617. The margin identifies "Newmarke Castle," but J. B. Nichols does not name the castle (*The progresses, processions and magnificent festivities of King James* . . . . [London: 1828; rpt. 1970], 3:268).

239. a perspectiue. Any optical instrument used to make objects appear larger (*OED*).

240. Beuer and Lyncolne. Two castles, Belvoir and Lincolne, the former south of Newark, the latter northeast. Our travelers appear to be deciding which way to go (B&TR).

247. Loughborough. South-southwest of Newark. They are turning for home.

250. iades. Horses of inferior breeding (*OED*).

290. Bosworth. Bosworth Field is near the town of Market Bosworth, twelve miles west of Leicester.

295. Forrest [margin "Lester fforrest"]. The forest of Charley or Charnwood (B&TR 123).

296. Beuis. Reference to the romance of *Beves of Hamtoun*.

298. Knight O' the Sun. *El Donzel del Febo* (squire of Phoebus), hero of a Spanish romance, *The Mirror of Knighthood*. It was translated into English in 1578 (B&TR).

306. William. See. l. 117.

308. Puck. See l. 314.

314. Robin. Robin Goodfellow, i.e., Puck, "who misleads night-wanderers" (B&TR). He is a very familiar character in English folklore; however, based on the reference to Shakespeare's *Richard III* (l. 351), Corbett may have been thinking of *A Midsummer Night's Dream*.

319. a gentle Keeper. B&TR use the gloss in the Holgate marginalia to identify this character: "Groby Park is three miles north-west of Leicester" (124).

329. til'de. tiled.

346. the play. *Richard III.*

352. Burbidge. Richard Burbage (1567?–1619). Richard III was one of his most famous roles.

361. The Keeper of the Castle. Sir Robert Dudley, self-proclaimed Duke of Northumberland and Earl of Leicester. In 1605, he moved permanently to Italy (B&TR 124–25).

364–66. My Lord of Leisters Man . . . bauderye. The reference here is unclear. According to B&TR, Gilchrist believed this to be one John Bust, a "clerical profligate."

369. an humble shrine. A well-known shrine of Guy of Warwick (cf. l. 145). It was believed Guy of Warwick saved England from the Danes.

378. A pillar stands. There is a Guy's Cliff in Warwick.

382. our Inn. Bodleian MS Rawl. poet 206 identifies the inn as "The Swan" (B&TR 125).

393. Theorbo. A double-necked lute, or arch-lute.

420. Sr Francis Grivell [margin]. Sir Fulke Greville. He was granted Warwick Castle by James I in 1604, but because it was in poor condition, he had to restore it. His writing was published posthumously from manuscripts found in the castle (Baker 4).

430. Archdeacon Burton [margin]. Samuel Burton, rector of Dry Marston, archdeacon of Gloucester. He, too, was a Christ Church man.

432. Lord Abbot. George Abbot (1562–1633), Archbishop of Canterbury, known as a Puritan Archbishop, famous for his disputes with Archbishop Laud.

443. feast of Bartholmew. B&TR suggest this might be a reference to Jonson's *Barthol'mew Fayre* (126).

446. The Alter was translated to an Inn. Apparently, an altar stone was set on the tavern door.

465. Mr Wheatly's sake. William Whately (1583–1639) was Vicar of Banbury. He was a Puritan, author of *The Redemption of Time* (1606) and *The New Birth, or A Treatise of Regeneration* (1618).

483. The Puritane, the Anabaptist, Brownist. Banbury was known as a center for puritanism. Anabaptists rejected Anglican doctrines on the sacraments and holy orders. Brownists were followers of Robert Brown, an English Puritan.

484. grandsallet. A large salad.

485. The Crosses alsoe. The crosses in Banbury were destroyed by the Puritans. The incident is the subject of a children's nursery rhyme, "Ride a Cock Horse to Banbury Cross."

488. Crist hath nere descended into Hell. Corbett became known as an Arminian after a sermon on this subject, 1613. He believed that the Puritans perverted the true meaning of this article of faith.

498. Apocriphall. Most Puritans objected to the Apocrypha. An exception, of course, was John Milton.

500. Kate Stubbs. The wife of Puritan pamphleteer Phillip Stubbs, who wrote a popular life of her, *A Christal Glasse for Christian Women* (1591).

500. Anne Askew. According to a Roxburghie Ballad, she was burned at the stake because she refused to attend mass (*Roxburghe Ballads*, ed. W. Chappell and J. W. Ebsworth., 9 vols. [Hertford: Steven Austin and Son, 1871–1899], 1:29; B&TR 128).

506. Rawleigh from his voayge. Ralegh returned from Guiana in June 1618. He was executed 29 October 1618. He is the subject of the next poem, **HolM 26.**

✦ Manuscripts: Crum F578. Beal Vol. II, pt. 1, CoR 279–315. Yale F0524 ✦ *Aberdeen University Library:* MS 29 (pp. 1–15); *Bodleian:* MS Eng. poet. e. 14 (ff. 2–8ᵛ); MS Eng. poet. e. 97 (pp. 14–25); MS Ashmole 47 (ff. 8–16ᵛ); MS Eng. poet. c. 50 (ff. 47–51ᵛ); MS Rawl. poet. 172 (ff. 143–58); MS Rawl. poet. 206 (pp. 1–16); MS Wood D. 19 (ff. 72–79ᵛ); *Bradford District Archives:* Hopkinson MSS, Vol 34 (pp. 138–50); *British Library:* MS Harley 6931 (ff. 39–48); Add. MS 4457 (ff. 7–14ᵛ); Add. MS 37683 (f. 1–1ᵛ); Add. MS 58215 (pp. [51–71]); Egerton MS 2725 (ff. 47ᵛ–54); MS Sloane 542 (ff. 29ᵛ–36); MS Sloane 1446 (ff. 2–9); MS Sloane 1792 (ff. 28–38); *Folger:* V.a. 97 (pp. 45–51); V.a. 170 (pp. 106–26); MS J.a. 1 (ff. 93–99ᵛ); V.a. 125, pt. I (pp. 45–51); *Huntington Library:* HM 198, pt. 2 (pp. 109–13); *New York Public Library:* Arents Collection, Cat. No. S191 (ff. 4ᵛ–14ᵛ [rev]); Arents Collection, Cat. No. S288 (pp. 54–67); *University of Newcastle upon Tyne:* MS Bell/White 25 (ff. 1–8); *University of Nottingham:* Portland MS Pw V 37 (pp. 323–30); *Rosenbach:* MS 239/27 (pp. 226–39); MS 239/22 (ff. 28–35ᵛ); MS 240/2 (pp. 101–16); MS 1083/16 (pp. 210–26); *St. John's College, Cambridge:* MS S. 23 (James 416) (ff. 4–14ᵛ); *Trinity College, Cambridge:* MS B 14.22 (James 307) (ff. 62–71); *Victoria and Albert Museum:* Dyce Collection, Cat. No. 18 (Pressmark 25.F.17) (ff. 65–71ᵛ); *Westminster Abbey:* MS 41 (ff. 3–9ᵛ); *Dr. Williams's Library:*

MSS 12.54 (ff. 1–7ᵛ); *Yale*: Osborn b 356, p. 49. N.B. Beal CoR 315: "This description given in Janus Albinus, *Catalogus . . . liborum* (Dordrecht, 1696), p. 325, as item 41 in the section 'Libri Manuscripti in Folio' [exemplum of this catalogue in the British Library, Department of Printed Books, 126.a.18]." Unlocated.

✦ B&TR, xx–xxi, 31–49, 118–28. See also Mary Hobbs, "Early Seventeenth-Century Verse Miscellanies and Their Value for Textual Editors," *English Manuscript Studies, 1100–1700*, 1 (1989), 182–210.

• • •

26. Anon., "On the death of Sʳ W: R:.," 36. Pr. *Wits Recreations* (1641), Epitaph 148; John Shirley, *Life of Raleigh* (1677), 239.

Although this short essay was frequently attributed to John Gill, no positive attribution can be made. (There is no ascription to the poem in Shirley's *Life of Raleigh*.) Ralegh was executed 29 October 1618, after his unsuccessful expedition to Guiana. His death was apparently brought about by the Spanish Ambassador, Diego Sarmiento de Acuña, Conde de Gondomar. Ralegh was strongly anti-Catholic. James acceded to the Spanish demand for Ralegh's execution because at the time James hoped the Spanish Infanta would marry his eldest son, Charles.

As the poem describes, Ralegh's death is noteworthy in that he comported himself so bravely on the scaffold (Morfill 261).

Note the reference to Ralegh that concludes the previous poem, **HolM 25**, line 506.

The deleted majuscule "P" at the end of l. 8 suggests that someone else was reading this poem to the transcriber as he/she transcribed it. Line 9 starts with the word "Pale." Had the scribe been reading the text, he/she more than likely would have seen that "Pale" starts the next line.

Note also that the only line that is not part of a rhymed couplet is l. 7, which reads "Else what a miracle is wrought?" Collation reveals that the Holgate is missing *Wits Recreations* l. 8, which reads "To triumph both in flesh and thought?" The final word "thought" would have completed the couplet in Holgate's l. 7 last word, "wrought."

> ✦ Collation: *Wits Recreations* (1641) *WR*. Title: On the death of Sr: W: R:] On Sir Walter Rawleygh at his execution *WR* ; 4 free] freed *WR* ; 5 didst] dyest *WR* ; quit] quit'st *WR* ; 7 is] were *WR* ; *after l. 7* To triumph both in flesh and thought? *WR* ; 9 thy] (10) thine *WR* ; 10 The Legacie thou gaust vs then] Th' example that thou left'st was then *WR* ; 11 Wee'le sue] Wee looke *WR*

> ✦ Manuscripts: Crum G504; Yale G0457 ✦ **Bodleian:** MS Eng. Hist. C. 272 (p. 51, Captaine Kinge); MS Eng. poet. e. 14 (f. 98ᵛ [rev]); MS Rawl. D. 954 (f. 35); MS Rawl. poet. 26 (f. 49ᵛ); MS Rawl. poet. 209 (f. 10); MS Tanner 306 (f. 251); **British Library:** Add. MS 33998 (f. 96ᵛ); MS Harley 791 (f. 49); Lansdowne MS 777 (f. 64); Stowe MS 962 (f. 71ᵛ); **National Library of Scotland:** Hawthornden VIII MS 2060 (f.2); (p. 71b); **Rosenbach:** MS 239/27 (p. 357); MS 1083/17 **Folger:** V.a. 103, pt. I (f. 3ᵛ); V.a. 125, pt. II (f. 7ᵛ, IoGill); V.a. 262 (p. 262); V.a. 308 (f. 128ᵛ); V.a. 418 (f. 5); V.b. 43 (f. 32, I:G:); **Yale:** Osborn b 54 (p. 877); Osborn b 197 (p. 47, Mr. Cicill); Poetry Box VI/107.

✦ *Ballads from Manuscripts*, ed. W. R. Morfill (1873; rpt. 1968), pt. 1, 260–62, 269; *Courtly Poets*, ed. John Hannah (London, 1870); *New Oxford Book of Seventeenth Century Verse*, ed. Alistair Fowler (Oxford: Oxford Univ. Press, 1991), no. 556.

• • •

27. William Holgate (?). "An Elegie vppon the worshipfull his deceased Scholmaster Mr Richard Lucey," subscribed "W: H:," 37–39. Unprinted.

This is the last poem in the miscellany ascribed to "W. H.," probably William Holgate. Unfortunately, there is no way to know anything about his relationship to Richard Lucey. A Richard Lucy was associated with St. Peter's Church, Cornhill, but that Richard Lucy died in 1667 (*Church parish register*, p. 36). Line 15 suggests that Richard Lucy was William Holgate's teacher. However, nothing is known about William Holgate's education.

> **32. semor.** Possibly as in "seemly."
> **68. Tennis-ball-like.** Cf. **HolM 112.**
> **73. et** Perhaps "and" or an error for "yet".

• • •

28. Richard Corbett (1582–1636), "An Elegie on the Lady," 39–41. Pr. *CEP*, 43–44; *Poëtica Stromata* (n. p., 1648).

For details about Corbett, see **HolM 11 notes.** Lady Elizabeth Haddington died 6 December 1618. She was the wife of Viscount Haddington, later Earl of Holdernesse. Her husband was given the title of Viscount by James I in reward for his aid in foiling the Gowrie Conspiracy (1600), when Haddington may have saved James's life (F. P. Wilson, *The Plague Pamphlets of Thomas Dekker* [Oxford: Oxford Univ. Press, 1925], 126–30). Ben Jonson wrote *The Haddington Masque* (Orgel 107–21) to honor their wedding, Shrove Tuesday, 1607/8.

According to the title of the poem in *CEP*, Lady Haddington died of smallpox.

As previously stated, Corbett's poetry was very popular during the seventeenth century. The large number of existent texts and the many variants between the Holgate text and *CEP* suggest that there must have been numerous copies of this poem, most of which are surely lost.

> **15. highly borne.** Her father was Robert, fifth Earl of Sussex.
> **26. deuorce.** Apparently this refers to Frances, Countess of Essex, who sued for divorce to marry Robert Carr, Viscount Rochester, alleging that her husband was impotent, but only with her. Her ex-husband, Essex, later remarried and became a father (B&TR 135).
> **30–31. Barren embraces . . . Twice pretty-ons thrice worthier. . . .** Lady Haddington had two sons and a daughter, none of whom survived infancy (B&TR 135).
> **38. chanell.** Unclear usage. "Changed" is clearly correct, as in *CEP*.
> **59. O thou deform'ed, vnwomanly disease.** Reference to her smallpox.
> **69–70. Amongst the gamsters where thy name the tricke / At the last maine, or last pockey nicke.** These are gaming references. "Maine" is the number called in hazard before the dice is thrown; "nick" is the same as the maine or equal to it; "pockey" refers to the disease but is probably a metaphor for the dice. Also, note the Holgate's margin notation.
> **71. Clyen'd.** Client or client's.
> **74. Boxe.** The *OED* does mention a dice-box, a possible interpretation.
> **90. te.** To.
> **90. Pyramis of Iet.** "Pyramis" is the earliest spelling of "pyramid." "Iet" is probably "jet black," but the next line, "And put out fier" might suggest a jet stream of water. Either would be contemporary usages (*OED*).
> **91. didge.** Dig.

✦ Manuscripts: Crum D106; Beal, Vol. II, pt. 1, CoR 127–162; Yale D0115 ✦ *Bodleian:* MS Ashmole 47 (f. 116); Don.d.58 (ff. 5–6); MS Eng. poet. e. 97 (pp. 65–67); MS Malone 21 (ff. 17ᵛ–19); MS Rawl. poet. 117 (ff. 18ᵛ–19); MS Harley 6931 (ff. 76ᵛ–78); *British Library:* Add. MS 10308 (ff. 145ᵛ–47); Add. MS 21433 (ff. 172ᵛ–74ᵛ); Add. MS 25303 (ff. 100ᵛ–2); Add. MS 27408 (ff. 167–68); Add. MS 58215 (pp. [76–79]; MS Harley 3910 (ff. 33ᵛ–35); MS Sloane 1446 (ff. 14ᵛ–15ᵛ); MS

Sloane 1792 (ff. 47^v–49^v, 54); Stowe MS 962 (ff. 45^v–47); **Corpus Christi College, Oxford:** MS 328 (ff. 53–54); **Folger:** V.a. 96 (ff. 28^v–29^v); V.a. 170 (pp. 216–20); V.a. 262 (pp. 46–49); V.a. 345 (pp. 84–85); V.a. 339 (253^v–54^v); **Huntington Library:** EL 8798; HM 172 (69–70); HM 198 pt. I (pp. 97–98); **Leicestershire Record Office:** DG.9/2796 (p. 50); **Rosenbach:** MS 239/22 (ff. 37^v–38^v); MS 239/27 (pp. 183–84 *final 42 lines*, pp. 341–42); MS 1083/17 (pp. 8–11); MS 652 (ff. 361^v–62^v); **Westminster Abbey:** MS 41 (ff. 19–20, 25); **Yale:** Osborn b 62 (pp.106–7); Osborn b 197 (pp. 163–65); Osborn b 356 (p. 13).

✦ B&TR, 59–62, 134–35; *The Complete Masques.* ed. Stephen Orgel (New Haven: Yale Univ. Press, 1969).

• • •

29. Sir Walter Ralegh ([?], 1554–1618. "The Lie"). 42. Pr. Francis Davison, *A Poetical Rapsodie* (London, 1608), 17–19; Joshua Sylvester, *Postumi* (1633), 642; *P&R*, 104.

Ralegh was a soldier, diplomat, MP, explorer, historian, and poet. He was born in Devonshire, attended Oriel College, Oxford, but apparently he did not graduate. His first career was as a soldier. Based on comments in his own *History of the World* (1614), he served with the French Huguenots in 1569. In 1575, he was at the Middle Temple. By 1587, he became captain of the Queen's Guard. He also fought with the Dutch against the Spanish, with Sir Francis Drake against the Spanish Armada, and with Essex (his chief rival for the Queen's favor) at Cadiz and in the Azores.

Ralegh is well-known as a courtier. He became a favorite of Elizabeth, whose patronage led him to great wealth. He fell from favor and was imprisoned after he seduced and married a lady of the court, Elizabeth Throckmorton. He was also falsely accused of being an accomplice in Essex's rebellion. Among the many charges brought against him was that he was a Puritan.

With the advent of James in 1603, life became even more difficult for Ralegh. He was accused of conspiracy with Spain to place a Roman Catholic on the English throne and spent thirteen years in the Tower. He was released on the instigation of Buckingham, by then the King's favorite. In 1617, he made a final expedition to Guiana, which failed. When he returned to England, he was executed at the instigation of Spain. Although "The Lie" was circulating in the 1590s, Ralegh was dead when this text was copied into the manuscript.

Certain elements of Ralegh's career bear mention in the context of the Holgate manuscript. He was a favorite of Prince Henry, who encouraged Ralegh to write *The History of the World*. The Holgate includes several poems dedicated to Prince Henry, including a sequence of elegies commemorating his death (**HolM 101–5**). Also Buckingham, who urged James to release Ralegh from prison, is the subject of several poems found in the Holgate, especially those that involve Buckingham's trip to Spain (**HolM 72–73, 146**).

The Ralegh canon is problematic at best. Michael Rudick's *The Poems of Sir Walter Ralegh* is the most recent edition of his poems, but there remains much disagreement as to what Ralegh actually wrote, and there are many variant readings of any text associated with his poetry.

Pierre Lefranc does not accept that this poem was written by Ralegh (86–87). He believes that it is a mediocre poem, that its sentiments are decidedly puritan. He also believes that the poem was ascribed to Ralegh, not by mistake, but because his enemies wanted to associate him with the ideas that would have gotten him into trouble. Stephen Greenblatt, however, has specifically argued against Lefranc (171–76). He considers the poem a satire. Rudick discusses Lefranc's interpretation extensively, xlii–xlvii.

A Poetical Rapsodie reveals the Holgate is missing stanza 8. It reads: "Tell wit how much it wrangles / In tickle points of nycenesse, / Tell wisedome she entangles / her selfe in ouer wisenesse. / And when they do reply / straight giue them both the lie." *P&R* also is missing stanza 6. It reads:

"Tell wit it wants Devotion / tell love it is but Lust. / Tell time it is but motion, / tell flesh it is but Dust. / And with them not reply, / For thou must give the lye."

♦ Manuscripts: Crum G205; Beal Vol. I, pt. 2, RaW 147–177; Yale G0180 ♦ *All Souls College, Oxford:* MS 155 (ff. 18ᵛ–19ᵛ); *Bibliothèque Nationale, Paris:* Department de la Musique, Conservatoire MS 2489 (f. 73); *Bodleian:* MS Ashmole 51 (f. 6); MS Douce f (ff. 11–12); MS Eng. poet. d. 3 (f. 2ᵛ); MS Firth e. 4 (pp. 3–5); MS Rawl. poet. 172 (f. 12ᵛ); MS Rawl. poet. 212 (ff. 88–90, D:Lat); MS Tanner 306 (f. 188); *Bradford Central Library:* Hopkinson MSS, Vol 34 (pp. 9–11); *British Library:* Add. MS 5832 (ff. 218–19, Ralegh); Add. MS 29764 (f. 9, Raleigh); MS Harley 2296 (f. 135); MS Harley 6910 (ff. 141ᵛ–42); *Cambridge:* MS Add. 4138 (f. 46, Doctor Latworth); *Chetham's Library, Manchester:* Mun. A. 4.15 (p. 103 seq, Raleigh); *Folger:* V.a. 103, pt. I (f. 67, Dr. Lateware), V.a. 345 (pp. 176–77, Rawley); V.b. 198 (f. 2, Lady Anne Southwell); *Huntington Library:* HM 198, pt. 1 (f. 1); *National Library of Wales:* Southeby MS B2 (pp. 131–33); *University of Nottingham:* Portland MS Pw V 37 (pp. 138–39, Dr. Latewarr); *Princeton:* Robert Taylor Collection; *Rosenbach:* MS 239/27 (pp. 175–77, Sr.W.R.); MS 1083/16 (ff. 16ᵛ–17); *St. John's College, Cambridge:* MS U. 26 (James 548) (p. 43); *Texas Tech:* Dalhousie I (ff. 57ᵛ–58); Dalhousie II f. 30); *Trinity College, Dublin:* MS 877, (ff. 216–17); *Dr. Williams's Library:* MS Jones B.60 (pp. 257–60); *Yale:* Osborn b 356 (p. 133).

♦ Latham, 45–47, 128–38; Rudick, xlii–xlvii, 30–44. Stephen J. Greenblatt, *Sir Walter Ralegh, The Renaissance Man and His Roles* (New Haven and London: Yale Univ. Press, 1973), 171–76; Pierre Lefranc, *Sir Walter Ralegh, Ecrivain, l'œuvre and les idées* (Paris: Librairie Armand Colin, 1968), 86–87.

• • •

30. Anon., "A Paradox in praise of a painted fface:." 43–45. Pr. *Parnassus Biceps* (1656), 97–100; *P&R*, 93–95; *Le Prince d'Amour* (1660), 99.

Grierson reprints this poem because of its attribution to Donne in some manuscripts. Also, it is ascribed "I. D." in *Le Prince d'Amour*. However, it is attributed to James Shirley in two manuscripts and William Baker in two others (see below). To the present editor it seems to be an imitation of Donne rather than a poem by him.

The text, however, contains a curious transcription question. Holgate repeats ll. 13–14 at ll.27–28, but only as half lines. Thus, ll. 13–14 read "Giue mee a face thas is as full of lyes / As Gypsies or your runinge Lotteries;" but ll. 27–28 read "Giue me a face:— / As Gypsies &—." **HolM 30,** ll. 13–14, are the same as *Parnassus Biceps,* ll. 25–26. If **HolM 30** ll. 13–14 did not exist, then the half lines (now ll. 27–28) would be situated exactly as they are in *Parnassus Biceps.* This suggests that somewhere in this stemmatic group, ll. 25–26 were copied incorrectly as ll. 13–14, and that the scribe, when he/she realized the mistake, decided to highlight the proper transcription by writing only half the line. To us, that would be an unsatisfactory way to handle such a mistake because it would be simpler to cross out the misplaced line and then continue to transcribe the lines in their proper sequence. What is interesting, however, is that in miscellanies like the Holgate, deleting entire lines is rare. For example, in the Holgate there is no instance of an entire line being removed. Also, there are no arrows drawn on any page to indicate that line "x" should follow line "y," which would be another solution to the problem. There are, of course, many corrections made in individual words or even phrases, but not when the entire line needs to be changed. It would be helpful to find other texts with this same textual error. Redding (84) collates *Parnassus Biceps,* Rosenbach MSS 189 and 1083/16; Folger MS V.a. 245; and *P&R,* none of which share this problem.

10. St Georges day. April 23rd. Cf. **HolM 62**, l.14.

15. <fucos> & paint. Rosenbach MS 1083/16 reads "fucus and cerusse." "Fucus," commonly used in the seventeenth century, a cosmetic or paint used to beautify the skin. "Cerusse," also known as white lead, is a compound used as a cosmetic (*OED*).

36. Candean wines. Refers to Candia (obsolete form of Crete), which produces wines.

37. Ciuett. A substance used to make perfume. It has a musky smell. It comes from animals of the civet family (see l.39).

38. Muscatts nose. Muscat is a type of wine. Here the poet means "muskrat," a type of animal from which musk is obtained. It is not a civet.

39. a baser place. Civet, the substance, comes from the anal sac.

46. pyde. Variously colored.

51. Cordouant. Spanish leather. Redding glosses this as a glove made of scented Cordovan (86).

+ Manuscripts: Crum N372; Yale N0337 + **Bodleian:** MS Eng. poet. e. 14 (f. 83[rev]); MS Malone 21 (ff. 74–75); MS Malone 117 (f. 29ᵛ, WmBaker); **Bradford Central Library:** Hopkinson MSS, Vol 34 (pp. 63–64); **British Library:** Egerton MS 2230 (f. 24); MS Harley 3910 (ff. 20ᵛ–21ᵛ); Stowe MS 961 (f. 70); Stowe MS 962 (ff. 49–59); **Cambridge:** MS Ee. 4.14 (ff. 77–78ᵛ); **Corpus Christi College, Oxford:** MS 327 (f. 15ᵛ, Sherly); MS 328 (f. 32); **Folger:** V.a. 97 (pp. 165–67, F. Sherly); V.a. 245 (ff. 7ᵛ–9); V.a. 322 (pp. 130–34); W.a. 118 (f. 6ᵛ); **Harvard:** MS Eng. 966.6 (pp. 326–30); **New York Public Library:** Arents Collection, Cat. No. S191 (ff. 16–17[rev], Baker); **Rosenbach:** MS 189 (p. 417); MS 1083/16 (pp. 24–27); **Texas Tech:** Dalhousie I (f. 28); Dalhousie II (ff. 244–45ᵛ); **Yale:** Osborn b 205 (ff. 30–31).

+ Redding, 81–86; Grierson, 1:456–59.

• • •

31. Sir George Radney (also Rodney: 1575–1601), "Radneys verses before hee kild himself," 45. Pr. *Wits Interpreter* (1655), 69, 2nd numbering.

Little is known about Radney's life except the unfortunate circumstances of his death. He was the son of Morris Rodney, gentleman, and Joane Dyer, the sister of Sir Edward Dyer, courtier and poet. In 1599, he began to court the widow of a wealthy vinter, Frances Pranell, who refused to marry him.

Frances Pranell was born Frances Howard, the only daughter of Thomas Howard, first Viscount Bindon, by his third wife, Mabel Burton. By age four, both her parents were dead, and she became a ward of her cousin Thomas Howard, Baron de Walden, later first Earl of Sussex. The exact date and circumstances of her wardship are unknown. At age thirteen, Frances married Henry Pranell. This created a scandal because Queen Elizabeth wanted William Cecil, Lord Burghley, to decide whom the members of the Howard family were to marry. Pranell was imprisoned for marrying Frances Howard, but was released when he wrote a letter of apology to Cecil (Foster 74–75). It should be pointed out that it was a different Frances Howard, actually her younger cousin, who was later involved with Lord Robert Carr, an affair which led to the death of Sir Thomas Overbury (Foster 72–74).

Apparently, the Pranell marriage was not a happy one, and Frances fell in love with Henry Wriothesley, third Earl of Southampton (Foster 76), who has, of course, been suggested as the Mr. W. H. of Shakespeare's *Sonnets*. Sometime thereafter, Pranell went on a business trip and apparently died. Frances Pranell had her husband declared dead by 20 December 1599 (Foster 81).

Frances Pranell was a wealthy, young, and apparently quite attractive widow with several suitors. Wriothesley decided he did not want to marry her. Among her other suitors were Sir William Woodhouse; Sir William Evers; Edward Seymour, Earl of Hertford, whom she later married; and Sir George Radney, who wrote the present poem.

Radney was unable to cope with his failed suit. In a letter to Sir Dudley Carlton (3 February 1601) Sir John Chamberlain wrote that "One Radney of Somersetshire, nephew to Sir Ed: Dier was lately knighted, but whether he were overjoyed with that dignitie or overawed with the love of Mistris Pranell (whom he woed and could not obtaine) or as some way so doted upon a greater mistris, that his braines were not able to beare the burthen, but have plaide banckrout and left him raving" (Chamberlain 1.116; Foster 86).

Upon the marriage of Frances Pranell to Edward Seymour, Radney followed the newlyweds to their estate and composed a verse epistle—in blood no less—to Frances, "From one that languisheth in discontent" (Crum F723). In it he describes the death of the Petrarchan lover (Pr. in Foster 89). Her answer to that poem is her only known poetry, "Divided in your sorrows have I strove" (Crum D344). In the poem she rejects the idealizations of Petrarchan love.

After receiving her response, Radney, unable to cope with her rejection, composed the poem found in the Holgate manuscript and then committed suicide.

> **3, 13. Ay.** Foster believes that Radney is responding to l. 136 in her poem, "To corrupt trust in sonneting *ay-mes*," which is often spelled "I me" (98n).

> ✦ Manuscripts: Crum W670 ✦ **Bodleian:** MS Rawl. poet. 172 (f. 11ᵛ); **British Library:** Add. MS 25707 (f. 4ᵛ); Add. MS 30982 (f. 140ᵛ); MS Sloane 1446 (f. 66ᵛ); MS Sloane 1792 (f. 121ᵛ); **Corpus Christi College, Oxford:** MS 328 (f. 90); **Folger:** V.a. 345 (p. 61); **Rosenbach:** MS 239/27 (p. 209).

✦ Donald W. Foster, " 'Against the perjured falsehood of your tongues': Frances Howard on the Course of Love," *English Literary Renaissance* 24 (Winter 1994), 72–103.

• • •

32. Sir Walter Ralegh (1554–1618), "Of Man:," 45. Pr. Orlando Gibbons, *The First Set of Madrigals and Motets* [musical setting] (London, 1612). Richard Brathwaite, *Remains After Death* (London, 1618), sig. L2ᵛ.

For biographical information about Ralegh, see **HolM 29 notes**.

Like most poems associated with Ralegh, this one poses daunting textual problems. Latham used Orlando Gibbons's musical setting for her copy-text, but there is no evidence that this was Ralegh's authorized or original lyric. The poem is found in many verse miscellanies, but there is little textual agreement between any two of them. Latham says she has seen no two texts alike (144), and Michael Rudick (1986) has seen verbal similitude in only two (77). Rudick has attempted to reconstruct Ralegh's original poem by coalescing textual variants with logical analysis of the poem's meaning. His conclusions are fascinating, but he assumes a logical structure the poem may never have had.

However, to suggest a textual history that may lead to the Holgate, Rudick believes that the final couplet, "Thus march we playing to our latest rest, / Onely we dye in earnest, that no Iest" (Gibbons, Latham, et al., but absent in the Holgate) was not written by Ralegh because its meaning is incongruous with the rest of the poem, especially the sense that life is a "play of passion." Moreover, the final couplet does not follow from ll. 7–8, nor does the triviality suggested by the couplet work with the overall tone and meaning of the poem.

If Rudick's argument is correct, then the Holgate's transcription is unrelated to Gibbons's musical setting. The earliest manuscript that ascribes the poem to Ralegh is Marsh's Library, MS Z 3.5.2. It is described as a late Elizabethan-early Jacobean text. Like the Holgate, it does not include the final couplet. Its principal difference in terms of meaning is l. 4, "tragedye" instead of "comedie." 'Tragedye' is more closely related to the tone and meaning of the poem than is "comedie," a word that appears in many of the manuscripts.

It is clear that the Holgate text is unrelated to Gibbons's musical text. Its structure suggests an early original, but one where changes were made that were compounded over the years until they appeared in the Holgate. Rudick's analysis suggests the parameters of how complicated this textual history is, and how the Holgate version came to exist.

> **1. play of passion.** A passion play, in accord with the poem's theatrical conceit.
> **2. diuision.** In music, a run, a quick-paced variation on a theme (*OED*).

✦ Manuscripts: Crum W527, W524, W529, W547; Beal RaW 224–293; Yale W0463 ✦ *Aberdeen University Library:* MS 29 (p. 141); *Bodleian:* MS Ashmole 36/37 (f. 35); MS Ashmole 38 (p. 154); MS Ashmole 47 (ff. 51ᵛ–52); Don.c.54 (f. 3ᵛ, 11); Don.c.57 (f. 38ᵛ) *musical setting*; MS Douce f (f. 5); MS Eng. poet. e. 14 (f. 101); MS Eng. poet. f. 10 (f. 92ᵛ); MS Eng. poet. f. 27 (p. 91); B58: (f. 11, fol. 33) *musical setting*; MS Rawl. poet. 65 (f. 92); MS Rawl. poet. 117 (f. 271 [rev]); MS Rawl. poet. 172 (f. 8); *Bradford Central Library:* Hopkinson MSSS, Vol 34 (p. 31); *British Library:* Add, MS 15227 (f. 14ᵛ, Tho: Dod, Jesu); Add. MS 18044 (f. 154ᵛ, Raleigh); Add. MS 21433 (f. 113ᵛ, Ralegh); Add. MS 25303 (f. 118ᵛ); Add. MS 25707 (f. 7ᵛ); Add. MS 30982 (f. 139 [rev]); Egerton MS 923 (f. 8); Egerton MS 2230 (f. 7ᵛ); Egerton MS 2725 (f. 60ᵛ); MS Harley 3511 (f. 1); MS Harley 6057 (f. 14ᵛ); MS Harley 7332 (f. 215,Rauleigh); Lansdowne MS 498 (f. 60); Lansdowne MS 777 (f. 70); MS Sloane 1489 (f. 21ᵛ, Ralegh); MS Sloane 1792 (f. 56, 113); *Chetham's Library, Manchester:* Mun. A 3.47 (f. [30ᵛ]); *Corpus Christi College, Oxford:* MS 176 (f. 7ᵛ); MS 328 (f. 19); *Folger:* V.a. 97 (p. 7); V.a. 162 (f. 32); V.a. 170 (p. 44); V.a. 245 (f. 41ᵛ); V.a. 262 (p. 82); V.a. 319 (f. 2, Raughly); V.a. 339 (f. 18); V.a. 345 (p. 14); *Harvard:* MS Eng. 686 (f. 17, 67ᵛ); MS Eng. 703 (f. 15ᵛ); *Owned by Sir Geoffrey Keynes:* Bibliotheca Bibliographici No. 1863 (f. 2); *John Rylands University Library of Manchester:* Rylands English MS 410 (f. 20); *Leeds Archives Department:* MX 237 (f. 7ᵛ, Tho: Harding); *Leicestershire Record Office:* DG.7/Lit. 2 (f. 342ᵛ); DG.9/2796 (p. 67); *Marsh's Library, Dublin:* MS Z 3.5.21 (f. 126, Rawly); *National Library of Wales:* NLW.MS 12443A, pt. ii (pp. 9–20); *University of Nottingham:* Portland MS Pw V 37 (p. 169, Benjamin Stone); *Rosenbach:* MS 239/23 (p. 182); MS 239/27 (p. 187); MS 243/4 (p. 49, John Donne); MS 1083/16 (p. 5); MS 1083/17 (f. 80ᵛ); *St. John's College, Cambridge:* MS S. 32 (James 423) (f. 4); *South African Library, Cape Town:* MS Grey 7 a 29 (p. 139); *University of Texas at Austin:* MS File/Herrick, R)Works B (p. 113); *Victoria and Albert Museum:* Dyce Collection, Cat. No. 44 (Pressmark 25.F.39) (f. 70ᵛ); *Westminster Abbey:* MS 41 (f. 32); *Yale:* Osborn b 62 (pp. 46–47); Osborn b 200 (pp. 112–13); Osborn b 205 (f. 44); Osborn b 208 (p. 59); Osborn fb 69, p. 204.

✦ Latham, xiii–lvi, 51, 143–45; Rudick li–liv, 69–70, 165. Also see Rudick, "The Text of Ralegh's Lyric, 'What is our life?'" *Studies in Philology* 83 (Winter, 1986), 76–87.

• • •

33. Benjamin Stone (?). "On Samburne the Shreife of Oxford: A: Dī: 1609," 46–47. Pr. *Parnassus Biceps*, 22–23; *J. Cleaveland Reviv'd* (London, 1659), 79–81; *London Drollery* (London, 1673), 89.

C. F. Main, on the basis of an ascription in Harvard MS 686, attributes this poem to Benjamin Stone. Although several other manuscripts attribute the poem to Stone, it is not certain that the attribution is correct (see list of manuscripts below).

Benjamin Stone received his B. A. from New College, Oxford, in 1609. He came from Somerset (Redding 277). The poem is obviously satiric, describing events at Oxford, 1609, when "Henry
Samborne, of Moulsford in Berkshire, sheriff of Oxfordshire . . . offended the undergraduates by
his stinginess in providing refreshments at the Lenten assizes" (Main 448). Lines 43–46 were often
printed as a separate epigram, "Our Oxford sheriff of late is grown so wise" (Crum O–1310).

> **6. beeues.** Poetic for cattle (*OED*).
>
> **23. Syze.** Assize. Main describes this as the Lenten assizes, but there is no contextual evidence
> to support that assertion. There were many assizes, among them accessing the cost of bread and
> wine (*OED*).
>
> **26. ferkin.** A small cask for liquids holding a quarter of a barrel or half a kilderkin.
>
> **26. Kilderken.** Half a barrel. Redding says it is the equivalent of sixteen to eighteen barrels
> (481).
>
> **48. Cut . . . long tayle.** Of animals that have long tails, they have been either "cut" or remain
> "long tayle" (*OED*).

✦ Manuscripts: Crum F293; Redding: No. 243; Yale: F0263 ✦ *Bodleian:* MS Douce f (f. 17);
MS Malone 19 (p. 62); MS Malone 21 (f. 62, Ben Stone); MS Rawl. poet. 117 (f. 190ᵛ[rev]);
MS Rawl. poet. 199 (p. 42, Ben Stone); Egerton MS 923 (f. 14); Egerton MS 2421 (f. 20); MS
Sloane 542 (f. 28ᵛ); *Corpus Christi College, Oxford:* MS 328 (f. 5ᵛ); *Folger:* V.a. 97 (p. 119,
Stone); V.a. 103, pt. I (f. 70, Stone); V.a. 124 (f. 26ᵛ); V.a. 262 (pp. 94–96, Ben Stone); *Harvard:*
MS Eng. 686 (pp. 36–37, Ben Stone); *Rosenbach:* MS 239/27 (p. 174); MS 1083/16 (f. 76); MS
1083/16 (pp. 170–71); *Owned by Edwin Wolfe II:* MS (pp. 127–30); *Yale:* Osborn b 137 (p.
176); Osborn b 200 (pp. 4–6); Osborn b 208 (p. 58).

✦ C. F. Main, "Notes on Some Poems Attributed to William Strode," *Philological Quarterly* 34.4
(October 1955), 444–48; Redding, 227, 477–81.

• • •

34. Thomas Carew (1595?–1640). "On a Sigh," 47. Pr. Thomas Carew, *Poems* (London, 1640), 17;
Poems: written by Wil Shake-speare. Gent. (London, 1640).

The theme of Carew's poem is from Petrarch, *Rime-sparse*, no. 153, "Ite, caldi sospiri, al fredo core."

The printed version of this poem is thirty-two lines; Holgate's text deletes the most sexually
explicit references. The Petrarchan *rime* lacks the overt sexuality.

For biographical and critical information on Carew, see **HolM 59 notes.**

> **9. Hibla.** A town in Sicily known for the honey produced on its neighboring hills.

✦ Manuscripts: Crum G215, G201, G233; Beal Vol. II, pt 1, CwT 545–593; Yale G0184 ✦
Aberdeen University Library: MS 29 (pp. 172–73); *Bodleian:* MS Ashmole 47 (f. 36ᵛ); Don.b.9
(ff. 20ᵛ–21ᵛ); Don.c.57 (f. 72)*; Don.d.58 (f. 23ᵛ); MS Eng. poet. c. 50 (ff. 115ᵛ–16, f. 127); MS
Eng. poet. e. 37 (f. 78); MS Eng. poet. e. 112 (f. 80); MS Eng. poet. f. 27 (pp. 176–77); MS Firth
e. 4 (p. 116); MS Malone 16 (p. 11); MS Rawl. poet. 209 (f. 5); *British Library:* Add. MS 11811
(f. 7); Add. MS 21433 (f. 141); Add. MS 25303 (f. 153ᵛ); Add. MS 30982 (ff. 145–44ᵛ [rev]);
Add. MS 53723 (f. 96)*; MS Harley 3511 (f. 65); MS Sloane 1446 (f. 74); MS Sloane 1792 (ff.
130–31); *Corpus Christi College, Oxford:* MS 176 (f. 18); MS 328 (ff. 19ᵛ–20); *Edinburgh University Library:* MS H.-P. Coll. 401 (f. 102ᵛ); *Folger:* V.a. 96 (ff. 46ᵛ–47ᵛ); V.a. 97 (p. 61); V.a.
319 (f. 33ᵛ); V.a. 322 (p. 87); V.a. 345 (p. 10); V.b. 43 (f. 6); *Harvard:* fMS 626 (ff. 73ᵛ–74); MS
Eng. 686 (f. 51); MS Eng. 703 (f. 22); *Huntington Library:* HM 116 (73–75); HM 46323 (p. 2);
Leeds Archives Department: MX 237 (f. 16ᵛ); *New York Public Library:* Music Division, Drexel

MS 4257 (No. 31); **Rosenbach:** MS 239/27 (p. 49); MS 240/7 (pp. 47–48, 88); MS 243/4 (pp. 110–11); MS 1083/17 (pp. 27–28); **South African Library, Cape Town:** MS Grey 7 a 29 (pp. 78–79); **Owned by Edwin Wolfe II:** MS (pp. 1–11); **Yale:** Osborn b 205 (f. 75).

    * Musical setting

♦ Dunlap, 11–12, 219–20, 289–90.

• • •

35. Richard Corbett (1582–1636), "D.C: to yᵉ M:B: 1622:," 47. Pr. *Poëtica Stromata* (n. p., 1648), 23–24.

    The title of the poem is noteworthy: only six known manuscript copies refer to Buckingham as a Marquis, which in 1622 was correct. Generally, manuscripts of this poem identify Buckingham as a Duke. He did not become a Duke until 18 May 1623. Buckingham, of course, was very famous, so it is fair to assume that the copy-text identified the correct title or that the scribe wanted this copy of the poem to identify Buckingham's title when the poem was actually written. However, based on the time sequence of many of the poems transcribed in the manuscript, the poem was most likely transcribed between New Year's Day, 1622 and 18 May 1623.

    The exact occasion of this poem is unknown; however, poems written as New Year's gifts were quite common (Kerrigan 336). Corbett was made Dean of Christ Church, 24 June 1620. As the poem makes clear, Corbett "regarded Buckingham as the agent for his securing the deanery" (*ODNB*).

    The *Poëtica Stromata* text has twenty-two lines not found in the Holgate text. They help clarify the political significance of this poem.

> „For, when as goodnesse doth so overflow,
> „The conscience bindes not to restore, but owe: *10*
> Requitall were presumption; and you may
> Call me ungratefull, while I strive to pay.
> Nor with a morall lesson doe I shift,
> Like one that meant to save a better gift;
> Like very poore, or conterfeite poore men,
> Who to preserve their Turky, or their hen,
> Doe offer up themselves: No, I have sent
> A kind of guift, will last by being spent,
> Thankes sterling: far above the Bullion rate
> Of horses, hangings, iewells, or of plate. *20*
> O you that know the choosing of that One,
> Know a true Diamond from a Bristow stone;
> You know those men alwaies are not the best
> In their intent, that lowdest can protest:
> But that a Prayer from the Convocation,
> Is better then the Commons Protestation.
> Trust those that at the test their lives will lay,
> And know no Arts, but to Deserve, and Pray:
> Whilst they, that buy preferment without praying,
> Begin with broyles, and finish with betraying.

The Commons Protestation mentioned in l. 26 (above) occurred in December 1621 when the House of Commons asserted its right to free speech, especially with regard to religion and foreign policy. James quashed the issue by dissolving Parliament and removing the Protestation from the official journals. Afterwards, several leading members of Commons were punished: some were imprisoned, others sent to Ireland or the Palatinate. Conrad Russell writes: "The fiasco of the second session of 1621 had many consequences. One of the most important . . . is that it did a great deal to increase distrust of Buckingham. In the next Parliament, when Buckingham did want war with Spain, he found that a number of people were surprisingly reluctant to believe him" (144). From his later writings, there is no evidence that Corbett ever came to accept that view.

No other surviving text is abridged in this manner. Most Corbett poems found in the Holgate have many more substantive variants when compared to the seventeenth-century print editions of his poems, *CEP* and *Poëtica Stromata*.

For biographical information on Richard Corbett, see **HolM 11** notes.

✦ Manuscripts: Crum W1163; Beal Vol. II, pt. 1, CoR 389–408; Yale W1033 ✦ *Aberdeen University Library:* MS 29 (pp. 24–25); *Bodleian:* MS Ashmole 47 (f. 91); MS Eng. poet. e. 14 (f. 9ᵛ); MS Eng. poet. e. 97 (p. 154); MS Rawl. poet. 26 (f. 60); MS Rawl. poet. 152 (ff. 17ᵛ–18); MS Rawl. poet. 199 (pp. 28–29); *Bradford Central Library:* Hopkinson MSS, Vol 34 (p. 33); *British Library:* Add. MS 30982 (f. 57); MS Harley 1221 (f. 75ᵛ); MS Harley 6038 (f. 19ᵛ); MS Harley 6931 (f. 21ᵛ); MS Sloane 1792 (ff. 49ᵛ–50); *Folger:* V.a. 345 (p. 124); V.b. 43 (f. 25); *Huntington Library:* HM 198, pt. 1 (p. 173); *University of Texas at Austin:* MS File/ (Herrick, R) Works B (pp. 251–52); *Westminster Abbey:* MS 41 (f. 20); *Yale:* Osborn b 200 (p. 215).

✦ B&TR, 71–72, 143. Conrad Russell, *Parliaments and English Politics, 1621–1629* (Oxford: Clarendon Press, 1979); John Kerrigan, "Thomas Carew," *Proceedings of the British Academy* 74 (1988), 311–50. For extended discussion of the political history surrounding the poem, see Robert Zaller, *The Parliament of 1621* (Berkeley: Univ. of California Press, 1971).

• • •

36. Barton Holyday [?] (1593–1661)."Mʳ: B. H: verses to the Q: A: as shee past by Oxford," 48–50. Unprinted.

The poem is ascribed to Corbett in Rosenbach MS 1083/16, but that ascription is rejected by B&TR (174).

Redding suggests that the Holgate ascription to "Mr B: H:" probably refers to Barton Holyday, who was at Oxford in 1617. He wrote a play, *The Marriage of the Arts* (1621) that James did not like (450). He also translated Persius, Juvenal, and Horace. Holyday was admitted to Christ Church in 1605, received his B.A. in 1612, M.A. in 1615, and D.D. in 1642. He was appointed vicar of Ashelworth, Gloucester, and Brize Norton, Oxfordshire, in 1623. He was made archdeacon of Oxford in 1625, also rector of Emmington in 1638, of Cromwell, Oxfordshire (date unknown), and of Chilton, Berkshire in 1656. A noted cleric, Holyday also served as a chaplain to Charles I (Turner 2, 320).

Anne of Denmark (1574–1619) was the queen consort of James I. She was the daughter of Frederick II of Denmark and Norway. She married James in 1589. She later converted to Catholicism, but officially she was a Protestant. The Queen traveled through Oxford on her way to meet the King, who was returning home after his visit to Scotland. James made only this one visit to Scotland after being crowned King of England, stopping at Woodstock (l. 15) on the return journey. **HolM 62,** Corbett's "To the Lord Mordent," also involves James's return from Scotland.

The "Saints" mentioned in the poem (l. 18) are chapels and churches in Oxford, each one wanting to hold the appropriate ceremony to celebrate the Queen's visit. Unless otherwise noted, all annotations below are based on *Survey of the Antiquities of the City of Oxford Composed in 1661–66 by Anthony á Wood*, ed. Andrew Clark, vol. 2, *Churches and Religious Houses* (Oxford: Clarendon Press, 1890).

> **26. Sᵗ Friswid.** Founded A.D. 727, as the poem states, it is located near the South Gate (58–62).
>
> **29. Sᵗ Aldate.** Built "a little after the first coming of the Saxons," it is on the west side of Fish Street, within the wall (33–39).
>
> **36. Broad-gates.** Broadgate College, the forerunner of Pembroke College (Redding 450).
>
> **37. Sᵗ Ebbs.** Predates the Norman Conquest, found on the west side of Penifarthing Street, "not far from the west gate" (52–55).
>
> **43. Sᵗ Thomas.** Founded A.D. 1141, it is within the limits of Osney Abbey, on the west end of the city (112–17).
>
> **55. Sᵗ Marten.** It is in the middle of the city at Carfax. Named for the Bishop of Tours (also known as St. Martin of Tours) in France, who died "anno 399. . . and its dedication day was <27 January> on the 6 of the calends of February being St. Julian's Day" (80–85).
>
> **61. Sᵗ Michaell.** Oxford has two St. Michaels, one at the North Gate (86–90), the other at the South Gate (91–93).
>
> **66. Sᵗ Maries.** Mary Magdalen was "without the North Gate" (74–80).
>
> **73. Sᵗ Giles.** Also without the North Gate, founded ca. A.D. 1120 (65–70).
>
> **85. Sᵗ Peter.** As the poem says, there are two St. Peters: one near the East Gate (97–102), the other, St. Peter in the Bayle, near the West Gate (102–6).
>
> **110. Holy-well.** St. Cross's church, or St. Crosse of Halywell, is at the east end of Holywell Street, built around the time of William the Conqueror (50–52).
>
> **115. Sᵗ Clement.** Without the East Gate on Brugsut Street, it was confirmed by Henry I in 1122 (48–50).

✦ Manuscripts: Crum I–133 ✦ ***Bodleian:*** MS Rawl. D. 1048 (f. 66); ***Rosenbach:*** MS 1083/16 (p. 150, Dr. Corbett).

This and the next poem, **HolM 37**, follow sequentially in MS Rawl. D. 1048. They both concern Queen Anne's passing through Oxford on her way to meet James at Woodstock, September 1617. Most likely, the poems were copied after 1619 when Anne died because **HolM 15**, "In obitū – Annæ Reginæ" is a Latin elegy on her passing, and **HolM 38**, "You towringe spiritts whose Art-irradiate eyne," is also occasioned by her death.

✦ Redding, 442–50. Alberta T. Turner, "The Oxford and Cambridge Poetical Miscellanies, 1600–1660" (Diss. The Ohio State University, 1947).

• • •

37. Anon., "To Q: A most excellent Maiestie," 50–51. Unprinted.

The anticipation described in **HolM 36** must have been frustrated by the Queen's short visit to Oxford. The Bodleian manuscript is headed "To Queen Anne on her visit to Oxford, September 1617." For further commentary, see **HolM 36 notes.** For James's visit to Scotland, see **HolM 62 notes.**

> **16. Hyperborean Axeltree.** Axeltree is simply an axle, but in this context it means axis, as solar rotation, implied by l. 17, "for halfe the yeere they see no day." In Greek mythology, Hyperboreans were a legendary race of Apollo worshipers who lived in the far north (*OCD*).

✦ Manuscripts: Crum A1288 ✦ ***Bodleian:*** MS Rawl. D. 1048 (f. 69).

38. Robert Fletcher [?], fl. 1586), "An Elegie vppon the death of Q: A:," 52–54. Unprinted.

The attribution to Robert Fletcher is based on the initials found in BL Add. MS 21433 and BL Add. MS 25303, and that there are no other candidates. R. W. Saunders identifies no other poets with those initials. Very little is known about Robert Fletcher. He was from Warwickshire, studied at Merton College, later became a schoolmaster and clergyman in Taunton. His two published works were *An Introduction to the Looue of God* (1581) and *The Song of Solomon* (1586) (Saunders 52–53).

This is the third funeral elegy to Queen Anne found in the Holgate manuscript, but unlike other royal family members who have their elegies grouped together, Prince Henry **HolM 101–5,** and James **HolM 149–151,** Anne's funeral elegies are separate, **HolM 2, HolM 15,** and the present entry. This poem does, of course, follow two poems concerning her visit to Oxford in 1617.

Anne of Denmark (1574–1619) married James in 1589, fourteen years before he became King of England. Her brother was King Christian of Denmark (1588–1648). In England, she became active in courtly entertainments. She commissioned two masques by Samuel Daniel and four by Ben Jonson. She actively collected art and books. She also patronized an acting company for children, the Children of the Queen's Revels (*ODNB*).

Although Anne's true sympathies were generally believed to have been with the Catholic Church, she was publicly a Protestant, and on her deathbed, in the presence of the King and the Archbishop of Canterbury, she professed Protestantism (*ODNB*).

For further discussion of the circumstances of her death, see **HolM 2 notes.**

> **3. Crimtts.** Comets, see **HolM 2.**
> **8. Iacobs staffe.** James.
> **77. viduate.** Destitute or widowed (*OED*).
> **93. Charle-Maine Eliza.** Her daughter Elizabeth was the Princess of the Palatine (l. 94).

✦ Manuscripts: Crum Y383 ✦ *Bodleian:* MS Firth d. 7 (f. 140); *British Library:* Add. MS 21433 (ff. 178ᵛ–81, R:ff:L); Add. MS 25303 (ff. 127–28ᵛ, R.ff); *Cambridge:* MS Add. 4138 (ff. 44ᵛ–45ᵛ).

✦ R. W. Saunders, *A Biographical Dictionary of Renaissance Poets and Dramatists, 1520–1650* (Sussex: Harvester Books, 1983).

• • •

39. William Lewis (1592–1667), "Verses made on Sr ff. B: when hee was Lord Chancellor," 55–59. No seventeenth-century printings.

Lewis is the best and only candidate for the authorship of this poem, and there is no reason to dispute the poem is his. He received a B. A. from Hart Hall, Oxford (1608), and an M. A. from Oriel College, Oxford (1612). He then took holy orders and became chaplain to Sir Francis Bacon, Lord Chancellor. He was an Arminian. In 1618, he returned to Oriel College as Provost, being elected to that position through Bacon's influence. He served as Provost until 1621 when Bacon was removed from office. Lewis then proceeded to Paris on a diplomatic mission but returned to England to become chaplain and secretary to George Villiers, Duke of Buckingham. After Buckingham's assassination in 1628, he was appointed chaplain to Charles I, this last at the urging of William Laud. During the Commonwealth, he was forced to live abroad where his two sons converted to Roman Catholicism (*DNB*).

Sir Francis Bacon (1561–1626) became Lord Chancellor in January 1618. His term ended in May 1621, when he was impeached. At question were monopolies and letters patent which granted individuals or groups exclusive rights to operate certain businesses or even carry on certain legal functions, such as the right to probate wills. The House of Commons accused Bacon of taking bribes. Roger Lockyer writes that the King did not support Bacon because he wanted to appear in favor of reform (99). Unfortunately, the charges against Bacon were true, and he decided not to fight them. He was fined £40,000, sent to the Tower, and barred from holding any future office.

Buckingham was Bacon's protegé. They frequently corresponded, and with the King's consent, Bacon acted as Buckingham's tutor when the favorite first gained access to high political circles (Lockyer 29). During the scandal Buckingham supported his mentor but was unable to help him because of the clear evidence against Bacon.

The title of the Holgate text implies no criticism of Bacon; however, not all exemplars of this poem are so neutral. Morfill prints a title from British Library Add. MS 25303, which is clearly derogatory. His text, however, comes from British Library MS Sloane 826. Its title reads: "Certen verses made in the behalfe of Sr Francis Bacon, whoe was Lorde Keeper of Englande Anno 1620; but then put off by the Parlement howese for some occations to me vnknowen" (Morfill 271).

> **75. cleased.** Error for "clensed."
> **95. predecessor's Ghost.** Bacon's predecessor as Lord Chancellor was Sir Thomas Egerton, Lord Ellesmore. At Egerton's death in 1617, Bacon asserted that it was Egerton's wish that he, Bacon, might become Lord Chancellor (*DNB*).
> **126. seild.** Seld, seldom.
> **133. patent.** Letters patent.
> **137. referrers.** Referees. Before a patent could be approved, it was first submitted to referees, who, upon approval, sent it to the King for formal approval.

✦ Manuscripts: Crum W1641, W1635; Yale W1471 ✦ **Bodleian:** MS Ashmole 38 (pp. 10–12); MS Eng. poet. f. 10 (f. 104, William Lewis); MS Rawl. B. 151 (f. 101); MS Rawl. poet. 26 (f. 101); MS Rawl. poet. 84 (f. 64ᵛ [rev]); MS Rawl. poet. 160 (f. 25); **British Library:** Add. MS 10308 (ff. 128ᵛ–32); Add. MS 25303 (ff. 83–86, Mor); Add. MS 29303 (f. 3ᵛ, Mor); Egerton MS 2725 (ff. 43–45); MS Harley 2127 (ff. 27ᵛ, 77); MS Sloane 826 (ff. 4, 5, 8); MS Sloane 1489 (f. 46ᵛ); MS Sloane 1792 (f. 109, Mor); Stowe MS 962 (f. 52ᵛ, Will Lewes); **Folger:** V.a. 192, pt. II (f. 7); V.a. 162 (f. 2); V.a. 345 (p. 127, Mr. Lewis); **Huntington Library:** HM 198, pt. 1 (pp. 37–40); **Leeds University:** Brotherton Collection, MS Lt. q 44 (ff. 10–12ᵛ); **National Library of Scotland:** Hawthornden VIII MS 2060 (ff. 53–59); **Yale:** Osborn b 197 (pp. 139–43); Osborn b 200 (pp. 19–23); Osborn fb 23 (p. 269).

"There is also another [text] among the Jackson MSS presented to the University of Edinburgh by Mr. Halliwell (p. 82), this headed 'In laudem Francisci Baconis olim totius Angliæ cancellar'" (Morfill 270).

✦ W. R. Morfill, ed., *Ballads from Manuscripts*, II (Hertford and London: The Ballad Society, 1873; rpt. New York: AMS, 1968), 270–76. Also see Roger Lockyer, *Buckingham* (London and New York, 1981), especially 90–100; Marotti, 105.

• • •

40. William Herbert, Earl of Pembroke [?] (1580–1630). Untitled, "Muse gett thee to a Cell, and wont to singe," 59. Pr. *P&R*, 28.

It is impossible to say with certainty who wrote this poem: Margaret Crum attributes it to "Sir G. H." on the basis of its ascription in Bodleian MS Eng. poet. e. 14. Gary Waller ascribes it to William Herbert because it is included in the first fifty-four pages of *P&R*. That volume, printed thirty years after Pembroke's death, purports to be a collection of poems by William Herbert and his friend

Sir Benjamin Rudyerd. The transmission of some texts in this printed edition may be connected with sources used by the Holgate scribe. The manuscript contains nineteen poems later printed in *P&R*, some of which are very similar to the printed copies.

William Herbert was the son of Henry Herbert, second Earl of Pembroke, and Mary Sidney, sister of Sir Philip Sidney. He was the first cousin of Lady Mary Wroth, by whom he fathered two children, William and Katherine. As a child, his tutor was Samuel Daniel. He matriculated at New College, Oxford at the age of thirteen. He was imprisoned but later rusticated by Queen Elizabeth (1601) because he impregnated one of her ladies in waiting, Mary Fitton, whom he refused to marry. The child died soon after its birth. He regained favor during the reign of James I, becoming Lord Warden of the Stanneries (1604), Lord Lieutenant of Cornwall (1605), Warden of the Forest of Dean (1608), Privy Councillor (1611), and Lord Chamberlain of the Royal Household (1615). He also became Lord Chancellor of Oxford (1617), a post he held until his death. After he died, Broadgates College was renamed Pembroke College. In politics, he was considered anti-Spanish (*ODNB*).

Herbert was a prominent literary patron. Jonson dedicated his Epigrams to him. William Browne lived in his home, Wilton House. Chapman dedicated a sonnet to him in his translation of the *Iliad*. Shakespeare's First Folio (1623) is dedicated to William Herbert and his brother Philip. He is also a candidate for the famous "W. H." of Shakespeare's *Sonnets*.

Herbert's poems were published in 1660 by John Donne, Jr. The full title of the volume is *Poems, Written by the Right Honorable William Earl of Pembroke, Lord Steward of his Majesties Houshold. Whereof Many of which are answered by way of Repartee, by Sr. Benjamin Ruddier, Knight. With several Distinct Poems, Written by them Occasionally and Part.* The volume is commonly referred to as *Pembroke and Ruddier* (*P&R*). Unfortunately, the book was very poorly edited, and we have no assurance about who wrote which poems. In addition to the two named authors, the volume includes poems by Sir Walter Ralegh, Thomas Carew, Christopher Brooke, John Donne, Dudley North, Michael Drayton, Sir Henry Wotton, and William Strode (Waller 164). More important to know, however, would be how the poems were selected. *P&R* was edited by Donne through the patronage of the Countess of Devonshire. She had been a friend of William Herbert and, in fact, was with him the night before he died. Waller believes that at least some of the poems came from her own collection (163). Moreover, in the dedication to the 1660 edition, Donne writes that two musicians, Henry Lawes and Nicholas Lanier, contributed lyrics to *P&R*. It is a collection of royalist poetry published to celebrate the return of Charles II (Marotti, 277–78). By examining the organization of the text, Gary Waller infers that the poems written by William Herbert are found in the first fifty-four pages of the edition, and that for the remainder of the text, Donne added whatever he thought appropriate to complete the text as it now appears (163–65). The Herbert poems include four debate poems he had written with Benjamin Rudyerd (c. 1602) when they were together at the Inns of the Court (see **HolM 120–21**). Waller writes that the declamatory style of these poems lends itself to the speaking voice (173).

This is the first of several poems found in the Holgate that bear a striking resemblance to poems found in British Library Add. MS 23229. It is in hand A as described in the Introduction, p. sviii–xx. Collation indicates the similarity between the two manuscripts and the text of the poem as it later appeared in *P&R*.

+ Collations: *P&R* / BL Add. MS 23229 (hand A) *BL–A* 3 thy] thine *P&R*, *BL–A* ; 9 sighs] sights *BL–A* ; 13 by] with (*corrected in HolM text margin*) *P&R* ; 14 the] your *P&R*

+ Manuscripts: Crum M547a + **Bodleian:** MS Eng. poet. e. 14 (f. 32); **British Library:** Add. MS 23229 (f. 54); **Huntington Library:** HM 198, pt. 2 (f. 54).

+ Waller, 53–92, 158–87; Marotti, 277–78.

41. Anon., untitled, "Is shee not wondrous faire? O but I see," 60. Pr. "A Lovers passion," *Wits Interpreter* (1655), 15–16 (2nd numbering); *Cupid's Master-Piece* (1656?), sig. B3.

Thomas Carew's modern editor, Rhodes Dunlap, includes this sonnet in his section of poems of "Uncertain Authorship." Four manuscripts ascribe it to William Lewis, who wrote **HolM 39**, which concludes on the previous page.

For further commentary, see **HolM 42 notes**.

✦ Manuscripts: Crum I–1750, W50; Yale I–1460 ✦ *Bodleian:* MS Ashmole 38 (p. 155); MS Ashmole 47 (f. 38); Don.d.58 (f. 84ᵛ); MS Douce f (f. 20ᵛ); MS Eng. poet. e. 97 (p. 187, Dr. Lewes); MS Malone 16 (p. 20); MS Rawl. poet. 84 (f. 93ᵛ [rev]); MS Rawl. poet. 153 (f. 15); *British Library:* Add. MS 15227 (f. 12, W.S.); Add. MS 30982 (f. 155); MS Harley 1631 (f. 2); MS Sloane 1446 (f. 76); MS Sloane 1792 (f. 21); *Folger:* V.a. 97 (p. 64); V.a. 162 (f. 91ᵛ); V.a. 170 (p. 43, Mr Lewis); V.a. 245 (f. 41, Mr. Lewis of Oriall); V.a. 262 (p. 50); V.a. 322 (p. 53); V.a. 345 (p. 59, Mr Lewes of Oriel); V.a. 319 (f. 28); *Harvard:* MS Eng. 626 (ff. 2ᵛ–3); *Huntington Library:* HM 116; *Rosenbach:* MS 239/23 (p. 72); MS 239/27 (p. 41); MS 243/4 (p. 89); MS 240/7 (p. 84); MS 1083/17 (p. 116); *St. John's College: Cambridge:* MS S. 32 (James 423) (f. 41ᵛ, Th: Ca:; f. 9ᵛ, Tho: Cary); *Yale:* Osborn b 200 (p. 47); Osborn b 205 (f. 34).

✦ Dunlap, 192; Thompson, 115, 522.

• • •

42. Anon., untitled, "Nor teares shall lessen greife, nor sighes impart," 60. Unprinted.

This poem is not found in any other known miscellany. However, note its similarity—both textually and stylistically—to the poem it follows (**HolM 41**). The text of each is transcribed in a broad, sweeping hand. The entire page uses only twenty-six lines, whereas pages in the Holgate typically use between thirty and forty. The handwriting on this page is more florid than usual. Broad ascenders and descenders typify each transcription. For example, *shee*, 41.1, and *shall*, 42.1: the *h* in both words extends far above the line and crosses back over the preceding *s*. In the final line of each poem, *againe*, 41.14, and *away*, 42.12, each word's respective descenders, *g* and *y*, sweep atypically far to the left. The capital letters that begin each individual line in both poems are broad and extend dramatically toward the left margin.

The vocabulary in each poem is similar. Many words have only one syllable. The poems have an open declamatory style. Both are sentimental and utilize Renaissance commonplaces. Both are structured around typical dialectical inner monologues.

• • •

43. John Donne, "Twicknam Garden," untitled, "Blasted with sighes and surrounded with teares," 61. Pr. *Poems*, 218–19.

Twickenham Park, on the Thames, was the home of Lucy, Countess of Bedford, Donne's friend and patroness. It had previously been owned by Francis Bacon (Bald 172). There is, however, no known connection between the poem and the countess. Lady Bedford resided at Twickenham Park from 1607–1618, so the poem was most likely written during that period (Smith 403).

> **7. cannot.** This is a crucial error in the transcription because it changes the meaning of ll. 6–9.
> **6–9. The spider Loue. . . I have the serpent brought.** Spiders were thought to transform anything they ate into poison. The image reverses the Eucharist, which turns bread into the body of Christ. Here "manna" is turned into "gall," thus the serpent (l. 9) destroys "True Paradise."
> **17. Mandrake . . . grow.** Gardner uses "grow" in her edition whereas Grierson reads "groane." The image makes better sense with "groane" because mandrakes were thought to groan when

pulled from the ground. Gardner rejects this reading because "the mandrake was not held to groan when *in situ*; it only groaned when it was turned up" (216), which contradicts the meaning of the image because the poet may not "leave this garden." "Grow" is found in several manuscripts collated by Shawcross: Cambridge MS Add. 5778; Trinity College, Cambridge MS R 3.12 (James 307); Harvard fMS Eng 966.4; Harvard MS Eng 966.5. It is also found in *Poems* (1633).

19. Cristall Vialls. It was believed that in ancient times mourners collected their tears in bottles and buried them with the dead.

✦ Manuscripts: Crum B392; Beal Vol. I, pt. 1, DnJ 3639–3684; Yale B0362 ✦ *Bodleian:* MS Eng. poet. c. 50 (f. 64); MS Eng. poet. e. 112 (f. 115); MS Eng. poet. f. 9 (p. 37); MS Rawl. poet. 117 (f.66); *British Library:* Add. MS 18647 (ff.14ᵛ–15); Add. MS 25707 (f. 32); MS Harley 3511 (f. 40); MS Harley 3991 (f. 113); MS Harley 4064 (f. 259); MS Harley 4955 (f. 120); Lansdowne MS 740 (f. 107ᵛ); Stowe MS 961 (f. 87); Stowe MS 962 (ff. 91ᵛ–92); *Cambridge:* MS Add. 29 (f. 16ᵛ); MS Add. 5778 (f. 60ᵛ); MS Ee. 4.14 (p. 1); *Edinburgh University Library:* MS La. III 493 (f. 88); *Emmanuel College, Cambridge:* MS 1.3.16 (James 68) II (f. 6); *Folger:* V.a. 103, pt. I (ff. 39ᵛ–40); *Harvard:* fMS Eng. 966.1 (20ᵛ–21); fMS Eng. 966.3 (ff. 28ᵛ–29); fMS Eng. 966.4 (f. 183ᵛ); MS Eng. 966.5 (f. 128ᵛ); MS Eng. 966.6 (f. 160); *Huntington Library:* EL 6893 (ff. 89ᵛ–90); HM 198, pt. 2 (f. 28ᵛ); *Owned by Sir Geoffrey Keynes:* Bibliotheca Bibliographici No. 1860 (ff. 86ᵛ–87); Bibliotheca Bibliographici No. 1861 (f. 102ᵛ); *Leeds Archives Department:* MX 237 (ff. 66ᵛ–67); *National Library of Scotland:* MS 6504 (f. 24ᵛ, 31); *National Library of Wales:* Dolau Cothi MS (pp. 83–84); *New York Public Library:* Arents Collection, Cat. No. S191 (Miscellania 54–55); *University of Nottingham:* Portland MS Pw V 37 (p. 73); *St. John's College, Oxford:* Crynes volume (pp. 218–19); SPC; SAL (pp. 90–91); *Texas Tech:* Dalhousie I (f. 45); *Trinity College, Cambridge:* MS R 3.12 (James 307) (p. 32); *Trinity College, Dublin:* MS 877 (I) (f. 41ᵛ), (II) (f. 246); *Victoria and Albert Museum:* Dyce Collection, Cat. No. 18 (Pressmark 25.F.17) (ff. 33ᵛ–34); *Yale:* Osborn b 114 (p. 258); Osborn b 148 (56–60).

✦ Gardner (1965), 83–84, 214–16; Grierson, 1: 28–29; Shawcross, 115–16, 450–51; A. J. Smith, ed. *John Donne: The Complete Poems* (London: Penguin, 1987), 82, 403–4. For a discussion of Donne's relationship with the Countess of Bedford, see Bald, 172–80.

• • •

44. John Donne, "Woman's Constancy," untitled, "Now thou hast lou'd mee one whole day," 61–62. Pr. *Poems*, 197–98.

Helen Gardner describes this dramatic monologue as the first example in English of the verse paragraph (166). Traditionally, however, the verse paragraph employs blank verse, while this poem is in rhyme.

14. Wayne. A variant of vain (*OED*).

✦ Manuscripts: Crum N577; Beal Vol. I, pt. 1, DnJ 3969–3997; Yale N0517 ✦ *Bodleian:* MS Ashmole 381 (f. 104ᵛ); MS Eng. poet. f. 9 (pp. 105–6); *British Library:* MS Harley 3991 (f. 113); MS Harley 4064 (f. 288ᵛ); MS Harley 4955 (f. 114); Add. MS 18647 (f. 22); MS Lansdowne MS 740 (f. 125); Stowe MS 962 (f. 159); *Cambridge:* MS Add. 5778 (f. 53); *Corpus Christi College, Oxford:* MS327 (ff. 7ᵛ); *Harvard:* fMS Eng. 966.3 (f. 37); fMS Eng. 966.4 (f. 207); MS Eng. 966.5 (f. 130); MS Eng. 966.6 (f. 131); *Huntington Library:* EL 6893 (f. 22); HM 198, pt. 2 (ff. 19ᵛ–20); *Owned by Sir Geoffrey Keynes:* Bibliotheca Bibliographici No. 1860 (f. 74ᵛ); Bibliotheca Bibliographici No. 1861 (f. 103ᵛ); *National Library of Scotland:* MS 6504 (f. 48ᵛ); *National Library of Wales:* Dolau Cothi MS (p. 70); *St. Paul's Cathedral:* MS 49.B.43;

South African Library, Cape Town: MS Grey 7 a 29 (p. 67); *Texas Tech:* Dalhousie I (f. 56); Dalhousie II (f. 29ᵛ); *Trinity College, Cambridge:* MS R 3.12 (James 307) (p. 49); *Trinity College, Dublin:* MS 877 (I) (f. 49ᵛ), (II) (f. 203); *Yale: Osborn b 148* (pp. 108–9).

✦ Gardner (1965), 42–43, 166; Grierson, 1:9; Shawcross, 91–92, 445.

• • •

45. John Donne, "The Expiration," "Goe, go, &," subscribed "I: D:," 62. Pr. Alfonso Ferrabosco, *Ayres* (London, 1609), no. vii; *Poems*, 295.

This was the first poem by Donne to be printed. The song was written for voice and lute. Unfortunately, there is no way to know if the transcriber of the Holgate thought of it as a poem or a song.

The music to accompany these lyrics can be found in Gardner (1965), 242, and Shawcross 147. Bodleian MS Mus. Sch. 575 contains an anonymous musical setting, also for lute and voice (Gardner 242).

> **1. leaue.** This reading agrees with Ferrabosco, not *1633*. It is more musical, but less powerful than the *1633* use of "breake." Most manuscripts have "leave."
>
> **2. sucks two soules.** The idea is that souls, not bodies, meet in kisses. Donne refers to this Platonic notion in a sermon, "Kiss the Son, lest he be angry" (*Sermons*, III, 320). The idea is also used in Castiglione, *The Courtier*, Book IV (trans. T. Hoby, 1561), sig. 2ᵛ–4ᵛ.

> ✦ Manuscripts: Crum S885; Beal Vol I, pt. 1, DnJ 1188–1214; Yale S0851 ✦ *Bodleian:* MS Eng. poet. f. 9 (p. 106); MS Eng. poet. c. 50 (f. 65); MS Mus. Sch. F. 575 (f. 8ᵛ); *British Library:* Add. MS 18647 (f. 55); Add. MS 25707 (f. 18); Stowe MS 961 (f. 69ᵛ); Stowe MS 962 (ff. 87ᵛ–88); *Cambridge:* MS Add. 29 (f. 6); *Corpus Christi College, Oxford:* MS 327 (f. 17); *Harvard:* fMS Eng. 966.3 (f. 72); fMS Eng. 966.4 (f. 187ᵛ); MS Eng. 966.5 (f. 146ᵛ); MS Eng. 966.6 (f. 151ᵛ); MS Eng. 966.7 (f. 47); *Huntington Library:* EL 6893 (f. 23); HM 198, pt. 2 (f. 23); *Owned by Sir Geoffrey Keynes:* Bibliotheca Bibliographici No. 1861 (f. 117ᵛ); *National Library of Wales:* Dolau Cothi MS (pp. 86–87); NLW.MS 5308E (f. 5ᵛ); *University of Newcastle upon Tyne:* MS Bell/White 25 (f. 20); *New York Public Library:* Arents Collection, Cat. No. S191 (Miscellanea, p. 43); TCC 3 (p. 119); *Trinity College, Dublin:* MS 877 (I) (f. 89ᵛ); *Victoria and Albert Museum:* Dyce Collection, Cat. No. 18 (Pressmark 25.F.17) (f. 30ᵛ); *Yale:* Osborn b 114 (pp. 311–12); Osborn b 148 (p. 109).

✦ Gardner (1965), 36–37, 159–60, 238–47; Grierson, 1: 68; Shawcross, 147, 457. Also see Doughtie, 294–95, 564.

• • •

46. John Donne, "Witchcraft by a Picture," untitled, "I fixt mine eye on thine, and there," 62. Pr. *Poems*, 189.

The conceit here is that the image she holds of him in her eye is washed away by tears. Lack of this poem's famous title alters its dramatic focus.

> **8. sweetest.** Although she uses the phrase "sweet salt teares" in her text of this poem, Gardner notes other manuscripts' use of the word "sweetest" and suggests that it is perhaps "the true reading and that 'sweet salt teares' is due to reminiscence of [line 16] in 'The Anniversary'"(160). "Sweetest" agrees with Group III manuscripts, Harvard fMS Eng 966.4, Harvard MS Eng 966.5, and Huntington HM 198, pt. 2.
>
> **9. powre.** Pour.

✦ Manuscripts: Crum I–166; Beal Vol. I, pt. 1, DnJ 3945–68; Yale I–0136 ✦ **Bodleian:** MS Eng. poet. f. 9 (pp. 34–35); MS Rawl. poet. 31 (f. 39b); **British Library:** Add. MS 18647 (f. 44^v); MS Harley 4064 (f. 278); Stowe MS 961 (f. 59^v); Stowe MS 962 (f. 161^v); **Harvard:** fMS Eng. 966.1 (f. 23^v); fMS Eng. 966.3 (f. 65); fMS Eng. 966.4 (f. 163); MS Eng. 966.5 (f. 139^v); **Huntington Library:** EL 6893 (f. 15); HM 198, pt. 2 (f. 23); **Owned by Sir Geoffrey Keynes:** Bibliotheca Bibliographici No. 1860 (ff. 63^v–64); Bibliotheca Bibliographici No. 1861 (f. 113); **National Library of Scotland:** Hawthornden VIII MS 2060 (f. 247); MS 6504 (f. 37^v); **National Library of Wales:** Dolau Cothi MS (p. 58); **New York Public Library:** Arents Collection, Cat. No. S191 (Miscellanea, p. 72); **South African Library, Cape Town:** MS Grey 7 a 29 (p. 63); **Trinity College, Cambridge:** MS R 3.12 (James 307) (p. 98); TCD (I) (f. 81); **Victoria and Albert Museum:** Dyce Collection, Cat. No. 18 (Pressmark 25.F.17) (f. 40); **Yale:** Osborn b 148 (pp. 54–55).

✦ Gardner (1965), 37, 160; Grierson, 1.45–46; Shawcross, 82, 442.

• • •

47. Sir Henry Wotton (1568–1639), "'On his Mistris Inconstancie' By S^r H: Wotton:," 63. Pr. Francis Davison, *Poetical Rapsody* (London, 1602), 218; *Reliquiæ Wottonianæ* (London, 1651), 516; *P&R*, 34–35. Also see Dyce1.

Wotton was born in Kent, educated at Winchester and New College, and later at Queens College, Oxford, where he wrote a tragedy, *Tancredo*, now lost. He became Provost of Eton College in 1624, a position he held until his death in 1639. He was one of the best known and highly regarded figures of the early seventeenth century. His biography appears as the second chapter of Izaak Walton's *Lives*. Although he wrote few poems, his verse was extremely popular, appearing in many miscellanies. Most frequent are those poems commonly titled "On his mistriss, the Queen of Bohemia" (**HolM 60**) and "The Character of a Happy Life" (**HolM 118**). In addition to writing poetry, he was a courtier, diplomat, MP, and educator. He also wrote *The Elements of Architecture* (1624). His poems were collected and published posthumously in *Reliquiæ Wottonianæ* (1651). He was a friend of John Donne, who wrote four verse letters to Wotton: "Here's no more newes, then vertue, I may as well"; "Sir, more then kisses, letters mingle Soules"; "Went you to counquer? And have so much lost"; and "After those reverend papers, whose soule is".

In *Reliquiæ Wottonianæ*, this poem is headed "A Poem Written by Sir Henry Wotton in His Youth." However, it is ascribed to Benjamin Rudyerd in *P&R*; Gary Waller accepts as correct the ascription of any poem found in the first fifty-four pages of that volume (164), and this poem is found on page 34. For information on Bejamin Rudyerd, see **HolM 40 notes.**

✦ Collation: *P&R.* Title: On his Mistris Inconstancie] Verses made by Sir B. R. *P&R*; **5** desires] desire *P&R*; **15** was] is *P&R*; **21** her] my *P&R*; **23** not thy] not now thy *P&R*; **25** shames] shame *P&R*.

✦ Manuscripts: Crum O–362; Beal Vol. I, pt. 2, WoH 134–157; Yale O–0292 ✦ **Bodleian:** MS Eng. poet. f. 9 (pp. 193–94); MS Rawl. poet. 31 (ff. 5^v–6); MS Rawl. poet. 147 (p. 174); **British Library:** Add. MS 11811 (ff. 31^v–32); Add. MS 33998 (f. 31^v); Egerton MS 923 (f. 17); Egerton MS 2725 (f. 102); MS Harley 4064 (f. 235); Loan MS 15/pt 2 (ff. 19^v–20); Stowe MS 962 (f. 170); **Cambridge:** MS Add. 5778 (f. 85); **Corpus Christi College, Oxford:** MS 318 (f. 43); **Derbyshire Record Office:** D258/31/16 (p. 12); **Dorset Record Office:** D51/5 (p. 211); **Folger:** D347 (pp. 4–5); V.a. 276, pt. II (ff. 15^v–16); **Harvard:** MS Eng. 703 (f. 19^v); **Huntington Library:** HM 198, pt. 2 (f. 46); **National Library of Scotland:** MS 6504 (f. 85); **National Library of Wales:**

NLW.MS 12443A, pt. ii (pp. 52–3); Peniarth MS 500B (pp. 18–20); TCD (f. 232); **Yale:** Osborn b 148 (pp. 142–43).

✦ Wotton's prose writing has been collected in Logan Pearsall Smith, ed., *The Life and Letters of Sir Henry Wotton*, 2 vols. (Oxford: Clarendon Press, 1907). There is no modern, critical edition of Wotton's verse. Also see Izaak Walton, *Lives* (London: Oxford Univ. Press, 1927; rpt. 1956).

• • •

48. Sir Francis Beaumont [?], untitled, "Why should not Pilgrims to thy body come," 63–64. Pr. *Love and Drollery* (London, 1669), no. 213.

Ascription to Beaumont rests on the ascriptions to "F. B." in four manuscripts: Bodleian MS Eng. Poet. E. 37; Bodleian MS Eng. poet. f. 9; Harvard MS Eng 966.7; and Yale Osborn b 148. Ringler argues, however, that attribution by initials is problematic (123). The poem is not included in Dyce2 or any other collection of Beaumont's verse.

For information on Francis Beaumont, see **HolM 64 notes**.

Stylistically, this poem can be compared to Beaumont's "Elegie on the Death of the Lady Marcum" (**HolM 64**).

> **24. conuent.** A transcription error. It should be *convert*.
> **25. Due.** The spelling here is probably intentional. Cf. l. 26, "doe."

✦ Manuscripts: Crum W2407; Beal Vol. I, pt. 1, BmF 144–50; W22241 ✦ **Bodleian:** MS Eng. poet. e. 37 (p. 30, F.B.); MS Eng. poet. f. 9 (pp. 206–7, ff B); **British Library:** Add. MS 25707 (f. 60ᵛ, I.D.); **Harvard:** MS Eng. 966.7 (f. 16, F.B.); **Trinity College, Dublin:** MS 877 (ff. 234ᵛ–35); **Yale:** Osborn b 148 (p. 150, F.B.).

✦ Ringler, 120–40.

• • •

49. Sir Francis Beaumont [?], untitled, "Good Madam Fowler doe not trouble mee," 64. Pr. *Wits Interpreter* (1655), 52 (2nd numbering).

This poem is ascribed to Beaumont in the following manuscripts: British Library Add. MS 33998; British Library Egerton MS 2026; British Library MS Harley 6993; Rosenbach MS 243/4; Trinity College, Dublin MS 877; and Yale Osborn b 200. It is attributed to "F. B." in Bodleian MS Eng. Poet. e. 37, Huntington HM 198, pt. 2, and Yale Osborn b 148. There is no autograph of the poem, and it is not included in any of the printed collections of Beaumont's verse.

For information on Francis Beaumont, see **HolM 64 notes**.

Also, like the previous poem, the humor of this verse is similar to Beaumont's "An Elegie on the Death of the Lady Marcum," **HolM 64**.

✦ Manuscripts: Crum G395; Beal Vol. I, pt.1, BmF 117–132; Yale G0305 ✦ **Bodleian:** MS Eng. poet. e. 37 (p. 29, F.B.); MS Eng. poet. f. 9 (pp. 136–37); MS Rawl. poet. 31 (f. 48); **British Library:** Add. MS 22603 (ff. 7ᵛ–8); Add. MS 33998 (ff. 70ᵛ–71, ffran. Beaumont); Egerton MS 2026 (f. 67, F.Beo.); MS Harley 3910 (f. 17); MS Harley 4064 (f. 292); MS Harley 6931 (f. 70, F.Beaumont); **Huntington Library:** HM 198, pt. 2 (ff. 10ᵛ–11, F.B.); **Rosenbach:** MS 243/4 (p. 13, Francis Beaumont); MS 1083/16 (pp. 275–76); **Trinity College, Dublin:** MS 877 (I) (f. 234, Francis Beaumont, *Grossart copy-text*); **Yale:** Osborn b 148 (p. 133, ff.B); Osborn b 200 (p. 218, ffrancis Beaumont).

✦ Ringler, 120–40; Alexander B. Grossart, "Literary Finds in *Trinity College*, Dublin, and Elsewhere," *Englische Studien* 26 (1899), 8.

• • •

50. John Donne, "A Fever," untitled, "Oh doe not dye for I shall hate," 64–65. Pr. *Poems*, 209–20; *Wits Interpreter* (London, 1655), 4.

This poem is based on the Petrarchan conceit that the world will be destroyed with the death of his mistress.

> **25. loosinge.** "Seizing" is the accepted reading. No other manuscript has this particular reading. The entire stanza loses its irony with Holgate's transcription.

✦ Manuscripts: Crum O–334; Beal Vol. I, pt. 1, DnJ 1305–1337; Yale O–0275 ✦ ***Bodleian:*** MS Eng. poet. e. 99 (f. 110); MS Eng. poet. f. 9 (pp. 72–73); MS Harley 4064 (f. 279); MS Harley 4955 (f. 117); ***British Library:*** Add. MS 18647 (f. 46); Lansdowne MS 740 (f. 126^v); Stowe MS 961 (f. 56^v); Stowe MS 962 (f. 125); ***Cambridge:*** MS Add. 5778 (f. 57); ***Harvard:*** fMS Eng. 966.1 (f. 39); fMS Eng. 966.3 (f. 66); fMS Eng. 966.4 (f. 200); fMS 966.6 (f. 149); MS Eng. 966.5 (f. 137); MS Eng. 966.7 (ff. 39^v–40); ***Huntington Library:*** EL 6893 (f. 16); HM 198, pt. 1 (p. 70); HM 198, pt. 2 (f. 20^v, 120); ***Owned by Sir Geoffrey Keynes:*** Bibliotheca Bibliographici No. 1860 (ff. 81–82); Bibliotheca Bibliographici No. 1861 (f. 110^v); ***National Library of Scotland:*** MS 6504 (ff. 37^v–38); ***National Library of Wales:*** Dolau Cothi MS (pp. 70–71); ***New York Public Library:*** Arents Collection, Cat. No. S191, Miscellanea, p. 50); ***St. John's College, Oxford:*** [No ref. no.] (p. 210); ***St. Paul's Cathedral:*** MS 49.B.43; SAL (p. 100); ***Trinity College, Cambridge:*** MS R 3.12 (James 307) (pp. 101–2); TCD–I (f. 82); TCD–II (f. 228); ***Victoria and Albert Museum:*** Dyce Collection, Cat. No. 18 (Pressmark 25.F.17) (f. 32); ***Yale:*** Osborn b 148 (pp.87–88).

✦ Gardner (1965), 61–62; Grierson, 1:21; Shawcross, 103–4, 448.

• • •

51. John Donne, "D^r D:" [The Legacie"], 65–66. Pr. *Poems*, 208–9.

Helen Gardner writes that this was the first of the *Songs and Sonnets* to be quoted. It was used by Katherine Thimelby (circa 1635) in a letter to her lover: "How infinite a time will it seme till I see you: for lovers hours are full eternity. Doctor Dun sayd this, but I think it" (*Tixall Letters*, ed. A. Clifford [1815], 1. 147, as quoted in Gardner [1965], 172).

> **16. couzen.** Cozen, to deceive.
> **18. coulours it and coruers had.** Gardner, et al., suggest false colors and dark corners. The manuscript's initial transcription of "corners" is probably influenced by "coulours." The superscribed "r" is clearly added later.

✦ Manuscripts: Crum W1165; Beal Vol. I, pt. 1, DnJ 1816–1857; Yale W1038 ✦ ***Bodleian:*** MS Eng. poet. e. 99 (ff. 109^v–10); MS Eng. poet. f. 9 (pp. 63–64); MS Rawl. poet. 116 (f. 52^v); MS Rawl. poet. 117 (ff. 65^v–66); ***British Library:*** Add. MS 18647 (ff. 10^v–11); Add. MS 25707 (f. 33^v); Egerton MS 2230 (f. 17^v); MS Harley 4064 (f. 272); MS Harley 4955 (f. 117); Lansdowne MS 740 (f. 106); Stowe MS 961 (f. 78^v); Stowe MS 962 (f. 122); ***Cambridge:*** MS Add. 5778 (ff. 56^v–57); ***Edinburgh University Library:*** MS La. III 493 (f. 89^v); ***Emmanuel College, Cambridge:*** MS 1.3.16 (James 68) II (ff. 4^v–5); ***Folger:*** V.a. 345 (p. 74); ***Harvard:*** fMS Eng. 966.1 (f. 37^v); fMS Eng. 966.3 (f. 25); fMS Eng. 966.4 (f. 209); MS Eng. 966.5 (f. 132); MS Eng. 966.6 (f.

132ʸ); MS Eng. 966.7 (f. 4); *Huntington Library:* EL 6893 (f. 58ʸ); HM 198, pt. 2 (ff. 28ʸ–29); *Owned by Sir Geoffrey Keynes:* Bibliotheca Bibliographici No. 1860 (ff. 80ʸ–81); Bibliotheca Bibliographici No. 1861 (f. 105ʸ); Bibliotheca Bibliographici No. 1863 (ff. 30ʸ–31); *National Library of Scotland:* MS 6504 (f. 21); *National Library of Wales:* Dolau Cothi MS (p. 76); NLW.MS 5308E (f. 4); *Rosenbach:* MS 1083/16 (pp. 204–5); *Saint John's College, Oxford:* [no reference number] (p. 208); *St. Paul's Cathedral:* MS 49.B.43 (n.p.); *South African Library, Cape Town:* MS Grey 7 a 29 (pp. 66–67); *Texas Tech:* Dalhousie I (f. 44); Dalhousie II (f. 22ʸ); *Trinity College, Cambridge:* MS R 3.12 (James 307) (pp. 22–23); TCD–I (f. 37ʸ); TCD–II (f. 202ʸ); *Yale:* Osborn b 114 (pp. 285–87); Osborn b 148 (p. 79).

✦ Gardner (1965), 50, 171–72; Grierson, 1:20; Shawcross, 50.

• • •

52. John Donne, "Off on that was betrayd by a p[er]fume" ["The Perfume"], 66–68. Pr. *Poems,* 49–51.

Although the Holgate is not considered a Group I manuscript, it follows the Group I characteristic of omitting ll. 7–8, "Though he had wont to search with glazed eyes, / As though he came to kill a Cockatrice." *Poems* shares this same omission. Shawcross lists two other manuscripts that do not have these lines, Cambridge Add. MS 5778 (Group I) and the National Library of Wales Dolau Cothi manuscript (Group II).

Donne wrote this Ovidian elegy between 1593 and 1596, when he was at Lincoln's Inn.

> **2. scapes.** Trysts.
> **6. Hydroptique.** Dropsical.
> **19. lounge.** Read "long."
> **25. little brethren.** Helen Gardner points out that "little brethren" combines with "seruing-man," l. 29, to create a compound subject for "could," l. 29. The Holgate scribe must have missed this subtle grammatical point because there is a period inserted after "there," l. 36.
> **45. as . . . Ile.** Two readings are possible here. If "as" introduces a simile, then "Ile" is an imaginary island. If "as" is a subordinate conjunction, then "Ile" is England.
> **47. pretious Vnicornes, strange, Monsters call.** (See text note) According to A. J. Smith, unicorns were often confused with rhinoceroses. The horn of a unicorn "possessed magical and medicinal properties." The horn of a rhinoceros, however, was used as an aphrodisiac (418–19).
> **62. substantiall.** Something real as opposed to things that "seeme."

✦ Manuscripts: Crum O–1112; Beal Vol. I, pt. 1, DnJ 2537–2583; Yale O–0951 ✦ *Aberdeen University Library:* MS 29 (pp. 63–65); *Bodleian:* MS Eng. poet. e. 14 (ff. 34ʸ–35ʸ); MS Eng. poet. e. 99 (ff. 17ʸ–18ʸ); MS Eng. poet. f. 9 (pp. 83–86); MS Malone 19 (p. 81); MS Rawl. poet. 117 (ff. 212–11 [rev]); *British Library:* MS Harley 3991 (f. 114); MS Harley 4955 (ff. 97ʸ–98ʸ); Add. MS 18647 (ff. 4ʸ–5ʸ); Add. MS 25707 (ff. 8ʸ–9); Lansdowne MS 740 (f. 83); Stowe MS 961 (ff. 28–29); Stowe MS 962 (ff. 128ʸ–29ʸ); MS Sloane 1792 (ff. 38ʸ–39ʸ); *Cambridge:* MS Add. 29 (f. 3); MS Add. 5778 (ff. 27ʸ–28ʸ); *Corpus Christi College, Oxford:* MS 327 (ff. 2–3); *Emmanuel College, Cambridge:* MS 1.3.16 (James) II (ff. 5–6); *Folger:* V.a. 125, pt. I (f. 32ʸ); *Harvard:* fMS Eng. 966.1 (ff. 17–18); fMS Eng. 966.3 (ff. 19–20); fMS Eng. 966.4 (ff. 146–47); MS Eng. 966.5 (ff. 61–2); MS Eng. 966.6 (ff. 94ʸ–95ʸ); MS Eng. 966.7 (ff. 84–85); *Huntington Library:* EL 6893 (ff. 92–93); *Owned by Sir Geoffrey Keynes:* Bibliotheca Bibliographici No. 1860 (ff. 25ʸ–27); Bibliotheca Bibliographici No. 1861 (ff. 24–25); *Meisei University Library, Tokyo:* Crewe Ms, formerly Monckton Milnes MS (pp. 10–11); *National Library of Scotland:* Hawthornden XV MS 2067 (ff. 30–31ʸ); MS 6504 (ff. 39–40); *National Library of Wales:*

Dolau Cothi MS (pp. 28–31); Peniarth MS 500B (pp. 20–24); **New York Public Library:** Arents Collection, Cat. No. S191 (Elegies, pp. 7–10); Berg Collection, Westmoreland MS: **Rosenbach:** MS 239/22 (ff. 51ᵛ–52ᵛ); MS 1083/16 (pp. 303–4); MS 1083/17 (ff. 136ᵛ–38); **St. John's College, Oxford:** Crynes volume (p. 49); **St. Paul's Cathedral:** MS 49.B.43; **Texas Tech:** Dalhousie I (f. 31); Dalhousie II (f.15); **Trinity College, Cambridge:** MS R 3.12 (James 307) (pp. 8–10); TCD–I (ff. 32ᵛ–33ᵛ); **Victoria and Albert Museum:** Dyce Collection, Cat. No. 18 (Pressmark 25.F.17), (ff. 20ᵛ–21); **Westminster Abbey:** MS 41 (ff. 32ᵛ–33); **Yale:** Osborn b 148 (pp. 95–96).

✦ Gardner (1965), 7–9, 122–24; Grierson, 1:84–86; Shawcross, 49–51, 435–36; Smith, 98–100, 418–19; *Variorum* 2:74–97, 568–96.

• • •

53. Anon., "In Obitum Ducis Leñoxiæ," 68. Pr. Camden's *Remaines* (1636), 400.

There is no further evidence to support the attribution to either Sir John Eliott in Bodleian MS Eng. poet c. 50 or Ben Jonson in Rosenbach MS 239/27. Ludovick Stuart, second Duke of Lennox and Duke of Richmond (1574–1624), died on the opening day of Parliament, 16 February 1624.

Lennox was a lifetime friend of King James. Before the birth of Henry, James's first son, Lennox was next in line to the Scottish throne. He accompanied James to England in 1603 when James ascended to the British throne. In the same year, he was naturalized in England and made a gentleman of the bedchamber and a member of the Privy Council. In 1607 he became high commissioner of the King to the Scottish Parliament (*DNB*). In 1617, he attended the king on the one trip James made to Scotland while he was king of England (see **HolM 62**).

This poem is followed by a second epitaph to Lennox, **HolM 54**. Both are found in British Library Stowe 962, but in reverse order.

✦ Manuscripts: Crum A1375; Yale A1292 ✦ **Bodleian:** MS Ashmole 38 (p. 173); MS Ashmole 47 (f. 59); MS Eng. poet. c. 50 (f. 59); MS Eng. poet. e. 14 (f. 24); MS Eng. poet. f. 10 (f. 116ᵛ); MS Rawl. poet. 147 (p. 42); MS Rawl. poet. 160 (f. 23ᵛ); MS Tanner 465 (f. 73ᵛ); **British Library:** Add. MS 15227 (f. 97); Add. MS 22118 (f. 36); MS Harley 791 (f. 69); MS Harley 6057 (f. 15ᵛ); Stowe MS 962 (143ᵛ); **Folger:** V.a. 125, pt. II (f. 8); V.b. 43 (f. 31ᵛ); W.b. 455 (p. 47); **Leeds University:** Brotherton Collection, MS Lt. q 44 (f. 57); **New York Public Library:** Arents Collection, Cat. No. S288 (pp. 87–88); **Rosenbach:** MS 239/27 (p. 327, Ben Ionson); MS 1083/16 (p. 89); **Yale:** Osborn b 356 (p. 250); Osborn fb 143 (p. 27).

• • •

54. Anon., "Epitaph," 68. Unprinted.

This is the second of two consecutive epitaphs on Ludovick Stuart, Duke of Richmond and Lennox. For more information concerning Lennox, see **HolM 53 notes**.

In MS Stowe 962 the poem is headed "Vppon ye Death of Lodwicke Duke of Richmond who died soddenly that morninge he was to goe wᵗʰ ye Kinge to Parliament 16° ff 1623."

✦ Manuscripts: **British Library:** Stowe MS 962 (f. 143ᵛ).

• • •

55. Anon., untitled, "Like to a thought slipt out of minde," 68.

This poem follows the pattern of verse used by Francis Quarles in his poem "Like to the Damaske Rose you see," **HolM 56,** and by William Strode in "Like to a rowling of an eye," **HolM 165**. The pattern was frequently imitated: its chief characteristic being the extended use of simile. These poems all express a similar theme: everything in life passes. Saintsbury prints several of these poems under the genre of "Sic Vita" poems. He credits another "Sic Vita" poem, "Like to the falling of a star" (not in the Holgate) as probably the first and best of such poems. He attributes that poem to either Henry King or Francis Beaumont (236).

♦ Manuscripts: **Harvard:** MS Eng. 703 (p. 17).

♦ Saintsbury, 236–37.

· · ·

56. Anon. (see below), "Of Mans Life," 69. Pr. William Pulley, *The Christians Taske: Shewing The Matter Measure Reward Manner of his Salvation* (London, 1619), 302; F. Quarles, *Argalus and Parthenia* (London, 1629), 161; Simon Wastrell, *Microbiblion or The Bibles Epitome* (London, 1629), [p. 512]; *Thankfull remembrances of Gods wonderful deliuerances with other prayers* (1628, 1629, STC 23016, 23016.5), sig. O8–8ᵛ; M. Sparke, *Crums of Comfort*, 10ᵗʰ ed. (London, 1629).

> *Thankfull remembrances . . .* is part of the 1628 edition of *The Crums of Comfort*, published anonymously for M. Sparke (STC 23016). The first edition of the series was entered 7 October 1623, but all editions from the first through the 1628 edition apparently have been lost (Ault 475n). The 1629 edition is reproduced on UMI Reel 1220 as *STC23028a*.

Although Francis Quarles claimed to have written this poem (see below), it was first printed anonymously in *The Christians Taske* (1619). Dubinsky (1692.5) says it is a translation from the Latin by Cornelius Schonaeus.

Francis Quarles (1592–1644) is best known for his *Emblems* (1635), a collection of religious poetry printed with elaborate plates depicting the scenes described in the poems. He was educated at Christ College, Cambridge (B.A. 1608), then studied law at Lincoln's Inn. He was in the service of the Earl of Arundel at the marriage of James's daughter Elizabeth to the Elector Palatinate (1613). He also served in Dublin as secretary to James Usher, Archbishop of Armagh. In 1639, he became Chronologer of London. During the Civil War, he supported the Royalists.

Argalus and Parthenia (1629) is a prose romance based on Sidney's *Arcadia*. Following the romance, Quarles added this poem with the inscription "Hos ego versiculos," ('These are my verses.') With this inscription, he implies that the verse as it appears in his own text is what he wrote and that imitators have used the poem as a paradigm to write their own poems. One possible example is **HolM 55**, "Like to a thought slipt out of minde." From the date of *The Christians Taske* (1619, see note above), the poem was probably written in the late 1610s. Ault also adds that Hazlitt cites a 1622 edition of *Argalus and Parthenia*, but Ault was unable to locate that edition (475n). Freeman writes on this poem, "This, Quarles's most widely anthologized poem, may well have started the *sic vita* fashion in verse in the second quarter of the seventeenth century" (222). He also cites Hebel that the poem may have appeared in manuscript prior to its attachment to *Aragalus and Parthenia* (1023).

For a similar poem, see **HolM 165**.

For the link between the Quarles and Holgate families, see Introduction, p. xiv, n.13.

♦ Manuscripts: Crum L409–411, L383; Yale L0390 ♦ **Bodleian:** MS Eng. poet b (p. 30); MS Malone 16 (p. 54); MS Malone 19 (p. 11); MS Rawl. B. 947 (f. 3); MS Rawl. D. 859 (f. 158); MS Rawl. poet. 117 (f. 162 [rev]); MS Top. gen. e. 32 (f. 74); **British Library:** Add. MS 52585 (f. 19ᵛ); Egerton MS 923 (f. 24ᵛ); Landsdowne MS 777 [W. Browne]; MS Sloane 1489 (f. 17); Stowe MS 962 (f. 141); **Folger:** V.a. 162 (f. 63); V.a. 275 (pp. 180, 181); V.a. 339 (f. 220, SW); V.a. 345

(p. 1); V.a. 423, pt. I (f. 50); **Harvard:** MS Eng. 703 (p. 17); **Huntington Library:** HM 106 (p. 82); **Rosenbach:** MS 240/2 (p. 95); MS 243/4 (p. 106); **Yale:** Osborn b 4 (p. 9).

✦ *English Religious Poetry: Printed 1477–1640: A Chronological Bibliography with Indexes*, ed. Roman R. Dubinski (Waterloo, Ont.: North Waterloo Academic Press, 1996). See also Saintsbury, 236–37; Ault, 475; Hebel, 749; *The New Oxford Book of Seventeenth-Century Verse*, ed. Alastair Fowler (New York: Oxford Univ. Press, 1991), no. 359; Alexander B. Grosart, *The Complete Works in Prose and Verse of Francis Quarles*, 3 vols. (New York: AMS, 1967), 3:285. *Argalus and Parthenia*, ed. David Freeman, Renaissance English Text Society (Washington, D. C.: Folger Books, 1986), 180, 222–23.

• • •

57. Anon., untitled, "I may forgett to eate, to Sleepe, to Drinke," 69. Unprinted.

Beal (Vol. I, pt. 1, BmF 49) incorrectly describes this as an eighteen-line version of **HolM 96**, Francis Beaumont's "An Elegie on the Death of the Countess of Rutland." The comparison must be restricted to line 1, which in the Beaumont poem reads: "I may forgett to Eate, To Drinke to Sleepe." What follows are two very different poems. It is possible that one of the two poets used the first line of the *other* poem as a model and then proceeded to create his/her own poem.

The similarity between the Holgate and British Library Add. MS 23229 text is noteworthy. Even the parentheses at l. 7 are identical. Add. MS 23229 is described by Beal as "a composite volume of verse among the 'Conway papers' chiefly descended from Sir Edward Conway, Viscount Conway (d. 1631)" (BmF 33). **HolM 57–60** are all found in close proximity to one another in Add. MS 23229, and all transcribed by hand B (see the Introduction, pp. xviii–xx).

The poem has eighteen lines of nine iambic pentameter couplets. What is noteworthy, however, is that the shifting conceptual focus and indented concluding couplet makes it appear like a sonnet. The final couplet is similarly indented in BL Add. MS 23229. Also, like many sonnets, the poet makes reference to his/her own death (line 11). It is at least worth conjecture that Beaumont was alluding to this poem when he wrote his first line (**HolM 96**), and that the poet of this verse is Elizabeth, Countess of Rutland. Line 206, *Conversations with Drummond*, reads "The Countess of Rutland was nothing inferior to her father, S[ir] P. Sidney, in poesy." (See **HolM 96 notes**.)

   ✦ Collation: Add. MS 23229 (hand B) *BL-B.* 18 *second* thy] my *BL-B*

   ✦ Manuscripts: **British Library:** Add. MS 23229 (f. 62ᵛ).

• • •

58. Anon., "'Written to a friend in the Lowe-Cuntries:' By: H: H:," 70. Unprinted.

The identity of "H. H." is unknown, but the personal quality of this verse epistle suggests that at the time it was written his identity was known. Hugh Holland (d. 1633) is surely a possibility. However, neither Holland nor any other contemporary poet with the initials H. H. is known to have been imprisoned for debt (Redding 680). He wrote the sonnet to Shakespeare published in the First Folio, "Those hands, which you so clapt, go now, and wring." In 1625, he published *A Cypress Garland* on the death of James I (*ODNB*). A second poem by "H: H:" with a similar colloquial tone is **HolM 100**. For more information on Hugh Holland, see especially the notes to **HolM 104** and **HolM 103**.

This is the second of four poems found together in the Holgate manuscript and Add. MS 23229 (hand B). Except for spelling, capitalization and some punctuation, the texts of the two manuscripts are identical. For discussion on the two miscellanies and this poem, see Introduction, pp. xviii–xx.

   ✦ Manuscripts: **British Library:** Add. MS 23229 (f. 63, H.H); **Rosenbach:** MS 1083/16 (p. 260, H:H:).

59. Thomas Carew (1595?–1640), "'A Winters Entertainement at Saxam' written by: T: C:," 70–71. Pr. Thomas Carew, *Poems* (London, 1640), 45–47.

Thomas Carew was an intimate of Charles I. His father, Sir Matthew Carew, was a Doctor of Civil Law and Master in Chancery. Thomas graduated Merton College with a B.A. in 1611. He then studied law at the Middle Temple, but according to his father his son "hath a chamber and studye, but I feare studiethe the lawe very litle" (*ODNB*). He entered the Venetian embassy of Sir Dudley Carleton (see **HolM 79 notes**). Carew also accompanied Carleton on an embassy to the Netherlands in 1616, but was dismissed, *possibly* because he made unflattering written and spoken comments about Carleton and his wife. The exact circumstances of his dismissal are unknown (Dunlap xxi–xxii).

In 1619, Carew accompanied his friend Lord Herbert of Cherbury to France. It was here that he met John Crofts (see below), whose verse, like Carew's, was set to music by Lawes. In Paris, he began writing verse and was known among literary circles. On his return to England in 1624, he made friends with Ben Jonson, William Davenant, and Aurelian Townshend. He also became well-known at Court. Clarendon wrote, "He was very much esteemed by the most eminent Persons in the Court, and well looked upon by the King himself" (as qtd. in Sharpe 111). In 1630, he became a Gentleman of the Privy Chamber extraordinary, and then Sewer in Ordinary to the king, the king's personal waiter. He died while accompanying Charles in the first Bishops' War against Scotland, probably from the severe physical hardships of the expedition (Dunlap xli).

Modern investigation into the manuscript tradition is leading to a reappraisal of Carew's poetry. John Kerrigan writes that "an intelligible Carew emerges only when early printed texts . . . are supplemented by, often subordinated to, manuscript. As well as recovering a poet peculiarly sensitive to what it means to be read—alert to the way in which script, music and print modify the significance of language—Carew then shows himself capable of intricate development" (318).

Carew is perhaps the best known of the so-called Cavalier poets, who have been seen more as court flatterers than serious poets. But Edward I. Selig, among others, has recognized the difference between court flattery and court compliment, the latter being far more characteristic of Carew. Selig writes: "It may now be useful to draw a line between flattery and compliment. . . . The former usually occurs in a situation of inequality, the flatterer prostrating himself before his superior with intent to gain some advantage by his dissembling. But compliment must pass from one compeer to another as an ingenuous and disinterested expression of good will" (23).

In this light, it is helpful to compare Carew's poetry to Corbett's, especially Corbett's New Year's gift to Buckingham (**HolM 35**), which, as it appears in this manuscript, is more flattery than compliment. Unfortunately, Carew is generally compared to Donne, who is actually part of the earlier generation of seventeenth-century poets. Carew's modern association with Donne derives from the subject of his best-known poem, "Elegy Upon the Death of the Dean of St. Paul's, Dr. John Donne."

Saxham, or Little Saxham, near Bury, was the home of Sir John Crofts (1563–1628). His son John traveled with Carew in France in 1619. Carew also wrote a poem to be read by John Crofts, "To the King at his entrance into Saxham, by Master Io. Crofts" (Dunlap 30–31). Like that poem, more than likely "To Saxham" was read at a large banquet. Carew also wrote five other poems that can be associated with the Crofts family (Dunlap 225). "To Saxham" was probably written in the 1620s (Sharpe 130).

> **11. starud.** "Sterv'd" (1640) means "to die" in both English and Dutch. "Sterved" is the more commonly accepted reading.
> **18. volery.** An aviary.
> **40. fairely welcome.** Courteously (Baker 225).
> **42. hinde.** Servant (Baker 225).

This poem follows **HM 58** sequentially in BL Add. MS 23229. Despite the length of this poem, the two transcripts are virtually identical. For discussion, see Introduction, pp. xviii–xx, and collation.

> ✦ Collation: BL Add. MS 23229 (hand B) *BL-B.* 2 dores] dore *BL-B* ; 39 refresht] refreshd (*accidental*) *BL-B*

> ✦ Manuscripts: Crum T2348; Beal Vol. II, pt. 1, CwT 1112–1132; Yale T2195 ✦ *Aberdeen University Library:* MS 29 (pp. 41–42); *Bodleian:* Don. b. 9 (14ᵛ–15ᵛ) (facsimile in Dunlap); MS Rawl. poet. 142 (f. 44); MS Rawl. poet. 199 (pp. 81–83); MS Rawl. poet. 209 (f. 1); *British Library:* Add. MS 11811 (f. 9); Add. MS 22118 (ff. 44ᵛ–45ᵛ); Add. MS 23229 (63ᵛ–64ᵛ); Add. MS 30982 (ff. 154–53 [rev]); Add. MS 33998 (f. 72); MS Harley 6931 (ff. 24ᵛ–25ᵛ); MS Sloane 1792 (ff. 66ᵛ–67ᵛ); *Huntington Library:* HM 198, pt. 1 (pp. 148–49); JS1; *Rosenbach:* MS 239/27 (276–77); MS 1083/17 (ff. 69ᵛ–70ᵛ); *St. John's College, Cambridge:* MS S. 32 (James 423) (ff. 36–37); *Westminster Abbey:* MS 41 (ff. 58ᵛ–59ᵛ); *Owned by Edwin Wolfe II:* MS (pp. 66–68); *Yale:* Osborn b 200 (pp. 232–33).

✦ Dunlap, 27–29, 225–26; Baker, 225. For critical commentary, see Edward I. Selig, *The Flourishing Wreath* (New Haven: Yale Univ. Press, 1958); Kevin Sharpe, *Criticism and Compliment* (Cambridge: Cambridge Univ. Press, 1987), 109–51; John Kerrigan, "Thomas Carew," *Proceedings of the British Academy*, 74 (1988): 311–50.

• • •

60. Sir Henry Wotton (1568–1639), "'Uppon the Queene of Bohemia,' Sʳ. H. Wotton," 72. Pr. Michael East, *Sixt Set of Bookes* (London, 1624), with musical setting; *Wits Recreations* (1640), No. 472; *Reliquiæ Wottonianæ* (London, 1651), 518.

For further information about Wotton, see notes to **HolM 47** and **HolM 118**.

This is one of the most commonly-found lyrics in seventeenth-century verse miscellanies. It is written for the Lady Elizabeth, daughter of James I, wife to Frederick, the Elector Palatine. Frederick had been chosen King of Bavaria in 1619, but was forced from the throne by the Bohemians, an event that started the Thirty Years' War. Wotton visited the King and Queen at Heilbronn, after which he wrote this poem (*ODNB*). The lyric is identified in a letter from Sir Henry Mainwaring to Lord Zouche dated 12 June 1620. "He [Wotton] made a sonnet to the Queen of Bohemia which he sent by me to the Lady Wotton; the copy I have sent your Lordship. It will be a good exercise for your lordships two choiristers, Mr. Fooks and Mr. North, to set it to a sound" (qtd. in Leishman 99).

The musical setting to this poem was printed in 1624 by Michael East. *Reliquiæ Wottonianæ* was published in 1651, thirteen years after Wotton's death. Leishman argues that the two texts represent separate lines of descent in the poem's transmission, their principal differences being the reversal of the second and third stanzas and the substitution of "moone" for "sun" in l. 5. From that perspective, it is clear that the Holgate transcription follows stemmatically from the earlier musical setting rather than the poem's later printed version. Douglas Hamer agrees that the musical setting is closer to the original text and that, by 1651 when *Reliquiæ Wottonianæ* was published, the poem had accrued "decadence" (46). Unfortunately, there is no indication in the Holgate that the verse was used musically.

The poem makes better sense in the stanzaic order seen in the Holgate. It reads stanza 1 (night), stanza 2 (day), stanza 3 (dusk). See collations.

> This is the last of four poems (**HolM 57–60**) found in similar sequential order in British Library Add. MS 23229 (hand B). The texts found in the two manuscripts are virtually identical. In Add. MS 23229, l. 7, the word "best" is clearly added in front of the line. It would appear from the microfilm to be in the original hand. Also in Add. MS 23229, l.

19, "Designed," the final "d" does not appear connected to the root of the word and may have been written at a later date. Regardless, it is clear from this and the preceding three poems that the two miscellanies are very closely aligned. For discussion, see Introduction, pp. xviii–xx.

✦ Collation: BL Add. MS 23229-(hand B) *BL-B*. 7 (*see commentary notes*) ; 19 Designe] Designed (*possibly added to text, see notes*) BL-B

✦ Manuscripts: Crum Y301, Y57, Y83, Y150, Y264, Y384; Beal Vol. I, pt. 2, WoH 62–133.5; Yale Y–0350, Y–0532 ✦ **Bodleian:** MS Ashmole 38 (p. 118); Ashmole 788 (f. 21ᵛ); Don.c.57 (f. 39); Don.d.58 (f. 21); MS Douce 357 (f. 19, followed by Latin version); MS Eng. poet. c. 50 (f. 77); MS Eng. poet. e. 14 (f. 68ᵛ); MS Eng. poet. f. 27 (p. 198); MS Malone 19 (p. 37); MS Rawl. poet. 142 (f. 46); MS Rawl. poet. 159 (f. 142); MS Rawl. poet. 160 (f. 109); MS Rawl. poet. 199 (p. 2); MS Tanner 465 (f. 43); **Bradford Central Library:** Hopkinson MSS, Vol 17 (ff. 122ᵛ–23); **British Library:** Add. MS 11608 (ff. 52, 52ᵛ); Add. MS 15227 (f. 76); Add. MS 22118 (f. 37); Add. MS 23229 (f. 62ᵛ); Add. MS 30982 (f. 145ᵛ [rev]); Add. MS 44963 (ff. 21ᵛ–22); Add. MS 47111 (f. 7); Add. MS 58215 (pp. 192–93); Loan MS 15/pt 2 (ff. 25ᵛ–26); MS Sloane 1446 (ff. 43ᵛ–44); MS Sloane 1792 (f. 2); **Cambridge:** MS Add. 79 (f. 11); CL2 (Cantus 3, ff. 35, 52); **Corpus Christi College, Oxford:** MS 328 (f. 79ᵛ); **Dorset Record Office:** D51/5 (p. 211); **Edinburgh University Library:** MS La. III 436 (pp. 24–25); MS La. III 483 (musical setting) (see pp. 185, 192–93, 194, 202); MS La. III 490 (pp. 63–64); **Folger:** V.a. 103, pt. I (f. 53, followed by Latin version); V.a. 148, pt. I (f. 48); V.a. 162 (f. 79); V.a. 169, pt. II (ff. 16, 19ᵛ); V.a. 170 (pp. 43, 100–1); V.a. 245 (f. 42ᵛ); V.a. 262 (p. 88); V.a. 319 (f. 32); V.a. 322 (p. 56); V.a. 345 (pp. 148–49); **Harvard:** fMS 626 (f. 8); MS Eng. 686 (ff. 9ᵛ–10, 84); MS Eng. 703 (ff. 32ᵛ–33); **Hatfield House:** Cecil Papers 206 (p. 6); **Owned by Sir Geoffrey Keynes:** Bibliotheca Bibliographici No. 1863 (f. 2ᵛ); **Leicestershire Record Office:** DG.7/Lit. 2 (f. 336ᵛ); **Mitchell Library, Glasgow:** 308897 (pp. 21–22); **National Library of Scotland:** Adv. MS 5.2.14 (f. 10); **National Library of Wales:** MS 5390D (p. 152); **New York Public Library:** Music Division, Drexel MS 4257 (No. 98); Music Division, Drexel MS 4175 (No. i); **University of Nottingham:** Portland MS Pw V 37 (p. 110, followed by Latin version); **Rosenbach:** MS 239/27 (pp. 33–34, followed by Latin version); MS 243/4 (p. 48); MS 1083/17 (f. 136); **Sandman Library, Perth:** N16 (No. liv.); **Trinity College, Dublin:** MS 412 (f. 46ᵛ); MS 877 (ff. 162ᵛ, 192); **Owned by Edwin Wolfe II:** MS (pp. 3, Latin version, 14); **Westminster Abbey:** MS 41 (f. 48); **Yale:** Osborn b 4 (f. 39); Osborn b 150 (pp. 205–6); Osborn b 197 (pp. 44–45); Osborn b 213 (28–29).

✦ Dyce1, 10–12; Douglas Hamer, "You Meaner Beauties of the Night," *N&Q* 163 (1932), 45–47; J. B. Leishman, "'You Meaner Beauties of the Night': A Study in Transmission and Transmogrification," *The Library*, 4ᵗʰ series, 26 (1945): 99–121. Both Hamer and Leishman discuss later editions of the poem.

• • •

61. Anon., "An Epitaph on the Lady May and Natt: feild yᵉ player," 72. No seventeenth-century printings. Pr. John Payne Collier, *Memoirs of the Principal Actors in the Plays of Shakespeare* (London, 1846), 217.

Like several poems in the Holgate this epitaph relates to a scandal. Nathan Field (1587–1619/20) was a player in Shakespeare's company. He was the son of John Field, a puritan minister who hated stage plays; his brothers were Theophilus Field, Bishop of Llandaff, and Nathaniel, a stationer. Nathan Field was a leading actor in Lady Elizabeth's Men, and later with the King's Men, which he joined in 1616, possibly as a replacement for Shakespeare himself. With Burbage, he was considered one of the great actors of his day. He wrote two comedies, *A Woman is a Weather-coke*

(1612) and *Amends for Ladies* (1618). He also collaborated with both Massinger and Fletcher writing plays (*ODNB*).

As the poem suggests, Field was accused of sexual indiscretion. A letter found among the papers of James Hay, Earl of Carlisle, from William Trumbull, Ambassador to Holland, says that the Earl "was privy to the payment of 15 to 16 poundes sterling to one of your lordships Trayne called Wisedome for the noursing of a childe which the world sayes is daughter to my lady [Argyll] and N[at] Feild the Player" (Brinkley 42). The "Lady Argyll" was Anne, the daughter of Sir William Cornwallis of Brome. It is not known why she is referred to as the "Lady May" in the poem.

However, Brinkley does not believe Field was involved in the scandal, noting that in Collier, *History of English Dramatic Poetry and Annals of the Stage*, 3.434–35, Field's name is spelled "Feild" rather than "Field." Unfortunately, the Brinkley citation is incorrect, so that claim could not be substantiated. However, in a later Collier text, *Memoirs of the Principal Actors*, the name is spelled "Field." Regardless, the spelling is insignificant; as is well known, Shakespeare himself spelled his own name in several ways.

Bodleian MS Ashmole 47, f. 49 is headed: "On Nathaniell ffeild suspected for too much Familiarity with his Mrs. Lady May." The four Rosenbach miscellanies (listed below) also identify Field and the so-called Lady May as the subjects of this poem.

◆ Manuscripts: Crum T1980 ◆ *Bodleian:* MS Ashmole 47 (f. 49); Don.d.58 (f. 44a^v); MS Eng. poet. e. 14 (f. 52); *Rosenbach:* MS 239/27 (p. 183); MS 243/4 (p. 17); MS 1083/16 (p. 123); MS 1083/16 (p. 48).

◆ For critical and biographical information on Field, see Roberta Florence Brinkley, *Nathan Field, The Actor-Playwright* (New Haven and London: Yale Univ. Press, 1928), especially 42.

• • •

62. Richard Corbett (1582–1636), "D^r: C: of Oxfoord beinge kept out of the Haule on St George his day at Windsor by the Guard, wrote the verses vnto the Lord Mordent," 73–77. Pr. *CEP* (London, 1647), 33–40.

James I made his only visit to Scotland during his reign as King of England in March 1617. His trip forced postponement of the Order of the Garter's Saint George's feast, scheduled for Saint George's Day, 23 April. Instead, the feast was held 13 or 14 September 1617, at Windsor. This poem describes Corbett's visit to that feast.

John, fifth Baron Mordaunt, travelled with James to Scotland. His exact duties are unknown, but at the time he was only nineteen years old. He was born into a Catholic family. His father had been suspected of conspiring in the Gunpowder Plot and was put in the Tower. John, too, was raised a Catholic, but "converted by a disputation at his house between a Jesuit and Archbishop Usher" (Nichols 3:220n). In 1627, he became Earl of Peterborough.

B&TR suggest that Corbett wrote this poem as "poetical flattery" (xix) and point out that Mordaunt married Elizabeth Howard, the granddaughter of the Earl of Nottingham, Lord High Admiral. Their marriage, however, did not take place until 1621 (Chamberlain 2: 349n). The poem describes a comic event in a familiar tone. It is typical of the colloquial humor for which Corbett was known.

There are many variants between the Holgate text and the poem's first printing in Corbett's *CEP*.

For further information on Richard Corbett, see the notes to **HolM 11** and **HolM 78**.

3. Northerne winde. Scotland.

8. woodstocke. James left Compton Wingate, 6 September for the royal palace of Woodstock and remained there until 10 September (Nichols 3: 435–36).

9. Contagion. Lord Mordaunt must have been ill while in Scotland. This may in part explain why Corbett wrote the poem.

12. Buck was out. It was illegal to hunt buck or hart from 14 September to 24 June (B&TR 116).

13. holy Roode. 14 September, the Feast of the Exultation of the Cross (ibid.).

17. Red Inke. The Church Calendar (ibid.).

28. praies in a strange tongue. The prayer book for the Garter was the Book of Common Prayer. This must refer to the motto, l. 30.

30. Hony Soit Qui Mal y Pense. No one knows the true source of the motto of the Order of the Garter. The story is that during a ball held in Calais, Joan, Countess of Salisbury, dropped her garter. King Edward III, when he saw it fall, put it on his own leg and said 'Hony Soit Qui Mal y Pense.' "Evil (or ashamed) be he that thinks evil of it" (Begent, n. p.).

32. Buckle is Prophane. Elias Ashmole (. . .*Order of the Garter*, see description of citations below) does not mention the buckle as part of the garments worn by members of the Garter.

34. Precession. *OED* suggests that this is a common error for "procession."

38. knocks. John Knox was the sixteenth-century founder of Scottish Presbyterianism.

45. St. George. St. George is the patron saint of the Order of the Garter. He is a Saint of the Eastern Church.

50. Betwixt the Kinge. . . . B&TR suggest that the ceremony described is "The Offering of the Gold and Silver" (see Ashmole, 21, sect. 5).

54. poore Knights. Retired military officers (Begent, n. p.).

98. Recusant. A term most often used to refer to Roman Catholics who refused to attend the services of the Church of England (*OED*).

101. Clarke o'the Check. "The officer who keeps the check-roll of the yeomen of the guard" (B&TR 116).

107. Hangings. The hangings are depicted in Ashmole, p. 592.

113. mulckt. A fine or penalty (*OED*).

128. Priuie Chamber. The sovereign's personal quarters in a royal palace. This line should probably read "The [P]resence [or] the Priuie Chamber doore." A monarch would receive visitors in the Presence Chamber.

132. Iohn Dory. A Scottish ballad; Corbett here makes it sound like a drinking song. See Child, no. 284.

134. Cheuy. "The ballad of Chevy Chase," in Child, no. 162.

150. Two Capitall Letters. Guards wore the initials of the reigning sovereign. This particular guard seems to have been wearing an old uniform.

152. Bumbard. A leather container for liquor.

153. Ironside. The guard must have worn a sword.

156. halfe a Barr. This is an unclear reference, possibly a barrier, or perhaps the bar on a cask of liquor (*OED*).

161. Nicholas. The patron saint of scholars, also schoolboys.

162. Hercules did Cacus. Hercules slew Cacus after the latter had stolen his cattle (*OCD*).

172. How Esope hath it and how Alciat. Andrea Alciati created the first emblem book. He borrowed from Æsop (B&TR 117).

185. St. Arche, or Garret. Two court jesters. "Sir" Archibald Armstrong (Arche) was Scottish. He accompanied James from Scotland when James claimed the English throne (B&TR 117).

186. cheat lofe. Second quality wheaten bread coursely sifted; ant. "mabchet" (*OED*).

189. Bloxfoord Man. Sarcastic colloquial description of an Oxford man.

194. Holberds. Halberds, combination spears and battle-axes.

202. Noble ffenton. Sir Thomas Erskine; he was a lifetime friend of James, Captain of the yeoman of the Guard (1603–1617), and was installed in the Order of the Garter (1615).

205. Pembrooke. William Herbert, third Earl of Pembroke, Lord Chamberlain (1616), also Chancellor of Oxford (1616). For further information, see **HolM 40 notes**.

214. St Paule hath fought with Beasts at Ephesus. 1 Corinthians 15.32. Paul is associated with the city of Ephesus in several biblical references; see Acts 19.1–41; 20.17–35; 1 Cor.16.8.

✦ Manuscripts: Crum M777; Beal Vol. II, pt. 1, CoR 630–47 ✦ *Aberdeen University Library:* MS 29 (pp. 15–21); *Bodleian* MS Ashmole 47 (ff. 17–21); MS Eng. poet. e. 97 (pp. 44–48); *Bradford District Archives:* Hopkinson MSS, Vol. 34 (pp. 57–62); Spencer-Stanhope MSS, Calendar No. 2795 (Bundle 10, No. 34) (ff. 2ᵛ–5); *British Library:* MS Harley 6931 (ff. 83–86ᵛ); MS Sloane 1792 (ff. 76ᵛ–80ᵛ); Stowe MS 962 (ff. 72–75ᵛ); Add. MS 10309 (ff. 112–17); *Huntington Library:* HM 198, pt. 1 (pp. 108–9); *Kent Archives Office:* U 1121 Z9; *University of Notthingham:* Portland MS Pw V 37 (pp. 307–12); *Rosenbach:* MS 239/22 (ff. 14–17ᵛ); MS 239/27 (pp. 136–42); MS 1083/16 (pp. 227–35); MS 652 (ff. 359–60ᵛ); *Dr. Williams's Library:* MSS 12.54 (ff. 9–12ᵛ).

✦ B&TR, 23–32, 115–18. See also Elias Ashmole, *The institution, laws & ceremonies of the most noble Order of the Garter,* 1672 (rpt. Baltimore: Geneological Publishing, 1971); Peter J. Begent, *The Most Noble Order of the Garter: Its History and Ceremonial* (London: Spink, 1999); F. J. Child, *English and Scottish Popular Ballads,* 8 vols. (1883–1898): 4 vols., ed. Mark F. and Laura Sexton Heiman (Northfield, MN: Loomis House Press, 2001–2008); John Nichols, *The Progresses, Processions and Magnificent Festivities of King James the First* (London, 1828; rpt. New York: Burt Franklin, no. 118, 1967).

⋯

63. Thomas Carew (1595?–1640), "Of the Springe" ["The Spring"], 78. Pr. Thomas Carew, *Poems* (London, 1640), 1–2.

For information on Thomas Carew, see **HolM 59 notes**.

This poem recreates a familiar Renaissance theme: the weather has turned warm but the poet's mistress is as cold as ice. It is the first poem printed in Carew's posthumous collection, *Poems* (1640). The volume was published immediately after his death. Clear influences for this type of poem are Petrarch, Virgil, and Ronsard. Dunlap cites Carew's literary sources in detail, pp. 215–16.

As with several poems in the Holgate, this entry shares a distinct correlation with the same poem in British Library Add. MS 23229. For discussion, see Introduction, pp. xviii–xx, and collation.

3. Candies the grasse. Covers with ice.
6. second. "Sacred" is the more accepted reading.

• Collation: BL Add. MS 23229 (hand A) *BL-A.* 7 wake] wakes *BL-A*

✦ Manuscripts: Crum N–563, N–515; Beal Vol. II, pt. 1, CwT 967–81; Yale N–0502 ✦ *Bodleian:* MS Eng. poet. f. 25 (ff. 13ᵛ–14); MS Malone 21 (f. 45); *British Library:* Add. MS 11811 (f. 4); Add. MS 23229 (f. 53); Add. MS 25303 (f. 174); MS Harley 3511 (f. 55ᵛ); MS Harley 6057; *Corpus Christi College, Oxford:* MS 328 (f. 19ᵛ); *Edinburgh University Library:* MS La. III. 468; *Emmanuel College, Cambridge:* MS 1.3.16 (James) VI (No. 17); *Huntington Library:* HM 198, pt. 1 (pp. 130–31); *Rosenbach:* MS 239/27 (pp. 264–65); MS 1083/17 (p. 15); *Owned by Edwin Wolfe II:* MS (pp. 95–96); *Yale:* Osborn b 200 (p. 113).

✦ Dunlap, 215–16. For critical commentary, see Edward I. Selig, *The Flourishing Wreath* (New Haven: Yale Univ. Press, 1958), 120–25.

64. Francis Beaumont (1584–1616), "An Elegie on the death of the Lady Marcum," subscribed "F: B:," 78–80. Pr. *Poems: By Francis Beaumont* (London, 1640), sig. H2ʳ–H3ᵛ: *Love and Drollery* (1673).

Beaumont was the son of Francis Beaumont (d. 1598), a judge, and younger brother of Sir John Beaumont (d. 1627). He attended Broadgates College, Oxford, but left school without graduating at the death of his father. He entered the Inner Temple in 1600, but he did not take up legal studies. While there, he befriended members of the so-called Mermaid group, which included Ben Jonson, his own brother Sir John Beaumont, William Browne, and Michael Drayton. At this time he began writing verse, including *Salmacis and Hermaphroditus* (1602). He is best known for his association with John Fletcher (1579–1625), with whom he shared great success as a playwright.

Concerning the 1640 printed edition of Beaumont's poems, Ringler writes "This is the only poem in [16]40 whose attribution to Beaumont is adequately substantiated from other sources" (129).

Bridget Markham died 4 May 1609 at Twickenham. She was the daughter of Sir James Harrington and wife of Sir Anthony Markham as well as a cousin to Lucy, the countess of Bedford, daughter of Sir John Harrington. She was also a Lady of Queen Anne's Bedchamber. For Donne's elegy on her death, "Man is the world and Death the Otian," see **HolM 92**.

The Holgate text collates very closely with British Library Add. MS 23229. However, this is neither hand A nor B. For discussion, see Introduction and collation. It is the same hand for **HolM 96**.

> ✦ Collation: BL Add. MS 23229 *BL*. 26 bar] beare (*accidental?*) *BL* ; 32 Supper] suppe *BL*

> ✦ Manuscripts: Crum A1708; Beal Vol. I, pt. 1, BmF 56–83; Yale A1687 ✦ *Bodleian:* MS Ashmole 38 (pp. 76–77, FB); MS Eng. poet. f. 9 (pp. 199–202, J.D.); MS Rawl. poet. 117 (f. 193 [rev]); MS Rawl. poet. 160 (ff. 27ᵛ–28); *Bradford Central Library:* Hopkinson MSSS, Vol 34 (pp. 109–10); *British Library:* Add. MS 23229 (f. 66ᵛ); Add. MS 25707 (f. 30, F.B.); Add. MS 30982 (ff. 49ᵛ–50, Beaumont); Egerton MS 2230 (ff. 3ᵛ–4ᵛ); MS Sloane 1446 (ff. 72ᵛ–73); Stowe MS 961 (ff. 19–20); Stowe MS 962 (ff. 81–82ᵛ, Beaumont); *Cambridge:* MS Add. 29 (f. 16); MS Add. 5778 (ff. 83ᵛ–84ᵛ); EDU 8 (ff. 97–98); *Folger:* V.a. 125, pt. II (f. 19); V.a. 160 (pp. 10–11, starts at l. 49); *Harvard:* fMS Eng. 966.1 (47ᵛ–48); MS Eng. 966.6 (ff. 90–91ᵛ); *Huntington Library:* HM 198, pt. 1 (pp. 10–11, Beaumont); *Leeds Archives Department:* MX 237 (f. 8); *Leeds University:* Brotherton Collection, MS Lt. q 11 (No. 50); *Leicestershire Record Office:* DG.9/2796 (pp. 72–77); *University of Nottingham:* Portland MS Pw V 37 (pp. 21–22); *Rosenbach:* MS 1083/16 (pp. 110–12); *Yale:* Osborn b 148 (146–47); Osborn b 197 (pp. 49–51). Beal cites an unlocated MS of ll.49–68 found among papers of Sir Kenelm Digby, "printed from this MS in *Poems from Sir Kenelm Digby's Papers, in the possession of Henry A. Bright,* Roxburghe Club (London, 1877), 29" (Beal BmF 83).

✦ Ringler, 129. See also Dyce2, 11:503–5; Grierson, 2:cii.

• • •

65. Anon., untitled, "From such a face whose excellence," 80–81. No seventeenth-century printings. Pr. *Works of William Drummond* (Edinburgh, 1711), "Poems," 55.

This poem is ascribed to William Drummond of Hawthornden (1585–1649) in *The Works of William Drummond of Hawthornden.* However, L. E. Kastner, editor of *The Poetical Works of William Drummond of Hathornden,* reprinted it among "Poems of Doubtful Authenticity." National Library of Scotland Adv. MS 19.3.8 is the source for the original ascription, where the poem appears in Drummond's hand, but with no identification of the poet. Since Drummond himself supervised the manuscript, it is doubtful that he is the poet (see Beal, Vol. 1, pt. 1, 18; also Gilbert; Main).

A fragment of the poem was found among the papers of Alexander Gil, who was questioned after the 1628 assassination of Buckingham. Gil was fined and sentenced to the loss of his ears because of statements he made approving Buckingham's assassination. Buckingham was assassinated by John Felton.

The poem corresponds to Ben Jonson's "The Five Senses," **HolM 66**, written for *The Gypsies Metamorphosed*, a masque performed before King James in 1621. The two poems appear sequentially in only one other manuscript, National Library of Wales MS 12443A, pt. ii. The poem is generally accepted as a parody of Jonson's genial complaint to the King, **HolM 66** (see Main); however, it is at least possible this poem predates Jonson's masque, making it a corrective of an earlier, anonymous complaint (Gilbert). Jonson visited Drummond in 1619, two years before the writing of *The Gypsies Metamorphosed*.

The poem is a "libel," a scathing attack on another person, in this case James I. Since the Jonson masque was performed by Buckingham before James, Buckingham can also be taken as a target of the libel. Also, because both poems have similar metrical patterns, it is possible this version was sung to a familiar melody.

> **4. Phayetone** (Phaethon). Son of Helios and Clymene. In Greek mythology, he was permitted by Helios to drive the solar chariot, but he was too weak to do so properly. Zeus, lest Phaethon burn up the world in his recklessness, killed him (*OCD*).
>
> **19. Spanish Treates.** Probably an allusion to the proposed marriage of Prince Charles and the Spanish Infanta, daughter of King Philip IV. Buckingham accompanied Charles on his trip to the Spanish court (see **HolM 72, 73, 146**).
>
> **29–32. from the Labourers . . . those strangled.** A political complaint. See also ll.74–77.
>
> **33–35. Candied poysond baytes . . . Romish Drugges.** Strong anti-Catholic sentiment.
>
> **36. Dugges** (*Dugs*). Teats or nipples of female mammals. A contemptuous usage, the word was unknown before the sixteenth century.
>
> **38. the dangerous figg of Spaine.** Clear reference to the proposed marriage.
>
> **45. beardless chinn.** James was rumored to be partial to beardless youths (Main 389).
>
> **59–66. next I craue. . . and his smellinge.** Buckingham and James were rumored to have had an immoral relationship (see Bergeron).
>
> **61. Gānymeade.** A cupbearer to Zeus, but also a boy used by a pederast.
>
> **72. houndes.** James was considered to be overly fond of hunting (Main 389).

✦ Manuscripts: Crum F751; Beal (See Vol. I, pt. 2, p. 18); Yale F0713 ✦ *Bodleian:* MS Eng. poet. c. 50 (f. 25); MS Eng. poet. e. 37 (p. 72); MS Malone 23 (p. 28); MS Rawl. poet. 26 (f. 72); MS Rawl. poet. 117 (ff. 23ᵛ–24ᵛ); MS Rawl. poet. 160 (f. 14ᵛ); MS Tanner 465 (f. 97); *Bradford Central Library:* Hopkinson MSS, Vol 34 (pp. 65–66); *British Library:* Add. MS 23229 (ff. 99–100); Add. MS 25303 (ff. 133–34); Egerton MS 923 (f. 30); MS Harley 367 (f. 153); Stowe MS 962 (ff. 144ᵛ–46); MB1 (Appendix, p. 204); *Chetham's Library, Manchester:* Mun. A 3.47 (ff. 1–2); *Downing College, Cambridge:* Bowtell Collection, MS Wickstede Theasaurus, pt. II (ff. 106ᵛ–7ᵛ); *Durham Cathedral:* Hunter MS 27 (ff. 94ᵛ–95); *Edinburgh University Library:* MS H.-P. Coll. 401 (f. 51); *Folger:* V.a. 275 (p. 175); V.a. 276, pt. II (f. 40ᵛ); V.a. 339 (f. 256); V.a. 345 (pp. 59–61); MS Xd 235; *Harvard:* MS Eng. 686 (ff. 59ᵛ–60); *Hatfield House:* Cecil Papers 206 (pp. 252–53); *Huntington Library:* HM 198, pt. 1 (pp. 30–32); *Leeds University:* Brotherton Collection, MS Lt. q 44 (ff. 1–2); *Leicestershire Record Office:* DG.7/Lit. 2 (ff. 333ᵛ–34ᵛ); *National Library of Scotland:* Adv. MS 19.3.8 (ff. 47–48ᵛ); *National Library of Wales:* MS 12443A, pt. ii (pp. 125–30); *University of Nottingham:* Portland MS Pw V 37 (pp. 198–200); *Rosenbach:* MS 239/27 (p. 58bis.); MS 1083/16 (pp. 84–87); *St. John's College, Cambridge:* MS S. 32 (James 423) (ff. 31–32); *Somerset Record Office:* DD/SF C/2635, Box 1;

University of Texas at Austin: MS File/ (Herrick R.) Works B (pp. 525–27), facsimile in *Texas Quarterly* 16 Supplement (1973), 136–41; *Westminster Abbey:* MS 41 (ff. 21–22); *Yale:* Osborn b 54 (p. 877).

✦ L. E. Kastner, ed., *Poems of Drummond* (Scottish Text Society, n. s. 4, 1913), 2:296; David M. Bergeron, *King James & Letters of Homoerotic Desire* (Iowa City: Univ. of Iowa Press, 1999). For critical commentary, see Allan H. Gilbert, "Drummond or Gil on the King's Senses," *Modern Language Notes,* 62 (1947), 35–37; Robert H. MacDonal, "Amendments to L. E. Kastner's Edition of Drummonde's Poems." *Studies in Scottish Literature* 7 (1969), 102–22; C. F. Main, "Ben Jonson and an Unknown Poet on the King's Senses," *Modern Language Notes* 74 (1959): 389–93.

• • •

66. Ben Jonson (1572–1637), untitled, "From a Gypsie in the morninge," 82–83. The Patrico's song from *The Gypsies Metamorphos'd* (1640), 97–100.

Although *The Gypsies Metamorphos'd* was performed three times before King James, at Burley-on-the-Hill, Belvoir Castle, and Windsor Castle, August–September 1621 (H&S 7.541), the Patrico's song was performed only at Windsor, the last of the three performances.

It is noteworthy that there are fewer extant manuscript copies of this poem than the previous, **HolM 65,** which is far more satiric about James than this poem.

The Gypsies Metamorphos'd was written to be performed by a specific cast, at a specific castle, with a specific audience (Randall 68). The first performance was at Burley, the home of George Villiers (Buckingham). The First Gypsie, or Captain, was played by Buckingham himself; the Second Gypsie was William, Baron Fielding, Buckingham's brother-in-law; the Third Gypsie was Endymion Porter, a poet associated with Buckingham; the Fourth Gypsie was possibly played by Buckingham's brother John, Viscount Purbeck. The Fifth Gypsie may have been played by a lord named Gervase. His identity is unknown (Randall 124–36). During the course of the action, the King's fortune is told by the First Gypsie, the Prince's fortune by the Second, the Lady Marquess Buckingham's and the Countess of Rutland's by the Third, etc., to include several distinguished members of the court.

At the end of the masque, the gypsie performers are all metamorphosed into the fine gentlemen who were actually playing the roles. Among the songs and dances of praise at the end of the masque is the Patrico's song, herein transcribed. The Patrico was a priest, thus explaining the prayer-like quality of the song. The Patrico was played by a professional actor.

> **7–8. A Smocke rampant . . . on the britches.** A woman who controls her husband (Orgel, H&S).
> **11. serious toyes.** An oxymoron. Orgel glosses as "solemn nonsense."
> **15. tongue with out a file.** Nonstop talking.
> **19. Loughburie.** Section of London known for its foundries.
> **20. Banburie.** Puritan area of Oxfordshire.
> **25–26. from a Lady . . . vnderneath.** Cf. King James's "Invective Against Women," **HolM 13.**
> **28. Beares Colledge.** "The bears at the Paris Garden in Southwark" (H&S).
> **29. Tobacco.** James despised tobacco, attacking it in his *A Counter-blaste to Tobacco* (1604).
> **43. Doxie.** A prostitute.
> **47. Sᵗ Anthonies old fire.** Erysipelas, a disease characterized by inflammation and fever.
> **48. neild.** A needle, but the spelling appears unique. It is possibly a transposed *l* and *d.*

✦ Manuscripts: Crum F641; Beal Vol. I, pt. 2, JnB 654–670.5 ✦ *Aberdeen University Library:* MS 29 (pp. 80–82); MS Ashmole 47 (ff. 90–91); MS Eng. poet. f. 16 (f. 9); *Bradford Central Library:* Hopkinson MSS, Vol. 34 (pp. 67–68); *British Library:* Add. MS 30982 (ff. 155–54ᵛ

[rev]); MS Harley 4055, a copy of the entire masque, with a text of **HolM 66** on f. 27; MS Sloane 1792 (ff. 64–66); *Folger:* V.a. 125, pt. I (f. 21ᵛ); V.a. 170 (pp. 67–68bis); V.a. 245 (f. 62); **University of Nottingham:** Clifton MS C1 LM 43; Portland MS Pw V 37 (pp. 197–98); **Rosenbach:** MS 239/27 (pp. 60–62); **St. John's College, Cambridge:** MS S. 32 (James 423) (ff. 27ᵛ–28ᵛ); **Scottish Record Office:** GD 34/996; **Westminster Abbey:** MS 41 (ff. 27ᵛ–28ᵛ); **Owned by Edwin Wolfe II:** MS (p. 47). Beal notes also (JnB 670.5), a "Copy in a miscellany (pp. 27–28) probably compiled by one or two members of the Calverley family, ca. 1623–30s. Christie's, 13 June 1979 (Arthur A. Houghton, Jr. sale), Lot 135, sold to Maggs; thence to Huntington."

✦ See George Watson Cole, ed. *The Gypsies Metamorphosed, Ben Jonson, a Variorum Edition.* (New York: MLA, 1931); H&S 7; Stephen Orgel, *Jonson: The Complete Masques* (New Haven and London: Yale Univ. Press, 1969), xx. For critical commentary on the masque, see Dale B. J. Randall, *Jonson's Gypsies Unmasked* (Durham, NC: Duke Univ. Press, 1975). For a textual study, see W. W. Greg, *Jonson's 'Masque of Gipsies.'* (London, Oxford Univ. Press, 1952).

• • •

67. Anon., "A man, and two Maides in a Boate at Sea," 83–84. Unprinted.

The poem might be described as a verse joke. The only other extant copy is in BL Add. MS 23229. For a discussion of the relationship between these two miscellanies, see Introduction, pp. xviii–xx, and collation.

19. Idde. Probably a vulgar form of *idea*, as in Platonic *idea*. *OED* spells this usage *idee*.

✦ Collation: MS 23229 (hand B) *BL-B*. (Collation is for ll.1–32 only. Leaf missing from Add. MS 23229 [f. 65]. The catch words at f. 64ᵛ are "the pen." Holgate l. 33 begins "The Pensive."; 1 From] ffor *BL-A*.
✦ Manuscript: **British Library:** Add. MS 23229 (f. 64ᵛ).

• • •

68. Anon., untitled, "This Night is blacke, but blacker is my soule," 84. Unprinted.

There is no other known copy of this poem.

• • •

69. Anon., "The Question of a Garland" and "The Answere," 85. Pr. *Wits Recreations* (1641), sig. T7ᵛ; *Wits Interpreter* (1655), 295.

This poem can be compared qualitatively and thematically to **HolM 67**. Humorous poems such as these are quite common in verse miscellanies, but less frequent in the Holgate.

✦ Manuscripts: Crum B346, B355; Yale B0328 ✦ **Bodleian:** Ashmole 781 (p. 144); MS Eng. misc. f. 49 (f. 28ᵛ); **British Library:** Stowe MS 962 (f. 184); **Folger:** V.a. 339 (f. 233); V.a. 399 (f. 65ᵛ); **Yale:** Osborn b 197 (p. 212).

• • •

70. Anon., "A Meditation," 85. Unprinted.

Unfortunately, Lord David Cecil, editor of the *Oxford Book of Christian Verse*, included this poem in the volume without identifying his copy-text. In British Library Add. MS 34692, the lyric is among a group of poems attached to a sermon by Thomas Lenthall, Fellow of Pembroke College, Cambridge. Its concluding motto in that manuscript is "Crux Christi nostra Corona est."

The poem is more overtly Catholic than most religious poems found in the Holgate; however, it can be compared to John Donne's "The Crosse," **HolM 88**.

The late W. H. Kelliher, former Curator of Manuscripts, British Library, suggested that this poem was written between 1600–1625. I am indebted to Mr. Kelliher for his help in identifying this poem.

◆ Manuscripts: Crum R–234 ◆ *Bodleian:* MS Rawl. poet. 200 (f. 126); *British Library:* Add. MS 34692 (f. 30); *Harvard:* MS Eng. 613 (f. 6); *Rosenbach:* MS 239/16 (p. 19); *Yale:* Osborn b 150 (p. 263).

◆ David Cecil, ed. *The Oxford Book of Christian Verse* (Oxford: Clarendon Press, 1940), No. 189.

· · ·

71. John Donne, untitled ["The Anagram"], "Mary and Loue thy Flauia for shee," 86–87. Pr. Elegie II, *Poems*, 43–45.

This is one of the most frequently copied poems found in seventeenth-century verse miscellanies. Its theme, in praise of the "ugly" woman, was commonly used by several European poets, including Berni and Tasso.

Donne wrote his elegies in the 1590s. Leishman believes Donne learned his witty, paradoxical style in Italy, where he had traveled (84).

19, 21. Gam-vt. A scale of seven notes used on the ancient hexachord.

35. husbands. Both spouses and farmers.

37. Plaister. A remedy.

40. Marmosit. A weasel.

41. Belgias Cities. Lowlands.

47. stews. Brothels.

50. Tympanie. An abdominal swelling.

53–54. whom Dildoes beadstaues and her velvett glass . . . as Ioseph was. Paraphernalia of female masturbation, i.e., a phallus, her bedboard, and a velvet covered hand mirror. Helen Gardner says that these two lines were omitted from the 1633 edition of Donne's poems because they were indecent. They were first printed in 1669, but they are found in all known manuscripts (139).

54. Ioseph. This is the Old Testament Joseph. He refused to sleep with the wife of his master, Potiphar (Genesis 39:7–20).

◆ Manuscripts: Crum M207; Beal Vol. I, pt. 1, DnJ 31–99; Yale M0161 ◆ *Aberdeen University Library:* MS 29 (pp. 169–71); *Bodleian:* MS Add. B. 97 (ff. 55ᵛ–56); Don.d.58 (f. 48); MS Eng. poet. e. 14 (ff. 29ᵛ–30); MS Eng. poet. e. 37 (pp. 31–32); MS Eng. poet. e. 99 (ff. 15ᵛ–16ᵛ); MS Eng. poet. f. 9 (pp. 116–18); MS Eng. poet. f. 27 (pp. 113–14); MS Rawl. poet. 117 (f. 224 [rev]); MS Rawl. poet. 160 (f. 104); *British Library:* Add. MS 18647 (f. 1); Add. MS 22118 (f. 7ᵛ); Add. MS 25707 (f. 12); Add. MS 30982 (ff. 81–82); Egerton MS 2421 (f. 35); MS Harley 4955 (ff. 96ᵛ–97); Lansdowne MS 740 (f. 97); MS Sloane 542 (ff. 53ᵛ–54); MS Sloane 1792 (ff. 83–84); Stowe MS 961 (f. 53); Stowe MS 962 (ff. 127ᵛ–28ᵛ); *Cambridge:* MS Add. 29 (f. 39ᵛ [rev]); MS Add. 5778 (ff. 26–27); MS Ee. 4.14 (f. 76ᵛ); *Chetham's Library, Manchester:* Mun. A 4.15 (pp. 95–97); *Derbyshire Record Office:* D258/60/26a (ff. 35–36); *Emmanuel College, Cambridge:* MS 1.3.16 (James) VI (f. 3ᵛ); *Folger:* V.a. 97 (pp. 42–43); V.a. 125, pt. I (f. 54); V.a. 170 (57–59); V.a. 245 (f. 47); V.a. 319 (ff. 44ᵛ–45); V.a. 322 (pp. 39–41); V.b. 43 (ff. 9ᵛ–10); W.a. 118 (f. 6); *Harvard:* fMS Eng. 966.1 (ff. 13ᵛ–14ᵛ); fMS Eng. 966.3 (ff. 16ᵛ–17ᵛ); fMS Eng. 966.4

(f. 145); MS Eng. 686 (f. 61ᵛ, 78ᵛ); MS Eng. 966.5 (ff. 68–69); MS Eng. 966.6 (ff. 82ᵛ–84); MS Eng. 966.7 (ff. 6ᵛ–7, 89ᵛ–90); *Huntington Library:* EL 6893 (ff. 60–61); **Owned by Sir Geoffrey Keynes:** Bibliotheca Bibliographici No. 1860 (ff. 23–24ᵛ); Bibliotheca Bibliographici No. 1861 (ff. 30ᵛ–31ᵛ); Bibliotheca Bibliographici No. 1863 (ff. 3ᵛ–4); *Meisei University Library, Tokyo:* Crewe MS, formerly Moncton Milnes MS, (pp. 16–18); *National Library of Scotland:* MS 6504 (ff. 18ᵛ–19ᵛ); *National Library of Wales:* Dolau Cothi MS (pp. 21–23); *New York Public Library:* Arents Collection, Cat. No. S191 (Elegies, pp. 20–21); Berg Collection, Westmoreland MS; *University of Nottingham:* Portland MS Pw V 37 (pp. 112–13); *Rosenbach:* MS 239/22 (ff. 4ᵛ–5); *St. John's College, Cambridge:* MS U. 26 (James 548) (pp. 92–94); *St. John's College, Oxford:* Crynes volume (p. 47); *St. Paul's Cathedral:* MS 49.B.43; SPC2; *South African Library, Cape Town:* MS Grey 7 a 29 (pp. 57–58); *Texas Tech:* Dalhousie I (f. 16); Dalhousie II (f. 31); *Trinity College, Cambridge:* MS R 3.12 (James 307) (pp. 1–2); TCD-I (ff. 29ᵛ–30); *Victoria and Albert Museum:* Dyce Collection, Cat. No. 18 (Pressmark 25.F.17) (ff. 24–25); *Westminster Abbey:* MS 41 (f. 14); *Yale:* Osborn b 148 (pp. 115–16). Osborn b 205 (ff. 32ᵛ–33). Beal notes an unlocated manuscript formerly owned by John Sparrow (DnJ 98).

✦ Gardner (1965), 21–22, 137–39; Grierson, 1:80–82; Shawcross, 60–62, 438–39; *Variorum 2,* Elegy 10.217–47, 757–77.

• • •

72. Richard Corbett (1582–1636), "Dʳ Corbet to the Duke of Buckingham in Spaine: 1623," 87–89. Pr. *CEP* (London, 1647), 40–43.

For biographical information on Corbett, see **HolM 11 notes.**

This poem was written in late summer 1623 when Corbett was still Dean of Christ Church. Buckingham was Corbett's patron. Corbett was criticized for writing this poem. It was believed that its flattery was more appropriate to a courtier than to "the poet of the taphouse" (B&TR xxv). Some contemporaries did not accept the Corbett attribution. For example, a poem beginning "False on his [my] deanery? false? nay more I'll lay" (see l. 59) is answered in Folger V.a. 345 "An Apologetick Rime vindicating D.C. deane of C.C. from ye aspersion of lat Adulatory verses published under his name." In Folger V.a. 262, the Corbett poem is followed by the answer poem, "ffalse on his Deanry," most of which appears as **HolM 134.**

James wanted his son Charles to marry the Spanish Infanta, Maria, daughter of Philip III, and dispatched Charles and Buckingham to Spain in order to negotiate the match. They departed England on 18 February 1623, presumably in secret, but their trip soon became common knowledge. English Protestants were alarmed over the proposed match. James's anti-Catholicism was never fully accepted; thus it was commonly believed the match would lead England into popery.

James had actually been planning the match for ten years. His daughter Elizabeth had married Elector Frederick of the Palatinate, a Protestant. James wanted to moderate the conflict between Catholics and Protestants, who, by 1623, were engaged in the Thirty Years' War (Lockyer 19). But the trip was not purely diplomatic. Charles, though he had never seen the Infanta, fell in love with her and instigated the trip himself (Sharpe 4). The entire mission was a failure because Spain insisted that Charles convert to Catholicism, which he was unwilling to do.

The trip was also important because, while traveling, Charles and Buckingham (James's favorite) became friends. Buckingham would later play an important role in the early years of Charles's reign. James created Buckingham Duke while in Spain.

For other poems related to this famous incident, see **HolM 73** and **HolM 146.**

There are many variants between the Holgate manuscript and *CEP.*

1–2. Ilands floatinge and remou'd in Ouids time. Ovid, *Metamorphosis* 6.334.

9. the Card. The map.

14. Black friers. A district in London.

15. Smyths. Buckingham and Charles left London in disguise, calling themselves Tom and Jacke Smith (Cf. **HolM 146**).

16. Paules. Paul's walk (see **HolM 152**).

17. Legend of each Day. Rumors.

20. Madrill. A forced rhyme, Madrid.

25. Chapline. Two or three chaplains were sent with Charles to Spain, but the Spanish would not allow them to hold their services (B&TR 147–48).

28. vitailes. The margin note is clearly French. Perhaps Holgate was correcting a misreading from his copy-text, or perhaps he wanted to stress a European sound.

38. Sacko. Sack, a white Spanish wine.

39. Pulletts. Young chickens.

52. the middle Ile. The middle aisle of St. Paul's, see l. 16n.

53. Duke Humpheries mess. B&TR relate the proverb "'to dine with Duke Humphrey'–to go dinnerless." It was believed that the Duke was buried in St. Paul's (148).

56. Gleeke. A card game. The Spaniards were believed to enjoy playing cards.

59. False on my Denerie. A comma after "false" would make this clearer. As the Dean of Christ Church, Corbett is swearing on his Deanery. For textual references to this line, see commentary above and **HolM 134 notes**.

60. Conde De Oleuares. Olevares was the most influential man in the Spanish court, thought responsible for making the marital negotiations fail. He opposed the marriage of Charles and the Infanta (Lockyer 130).

71. Carantoes. Gazettes.

71. Packetts. Probably a small package or parcel of letters, but possibly a packet of lies.

73. Belgicke Pismire. A pismire is an ant. "The Belgicke Pismire" was a tract favoring an alliance with the Dutch and against the Spanish Match. Many such tracts were written, some anonymously by Thomas Scott, who compared the Lowlanders (Belgics) to Pismires (B&TR 149).

78. Mother Zebedee. Zebedee was the father of James and John. His wife was Salome. (Matthew 20.20–21).

✦ Manuscripts: Crum I–1920; Beal Vol. II, pt. 1, CoR 342–371; Yale I–1601, I–1609 ✦ *Aberdeen University Library:* MS 29 (pp. 21–24); *Bodleian:* MS Ashmole 47 (ff. 83ᵛ–85ᵛ); MS Malone 19 (pp. 27–30); MS Rawl. D. 1048 (ff. 51ᵛ–52ᵛ); *Bradford Central Library:* Hopkinson MSS, Vol 34 (pp. 49–51); *British Library:* Add. MS 22603 (ff. 39ᵛ–41); Add. MS 33998 (ff. 8ᵛ–10); MS Harley 6931 (ff. 6–7ᵛ); MS Sloane 1792 (ff. 42–43ᵛ); *Corpus Christi College, Oxford:* MS 176 (f. 2); *Owned by H. M. Fitz-Roy Newdegate:* A414 (pp. 252–55); *Folger:* V.a. 125, pt. I (ff. 22ᵛ–23ᵛ); V.a. 162 (f. 66ᵛ–68); V.a. 262 (pp. 61–64); V.a. 345 (pp. 135–36); *Harvard:* MS Eng. 686 (ff. 5–6); *Huntington Library:* HM 198, pt. 1 (pp. 6–8); *New York Public Library:* Arents Collection, Cat. No. S191 (f. 2 [rev]); *University of Nottingham:* Portland MS Pw V 37 (pp. 317–19); *Rosenbach:* MS 239/22 (ff. 36–37); MS 239/27 (pp. 11–13); *St. John's College: Cambridge:* MS S. 32 (James 423) (ff. 38ᵛ–39ᵛ); *Sheffield Central Library:* Wentworth Woodhouse Muniments Str. 40–91; *University of Texas at Austin:* MS File/Herrick, R) Works B (pp. 348–50); *Trinity College, Dublin:* MS 877 (ff. 193–95); *Westminster Abbey:* MS 41 (ff. 12ᵛ–13ᵛ); *Yale:* Osborn b 197 (pp. 119–21); Osborn b 200 (pp. 24–27); Osborn b 208 (pp. 252–55).

✦ B&TR, xxiii–xxvi, 76–79, 146–49. For a related history of the incident, see Roger Lockyer, *Buckingham* (London: Longman, 1981), 16–19, especially 125–165; Kevin Sharpe, *The Personal Rule of Charles I* (New Haven and London: Yale Univ. Press, 1992), 3–6. The most recent history on the Spanish Match is Glyn Redworth, *The Prince and the Infanta* (New Haven and London: Yale Univ. Press, 2003).

• • •

73. John Grange (b. 1586/7 [?]), "Vppon Prince Charles his cominge home out of Spaine: 1623," subscribed "I: G:," 89. Pr. *P&R*, 63–64.

Calendar of State Papers Domestic identifies John Grange as the poet. There are no other candidates. Very little, however, is known about him, and certainly there can be no assurance that he wrote this poem. Mary Hobbs, in her facsimile edition of the Stoughton Manuscript, says Grange was "educ. Balliol College, Oxford (matric 1604); Lincoln's Inn, 1604. Six of his fourteen poems were set to music by Henry Lawes" (p. 311).

For information about Charles's trip to Spain to marry the Spanish Infanta, see **HolM 72 notes**.

The Holgate version, although lacking two lines found in the other sources, is quite similar to that in the *State Papers Domestic* (see collation). That manuscript is described as being a part of the Conway Papers. Another Conway manuscript is British Library Add. MS 23229, a miscellany clearly related to the Holgate. The handwriting of the manuscript collated below is the same as the hand B in Add. MS 23229. A second poem also found in the same grouping in *State Papers Domestic* is **HolM 134**. It, too, is in the same hand B. For discussion of British Library Add. MS 23229, see Introduction.

A second poem ascribed to "I: G:" is **HolM 81**.

   ✦ Collations: *P&R* / SP 153/113 SP. Title: Vppon Prince Charles his cominge home out of Spaine: 1623] Benj. Rudier to the Prince At his Return from Spain *P&R* ; 8 tryumph] triumphs *P&R*, SP; *P&R* ll. 9–10, *om.* Holgate. So open hearted men were, as 't'had been / No point of faith to think excess a sin. ; 20 that wine] what wind *P&R* ; 24 mee that doth] them that do *P&R* ; 26 no] a *P&R* ; 26 farther] further SP

   ✦ Manuscripts: Crum S–744 ✦ **Bodleian:** MS Eng. poet. c. 53 (f. 7ʳ); Public Record Office: SP 153/113 (**State Papers Domestic**).

✦ Mary Hobbs, ed., *The Stoughton Manuscript*, facsimile (Hants and Aldershot, UK: Scolar Press, 1990).

• • •

74. Anon., "Vppon a false report of my Ld of Kenzington And Sʳ George Geringe," 89. Pr. *Wits Recreations* (1640), no. 135.

This poem presents a problem for this edition because it *may* describe an event that occurred in 1637. More than likely, however, it was written in the early 1620s, the time frame of the two previous poems. Like several poems in the manuscript, it concerns the Spanish Match. Fortunately, two contemporaneous monographs survive that detail the events of the 1637 Siege of Breda, William Lithgew's *A True and Experimental Discourse, . . . of the last siege of Breda* and Henry Hexham's *A True and Brief Relation of the famous Seige of Breda*.

The date 1637 for this poem comes from Margaret Crum, *First-Line Index of Manuscript Poetry in the Bodleian Library*, I–185. The date is also asserted in the Yale Index. Crum's title for the poem reads: "'Upon the death of Sir G. Goring and the Earl of Kensington Falsely rumored', at the siege of Breda, 1637." Crum does not specify which Bodleian manuscript uses this title, but it is not MS

Rawl. poet 160, where it is entitled "On the report of ye death of the Earl of Kensington & Sr Georg Goring." In the Osborn b 197, it is entitled "Vpon the report of ye death of the Earle of Kensin?gton & Sr George Goringe." That manuscript was created in the late 1630s, but it does contain several poems about the Spanish Match. Crum explains her recreation of manuscript titles in the following manner: "Titles and notes in inverted commas are quoted exactly from the manuscript. Information derived from the manuscripts, but not quoted literally, is given without inverted commas" (1:ix). Crum does not put the notation "at the siege of Breda, 1637" in inverted commas; therefore, the place and date must come from one of the other two manuscripts.

The primary reason this poem is associated with the siege of Breda is that George, Lord Goring (1608–1657), was seriously injured at Breda in 1637. He was the son of George Goring, Earl of Norwich (1583?–1663). The *DNB* says he "became famous as the most brilliant and prodigal of the younger courtiers" (*DNB*, 1890 ed, 248a). He was shot in the leg by a "sling bullet" on 31 August 1637 while attempting "to lay a Damme of Rize-Bushes ouer a moate of the Horne-worke, in the French Approach" (Hexham 20). His injury was very serious and he nearly lost his leg.

William Davenant wrote a poem based on the belief that Goring had been killed, "Written, When Collonell Goring Was beleev'd to be slaine, at the siege of Breda." See *Sir William Davenant, The Shorter Poems, and Songs from the Plays and Masques*, ed. A. M. Gibbs (Oxford: Clarendon Press, 1972), 69–73. There is no mention of a Lord Kensington in the Davenant poem. Goring later fought as a Royalist in the Bishop's War and the Civil War.

Although Goring's injury is evidence that this poem was written after 1637, there are several reasons to question that date. First, Henry Hexham's account of the Seige of Breda includes a list of "Officers Slaine and Hurt of the English Tercia," or infantry (17–18, see below), but no Lord Kensington is mentioned in the list. Second, there are two candidates for Lord Kensington—Robert Rich, Earl Holland and Baron Kensington, born c. 1620, styled Lord Kensington, 1624–1649; or his father, Henry Rich (1590–1649), first Earl of Holland, also Lord Kensington. Of the two, the father was far better known. He was made Gentleman of the Bedchamber to Charles, Prince of Wales, in 1617. In February 1624, after it was decided that Charles would not marry the Spanish Infanta (see **HolM 72–73, 146**), Rich was sent to Paris to investigate a proposed marriage between Charles and Princess Henrietta Maria. In 1627, he was placed in command of a fleet sent to the Isle of Rhé. At Buckingham's death, Kensington became Chancellor of Cambridge University. If this Lord Kensington had been at the siege of Breda, Hexham would have (or at least should have) recorded it. His son, Robert Rich, is a possibility, but he would have only been about seventeen years old at the time. Niether the *DNB* or *ODNB* has an entry for Robert Rich.

In addition to the two Lord Kensingtons, there were also two George Gorings. George Goring, Earl of Norwich (1583?–1663) was the father of the George Goring injured at Breda. In 1610, he was appointed to the privy chamber for Henry, Prince of Wales. In 1623, he attended Charles on his trip to Spain to help complete the wedding match of Charles and the Spanish Infanta. In the following year, he helped negotiate the marriage treaty between Charles and Princess Henrietta Maria. He was made Baron Goring in 1628.

This George Goring is the probable subject of this poem because, not only was he a well-known person connected to many of the events described in the Holgate, he was also an associate of Henry Rich, Lord Kensington. For example, the *Calander of State Papers Domestic* for April 1623 (vol. 142), the approximate date for the two poems immediately preceding **HolM 74**, contains three entries that mention Kenington and Goring together. They are: "The Prince has sent for Lord Kenzington, Sir George Goring, and Sir Thos. Germain" (April 5, no. 38); "Note of safe conduct for Hen. Lord Kensington, Captain of the Guard, and Sir George Goring, Lieutenant of the Pensioners to go to Spain to the Prince" (April 9, no. 48, Chamberlain to Carlton); "Lord Kensington and Sir George

Goring's trunks and servants to be sent after them in the ships" (April 19, Conway to Vane). There is no information to suggest that Goring and Kensington fell into trouble during their trip to Spain, but it is certainly possible. A related journey to Spain is described in **HolM 146**.

Another reason for possible confusion around this poem is that there were two sieges of Breda, the first occurring in 1625. Circumstances leading up to that siege are described in **HolM 107**. There is no information that any of the four people described above were involved.

There is little positive evidence to suggest that the siege of Breda in 1637 had anything to do with this poem. The confusion comes from Davenant's poem and the fact that George Goring, the son, was injured there.

In terms of the Holgate, had the poem been written after 1637, it would be completely out of place. With the exception of **HolM 182**, no other poem in the miscellany describes any event that occurred in the 1630s. Moreover, it sequentially follows two poems that do concern negotiations for the proposed Spanish Match, which did involve the two fathers in question. For further discussion, see Introduction, p. xix.

There is one other remote explanation for this problem. The handwriting for this poem is slightly smaller than the writing on the rest of this page. It is possible that the scribe transcribed this poem later than the other poems found on this page and squeezed it into a small space that he had left open.

✦ Manuscripts: Crum I–185; Yale I–0154 ✦ ***Bodleian:*** MS Firth e. 4 (p. 6); MS Rawl. D. 398 (f. 228ᵛ); MS Rawl. poet. 160 (f. 23); ***Yale:*** Osborn b 197 (p. 130).

✦ The second siege of Breda must have created much excitement. Two contemporary accounts were published, William Lithgew's *A True and Experimental Discourse, upon the begining, proceeding, and Victorious event of the last seige of Breda* (London, 1637), and Henry Hexham's *A True and Brief Relation of the famous Seige of Breda*, (London, 1637). The latter details Goring's injury. The list of "Slaine and Hurt," discussed above, is found in what appears to be an appendix to the book entitled "The Articles of Composition." The appendix has its own pagination.

. . .

75. Sir Francis Hubert (1568?–1631), "Noli peccare," 90. Pr. *The Historie of Edward the Second, surnamed Carnavon, one of our English Kings: together with the fatall Downfall of his two Vnfortunate Favorites, Gaveston and Spencer* (London, 1629), 166–68.

Like William Holgate, Sir Francis Hubert was from Essex. His father was probably Edward Hubert, a Six Clerk in Chancery. The Six Clerks held very lucrative positions, serving as the official intermediaries between the solicitors and the court itself.

Hubert matriculated at Hart Hall, Oxford, 5 June 1584, but did not graduate. He was admitted to Lincoln's Inn, 16 October 1587 (Mellor xiv–xv). He also served as one of the Six Clerks in Chancery, 1601–1603, and was knighted shortly after his appointment (*ODNB*).

Hubert's political narrative, *The Historie of Edward the Second*, was written late in the reign of Elizabeth. It was suppressed because it dealt with the deposition of a monarch. The poem, however, survived in manuscript, and in 1628, one year prior to Hubert's death, an unauthorized version was published. Thereafter, in 1629, Hubert issued his own text of the poem, which the frontispiece describes as "according to the true Originall Copie." It is in this edition that the poem "Noli peccare" was published.

There are no other known manuscript copies of this poem, nor is it included in any manuscript of *Edward the Second*.

✦ *The Poems of Sir Francis Hubert*, ed. Bernard Mellor (Oxford: Oxford Univ. Press, 1970), xi–xlvi, 170–71. For historical criticism of Hubert's poetry, see Homer Nearing, Jr., "English Historical Poetry, 1599–1641" (Diss., U of Pennsylvania, 1945), 70–77. Nearing believes the poem was completed in 1608 or 1609 (70).

• • •

76. Anon., untitled, "Wett eyes (yet great wth teares) why weepe you so?," 91. Unprinted.

Research has revealed no other copy of this poem. Stylistically, it seems similar to the previous poem, **HolM 75**, but it is not found among the known works of Sir Francis Hubert.

• • •

77. William Herbert (1580–1630), "I lost you & now the gaine is double to mee," 91. Pr. *P&R*, 25.

Gary Waller ascribes this poem to Pembroke on the basis of its inclusion in the first fifty-four pages of *P&R* (165). Unfortunately, he comments only briefly on this poem, saying that when a woman acts independently of a man, his regaining her is used to reassert and even "double" (see inscription) his authority over her. Waller's comments are significant to this edition because the miscellany tradition is overwhelmingly male, the predominant point of view being what Waller calls "late Petrarchan."

The Holgate text is similar to *P&R*, suggesting that the original source for it was close to the coterie in which Herbert's text circulated (see collation). "Hands," rather than "shades," l. 4, sounds correct, but it may be a transcription error. The number of variants in the Rosenbach text suggests that several manuscripts containing this poem have been lost.

For a discussion of William Herbert and *P&R*, see **HolM 40 notes**.

> ✦ Collation: *P&R*. Inscription: I lost you & now the gaine is double to mee] I left you, and now the gain of you is to me a double gain. *P&R* ; 4 hands] shades *P&R*
> ✦ Manuscripts: Crum D–161 ✦ **Bodleian:** MS Ashmole 47 (f. 42); **New York Public Library:** Arents Collection, Cat. No. S288 (pp. 77–78); **Rosenbach:** MS 1083/16 (p. 255).

✦ Redding, 665–66; Waller, 159–88.

• • •

78. Richard Corbett (1582–1636), "A Letter from D^r: C: to a friend," 92–93. Pr. *CEP* (1647), 31–33.

The "friend" is Sir Thomas Aylesbury, secretary to the Lord High Admiral Charles Howard, the Earl of Nottingham; Aylesbury later became secretary to George Villiers, the Duke of Buckingham, after Buckingham replaced Nottingham as the Lord High Admiral. The comet (line 10) appeared over England 18 November 1618. It is the principal image in "Uppon Queene Anne," by King James (**HolM 2**). Corbett used the same image in his "Elegy Upon the death of Queene Anne."

Corbett was part of a coterie of Christ Church friends that included Aylesbury and Sir Francis Stuart (see **HolM 146 notes**), a relative of both King James and Lord Admiral Nottingham. Aylesbury and Stuart, in turn, were friends of Thomas Harriot, astronomer and mathematician.

The poem appears to have been written in 1618, near the time Buckingham replaced Nottingham as Lord Admiral. Buckingham was an intimate friend of the King. Indeed, a year earlier James had told his privy councilors that "he loved the Earl of Buckingham more than any other man" (*Documentos ineditos para la historia de Espana*, 1936–45, 1:101–2, qtd. in *ODNB*). Buckingham's advance included his doling out patronage as a means to gather power for himself.

Corbett frequently used poetry as a way to solicit patronage. In 1618, he was still a proctor at Christ Church, Oxford. He wanted, however, to "become a bishop 'or at least a dean of a rich church'" (B&TR xix). To this end he had written an elegy on the death of Lord Howard of Effingham and a poem praising Lord Mordaunt (**HolM 62**).

> **3–5. Sʳ Francis . . . Imparted his returne.** Sir Francis Stuart (see above) accompanied Gondomar, the Spanish Ambassador, back to Spain. James had sought to mediate the conflict between Frederick, the Elector Palatine, and Matthias, the Emperor of Bohemia, at the beginning of the Thirty Years' War. Matthias was a Hapsburg and a client of Philip III of Spain. James hoped to keep Spain out of the war, and he also hoped that his son Charles would marry the Spanish Infanta. Frederick was James's son-in-law. Philip did not take James's offer of mediation seriously but sent Gondomar to England as a way to placate James and make him feel important (Bald 338–39).
>
> **5. (Deer Charle).** *CEP* prints "churle," B&TR "Churle." Perhaps a name or nickname, but Aylesbury's name was Thomas. If "churle," the use is ironic, a man of low estate, a villain, but also someone stingy or niggardly.
>
> **12. Sion.** Syon House was the home of the Earl of Northumberland, patron of both Aylesbury and Harriot.
>
> **14. Twixt Barnauell and vniuersall Grace.** Jan van Oldenbarneveldt, a Dutch statesman, was arrested and interrogated by the States-General. Universal grace was an Arminian tenet. Corbett was an Arminian.
>
> **16. Lerma-Duke and Cardinall.** Spanish Premier during the reign of Philip III. He controled the Spanish government.
>
> **21–22. And though wee vse . . . porcters to the Kinge.** He means "proctors." According to B&TR (136), this is an Oxford joke at the expense of Cambridge. A Cambridge proctor by the name of Singleton preached before the King on the subject of universal grace. The King, however, was so displeased that Singleton had to be censured and converted.
>
> **38. Ho boyes.** Hautboys or hoboys. A high-pitched reed instrument. An oboe.
>
> **38. Iacobs staues.** Instruments to measure the location of the sun.
>
> **39. Gunter.** Edmund Gunter (1581–1626). A noted mathematician, he studied with Corbett at both Westminster and Christ Church. He is known for his study of logarithms and the application of mathematical instruments for astronomy and navigation (*ODNB*).
>
> **41. Guy.** An Oxford carrier.
>
> **42/43. Charles waine.** Seven bright stars in the constellation Great Bear (or Big Dipper).
>
> **47. Heriots minde.** Thomas Harriot (see note above) was noted for his expertise in mathematics and navigation.
>
> **52. doth hee rule a boue the Moone.** Apparently, there was much discussion about the nature of comets. A Mr. Briggs, Lecturer at Gresham College and later at Oxford, argued that perfect comets flew above the moon, in contradistinction to a belief of Aristotle (B&TR 138).

✦ Manuscripts: Crum M599; Beal Vol. II, pt. 1, CoR 316–341 ✦ *Aberdeen University Library:* MS 29 (pp. 78–80); *Bodleian:* MS Ashmole 313 (ff. 32ᵛ–33); MS Smith 17 (pp. 140–41); MS Tanner 306/2 (f. 251); Hopkinson MSSS, Vol 34 (pp. 37–38); *British Library:* Add. MS 21433 (ff. 103–4ᵛ); Add. MS 22602 (f. 9); Add. MS 25303 (ff. 107ᵛ–8ᵛ); Add. MS 30982 (f. 80); Add. MS 33998 (f. 10); Add. MS 58215 (pp. 14–15); MS Harley 3910 (ff. 58–59); MS Sloane 1792 (ff. 68–69); *Folger:* V.a. 170 (pp. 242–44); V.a. 345 (pp. 113–15); *Huntington Library:* HM 198, pt. 1 (pp. 105–6); *National Library of Wales:* Peniarth MS 500B (pp. 1–4); *New York Public Library:* Arents Collection, Cat. No. S191 (ff. 3–4 [rev]); *University of Nottingham:* Portland MS Pw V 37 (pp. 312–13); *Rosenbach:* MS 239/22 (ff. 17ᵛ–18ᵛ); MS 239/27 (pp.

142–43); ***Victoria and Albert Museum:*** Dyce Collection, Cat. No. 18 (Pressmark 25.F.17) (f. 72); ***Westminster Abbey:*** MS 41 (ff. 66^v–67); ***Dr. Williams's Library:*** MSS 12.54 (ff. 13–14); YAS1. Also ***State Papers Domestic:*** Jac. I, Dec. 9, 1618, no. 17.

✦ B&TR, xvii–xx, 63–65, 135–38.

• • •

79. Thomas Carew (1595?–1640), "Excuse of Absence," 93. Pr. *Wits Recreations* (1641), Sig. V3^v.

This poem is based on Guarini's Madrigal XCVI (*Rime*, 1598, 105^v). The madrigal is printed in Dunlap, 272.

Carew traveled with the embassy of Sir Dudley Carleton to Italy, 1613–15. A letter from Carew to Carleton dated 2 September 1616 indicates that he learned "languages" while there (Dunlap 202). It is surely possible that this and the following poem were written during that time period.

✦ Manuscripts: Crum Y404; Beal Vol. II, pt. 1, CwT 205–234 ✦ ***Bodleian:*** MS Ashmole 47 (f. 41^v, Dun); Don.d.58 (f. 45, Dun); MS Eng. poet. c. 50 (f. 116^v); MS Eng. poet. d. 152 (f. 108); MS Eng. poet. e. 37 (p. 75, Dun); ***British Library:*** Add. MS 30982 (f. 11, Dun); MS Eng. poet. f. 25 (f. 19^v); MS Eng. poet. f. 27 (p. 232); MS Rawl. poet. 160 (f. 106^v); MS Rawl. poet. 209 (f. 4^v, Dun); Add. MS 15227 (f. 96^v); Egerton MS 2421 (f. 4, Dun); Egerton MS 2725 (f. 62^v); Lansdowne MS 777 (f. 68, Dun); ***Corpus Christi College, Oxford:*** MS 328 (f. 83); ***Folger:*** V.a. 96 (ff. 49^v–50); V.a. 308 (f. 33^v); V.a. 345 (p. 28); V.a. 399 (f. 233^v); V.b. 43 (f. 7); ***Harvard:*** fMS 626 (f. 76); MS Eng. 686 (f. 91); ***Leeds Archive Department:*** MX 237 (f. 7^v); ***University of Newcastle upon Tyne:*** MS Bell/White 25 (ff. 52^v–53); ***Rosenbach:*** MS 239/23 (pp. 44–45); MS 239/27 (p. 39); MS 1083/17 (f. 43^v); ***Yale:*** Osborn b 62 (pp. 32–33); Osborn b 197 (p. 237); Osborn b 205 (f. 45^v).

✦ Dunlap, 131, 272.

• • •

80. Thomas Carew (1595?–1640), "A Laydes Prayer to Cupid," 93. Pr. *The Academy of Complements* (1650); *Wits Interpreter* (1655), 116.

This and John Donne's "Break of Day" (**HolM 126**) are the two poems in the manuscript narrated by a woman. It translates Guarini's Madrigal CIX (*Rime*, 1598, 112^v).

✦ Manuscripts: Crum S–546; Beal Vol. II, pt. 1, CwT 389–392 (excludes Holgate) ✦ ***Bodleian:*** MS Ashmole 47 (f. 41); MS Eng. poet. e. 37 (p. 56); MS Rawl. poet. 209, f. 4^v (Dun); ***British Library:*** MS Harley 6057 (f. 45); ***New York Public Library:*** Arents Collection, Cat. No. S288 (p. 77).

✦ Dunlap, 131, 272.

• • •

81. John Grange (?), "Of one braginge of his Auncestors," subscribed "I: G:," 94. Unprinted.

Consensus has it that this poem was written by someone named John Grange, but beyond that very little can be said. There was a sixteenth-century poet named John Grange (b. 1556/57), who wrote *The Golden Aphroditis* (1577). Although there appears to be no correlation between that poetry and what is found in the Holgate, the entry for John Grange in the *ODNB* notes that his parents were plebian, perhaps suggesting the subject of this poem.

"Vppon Prince Charles his comminge home out of Spaine: 1623" (**HolM 73**), is subscribed "I: G:". The date and the subject matter of that poem would surely indicate a different person from the Elizabethan poet. Both manuscripts listed below attribute this poem to "Io: Grange."

For possible information on John Grange, see **HolM 73 notes**.

✦ Manuscripts: *British Library:* Add. MS 33998 (f. 81, Io: Grange); *Folger:* V.a. 96 (f. 70, Mr. Io: Grange).

• • •

82. Ben Jonson (1572?–1637), "An Epitaph," subscribed "B: I.", 94. Pr. John N. Harper, "Ben Jonson and Mrs. Bulstrode," *N&Q,* 3rd Ser. 4 (1863), 198–99.

The subject of this epitaph is Cecelia Bulstrode. Jonson included it in a letter to a friend, George Garrard, printed in H&S, 8:372.

Cecelia Bulstrode died at Twickenham Park, 4 August 1609 at the age of twenty-five. She was the daughter of Hedgerley Bulstrode and cousin to Lucy, the Countess of Bedford. Several poets wrote verses on her passing, including Donne, "Elegie upon the death of Mrs. Boulstread," and an epitaph by Lord Herbert of Cherbury (see Moore Smith, 20–21). Donne describes her painful death in a letter to Henry Goodyere (*Letters to Severall Perrsons of Honour,* 1651, 215–16).

This is the second poem Jonson wrote about Cecelia Bulstode. Twice in *Conversations with Drummond* (ll. 88–89, 569–71) Jonson identifed her as the subject of "An Epigram on the Court Pucell" (*The Under-wood,* xlix). A pucelle is a courtesan (*OED*). It is generally assumed that this epitaph was meant by Jonson to counterbalance his attack on her in the earlier poem. In l. 3, Jonson refers to her as a "virgin."

> **6. Graces fowre.** In his letter to Garrard, Jonson says he wrote this poem in a hurry. There were actually three Graces, the daughters of Zeus.
> **7. Pallas, Language.** Parfitt writes that she "came to be regarded as the patronese of arts and crafts, and hence as the goddess of wisdom" (558).
> **7. Cinthea Modestie.** Cynthia was the Goddess of Chastity.
> **12. sett boulstred.** Her name. It should read "Sell," for "Cecelia."

✦ Manuscripts: Crum S1178; Beal Vol. I, pt. 2, JnB 102–121; Yale S1093 ✦ *Bodleian:* MS Ashmole 38 (p. 187); MS Rawl. poet. 31 (f. 36); MS Rawl. poet. 116 (f. 55ᵛ); MS Rawl. poet. 160 (f. 25ᵛ); *British Library:* Add. MS 33998 (f. 33); Egerton MS 2230 (f. 35ᵛ); MS Harley 4064 (f. 261ᵛ); MS Harley 6057 (f. 33ᵛ); Stowe MS 962 (f. 90ᵛ); *Chetham's Library, Manchester:* Mun. A 4.15); *Edinburgh University Library:* MS La. III 493(f. 94); *Folger:* V.a. 96 (f. 76); *Huntington Library:* EL 6893 (f. 26); HM 198, pt. 2 (f. 113ᵛ); MS Eng. 966.5 (f. 87); *Owned by Sir Geoffrey Keynes:* Bibliotheca Bibliographici No. 1860 (f. 49ᵛ); *National Library of Scotland:* Hawthornden VIII MS 2060 (f. 164); *Rosenbach:* MS 1083/16 (p. 274); *Yale:* Osborn b 356 (p. 99).

✦ H&S, 8:371–72; 9:130–31. Beal writes in JnB 102: "Autograph fair copy, in a letter to George Garrard: [1609]. Harvard, Lowell autography." This is copy-text for H&S. (See *TLS,* 6 March 1930.) See also *The Poems, English and Latin, of Edward Herbert of Cherbury,* ed. G. C. Moore Smith (Oxford: Clarendon Press, 1923); "Conversations with William Drummond of Hawthornden," in *Ben Jonson, The Complete Poems,* ed. George Parfitt (New Haven and London, Yale Univ. Press, 1975), 273, 459–80, 558. For additional commentary, see Grierson, 2:212–14.

83. Anon., untitled, "Cease bootless teares, weepe not for him whose Death," 94.

Michael Rudick describes this poem in his edition of Ralegh's poems as a "Verse Testimonial" to Ralegh. He uses the Holgate as his copy-text, emended from that version in PRO SP 46/64, f. 163.

> **9. Eueinge.** The scribe clearly intended "Eveninge," but he omitted the first *n*. This is typical in the manuscript. Many 'ing' endings are written to look like 'nig'; the dot above a lowercase "i" is frequently omitted. This edition corrects that mistake, but in this case the missing letter is omitted.

✦ Rudick, 194.

• • •

84. Anon., untitled, "I wonder how my Turtle can deny," 95–96. Unprinted.

No other copy of this poem has been found.

> **16. Gnomen.** A jocular reference to the nose and/or the arm of a sundial. Spelling in *OED* is "gnomon."
> **60. venter.** Venture, spelled 'venter' through the sixteenth century, to hazard or risk (*OED*).

• • •

85. William Shakespeare, "On his Mistris Beauty" [Sonnet 106], 96. Pr. *Shake-Speares Sonnets* (1609).

We do not know why Shakespeare's sonnets are not better represented in surviving manuscripts. Of the sonnets, only twelve are transcribed: nos. 1, 2, 8, 32, 33, 68, 71, 106, 107, 116, 128, 138. Sonnet 106 is found in Rosenbach MS 1083/16 but attached to a second poem, "When mine eies, first admiringe your rare beauty," which coincidentally is **HolM 125**. By its variants, the poem does not appear to be part of a family stemma that originated with the 1609 edition. Peter Beal writes: "It is, however, known that at least some of the Sonnets had a MS circulation in the 1590s: among the works of the 'mellifluous & hony-tongued Shakespeare' which Francis Meres praises in *Palladis Tamia* (London, 1598), 281–82, are 'his sugred Sonnets among his priuate friends'. It is at least a possibility that certain of the texts found in miscellanies of the 1620s and 1630s ultimately derive from early MS copies of individual sonnets and have no connection whatever with the 1609 edition" (450).

It should be noted that William Holgate has been suggested as one of the many possible persons to whom the sonnets were dedicated, "Mr. W. H." There is nothing besides the inclusion of this poem in the manuscript coupled with the coincidence of William Holgate's initials that would suggest such a possibility. For discussion, see Rollins 2:225–26.

The sonnet as transcribed from the Holgate text is printed in Rollins 1:260.

Shakespeare's acting company, The King's Men, visited Saffron Walden, the home of the Holgate family, in 1605 (Kernan 205).

> **12. skill.** Modern editions have generally adapted this improved reading (cf. 1609, 'still') (Booth 341–42).

✦ Manuscripts: Beal Vol. I, pt. 2, ShW 25–66 ✦ ***Rosenbach:*** MS 1083/16 (pp. 256–57).

✦ See *A New Variorum of Shakespeare: The Sonnets*, ed. Hyder Edward Rollins (Philadelphia: Lipponcott, 1944), 1:260, 2:225–26; *Shakespeare's Sonnets*, ed. Stephen Booth (New Haven and London: Yale Univ. Press, 1978), 93, 340–42, 545–48; *"The Sonnets" and "A Lover's Complaint,"* ed.

John Kerrigan (Harmondsworth and New York: Viking, 1986), 129, 443–44, 451; Alvin Kernan, *Shakespeare, the King's Playwright* (New Haven: Yale Univ. Press, 1995).

For critical commentary, Patrick Cheney, "Shakespeare's Sonnet 106, Spenser's National Epic, and Counter-Petrarchism," *English Literary Renaissance* 31 (2001), 331–64.

• • •

86. John Donne, "Dᴿ D: at his goinge into Bohemia: A Himne to Christ," ["A Hymne to Christ, at the Authors last going into Germany"], 97. Pr. *Poems*, 304–5.

Donne was appointed by James as chaplain to the Lord of Doncaster. Doncaster was sent to the continent to mediate the conflict between Ferdinand of Styria and the Bohemian Protestants, who refused to accept Ferdinand's appointment as their ruler. Ferdinand had been appointed by Matthias, king of Bohemia. James was responding to the entreaties of his son-in-law, Frederick, the Elector Palatine, who supported the Protestants. James hoped to maintain neutrality because he did not want to antagonize Spain, which supported Ferdinand. James wanted his son Charles to marry the Spanish Infanta (see **HolM 72, 73**). The refusal by the Protestants to accept Ferdinand is considered the beginning of the Thirty Years' War (Bald 338–40).

Donne left England 12 May 1619 in poor health (Bald 340, 343). Bald argues that this accounts for the sense of doom and shipwreck that pervades the poem.

This is the latest poem written by Donne that is found in the Holgate. In 1622, he was made Dean of St. Paul's with Buckingham's support.

2. Emblim of thy Arke. Ark of the Covenant, but Noah's ark is a possible interpretation.

✦ Manuscripts: Crum I–1646; Beal Vol. I, pt. 1, DnJ 1550–1564 ✦ *Bodleian:* MS Eng. poet. f. 9 (pp. 6–7); MS Rawl. poet. 160 (f. 51); *British Library:* Add. MS 18647 (ff. 90ᵛ–91); MS Harley 6057 (f. 33ᵛ); Stowe MS 961 (ff. 109ᵛ–10); *Cambridge:* MS Add. 5778 (f. 81ᵛ); *Harvard:* fMS Eng. 966.3 (f. 1 12ᵛ); fMS Eng. 966.4 (f. 93); MS Eng. 966.5 (f. 20); *Huntington Library:* EL 6893 (f. 140). *Owned by Sir Geoffrey Keynes:* Bibliotheca Bibliographici No. 1861 (f. 98); *Trinity College, Cambridge:* MSR 3.12 (James 307) (p. 199); *Trinity College, Dublin:* MS 877 (I) (f. 134ᵛ); *Yale:* Osborn b 148 (p. 2).

✦ For extensive commentary on Donne's trip to Germany, see Bald, 338–65. See also Grierson, 352–53; Gardner (1978), 48–49, 106–7; Shawcross, 387–88.

• • •

87. John Donne, "Dᴿ D: to his freinde of a storme at sea," ["The Storme"], 98–99. Pr. *Poems*, 56–59.

Donne had accompanied the English fleet on its successful attack on the Spanish Armada at Cadiz, 21 June 1596. Apparently, he did not see any battle action. When Philip II fortified the Armada, the British countered by assembling a second fleet with the Earl of Essex as commander-in-chief, Lord Thomas Howard, vice-admiral, and Ralegh, rear-admiral (Bald 82–86). Donne again volunteered. The British fleet set sail for the Azores on 5 July 1597, but within a few days encountered a violent storm, the occasion of this poem. Donne also wrote a prose letter (see *Prose Works*, ed. Simpson, 284–86), in which he describes the misery the troops confronted during this aborted voyage.

"The Storme" is a verse letter to Christopher Brooke (d. 1628), one of Donne's closest friends. They shared chambers at Lincoln's Inn. Brooke was imprisoned for his part in Donne's secret wedding in 1602. Later, Brooke became MP for York (1604–26). See also **HolM 99 notes**.

"The Storme" is generally associated with a second verse letter to Christopher Brooke, "The Calme," which Donne wrote while the fleet was sailing to the Azores. "The Calme" is not in the Holgate.

> **1. Thou that art I.** Donne sets up Brooke as his alter ego in this poem (Marotti 114–15).
>
> **14. Æyres middle Marble rounde.** The accepted reading is "room" not "rounde," which makes far better sense. Shawcross records no other text with this reading. Hail and snow were engendered from the middle regions of the air (Milgate 204). The air in this region was thought to be extremely cold, i.e., as cold as marble (Smith 517).
>
> **32. A non.** Anon.
>
> **60. striues.** According to Milgate, "strive" (1633) is correct because "ordinance" is used as a plural. The later editions of Donne's *Poems* all use "strives."

✦ Manuscripts: Crum T2295; Beal Vol. I, pt. 1, DnJ 3047–3087 ✦ *Bodleian:* MS Eng. poet. e. 14 (ff. 41–42); MS Eng. poet. e. 99 (ff. 30ᵛ–31ᵛ); MS Eng. poet. f. 9 (pp. 41, 213–15); MS Rawl. poet. 117 (ff. 26–27); *British Library:* Add. MS 25707 (f. 55); MS Harley 3511 (ff. 19ᵛ–20); MS Harley 4955 (ff. 102–3); Lansdowne MS 740 (ff. 95–96); Stowe MS 962 (ff. 55ᵛ–56ᵛ); *Cambridge:* MS Add. 5778 (ff. 33–34); MS Ee. 4.14 (ff. 72ᵛ–73ᵛ); *Edinburgh University Library:* MS La. III 493 (ff. 108–9); *Harvard:* fMS Eng. 966.1 (ff. 24ᵛ–25ᵛ); fMS Eng. 966.3 (ff. 14ᵛ–15ᵛ); fMS Eng. 966.4 (ff. 172–73); MS Eng. 966.5 (ff. 118–19ᵛ); MS Eng. 966.6 (ff. 105ᵛ–7); MS Eng. 966.7 (ff. 13ᵛ–14ᵛ); *Huntington Library:* EL 6893 (ff. 103–4); HM 198, pt. 2 (f. 12); *Owned by Sir Geoffrey Keynes:* Bibliotheca Bibliographici No. 1860 (ff. 35ᵛ–37); Bibliotheca Bibliographici No. 1861 (ff. 79–80); *National Library of Scotland:* Hawthornden XV MS 2067 (ff. 23ᵛ–25); MS 6504 (ff. 12–13); *National Library of Wales:* Dolau Cothi MS (pp. 38–41); NLW.MS 5308E (ff. 8ᵛ–9); NLW.MS 12443A, pt. ii (pp. 105–19); *New York Public Library:* Arents Collection, Cat. No. S191 (Satires, pp. 38–40); Berg Collection, Westmoreland MS; *St. John's College, Oxford:* Crynes volume (pp. 56–58); *St. Paul's Cathedral:* MS 49.B.43; *Texas Tech:* Dalhousie I (f. 38); Dalhousie II (f. 18); *The Queen's College, Oxford:* MS216 (ff. 207–8); TCD-I (ff. 27ᵛ–28ᵛ); *Victoria and Albert Museum:* Dyce Collection, Cat. No. 17 (Pressmark 25.F.16) (ff. 12–13); Dyce Collection, Cat. No. 18 (Pressmark 25.F.17) (ff. 16ᵛ–17); *Yale:* Osborn b 114 (pp. 221–26); Osborn b 148 (pp. 59–60). Also *Owned privately in England:* Heneage MS (Beal DnJ 3074).

✦ For discussion of Donne's military service, see Bald, 80–92. Also see Grierson, 1:175–77; Milgate, 54–57, 203–6; Shawcross, 189–91, 464–65; *Prose Works*, ed. Evelyn Simpson, 2ⁿᵈ ed. (Oxford: Clarendon Press, 1924), 284–86; Smith, 197–99, 516–18.

• • •

88. John Donne, "'The Crosse' by Dʳ: D:," 99–100. Pr. *Poems* (1633), 64–66.

This is not a good text. Several errors are described in the notes below. Shawcross does not cite any text of this poem with similar errors, which at least suggests that this is a poor transcription. There are several types of errors, including omission of lines, misread words, and combining two lines into one.

The cross, as a symbol, was associated with Roman Catholicism. Puritans called for the abolition of its use in baptism (Smith 646). They petitioned James with the Millenary Petition (1603), but at the Hampton Court Conference (1604), James decided that the Roman Church did not misuse the cross. Donne clearly supported the use of the cross in religious practice.

Unfortunately, the composition date of this poem is unknown. Gardner believes that because of its popularity and style, the poem is probably an early one.

16. drau'd one. The rendering here is certainly awkward. The standard reading is "dew'd," from *The Book of Common Prayer*, "pour upon them the continual dew of thy blessing" (Smith 647). It is impossible to say if the scribe intended "one" to mean "on" or "one."

22. saisd. Clearly a transcription error. It should read "raisd." The initial letter "s" is identical to the initial letter "s" in "seest," in the same line.

26. Chimicks. Chemicals. The word belongs in the next line, as in 1633. According to Shawcross, the omission of ll. 27–28 is unique.

50. points downewards when it downe wards bends. Two lines have become one, the first part of the first, the second part of the second. Shawcross records no other example of this error. "Bends" is found in Harvard fMS 966.4. See also the text note.

✦ Crum S514; Beal Vol. I, pt. 1, DnJ 775–805; Yale S0542 ✦ *Bodleian:* MS Eng. poet. e. 99 (ff. 46–47ᵛ); MS Eng. poet. f. 9 (pp. 220–22); MS Rawl. poet. 117 (ff. 203 [rev]); *British Library:* Add. MS 18647 (ff. 89–90); Add. MS 25707 (ff. 61ᵛ–62); MS Harley 3511 (ff. 19ᵛ–20); MS Harley 4955 (ff. 104–5); Stowe MS 962 (ff. 118ᵛ–19ᵛ); *Cambridge:* MS Add. 5778 (ff. 36–37); *Corpus Christi College, Oxford:* MS 327 (ff. 6ᵛ–7); *Edinburgh University Library:* MS La. III 493 (ff. 104ᵛ–5ᵛ); *Harvard:* fMS Eng. 966.3 (f. 111); fMS Eng. 966.4 (f. 92); MS Eng. 966.5 (ff. 9ᵛ–10ᵛ); MS Eng. 966.6 (ff. 145–46ᵛ); MS Eng. 966.7 (ff. 31–32); *Huntington Library:* EL 6893 (ff. 4–5); HM 198, pt. 2 (ff. 117ᵛ–18ᵛ); *Owned by Sir Geoffrey Keynes:* Bibliotheca Bibliographici No. 1860 (ff. 40–41ᵛ); Bibliotheca Bibliographici No. 1861 (ff. 6ᵛ–7ᵛ); Bibliotheca Bibliographici No. 1863 (ff. 10ᵛ–11); *National Library of Scotland:* MS 6504 (ff. 29ᵛ–30); *National Library of Wales:* Dolau Cothi MS (pp. 123–25); *New York Public Library:* Arents Collection, Cat. No. S191 (Miscellanea, pp. 108–10); *St. Paul's Cathedral:* MS 49.B.43; *South African Library, Cape Town:* MS Grey 7 a 29 (pp. 93–94); *Trinity College, Cambridge:* MS R 3.12 (James 307) (pp. 195–97); TCD-I (ff. 133–34); *Victoria and Albert Museum:* Dyce Collection, Cat. No. 18 (Pressmark 25.F.17) (ff. 52ᵛ–53); *Yale:* Osborn b 148 (pp. 86–87); Osborn b 200 (p. 92).

✦ See Gardner (1978), 26–28; Shawcross, 351–53; Smith, 326–27.

• • •

89. John Donne, "Dʳ: D:" ["Song"], 101. Pr. *Poems* (London, 1633), 96–97.
Some contemporary manuscripts have musical settings (Gardner 238–47; Shawcross, 91).

10. to see. The Holgate agrees with *Poems* (1633). Groups I and II generally omit "to." Gardner believes it should read "goe see," as in the 1669 edition of Donne's poems, thus retaining the poem's imperative mood (153). Two Group III manuscripts support this reading, British Library MS Stowe 961 and Harvard fMS 966.4.

✦ Manuscripts: Crum G118, G136; Beal Vol I, pt. 1, DnJ 2897–2941; Yale G0124, G0129 ✦ *Bodleian:* MS Eng. poet. e. 37 (p. 58); MS Eng. poet. e. 99 (ff. 103ᵛ–4); MS Eng. poet. f. 9 (pp. 44–45); MS Rawl. poet. 117 (f. 217[rev]); *British Library:* Add. MS 5956 (f. 37ᵛ); Add. MS 18647 (f. 21); Add. MS 25707 (f. 61); Egerton MS 2013 (f. 58ᵛ, musical setting); MS Harley 4064 (ff. 286ᵛ–87); MS Harley 4955 (f. 113ᵛ); Lansdowne MS 740 (f. 122); Stowe MS 961 (f. 75ᵛ); Stowe MS 962 (f. 65); *Cambridge:* MS Add. 29 (f. 19); MS Add. 5778 (ff. 52ᵛ–53); MS Ee. 4.14 (f. 61); *Folger:* V.a. 103, pt. I (f. 74); V.a. 162 (f. 25ᵛ); *Harvard:* fMS Eng. 966.1 (ff. 33ᵛ); fMS Eng. 966.3 (ff. 36ᵛ–37); fMS Eng. 966.4 (f. 203); MS Eng. 966.5 (f. 149ᵛ); MS Eng. 966.6 (f. 124); *Huntington Library:* EL 6893 (f. 21); HM 198, pt. 2 (f. 21ᵛ); *Owned by Sir Geoffrey Keynes:* Bibliotheca Bibliographici No. 1860 (ff. 73ᵛ–74ᵛ); Bibliotheca Bibliographici No. 1861 (f. 120); *National Library of Scotland:* MS 6504 (f. 43); *National Library of Wales:* Dolau Cothi MS (pp. 104–5); NLW.MS 5390D (pp. 6–7); *New York Public Library:* Arents

Collection, Cat. No. S191 (Miscellanea, p. 51); ***Owned privately in England:*** Monckton Milnes MS (p. 52); ***Rosenbach:*** MS 240/7 (p. 78); MS 243/4 (p. 21); ***St. Paul's Cathedral:*** MS 49.B.43; ***South African Library, Cape Town:*** MS Grey 7 a 29 (p. 145); ***Texas Tech:*** Dalhousie I (f. 54); Dalhousie II (f. 28); ***Trinity College, Cambridge:*** MS R 3.12 (James 307) (pp. 46–47); TCD-I (f. 49); ***Victoria and Albert Museum:*** Dyce Collection, Cat. No. 18 (Pressmark 25.F.17) (f. 32ᵛ); ***Westminster Abbey:*** MS 41 (f. 70); ***Yale:*** Osborn b 148 (pp. 66–67); Osborn b 200 (p. 92).

✦ Grierson, 1:8–9; Gardner (1965), 29–30; Shawcross, 90–91.

• • •

90. John Donne [?], "Dr: D:", 101–2. No seventeenth-century printings.

There is no way to know if this poem is actually by Donne. Shawcross prints it without comment. Chambers, however, seems quite positive about the attribution. He writes, "I think there can be no doubt that this is Donne's. It may be conjectured that he laid it aside, and used some of the notions for other elegies inspired by the same woman or the same theme" (71). Chambers then compares passages in this poem with passages in Elegy VI, "Oh, let mee not serve so, as those men serve," and Elegy VII, "Natures lay Ideot, I taught thee to love." Neither Elegy VI nor VII is in the Holgate.

Both Chambers and Bennett use the Holgate version as their copy-text.

> **2. sigh's.** In his collation, Shawcross reads this word as "sigh'ts," but the scribe deleted the "t". "Sigh's" clearly makes better sense, although it is noteworthy that here an apostrophe is used to replace an "e".

> ✦ Manuscript: ***Huntington:*** HM 198, pt. 2 (f. 50ᵛ).

✦ See E. K. Chambers, "An Elegy by John Donne," *Review of English Studies* 7 (1931), 69–71. Shawcross, 153–54, 458–59. Pr. *The Complete Poems of John Donne*, ed. Roger E. Bennett (Chicago: Packard, 1942), Elegy 21.

• • •

91. Anon., untitled, "Groane senceless earth to heare my burdenous woes," 102. Unprinted.

There is no other known copy of this poem; however, its tone resembles that of Donne's religious poetry. If **HolM 90** is an imitation of Donne, this might be a second poem by the same writer.

> **4. muringe.** An odd use of the word *mure*, to wall up, as if from the grave.

• • •

92. John Donne, "Dr. D:" ["Elegy on Lady Markham"], 103–4. Pr. *Poems*, 66–68.

Lady Bridget Markham, wife of Sir Anthony Markham, died 4 May 1609. She was the daughter of Sir James Harrington, first cousin and friend of Lucy, Countess of Bedford, at whose estate she died. Many poets wrote elegies on her death, including Francis Beaumont, "As unthrifts groane in straw for their pawnd beds," **HolM 64.** She was a Lady of Queen Anne's Bedchamber.

No particular relationship between Donne and Lady Markham is noted in the literature. She was, however, a friend of the Countess of Bedford, Donne's friend and patron (Bald 177–79).

For extensive annotation on this complex poem, see Milgate, 176–82.

> **5. pretend.** "To hold out or extend in front of or over a person or thing, especially as a covering or defense. *Obs.*" (*OED*, but cites sixteenth- and seventeenth-century usage).
> **7–8. land waters (teares of passion) . . . waters then aboue our firmament.** Milgate glosses: "The little world (l. 1) of man has "waters" (tears) corresponding to the two kinds of waters in

the macrocosm: those that flow through and from the "land," and the "seas above the firmament" (Genesis 1. 7–9).

11. teares which should wash sinners sinnes. This is a less complex reading than 1633, "teares, which wash sin, are sin." Milgate writes: "In those grieving for Lady Markham, tears of contrition are confused with tears for worldly losses, and are tainted with the saltiness of the 'Ocean' of death; thus their spiritual life is invaded by griefs which belong to man's 'lower parts.'"

12. Gods Noah. The reference to Noah has been disputed. A. J. Smith transcribes this as "God's 'No.'" He writes: "But the sense is that we now sinfully drown ourselves out of despairing grief, although God has forbidden us to take our own lives." Both Milgate and Grierson transcribe "Noe," meaning "Noah."

22. purslane. Porcelain.

24. mindes. Read "mine." Probably an accidental, Scotch "mynd." Precious metals, "hyperbolically, an abundant mass of gold" (*OED*).

35. vnabnoxious. The OED reports a 1649 usage of abnoxious as "incorrect"; however, the Holgate's "a" is quite clear. Not exposed to harm (*OED*).

42. christall glass. Milgate writes: "Crystal glass was made in Venice; glass with an infusion of clay, made in Florence, was called porcelain (see note 1. 22). Perhaps, too, paronomasia on "Christ."

47. Makeinge omissions ac kes. Should read "acts." Not to speak is as much an act as it is to speak. Lady Markham would omit things, then call them lies. See textual note.

57. froward. Presumptuous (*OED*).

57. heresie. Neo-Platonic commonplace that women were incapable of friendship.

◆ Manuscripts: Crum M106; Beal Vol. I, pt. 1, DnJ 1050–1089; Yale M0083 ◆ **Bodleian:** MS Eng. poet. e. 99 (ff. 24ᵛ–26); MS Eng. poet. f. 9 (pp. 124–26); **British Library:** Add. MS 18647 (ff. 11ᵛ–12ᵛ); Add. MS 19268 (f. 36ᵛ); Add. MS 25707 (f. 29); Add. MS 30982 (ff. 47ᵛ–48ᵛ);MS Harley 4064 (ff. 274ᵛ–75ᵛ); MS Harley 4955 (f. 105); Lansdowne MS 740 (f. 113); Stowe MS 961 (ff. 20ᵛ–21ᵛ); Stowe MS 962 (ff. 48–49); **Cambridge:** MS Add. 29 (ff. 15ᵛ–16); MS Add. 5778 (ff. 37–38); **Edinburgh University Library:** MS H.-P. Coll. 401 (f. 70ᵛ); MS La. III 493 (ff. 94ᵛ–95ᵛ); **Harvard:** fMS Eng. 966.1 (ff. 93–94); fMS Eng. 966.3 (ff. 25ᵛ–26ᵛ); fMS Eng. 966.4 (f. 140); MS Eng. 966.5 (ff. 82ᵛ–83); **Huntington Library:** EL 6893 (ff. 100–1); **Owned by Sir Geoffrey Keynes:** Bibliotheca Bibliographici No. 1860 (ff. 41ᵛ–43); Bibliotheca Bibliographici No. 1861 (ff. 4ᵛ–6); **National Library of Scotland:** MS 6504 (ff. 26ᵛ–27ᵛ); Hawthornden VIII MS 2060 (f. 247ᵛ); **National Library of Wales:** Dolau Cothi MS (p. 109); **New York Public Library:** Arents Collection, Cat. No. S191 (Miscellanea, pp. 96–97); Arents Collection, Cat. No. S288 (pp. 104–6); **University of Nottingham:** Portland MS Pw V 37 (pp. 23–24); **St. John's College, Oxford:** Crynes volume (p. 67); SPC; **South African Library, Cape Town:** MS Grey 7 a 29 (pp. 54–55); **Texas Tech:** Dalhousie I (ff. 48ᵛ–49); **Trinity College, Cambridge:** MS R 3.12 (James 307) (pp. 24–26); TCD-I (ff. 38–39); TCD-2 (ff. 258ᵛ–60); **Victoria and Albert Museum:** Dyce Collection, Cat. No. 18 (Pressmark 25.F.17) (ff. 48–49);**Yale:** Osborn b 114 (pp. 129–34); Osborn b 148 (pp. 119–21).

◆ Grierson, 1:279–81; Milgate, 57–59, 176–82; "Donne's Views on the State of the Soul after Death," in Gardner (1978), 114–17; Shawcross, 250–52, 405, 475–76; Smith, 247–49, 273–75; *Variorum* (*The Anniversaries and the Epicedes and Obsequies*), 6:112–28, 551–62.

• • •

93. William Herbert, Earl of Pembroke (1580–1630) and/or Sir Benjamin Rudyerd (1572–1658) or John Grange [?], "A Dialogue betwixt a Man and a woman," 104. Pr. *P&R*, 59–60; Henry Lawes, *The Second Book of Ayres and Dialogues* (1655), 10.

Although this poem was printed in *P&R*, we cannot assert that it was written by either or both poets: the edition contains poems that were not written by either. Gary Waller says it was probably written by John Grange but does not explain why (171). However, collation reveals that the text as it appears in the Holgate is much like the text as it was printed in 1660 (cf. **HolM 77, HolM 98, HolM 123**). Ault dates the poem to 1640, but David Coleman Redding has shown that it must have been written before 1631, the date of the Bishop miscellany, Rosenbach MS 1083/16 (Redding, 682).

The poem was set to music by Lawes (Redding, op cit., citing Day and Murrie, *English Song-Books*. According to John Donne, Jr., editor of *P&R*, Lawes contributed lyrics included in that edition (see **HolM 40 notes**).

The text as it appears in the Holgate suggests the possibility that this lyric was sung as a duet. The parts are clearly delineated in the margin and the stanzas are separated by lines drawn across the page.

> • Collation: *P&R* Title: *P&R*, "A Dialogue." (Stanzas in both texts are identical, but *P&R* identifies poets respectively as "Man, P"[embroke] and "Woman, R"[uddier]). 2 tasted] basted *P&R*; 5 whole] who'l *P&R*; 8 smell, or looke] smelt, or look't *P&R*; 10 vsiall] useless *P&R*.

> • Manuscripts: **British Library:** Add. MS 25707 (Ault copy-text); Egerton MS 2421 (f. 25ᵛ); **Rosenbach:** MS 1083/16 (pp. 261–62).

• Ault, 681–82; Cyrus L. Day and Eleanore B. Murrie, *English Song-Books 1651–1702: A Bibliography with a First-Line Index of Songs* (London: Oxford Univ. Press, 1940); Waller, 163–71.

• • •

94. Francis Beaumont, "To the Countess of Rutland," subscribed "F:B.," 105–6. Pr. "An Elegie by F.B.," *Certain Elegies. Done by Sundrie Excellent Wits* (1618), sig. A2–3; *Sir Thomas Ouerbury His Wife* (1622), "Ad Comitissam Rutlandiae," sig. C4–5; *The Harmony of the Muses* (1654), 29–31; Dyce2, 11: 505–7.

This is one of two poems about Elizabeth, Countess of Rutland, commonly attributed to Beaumont (see **HolM 96**). She was the only child of Sir Philip Sidney and wife of Roger, 5th Earl of Rutland.

The Rutlands had risen to prominence during the Tudor period. Their fortune, however, was jeopardized when Roger was imprisoned in the Tower by Queen Elizabeth for his role in Essex's unsuccessful rebellion on 8 February 1601. His fortunes were later restored by James, who generally favored Essex and his adherents. Rutland's niece, Lady Katherine Manners, married George Villiers, the Kings favorite, later Duke of Buckingham (Lockyer 58).

The poem is ascribed to "Fr. Beau." in *Certain Elegies. Done by Sundrie Excellent Wits* (1618), one of only three poems in print ascribed to Beaumont during the seventeenth century (Ringler 121).

For information on Francis Beaumont, see **HolM 64 notes**. For information on the Countess of Rutland, see **HolM 96 notes**.

> **16. diamound.** An instrument used for cutting glass (*OED*).
> **23. the little Taylor.** Obviously, a specific but unknown reference.

> • Manuscripts: Crum M37, Beal Vol. I, pt. 1, BmF 1–26. • **Bodleian:** Don.b.9 (ff. 56ᵛ–57ᵛ); MS Eng. poet. c. 53 (f. 13); MS Rawl. poet. 31 (ff. 37ᵛ–39); **British Library:** Add. MS 25303 (ff. 102ᵛ–3ᵛ, Fra.Be.); Add. MS 25707 (f. 31, F.B.); Egerton MS 2230 (ff. 8ᵛ–9ᵛ); MS Harley 1221 (ff. 79ᵛ–80); MS Harley 3910 (ff. 15ᵛ–16ᵛ, Fr.B.); MS Harley 4064 (ff. 268–69); MS Harley 6038 (ff. 24–25); Lansdowne MS 740 (f. 120); MS Sloane 1446 (ff. 73ᵛ–74); Stowe MS 962 (ff. 88–89); **Derbyshire**

Record Office: D258/60/26a (ff. 40ᵛ–41); *Edinburgh University Library:* MS La. III 493 (ff. 98–99); *Harvard:* fMS Eng. 966.3 (ff. 31–32); MS Eng. 966.7 (ff. 63ᵛ–64ᵛ, ff.B); *Huntington Library:* HM 198, pt. 1 (pp. 205–6); HM 198, pt. 2 (f. 114); *University of Kansas:* MS 4A:1 (pp. 56–57); *Leeds Archives Department:* MX 237 (f. 9); *Leicestershire Record Office:* DG.9/2796 (pp. 24–28); *Texas Tech:* Dalhousie I (ff. 52ᵛ–53); Dalhousie II (ff. 26–27).

✦ Ringler, 120–40. See also Roger Lockyer, *Buckingham* (London and New York: Longman, 1981), especially 55–61.

• • •

95. Anon., untitled, "Fond world in thee who putteth any trust," 106. Unprinted.
 A graceful and elegant poem, unknown except in this manuscript.

• • •

96. Francis Beaumont (1584–1616), "An Eligie on the Death of the Countess of Rutland," subscribed "F: B:", 107–9. Pr. *Sir Thomas Ouerbury His Wife. With Addition of many new elegies vpon his untimely and much lamented death* (1616), sig. A5ᵛ–A7ᵛ; Dyce2, 11:507–11.
 This is the second of two poems that concern Elizabeth, the Countess of Rutland. The first, **HolM 94**, is a verse epistle to her. This is an elegy on her death, 1 September 1612.
 Ascription to Beaumont is generally accepted. Both Ben Jonson and John Earle write that Beaumont wrote an elegy to the Countess (Ringler 122). *Conversations with William Drummond* includes the following comment: "The Countess of Rutland was nothing inferior to her father, S[ir] P. Sidney, in poesy. Sir Th. Overbury was in love with her, and caused Ben to read his *Wife* to her, with excellent grace, did, and praised the author. That the morn thereafter he discorded with Overbury, who would have him to intend a suit that was unlawful. The lines my lady kept in remembrance. 'He comes to near, who comes to be denied'. Beaumont wrote that elegy on the death of the Countess of Rutland, and in effect her husband wanted the half of his in his travels" (ll. 206–14). See *Ben Jonson, The Complete Poems*, ed. George Parfitt, The English Poets Series (New Haven: Yale Univ. Press, 1975), 466.
 For information on Francis Beaumont, see the notes to **HolM 63** and **HolM 94**.
 This poem is found in British Library Add. MS 23229, ff. 65–66. It is neither hand A nor B; however, it is the same hand for **HolM 64**. Unfortunately, the leaves of the British Library manuscript are damaged, and a true collation is extremely difficult. However, there are no substantive variants for either text in ll. 1–11. For comments on the significance of this manuscript, see Introduction.

> **15. three days since.** From this, the poem must have been written on or close to 4 September 1612.
> **50–51. thy noble ffather fell in a dull Clime.** Sidney died from a battle wound at Zutphen, The Netherlands, 1586.
> **92. Anothomies.** The *OED* records this spelling of "anatomy" in the sixteenth century.
> **108–9. Penelope . . . Queene of Sheba.** As aristocratic and noble, Penelope and the Queen of Sheba are comparable in station to the countess. If those ladies had been "dissected," the countess's doctors should have been able to treat her better than they did.

✦ Manuscripts: Crum I–337; Beal, Vol. I, pt. 1, BmF 27–55; Yale: I–0266 ✦ *Bodleian:* MS Douce f (f. 35); MS Eng. poet. e. 37 (pp. 35–38, F.B.); MS Eng. poet. f. 9 (pp. 139–43, I.D.); MS Rawl. poet. 117 (ff. 185ᵛ–84 [rev]); MS Rawl. poet. 160 (ff. 20ᵛ–21ᵛ, Fran.Beaumont); *Bradford Central Library:* Hopkinson MSS, Vol 34 (pp. 45–47); *British Library:* Add. MS 23229 (ff. 65–66, F.B.); Add. MS 25707 (ff. 62–63); Egerton MS 2230 (ff. 4ᵛ–6ᵛ); MS Harley 1221 (ff. 78–79); MS Harley 6038 (ff. 22ᵛ–23ᵛ, F.B.); Stowe MS 962 (ff. 40ᵛ–42ᵛ, Beaumond); **Cambridge:** MS Add. 5778 (ff. 82–83ᵛ); **Derbyshire Record Office:** D258/28/5i (ff. 4ᵛ–5ᵛ); **Edinburgh University Library:** MS La. III 493 (ff. 109ᵛ–11); **Folger:** V.a. 319 (ff. 7–9); V.a. 322 (pp. 29–31, Fran:Beamont); **Harvard:** fMS Eng. 966.1 (ff. 46–47ᵛ); **University of Kansas:** MS 4A:1 (pp. 50–53); **Leeds Archives Department:** MX 237 (ff. 91–92ᵛ); **National Library of Wales:** MS 5308E (ff. 10–11); **Rosenbach:** MS 239/22 (f. 27); MS 239/27 (pp. 328–30); TCD-? (ff. 254ᵛ–57, Beaumont); **Yale:** Osborn b 148 (pp. 136–38); Osborn b 197 (pp. 65–68).

Beal includes **HolM 57** among texts of BmF 49; however, only the first line of each poem is similar (see **HolM 57 notes**).

✦ See Ringler, 120–40.

• • •

97. Francis Beaumont [?], "To Mʳ B: I:.," subscribed "F B:", 110.

This poem is noteworthy because it contains one of the few surviving contemporary references to Shakespeare in verse (l. 18). This reference, plus the inclusion of Sonnet 106 (**HolM 85**), makes the Holgate important to Shakespearean studies. E. K. Chambers includes the poem in *William Shakespeare* (see below). His eclectic text is based on the Holgate version and that in British Library Add. MS 30982. Concerning the two texts, Chambers writes, "The Holgate MS is a good text, the Addl. MS much less good, but identical errors in l. 17 and l. 30 suggest a common origin."

Jonson and Beaumont were friends. They met when Beaumont was at the Inner Temple, circa 1600.

Ringler describes the attribution to Beaumont as "doubtful" (123), but Chambers accepts it on the basis that Beaumont wrote another well-known verse epistle to Jonson, and that it would be natural for Beaumont to know the theatrical allusions in l. 31 (233). They are described in the notes.

> **11–12. post of Douer**. Chambers believes this is an allusion to Anthony Nixon's *A Straunge Foot-Post* (1613). It was reissued as *The Foot-Post to Dover* (1616).
>
> **12. Carriers pist-ling ghost**. Chambers believes this refers to G[ervase] M[arkham's] *Hobsons Horse-load of Letters: or A President of Epistles* (1613). Thomas Hobson was a Cambridge carrier. He was frequently written about—for example, in Milton's "On the University Carrier."
>
> **26. tawny**. An orange and brown color, but can be used with the names of other colors to express how the primary color was modified by tawny, as in this example, "Orrenge tawny" (*OED*). Tawny was also the color worn by officials of the ecclesiastical court, which may explain this reference. Note "ordainde," l. 30.
>
> **27. at Windsor**. Chambers takes this as reference to an installation of the Order of the Garter (223).
>
> **30. geinne**. Chambers transcribes this as "grinne" (p. 225).
>
> **31. fawne**. Chambers says this refers to Marston's play *The Fawn* (1604–6).
>
> **31. fleere**. Edward Sharpham's *The Fleire* (1606).
>
> **42. Bretons Comõn talke**. Chambers writes that Nicholas Breton did not write a book called *Common Talke*, "although the description might serve for many of his compilations, including the *Wits Private Wealth*, of which a new edition appeared in 1613" (2.223). Chambers also suggests that the reference may be to a legal text concerning common pleas by John Breton, circa 1540, entitled *Britton,* and *Common Talke*. Beaumont did study at the Inner Temple, so he may have had knowledge of that text.

✦ Manuscripts: Beal Vol. I, pt. 1, BmF 137–40 ✦ **British Library:** Add. MS 30982 (ff. 75ᵛ–76); **Folger:** V.a. 96 (f. 70ᵛ–71ᵛ, Fran:Beaumont); **Huntington Library:** HM 198, pt. 2 (f. 116).

✦ See E. K. Chambers, *William Shakespeare: A Study of Facts and Problems* (Oxford: Clarendon Press, 1930), 2:222–25; H&S, 9:377–79; Ringler, 120–40.

• • •

98. Rowland Woodward (1573–1637) [?], "Off Freindshippe," 111. Pr. *P&R*, 48.

Marotti gives this poem to Woodward, evidentially on its attribution in Huntington HM 198 (71). Woodward was a close friend of Donne, who sent several verse epistles to him. They became friends when both attended Lincoln's Inn (ca. 1592). Woodward transcribed the Westmoreland Manuscript, housed at the New York Public Library.

P&R was very poorly edited by John Donne Jr. (see **HolM 40 notes**). The poet is not identified in that text, but it follows two poems ascribed to Sir Benjamin Rudyerd, creating the impression that Rudyerd was the poet. There is, however, no direct evidence to support that attribution. It is ascribed to Donne in Ashmole 36/37.

> **2. North East passage.** From the fifteenth century, western explorers hoped to find a route to India and Cathay through the Arctic.
> **4. latter'de.** "Tatter'd" *P&R* is probably correct (see collation). Unfortunately, the handwriting is unclear here. A possible interpretation of "latter'de," from latten, a yellow alloy similar to brass.
> **9. nealled.** From annealed, a method of baking in colors on earthenware.
> **22. fort.** Read "for it" or "for't."

✦ Collation: *P&R*. 4 latter'de] tatter'd *P&R* ; 8 vanish] tarnish *P&R* ; 9 affectction] affliction *P&R* ; 22 fort] for't *P&R*

✦ Manuscripts: Crum F633 ✦ **Bodleian:** MS Ashmole 36/37 (f. 124, Dr. Donne); Ashmole 781 (p. 162); MS Rawl. poet. 117 (f. 270 [rev]); **British Library:** Add. MS 10809 (f. 110); MS Sloane 1446 (f. 88ᵛ); **Huntington Library:** HM 198, pt. 1 (p. 174, R.W.); **Rosenbach:** MS 243/4 (p. 113).

• • •

99. Christopher Brooke (d. 1628) [?], "Dʳ: B: of teares:," 112–13. Pr. *Reliquiæ Wottanianæ* (1654), 534–536; *P&R*, 46.

Brooke is best known as a friend of John Donne. They met at Lincoln's Inn, where they shared chambers. Brooke was educated at Trinity College, Cambridge. His father was a merchant and Lord Mayor of York. Brooke himself served as MP for York (1604, 1614, 1620, 1624, 1625, and 1626). Donne's verse epistle to Brooke is "The Storme," **HolM 87**.

The only evidence that Brooke wrote this poem is that it is ascribed to him in several manuscripts. It is noteworthy that the sea imagery and the sense of loss mirror the Donne poem.

✦ Collation: *P&R* Heading: Dʳ: B: of teares] Benj. Rudier of Tears *P&R* ; 10 those] these *P&R* ; 12 those] these *P&R* ; 21 dashing] dash in *P&R* ; 29 hope] hopes *P&R* ; 37 sterue] starve *P&R*

✦ Manuscripts: Crum W2203 ✦ **Bodleian:** MS Rawl. poet. 160 (f. 85ᵛ, Dr. Brookes); MS Tanner 466 (f. 5ᵛ); **British Library:** Add. MS 25707 (pp. 174–75, Dr Brookes); **Folger:** V.a. 276, pt. II (ff. 25ᵛ–26, Dr Brookes).

✦ The poem is not found in Brooke's collected works. See *The Complete Poems of Christopher Brooke*, Prtd. for private circulation, 1872, in *Miscellanies of the Fuller Worthies' Library*, ed. A. B. Grosart (Blackburn 1870–1876) 4: [9]–238.

• • •

100. Anon., "A Letter from H: H of London to H: L: in the Cuntry," 113. Unprinted.

This is the second of two verse letters ascribed to "H: H:," who very well may be Hugh Holland, but without more information, no true ascription can be made (cf. **HolM 58**). The first name of the addressee is "Henry," l. 25.

27. Lurden. Variant of "lurdan," a term of opprobrium; dullness or laziness *OED*).

• • •

101. Anon., "'An Elegie on Prince Henry,' by Mr. Thoris, An Italian [?]," 114–16. Unprinted.

The only other known text of this poem is in Huntington MS HM 198, pt. 2, where it is transcribed without attribution. There are two likely candidates for "Mr. Thoris, An Italian." One is Raphael Thorius, MD (d. 1625). He is the best candidate simply because his first name sounds Italian, although he was actually born in Flanders. Several of his poems are found in British Library Sloane MS 1768, but this poem is not among them. Most of his poems are in Latin (*ODNB*). A second possibility is John Thorie. He was a friend of Gabriel Harvey, whose home was next door to an inn owned by the Holgate family. Harvey was attacked by Thomas Nashe in *Have with you to Saffron Walden* (1596). Harvey included in his reply to Nashe, *Pierce's Supererogation* (1596) letters and poems written by John Thorius (*ODNB*).

Henry, Prince of Wales (1594–1612), was the eldest son of James I and Queen Anne. This is the first of five poems dedicated to Prince Henry's memory (**HolM 101–105**); also see **HolM 3** and **HolM 5**.

Among the many poets who wrote funeral elegies for Henry were John Donne, Joshuah Sylvester, Thomas Campion, John Davies of Hereford, George Chapman, William Drummond, and John Taylor, (Edmond 141–58; Wilson 128–76). None of their elegies is found in the Holgate. Sylvester dedicated a section of his *Du Bartas* to Prince Henry.

Henry was invested Prince of Wales in 1610. He was extremely popular, in fact, more popular than his father. Gardiner writes the following on Henry's death: "Throughout the whole of England the sad news was received with tears and lamentations. Never in the long history of England had an heir to the throne given rise to such hopes, or had, at such an early age, inspired every class of his countrymen with love and admiration" (2.158).

99. brickle. *Brittle* in HM 198, pt. 2, but neither is a variant spelling of the other (*OED*).

✦ Manuscript: **Huntington Library:** HM 198, pt. 2 (ff. 54ᵛ–56).

✦ John Philip Edmond, "Elegies and Other Tracts Issued on the Death of Henry, Prince of Wales, 1612," *Publications of the Edinburgh Bibliographical Society*, 6 (1906): 141–58; Samuel R. Gardiner, *History of England from the Accession of James I to the Outbreak of the Civil War, 1603–1642*, Fifth Impression, (London, 1899), 2:157–59. For a detailed discussion of elegies written on the occasion of Prince Henry's death, see Elkin Calhoun Wilson, *Prince Henry and English Literature* (Ithaca: Cornell Univ. Press, 1946), 128–76.

102. Stephen Haxby (dates unknown), "An Epitaph on Prince Henry:," 116. Pr. *Epicedium Cantabrigiense in obitum immaturum semperque deflendum Henrici illustrissimi Principis Walliæ* (1612), 101.

Epicedium Cantabrigiense (STC 4481) identifies the poet as "Stephen Haxby, Coll. Io." Since this book was published by Cambridge University to honor Prince Henry, the attribution is probably correct. *Alumni Cantabrigienses* describes him as: "B. A. from St. John's, 1604–5. Of Yorkshire, MA 1608: BD 1616. Fellow, 1607. R.[ector] of Bodney, Norfolk, 1611. Preb.[end] of Lichfield, 1619–22. R.[ector] Coppenhall, Cheshire, 1621–7 (E. Axon)."

Giles Fletcher's "Miraris qui saxa loqui didicere, Viator" is also in the same printed book. **HolM 5** is an English translation of Fletcher's poem.

For details on Prince Henry, see **HolM 101 notes**.

>   **2. Ida.** Highest mountain on Crete.
>   **2. Callidonian wood.** The Scottish Highlands, but sometimes used adjectively for inland Northern Britain (*OCD*).
>   **5. Cyrus.** Probably Cyrus I, founder of the vast Achaemenid Persian empire.
>   **6. Solls watry bed.** Image of sunset at sea.

>   ✦ Manuscript: ***British Library:*** Add. MS 15226 (f. 4ʳ).

• • •

103. Hugh Holland [?], "'An other:' by H: H:," 116. Pr. *Wits Recreations* (1640), Epitaph 102.

Wilson reprints this poem from the version in *Inedited Poetical Miscellanies, 1584–1700*. He writes, "A certain 'T. S.' catches the spirit in the . . . epitaph" (159). The poem is also attributed to "T. S." in the Rosenbach manuscript. Lansdowne MS 777 is in the hand of William Browne. The Lansdowne text is identical to that found in the Holgate manuscript. If "H. H." stands for Hugh Holland, then it is likely he wrote two poems on the death of Prince Henry, this one and the following, **HolM 104**. However, the attribution is disputed by evidence from these primary sources.

For details about Prince Henry, see **HolM 101 notes**. For details about Hugh Holland, see the **HolM 104 notes**. Also see **HolM 58** and **HolM 100**.

>   ✦ Manuscripts: Crum L509 ✦ ***Bodleian:*** MS Eng. poet. c. 50 (ff. 23, 59); ***British Library:*** Add. MS 33998 (f. 85ʳ); Lansdowne MS 777 (f. 66, Hugh Holland); ***Rosenbach:*** MS 240/2 (p. 39, T.S.).

Inedited Poetical Miscellanies, 1584–1700, ed. William Carew Hazlitt and Henry Huth, (London, 1870); Elkin Calhoun Wilson, *Prince Henry and English Literature* (Ithaca: Cornell Univ. Press, 1946), 159; Geoffrey Grigson, ed., *Faber Book of Epigrams and Epitaphs* (London: Faber, 1977).

• • •

104. Hugh Holland [?], "'An Elegie on Prince Henry,' by H: Holland:," 117–20. Pr. *Sundry Funeral Elegies on the Vntimely Death of the most excellent Prince, Henry; Late, Prince of Wales*, appended to *Lachrimæ Lachrimarum, or the Spirit of Teares, distilled for the vn-tymely death of the incomparable Prince, Panaretus*, by Joshua Sylvester (1612), sig. D2.

The 1612 edition of *Lachrimæ Lachrimarum* was entered in the Stationers' Register 27 November 1612, actually before the funeral of Prince Henry (Bald 268–69). *Sundry Funerall Elegies* is appended to the third edition of *Lachrimæ Lachrimarum*. It has its own title page. It comprises poems by Sir Peter Osborne, George Garrard, Sir William Cornwallis (**HolM 105**), Sir Edward Herbert, Sir Henry Goodyer, and Henry Burton.

The ascription in *Sundry Funerall Elegies* indicates that this poem actually was written by Holland. He was educated at Westminster School; later he became a fellow at Trinity College, Cambridge

(l. 131). After leaving Cambridge, the *DNB* describes his life as follows: ". . . he went abroad, travelling as far as Jerusalem. It was insinuated that he was made a knight of the Sepulchre; he certainly embraced the Roman Catholic faith, and suffered in some way at Rome for indulging in free expressions concerning Queen Elizabeth." He was patronized by George Villiers, Duke of Buckingham, but he never attained preferment from James. He was buried in Westminster Abbey, 23 July 1633. In addition to the elegy on Shakespeare printed in the First Folio (1623), he wrote commendatory verses for Farnaby's *Canzonets* (1598), Ben Jonson's *Sejanus* (1605), and Bolton's *Elements of Armory* (1610). He was also a member of the Mermaid Club (*ODNB*).

Holland's writing about Henry is notably passionate, but his references are not always clear. Some references in this poem remain obscure.

Both this and the following poem, **HolM 105**, appear in *Sundry Funeral Elegies*. For further information on Hugh Holland, see **HolM 58 notes**, and for Prince Henry, **HolM 101 notes**.

> **4. Tiburne**. Tyburn, place in London for public executions (*OED*).
> **33. Catesby . . . ffaulx . . . Percy.** All were Gunpowder Plot conspirators. William Catesby (b. in or after 1572, d. 1605); Guy Fawkes (bap. 1570, d. 1606); Thomas Percy (1560–1605). (*ODNB*)
> **38–40. Nouember . . . fifth . . . sixt.** Comparing, respectively, Guy Fawkes Day and the date of Henry's death 6 November 1612.
> **45. Tilt and Ringe**. As practice for the tilt (jousting), riders attempted to catch on their lances a ring suspended on a string or ribbon as they rode past it.
> **89. Lee**. An obscure reference, possibly the lee-anchor. "Lee" as a nautical term implies the side of a vessel safe from the wind.
> **92. Humber**. Estuary of the Trent and Ouse Rivers, between Yorkshire and Lincolnshire.
> **109. Costing**. The scribe's writing actually looks like "Costnig." In words that end in "ing," he frequently puts the dot over the "n" rather than the "i." Here, however, his "nig" is quite pronounced, but it makes no sense.
> **138. Grant and Theames**. "Granta" is an alternate name for the River Cam in Cambridge; "Theames" is likely the Thames. The context relates to Cambridge and Oxford universities.

✦ Manuscripts: Crum H415 ✦ *Bodleian:* MS Eng. poet. e. 37 (p. 52).

• • •

105. Sir William Cornwallis (1579?–1614?), "On Prince Henrye," 121–24. Pr. *Sundry Funerall Elegies . . .* , annexed to *Lachrymæ Lachrymarum*, by Joshuah Sylvester (London, 1613), sig. E3–F2.

Cornwallis is best known for his *Essayes*, written in the style of Montaigne. He was a friend of Wotton and Donne. The *DNB* reports that he commissioned Jonson's masque *Panates*, but this claim has been disputed (Allen x–xi). His father, Sir Charles Cornwallis, was appointed Ambassador to Spain (1605). William was elected MP of Orland in Suffolk. He was also employed by his father to carry messages between England and Spain. Despite his privileged family status, he spent most of his life in poverty (Allen ix–xviii).

Cornwallis is considered an indifferent essayist, more an imitator of Montaigne than a unique contemporary voice. With Bacon, he was among the first English writers in this genre.

Five of Cornwallis's poems are found in Bodliean MS Tanner 306, including one inscribed "to Mr. John Done Secretary to my Lorde Keeper" (Crum A1574), but none of these poems appears in the Holgate manuscript. He is also said to have introduced Sir Thomas Overbury to Robert Carr (*ODNB*). For details about Prince Henry, see **HolM 101 notes**, and for *Sundry Funerall Elegies*, see **HolM 104 notes**.

5. Lowte. Lout, a bumpkin or clown, used here to contrast with 'Lord'; both the highest and lowest in society grieve for Henry.

7. Curious. Observant, especially with hand or eye (*OED*).

20. p¹aine. the "l" is clearly inserted. The 1613 text has "Plain," abbreviated or poetic for "complain" (*OED*).

49. Phillips sonne. Charles II of Spain. He did not succeed his father, Philip IV, until 1661.

63. tennis Balance. Henry was known to play tennis. In fact, it was believed that his fatal illness became worse after playing (Gardiner 2:157).

73. Carpet Knight. A Knight of the Carpet (obsolete). A knight so described because he kneels while the king sits (*OED*).

79. But runing swiminge, and such exercise. Henry was known for his athleticism.

82. pedint arts. Book learning.

95. Ligement. The anatomical use of the word was established by the early fifteenth century.

99. entralls. The allusion to faculty psychology in the following line suggests "entralls" as the inner parts of the body, the seat of emotions (*OED*).

124. Only one Phœnix. An allusion to Christ.

133. Brothers iests. "Brothers" is possessive; "iests" means "gests," i.e., deeds. Charles was then twelve years old.

169. Ilande. England.

✦ Manuscript: *Huntington Library:* HM 198, pt. 2 (ff. 77–79).

✦ See Sir William Cornwallis the Younger, *Essayes*, ed. Don Cameron Allen (Baltimore: Johns Hopkins Press, 1946); Ruth Wallerstein, *Studies in Seventeenth-Century Poetic* (Madison and Milwaukee, Univ. of Wisconsin Press, 1965), 59–95. For extended biographical comment, see P. B. Whitt, "New Light on Sir William Cornwallis, the Essayist," *Review of English Studies* 8 (1932): 155–69. On the death of Prince Henry, see Samuel R. Gardiner, *History of England from the Accession of James 1 to the Outbreak of the Civil War, 1603–1642* (London, 1884; rpt. New York: AMS Press, 1965) 2:157–58.

• • •

106. John Donne, "His Passion for a lost Chaine of Gould" [The Bracelet], 125–27. Pr. Elegie XII, "The Bracelet," *Poems* (London, 1635).

This poem was first published in 1635, the second edition of Donne's poems. Gardner says that the copy-text for 1635 was a poor text (111).

To judge from its topical references, the poem was written about 1593 when Donne was at Lincoln's Inn. Based on work by Grierson, Gardner (1965) argues that Thomas Kyd's *Solimon and Perseda* was the inspiration for this poem. A lost chain is the principal action in the first two acts of the play. Possible allusions to Kyd's arrest for libel are made in ll. 99–100.

7. seauen fould Chaine. There are seven links to the chain.

9. twelue righteous Angells. The angel was a gold coin named for the image of the archangel Michael stamped upon it.

10. vilde fodder. Vile soder. Soder is "A fusible metallic alloy used for uniting metal surfaces or parts" (*OED*). Despite the similarities between "f" and "s," the "f" here is clear. This, to the knowledge of the present editor, is the only manuscript with this error.

11. strid. Strayed.

22. their naturall Cuntrie rott. Syphilis, known as "the French disease" or "French crown" (l. 21).

24. Soe leane, soe lame, soe ruinous. The Holgate manuscript omits "pale," which is in the 1635 version. The passage describes French coins, thought to be thin (leane), made of pale metal (pale), and clipped (lame); the image continues the syphilis metaphor.

28. Catholike. A pun—the Spanish king was, of course, Catholic, but Spanish coin was thought to be everywhere, a common complaint.

29. vnlike. Unlicked.

29. vnfield. Unfiled.

32. Iegaries. This is not a word; it should read "figures." "Manie Angled" figures are five-pointed stars used in conjuring.

42. Chimiks. Alchemists.

44. durtely. Dirtily.

53. Lou'de Squeaking Cryer. Criers advertised goods or sought the recovery of lost property. In Kyd's *Solimon and Perseda*, a crier is sent to recover a lost chain of gold.

60. rents. A pun, the rents for the tenements and the rents, or gaps, left in the skies by the astrologer.

62. rome. Room.

75–76. pittie the Angells yett their dignities / pass vertus, powrs, and principalities. Gardner (1965) reads "yett," as pity the angels while there is still time. A more accepted reading, however, is that his good angels have more dignity than the virtues, powers, and principalities of bad angels (117–18).

95. forren. Foreign.

99–100. Or some libell . . . / . . . may thy ruine bringe. Kyd was arrested on 12 May 1593 for libeling the state. When his rooms were searched, papers were found that led authorities to suspect he was an atheist. For this, he was tortured.

✦ Manuscripts: Crum N397, N361; Beal Vol. I, pt. 1, DnJ 357–413; Yale N0359 ✦ *Bodleian:* MS Ashmole 36/37 (f. 61ᵛ); Don.c.54 (ff. 24ᵛ–25); MS Eng. poet. e. 99 (ff. 13–14ᵛ); MS Eng. poet. f. 9 (pp. 209–13, 44); MS Malone 19 (p. 150); MS Malone 23 (p. 220); MS Rawl. poet. e. 14 (ff. 30ᵛ–32); MS Rawl. poet. 117 (ff. 225ᵛ–24 [rev]); MS Rawl. poet. 160 (ff. 171ᵛ–72ᵛ); MS Rawl. poet. 212 (f. 152ᵛ[rev]); *British Library:* Add. MS 25707 (ff. 5ᵛ–6ᵛ); Egerton MS 2230 (ff. 15–16ᵛ); MS Harley 3991 (f. 114); MS Harley 4955 (ff. 94–95ᵛ); Lansdowne MS 740 (ff. 66–67ᵛ); MS Sloane 1792 (ff. 39ᵛ–41); Stowe MS 961 (ff. 94ᵛ–96); Stowe MS 962 (ff. 214ᵛ–16ᵛ); *Cambridge:* MS Add. 29 (ff. 1–2); MS Add. 5778 (ff. 23ᵛ–25); MS Ee. 4.14 (ff. 67–68); *Corpus Christi College,Oxford:* MS 327 (f. 5); *Derbyshire Record Office:* D258/60/26a (ff. 33ᵛ–35); *Edinburgh University Library:* MS La. III 493 (ff. 92ᵛ–94); *Folger:* V.a. 170 (pp. 200–3); V.a. 262 (p. 12); *Harvard:* fMS Eng. 966.1 (ff. 5–6); fMS Eng. 966.3 (ff. 12ᵛ–14ᵛ); fMS Eng. 966.4 (ff. 162–63ᵛ); MS Eng. 686 (f. 14); MS Eng. 966.6 (ff. 80ᵛ–81ᵛ); MS Eng. 966.6 (ff. 79ᵛ–82); MS Eng. 966.7 (ff. 61ᵛ–63); *Huntington Library:* EL 6893 (ff. 76ᵛ–78ᵛ); HM 198, pt. 1 (pp. 35–37); HM 198, pt. 2 (ff. 112ᵛ–13ᵛ); *Owned by Sir Geoffrey Keynes:* Bibliotheca Bibliographici No. 1860 (ff. 17ᵛ–20ᵛ); Bibliotheca Bibliographici No. 1861 (ff. 43–44ᵛ); Bibliotheca Bibliographici No. 1863 (ff. 7–8); *Leeds Archives Department:* MX 237 (f. 6); *Owned privately in England:* Monckton Milnes MS (pp. 23–27); *National Library of Scotland:* MS 6504 (ff. 40ᵛ–42ᵛ); *National Library of Wales:* Dolau Cothi MS (pp. 32–35); NLW.MS 5390D (pp. 444–42 [rev]); *New York Public Library:* Arents Collection, Cat. No. S191 (Elegies, pp. 1–5); Berg Collection, Westmoreland MS; *Rosenbach:* MS 239/22 (ff. 44–45ᵛ); *St. John's College, Cambridge:* MS U. 26 (James 548) (pp. 94–98); *St. Paul's Cathedral:* MS 49.B.43; *Texas Tech:* Dalhousie I (f. 27); Dalhousie II (ff. 9–10); *Trinity College Library, Dublin:* MS 877 (ff. 25ᵛ–27); *Victoria and Albert Museum:* Dyce Collection, Cat. No. 18 (Pressmark 25.F.17) (ff. 18ᵛ–19ᵛ); *Westminster Abbey:* MS 41 (ff. 30ᵛ–32); *Yale:* Osborn b 114 (pp. 98–105); Osborn b 148 (pp. 64–66).

✦ Gardner (1965), 111–19; Grierson, 1:96–100; Shawcross, 43–46, 434–35; Smith, 427–30; *Variorum* 2, Elegy 1:4–50, 513–44.

• • •

107. Anon., pseud., "On the Money Newes so generally Currant in Frankendale about Iune: 1621:," subscribed "Iacobus Dei gratia," 128–31. Unprinted.

Among the many fascinating things about this poem is that it, too, is found in British Library Add. MS 23229 (hand B). Unfortunately, only the last page of that transcription survives. The Add. MS text begins at l. 129 (see collation). From that point forward, the two texts are virtually alike, including a broad sweeping signature at the end of the poem and the marginalia in the lower left-hand corner. It is, of course, possible that both texts were transcribed from a common printed text, but the two signatures "Iacobus Dei gratia" seem imitative of each other. For a discussion concerning the similarities of these two manuscripts, see Introduction, pp. xiii–xx.

The poem describes events that occurred during a cease fire reached at Mainz between Protestant and Catholic forces early in the Thirty Years' War. James hoped to settle hostilities by diplomatic efforts, mainly through the proposed marriage of his son Charles to the Spanish Infanta. His intention was to restore the Palatinate to his son-in-law Frederick in exchange for his own prior claims to Bohemia. Part of the agreement entailed the disbanding of the Protestant Union in return for which Protestant territories would not be attacked. Archduchess Isabella of the Spanish Netherlands took advantage of the cease fire and, at the death of Philip III of Spain in March 1621, laid siege to Frankenthal, one of three Protestant fortresses (Parker 64). In charge of the siege was General Ambrogio Spinola, corrupted to Spinla (l. 148).

Frankenthal is south of Mainz, northwest of both Mannheim and Heidelberg. In 1621, it was part of the Rhenish or Lower Palatinate. The name "Franken*dale*" (in title) is satiric as an Anglicized corruption of the German name, "Franken*thal*." Clearly, from the poem, conditions for English soldiers fighting in the Thirty Years' War were deplorable. The results of these conditions were described by Samuel R. Gardiner:

> In those terrible years, no army marched into the field without perpetrating horrors which in our day even the most depraved outcasts could not look upon without a shudder. Liable to dismissal at any moment, the soldier thought it no shame to transfer his services from one side to the other with reckless impartiality. No tie of nationality kept him faithful to the cause which he happened to be serving for the moment, and against which he might be fighting to-morrow. Even military pride, which has sometimes been known almost to replace that lofty and patriotic feeling, was wanting to him. He knew that he had sold himself, body and soul, to his hirer for the time being, and according to the law of our nature all other vices followed in the train of that last degradation of which man is capable. In those camps robbery, cruelty, and lust reigned supreme. Smiling fields and pleasant villages were made hideous by their presence. Blazing farmsteads marked the track of their march, and the air was tainted by the mouldering corpses, not of armed men, but of helpless peasants–of tender babes and of delicate women, fortunate if they had escaped by the sharp remedy of the sword a fate more horrible still. (4:196)

The siege at Frankenthal actually lasted until April 1623. In a letter dated 10/20 July 1622, the English ambassador wrote, "It grieves me to behold the waste and ruin of so many towns, boroughs and villages which were lately rich and prosperous, and to hear of the intolerable oppression and rapine committed upon the poor people that are left, by the soldiers as well of our army as that of the enemies" (Chichester to Calvert, Public Record Office, *S. P. German States*, 36. F. 75, quoted in the *New Cambridge Modern History*, 4:317).

The poem is replete with local idioms. Some of the slang would be known only to members of this poet/soldier's regiment.

◆ Collation: Add. MS 23229 (hand B), f. 62 *BL-B*. 165 then vocation] then thy vocation *BL-B*

◆ Manuscript: **British Library:** Add. MS 23229 (ff. [?]–62).

◆ For information on the Thirty Years' War, see Samuel R. Gardiner, *History of England from the Accession of James I to the Outbreak of the Civil War, 1603–1642*, 10 vols.; Geoffrey Parker, *The Thirty Years' War* (London: Routeledge, 1984), 61–71; *The New Cambridge Modern History* vol. 4, *The Decline of Spain and the Thirty Years' War, 1609–48/59*, ed. J. P. Cooper (Cambridge: Cambridge Univ. Press, 1971).

• • •

108. William Herbert (1589–1630), "To his Mistris in his Death:," 132. Pr. *P&R*, 52.

Gary Waller writes that this is one of the poems that Lawes supplied to John Donne Jr. for the publication of *P&R* (171, see **HolM 40 notes**). Waller describes a social function for this type of verse: "The poem suggests a civilized, courtly occasion, asking for verse and a musical setting that move elegantly, simply, and without disrupting the atmosphere, which is designed to soothe and relax" (171).

There is no evidence in the Holgate manuscript that this lyric was sung. Noteworthy, however, is l. 11, with "not" superscribed above "that," which is not cancelled. This is a rare circumstance in the manuscript. Normal procedure throughout the manuscript is to superscribe over a cancellation. The scribe may have written the line as he preferred, but preserved the line as it appeared in the copy-text; or perhaps (if sung) the verse was changed when repeated.

◆ Collation: *P&R*. Title: in] on *P&R* ; 2 springes] strings; *P&R* ; 10 miserable] miserably *P&R* ; 11 this that/not (*see commentary note above*)] This, that *P&R*
◆ Manuscript: **Rosenbach:** MS 1083/16 (p. 290).

◆ Redding, 746; Waller, 159–88.

• • •

109. Ben Jonson (1573?–1637), "Of the Sand runinge in an hower Glass," 132. Pr. *The Vnder-wood* (1640), viii. This poem is based on *Horologium Pulvuerum* by Girolamo Amaltei. See Gherus, *Delitiæ cc Italorum Poetarum* (1603), 1:73.

Jonson sent a copy of this poem to Drummond (*Conversations*, 1: 679). Drummond refers to it as a madrigal.

◆ Manuscripts: Crum D353, C695; Beal Vol. I, pt. 2, JnB 270–307; Yale D0343. ◆ **Bodleian:** MS Ashmole 36/37 (f. 257); MS Eng. poet. c. 50 (f. 113); MS Eng. poet. f. 25 (f. 19ᵛ); MS Eng. poet. f. 27 (p. 66); MS Firth e. 4 (p. 51); MS Rawl. poet. 172 (f. 74ᵛ); **British Library:** Add. MS 11811 (f. 31); Add. MS 15227 (f. 96ᵛ); Add. MS 19268 (f. 4ᵛ); Add. MS 22603 (f. 49); Add. MS 33998 (f. 14); Egerton MS 2725 (f. 112ᵛ); Stowe MS 961 (f. 69ᵛ); Stowe MS 962 (f. 144); **Carlisle Cathedral:** Dean & Chapter of Carlisle MSS, (Box B1, Altus and Bassus, p. 8); **Corpus Christi College,Oxford:** MS 176 (f. 8); **Derbyshire Record Office:** D258/31/16 (p. 9); **Edinburgh University Library:** MS Dc.7.94 (f. 17ᵛ); **Folger:** V.a. 162 (f. 90); V.a. 170 (p. 76); V.a. 245 (f. 55ᵛ); V.b.

43 (f. 9ᵛ); *Harvard:* fMS 626 (f. 73); MS Eng. 966.6 (f. 139ᵛ); MS Eng. 966.7 (f. 32); *Hunting-ton Library:* HM 198, pt. 1 (p. 53); *Owned by Sir Geoffrey Keynes:* Bibliotheca Bibliographici No. 1861 (f. 113); *Leeds Archives Department:* MX 237 (f. 34); *Rosenbach:* MS 1083/16 (p. 291); MS 1083/17 (p. 15); *St. John's College, Cambridge:* MS S. 32 (James 423) (f. 7ᵛ); *Scottish Record Office:* GD 18/4312; *South African Library, Cape Town:* MS Grey 7 a 29 (p. 75); *Yale:* Osborn b 197 (p. 59); Osborn b 205 (f. 73ᵛ). Beal writes in JnB 307: "Copy in a MS collection once owned by Sir Kenelm Digby. . . Printed . . . in *Poems from Sir Kenelm Digby's Papers . . .* Roxburghe Club (London, 1877), 31, collated . . . in H&S. Unlocated."

✦ H&S, 8:149–50; 11:53–54.

• • •

110. Anon., untitled, "Goe make thy will, and dye sad soule consumde with Care," 132–33.
Again, the similarity between texts in the Holgate manuscript and Add. MS 23229 is notewor-thy (see collation). They are also the only two known manuscripts of this poem. For discussion, see Introduction, pp. xviii–xx.

✦ Collation: BL Add. MS 23229 (hand A) *BL-A.* 14 liuing] liuely *BL-A* ; 20 fall] for *BL-A*

✦ Manuscript: *British Library:* Add. MS 23229 (f. 51).

• • •

111. Dudley, Third Baron North (1581–1666), "That Lust is not his Aime:," 133. Pr. *A Forest of Varieties* (1645), 46; *P&R*, 33–34.
Dudley North, a courtier, is best known for discovering the waters at Tunbridge Wells. His life was marked by a series of failures and dwindling expectations. He was educated at Cambridge but did not graduate. By the arrangement of his grandfather, Roger Second Baron North, he mar-ried Frances Brockett, daughter of Sir John Brockett, but the marriage was not successful. North described his own nature as sanguine but felt constrained by his marriage. He was also plagued by financial problems. The result was a persistent melancholia and illness. North described his own sense of failure in *A Forest of Varieties* (see Randall 19–20).
However, what distinguishes North is his critical commentary, especially as it relates to his own poems in the new age of print media. Clearly, he was unhappy with changes modern technology advanced. He wrote:

> They meet with an unfriendly time, and though my selfe have kept them [his poems] these late years of our troubles, like a candle under a bushel, without so much as casting my own eye upon them; I feare you will admit others, perhaps, neither friends to you nor mee; which if against my will you do, I have taught them to say something for themselves, and here and there they will return a troth; they were designed, as they tell you, to a domestique confinement, impatient of publique view, and still of shop mart and residence; whosoever censures, shall not be entitled to it as of publique stage-playes, for his money, whereupon I hope he will bee the more modest and indulgent: But now meeting with this plundering age, if they venture not to undergo the Presse, they are obnoxious to sodain destruction. . . . (North A2)

North published *A Forest of Varieties* in 1645. It is a compilation of his essays, letters, character descriptions, and poems. The poems, as the previous quotation suggests, were written somewhat earlier.
For further critical commentary, see **HolM 127 notes**.

✦ Collation: *P&R* 3 moue] me *P&R* ; 19 commandes] command *P&R*

✦ Manuscripts: Crum O–340 ✦ **Bodleian:** MS Eng. poet. c. 50 (f. 68ᵛ, Sir G.H.); MS *North e. 41 (f. 43ᵛ, corrected by author).

✦ Dudley North, *A Forest of Varieties* (London, 1645). See also the biography of Dudley North's son: Dale B. J. Randall, *Gentle Flame, The Life and Verse of Dudley, Fourth Lord North (1602–1677)* (Durham, NC: Duke Univ. Press, 1983), 11–27.

•••

112. Edward DeVere, seventeenth Earl of Oxford, "'Of playing at Tenis' by Sʳ E: D:," 134. Pr. *Wits Interpreter* (1655), 6–7 [2nd numbering].

Steven May (1980) includes this poem among the verse written by Edward DeVere, seventeenth Earl of Oxford. Joseph Frank describes the poems of *Wits Interpreter* as anonymous and predating 1640, the book's purpose being "Didactic: intended to serve as a handbook for courtly expression, especially in regard to love" (Frank 343).

> **9. Iutties.** Not a term of the game, simply something thrown or projected.
> **10. stoppers.** *OED* quotes Higgins, *Iunius' Nomenclature* (1585), "the stopper, or he that marketh the chase in playing, at tennise specially."
> **11. Sr Argus.** (Argos) Mythical monster variously described as having anywhere from four eyes to many (*OCD*).
> **23. A bandy ho.** May (1980) cites "*OED* 'to bandy, a particular way of playing at Tennis, the nature of which is not now known.' Apparently a point was lost if the ball touched the wall while bandying. The definition of *bander* in Randle Cotgrave's *Dictionarie of the French and English Tongues* (1611), suggests the added excitement of bandying: 'To bandy against, at Tennis; and (by metaphor) to pursue with all insolencie, rigour, extremitie'" (77).

✦ Manuscripts: **Huntington Library:** HM 198, pt. 1 (f. 45); **Marsh's Library:** MS 183, f. 20; **British Library:** Add. MS 19269, ff. 202–3.

✦ Joseph Frank, *Hobbled Pegasus* (Albuquerque: Univ. of New Mexico Press, 1968). Steven W. May, *The Elizabethan Courtier Poets* (Columbia, MO and London: Univ. of Missouri Press, 1991), 269–86; Steven W. May, "The Poems of Edward DeVere, Seventeenth Earl of Oxford and of Robert Devereux, Second Earl of Essex," *Studies in Philology* (1980), especially 35, 75–78, 120.

•••

113. Sir Robert Ayton (1569–1638), untitled, "Wrong not deere Empress of my heart," 134–35. Pr. John Cotgrave, ed. *Wits Interpreter* (1655), 40–41, 68 [both of the 2nd numbering]; *P&R*, 35–36.

A Scottish gentleman, diplomat, and poet, Sir Robert Ayton came to reside in England in 1615, but he had been appointed Groom of the Privy Chamber as early as 1608. Also, he had been sent by James to Protestant princes in Germany to explain James's book, *Premonition to all most Mighty Monarchs, Kings, Free Princes and States of Christendom* (1609), in which James claimed authority to demand sworn allegiance from all his subjects, regardless of their individual religions. Ayton was also Secretary and Master of Requests to Queen Anne until her death in 1619. Ayton was appointed Private Secretary to Queene Henrietta Maria by Charles I in 1625 after a dispute between Charles and her French household. He was an associate of George Villiers, Duke of Buckingham, from whom he sought patronage. He was a friend of Ben Jonson, Thomas Hobbes, and William Drummond of Hawthornden. Among his Latin poems is one dedicated to Buckingham, "Buchiniamus Io est praefectus, et idem."

The poem has a complex textual history. It is most frequently attributed to Sir Walter Ralegh; however, Gullans argues that it was written by Ayton. Michael Rudick accepts Gullans's explanation (lx–lxi). In several manuscripts, the poem begins with a stanza—probably by Ralegh, "Passions are lik'ned best to flood and streams." *Wits Interpreter* (1655) prints both versions. Six of the nine manuscripts that attribute this poem to Ralegh have the first stanza "Passions are . . ."; however, this stanza has a different scansion and rhyme scheme than the poem as it appears in the Holgate. Gullans writes that C. F. Main has suggested that the two poems were transcribed sequentially into one manuscript under a common heading, "such as Woman's Love or in this instance, Passions," and that thereafter, whenever copied, were thought of as one poem (325). Primary evidence that this poem is by Ayton is its occurrence in British Library Add. MS 10308 and Add. MS 28622, both of which are compilations of Ayton's poetry.

Gullans dates the poem circa 1610. He writes: "I believe this poem to have been written after 1603 and before 1612. The outside dates are based on the assumption that the poem was addressed to Princess Elizabeth, the daughter of James I. Several manuscripts say that the poem was addressed to 'Princess Elizabeth' and in other manuscripts this was transformed to 'Queen Elizabeth'" (260).

Collation demonstrates that this text is similar to that in *P&R*. That edition was printed from documents collected from people closely associated with William Herbert, Earl of Pembroke. The text is also similar to the poem as it appears in British Library Add. MS 23229. See Introduction, pp. xviii–xx.

> ✦ Collations: *P&R* / BL Add. MS 23229 (hand A) *BL-A.* 3 which thinketh] with thinking *P&R BL- A* ; 5 of] if *P&R*

> ✦ Crum W2846 (also O–1317, P–67); Beal Vol. I, pt. 2, RaW (Ralegh) 500–542; Yale: W2634; Gullans, Notes to the Text, 319–321. ✦ *Bodleian:* MS Ashmole 381 (p. 143, Lord Walden); Don.d.58 (f. 22ᵛ); MS Eng. poet. e. 14 (f. 19); MS Eng. poet. f. 9 (p. 6); MS Rawl. poet. 160 (f. 117, Sir Walter Ralegh to Queene Elizabeth); *British Library:* Add. MS 10308 (ff. 9ᵛ–10); Add. MS 21433 (ff. 112ᵛ–13ᵛ, Sir W:R:); Add. MS 22602 (ff. 30ᵛ–31, Sir Walter Ralegh to yᵉ Queen); Add. MS 23229 (f. 54); Add. MS 25303 (f. 118, Sir W:R:); Add. MS 27407 (f. 129); Add. MS 28622 (f. 18); Egerton MS 2560 (f. 114); MS Harley 3511 (ff. 12ᵛ–13); MS Harley 6057 (f. 18, Sir Walter Rawleigh); Lansdowne MS 777 (f. 63, Sr.Wa. Raleigh); Stowe MS 962 (f. 185, Lord Walden); *Cambridge:* MS Ee. 5.23 (pp. 6–7); *Corpus Christi College, Oxford:* MS 327 (f. 10ᵛ); MS 328 (f. 78); *Edinburgh University Library:* MS La. III 436 (pp. 20–21); *Folger:* V.a. 103, pt. I (f. 30, Sr Wa:Ral:); V.a. 345 (p. 90); V.a. 96 (f. 62); *Huntington Library:* HM 116 (pp. 16–18, Sr Gwalter Raleigh to yᵉ sole Governesse of his Affection); HM 198, pt. 2 (ff. 52ᵛ–53); *Rosenbach:* MS 239/27 (pp. 50–51); MS 240/2 (p. 5); MS 243/4 (p. 7); MS 1083/16 (p. 49); *Yale:* Osborn b 197 (p. 212, Lo:Wal:); Osborn b 200 (pp. 78–79).

✦ *The English and Latin Poems of Sir Robert Ayton* ed. Charles B. Gullans, Scottish Text Society, 4th Ser. no. 1 (Edinburgh and London: William Blackwood & Sons, 1963); Latham, 18–19; Rudick, lx–lxi, 106–9.

• • •

114. Anon., untitled, "This blacke Night represents my blacker woe," 135. Unprinted.

This is the first of four anonymous love poems found on pp. 135–36. To this reader, they appear of equal quality and may be by the same poet. No other copy of this poem has been found.

115. Anon., untitled, "Art thou so fond to thinke I can bee thine," 135. Unprinted.

No other copy of this poem has been found.

• • •

116. Anon., untitled, "I labor still in vaine," 136. Unprinted.

This is the third of four poems belonging to this group, and the only one known to appear in another miscellany. There is only one variant between the two manuscript texts.

✦ Manuscript: *Huntington Library:* HM 198, pt. 2 (f. 51).

• • •

117. Anon., untitled, "O clearest Moone why dost thou shew thy face," 136. Unprinted.

No other copy of this poem has been found.

• • •

118. Sir Henry Wotton (1568–1639), untitled, "Sʳ Henry Wotton," 137. Pr. Sir Thomas Overbury, *A Wife* (London, 1614), sig. F3ᵛ; *Reliquiæ Wottonianæ* (London, 1651), 522–23; *Le Prince d'Amour* (1660), 134–35; Dyce1, 5–7.

For further information on Wotton, see the notes to **HolM 47** and **HolM 60**.

A well-known anecdote helps explicate this popular lyric. In 1612, two years before the poem's first printing, Wotton, while visiting Germany on a diplomatic mission, was asked by a Christopher Fledamore to write a sentence in his personal album. Wotton wrote, "Legatus est vir bonus peregre missus ad mentiendum Reipublicæ causâ" ("An ambassador is an honest man sent to lie abroad for the good of his country"). In 1618, Fledamore's album was used by Gaspar Scioppius, a Catholic pamphleteer, who incorporated Wotton's sarcastic passage in two invectives against King James. James, upon hearing of the incident, chastised Wotton, but forgave him after Wotton wrote James two separate apologies (Nichols, 2:468–70).

There are no autograph copies of this poem, so critics have attempted to establish Wotton's original text. C. F. Main has followed J. B. Leishman's analysis of "You meaner beauties of the night" (**HolM 60**) by collating the known printed versions. *Reliquiæ Wottonianæ* was printed thirteen years after Wotton's death; Overbury's *Wife* was printed perhaps no more than two years after the poem was written. It stands to reason, then, especially when we consider the reversed stanzas, that the copy-text for *Reliquiæ Wottonianæ* was an alternate later version of the poem. Also, it is clear that the Holgate text is more closely aligned to the earlier printing than the later.

Ted-Larry Pebworth has analyzed this poem textually. He claims that both the Dulwich College MS and MS Phillipps 12341 (now at the University of Texas at Austin, see below) are older than the text in Overbury's *Wife*. They read at line 17 (modern spelling): "Who God doth late and early pray," a reading in neither Overbury's *Wife* nor the Holgate, which reads "who vnto God doth Late and early pray." Pebworth believes that the latter reading is an improvement in meaning, but it also intrudes "a pentameter line into an otherwise uniformly tetrameter poem," thus indicating a later emendation of the poem. Pebworth also collates the entire fourth stanza from the two earlier manuscripts with Overbury's *Wife*, ll. 13–16. They read (here from the Phillipps MS):

> Who envies none whom chance doth raise
> Or vice, who never vnderstood,
> How sword giues lighter wound, then praise
> nor rules of state, but rules of good.

Overbury's *Wife* reads:

Who enuieth none whome chaunce doth raise,
or Vice, who neuer vnderstood:
How deepest wounds are giuen with praise,
Not rules of state, but rules of good.
And the Holgate:
who Enuieth none whom Chance doth raise
NOr vice who neuer understood
how deepest wounds are giuen with praise
nor rules of state, but rules of good

Pebworth argues persuasively that the colon after "understood," l. 14, endstops the meaning of the first two lines of the stanza and leaves the final couplet without reference, thus without meaning. He also glosses "sword" (Phillipps, l. 15), to mean "rebuke," so that the entire stanza carries three separate notions: He is happy who envies not those raised up by chance or vice; he is happy who does not understand that it is kinder to rebuke one for his faults than praise one for his virtues; he is happy who does not understand that the rules of state can be different than the rules of morality. All these interpretations can be seen in the Phillipps manuscript, but not in Overbury's *Wife*, and by extension, in the Holgate manuscript.

The three stanzas, taken together, give us an opportunity to examine the scribe as a reader. In general, he uses very little punctuation, therefore letting his ideas run together so that they can naturally affect one another. His reading is superior to Overbury's *Wife* because he has not separated "who never understood" from the remaining couplet. "Nor" at the start of l. 16 also tends to pull the stanza together because it more naturally connects ll. 15–16. (Overbury's *Wife* is the only known text without this word.) Line 15, of course, is the key line. It is simpler, less meaningful, and far more conversational. If Pebworth's hypothesis is accepted, that the two manuscripts antedate Overbury's *Wife*, then somehow the Holgate comes between them. Moreover, if the trend in texts such as this is toward simplicity and conventionality, then it becomes even more difficult to comprehend the complexity of any particular textual moment.

Le Prince d'amour (1660) was edited by Sir Benjamin Rudyerd to commemorate the restoration of the monarchy (Marotti 277–78). **HolM 30** is also found in that volume.

✦ Manuscripts: Crum H1407; Beal Vol. I, pt. 2, WoH 1–48; Yale H1286 ✦ *Bodleian:* MS Ashmole 47 (f. 29ᵛ); Broxbourn R 359 (No 118) [f. 40ᵛ]; Don.c.57 (f. 51ᵛ); MS Malone 13 (p. 11); MS Malone 19 (p. 146); MS Rawl. D. 1048 (f. 58); MS Rawl. poet. 26 (f. 1ᵛ); MS Rawl. poet. 31 (f. 5); MS Rawl. poet. 66 (f. 55); MS Rawl. poet. 208 (f. 1); MS Rawl. poet. 212 (f. 150 [rev]); *Bradford Central Library:* Hopkinson MSS, Vol 17 (f. 124); Hopkinson MSS, Vol 34 (p. 44); *British Library:* Add. MS 21433 (ff. 115ᵛ–16); Add. MS 25303 (f. 121); Add. MS 25707 (f. 34ᵛ); Add. MS 29921 (f. 42); Add. MS 30982 (f. 160); Egerton MS 2026 (f. 11ᵛ); Egerton MS 2230 (f. 20ᵛ); MS Harley 1576 (f. 2); MS Harley 4064 (f. 234ᵛ); MS Harley 6057 (f. 18); Lansdowne MS 777 (f. 65); MS Sloane 3769 (f. 2); Stowe MS 962 (f. 176 [rev]); *Cambridge:* MS Ee. 4.14 (f. 76); *Dulwich College:* Alleyn Papers, Vol. I, No. 136 (f. 259); *Folger:* D347 (pp. 5–6); V.a. 103, pt. I (f. 77); V.a. 262 (p. 89); V.a. 345 (p. 63); V.b. 296 (f. 332); Y.d. 24 14B (74); *Harvard:* MS Eng. 686 (ff. 15ᵛ–16); MS Eng. 966.7 (f. 17ᵛ); MS Eng. 1035 (f. 10); *Huntington Library:* HM 93 (p. 183); *Leeds University:* Brotherton Collection, MS Lt. 25 (f. 7); MS Lt. 48 [f. 48]; *Leicestershire Record Office:* DG.7/Lit. 2 (f. 278); *National Library of Scotland:* MS 6504 (f. 85ᵛ); *University of Nottingham:* Portland MS Pw V 37 (p. 169); *University of Texas at Austin:* MS File (Herrick, R) Works B (pp. 78–79); *Rhode Island Historical Society:* John Saffin Miscellany; *Rosenbach:* MS 230/16 (p. 18); MS 239/22 (f. 25ᵛ); *Texas Tech:* Dalhousie

I (f. 11); *Trinity College, Dublin:* MS 877 (ff. 165ᵛ–66); MS 877 (ff. 261ᵛ–62); *Yale:* Osborn b 197 (p. 49); Osborn b 356 (p. 135).

✦ C. F. Main, "Wotton's 'The Character of a Happy Life,'" *The Library*, 5th Ser. 10 (1955): 270–74; Ted-Larry Pebworth, "New Light on Sir Henry Wotton's 'The Character of the Happy Life,'" *The Library*, 5ᵗʰ Ser. 33 (1978): 223–26. Also see, John Nichols, *The Progresses, Processions, and Magnificent Festivities of King James the First*, 4 vols. (London, 1828; rpt. New York: Burt Franklin, 1967), Research and Source Works Series, #118.

• • •

119. Anon., untitled, "Sweet stay a while, why will you rise," 137. Pr. John Dowland, *A Pilgrim's Solace* (London, 1612), two-stanza version; Orlando Gibbons, *The First Set of Madrigals and Mottets* (London, 1612); John Donne, *Poems* (London, 1669), sig. C1, (first stanza prefixed to Donne's "Break of Day").

It is highly doubtful that this poem is by John Donne. Its first stanza was printed as the first stanza of Donne's "Break of Day" (**HolM 128**) in *Poems* (1669). The two poems, however, have different meters. Moreover, the narrator of "Break of Day" is a woman, while the narrator of this poem is a man. Gardner (1965) suggests that the lyric may be by Dowland himself, who first published it in 1612 (230).

8. ffarr sweeter then the Phenix nest. The phoenix nest was made of spices (Doughtie 611).

✦ Manuscripts: Crum S1149, A762; Beal Vol. I, pt. 1, DnJ 2942–2983 ✦ *Aberdeen University Library:* MS 29 (pp. 185–86); *Bibliotheque Nationale, Paris, Department de la Musique:* Conservatoire MS 2489 (p. 269/f. 10ᵛ); *Bodleian:* MS Ashmole 47 (f. 73); Don.c.57 (f. 29ᵛ); MS Eng. poet. f. 9 (p. 19); MS Eng. poet. f. 25 (f. 11); MS Mus. f (ff. 20–24); MS Mus. f. 20 (f. 56ᵛ); MS Rawl. poet. 117 (f. 220ᵛ [rev]); MS Rawl. poet. 214 (f. 81ᵛ [rev]); *British Library:* Add. MS 10337 (ff. 20ᵛ–21); Add. MS 19268 (f. 19); Add. MS 25707 (f. 18ᵛ); Add. MS 29481 (f. 9); Add. MS 53723 (f. 10ᵛ); MS Sloane 542 (ff. 11ᵛ–12); MS Sloane 1792 (f. 12); Stowe MS 961 (f. 71ᵛ); *Cambridge:* MS Add. 7196 (f. 18ᵛ [rev]); *Corpus Christi College, Oxford:* MS 328 (f. 47ᵛ); *Folger:* V.a. 97 (p. 70); V.a. 262 (p. 102); V.a. 319 (f. 31ᵛ); V.a. 322 (p. 55); V.a. 345 (p. 237); *Harvard:* MS Eng. 686 (f. 94ᵛ); MS Eng. 966.6 (f. 146ᵛ); *Hertfordshire Record Office:* 19061; *Huntington Library:* HM 198, pt. 2 (f. 42ᵛ); *Owned by Sir Geoffrey Keynes:* Bibliotheca Bibliographici No. 1861 (f. 117ᵛ); *Leeds Archives Department:* MX 237 (f. 66ᵛ); *Leicestershire Record Office:* DG.9/2796 (p. 56); *National Library of Scotland:* Adv. MS 19.3.4 (f. 9ᵛ); *New York Public Library:* Arents Collection, Cat. No. S288 (p. 48); Music Division, Drexel MS 4175 (No. vi); *Rosenbach:* MS 239/18 (p. 106); MS 239/27 (pp. 51–52); MS 243/4 (p. 73); MS 1083/17 (f. 135); WCI1 (f. 16ᵛ); *Yale:* Osborn b 148 (p. 5); Osborn fb 88 (f. 120).

✦ For more information about this poem, especially the 1612 text, see Doughtie, 402–3, 608–11. See also Gardner (1965), 198 (dubia); and Grierson, 1:432, who attributes the poem to Dowland. Not in Shawcross.

• • •

120. Anon. "Verses made by the E: of P:," 138. Pr. John Donne, *Poems* (1635), 195–96; *P&R*, 3–4.

This and the following poem (**HolM 121**) usually appear as companion works. Identification of the poets, however, varies. By using the word "Verses" in the heading for both poems, the Holgate text identifies Pembroke as the author of both. The poems were printed in all but the first edition of John Donne's *Poems* (1635–1669). In those editions, Henry Wotton was presumed to have written one of the verses.

For textual information and sources concerning both poems, see **HolM 121 notes**.

✦ Collation: British Library Add. MS 23229 (hand A) *BL-A*. Headed: E: of P:] Earle of Pembroke *BL-A* ; 4 shall] sell *BL-A*

✦ Manuscripts: Crum I–798; Yale I–0597 ✦ ***Bodleian:*** MS Eng. poet. f. 9 (p. 133, Earle of Pembroke); MS Rawl. poet. 31 (f. 30, P.); MS Rawl. poet. 116 (f. 50, Pemb); MS Rawl. poet. 117 (f. 199ᵛ [rev], Sir H. Wootan); MS Rawl. poet. 147 (p. 81, P. altered to Sr. H.W.); ***British Library:*** Add. MS 10308 (f. 109ᵛ); Add. MS 23229 (f. 52ᵛ); Egerton MS 2725 (ff. 91ᵛ–92); Stowe MS 962 (f. 111); ***Cambridge:*** MS Add. 4138 (f. 49ᵛ); ***Folger:*** V.a. 125, pt. I (p. 51); ***Harvard:*** MS Eng. 966.1 (f. 41ᵛ); ***Huntington Library:*** HM 198, pt. 1 (p. 138); ***Yale:*** Osborn b 148 (p.13).

· · ·

121. Anon. "The Answeare," 138. Pr. John Donne, *Poems* (1635), 196; *P&R*, 4–5.

This poem and **HolM 120** almost always appear together, sometimes attributed to one of the two poets, William Herbert, Earl of Pembroke, and/or Sir Benjamin Rudyerd, but usually to both. More than likely they are the combined work of Herbert and Rudyerd. They were printed together in *P&R* but with the attribution only to Pembroke. That volume was carelessly edited by John Donne, Jr. to celebrate the return of the monarchy. Donne collected the poems from several sources, including and especially the Countess of Devonshire, a friend of Herbert, and from the musicians Henry Lawes and Nicholas Lanier, both of whom had set lyrics by Herbert to music. *P&R* contains nineteen poems that appear in the Holgate (see **HolM 40 notes**).

These debate poems were probably composed ca. 1602 when both Pembroke and Rudyerd were at Gray's Inn. In his critical study of William Herbert, Gary Waller describes the probable circumstances of the poems' composition: "In the records of Gray's Inn, Rudyerd is named as having written for the law students' annual entertainment, and the poems by him and Pembroke in 1660 may have been composed for a similar event. Written in heroic couplets, with wit that would have been appropriate for a mock-legal debate, they take sides over the question whether reason or love is to be preferred in a lover. Pembroke takes the part of love, arguing for its superiority over reason on conventional grounds" (Waller 176).

For further information on William Herbert, see **HolM 40 notes**.

Sir Benjamin Rudyerd was a well-known court figure. He was a friend of John Hoskins and the epigrammatist John Owen. Jonson addressed three epigrams to him, nos. 121–23 (*DNB*). He entered the Inner Temple and was admitted to the bar in 1600. He was knighted (1618) and made Surveyor of the Court of Wards, a lucrative post which he held until 1647. At different times he served as MP for Portsmouth, Old Sarum, Downton, and Wilton. He favored war with Spain and was opposed to the proposed marriage of Charles to the Spanish Infanta (cf. **HolM 72–73**). In 1660, he edited *Le Prince d'Amour*, a work celebrating the return of Charles II.

For a discussion of the similarity between the texts in the Holgate and British Library Add. MS 23229, see Introduction, pp. xviii–xx, and collations.

> **10. Caniculare.** Probably a pun, refers to the dog-days or dog-star, but also to dogs in general (see l. 11) or finally doggerel verse. Without this word, modern readers would miss the humor intended by these poems.

✦ **HolM 121** and Add. MS 23229 (hand A) are identical in all substantive variants. However, there are many substantive variants between the Holgate texts (**HolM 120** and **HolM 121**) and *P&R*, where they appear as one poem.

✦ Manuscripts: Crum T–2778; Yale T–2656 ✦ **Bodleian:** MS Eng. poet. f. 9 (p. 134, Ben Rudiar); MS Rawl. poet. 31 (f. 30ᵛ, R.); MS Rawl. poet. 116 (f. 50, Sir B.R.); MS Rawl. poet. 117 (ff. 119ᵛ, 200 [rev], Mr. Dunne); MS Rawl. poet. 147 (p. 81, Ben R. altered to Dr. D.); **British Library:** Add. MS 10308 (ff. 109ᵛ–10); Add. MS 23229 (f. 52ᵛ); Egerton MS 2725 (f. 92); Stowe MS 962 (f. 112); **Cambridge:** MS Add. 4138 (f. 49ᵛ); **Folger:** V.a. 125, pt. I (p. 51); **Huntington Library:** HM 198, pt. 1 (p. 138); HM 198, pt. 2 (p. 128); **Rosenbach:** MS 240/2 (p. 13); **Yale:** Osborn b 148 (p. 32).

✦ Waller, 159–88.

• • •

122. Anon., untitled, "Once Delia, on a Sunny banke her laide," 138. Unprinted.

Research has revealed no other copy of this poem; however, this type of light lyric is common to the miscellany tradition.

• • •

123. William Herbert (1580–1630), "That hee would not bee beloued," 139. Pr. John Dowland, *A Pilgrimes Solace* (1612), No. 1; Robert Chamberlain, *The Harmony of the Muses* (1654), 6; *P&R*, 5, 45 (see collations).

John Dowland's songbook *A Pilgrimes Solace* was dedicated to his employer, Theophilus Howard, Lord Walden, later Earl of Suffolk. Howard's home, Audley End, was near Saffron Walden, the home of William Holgate. The Dowland text organizes the words and music for four singing parts, headed Cantus, Tenor, Bassvs, and Altvs. No. 1 opens to B1ᵛ–B2ʳ. Holding the book in a normal manner, Cantvs and Tenor face toward the reader, Cantvs on the left, Tenor on the right. Bassus is above Tenor but faces to the right margin; while Altvs is upside down. In this manner, one text could be used simultaneously by four singers.

The close correlation of the Holgate text to the second text in *P&R* is noteworthy (see collations). Doughtie incorrectly thought that the Holgate was late seventeenth century. However, the latest this poem could have been transcribed in the Holgate manuscript is circa 1630. Had the Holgate entry been made after the publication of *P&R*, then the printed book might very well have been the copy-text. Since the Holgate clearly predates the printed text, the two transcriptions are probably of similar origin.

Waller attributes this poem to William Herbert. It valorizes desire for a woman over genuine affection. Waller's comments are relevant to the miscellany tradition as it must have been practiced, at least by the owner of this manuscript: "Like all of Pembroke's lyrics, its desired effect is to amuse, to pass the time pleasingly and make no further demand on its readers than, perhaps, memory (and desire for a repetition) of the pleasure to which it refers" (186). Waller's comments describe several of the poems found in the Holgate manuscript between pages 132 and 144, most of which comment on the nature of love (**HolM 108, HolM 110–117, HolM 119–144**).

For extensive textual variants, see Doughtie, 608. His collations indicate that Huntington HM 198, pt. 2 is similar to the Holgate. The two manuscripts differ only at l. 11: Holgate, "all though I"; HM 198, pt. 2 "though I do". Overall, HM 198, pt. 2 has much in common with *P&R* (Marotti 70–72).

See the collations for the Holgate text's variants from that in British Library Add. MS 23229. For further discussion of *P&R*, see **HolM 40 notes**.

✦ Collation: BL 23229 (hand A) *BL-A.* / *P&R* 5 / *P&R* 45   9 sighs] sights *BL-A* ; 10 mettell] mettles *P&R* 45 ; 11 Laugh] Laught *BL-A*, *P&R* 5

✦ Manuscripts: Crum D–327, Doughtie (p. 608) ✦ *Bodleian:* MS Rawl. poet. 116 (f. 53ᵛ); MS Rawl. poet. 160 (f. 103ᵛ, I.D.); *British Library:* Add. MS 22603 (f. 50ᵛ, J.D.); Add. MS 23229 (f. 52ᵛ); Egerton MS 2725 (f. 91ᵛ); Stowe MS 962 (f. 170ᵛ); *Corpus Christi College, Oxford:* MS 328 (f. 78); *Huntington Library:* HM 198, pt. 1 (p. 173); HM 198, pt. 2 (f. 42ᵛ).

✦ Doughtie, 402, 607–8; Waller, ch. 5, especially 185–87.

• • •

124. Anon., untitled, headed "Sʳ H:.N:," 139. Unprinted.

A handwritten modern pencil notation in the margin says "Henry Nevill of Billingbeare." However, the attribution is speculative. Henry Neville (1571/2–1615) was a courtier and diplomat. He had a son also named Henry Neville (d. 1629), but *ODNB* does not mention that either of them wrote poetry.

✦ Manuscript: *Huntington Library:* HM 198, pt. 2 (f. 38).

• • •

125. William Herbert (1580–1630), "The picture of his Mistris," 140. Pr. *P&R*, 54–55.

This is the last poem in *P&R* that Waller confidently ascribes to Pembroke (see **HolM 40 notes**). He describes its surface as being complimentary to the woman, but then analyzes the poem psychologically from the perspective of gender. Waller writes: "In terms of the sexual politics of late Petrarchism, however, it is far more revealing. Sight, and by extension rational visualization, is what is used to conjure up the power of the woman, even when she is absent. The lover freezes the beloved into an image, a statue, a picture, at a moment of his choice: 'It protects him from becoming conscious of some wishes and fantasies that would otherwise frighten and humiliate him.' To survive, he must divide and fetishize her. As Kaplan comments, in every perverse scenario, 'something or someone is treated as a fetish object, which is why fetishism is considered the prototype of all sexual perversions.'" (Waller 185 quoting Louise Kaplan, 124).

The sense of coterie poetry is emphasized at l. 15, "And in that secrett Closett still remaine." By extension, the world in which this and poems like it were exchanged was overwhelmingly male.

✦ Collation: *P&R* Title: The picture of his Mistris] *om. P&R* ; 6 scand] stand *P&R* ; 7 would] could *P&R* ; 9 place] part *P&R* ; 10 And did approud it] *concludes* l. 9 *P&R*

✦ Manuscript: *Rosenbach:* MS 1083/16 (pp. 256–57).

✦ Louise J. Kaplan, *Female Perversions: The Temptations of Emma Bovary* (New York: Doubleday, 1991); Waller, ch. 5, especially 184–85.

• • •

126. John Donne, untitled, "T'is true, t'is Day, What though it bee?" ["Breake of Day."], 140. Pr. William Corkine, *The Second Book of Ayres* (London, 1612), No. 4; *Poems*, 212.

The poem/setting is found in eleven extant manuscripts following "Sweet stay a while, why will you rise" (**HolM 119**). The poem is an aube, spoken by a woman. The musical setting was written for voice and viol. For what little is known about William Corkine, see *ODNB*.

Line 4 is omitted in the text of this famous poem, "Did we lie downe because 'tis night?" (as qtd. in Shawcross, 106). There is no way to know if the scribe considered this a poem or a song; however, it would be impossible to sing without l. 4.

The music that accompanies these lyrics can be found in Gardner (243) and Shawcross (107).

✦ Manuscripts: Crum T2871, T2851, L353; Beal Vol. I, pt. 1, DnJ 414–471; Yale T2756 ✦
Aberdeen University Library: MS 29 (pp. 184–85); *Bodleian:* Don.d.58 (f. 27); MS Eng. poet.
e. 99 (f. 111ᵛ); MS Eng. poet. f. 9 (pp. 208–9); MS Eng. poet. f. 25 (f. 11); MS Rawl. poet. 117 (f.
220ᵛ [rev]); *Bradford Central Library:* Hopkinson MSS, Vol 34 (p. 26); *British Library:* Add.
MS 10308 (f. 48ᵛ); Add. MS 15227 (f. 75); Add. MS 18647 (f. 8); Add. MS 25707 (f. 18ᵛ); Add.
MS 30982 (f. 52ᵛ); Egerton MS 2230 (f. 13); MS Harley 3511 (ff. 39ᵛ–40); MS Harley 4064
(f. 262ᵛ); MS Harley 4888 (f. 253); MS Harley 4955 (f. 118); Lansdowne MS 740 (f. 109ᵛ); MS
Sloane 1792 (ff. 11ᵛ–12); Stowe MS 961 (f. 71ᵛ); Stowe MS 962 (f. 130ᵛ); *Cambridge:* MS Add.
29 (f. 6); MS Add. 5778 (ff. 57ᵛ–58); MS Ee. 4.14 (f. 64); *Folger:* V.a. 97 (p. 70); V.a. 103, pt.
I (f. 74); V.a. 262 (p. 102); V.a. 319 (f. 31ᵛ); V.a. 322 (p. 55); V.a. 345 (p. 237); *Harvard:* fMS
Eng. 966.3 (f. 22ᵛ); fMS Eng. 966.4 (f. 203ᵛ); MS Eng. 966.5 (f. 130ᵛ); MS Eng. 966.6 (f. 134);
Hertfordshire Record Office: 19061; *Huntington Library:* EL 6893 (f. 91ᵛ); HM 198, pt. 2 (ff.
22ᵛ–23, 120); *Owned by Sir Geoffrey Keynes:* Bibliotheca Bibliographici No. 1860 (ff. 82ᵛ–83);
Bibliotheca Bibliographici No. 1861 (f. 104); *Leeds Archives Department:* MX 237 (f. 66ᵛ);
National Library of Scotland: MS 6504 (f. 46); *National Library of Wales:* Dolau Cothi MS
(p. 61); *New York Public Library:* Arents Collection, Cat. No. S191 (Miscellanea, p. 48); *University of Nottingham:* Portland MS Pw V 37 (p. 76); *Owned privately in England:* Monckton
Milnes MS (p. 64); *Rosenbach:* MS 239/27 (pp. 51–52); MS 243/4 (p. 73); MS 1083/17 (f.
135); *St. John's College, Oxford:* Crynes volume (p. 212); *St. Paul's Cathedral:* MS 49.B.43;
South African Library, Cape Town: MS Grey 7 a 29 (p. 74); *Texas Tech:* Dalhousie I (f. 46);
Dalhousie II (f. 23ᵛ); *Trinity College, Cambridge:* MS R 3.12 (James 307) (pp. 16–17); *Trinity
College, Dublin:* MS 877 (f. 36); *Victoria and Albert Museum:* Dyce Collection, Cat. No. 18
(Pressmark 25.F.17) (ff. 31ᵛ–32); Dyce Collection, Cat. No. 44 (Pressmark 25.F.39) (f. 78); *Yale:*
Osborn b 205 (f. 25); Osborn fb 88 (f. 120).

Beal writes in DnJ 471: "Copy, untitled, in a miscellany (p. 7) probably compiled by one or two members of the Calverley family; c. 1623–30s. Christie's, 13 June 1979 (Arthur A. Houghton, Jr. sale),
Lot 135, sold to Maggs; thence to Huntington."

✦ Doughtie, 389, 601–2; Gardner (1965), 35–36, 157–58, 238–47; Grierson, 1:23; Shawcross, 106–
7, 448–49.

• • •

127. Dudley, Third Baron North (1581–1666), untitled, "Queene of beauty most Diuine," 141. Pr. *A
Forest of Varieties* (1645), 17–18.

North privately printed *A Forest of Varieties* in 1645 during the Civil War. It contains essays,
letters, character descriptions, and poetry. His essays are interesting because of their critical commentary. He compares himself to other writers of his day: "These tormentors of thier owne and their
Readers braines I leave to bee admired in their high obscure flight, (while my selfe will bee happy,
if I can procure but a familiar delight to a superficiall reading) they affect to shew more wit then
love. . . ? (North, *Forest*, quoted in Randall, 25). He also described his own writing in the context of
his troubled times: "[T]*he direfull extremities and convulsions which my unhappy Country, and my self in
it have suffered these last yeeres make good with me the saying of* Ingentes curae stupent: *Partiality found
much, ingenuity little freedom: the first surprize was such as caryed me to an affectation of dissolution rather
then to endure the spectatorship of the growing miseries & approaching tragedies; nay, spectatorship was
not allowed*" (Randall, 21).

For further commentary on Dudley North, see **HolM 111 notes.**

✦ Manuscripts: Crum Q4 ✦ ***Bodleian:*** MS *North e. 41 (f. 14ʳ) (autograph); ***Huntington Library:*** HM 198, pt. 2 (f. 61).

✦ For a critical biography of Dudley North's son that contains commentary on North himself, see Dale B. J. Randall, *Gentle Flame: The Life and Verse of Dudley, Fourth Lord North (1602–1677)* (Durham, NC: Duke Univ. Press, 1983), 11–27.

• • •

128. Anon., untitled, "Thou foolish man, that louest to liue in bands," 142. Unprinted.
   No other copy of this poem has been found.

• • •

129. Anon., untitled, "Sweet Lady liue and liue in pleasure," 142–43. Unprinted.
   No other copy of this poem has been found. Its length is noteworthy: anonymous love poems are generally shorter than this.

• • •

130. Anon., untitled, "Why do wee loue these things which wee call weomen," 144. Pr. Robert Chamberlain, *The Harmony of the Muses* (1654), 26; *P&R*, 55–56.
   This poem is usually ascribed to Sir Benjamin Rudyerd based on its inclusion in *P&R*; however, that edition was so poorly edited that the ascription remains uncertain. Noteworthy, however, is how close the Holgate text is to the 1660 printed text (see collation). For a discussion of *P&R*, see **HolM 40 notes.**
   The Holgate text is better than the text in British Library Add. MS 23229. The omission of "loue," l. 15, in MS 23229 renders the line unintelligible (see collation). At l. 2, the MS 23229 scribe apparently mistook "like" for "lite." For a discussion of the potential relationship between these two manuscripts, see Introduction, pp. xviii–xx.

   ✦ Collations: *P&R*; British Library Add. MS 23229 (hand A) *BL-A* 2 like feathers] lite feathers *BL-A*; 10 yᵉ] *om. BL-A*; 12 sometime] sometimes *P&R*; 13 showres] flowers *P&R*; 15 Loue] *om. BL-A*

   ✦ Manuscript: ***British Library:*** Add. MS 23229 (f. 53ʳ).

✦ Pr. Ault, 438–39.

• • •

131. Anon., untitled, "Catch mee a starr yᵗˢ falling from the skie," 144. Pr. *Poems: By Francis Beaumont* (London, 1640); sig. I1ʳ; *Wits Recreations* (1640), sig. E3; *Wits Recreations* (1641), sig. D7.
   This poem has become associated with Francis Beaumont because of its inclusion in *Poems: By Francis Beaumont* (1640). It is, however, the only poem in that edition that was not reprinted in the second edition of Beaumont's poems in 1653 (Ringler 130). The poem is clearly a variant of John Donne's "Song," **HolM 89.**

   ✦ Manuscripts: Crum C104; Yale C0065 ✦ ***Bodleian:*** MS Ashmole 47 (f. 36); MS Malone 21 (f. 45ʳ); MS Rawl. poet. 153 (f. 8); ***British Library:*** Add. MS 30982 (f. 26); Egerton MS 2725 (f. 150ʳ); MS Harley 6057 (f. 15, Donne); MS Sloane 1867 (f. 24); Stowe MS 962 (f. 31ʳ); ***Corpus Christi College, Oxford:*** MS 328 (f. 19); ***Folger:*** V.a. 262 (p. 101); ***Harvard:*** MS Eng. 686 (f. 53ʳ); ***Huntington***

Library: HM 116 (p. 178); *New York Public Library:* Arents Collection, Cat. No. S288 (p. 30); *Rosenbach:* MS 240/7 (p. 78); *Yale:* Osborn b 62 (p. 38); Osborn b 200 (p. 3, Donne).

✦ Ringler 140. A short note on this poem appears in C. F. Main, "New Texts of John Donne," *Studies in Bibliography* 9 (1957), 231.

• • •

132. Anon., untitled, "There is a place where Care shall not molest," 145. Unprinted.
No other copy of this poem has been found.

• • •

133. Chidiock Tichborne, "A Song which Childock Tichborne traytor made of himselfe in the Towre yᵉ night before hee sufferd," 145. Pr. *Verses of Prayse and Joye . . . upon her Majesties preservation* (London, 1586), 4° [single sheet]; printed by John Wolfe.

This poem from the late-Tudor era was very popular during the early seventeenth century. In April 1586, Tichborne, a Catholic, became part of the Babington Conspiracy, a group that wanted to assassinate Elizabeth and free Mary Stuart. It was Mary's awareness of the plot that led to her own execution (Guy 334).

Tichborne was arrested 14 August 1586 along with two other co-conspirators. He pleaded guilty. While awaiting execution, he wrote a letter to his wife, printed in "The Works of Chidiock Tichborne," edited by Richard S. M. Hirsch (see below). According to Sir Stephen Powle, an agent for Sir Francis Walsingham and the Lord Treasurer Burghley, the poem was written three days before his execution, 19 September 1586 (Hirsch 305–6).

The poem was printed several times in the period following Tichborne's execution. After *Verses of Prayse and Ioy . . .* , it appeared in Huth's *Fugitive Poetical Tracts*, first series, No. 26; John Mundy, *Songs and Psalms* (London, 1594), 4° printed by T. Este, the assign of W. Byrd; Michael East, *Madrigales to 3, 4, and 5 parts apt for viols and voices* (London, 1604), 4° printed by T. Este. These publications, however, were not the source of the poem as it appears in the Holgate. Hirsch classifies these texts as branch β, which read at l. 7, "My tale was heard, and yet it was not told." This is the version printed by Hebel (196) and in *The New Oxford Book of English Verse*, edited by Dame Helen Gardner (Oxford, 1972), 59. The Holgate text, however, is terminal on branch α of Hirsch's stemma. It descends from Tichborne's holograph through the copy made by Sir Stephen Powle, now Bodleian MS Tanner 169, f. 69, collated below. According to Hirsch, Powle would have had access to the Tower at the time of Tichburne's imprisonment. Hirsch contends that from Powle's copy the text was transmitted through at least two lost intermediaries to MS Harley 6910. A third hypothetical source then transmitted the text to Trinity College, Cambridge MS 0127, from which descend the versions in Bodleian MS Eng. Poet. F. 10 and the Holgate manuscript.

Hirsch's article also includes the speech Tichborne made on the scaffold.

✦ Collation: Bodleian MS Tanner 169 (Hirsch 309–10; 314 *fac.*) Title: A Song which Childock Tichborne traytor made of himselfe in the Towre yᵉ night before hee sufferd] Tichbornes verses made by him selfe not three dayes before his execution || 5 fledd] gone || 8 be] are || 9 past] gone || 11 *second* is] was || 13 for] my || 14 yet] sawe || 15 ground] earth || 17 yet my] nowe the

✦ Manuscripts: Crum M863; Yale M0661 ✦ *Bodleian:* MS Ashmole 47 (f. 52); Ashmole 781 (p. 138, Chidiock Tichborne); MS Eng. poet. e. 97 (p. 215); MS Eng. poet. f. 10 (f. 93); MS Malone 19 (p. 54, Tychborne); MS Rawl. D. 859 (f. 143, Tichbourne); MS Rawl. poet. 172 (f. 7); Ms Rawl. poet. 200 (f. 2); MS Rawl. poet. 208 (f. 2); MS Tanner 169 (f. 79, Tichborne); MS Wood

460; **British Library:** Add. MS 30.076; Add. MS 30982 (ff. 24, 160); Add. MS 38823 (f. 30); Egerton MS 923 (f. 56ᵛ); Egerton MS 2642 (f. 256ᵛ); MS Harley 36 (f. 269ᵛ); MS Harley 6910 (f. 141ᵛ); Lansdowne MS 777 (f. 66ᵛ); Lansdowne MS 863; MS Sloane 1446 (f. 42); MS Sloane 3769 (f.10); **Christ Church, Oxford:** MS 184; **Corpus Christi College, Oxford:** MS 328 (f. 74ᵛ); **Edinburgh University Library:** MS Laing II, 69/24. **Folger:** V.a. 161, p. 12; V.a. 162 (f.32); V.a. 262 (f. 98); V.a. 345 (pp. 284–85); Harvard: MS 686 (f. 29); MS Eng. 749; **Huntington:** EL 6162; **National library of Wales:** Sotheby MS B2 (f. 65); **Trinity College, Cambridge:** MS 0127; **Yale:** Osborn fb 9 (f. 30).

✦ Richard S. M. Hirsch, "The Works of Chidiock Tichborne (text)," *English Literary Renaissance* 16 (1986), 303–18. See also Hirsch's correction of his commentary in "The Text of 'Tichborne's Lament' Reconsidered," *English Literary Renaissance* 17 (1987), 277. For commentary on the Babington Conspiracy, see John Guy, *Tudor England* (Oxford and New York: Oxford Univ. Press, 1988), 334–35.

• • •

134. Anon., "Natura negat facit indignator versum," 146–47. Unprinted.

The first lines of this text are omitted. The first line in the Holgate, "Has left his boys play, scornes to bee so base," is actually l.6. The scribe clearly knew he was omitting these lines because he left the appropriate space for them at the top of the leaf. He also indicated the missing lines with dots, each representing a missing line. Perhaps he hoped to complete his text using another manuscript, or he considered it too insulting to transcribe (see below). The opening of the poem reads as follows in Folger MS V.a. 262, pp. 64–65: "An Aunswer to Dr. Corbetts Verses to the Duke of Buckingham":

> ffalse on his Deanry; false nay more; Ile lay
> As many pounds; as hee and 's frends did pay
> Greate Phaebus darling for his dignitie,
> That no such thought abus'd his braine; that hee
> Is groun in witt, as well as beard, and place;

The poem responds to Corbett's "I'ue reade of Ilands floatinge and remou'd" (**HolM 72**), for which Corbett was frequently criticized. It was believed that the tone of that poem was more appropriate for a courtier than a cleric. Line 1 above, "ffalse on his Deanry," refers to l. 59 of the Corbett poem, "False on my Denerie."

The manuscript page found in *State Papers Domestic* is part of the Conway papers, and therefore can be aligned with British Library Add. MS 23229 (see Introduction, pp. xviii–xx). The handwriting of that manuscript page is the same as the manuscript collated with **HolM 73**, "Vppon Prince Charles his cominge home out of Spaine: 1623." It is also the same handwriting identified in this edition as hand B in British Library Add. MS 23229. The collation between these two texts is notably similar.

> **(5). Iet.** Probably should read "yet."
> **(21). Some Taylor or Some Fennor.** Refers to the 1614 controversy between two writer/entertainers (*ODNB*, 'John Taylor').
> **(22). clapp his name to theire Sale Poetrie.** The above-mentioned controversy.
> **(24). Wood stocke sceane.** Woodstock was a royal estate in Oxfordshire. At the time, Corbett was Dean of Christ Church, Oxford.
> **(34). second part of band stringe and the ringe.** In August 1621, Corbett preached before James at Woodstock. Corbett lost track of his sermon when he became focused on a ring James had given him which he had tied to the strings of his band (B&TR xxii). Corbett had also

written a poem, "The Ladyes Answer" (B&TR 91), in which he criticized the clothes worn by the ladies at court.

> Love-charmes have power to weave a string
>
> Shall tye you as you ty'd your ring.

The reference to "second part" is possibly a singing part.

(43). Mother Zebede. Salome. See **HolM 72**, l. 78 and comment.

(44). Leuies Lotte. The tribe of Levi, from which derived the sons of Aaron, Israel's priestly caste, possibly alluding to Dr. Corbett's clerical status. "Lotte'"suggests one's "lot" or role in life .

✦ Manuscripts: Crum F–136; Yale F–0092 ✦ *Bodleian:* MS Ashmole 36/37 (f. 155); Don.d.58 (p. 30); MS Rawl. D. 1048 (f. 53); *British Library:* Add. MS 21433 (f. 1206); Add. MS 25303 (ff. 131–32); *Folger:* V.a. 262 (p. 64); V.a. 345 (p. 133). **Yale:** Osborn b 200 (p. 29); Osborn b 208 (p. 255). Also *State Papers Domestic:* Jac. I, cliii, 113 [ll. 16–50].

✦ B&TR, xxii–xxv.

• • •

135. Francis Phelips, prose epistle:, "To the Kings most Excellent Maiestie. the humble petition of M^r. ffrauncis Phillippes Esquirer: in the behalfe of his Brother Sr Robert Phillipps: who was a Prisoner in the Tower of London: Anō Domi 1622," 153–57. Unprinted.

The *Calendar of State Papers Domestic* paraphrases a copy of this letter addressed to the King by Francis Phelips, probably the Auditor of the Exchequor, on behalf of his brother, Sir Robert Philips (1586?–1638), who at the time was MP from Bath. The *Calendar* dates the entry 12 April 1622. It reads: "[—Phelips] to the Same. Having no friend about Court, is compelled to address His Majesty direct; will not stand upon the goodness of his cause, but rather be a monument of sorrow and humility. Prays pardon for the earnestness with which he entreats his clemency, not for himself, but for his dear and only brother [Sir Robert Phelips], who, though walking in straightforward paths, yet having retired to his country house during the last recess of Parliament, was arrested by a serjeant-at-arms at Christmass, brought before the Council, and committed close prisoner to the Tower, where neither his wife nor himself can gain access to him. The commissioners sent to examine him have not been since the first week of his imprisonment, which has now lasted three months. Indorses, 'Petition to his Matie for ye release or enlargement of a Parliam^t man, close prisoner in ye Tower'" (*Calendar*, 375).

Robert Phelips was knighted during James's coronation in 1603. The same year he entered Parliament from East Looe, Cornwall. In 1614, he was elected MP from Saltash, Cornwall. He traveled to Spain in 1615 with Lord Digby as an early negotiator for the so-called Spanish Match, the proposed marriage of Charles I and the Spanish Infanta. Phelips, however, opposed the match.

Phelips was elected MP from Bath in 1621. On his motion, Parliament debated patent questions concerning gold and silver thread. He was also a supporter of Lord Bacon (see **HolM 39**). The *DNB* describes the circumstances of his arrest: "In November he warmly attacked Spain, and proposed to withhold commons' petition against the Catholics and the Spanish marriage. For his share in these proceedings he was on 1 Jan. 1622 arrested at Montacute, whither he had retired, and on the 12 imprisoned in the Tower. Here he remained in spite of his brother's petition until 10 Aug."

James wanted to exclude Phelips from the next parliament, 1623–24, but he was elected MP from Somerset.

✦ Manuscripts: *British Library:* Add. MS 25707 (ff. 138–41). Also *State Papers Domestic:* Jac. I, 129, 21.

136. Anon., pseudo., "Muld Sacke: or The Apologie of Hic Mulier: To the late declamation against her Exprest in a short declamation," 170. Pr. *Muld Sacke: or The Apologie of Hic Mulier* (1620), sig. A2. (STC 21538).

The complete title, *Muld Sacke: or The Apologie of Hic Mulier* (1620, entered in the Stationer's Register 29 April) is transcribed exactly on p. 170, ll. 1–6; the book's dedicatory poem follows. "Hic Mulier" is translated "Man-wife" or "this [masculine] woman." The book is an answer to a previous book, *Haec Vir or the Womanish Man* (1620), entered in the Stationers' Register to J. Trundle, 16 February 1620). There was, however, a previous edition of *Muld Sacke* which antedates the series, *Hic Mulier, or the Man-Woman* (registered to J. Trundle 9 February 1620).

There are no substantive variants in the transcription. More than likely, the scribe copied the poem from the book itself as indicated by the marginal note to the right of the title. In view of the stable copy-text, collation allows us an opportunity to access the scribe's transcription characteristics and orthography. Based on the evidence from this poem and the transcriptions from Tofte's *Blazon* (**HolM 1, HolM 4, HolM 7,** and **HolM 8**, the scribe of this manuscript was a very accurate copyist. For discussion of printed material used as copy-texts, see Introduction, p. xvii.

> **7–9.** These lines describe Muld Sack as depicted in a drawing on the book's title page.
> **9. spruse Bootes.** Leather boots.

✦ Collation (including accidentals) *Muld Sacke* (1620) *MS*. 1 heart] Heart *MS* ; 2 picture] Picture *MS* ; 3 Maides] Maydes *MS* ; 6 heart . . . selfe] Heart . . . Selfe *MS* ; name] Name *MS* ; 7 Vowinge] Vowing *MS* ; sword] Sword *MS* ; ffeather] Feather *MS* ; 8 Roses either] Roses, either *MS* ; 10 Loue] loue *MS*

• • •

137. Thomas Brewer [?], "Mistris Turners Repentance; Who, about the poysoning of that Ho: Knight Sir Thomas Ouerbury, was executed the 14ᵗʰ day of Nouember: 1615," subscribed "T. B.," 171–74. Pr. *Mistress Turners repentance, who, about the poysoning of Sir Thomas Overbury, was executed the 14ᵗʰ day of November, 1615* (London, 1615), single sheet folio for H. Gosson and J. White, entered November 23 (STC 3720); reprinted from the above text in *Fugitive Poetical Tracts Written in Verse* (1875), no. viii.

Holgate's three substantive variants from the 134 lines of verse edited in the *Fugitive Poetical Tracts* text offers strong evidence that the scribe copied from the 1615 broadside (cf. **HolM 136**). The Society of Antiquaries, London copy is listed in Robert Lemon, *Catalogue of a Collection of Printed Broadsides* (London, 1866). Noteworthy is the change in the title: "last" in the copy-text; "1615" in the Holgate. The Holgate scribe changed "last" in his anthology for future reference. See collation for the similarity of the two texts.

Although there were many broadside ballads printed at the time of Turner's execution, only two were signed, this one attributed to Thomas Brewer and "The Poysoned Knight's Complaint" by Samuel Rowlands. According to Allistair Bellany, "Brewer was the author of verse merriments, ballads and a murder tract" (128). However, the poem cannot with certainty be attributed to Brewer. The Brewer attribution was made by Robert Lemon for the above-mentioned 1866 *Catalogue* (*ODNB*).

Mistress Turner is Anne Turner (1576–1615), an accomplice in the murder of Sir Thomas Overbury. She was the widow of George Turner, M. D. (d. 1610). Her parents were Thomas Norton of Hinxton and Margaret, daughter and heir to Sir William Lowe of Somerset. Her brother Eustace was Falconer to Prince Henry (White 25). Her character, it would appear, may have been somewhat controversial: "After her husband's death she chose to make a living by pandering to the follies and vices of Court youths and maidens. At Mrs Turner's houses in Paternoster Row, or at

Hammersmith, illicit loves could be consummated in the appropriate atmosphere of secrecy and luxury. She was, besides, an arbiter of fashion, credited with the introduction of yellow starch for ruffs, which, stiffened and saffroned, made a gaudy setting for the fair skins and blonde curls of the Court ladies from the Queen downwards" (White 25–26).

Frances Howard and Anne Turner were friends, and together they plotted Overbury's death. Frances Howard hated Overbury because he had opposed her marriage to Robert Carr, formerly the King's favorite (see **HolM 147**). It was believed that Frances Howard wanted Carr to retaliate against Overbury, but he refused because Overbury and Carr had been involved in a plot to assassinate Henry, Prince of Wales (see **HolM 3, 5,** and **101–5**). James Franklin, described as a dependent of Frances Howard, concocted the poisons used to murder Overbury. Mixed in with Overbury's confectionary was a blend of arsenic, aqua fortis, mercury, powder of diamonds, lapis costitus, great spiders, and cantharides (*ODNB*, "Sir Thomas Overbury").

At trial, Anne Turner never admitted to her part in the murder; however, she was found guilty. As the poem indicates, she was hanged on 14 November 1615. A description of her execution sheds light on this poem.

> Realizing to the full her opportunities of moving a large and sympathetic audience, Mrs Turner made a devout end. On November 14th she was taken to Newgate in a coach and from there to Tyburn in a cart, casting money among the people as she went. "Men and women of fashion came in coaches to see her die, to whom she made a speech (probably composed by Whiting) desiring them not to rejoice at her fall, but to take example by her." The yellow ruff and cuffs worn by the hangman at Coke's command added a more gruesome touch to the occasion and finished for ever the fashion she had inaugurated. One John Castle—perhaps Dr. John Castle, Sir Henry Wotton's friend—was touched by her beauty and wrote that she went *a cruce ad gloriam*. (qtd. in White 125)

The poem also includes references to the religious controversies of the day. Turner was Catholic, but at her death received communion from the Church of England (White 124). It is interesting to note how up-to-date common knowledge was of this fact (ll. 119–22).

> **3. scrowle.** Scroll.
> **8. suspiration.** Sighing (*OED*).
> **21–22. may my sad end . . . how to mend.** See the description by Whiting above.
> **70 (margin). Doct:.** Reference to Dr. John Whiting (see above).

✦ Collation: *Fugitive Poetical Tracts FPT.* Title: 1615] last *FPT* ; 14 knee] knees *FPT* ; 26 Hells] Hell *FPT* ; 111 my] me *FPT* N. B. According to the *Catalogue of Printed Books in the British Museum*, the Brewer text was used as the copy-text for *Fugitive Poetical Tracts*. Since the texts are so similar, I assume that the Holgate transcribed the poem from the single sheet folio.

✦ See *Fugitive Poetical Tracts, 2nd ser., 1600–1700*, ed. William Carew Hazlitt and Henry Huth, *Fugitive Tracts Written in Verse* (London: Chiswick Press, 1875); Robert Lemon, *Catalogue of a Collection of Printed Broadsides in the Possession of the Society of Antiquaries* (London, 1866); also see Allistair Bellany, *The Politics of Court Scandal in Early Modern England* (Cambridge: Cambridge Univ. Press, 2002); Beatrice White, *Cast of Ravens* (London: John Murray, 1965), which contains a very helpful bibliography on Overbury's murder.

• • •

138. Anon., untitled, "Saint Thomas haueing lost his Master, sought about," 174. Unprinted.

No other copy of this epigram nor any information about it has been found. It concerns Saint Thomas the Apostle who doubted the Resurrection unless he could touch the wounds of Christ (John 20:25–28).

• • •

139. Anon., untitled, "With in this Rocke the Rock him selfe is layd," 174. Unprinted.
Like the preceding poem, this verse concerns the Resurrection.

Manuscript: *Folger:* V.a. 275 (p. 98).

• • •

140. Anon., untitled, "A one eyd boy borne of a halfe blind Mother," 175. Pr. Camden's *Remaines* (1637), 413; *Wits Recreations* (1640), No. 458; *Wits Interpreter* (1655), 276.
When first published in *Remaines*, this epigram appeared with what might be its Latin original.

Upon two beautiful children, a brother and sister, who wanted each of them an eye:
    Lumine Acon dextro caruit, Leonilla sinistro,
    Et potuit forma vincere uterque Deos:
    Parve puer, lumen quod habes concede sorori,
    Sic tu cæcus Amor, sic erit illa Venus.

Englished thus:
    Thou-one-ey'd Boy, whose sister of one mother,
    Matchlesse in beauty are, save one to th' other:
    Lend her thine eye, sweet Lad, and she will prove
    The Queen of Beauty, thou the God of Love.

✦ Manuscripts: Crum A324, A179, F53, H142, T2227 ✦ **Bodleian:** MS Ashmole 38 (p. 155); MS Eng. poet. c. 50 (f. 33ᵛ); MS Eng. poet. f. 10 (f. 114ᵛ); MS Eng. poet. f. 25 (f. 16ᵛ); MS Rawl. poet. 84 (f. 85); MS Rawl. poet. 116 (f. 54); MS Rawl. poet. 153 (f. 8); **British Library:** Add. MS 19268 (f. 24ᵛ); Add. MS 29492 (f. 5); Egerton MS 923 (f. 58); Egerton MS 2421 (f. 18); MS Sloane 1792 (f. 131ᵛ); MS Tanner 465 (f. 96ᵛ) **Corpus Christi College, Oxford:** MS 328 (f. 31); **Folger:** V.a. 97 (p. 155); **Yale:** Osborn b 62 (p. 137).

• • •

141. Francis Davison (fl. 1602), untitled, "Loue, if a God thou bee'st, then euer more bee mercifull & iust," 175. Pr. *A Poetical Rhapsody* (1602), first madrigal; Robert Jones, *First Set of Madrigals* (1607), v; *Wits Recreations* (1640).
Davison ascribed this poem to himself in the printed miscellany he compiled, *A Poetical Rhapsody* (1602, 1608, 1611). The poem was printed without ascription in the 1621 edition.
Davison was the son of William Davison, Elizabeth's Secretary of State. He entered Gray's Inn in 1593. Davison writes in his address "to the reader" that his poems were composed "six or seven years since" (ca. 1595) while traveling in Europe.
The lyric is actually translated from Luigi Groto, *Rime* (1583), 63. It was set to music by Robert Jones in his *First Set of Madrigals* (1607), v.

✦ Manuscripts: Crum L813; Yale L0638 ✦ **Bodleian:** MS Mus. Sch. F. 575 (p. 4, with melody and lute accompaniment); MS Harley 6057 (f. 45, Tho: Crosse); MS Rawl. poet. 153 (f. 21ᵛ); **British Library:** Egerton MS 2725 (f. 95ᵛ); Sloane 1792 (f. 11); **Folger:** V.a. 197 (pp. 243–44); V.a. 345 (p.

243); *Harvard:* Norton MS 4504 (p. 312); *Rosenbach:* MS 1083/16 (f. 70); *Trinity College, Dublin:* MS G.2.21 (p. 454, William Lewis); *Yale:* Osborn b 197 (p. 229).

✦ See *The English Madrigal School* 35, ed. E. H. Fellowes (London: Stainer and Bell, 1913–24), 24–28; Sanderson, 705; Hebel, 208.

• • •

142. Anon., untitled, "Loue whats thy name, a ffrenzy?," 175. Unprinted.

No other copy of this poem has been found.

• • •

143. Anon., "A renouation of an Auncient Bishp: wth will: yᵉ Conqr: out of St Pauls:," 175. Pr. Iohn Weever, *Ancient fvnerall monvments within the vnited monarchie of Great Britaine* . . . (1631), 362.

The entry includes a description of the poem by John Wale, a later owner of the miscellany. He wrote at the bottom of the page. "Gulielmᵘˢ Normannus Epus Londini obtained great Priuiledges of Willᵐ yᵉ Conquorr for ye City of London: in remembrance of whom, Sr Edwᵈ Barkham Ld Mayor erected a monumᵗ of Gratitude in Sᵗ Puls Church y[ar]d in yᵉ year 1622." John Weever's introduction to the poem confirms the information supplied by Wale.

The tablet in Saint Paul's memorializes the Bishop of London, identified in the poem as Bishop Norman (d. 1070). Weever reprints an inscription that was first erected in the Bishop's honor, then proceeds to describe this epitaph:

> But this tombe was long since either destroyed by time, or taken away vpon some occasion: yet howsoeuer the Lord Maior of London, and the Aldermen his brethren, vpon those solemne dayes of their resort to *Pauls*, do still vse to talke to the grauestone where this Bishop lyeth buried, in rememberance of their priuiledges by him obtained. And now of late yeares an Inscription fastened to the pillar next adioyning to his graue (called, The reuiuall of a most worthy Prelates remembrance, erected at the sole cost and charges of the right honourable and nobly affected Sir *Edward Barkham* knight, Lord Maior of the Citie of London, *Ann. 1622.*) thus speakes to the walkers in *Pauls* (362).

A second poem that refers to walking through St. Paul's Cathedral is Richard Corbett's "Elegy to Bishop Ravis," **HolM 152**.

I am grateful to W. H. Kelliher, the late Curator of Manuscripts, The British Library, for his help in identifying this poem.

✦ Manuscripts: Crum W–18 ✦ *Bodleian:* MS Ashmole 38 (pp. 187, 189); *Folger:* W.b. 455 (p. 28) [c. 1705].

• • •

144. Richard Martin, prose oration, "Mʳ Martins speech to yᵉ Kinge in yᵉ names of yᵉ Shreifs of London," 176–179. Pr. *A Speach delivered to the King's Most Excellent Maiestie, in the name of the sheriffes of London and Middlesex* (1603); John Nichols, *The Progresses Processions and Magnificent Festivities of King Iames the First* (1828), 1:128–32.

Information on this entry derives from Nichols, *Progresses of James I*. Martin was born in Otterton, Devonshire. He studied at Broadgate's College, Oxford, but he did not attain a degree. He then entered the Inner Temple, where he became an Inner Barrister. He was elected to Parliament (1601). Martin delivered this speech before the king at Stamford Hill, after which "James ever entertained the greatest esteem for him, being highly delighted with his facetiousness" (Nichols 1:128n). Martin was Lent Reader of the Inner Temple (1615) and was recommended by James to the City of London to be Recorder (1618). He died only a month after his election.

> **41. Gahazi.** 2 Kings 5:20–27.
> **57–58. Lazarus doggs . . . Princs soares.** Luke 16:1921.
> **72. vnder his owne oliue tree.** Micah 4:4.
> **78–86. Biblical allusions.** Numbers 22:24; John 2:12–22.

✦ Manuscripts: *British Library:* MS Harley 4106; *Cathedral Library at Exeter:* MS; *State Papers Doemstic: Jac.* I, i, 71 (7 May 1603). ✦ Calendar of *State Papers Domestic* (op. cit.) notices a second copy, (Dom. Eliz., vol., xlv, p. 131. Imperfect).

• • •

145. Walton Poole [?], subscribed "D: C: on a blacke Gentlewoman:," 180. Pr. *The Harmony of the Muses* (1654), 16–18; *Wits Interpreter* (1655), 53; *Parnassus Biceps* (1656), 75; *P&R*, 61.

This was a very popular seventeenth-century poem. Three surviving manuscripts attribute the poem to Donne, but the ascription is rejected by Grierson and all other editors. The two Jonson attributions are dismissed by H&S as "obviously wrong or absurd." B&TR describe the attribution to Corbett as "unconvincing" (173). The "D: C:" in the Holgate attribution is surely intended as Doctor Corbett (cf. **HolM 78**, et al.). Since it is not accepted as canonical for Donne, Jonson, or Corbett, a complete list of the extant manuscripts has never been compiled.

However, the poem is generally attributed to Walton Poole. In addition to the manuscripts that ascribe the poem to him, many manuscripts mention his wife Beata as the so-called "blacke Gentlewoman." Edwin Wolfe, II, who made a textual study of the poem, believes that Walton Poole was the second son of Sir Henry Poole of Okesey, Wiltshire, and that his wife Beata was the daughter of William Brydges, 4th Baron Chandos of Sudeley (835). He adds that they were married before 1616, that she died before 10 August 1637, and that the poem was written between 1615 and 1620, but gives 1630 as the last possible date it could have been written (836). There is no date in the Holgate manuscript.

Wolf argues the poem's popularity is due to the social standing of Beata Poole. He writes:

> Her brother, Grey, Lord Chandos, was one of the most frequent participants in the social functions of the court of James I, as witness his many appearances in masques and entertainments presented before the king, recorded in Nichols' *Progresses of King James*. His seat, Sudeley Castle, was the scene of such lavish entertainment that Chandos gained the title "King of the Cotswolds." His sister would certainly have taken a part in his social life, especially since she married into a family which with the Brydges had long been one of the leading families of Glousestershire (836).

The poem presents a complex set of questions concerning the difficulty of reading old texts. If the poem is indeed by her husband, then its suggestive sexual nature would seem inappropriate to publication, even within the cultural practice of manuscript transmission. As a transmitted document, the poem may suggest public foolishness on the part of its poet and his wife. It may have been written before they were married and later became a source of embarrassment for them. Also, even if it was not written by Poole, it was frequently accepted as having been written by him, so that, in terms of reception theory, it does not matter whether he wrote the poem or not. Its sexual connotations can also be seen as an extension of its implied racism.

> **14. Nigromancie.** Obsolete form of 'necromancy', here with a likely pun on 'Nigro/Negro', black.

✦ Manuscripts: (entries marked with * identify the "blacke Gentlewoman" as Beata Poole, wife of Walton Poole). Crum I–945; Yale I–0702 ✦ ***Bodleian:*** MS Ashmole 38 (p. 30); MS Ashmole 47 (f. 35); MS Douce f (f. 36); MS Eng. poet. c. 50 (f. 37ᵛ); MS Eng. poet. e. 14 (f. 82 [rev]); MS Eng. poet. e. 97 (p. 113*); MS Eng. poet. f. 10 (f. 91, Bi. Ox. Rich. Corbett); MS Eng. poet.f.16 (f. 5ᵛ, Dr. Donne); MS Eng. poet. f. 25 (f. 12, Dr.Dun); MS Rawl. poet. 117 (f. 175ᵛ [rev]); MS Rawl. poet. 142 (f. 27); MS Rawl. poet. 199 (p. 12); ***British Library:*** Add. MS 10308 (f. 47ᵛ); Add. MS 11811 (f. 33ᵛ, W.P. or Walton Poole); Add. MS 21433 (f. 109, Jonson); Add. MS 22118 (f. 6); Add. MS 25707 (f. 90); Add. MS 28644 (f. 74); Add. MS 30982 (f. 153 [rev]); Egerton MS 923 (f. 61ᵛ–62ᵛ); Egerton MS 2421 (f. 37); MS Harley 3910; MS Sloane 542 (f. 12ᵛ); MS Harley 6057 (f. 9ᵛ, Jonson); MS Harley 6931 (f. 8ᵛ, Poole); Lansdowne MS 777 (f. 71, Poole); MS Sloane 1446 (f. 71ᵛ, Mr.Walton Poole); MS Sloane 1792 (f. 23); Stowe MS 962 (f. 69v); ***Corpus Christi College, Oxford:*** MS 328 (f. 87ᵛ); ***Folger:*** V.a. 97 (p. 3, Walton Poole); V.a. 103, pt. I (f. 52ᵛ); V.a. 124 (f. 28); V.a. 125, pt. I (f. 24); V.a. 170 (p. 16*, W:P:); V.a. 245 (f. 36ᵛ–37); V.a. 262 (pp. 71–73); V.a. 275 (p. 111); V.a. 319 (f. 15); V.a. 322 (p. 31); V.a. 345 (p. 62*, DrCo); V.b. 43 (ff. 11ᵛ–12*, Walton Poole); ***Harvard:*** MS Eng. 686 (f. 95); ***New York Public Library:*** Arents Collection, Cat. No. S191 (f. 20–20ᵛ [rev]); ***Rosenbach:*** MS 239/18 (pp. 20, 44); MS 239/22 (f. 3ᵛ, Poole); MS 239/27 (p. 32*, Dr. Corbett); MS 240/2 (p.143); MS 240/7 (pp. 53*, 81*); MS 243/4 (p. 80, Wallton Poole); MS 1083/16 (p. 29*); MS 1083/17 (f. 86*); ***Trinity College, Dublin:*** MS G.2.21 (f. 428); ***Owned by Edwin Wolfe, II:*** MS (p. 18*); ***Yale:*** Osborn b 62 (p. 35, *incomplete*); Osborn b 200, (pp. 427–28*); Osborn b 205 (f. 34).

✦ Edwin Wolf, II, "'If Shadows Be a Picture's Excellence': An Experiment in Critical Bibliography," *PMLA* 63 (1948), 831–57. For discussion concerning the Donne attribution, see E. K. Chambers, *Poems of Donne* (1896), 2:279; C. F. Main, "New Texts of John Donne," *Studies in Bibliography* 9 (1957), 231.

• • •

146. Anon., "A Spanish Iournall: 1623: The Way," 181–89. Unprinted.

Although the poet is anonymous, there can be no doubt that it was written by someone with firsthand knowledge of the journey it describes. During the early 1620s, King James favored a match between Prince Charles and the Spanish Infanta. James hoped that the marriage would resolve the problems between Catholics and Protestants, whose differences set off the Thirty Years' War. Charles, for whatever reason, fell in love with the Infanta—literally sight unseen—and, with George Villliers, Duke of Buckingham, traveled to Spain to see her and negotiate the complicated terms of matrimony. Ultimately, the proposal failed because Charles refused to become a Catholic. Charles and Buckingham traveled incognito, departing 18 February 1623. For disguises, they put on hoods and false beards, and called themselves Thomas and John Smith (Lockyer 136). The journey described in this poem is the "after" journey, the one designed to send gifts to the Spanish court and bring Charles and the Infanta home to England. For further discussion on the so-called Spanish Match, see the notes to **HolM 72** and **HolM 73.**

Much of the information found in the poem is confirmed in the *Calendar of State Papers Domestic, James I.* For example, Sir Francis Steward wrote to Secretary Conway from the *St. George* on 22 April 1623, that he "Has been trying three days from morning to night, along with Capt. Love, to warp or sail their vessels over the chain, but cannot do it unless the easterly winds abate. Will do their best to convey the ship with the hackneys to St. Andrea" (142/40; cf. ll. 5–12).

Steward was the Lord High Admiral; Captain Love was captain of the *St. George.* On 24 April 1623 Lord Brooke wrote Secretary Conway that he "Has transferred the jewels and letters from Sir Fras. Steward to Sir John Wentworth. Capt. Wilbraham, with the ship that carries the geldings, has sailed, contrary to direction, into the Downs [l. 39 margin]. The Antelope and Sir Fras. Steward's ship have passed the chain [l. 14] to Gillingham [l. 12 margin], and to-morrow Capt. Love will sail for Spain, but he requires further directions on points specified, owing to the change of arrangements. Has examined into the stores of each ship, and sends a certificate of supplies needed" (*Calendar of State Papers Domestic, James I*, 142/61).

Among the many curiosities stimulated by the Spanish Match is that James himself wrote a poem about it, "Off Jacke and Tom," rpt. in Craigie 2:192 (cf. l. 1).

Many of the places mentioned are not found on modern maps; however, the basic itinerary will be clear from the glossary notes.

> **8–12. Rochester, Chattham, Gillingham.** Three coastal towns close by one another southeast of London.
> **29. Reculuers.** Reculver, coastal town in Kent.
> **53. Dongeynesse.** Dungeness, in the Strait of Dover. They traveled SSE down the English Channel and west across the southern coast of England.
> **61. wight.** Isle of Wight, approximately midway across the southern coast of England.
> **66 (margin). Cant Lizards.** Lizard Point, the southernmost land in England just east of Land's End.
> **78 (margin). Cape Ortegall.** West of the Bay of Biscay, at the northwest corner of Spain.
> **90 (margin). Feroll.** WSW of Cape Ortegall.
> **99 (margin). Galizia.** Region in northwest Spain.
> **129 Lugo.** They are moving inland toward Madrid. Lugo is a town southeast of Feroll.
> **202 (margin). Lyon.** Leon, aproximately one hundred miles ESE of Lugo.
> **274 Valdo lid.** Valladolid, another one hundred miles SSE of Leon, northwest of Madrid.

✦ For general discussion of the Spanish Match, see Roger Lockyer, *Buckingham: The Life and Political Career of George Villiers, First Duke of Buckingham* (London and New York: Longman, 1981), 125–67; Glyn Redworth, *The Prince and the Infanta: The Cultural Politics of the Spanish Match* (New Haven: Yale Univ. Press, 2003). See also *The Poems of James VI of Scotland*, ed. James Craigie, 2 vols. (Edinburgh: Scottish Text Society, 1955–58).

• • •

147. Anon., pseud. (?), "By Ld Carr: Earle of Som'sett: his owne verses," 190–91. Unprinted.

Knowledge of who wrote this poem and why it was written would help explain a long-standing mystery. It is virtually a confession that Lord Carr (ca. 1587–1645) was in part responsible for the death of Sir Thomas Overbury (see **HolM 137**). Carr and his wife were convicted of the murder but were later pardoned by King James. Carr, however, never confessed to the crime, so that if he did write the poem (or at least had it written), then the poem is a unique historical document. If he did not write the poem, then someone was clearly trying to make it look as if he did.

Lord Carr, or Ker, was a Scot. He was the son of Sir Thomas Ker, of Ferniehurst, Roxburghshire, by his second wife, Janet, sister of Sir Walter Scott of Buccleugh. As a youngster he was a page to King James I of Scotland and came to England when James became king of England. In England, Carr left the service of James and traveled to France. On his return, he was injured at a tilting match in the presence of James. When James recognized his former page, he took him back into favor (*DNB*). He then became the King's favorite, only to be replaced by Buckingham when Carr became involved in the murder of Overbury in 1613. Carr is considered James's most influential sexual favorite before Buckingham. He became a knight in 1607, Viscount Rochester in 1611, and Earl of Somerset in 1613.

Carr was a friend of Sir Thomas Overbury. However, their friendship broke when Overbury opposed Carr's intention to marry the then married Frances Howard, a woman whom Overbury considered of ill repute. She was the grand-niece of Henry Howard, the Earl of Northampton, who conspired with Carr to have Overbury placed in the Tower. James, apparently unhappy to see his favorite involved in such a scandal, wanted Overbury to accept a diplomatic mission out of the country. When Overbury declined, James had him committed to the Tower, 26 April 1613.

It is possible that Carr's first intention was to have Overbury removed from the scene until he could marry Frances Howard. She, however, was not so compromising, and instead had him murdered. Apparently, he was gradually poisoned over a three-month period, his death finally occurring 15 September 1613. All persons directly involved in the murder, including Anne Turner (see **HolM 137**), were executed.

After they were married, Lord Carr and Frances Howard were found guilty of murder; but James, perhaps out of his old affection for Carr, pardoned them. The evidence against Frances Howard was overwhelming, and she eventually confessed. There was, however, very little evidence against Carr, and he—despite the text of this poem—never confessed to the murder of Overbury. Because Carr was recalcitrant over the details of his pardon, James kept them confined to the Tower until 1622. She died in 1632, he in 1645. Their daughter, Lady Anne Carr, born soon after their marriage and in the midst of the scandal, married William, first Earl, and later first Duke of Bedford (White 178).

The details of the incident are, of course, far more complex than are described here. Carr was actually prosecuted by Sir Francis Bacon, who was an ally of Buckingham. Also, Henry Howard, who conspired with Carr to commit Overbury to the Tower, was the leader of the Catholic faction (*DNB*). Howard died 15 June 1614, after which Carr assumed his position as Lord Keeper of the Privy Seal. Like Howard, Carr advocated Catholic causes, and used his position as favorite to encourage alliance with Spain through royal marriage (see **HolM 72–73**). It is possible that lurking beneath the surface of this complicated political intrigue is nothing but religious politics.

There are several reasons not to believe Carr wrote this poem. If he had, his confession would have affected the history of the crime. Also, he is not known to have written poetry. Carr's only known connection to seventeenth-century poetry is his patronage of George Chapman (White 179).

> **10. Phaieton (Phaethon).** See **HolM 65**, note to l. 4.
> **14. best friend.** Overbury.

✦ For a detailed account of the entire affair, see Beatrice White, *Cast of Ravens* (London: J. Murray, 1965).

• • •

148. Anon., untitled, "Lifelesse my selfe, I keepe the life of all," 191. Unprinted.

There is no other known copy of this sonnet. In tone and quality of writing, it seems similar to the preceding poem, **HolM 147**. The poem is a riddle.

• • •

149. George Morley, Bishop of Winchester (1597–1684), "On Kinge Iames," 191–92. Pr. William Camden, *Remaines Concerning Britaine* (1636), 398–99; John Spottiswoode, *The History of the Church of Scotland* (1655), 547.

Like Richard Corbett and William Strode, Morley attended Westminster School and proceeded to Christ Church, Oxford. He graduated B.A. in 1618, M.A. in 1621, and D.D. in 1642. He was a Calvinist. In 1641, he was made a canon of Christ Church. He left England with Charles II in

1649 and did not return until the Restoration. He then became Dean of Christ Church, later Bishop of Winchester (*DNB*).

James I died 27 March 1625.

Remaines Concerning Britiane (1636) printed "On Kinge Iames" as two poems, the second immediately following the first. They correspond to Holgate ll. 1–22 and ll. 23–32 respectively. It appears, however, that the Holgate scribe thought of this as one poem. Dalhousie II (Texas Tech Univ.) also transcribes it as one poem. This includes the indentation the scribe inserted ll. 23–32 to separate what he interpreted as separate stanzas of the poem.

> **6. three Kingdomes.** England, Scotland and Ireland. Although this line says "three Kingdomes," l. 29 says "two." The following poem, **HolM 150**, l. 58, also says "two kingdomes." More than likely this is why the two sections of this poem have been read as different poems.
> **13. Naboth.** 1Kings 21.
> **15. Vriah.** 2 Samuel 11.
> **17. Sheme'is curses.** 2 Samuel 16:5–13.

Three manuscript texts begin at l. 23 of the Holgate version: Bodleian MS Ashmole 38, British Library Add. MS 30982, and Cambridge University Library, the Commonplace Book of Mary Browne (cited by Sir Geoffry Keynes, *Bibliotheca Bibliographici* [London: Trianon Press, 1964], 1301, pp. 46–47). The indentation of **HolM 149** at l. 23 (see p. 192) marks the poem's two parts.

✦ Manuscripts: Crum A1016 (inclusive), H421 (ll. 1–22), F498 (ll. 23–32); Sullivan, II, 34n (p. 208); Yale A0950 ✦ *Bodleian:* MS Ashmole 38 (p. 186, see note above); MS Eng. poet. c. 50 (f. 23ᵛ); MS Eng. poet. e. 14 (f. 10); MS Eng. poet. e. 97 (p. 10); MS Rawl. poet. 199 (pp. 61–62); Hopkinson MSS, Vol 17 (p. 150); Hopkinson MSS, Vol 34 (f. 24); *British Library:* Add. MS 11811 (f. 29ᵛ); Add. MS 15226 (f. 26); Add. MS 15227 (f. 91ᵛ); Add. MS 25707 (f. 79); Add. MS 27407 (f. 126); Add. MS 30982 (f. 59, G.Morly, see note above); Egerton MS 1160 (f. 89ᵛ); MS Harley 6917 (f. 72ᵛ, George Morly); MS Sloane 1792 (f. 44); Stowe MS 962 (f. 165); *Cambridge:* (see note above); *Chetham's Library, Manchester:* Farmer-Chetham MS 8012, A.4.15 (p. 165); *Corpus Christi College, Oxford:* MS 328 (f. 7); *Edinburgh University Library:* MS La. III 436 (pp. 25–26); *Folger:* V.a. 97 (p. 110, G. Morley); V.a. 162 (f. 89); V.a. 170 (p. 61, G:M); V.a. 245 (f. 51ᵛ, G. Morley); V.a. 345 (p. 16); V.b. 43 (f. 30, Mr. Morley); V.b. 303 (p. 261); *Harvard:* MS Eng. 686 (f. 68ᵛ); MS Eng. 703 (f. 54ᵛ); *University of Nottingham:* Portland MS Pw V 37 (p. 27); *Rosenbach:* MS 239/22 (p. 47); MS 239/27 (pp. 351–52); MS 240/7 (pp. 45–46); MS 1083/16 (f. 89, Corbet); *Texas Tech:* Dalhousie II (f. 34ᵛ); TCD-II (f. 184); *Westminster Abbey:* MS 41 f. 48ᵛ); *Yale:* Osborn b 200 (pp. 124–25); Osborn b 205 (f. 31ᵛ).

✦ Sullivan, 188.

• • •

150. Anon., "On King Iames," 192–93. Unprinted.

It is surprising there are so few extant copies of this poem, its subject matter being very common. Noteworthy is the number of kingdoms James is credited with combining. This poem says *two* at line 58, but the previous poem says *three* at line 6 but *two* at l. 29.

This is the second of three consecutive funereal poems for King James.

✦ Manuscript: *British Library:* Add. MS 33998 (f. 36ᵛ).

151. Anon., "On K: Iames," 193. Unprinted.

Examination of Folger MS V.a.124 reveals that this is an acrostic poem. The Holgate scribe does capitalize every first letter, but not in a manner that would call attention to the spelling of James's name on the left-hand margin. He may, of course, have known it anyway, or perhaps his copy-text did not emphasize the device. However, the Holgate text does not complete the acrostic, which should read "R-E-X" for lines 8–10; instead it reads "R-O-X".

> On yᵉ death of K: Iames
>
> I s he dead? No opinion aimes far wide
> A bÿt non obiit, he's but stept aside.
> C rownes yᵗ be earthy are but transitorie
> O ur Iames went hense to weare the crowne of glory.
> B ereft of life he endlesse life obtain'd
> V ertue still guard him & his blisse hath gained
> S ubstance for shadowes now he doth enioy
> R ich in his pleasure, free frõ worlds annoy:
> E ver belov'd, admired for gracious parts,
> X erxes though conquering never wonne more hearts.
>
> (Folger MS V.a. 124, ff. 25ᵛ–26)

✦ Manuscripts: Crum I–1728 ✦ *Bodleian:* MS Eng. poet. f. 10 (f. 92); *Folger:* V.a. 124 (ff. 25ᵛ–26).

• • •

152. Richard Corbett (1582–1636), "Dʳ: C: Elegy on Bp. Rauis of London who dyed 1607," 194. Pr. *CEP* (1647), 17–19.

For details about Corbett's life, see **HolM 11 notes**.

Dr. Thomas Ravis died in London, 14 November 1609. He became Bishop of London in 1607. The heading on this manuscript has the wrong year.

Dr. Thomas Ravis was Dean of Christ Church, 1596–1605. Like Corbett, he was educated at Westminster School. He also preceded Corbett to Christ Church, Oxford. He was elected proctor (1588) and vice-chancellor (1597). He was prebendary of Westminster (1592/93–1607). As a dean, he attended the Hampton Court conference (1604), a meeting designed to rectify the difference between the Scottish and English churches. He was appointed Bishop of Gloucester (1604) and Bishop of London in 1607. As Bishop, he persecuted nonconformists. He wrote, ". . . by the help of Jesus, I will not leave one preacher in my dioces that doth not subscribe and conform" (*ODNB*).

B&TR consider this poem the first in Corbett's "authentic canon" (xv).

> **1. Paul's . . . walk.** A busy meeting place and thoroughfare in the midst of St. Paul's Cathedral. It is described in John Earle's *Microcosmography* as ". . . a heap of stones and men, with a vast confusion of languages; and were the steeple not sanctified nothing liker Babel" (qtd. in Baker, 726). This section entitled "Pauls's Walk" in Earle's *Microcosmography* is not included in excerpts from it in **HolM 184**.
> **2. Britayne Sinners sweare and talke.** Earle: "The best signs of a temple in it is that it is the thieves' sanctuary, which rob more safely in the crowd than a wilderness, whilst every searcher is a bush to hide them" (Baker 726).
> **3. Harry Ruffians.** Swaggerers.
> **18. Bub & Alabaster boys.** Note the space after "Bub." Perhaps the scribe was confused and left space for a later correction. *CEP* has "bubbles," as do B&TR (who do not gloss this expression).

Perhaps "bubble" suggests "bubble over," but "bub" is a drinking term, a strong beer or the sound of drink (*OED*). "Alabaster" might suggest a container for wine, but such usage is not noted in the *OED* until the late eighteenth century. It might also suggest "ale." Regardless, this type of common humor is typical of Corbett's poetry. "Alabaster boys" could also refer to carved cupids or angels for an alabaster tomb (suggested by William Gentrup).

22. their Superscriptions. Their tombstones.

35. Chanclor. Lord Chancellor Chistopher Hatton's tomb was extremely ornate (Lockyer 42).

35. Pyramis. Pyramid.

✦ Manuscripts: Crum W1181; Beal Vol. II, pt. 1, CoR 163–85; Yale W1050 ✦ *Aberdeen University Library:* MS 29 (pp. 49–50); *Bodleian:* MS Eng. poet. e. 14 (f. 98 [rev]); MS Rawl. poet. 199 (pp. 53–54); *Bradford District Archives:* Hopkinson MSS, Vol 34 (p. 29); *British Library:* Add. MS 30982 (ff. 59ᵛ–60); MS Harley 1026 (f. 40ᵛ); MS Harley 6931 (ff. 55ᵛ–56); MS Sloane 1446 (f. 54); MS Sloane 1792 (ff. 65–66); *Folger:* V.a. 97 (pp. 126–27); V.a. 103, pt. I (f. 4); V.a. 125, pt. II (f. 13); V.a. 170 (pp. 85–86); V.a. 319 (f. 5); V.a. 322 (p. 28); V.a. 345 (p. 93); *Huntington Library:* HM 198, pt. 1 (pp. 104–5); *University of Nottingham:* Portland MS Pw V 37 (p. 6); *St. John's College, Cambridge:* MS S. 23 (James 416) (f. 58); *Westminster Abbey:* MS 41 (f. 10); *Yale:* Osborn b 200 (pp. 243–44); Osborn b 205 (ff. 80ᵛ–81).

✦ B&TR, xv, 3–4, 103.

• • •

153. Thomas Goffe [?], "A funerall Elegie, vppon the right Reuerand ffather in God Iohn King, Late Ld Bp: of London," subscribed "T. G.," 195–97. Unprinted.

T. G. may be Thomas Goffe (1591–1629). Goffe was from Essex, studied at Westminster School and Christ Church, Oxford. He became rector at East Clandon, Surrey. He wrote plays, among them *The Careless Shepherdess* (pub. 1656), *The Raging Turk*, and *The Courteous Turk*, both published posthumously (Saunders 59). In Bodleian MS D. 398, there are two copies (ff. 173, 174) of a verse epitaph for Henry King's wife Anne, née Berkeley (d. 1623/24) ascribed to Goffe (see *Crum* L–22).

The Holgate epitaph was written for Henry King's father, John, a noted cleric. Like Goffe, he studied at Westminster School and Christ Church, Oxford, receiving his B. A. in 1579–80 (*DNB*). He took holy orders, then became domestic chaplain to John Piers, Archbishop of York, and was collated to the archdeaconry of Nottingham in 1590. He then became chaplain to Sir Thomas Egerton, Lord Keeper of the Great Seal. In 1597, he entered the rectory of St. Andrew, Holborn, and in 1599, he became prebend of St. Paul's. He also acted as a chaplain to Queen Elizabeth. He received his D. D. from Oxford, 1601, and became Dean of Christ Church, Oxford in 1605. He was one of only four preachers to participate in the Hampton Court conference, 1604, where James hoped to rectify the differences between the English and Scottish churches.

John King was made Bishop of London by James in 1611. He died on Good Friday, 30 March 1621, and was buried in St. Paul's Cathedral (l. 97). At his death, a rumor circulated that he had pledged allegiance to the Roman church (ll. 108–25), but his son, Henry King (see **HolM 156** and **HolM 163**) denied it (*DNB*).

Among his literary connections, it should be noted that King ordained John Donne in 1615.

Curiously, the one other surviving manuscript of this poem, Rosenbach MS 1083, transcribes only the first six lines.

23–50. King was known as a great orator. The *DNB* quotes Anthony á Wood (*Athenæ Oxonienses*, 2:295): "He was a solid and profound divine, of great gravity and piety, and had so excellent a volubility of speech, that Sir Edward Coke would often say of him that he was the best speaker in the Star-chamber of his time."

60. Palatine. The *DNB*, citing Gardner (*History*, III, 341.2), is most helpful here: "On 26 March 1620 he pleaded in a sermon preached at St. Paul's Cross in the king's presence for contributions to the repair of St. Paul's Cathedral. James selected the text, and popular curiosity was excited by rumours that King was instructed to declare James's resolve to intervene in the German wars on behalf of his son-in-law, the King of Bohemia; but although one of the hearers wrote that the bishop's heart was in Bohemia, he made no reference to European politics." Frederick V was also the Elector Palatine.

66. Amittai's sonne. Jonah the prophet

69. Niniue's. Ninevah, capitol of Assyria, discussed in the Book of Jonah.

80. Isha'is. The prophet Isaiah. The prophecy of rebuilding the Temple is found in Isaiah 44:28.

78–81. Who shall now. . . and not Tombes. A reference to the Temple (see note to line 60).

104. Iezabel. 1 Kings 18–19; Rev. 2:20–23.

✦ Manuscript: **Rosenbach:** MS 1083/16 (p. 298, ll. 1–6).

✦ Redding, 767; R. W. Saunders, *A Biographical Dictionary of Renaissance Poets and Dramatists, 1520–1650* (Sussex: The Harvester Press, 1963), 59; Anthony á Wood, *Athenæ Oxonienses*, ed. Philip Bliss (London, 1813; rpt. Hildesbein, 1969), 2:295.

• • •

154. William Strode (1602?–1645), "On ye Death of M^ris Marye Prideaux," 198. No seventeenth-century printings.

William Strode was a very popular poet in the early seventeenth century. His work is commonly found in verse miscellanies. The Holgate manuscript contains fifteen of his poems, all between pages 198 and 216. Only John Donne wrote more poems found in this manuscript.

Strode's education can be closely aligned with Corbett's and Carew's. He studied at Westminster School and Christ Church, Oxford, where he graduated B.A. (1621), M.A. (1624), and B.D. (1631). He was chaplain to Richard Corbett, bishop of Oxford (1629). He became a canon of Christ Church and vicar of Blackbourton, Oxfordshire (1638). Besides his many poems, he wrote a tragicomedy, *The Floating Island*, performed by students of Christ Church before the King and Queen in 1636.

There are two important twentieth-century collections of Strode's poetry. *The Poetical Works of William Strode . . . to which is added The Floating Island* was edited by Bertram Dobell in 1907. It is not a critical edition, but instead was intended to introduce Strode to modern readers. It is an eclectic text based on two manuscripts now owned by the Folger Library, MS V.a. 170 and MS V.a. 245. The best critical edition, however, is Margaret Forey's unpublished thesis, "A Critical Edition of the Poetical Works of William Strode, excluding *The Floating Island*." This edition is mainly based upon Corpus Christi College, Oxford, MS 325, which is an autograph copy of many of Strode's poems. There is some evidence that the Holgate may be connected to MS 325 (see **HolM 174 notes**).

The present poem is one of two elegies Strode wrote on Mary Prideaux. The other is "Sleepe pretty one, oh sleepe while I" (Beal, StW 511–25). It is found in British Library Add. MS 30982, ff. 8^v–10.

Forey has untangled the complicated family of John Prideaux, Bishop of Worcester. He had nine children, all with his first wife, Anne, daughter of William Goodwin, Dean of Christ Church; his second wife was Mary, possibly the daughter of Sir Thomas Reynal. Mary Prideaux, the subject of this elegy, was Prideaux's eldest daughter. She was baptized at St. Michael's Church, Oxford, 10

February 1617 and buried at St. Michael's, 9 December 1624, the same year Strode received his M.A. (Forey 377–80). Mary's sister Anne is the subject of a second elegy found in the Holgate (**HolM 158**), "Nature in this small volume was about" by William Browne. Mary died only three months before Anne.

For biographical commentary on John Prideaux, see **HolM 158 notes**.

> **19. Seauen yeares shee liu'd.** See dates above.

✦ Manuscripts: Crum W194; Beal Vol. II, pt. 2, StW 555–564; Yale W0173 ✦ *Bodleian:* MS Rawl. poet. 84 (f. 60ᵛ [rev]); MS Rawl. poet. 206 (pp. 67–68); *British Library:* MS Sloane 1792 (ff. 98ᵛ–99); *Corpus Christi College, Oxford:* MS 325 (f. 70, autog.); MS 328 (28ᵛ–29, Stroud); *Folger:* V.a. 97 (pp. 12–13); V.a. 170 (pp. 80–81); *Yale:* Osborn b 205 (f. 52ᵛ). Beal identifies another manuscript, StW 562, "Owned formerly by John Sparrow: Unlocated."

✦ "The Poetical Works of William Strode, excluding 'The Floating Island'," ed. Margaret Forey, B. Litt. Thesis, St. Hilda's College, Oxford, 1966: 111, 278, 377–80; *The Poetical Works of William Strode (1600–1645)*, ed. Bertram Dobell (London, 1907), 58–59.

· · ·

155. Richard Corbett (1582–1636), "Butler of Ch:Ch: In Oxon: Iohn:," 198. Pr. *CEP* (London, 1647), 30.

For further details about Corbett's life, see **HolM 11 notes**.

According to British Library Add. MS 30982, John Dawson, butler of Christ Church, died in 1622. Corbett was Dean of Christ Church from 1620–1628, after which he became Bishop of Oxford.

This type of comic epitaph was particularly popular with university wits of the day. Corbett was one of the most famous of such wits.

There is a humorous difference between the Holgate manuscript and *CEP*. Line 13 includes the phrase "drink is bad," but *CEP* reads "beare was good."

> **7. Cheeses.** A curious image, the *OED* does not help, nor do B&TR. Corbett probably means that cheese ferments, like wine, thus those who attend the funeral will get drunk. This image may be an inside joke.
> **17. tiffe.** The *OED* quotes Corbett from this poem, "Liquor, especially poor, weak or 'small' liquor, 'tipple.'"
> **18. whiffe.** A sip, especially of liquor.
> **19. Rosemary.** An emblem worn at funerals (*OED*).

✦ Manuscripts: Crum D–49; Beal Vol. II, pt. 1, CoR 472–498; Yale D0039 ✦ *Aberdeen University Library:* MS 29 (pp. 122–23); *Bodleian:* Don.d.58 (f. 18); MS Douce f (ff. 3ᵛ–4); MS Eng. poet. c. 50 (f. 128); MS Eng. poet. e. 14 (f. 93 [ʳᵉᵛ]); MS Eng. poet. e. 97 (p. 170); MS Eng. poet. f. 27 (pp. 222–23); *British Library:* Add. MS 30982 (f. 4ᵛ); Egerton MS 2421 (f. 16); MS Sloane 1446 (f. 22ᵛ); *Folger:* V.a. 97 (p. 113 [bis]); V.a. 103, pt. I (f. 23, Mr. Stroude); V.a. 170 (pp. 66–67); V.a. 245 (f. 64ᵛ, W: Stroud); V.a. 262 (pp. 52–53); V.a. 345 (p. 147); V.b. 43 (f. 32ᵛ); *National Library of Wales:* Ottley (unnumbered bundle); *New York Public Library:* Arents Collection, Cat. No. S288 (p. 23); *University of Nottingham:* Portland MS Pw V 37 (p. 43); *Rosenbach:* MS 239/27 (p. 356); MS 240/7 (pp. 31–32); MS 1083/16 (p. 95); *Westminster Abbey:* MS 41 (f. 54ᵛ); *Yale:* Osborn b 205 (f. 80).

✦ B&TR, 72–73, 144.

156. Henry King, bishop of Chichester (1592–1669), untitled, "Let no prophaine ignoble foote tread neere," 199. Pr. Henry King, *Poems, Elegies, Paradoxes and Sonnets* (London, 1657), 51–52. Also, a variant version printed in Richard Corbett, *CEP* (London, 1647), 51.

Henry King was the son of John King, bishop of London (**HolM 153**). He is most famous for the poem he wrote on the death of his wife, "The Exequy," **HolM 163**. Like Corbett, Henry King was educated at Westminster School and Christ Church, Oxford. He became a canon of Christ Church (1623), Dean of Rochester (1638), and bishop of Chichester (1642). Like his father, he was a Royalist. One year after attaining the bishopric, he was removed by the Puritans but was reinstated during the Restoration.

Henry King was well-known in literary circles. He was a friend of Wotton, Jonson, and Donne. When Donne became ill in 1623, King wanted to have church monies made available to aid in his recovery. Donne, however, turned down the offer (Walton 57–59). He also knew and wrote elegies on George Sandys (author of *Europæ Speculum* and translator of Ovid's *Metamorphoses*) and Sir Henry Blount (explorer).

Richard Sackville, third Earl of Dorset, died 28 March 1624 at the age of thirty-five. He was the grandson of Thomas Sackville, co-author of *Gorboduc*. Like King, he studied at Christ Church, Oxford. He was also a friend of Donne, who sent him six of his Holy Sonnets (Grierson 2:226–28).

> **8. Who reconsiled the sword vnto the penn.** Sackville's wife, Lady Anne Clifford, wrote that he was "so great a lover of Scholars and Souldjers as that with an excessive bounty towards them . . . he did much diminish his estate" (Crum, *Poems of Henry King*, 196).

> ✦ Manuscripts: Crum L239; Beal Vol. II, pt. 1, KiH 273–301; Yale L356 ✦ **Bodleian:** MS Ashmole 38 (p. 167); MS Eng. poet. c. 50 (f. 59ᵛ); MS Eng. poet.* e. 30 (f. 26); MS Eng. poet. e. 97 (p. 28); MS Eng. poet. e. 127 (f. 16); MS Eng. poet. f. 27 (p. 155); MS Firth d. 7 (f. 169); MS *Malone 22 (f. 17); MS Rawl. poet. 209 (f. 9); MS Top. gen. e. 32 (f. 73); **British Library:** Add. MS 30982 (f. 156ᵛ); Add. MS 58215 (p. [6]); Add. MS 62134 (f. 12ᵛ); MS Harley 1026 (f. 40ᵛ); MS Harley 6931 (ff. 13ᵛ–14); MS Sloane 542 (f. 13); MS Sloane 1792 (f. 60); **Cambridge:** MS Add. 4138 (f. 51); GK5 (pp. 35–36); **Corpus Christi College, Oxford:** MS 328 (f. 11ᵛ); **Folger:** V.a. 125, pt. II (f. 4); V.a. 170 (pp. 220–21); V.a. 262 (pp. 36–37, Dr H. King); V.b. 43 (ff. 31ᵛ–32); **Leicestershire Record Office:** DG.9/2796 (pp. 59–60); **New York Public Library:** Arents Collection, Cat. No. S288 (p. 21); **Rosenbach:** MS 239/27 (p. 387); **Yale:** Osborn b 200 (pp. 220–21); Osborn b 356 (p. 259).

> Beal writes in "KiH 300: Owned formerly by John Sparrow, Oxford: Unlocated. Another owned by Rosemary Williams, Stoughton MS, pp. 220–21."

✦ *The Poems of Henry King*, ed. Margaret Crum (Oxford Univ. Press, 1965), 67–68, 196–97. Helpful biographical information is also found in Ronald Berman, *Henry King & the Seventeenth Century* (London: Chatto and Windus, 1964), 9–25; Izaak Walton, *Lives* (London: Oxford Univ. Press, 1927; rpt. 1956).

•••

157. George Morley, Bishop of Winchester (1597–1684) [?] or Brian Duppa, bishop of Winchester (1588–1662) [?], untitled, "Heer lies his Parent's hopes, and feares," subscribed "Morley," 199. Pr. *Musarum Deliciæ* (1655), 79–80 [2nd numbering].

Nothing can be said about this poem with any surety. Rosenbach MS 240/7, p. 184 and British Museum MS Lansdowne 777, f. 70, identify its subject as a son of John Prideaux (1578–1650), bishop of Winchester, 1640 (for more on Prideaux, see **HolM 158**). Prideaux had nine children with his first wife, Anne Goodwin. He had no children with his second wife, Mary Reynal. Of Prideaux's nine children, five were boys: William, John, Matthew or Matthias, Robert, and a second Matthew, born in 1625, soon after the first Matthew died. Line 9 of the poem says that the child who died was four years old. That might describe either the first Matthew (christened 1 September 1622 and buried 17 February 1625, aged 2½ years) or more likely Robert (christened 14 May 1624 and buried 14 September 1627, aged 3½ years), who, Margaret Forey says, died "after a short and painful illness" (379; note the reference to pain in l. 3). He is buried in the Exeter College Chapel, Oxford, where John Prideaux, his father, was rector.

Only George Morley and Brian Duppa are credited with this poem. George Morley graduated from Christ Church with a B.A. in 1616, an M.A. in 1621, and a D.D. in 1642. The *DNB* is unclear as to his whereabouts in 1625, but it does say "Remaining at Oxford, he made many friends. . . ." Brian Duppa received his D.D. from Oxford in 1625, became dean of Christ Church in 1628, and vice-chancellor in 1632. Both wrote poetry; each served as bishop of Winchester.

Two other epitaphs to Prideaux's children are found in the manuscript: **HolM 154** (Mary) and **HolM 158** (Anne). Of the three, only **HolM 154** identifies its subject. It is possible, of course, that the scribe knew—or knew about—the family, but without identifying each poem's subject, that is difficult to assert. It is also possible that he knew about whom the poems were written and didn't bother to record the information in the miscellany.

For information about John Prideaux, see **HolM 158 notes**.

✦ Manuscripts: Crum H760, H964; Yale H0747 ✦ ***Bodleian:*** MS Ashmole 47 (f. 38ᵛ); MS. poet. f.27 (f. 27); Lansdowne MS 777 (f. 70, Geo. Morley); MS Malone 21 (f. 6ᵛ, Duppa); ***British Library:*** Add. MS 15227 (f. 97); Egerton MS 923 (f. 52); ***Corpus Chrisiti College,*** MS 328 (f. 49ᵛ, Dr. Duppa); ***Folger:*** V.a. 124 (f. 43ᵛ); V.a. 262 (p. 37); ***Rosenbach:*** MS /7 (p. 17, Dr. Duppa; p. 184, Geo: Morley); ***Owned by Edwin Wolfe II:*** MS (p. 100); ***Yale:*** Osborn b 62 (pp. 22–23); Osborn b 356 (p. 258).

✦ For information about the family of John Prideaux, see above **HolM 154** and Forey, "The Poetical Works of William Strode," 377–80. See also Thompson, 287–88.

• • •

158. William Browne of Tavistock (1591–1643?), untitled, "Nature in this small volume was about," subscribed "Browne" 199. Pr. Camden's *Remaines* (London, 1636), 414; *Wits Recreations* (London, 1640); *Poems of W. Browne*, ed. G. Goodwin (1894), 2:287; *The Whole Works of William Browne*, ed. W. Carew Hazlitt, (1867) 2:337. Also Louise Brown Osborn, *The Life, Letters and Writing of John Hoskyns* (New Haven: Yale Univ. Press, 1937), 213.

Born at Tavistock in Devonshire, Browne studied at Exeter College, Oxford, then at Clifford's Inn and the Inner Temple. He became a tutor at Oxford in1624; thereafter, he became a tutor to the family of William Herbert, third Earl of Pembroke. He wrote *Britannia's Pastorals* (1613–16). He was a friend of George Wither, Christopher Brooke, and John Davies of Hereford, with whom he published *The Shepheard's Pipe* (1614). He is frequently described as a seventeenth-century Spenserian.

Inclusion of this epitaph in British Library MS Lansdowne 777 is strong evidence that this poem was written by William Browne. Folios 1–62ᵛ of that anthology comprise a large section of Browne's miscellaneous verse. The section concludes "ffinis W Browne." Its title page reads "Poems of Wᵐ Browne–of the Inner-Temple Gent. 1650." Beal suggests that the title page may have been added at a later date. There is no evidence that Browne actually owned this manuscript, rather the poems may have been transcribed from Browne's own manuscripts between 1637 and 1650 by someone from the Inns of Court (Beal 115).

Both Hazlitt and Gullans use Lansdowne 777 as their copy-text. It is headed "On Mrs. Anne Prideaux, daughter of Mr. Doctor Prideaux, Regius Professor. She dyde at the age of 6 years."

John Prideaux was appointed bishop of Worcester by Charles I in 1641. Beforehand, he studied at Exeter College, then became chaplain to Prince Henry and later to King James. He returned to Exeter College as rector, vice-chancellor, and finally Regius Professor of Divinity. As Regius Professor, Prideaux presided over theological disputations. He was considered a moderate, "without altogether alienating extremists on either side" (*DNB*). The *DNB* includes a comprehensive list of his writings.

There is some confusion about Prideaux's offspring. The *DNB* says that he had four children, none of whom was named Anne. Forey, however, argues convincingly that Prideaux had nine children, all with his first wife. Anne was their second daughter. Her baptism was recorded at St. Michael's Church, Oxford, 3 March 1618. She died in September 1624, three months before her elder sister, Mary (Forey 377–80).

An elegy to Mary Prideaux, "Weepe not because this child hath died so younge," by William Strode is **HolM 154**. An epitaph for Prideaux's son, "Heer lies his Parents hopes and feares" is **HolM 157**. A second poem by Browne, "Lydfoord Law in Deuonsheere," is **HolM 20**.

> ✦ Manuscripts: Crum N32; Beal Vol. I, pt. 1, BrW 108–43; Yale N0035 ✦ *Bodleian:* MS Eng. poet. c. 50 (f. 130^v); MS Eng. poet. e. 14 (f. 100^v); MS Eng. poet. e. 40 (f. 104); MS Eng. poet. e. 97 (p. 54, W: Stroad); MS Eng. poet. f. 27 (f. 109); MS Firth e. 4 (p. 110); MS Rawl. poet. 116 (f. 53); MS Rawl. poet. 199 (p. 4); MS Rawl. poet. 206 (p. 65); *British Library:* Add. MS 15227 (f. 89); Add. MS 25303 (f. 163); Egerton MS 923 (f. 65); Egerton MS 2421 (f. 2^v); MS Harley 3511 (ff. 71^v–72); MS Harley 3910 (f. 4); MS Harley 6917 (f. 62); Lansdowne MS 777 (f. 60^v); MS Sloane 1446 (f. 65); MS Sloane 1867 (f. 32); Stowe MS 962 (f. 151); *Corpus Christi College, Oxford:* MS 328 (f. 13^v); *Folger:* V.a. 97 (p. 58); V.a. 124 (f. 18^v); V.a. 125, pt. II (f. 9^v); V.a. 170 (pp. 48–49); V.a. 245 (f. 41); V.a. 262 (p. 128); V.a. 308 (f. 127^v); *Owned by Sir Geoffrey Keynes:* Bibliotheca Bibliographici No. 1863 (f. 22); *Rosenbach:* MS 240/7 (p. 78); MS 1083/17 (f. 72^v); *Trinity College, Dublin:* MS 877 (f. 254); *Worcester College, Oxford:* MSS 4.29 (ff. [10^v, 16]); *Yale:* Osborn b 62 (p. 132); Osborn b 205 (f. 33^v); Osborn b 356 (p. 250).

• • •

159. Sir John Davies (1569–1626), untitled, "As carefull Mothers to their beds doe laye," 199. Pr. Camden's *Remaines* (1637), 411; *Wits Recreations* (1640), sig. 2B4.

Sir John Davies was educated at Winchester School and Queen's College, Oxford. He became a barrister of the Inner Temple and member of a group at the Inns of Court that included John Donne, Henry Wotton, and John Hoskins (Saunders 37). He was disbarred from the Middle Temple, 1598–1601. He was appointed by King James Solicitor-General of Ireland. Also, he was elected speaker of the Irish Parliament in 1613. He was appointed Lord Chief Justice of England but died before he could assume office (Hebel 966).

As a poet, Davies is best known for *Orchestra* (1594). He also wrote *Hymns of Astrea*, a series of acrostic poems in praise of the Queen (1599); and *Nosce Teipsum*, a philosophical poem favored by King James (1599). Some of his poems were published in Davison's *Poetical Rhapsody* (1608) (Hebel 966).

This poem is attributed to Davies only in Bodleian MS Rawl. 117. Krueger, in *The Poems of Sir John Davies*, publishes it among "Poems Ascribed to Davies in Manuscripts." MS Rawl. poet 117 is his copy-text. It is headed "On the Deputy of Ireland his child Sir John Davis." MS Rawl. poet 117 was "compiled by someone at an Inn of Court" (Krueger 423). If the attribution to Davies is correct, the child is that of Arthur Chichester, Lord Deputy of Ireland, 1605–1616. He was Davies's superior at the time. Krueger accepts the attribution with qualification: it is the only poem in MS Rawl. poet 117 attributed to Davies, thus making positive attribution uncertain.

For a second poem by Davies, see the note to **HolM 8b**.

♦ Manuscripts: Crum A1464, A1613; Beal Vol. I, pt. 1, DaJ 161–221; Yale A1378 ♦ *Aberdeen University Library:* MS 29 (p. 136); *All Souls College, Oxford:* MS 174 (p. 34ᵛ); *Bodleian:* MS Ashmole 38 (pp. 168, 198); MS Ashmole 47 (f. 5ᵛ); MS Eng. poet. c. 50 (f. 130ᵛ); MS Eng. poet. e. 14 (f. 99 [rev]); MS Eng. poet. f. 27 (pp. 114–15); MS Firth d. 7 (f. 116); MS Rawl. poet. 84 (f. 85); MS Rawl. poet. 116 (f. 52ᵛ); MS Rawl. poet. 117 (f. 196ᵛ [rev], Sr. Joh. Davis); MS Rawl. poet. 206 (p. 65); MS Sancroft 59 (p. 45); MS Tanner 465 (f. 62); *British Library:* Add. MS 10308 (f. 135); Add. MS 15227 (f. 98); Add. MS 19268 (f. 11); Add. MS 29921 (f. 53); Add. MS 30982 (f. 2); Add. MS 44963 (f. 39); Add. MS 58215 (p. 17); Egerton MS 923 (f. 16); Egerton MS 2421 (f. 45ᵛ); Egerton MS 2725 (f. 59ᵛ); MS Harley 1221 (f. 70); MS Harley 6038 (f. 10); Lansdowne MS 777 (f. 70); MS Sloane 1792 (f. 6); Stowe MS 962 (f. 83); CL1 (p. 30); *Corpus Christi College, Oxford:* MS 328 (f. 49ᵛ); *Edinburgh University Library:* MS H.-P. Coll. 401 (f. 72ᵛ); *Folger:* MS E.a.6 (f. 7); V.a. 97 (p. 1); V.a. 103, pt. I (f. 2); V.a. 125, pt. II (f. 3ᵛ); V.a. 162 (f. 83); V.a. 170 (p. 38); V.a. 245 (f. 37ᵛ); V.a. 262 (p. 126); V.a. 319 (f. 25ᵛ); V.a. 345 (p. 4); *Harvard:* MS Eng. 686 (f. 52); *Leeds Archives Department:* MX 237 (f. 25ᵛ); *National Library of Wales:* Powis MSS (1959 deposit), series II, (Envelope) Bundle 26; *University of Nottingham:* Portland MS Pw V 37 (p. 4); *Rosenbach:* MS 239/16 (p. 9); MS 239/18 (p. 56); MS 239/22 (f. 8ᵛ); MS 239/27 (p. 355); MS 1083/16 (p. 94); MS 1083/17 (p. 5); *St. John's College, Cambridge:* MS S. 32 (James 423) (f. 2); *South African Library, Cape Town:* MS Grey 7 a 29 (p. 77); *Westminster Abbey:* MS 41 (f. 40ᵛ); *Worcester College, Oxford:* MSS 4.29 (f. 15ᵛ); *Yale:* Osborn b 62 (p. 132); Osborn b 200 (p. 219); Osborn b 205 (ff. 33ᵛ, 52ᵛ); Osborn fb 143 (p. 28); Osborn b 356 (p. 252).

♦ *The Works in Verse and Prose of Sir John Davis*, ed. Alexander Grossart, 3 vols. (London, 1869–76); Hebell, 966; *The Poems of Sir John Davies*, ed. Robert Krueger (Oxford: Clarendon Press, 1975); J. W. Saunders, *A Biographical Dictionary of Renaissance Poets and Dramatists, 1520–1650* (Sussex: Harvester Books, 1983), 37.

• • •

160. Anon., untitled, "Within this Marble casket lyes," 200. Pr. Camden's *Remaines* (1614), 382; Stowe's *Survey of London* (1618), 882; Camden's *Remaines* (1623), 345; *Recreation for Ingenious Headpieces* (1663), Epitaph 88.

When first printed in Camden's *Remaines* (1614), "Within this Marble casket lyes" appeared as the last four lines of an eighteen-line epitaph for Prince Henry beginning "Reader, wonder think it none." More than likely, its attachment to the epitaph was the result of a printer's error. The latter is a translation of a poem by Giles Fletcher which first appeared in *Epicedium Cantabrigiense, In obitum immaturum, semperq; deflendum Henrici, Illustrissimi Principis Walliæ, etc.* (1612), 13–14. A variant of that poem appears as **HolM 5**. Among its several headings in various texts are "on the L. Mary daughter to K. James," Bodleian MS Eng. poet. e. 14, f. 96ᵛ [rev], and "on Prince Henry," Bodleian MS Rawl. poet. 31, f. 2ᵛ (Marotti 128n).

"Within this Marble casket lies" is attributed to G: Morley in British Library Add. MS 30982, f. 2, and to Ben Jonson by W. R. Chetwood in *Memoirs of Ben Jonson, Esq.* (1756), 40. An extensive collation of manuscript variants is found in Redding, 269.

♦ Manuscripts: Crum W2690, I–1571; Yale W2524 ♦ *Bodleian:* MS Ashmole 38 (p. 168); MS Douce f (f. 17ᵛ); MS Eng. poet. c. 50 (f. 130ᵛ); MS Eng. poet. e. 14 (f. 96ᵛ [rev]); MS Rawl. poet. 31

(f. 2ᵛ); MS Rawl. poet. 117 (ff. 268ᵛ [rev], 183ᵛ [rev]); MS Rawl. poet. 212 (f. 151 [rev]); MS Sancroft 59 (p. 45); **British Library:** Add. MS 10809(f. 63); Add. MS 11811 (f. 2ᵛ); Add. MS 15227 (f. 11ᵛ); Add. MS 28644 (f. 76ᵛ); Add. MS 29921 (f. 39); Add. MS 30982 (f. 2, G.Morly); Egerton MS 923 (f. 15); MS Harley 1221 (f. 70); MS Harley 6038, (f. 10); MS Sloane 1792 (f. 22ᵛ); **Corpus Christi College, Oxford:** MS 328 (ff. 26ᵛ, 49ᵛ); **Folger:** V.a. 97 (p. 51); V.a. 103, pt. I (f. 5ᵛ); V.a. 125, pt. II (f. 3ᵛ); V.a. 162 (f. 27ᵛ); V.a. 262 (p. 130); V.a. 322 (p. 65); V.a. 345 (p. 5); **Harvard:** MS Eng. 686 (f. 11ᵛ); **Huntington Library:** HM 198, pt. 2 (f. 7ᵛ); **Rosenbach:** MS 239/16 (p. 10); MS 239/22 (f. 25ᵛ); MS 239/27 (p. 355); R8 (p. 355); MS 1083/16 (p. 152); MS 1083/16 (p. 95); MS 1083/17 (p. 96b); **Yale:** Osborn b 62 (p. 131).

• • •

161. Anon., untitled, "Hee that's imprisond in this narrowe roome," 200. Pr. *Parnassus Biceps* (1656), 95.

The first ten lines of this epitaph are carved above the south aisle of Canterbury Cathedral. More than likely, the person referred to is Sir Robert Berkeley (d. 1614), son of Sir Maurice Berkeley, Christ Church, Canterbury (Thompson 408, citing J. M. Cowper, *Memorial Inscriptions* [1897], 272). His daughter Anne (d. 1624) married Henry King, whose poem commemorating her death is "The Exequy," **HolM 163.**

It is noteworthy that pp. 195–202 of the Holgate manuscript include four poems associated with Henry King.

> ✦ Manuscripts: Crum H493; Yale H0461 ✦ **Bodleian:** MS Eng. poet. e. 14 (f. 99 [rev]); MS Rawl. C. 233 (f. 86 [rev]); MS Rawl. poet. 160 (f. 53); MS Rawl. poet. 206 (p. 65); **British Library:** Add. MS 11811 (f. 5); Add. MS 15227 (f. 84); Add. MS 21433 (f. 178); Add. MS 25303 (f. 121); Egerton MS 1160 (f. 222); **Folger:** V.a. 103, pt. I (f. 8ᵛ); V.a. 125, pt. II (f. 10); V.a. 162 (f. 88ᵛ); V.a. 262 (p. 41); V.a. 345 (p. 236); V.b. 43 (f. 32ᵛ); R5 (p. 9); **Rosenbach:** MS 239/27 (p. 384); MS 240/7 (p. 38); **Owned by Edwin Wolfe II:** MS (p. 5); **Yale:** Osborn b 62 (p. 57); Osborn b 356 (p. 258).

✦ Thompson, 407–8.

• • •

162. William Basse (1583?–1653), untitled, "Renowned Spenser, ly a thought more ny," *subscribed* "Bass," 200. Pr. *Donne* (1633), 149, sig. Y3; *Wits Recreations* (1640), sig. 2A2.

William Basse is best known for this poem. Chambers describes him as "an Oxford student and a retainer of Lord Wenman of Thame." The text in Folger V.a. 232 is headed "An Epitaph pʳpared for Shakespeare; if he had been buryed at Westminster." This suggests that Basse may have intended the poem to be inscribed on a tablet commemorating Shakespeare there. Other evidence for this can be seen in the heading of British Library MS Lansdowne 777, "On Mr. Wm. Shakespeare he dyed in Aprill 1616" (Chambers 226), and Rosenbach 239/23, headed "On Mr. Wm. shackspeare who dyed Aprill 1616" (Thompson 294). In his 1790 edition of Shakespeare's works, Edmond Malone writes: "From the words 'who died in April 1616' it may be inferred that these lines were written recently after Shakespeare's death, when the month and year in which he died were well known. At a more distant period the month would probably have been forgotten; and that was not an age of such curiosity as would have induced a poet to search the register at Stratford on such a subject. From the address to Chaucer and Spenser it should seem that when the verses were composed the writer thought a cenotaph would be erected to Shakespeare in Westminster Abbey" (qtd. in Thomspon 294–95, also Bond 113).

With greater surety, however, we can say the poem was written between April 1616 when Shakespeare died and 1623, the date of the First Folio, because Jonson's verse included in the First Folio refers to this poem.

> My Shakespeare rise; I will not lodge thee by
> > Chaucer, or Spenser, or bid Beaumont lye
> > > (see Chambers 207–9, especially 208, ll. 19–20)

12. The purpose of the question mark is unclear. To my knowledge, it is unique to this manuscript.

✦ Manuscripts: Crum R154, R151; Yale R0134 ✦ *Bodleian:* MS Ashmole 38 (p. 203, Dr. Doone); MS Eng. poet. c. 50 (f. 59ᵛ, Bass); MS Eng. poet. e. 14 (f. 98ᵛ [rev]); MS Malone 19 (p. 40, Basse); MS Rawl. poet. 117 (f. 16ᵛ, Basse); MS Rawl. poet. 160 (f. 13ᵛ); MS Rawl. poet. 199 (p. 54); Add. MS 10809(f. 119ᵛ); Add. MS 15227 (f. 77); Lansdowne MS 777 (f. 67); Stowe MS 962 (f. 78ᵛ); *Corpus Christi College, Oxford:* MS 328 (f. 59); *Folger:* V.a. 103, pt. I (f. 3ᵛ, Mr. Basse); V.a. 125, pt. II (f. 8); V.a. 232 (p. 62); V.a. 262 (pp. 57–58); V.a. 275 (p. 174); V.a. 319 (f. 6); V.a. 322 (p. 189, Basse); V.a. 345 (p. 74); R5 (p. 19, Basse); *Rosenbach:* MS 239/23 (p. 187, W:Basse); MS 1083/17 (p. 6); *Yale:* Osborn b 197 (p. 48, Bass); Osborn fb 143 (p. 20).

✦ *The Poetical Works of William Basse*, ed. R. W. Bond (London, 1893), 112–17; E. K. Chambers, *William Shakespeare: A Study of Facts and Problems* (Oxford: Clarendon Press, 1930), 2:226; Thompson, 294–95.

· · ·

163. Henry King (1592–1660), untitled [The Exequy], "Accept thou shrine of my dead saint," 201–2. Pr. Henry King, *Poems, Elegies, Paradoxes and Sonnets* (1657), 52–57.

For biographical information on Henry King, see **HolM 156 notes.**

Anne King was buried at St. Gregory's Church by St. Paul's Cathedral, 5 January 1623/24, near where she and her husband lived. She was the daughter of Sir Robert Berkeley, whose epitaph from a tablet in Canterbury Cathedral is **HolM 161.** At her death she was about twenty-four years old, but she had borne six children (Baker 191).

The theme of death dominates King's poetry, but this is by far his most impressive work. Poetically, he was clearly influenced by his close friend, John Donne. Ronald Berman calls "The Exequy" "a love poem on death," and after comparing it to some of the other great English elegies, he says "they try to form some kind of tenable synthesis on the meaning of living. This is a retreat to another world, the isolated microcosm of the two lovers so often imagined in the work of John Donne" (117).

Although the famous title of this poem is not in the Holgate, "exequy" means funeral rite or ceremony (*OED*).

28–29. thou scarce hadst seene soe manie yeares / As Day tells howres. She was twenty-four.

53. Calcine. An alchemical term, to reduce to quick-lime or some other similar substance through burning (*OED*).

✦ Manuscripts: Crum A633; Beal Vol. II, pt. 1, KiH 319–351; Yale A0621 ✦ *Bodleian:* MS Ashmole 36/37 (ff. 253–54); Don.d.58 (ff. 1–2ᵛ); MS Eng. poet. e. 37 (pp. 87–90); MS Eng. poet. *e. 30 (ff. 27–30ᵛ); MS Eng. poet. e. 127 (ff. 16ᵛ–19); MS Eng. poet. f. 27 (pp. 284–89); MS *Malone 22 (ff. 17ᵛ–19ᵛ); MS Rawl. D. 398 (ff. 175–76); MS Rawl. poet. 26 (ff. 149–50ᵛ); MS Rawl. poet. 160 (ff.

41^v–42^v); *British Library:* Add. MS 25303 (ff. 145^v–47); Add. MS 25707 (ff. 98^v–99^v); Add. MS 27408 (ff. 170–71); Add. MS 58215 (pp. [1–2]; Add. MS 62134 (ff. 13–14); Egerton MS 2725 (ff. 55–56^v); *Cambridge:* MS Add. 79 (ff. 35–36^v); Phillipps MS, *Sir Geoffrey Keynes Library, Bibliotheca Bibliographici* No. 2960, pp. 37–42; *Corpus Christi Library, Oxford:* MS 328 (ff. 93–94); *Folger:* V.a. 96 (ff. 29^v–32^v); V.a. 125, pt. II (ff. 14^v–16^v); V.a. 262 (pp. 30–34); V.a. 345 (pp. 104–6); V.b. 43 (f. 34); *Huntington Library:* HM 172 (pp. 71–74); HM 904 (ff. 146^v–49^v); *New York Public Library:* Arents Collection, Cat. No. S288 (pp. 17–20); *University of Nottingham:* Portland MS Pw V 37 (pp. 29–31); *Trinity College, Cambridge:* MS R 3.12 (James 307) (pp. 247–50); *Yale:* Osborn b 205 (ff. 84^v–87); Osborn b 356 (p. 126); Poetry Box VI/121 (formerly part of Phillipps MS 17696).

✦ Henry King, *Poems*, ed. Margaret Crum (Oxford: Clarendon Press, 1965), 68–72. For critical discussion, see Ronald Berman, *Henry King & the Seventeenth Century* (London: Chatto and Windus, 1964), 116–26.

• • •

164. Richard Corbett (1582–1636), "On Mris Mallett: R: C:," 202–3. Pr. *CEP*, 26–28; *Poëtica Stromata* (n. p., 1648), 6–7.

For biographical information on Corbett, see **HolM 11 notes.**

This poem was written circa 1612 when Corbett was a Junior Proctor at Oxford. Mrs. Helen Mallet was the widow of the Vice-Chancellor's servant. Apparently, she became infatuated with Corbett (among others), which Corbett claims not to have appreciated (B&TR xiv–xv).

The Cave Miscellany, New York Public Library, MS Arents, S191, f. 15 [rev], contains the following prose description of Mrs. Mallet, attributed to Corbett. It is also found in the Victoria and Albert Museum, Dyce Collection, Cat. No. 18 (Pressmark 2.F.17, f. 71). Neither Beal nor B&TR accept the attribution, Beal writing that the "attribution probably results from confusion with the poem." Regardless, in contemporary culture, it did become associated with Corbett and Mrs. Mallet.

> A femall which hath been long suspected for a woman (she is a so sufficiently proud and vainglorious) but vpon ye better discoverye is found to be a Heteroclite to ye kind both in wind and limbe. At Portugall voiage she made meanes to a Musitian against ye law of God to contracte a kind of matrimony (who indeed should haue been stoned for Buggerie) but hath noe issue by reason of the confusion of the species. Shee is now Dowager but would fayne to man againe wch might be easily purchased wth her rings and trappings, unlesse she were of herself detestably singuler. Her whole body is a pregnant scoff in which Nature tryumphs because noe art can imitate her. She is euer by herself though in a multitude and needs noe name to distinguish her. Loyola could not haue begott a Iesuite on her to hurt vs, the issue must needs be manifested by the damm. She is so exactly drye that a man may cutt her throate and not be guilty of bloodshed. Her hatt runs at tilt and her forehead serves for boyes of fifteen to play at speern point on. In breife her whole self is a Metaphore very impertinent, or a Parenthisis and may be left out. To conclude a Precisian may detest her with a safe Conscience and break her rack in ye feare of God.   R: Corbett

(Reprinted by permission of Arents Collections; The New York Public Library; Astor, Lenox and Tilden Foundations.)

8. Iesuits. See prose description above. Corbett was an Arminian.

13. Garnet. Henry Garnett, provincial of the Jesuits in England, executed 1606 for alleged complicity in the Gunpower Plot (B&TR 106).

36. Poet Pliny. Pliny the Younger, nephew of Pliny the Elder, the historian.

37. Hackluits. Richard Hakluyt (1552?–1616), English geographer and graduate of Oxford.

43. Antickt / Antichrist. B&TR agree with the margin note, "Antichrist."

45. Welcome. Unknown. B&TR describe him as an "itinerant showman."

✦ Manuscripts: Crum H315; Beal Vol. II, pt. 1, CoR 652–686; Yale H–0340 ✦ *Aberdeen University Library:* MS 29 (pp. 154–56); *Bodleian:* MS Ashmole 47 (ff. 69ᵛ–70); MS Eng. poet. e. 14 (f. 25); MS Eng. poet. f. 27 (pp. 92–93); MS Malone 21 (ff. 48ᵛ–49); MS Rawl. poet. 117 (f. 16); MS Rawl. poet. 199 (pp. 30–31); *Bradford Central Library:* Hopkinson MSS, Vol 34 (p. 82); *British Library:* Add. MS 10308 (ff. 107ᵛ–8ᵛ); Add. MS 19268 (ff. 42ᵛ–43); Add. MS 30982 (f. 138 [rev]); MS Harley 6931 (ff. 14–15); MS Sloane 542 (f. 17); MS Sloane 1792 (ff. 26–27); *Corpus Christi College, Oxford:* MS 328 (f. 12); *Folger:* V.a. 97 (pp. 11–12); V.a. 103, pt. I (ff. 71ᵛ–72); V.a. 125, pt. I (ff. 20ᵛ–21); V.a. 170 (p. 13); V.a. 245 (f. 40); V.a. 262 (pp. 126–28); V.a. 319 (pp. 46–47); V.a. 322 (pp. 41–42); V.a. 345 (pp. 123–24); V.b. 43 (f. 1); *Harvard:* MS Eng. 966.7 (ff. 64ᵛ–65ᵛ); *New York Public Library:* Arents Collection, Cat. No. S191 (f. 15ᵛ[rev]); Arents Collection, Cat. No. S288 (pp. 96–97); *University of Newcastle upon Tyne:* MS Bell/White 25 (ff. 15–16); *University of Nottingham:* Portland MS Pw V 37 (pp. 149–50); *Rosenbach:* MS 240/7 (pp. 93–94); *St. John's College, Cambridge:* MS S. 32 (James 423) (f. 44); *Westminster Abbey:* MS 41 (ff. 29ᵛ–30); *Owned by Edwin Wolfe II:* MS (pp. 70–72); *Yale:* Osborn b 200 (pp. 173–75); Osborn b 356 (p. 29).

✦ B&TR, 6–7, 105–6.

• • •

165. William Strode (1602?–1645), "Vppon Mortalitie" 203–4. Pr. John Hannah, ed. *Poems and Psalms by Henry King*, (Oxford and London, 1843), cxxii.

For biographical information on Strode, see **HolM 154 notes.**

British Library Add. MS 30982 is an important source for Strode's poems. Strode's signature appears as a witness to the authenticity of this volume. It was owned by Daniel Leare, a distant cousin of Strode. Besides its obvious importance to the Strode canon, this miscellany demonstrates important similarities to the Holgate manuscript in that they share forty-three separate poems, nearly one-quarter of all the poems found in the manuscript.

This poem appears in the manuscript as two poems, "Vppon Mortalitie" and "Vppon Resurrection," but examination of other texts has shown it to be one. It is known as a "Sic vita" poem, its chief characteristic being its extensive use of simile throughout the verse. Another example of this genre is Francis Quarles's "Like to a damaske Rose you see," **HolM 55** (also cf. **HolM 54**, "Like to a thought slipt out of minde.")

15. Ahabs. Ahaz would seem correct. Ahaz's watch is a sundial. 2 Kings 20.11: "And Isaiah the prophet cried unto the Lord: and he brought the shadow ten degrees backward, by which it had gone down in the dial of Ahaz." Ahab was King of Israel, ca. 873–851 BCE. He married Jezebel, a Sidonean princess.

16. gulfe. Suggesting a large body of water.

18. smothered. Concealed.

✦ Manuscripts: Crum L415; Beal Vol. II, pt. 2, StW 965–983; Yale L0391 ✦ *Aberdeen University Library:* MS 29 (pp. 133–34); *Bodleian:* MS Ashmole 47 (ff. 43ᵛ–44); MS Eng. poet. c. 50

(ff. 127ᵛ–28); MS Eng. poet. f. 27 (p. 105); MS Malone 16 (pp. 53–54); MS Rawl. poet. 199 (pp. 94–95); *British Library:* Add. MS 22118 (f. 26) Add. MS 30982 (f. 163ᵛ [rev]); MS Sloane 1792 (ff. 86ᵛ–87); *Cambridge:* MS Add. 8470 (f. 20); *Corpus Christi College, Oxford:* MS 325 (ff. 64ᵛ–65, autog.); MS 328 (f. 92); *Folger:* V.a. 170 (pp. 32–33); V.a. 245 (f. 44); V.b. 43 (f. 28); *University College of North Wales:* MS 422 (p. 16); *University of Nottingham:* Portland MS Pw V 37 (p. 193); *Yale:* Osborn b 200 (p. 228).

✦ Forey, 107–8, 276–77; Saintsbury, 3:237; Dobell, 50–51.

• • •

166. William Strode (1602?–1645), "Vppon Iustification," 204. No seventeenth-century printings. Clearly intended as a companion to the previous poem, **HolM 165.**

✦ Manuscripts: Crum S215; Beal Vol. II, pt. 2, StW 193–208; Yale S0225 ✦ *Aberdeen University Library:* MS 29 (pp. 134–35); *Bodleian:* MS Ashmole 47 (f. 44); MS Eng. poet. c. 50 (f. 129); MS Rawl. poet. 199 (p. 94); *British Library:* Add. MS 22118 (f. 22); Add. MS 30982 (f. 133 [rev]); Add. MS 33998 (ff. 80ᵛ–81); MS Sloane 1792 (f. 98ᵛ); *Cambridge:* MS Add. 8470 (f. 20); *Corpus Christi College, Oxford:* MS 325 (f. 65, autog.); *Folger:* V.a. 170 (pp. 42–43); V.a. 245 (f. 44ᵛ); *St. John's College: Cambridge:* MS S. 32 (James 423) (f. 21ᵛ); *Yale:* Osborn b 200 (p. 229). Also Beal StW 205: "Owned formerly by John Sparrow, unlocated."

✦ Forey, 109; Dobell, 55.

• • •

167. William Strode (1602?–1645), untitled, "I saw faire Cloris walke alone," subscribed "W: S:," 204. Pr. Walter Porter, *Madrigals and Ayres* (1632); *Wits Recreations* (1640), no. 180.
This is one of the most popular poems found in seventeenth-century verse miscellanies. It has been frequently set to music. Among the more noteworthy composers to have set this lyric are Henry Purcell and Henry Lawes (Main 446). The poem has also been translated and parodied. Among these is a Latin version, probably by Thomas Traherne, and a parody by Thomas Philipott, "On a sparke of fire fixing on a Gentlewomans brest," (*Poems*, 1646, p. 33).
The handwriting in BL Add. MS 23229 is neither hand A nor hand B as discussed in the Introduction, pp. xviii–xx. There are also many variants. Clearly, the Holgate scribe worked from a different copy-text.

✦ Manuscripts: Crum I–430, A1542; Beal Vol. II, pt. 2, StW 747–834; Yale I–0333 ✦ *Aberdeen University Library:* MS 29 (p. 164); Ajaaloo Museum, Reval/Tallin, Estonia, Fond 114; Bibliotheque Nationale, Paris, Department de la Musique, Conservatoire MS 2489 (p. 296); *Bodleian:* MS Ashmole 38 (p. 9); Don.c.57 (f. 60ᵛ); MS Douce f (f. 3ᵛ); MS Eng. misc.f.49 (f. 1ᵛ [rev]); MS Eng. poet. c. 50 (f. 34ᵛ); MS Eng. poet. e. 97 (p. 30); MS Eng. poet. f. 10 (f. 89); MS Eng. poet. f. 25 (f. 10); MS Eng. poet. f. 27 (p. 55); MS Firth e. 4 (p. 116); MS Lat. misc. c. (p. 421); B49A (p. 201); MS Malone 16 (p. 16); MS Rawl. poet. 116 (f. 42ᵛ); MS Rawl. poet. 117 (f. 163 [rev]); MS Rawl. poet. 153 (f. 8ᵛ); MS Rawl. poet. 160 (f. 113); MS Rawl. poet. 199 (pp. 3–4); MS Tanner 465 (f. 42ᵛ); *British Library:* Add. MS 11811 (f. 2ᵛ); Add. MS 15227 (f. 4); Add. MS 19268 (f. 23); Add. MS 22603 (ff. 8ᵛ–9); Add. MS 23229 (f. 46); Add. MS 25303 (f. 181); Add. MS 30982 (f. 158ᵛ [rev]); Add. MS 33998 (f. 62); Add. MS 44963 (f. 9ᵛ); Add. MS 47111 (f. 12ᵛ); Add. MS 58215 (p. [32]); Egerton MS 2013 (f. 23); Egerton MS 2421 (f. 3ᵛ); Egerton MS 2725 (f. 105ᵛ); MS Harley 3511 (f. 14); MS Harley 6396 (f. 9); MS Harley 6931 (f. 4); MS Sloane 1446 (f. 76ᵛ); MS Sloane 1454 (f. 26); MS Sloane 1792 (f. 10ᵛ); Stowe MS 962 (f. 179); *Cambridge:* MS Add. 8684 (f. 13ᵛ); CL1 (p. 9); *Corpus*

Christi College, Oxford: MS 325 (f. 64, autog.); MS 328 (f. 16); *Edinburgh University Library:* MS H.-P. Coll. 401 (ff. 56, 110); MS La. III 436 (p. 100); *Folger:* V.a. 124 (f. 20); V.a. 148, pt. I (f. 12); V.a. 162 (f. 81); V.a. 169, pt. II (f. 32); V.a. 170 (p. 48); V.a. 245 (f. 39ᵛ); V.a. 262 (pp. 76–77); V.a. 300 (f. 5ᵛ); V.a. 308 (f. 3ᵛ); V.a. 319 (f. 38); V.a. 345 (p. 145); V.b. 43 (f. 8ᵛ); *University of Glasgow:* MSS R.d. 58–61: (i, f. 8, ii, f.31ᵛ, iii, f. 17, iv, f. 29ᵛ); *Harvard:* MS Eng. 686 (f. 60ᵛ); *Huntington Library:* HM 116 (pp. 19–20, 86); LA (f. 41ᵛ); *Leicestershire Record Office:* DG.7/Lit. 2 (f. 350); MBh1 (p. 7 [rev]); *University of Newcastle upon Tyne:* MS Bell/White 25 (f. 40ᵛ); *University of Nottingham:* Portland MS Pw V 37; RP1 (p. 15); *Rosenbach:*MS 239/18 (pp. 43–44); MS 239/27 (p. 49); MS 243/4 (p. 133); MS 1083/17 (f. 134); *St. John's College, Cambridge:* MS S. 32 (James 423) (f. 9ᵛ); *South African Library, Cape Town:* MS Grey 7 a 29 (p. 89); TCD-? (ff. 166ᵛ–67, 224ᵛ–25, 272ᵛ); *Westminster Abbey:* MS 41 (f. 47); *Worcester College, Oxford:* MSS 4.29(f. [16]); *Yale:* Osborn b 62 (pp. 24, 138); Osborn b 200 (p. 12); Osborn b 209 (p. 56).

✦ For an extensive list of the many versions and settings of this poem, see C. F. Main, "Notes on Some Poems Attributed to William Strode," *Philological Quarterly* 34 (1955), 455. See also Ault, 478; Dobell, 41; Forey, 76–77, 254–55; Hebel, 636.

• • •

168. Anon., "On the standinge for a Beedells place," 204–5. Unprinted.

A beadle, as it applies in this poem, is "an apparitor or precursor who walks officially in front of dignitaries, a mace-bearer; a. *spec.* in the English universities . . . the name of certain officials, formerly of two ranks distinguished as *esquire bedels* and *yeoman bedels*, having various functions as officers of the University. Their duties are now chiefly processional" (*OED*).

The text in Folger MS V.a. 162 is headed "Uppon those that canvasd for Mr. Bell, the beedles place when hee was dangerously sick and by some supposed to bee dead." The key word, then, is "canvasd," (to solicit votes, OED) which is repeated in l. 57, "for indeed his wife canuasst." Clearly, Old John Bell was quite ill and believed dead. However, his friends must have wanted his position, even before he was dead. Among those caught in this net was John Prideaux (l. 48). See **HolM 154** and **HolM 158**.

From its jovial ironic humor, this ballad was probably sung, perhaps as a drinking song.

✦ Manuscripts: Crum N–262 ✦ *Bodleian:* MS Jones 27* (f. 18ᵛ); MS Tanner 306 (f. 302); *Folger:* V.a. 162 (ff. 42–43ᵛ); V.a. 170 (p. 237).

• • •

169. George Morley (1597–1684), "On the Nightingale," 205. Pr. *Musarum Deliciæ* (London, 1655), 76–77 [2nd numbering]; *Parnassus Biceps* (1656), 93.

For biographical information on George Morley, see the notes to **HolM 17**, **HolM 149**, and **HolM 157**.

✦ Manuscripts: Crum M769; Yale M–0596 ✦ *Bodleian:* MS Eng. poet. c. 50 (f. 133ᵛ); MS Eng. poet. e. 97 (p. 131, George Morley); MS Rawl. poet. 199 (p. 49, G.M.); *British Library:* Add. MS 30982 (f. 2ᵛ, Morly); *Folger:* V.a. 97 (p. 93); V.a. 125, pt. I (f. 29ᵛ, GM); V.a. 170 (p. 78, G.M.); V.a. 245 (f. 49ᵛ, G. Morley); V.a. 262 (p. 59); V.a. 319 (f. 35ᵛ), V.a. 322 (p. 37); V.a. 339 (f. 252ᵛ); *New York Public Library:* Arents Collection, Cat. No. S288 (p. 22); R5 (p. 456); *Rosenbach:* MS 243/4 (p. 100, George Marcham); *Yale:* Osborn b 62 (pp. 29–30); Osborn b 200 (pp. 199–200, Geo: Morley); Osborn b 205 (f. 55).

170. William Strode (1602?–1645), "On the Death of S^r Th: Pelham," 206. Pr. *Parnassus Biceps* (London, 1656), 72–73.

For biographical information on Strode, see **HolM 154 notes.**

Sir Thomas Pelham of Halland in Laughton, Sussex became sheriff of the county in 1589. He served as MP for both Lewes and Sussex. He died 2 December 1624. His father-in-law was Sir Thomas Walsingham, first cousin of Sir Francis Walsingham, Queen Elizabeth's Secretary of State (Forey 279).

Collation reveals that the Strode's autograph manuscript (MS 325) is much closer to the Holgate text than the printed version in *Parnassus Biceps.*

> **13. Three score and tenn is Natures date.** Psalm 90:10.
> **17–18. the Sun ne're stood . . . the peoples good.** Joshua 10:12–13.
> **35–36.** Margaret Forey suggests that the final couplet recalls the final couplet of **HolM 16,** a funeral elegy to Mr. Iohn Ryce, attributed in the Holgate manuscript to "GH" (for discussion, see **HolM 16 notes**).

> Sleepe, Sleepe: Good man and take thy Rest vppo'nt
> Sleep, Sleep; Thou hast had a Long iourney on't. (**HolM 16**, ll. 57–58)

✦ Manuscripts: Crum M333, Beal Vol. II, pt. 2, StW 573–591 ✦ *Aberdeen University Library:* MS 29 (pp. 101–3); *Bodleian:* MS Ashmole 47 (ff. 41, 51^v); MS Eng. poet. e. 97 (p. 118); MS Eng. poet. f. 27 (pp. 25–26); *British Library:* Add. MS 22118 (f. 19); Add. MS 30982 (f. 126 [rev]); *Cambridge:* MS Add. 8470 (ff. 9^v–10); *Corpus Christi College, Oxford:* MS 325 (ff. 81^v–82, autog.); MS 328 (f. 14); *Folger:* V.a. 97 (pp. 115–16, Strode); V.a. 170 (pp. 65–66, W.S.); V.a. 245 (f. 53); *National Library of Wales:* Powis MSS (1959 deposit), series II, (Envelope) Bundle 26; *New York Public Library:* Arents Collection, Cat. No. S288 (p. 77); *Rosenbach:* MS 239/27 (pp. 353–54); MS 240/7 (pp. 54–56, W.S.); *St. John's College, Cambridge:* MS S. 32 (James 423) (ff. 22^v–23).

✦ Dobell, 64–65; Forey, 114, 279–80; For the first printed text, see *Parnassus Biceps or Several Choice Pieces of Poetry (1656),* ed. G. Thorn-Drury (rpt. London: Frederick Etchells & Hugh Macdonald, 1927).

· · ·

171. William Strode (1602?–1645), "To his Sister," 207. Pr. *Wits Restor'd* (London, 1658), 83.

For biographical information on Strode, see **HolM 154 notes.**

This poem is not found in Corpus Christi College, Oxford MS 325, the autograph manuscript of Strode's poems. Its inclusion, however, in British Library Add. MS 30982 is strong evidence that it is Strode's because Strode is known to have witnessed that miscellany. The poem is attributed to "W. S." in Folger MS V.a. 170 and Folger MS V.a. 245, the two manuscripts that Dobell used as copy-texts.

Strode had one sister, Mary, baptized 25 July 1599. Nothing else is known about her.

Margaret Forey uses the Holgate manuscript as her copy-text for this poem. *Wit Restor'd* demonstrates several variants, including the omission of ll. 7–10.

> **4. pindust.** A dust from the filings of brass or other metals created in the manufacture of metal pins (*OED*).

✦ Manuscripts: Beal Vol. II, pt. 2, StW 1129–1137 ✦ *Bodleian:* MS Eng. poet. f. 27 (pp. 221–22); *British Library:* Add. MS 22602 (f. 16^v); Add. MS 30982 (f. 17^v); MS Sloane 1792 (f. 94); *Folger:*

V.a. 97 (p. 116); V.a. 170 (p. 64); V.a. 245 (f. 46). Beal also cites StW 1136, a manuscript owned formerly by John Sparrow of Oxford, unlocated.

✦ Dobell, 88; Forey, 198, 330–31.

• • •

172. William Strode (1602?–1645), "On a blisterd Lippe," 207. Pr. *Parnassus Biceps* (1656), 67–68. For biographical information on Strode, see **HolM 154 notes.**

This poem is not found in British Library Add. MS 30982. For discussion, see **HolM 165 notes.**

✦ Manuscripts: Crum C18; Beal Vol. II, pt. 2, StW 268–299; Yale C0151 ✦ *Aberdeen University Library:* MS 29 (pp. 197–98); *Bodleian:* MS Eng. poet. e. 14 (f. 14); *British Library:* Add. MS 22118 (f. 41); Add. MS 33998 (ff. 62ᵛ–63); Egerton MS 2421 (ff. 13ᵛ–14); MS Harley 6931 (ff. 9ᵛ–10); MS Sloane 542 (f. 61); MS Sloane 1792 (f. 86); CL1 (p. 11); *Corpus Christi College, Oxford:* MS 325 (f. 77, autog.); *Folger:* V.a. 103, pt. I (f. 35ᵛ); V.a. 170 (63–64); V.a. 245 (f. 54); V.a. 262 (pp. 92–93); *Harvard:* MS Eng. 686 (f. 71); *Huntington Library:* HM 116 (pp. 46–47); HM 198, pt. 1 (p. 153); *Leeds Archives Department:* MX 237 (f. 22ᵛ); *New York Public Library:* Arents Collection, Cat. No. S288 (pp. 12–13); *University of Newcastle upon Tyne:* MS Bell/White 25 (f. 19); *University College of North Wales:* MS 422 (pp. 66–67); *University of Nottingham:* Portland MS Pw V 37 (f. [lv], autog, facsimile in Beal); *Rosenbach:* MS 239/27 (p. 287); MS 243/4 (p. 157); MS 240/7 (pp. 36–37); MS 1083/17 (f. 154); *Westminster Abbey:* MS 41 (f. 55ᵛ); *Owned by Edwin Wolfe II:* MS (pp. 1–2), *Yale:* Osborn b 197 (pp. 156–57); Osborn b 200 (pp. 210–11); Osborn b 205 (ff. 60ᵛ–61).

Dobell, 28–29; Forey, 92–93.

• • •

173. William Strode (1602?–1645), "On the Bible," 208. Pr. *Parnassus Biceps* (London, 1656), 31–32. For biographical information on William Strode, see **HolM 154 notes.**

✦ Manuscripts: Crum B251; Beal Vol. II, pt. 2, StW 537–548; Yale B0203 ✦ *Aberdeen University Library:* MS 29 (pp. 126–28); *Bodleian:* MS Eng. poet. e. 97 (p. 141); *British Library:* Add. MS 30982 (f. 127ᵛ [rev]); *Corpus Christi College, Oxford:* MS 325 (f. 78, autog.); MS 328 (f. 91); *Folger:* V.a. 97 (p. 169); V.a. 170 (pp. 49–51); V.a. 245 (f. 45); *Leicestershire Record Office:* DG.7/Lit. 2 (f. 347); *Rosenbach:* MS 239/27 (pp. 167–68); *Owned by Edwin Wolfe II:* MS (pp. 25–26); *Yale:* Osborn b 205 (f. 61).

✦ Dobell, 51–52; Forey, 46–47.

• • •

174. William Strode (1602?–1645), "To a Gentle man, on a strange Cure," 209–10. Pr. *Parnassus Biceps* (1656), 104–6.

For biographical information on Strode, see **HolM 154 notes.** The autograph manuscript, Corpus Christi College, Oxford MS 325, identifies the addressee of this poem as "Mr. Rives." Nothing is known about him except what we learn from this poem. According to the poem, he suffered from what is described as an extra bone in his thigh (ll. 7–9). Forey suggests that it was most likely a calciferous cyst (228).

Dr. Bernard Wright was the surgeon who operated on Mr. Rives. He became a licensed surgeon in Oxford (1618) at the age of twenty-nine. He became an assistant in the Anatomy Lecture at Oxford when the lectureship was first founded in 1624. He was buried 3 August 1626.

Forey has discovered a perplexing textual problem concerning the Holgate version of the poem. Line 55 in this text ends "conuert," which she believes is an incorrect reading of the line. What is particularly interesting, however, is that the autograph copy, MS 325, also reads "conuert," but is corrected in Strode's hand to "translate." A caret was added in Strode's hand to identify the correct reading. "Translate" is clearly a better reading because the couplet is completed in l. 56 with "fortunate" (l. 55).

Forey suggests two possible explanations for this repeated error, both of which depend on when in the textual history of the poem the Holgate text was transcribed. It is possible that the Holgate was copied from MS 325 (or some ancestor derived from it) and that Strode corrected MS 325 at some point after his original transcription and after the error had been copied into the Holgate manuscript. Forey rejects this idea because she believes it was Strode's editorial practice to insert a caret only when he discovered a mistake at the time of his original transcription, thus making it unlikely that the two miscellanies would share a common error. Forey's alternative explanation of this problem is quite suggestive as to the nature of manuscript transmission. Both the Holgate and MS 325 derive from a common ancestor, a loose sheet, which Forey calls "γ". Strode, while copying the poem from γ to MS 325, copied the line as it appeared in his copy-text and then, realizing the mistake, immediately made his correction with the use of the caret. Moreover, Forey believes that Strode would not likely have been in the practice of transmitting his poems through the use of verse miscellanies, but would instead have transmitted his poem on a single sheet of paper. If that were the case, then γ was a loose sheet.

Another possibility concerns Strode as a poet. He was not a particularly artful rhymer, and indeed he also writes what best can be called "forced rhyme." In ll. 3–4, for example, Strode rhymes forth / Truth. It is possible, therefore, that while Strode was correcting a scribal error, he was also rewriting the poem.

> **11. Golgotha.** A graveyard (*OED*).
> **11. Charnel-house.** A place for dead bodies (*OED*).
> **21. Midmen.** Male midwives (*OED*). The image is completed in the next line.
> **22. Bacchus.** Semele, the mother of Bacchus, died when Zeus fulfilled his promise to let her see him in all his heavenly splendor. Before she died, he snatched the unborn child and kept it in his side until the child was born (Hamilton 64–67).
> **32. Van Otto.** James Van Otten (d. 1622) was Bernard Wright's partner.
> **37. Griffiths.** The reference is to a Mr. Griffiths, whom Dr. Wright had cured of a head injury (l. 40).
> **42. Paracelsus.** Philippus Aureolus Paracelsus (1493?–1541), a Swiss physician and alchemist who did not believe diseases were caused by the humours (see l. 8). Forey points out that Paracelsus thought life could be extended as it had been during the lives of the Old Testament patriarchs (see l. 43).
> **52. ring.** Probably a commemorative death ring which contained a skull or skeleton (Forey 230).

✦ Manuscripts: Crum W210; Beal Vol. II, pt. 2, StW 1139–1152; Yale W0179 ✦ **Aberdeen University Library:** MS 29 (pp. 61–63); Don.d.58 (ff. 46ᵛ–47); MS Rawl. poet. 206 (pp. 47–48); **British Library:** Add. MS 30982 (f. 135ʳ–ᵛ [rev.]); MS Harley 6931 (ff. 23–24); MS Sloane 1446 (ff. 21–22); MS Sloane 1792 (ff. 108–9); **Corpus Christi College, Oxford:** MS 325 (f. 62, autog. ll.13–66); **Folger:**

V.a. 97 (pp. 111–13); V.a. 245 (ff. 54ᵛ–55ᵛ); **University of Nottingham:** Portland MS Pw V 37 (p. 117); **Rosenbach:** MS 1083/16 (pp. 192–94); **Yale:** Osborn b 200 (pp. 229–32).

✦ Dobell, 95–97; Forey, 11–14, 228–30, 366–73; Edith Hamilton, *Mythology* (Boston: Little, Brown, 1998), 64–67.

• • •

175. William Strode (1602?–1645), "A Register for a Bible," 210. No seventeenth-century printings.

For biographical information on Strode, see **HolM 154 notes**. This and the following poem are generally found together in manuscripts. As used here, "register" means a bookmark.

✦ Manuscripts: Crum I–47, I–10, I–43; Beal Vol. II, pt. 2, StW 691–705; Yale I–0043 ✦ **Aberdeen University Library:** MS 29 (p. 128); **Bodleian:** MS Eng. poet. c. 50 (f. 127ᵛ); MS Eng. poet. e. 97 (p. 140); MS Rawl. D. 1092 (f. 270ᵛ); **British Library:** Add. MS 30982 (f. 128 [rev]); MS Harley 6931 (f. 8); MS Sloane 1792 (f. 93); **Corpus Christi College, Oxford:** MS 325 (f. 79, autog. with rev.); **Folger:** V.a. 170 (p. 56); V.a. 245 (f. 44ᵛ); R5 (f. 57); **Owned by Edwin Wolfe II:** MS (pp. 26–27); **Yale:** Osborn b 205 (f. 55). Beal StW 704: "Owned formerly by John Sparrow, Oxford, unlocated."

✦ Dobell, 52–53; Forey, 52, 249.

• • •

176. William Strode (1602?–1645), "Alias," following previous poem, 211. No seventeenth-century printings.

For biographical information on Strode, see **HolM 154 notes**. This is the companion piece to **HolM 175**. Lines 7–8 in this transcription are the same as ll. 7–8 of "Register for a Bible," Corpus Christi College, Oxford MS 325 and British Library Add. MS 30982.

Collation for this poem would not be helpful. Lines 1–2 are the same; the remainder of the poem is quite different. Holgate, l. 6, is the same as MS 325, l. 3. The text below is from Forey with the alternate text italicized. Forey suggests that the new lines found in the Holgate were written by another poet (250).

> I, your Memory's Recorder,
> Keepe my charge in watchful order.
> *My Strings divide the worde aright,*
> *Pressing the Text both day and night.*
> *And what the hande of God hath writt,*
> *Behold, my Fingers point at itt;*
> St. Peter cannot with his Keyes
> Unlock Heuv'n gate more sure then these.

9. Welch-men. Colloquial expression suggesting "thief" (Forey).
10. Heauen in a stringe. Death by hanging (Forey).

✦ Manuscripts: Crum I–638; Beal Vol. II, pt. 2, StW 2–16; Yale I–0477 ✦ **Aberdeen University Library:** MS 29 (p. 128); MS Eng. poet. c. 50 (f. 127ᵛ); MS Eng. poet. e. 97 (p. 140); **British Library:** Add. MS 30982 (f. 56ᵛ); MS Harley 6931 (f. 8ᵛ); MS Sloane 1446 (f. 24); MS Sloane 1792 (f. 93); **Corpus Christi College, Oxford:** MS 325 (f. 79, autog.); **Folger:** V.a. 125, pt. I (f. 7ᵛ); V.a. 170 (p. 56);

V.a. 245 (f. 44ᵛ); **Owned by Edwin Wolfe II:** MS (p. 27); **Yale:** Osborn b 205 (f. 55). Beal StW 15: Owned formerly by John Sparrow, Oxford, unlocated.

✦ Dobell, 53; Forey, 53, 250.

• • •

177. Anon., "Anagram: Iohn Portmane Mother no paine," 211. Unprinted.

Clearly, this is the same John Portman(e) Strode eulogized in the following poem, **HolM 178**. Portman lived in Orchard Portman, Somerset, and matriculated at Oxford in 1623. He was buried at Wadham College, Oxford, 23 December 1624 (Forey 278). The Wadham College chapel has a monument in his honor.

Anagrammatic poetry is common in the miscellany tradition, but there are only two in the Holgate, this and **HolM 14**.

✦ Forey, 278–79.

• • •

178. William Strode (1602?–1645), "On the Death of young Barronet Portman dyinge of an Impostume in his head," 211–12. No seventeenth-century printings.

For biographical information on Strode, see **HolM 154 notes**. For biographical information on John Portman, see **HolM 177 notes**.

"Impostume" is an archaic word for abscess (*OED*).

> **10. This vpper shoppe.** A metaphor for "head."
> **31. the widdowes Child.** 2 Kings 4: 18–20 (Forey).

✦ Manuscripts: Crum I–1719; Beal Vol. II, pt. 2, StW 598–604; Yale I–1436 ✦ *Aberdeen University Library:* MS 29 (pp. 99–101); *Bodleian:* Don.d.58 (ff. 12ᵛ–13); *British Library:* Add. MS 30982 (ff. 127–26ᵛ [rev]); *Corpus Christi College, Oxford:* MS 325 (ff. 80ᵛ–81ᵛ, autog.); MS 328 (ff. 54ᵛ–55); *Folger:* V.a. 170 (pp. 91–92); *Yale:* Osborn b 205 (ff. 61ᵛ–62ᵛ).

Dobell, 66–68; Forey, 112–13, 278–79.

• • •

179. William Strode (1602?–1645), untitled, "If Hercules tall stature might bee guest," 213. Pr. *Wit Restor'd* (1658), 90–91.

For biographical information on Strode, see **HolM 154 notes**. This is one of Strode's most successful poems. Since its conceit is based on the anatomical foot, the "thumb" (l. 2) refers to Hercules's big toe, an obsolete but alternate meaning for the word "thumb" (*OED*). Forey writes that the idea comes from Aulus Gellius, who reported that Pythagoras calculated the length of Hercules's foot by measuring the stadium at Olympia (*Noctes Atticæ*, 1.1.231).

> **13. roses.** A rose-shaped ribbon worn on shoes (*OED*).
> **20–22. clouen feete . . . vnhollowed creatures.** Christian iconography often represents Satan as cloven-footed. The idea follows the pagan myth of Pan, who was half goat (*OED*). In Old Testament dietary laws, Jews were allowed to eat animals that had cloven feet *and* chewed the cud, but were not allowed to eat animals that had cloven feet and did *not* chew the cud, or animals who chewed the cud but did not have cloven feet (see Leviticus 11: 1–8). Forey suggests that Strode was somewhat careless on this point because cloven-hoofed animals were permitted (232).

✦ Manuscripts: Crum I–799; Beal Vol. II, pt. 2, StW 442–468; Yale I–0598 ✦ *Aberdeen University Library:* MS 29 (pp. 123–25); *Bodleian:* MS Eng. poet. c. 53 (f. 3ᵛ); MS Eng. poet. e. 97 (p. 133); MS Eng. poet. f. 27 (pp. 214–15); MS Malone 21 (ff. 49ᵛ–50); *British Library:* Add. MS 19268 (f. 20); Add. MS 30982 (f. 15); Add. MS 33998 (ff. 76–77); MS Sloane 1446 (f. 78); *Cambridge:* MS Add. 8470 (ff. 13ᵛ–14); *Corpus Christi College, Oxford:* MS 325 (f. 71, autog.); MS 328 (f. 84); *Folger:* V.a. 97 (pp. 154–55); V.a. 124 (ff. 23ᵛ–24); V.a. 170 (pp. 59–60); V.a. 245 (ff. 50ᵛ–51); V.a. 262 (pp. 77–78); *Huntington Library:* HM 198, pt. 1 (pp. 151–52); *Leeds Archives Department:* MX 237 (ff. 40ᵛ–41); NLW9; *Rosenbach:* R5 (ff. 55ᵛ–56); MS 239/27 (pp. 220–21); MS 1083/17 (152ᵛ–53ᵛ); *Owned by Edwin Wolfe II:* MS (pp. 76–78); *Yale:* Osborn b 205 (f. 66). Beal StW 459: Owned formerly by John Sparrow of Oxford, unlocated.

✦ Dobell, 108–9; Forey, 16–17, 231–32.

• • •

180. William Strode (1602?–1645), "A translation of the Nightingale out of Strado," 214–16. No seventeenth-century printings.

For biographical information on Strode, see **HolM 154 notes.** This poem is a translation of Famianus Strada's (1572–1649) "The Nightengale," "Iam Sol à medio pronus deflexerat orbe." It depicts a song contest. Strada's poem was frequently translated, including English versions by Crashaw, "Now westward Sol had spent the richest beames," and John Ford, *The Lover's Melancholy,* Act I, scene 1 (Forey 253). The text found in Bodleian MS Eng. poet. c. 50 is followed by a second translation, "Now the declining sun his height had past" (Crum, *First-Line Index,* N–569). The two translations share a common heading, "Translated by two ffrendes."

> **25. keemes.** Obsolete form of "kemb," to comb or disentangle. Medieval pronunciation would have a short "e" (kemb or kemm,), so this spelling would stress a long "e."
> **28. points.** Early modern musical notations, either dots or marks (*OED*).

✦ Manuscripts: Crum N56;, Beal Vol. II, pt. 2, StW 1189–1205; Yale N0506 ✦ *Bodleian:* MS Eng. poet. c. 50 (f. 61, see note above); MS Rawl. poet. 160 (ff. 51ᵛ–52ᵛ); MS Rawl. poet. 199 (pp. 50–52); *British Library:* Add. MS 25303 (ff. 154–55); Add. MS 30982 (ff. 130–29 [rev]); MS Harley 3910 (ff. 113ᵛ–17); MS Harley 6931 (ff. 10–11ᵛ); *Corpus Christi College, Oxford:* MS 325 (ff. 74ᵛ–75ᵛ, autog. with rev.); *Folger:* V.a. 97 (pp. 141–43); V.a. 245 (ff. 48–49); V.a. 262 (pp. 27–30); *New York Public Library:* Arents Collection, Cat. No. S288 (pp. 15–17); *University College of North Wales:* MS 422 (pp. 16–18); *Rosenbach:* MS 1083/17 (ff. 139–40ᵛ); *Westminster Abbey:* MS 41 (ff. 57–58); *Yale:* Osborn b 200 (pp. 169–72).

✦ Crum, 569; Dobell, 16–18; Forey, 72–75, 253.

• • •

181. William Strode (1602?–1645), "On a ffountaine," 216. Pr. *P&R,* 107.

For biographical information on Strode, see **HolM 154 notes.** There is no autograph copy of this poem. It is transcribed in the Strode autograph collection, Corpus Christi College, Oxford MS 325, by William Fulman (1632–1688), who owned the manuscript after Strode's death. He used a now lost copy-text in Strode's handwriting.

✦ Manuscripts: Crum T1800, Beal Vol. II, pt. 2, StW 608–622 ✦ *Aberdeen University Library:* MS 29 P. 136); *Bodleian:* MS Eng. poet. c. 50 (f. 131); *British Library:* Add. MS 30982 (ff. 4ᵛ, 133ᵛ); Add. MS 33998 (f. 47ᵛ); MS Sloane 1446 (f. 23); MS Sloane 1792 (f. 86ᵛ); *Cambridge:*

MS Add. 8470 (f. 12ᵛ); ***Corpus Christi College, Oxford:*** MS 325 (f. 45, see n. above); ***Folger:*** V.a. 125, pt. I (f. 7ᵛ); V.a. 170 (p. 42); V.a. 245 (f. 47ᵛ); ***Leicestershire Record Office:*** DG.7/Lit. 2 (f. 346ᵛ); ***University College of North Wales:*** MS 422 (pp. 26–27).

✦ Collation: *P&R* 4 *Here from fishes doth*] Lo Here from fishes doth *P&R* ; 6 *where by*] by which *P&R*; 10 *waitinge*] wailing *P&R* ; 12 *giues*] give *P&R*

✦ Dobell, 46; Forey, 185.

• • •

182. Marchamont Nedham, "An Epitaph vpon Iames Duke of Hamilton: Año Domĩ 1649,'" 227–29. Pr. *Digitus Dei* (1649), 29–31.

Joseph Frank describes the first printed version of this poem as a "quadruple pamphlet" (*Pegasus*, 226). Its full title is "God's Iustice upon Treachery and Treason; Exemplifyed in the Life and Death of the late James, Duke of Hamilton." James Hamilton (1606–1649) was first heir to the Scottish throne after the descendants of James VI/I. He was born in Scotland; he later matriculated at Exeter College, Oxford. He became a gentleman of the bedchamber to Charles I in 1624 and was sworn to the Privy Council of Scotland in 1627. He raised an army of 6,000 men on behalf of Gustavus Adolphus during the Thirty Years' War, and saw action on the Continent in 1631–32. In 1638, he was sent by Charles to Scotland to appease the Covenanters, who resisted using the English prayer book, but instead he ended up trying to appease Charles. In 1643, he became Duke of Hamilton. The following year, he was expelled from Scotland for refusing to accept the Solemn League and Covenant, designed to establish a Presbyterian state church. On his return to England, he was imprisoned by Charles on suspicion of treachery. In 1648, he joined with the Scots fighting on Charles's behalf at the Battle of Preston but was defeated by forces led by Cromwell. He was executed 6 March 1649, only a few weeks before Charles himself was executed (*DNB*).

Marchamont Nedham was born in Burford, Oxfordshire, but was orphaned before he was two years old. He was accepted to an usher's place in the Merchant Taylors School, later becoming an under clerk at Gray's Inn. In 1647, he was imprisoned for making aspersions against Charles; however, upon his release he found favor with the King after they were introduced. He wrote *Mercurius Pragmaticus*, a satire against the Presbyterians, for which he was also imprisoned. He was released by John Bradshaw, president of the court of high justice, after which he wrote *Mercurius Politicus*, a tract politically opposite to *Mercurius Pragmaticus*. Frank describes the poem as printed in *Digitus Dei* as "the best example of negative portraiture in verse before Dryden that I know of" (*Pegasus*, 226). STC identifies Nedham as the author of *Digitus Dei*, although the book itself indicates no author on its title page.

The handwriting of this poem is larger and more carefully drawn than other poems in the manuscript, and it is placed eleven pages after the previous entry, **HolM 181**. Since the interceding texts written by John Wale were entered approximately fifty years later, the original scribe left ten pages blank when he entered this poem and approximately seventy pages after it. (An exact count is impossible because a few pages have been removed from the manuscript.) This entry proves that the principal Holgate scribe must have been alive in 1649, the date of this poem, and that for whatever reason, he had not added to the book for several decades.

Also significant here is that the scribe did not use *Digitus Dei* as his copy-text. *Digitus Dei* omits l. 22 (see manuscripts below), which is included in the Holgate text. With the exception of the title and l. 22 , the remainder of the text is identical with the printed copy. The scribe, then, may have known Nedham, or at least had access to an authorial text. With the *possible* exception of **HolM 74**, all the other poems found in the manuscript can be dated in the 1620s or before. Why the manuscript remained unused for so many years is impossible to say. For whatever reason, this poem has been invaluable in the attempt to discover the identity of the scribe. For extended commentary on his identity and the dates of this manuscript, see Introduction, pp. xii–xv.

⬩ Manuscripts: **British Library:** Add. MS 18044, f. 120ᵛ, ll. 1–22 .

◆ For general commentary on the role of newspapers in the seventeenth century, see Joseph Frank, *The Beginnings of the English Newspaper, 1620–1660* (Cambridge, Mass.: Harvard Univ. Press, 1961). For a descriptive bibliography of mid-seventeenth-century minor poetry, see Joseph Frank, *Hobbled Pegasus* (Albuquerque: Univ. of New Mexico Press, 1968). Both volumes include texts of this poem. For information on Marchamont Nedham, see Anthony á Wood, *Athenæ Oxonienses*, ed. Bliss, vol. 3.

⋯

183. William Cecil, prose epistle: "'Honos. alit artes' : R: C:," 303–6. The tract was first printed under the title "The Counsell of a Father to his Sonne, in ten seuerall Precepts (STC 4900.5, 1611). It was reprinted in "Certain Precepts for the Well Ordering of a Man's Life," STC 4897–4900 (four editions, 1617–37).

"R: C:" refers to the poem's addressee, Robert Cecil, son of William Cecil, Lord Burghley. William Cecil, first Baron Burghley (1520/21–1598), studied at St. John's College, Cambridge. He became Principal Secretary to Elizabeth when she became Queen, and Lord Treasurer in 1572. He died in 1598 (Wright xiii).

Robert Cecil followed in his father's political footsteps: he was a close advisor to both Elizabeth and James. For Elizabeth, he served as Principal Secretary, for James, Lord Treasurer (Wright xvii).

The letter is surely reminiscent of Polonius's advice to Laertes in *Hamlet*; but if Shakespeare knew of this letter, he must have encountered it in manuscript because the tract was first published more than a decade after the play appeared on stage.

From its location in the miscellany, the scribe wanted to have prose at the end of his miscellany and poetry at the beginning. Such division was fairly common practice. However, other prose works entered by the scribe in the poetry section are **HolM 135** and **HolM 144**.

✦ Manuscripts ✦ **British Library:** Stowe MS 143 (f. 321); **Folger:** V.a 143 (f. 100).

✦ For a critical text, see *Advice to a Son*, ed. Louis B. Wright (Ithaca: Cornell Univ. Press, 1962).

⋯

184. John Earle, prose commentary: "Mʳ Earl's Characters," 309–28. Pr. John Earle, *Micro-cosmographie or, A Peece of the World Discovered: In essayes and characters*, 2nd edition (1628).

Twelve editions of the *Microcosmography* were printed during the seventeenth century. Its success prompted Earle to expand it in its several editions through 1633. The second edition is the first in which all twenty-nine characters found in the Holgate manuscript appeared. Other manuscripts containing chapters from *Microcosmography* are Bodleian MS Eng. misc. f. 89; Bodleian MS Eng. poet. e. 112; British Library Add. MS 25303; British Library MS Stowe 962; Cambridge University Library MS Add. 6160; Durham Cathedral Hunter MS 130; Edinburgh University Library MS H.-P. Coll. 401; Folger MS V.a. 345; Harvard MS Eng. 686; Huntington HM 1338; Rosenbach MS 239/18; and a manuscript described in Beal EaJ 83, "in three hands."

John Earle was born in York, his father an ecclesiastical lawyer. He studied at Christ Church, Oxford, later became a fellow at Merton, and then chaplain to the Chancellor of Oxford University, Philip, fourth Earl of Pembroke. He was also a member of Lord Falkland's group of writers at Great Tew (Baker 723). In 1641, Charles made him tutor to the Prince of Wales. He was exiled during the Interregnum, but returned in 1660 when he was made Dean of Westminster, then Bishop of Worcester (1662), and finally Bishop of Salisbury (1663) (Baker, op. cit.).

Modern editions of Earle's *Microcosmography* are by Gwendolyn Murphy (Waltham St. Lawrence: Gold Cockerel, 1928); Harold Osborne (London: University Tutorial Press, 1933); and Alfred S. West (Cambridge: Cambridge Univ. Press, 1951).

A mere dull Physitian:
7. Alexis of Peckmount. Alexius Pedemontanus, a seventeenth-century Italian physician and alchemist.
15. vespatious. Vespasian, Roman emperor who taxed urine.
16. grine. Should read "gain."

The Comon vicars or singing men in Catherall Churches:
7. recidencer. Residencer, as pertaining to the Christian church, "A canon, incumbent, etc., in residence" (*OED*).

An Atturney:
2. Layer. Lawyer.

A younger Brother:
5–6. wch his eldest. Atypical of the Holgate, this phrase is repeated.

A Tauerne:
19. Smile. Simile.

An old Colledge Butler:
7. Gallo belgicus. An *Annual Register*, written in Latin, was published between 1598 and 1605.
11. vails. A tip or gratuity.
13. Keckerman. A Danish educator.
23. Cues & Cees. Q's and C's, the letters.
25. sconsinge. A university punishment for bad manners, usually a tankard of ale.
27. post & peare. A card game.

A Hansome Hostesse:
3. the cleuie. Probably should read "they cleave."

A Meere young Gentle man of ye Vniu'sitie:
14. Euphormio. Possibly a reference to John Barclay's *Euphormionis Satyricon* (1603?), a satire against the Jesuits.

For extended glossary notes on *Mr. Earle's Characters*, see *Character Writings of the Seventeenth Century*, ed. Henry Morley, vol. 14 of *The Carisbrooke Library* (London: George Routledge and Sons, 1891).

✦ Baker, 723.

Index of Authors

Attributions by the editor, not as they appear in the manuscript. Additional information in square brackets. Double quotes: "Titles" — Single quotes: 'First Lines'. HolM entry number.

First Line Index of Poetry

Renaissance English Text Society

INTERNATIONAL ADVISORY COUNCIL

Lukas Erne, University of Geneva
Sergio Rossi, University of Milan
Helen Wilcox, University of Wales, Bangor

Editorial Committee for The Holgate Miscellany: An Edition of Pierpont Morgan Library Manuscript MS 1057.
> *Steven May*, chair
> *Roy Flannagan*
> *Elizabeth H. Hageman*
> *Arthur F. Marotti*

The Renaissance English Text Society was established to publish literary texts, chiefly nondramatic, of the period 1475–1660. Dues are $50.00 per annum ($35.00, graduate students; life membership is available at $750.00). Members receive the text published for each year of membership. The Society sponsors panels at such annual meetings as those of the Modern Language Association, the Renaissance Society of America, and the Medieval Congress at Kalamazoo.

General inquiries and proposals for editions should be addressed to the president, Arthur Kinney, Massachusetts Center for Renaissance Studies, PO Box 2300, Amherst, Mass., 01004, USA. Inquiries about membership should be addressed to William Gentrup, Membership Secretary, Arizona Center for Medieval and Renaissance Studies, Arizona State University, Box 874402, Tempe, Ariz., 85287–4402.

Copies of volumes x–xii may be purchased from Associated University Presses, 440 Forsgate Drive, Cranbury, N.J., 08512. Members may order copies of earlier volumes still in print or of later volumes from xiii, at special member prices, from the Treasurer.

FIRST SERIES
VOL. I. *Merie Tales of the Mad Men of Gotam* by A. B., edited by Stanley J. Kahrl, and The History of Tom Thumbe by R. I., edited by Curt F. Buhler, 1965. (o.p.)
VOL. II. *Thomas Watson's Latin Amyntas*, edited by Walter F. Staton, Jr., and Abraham Fraunce's translation The Lamentations of Amyntas, edited by Franklin M. Dickey, 1967.

SECOND SERIES
VOL. III. *The dyaloge called Funus, A Translation of Erasmus's Colloquy (1534), and A very pleasaunt & fruitful Diologe called The Epicure, Gerrard's Translation of Erasmus's Colloquy (1545)*, edited by Robert R. Allen, 1969.
VOL. IV. *Leicester's Ghost* by Thomas Rogers, edited by Franklin B. Williams, Jr., 1972.

THIRD SERIES
VOLS. V–VI. *A Collection of Emblemes, Ancient and Moderne*, by George Wither, with an introduction by Rosemary Freeman and bibliographical notes by Charles S. Hensley, 1975. (o.p.)

FOURTH SERIES
VOLS. VII–VIII. *Tom a' Lincolne* by R. I., edited by Richard S. M. Hirsch, 1978.

FIFTH SERIES
VOL. IX. *Metrical Visions* by George Cavendish, edited by A. S. G. Edwards, 1980.

SIXTH SERIES

VOL. X. *Two Early Renaissance Bird Poems*, edited by Malcolm Andrew, 1984.

VOL. XI. *Argalus and Parthenia by Francis Quarles*, edited by David Freeman, 1986.

VOL. XII. Cicero's *De Officiis*, trans. Nicholas Grimald, edited by Gerald O'Gorman, 1987.

VOL. XIII. *The Silkewormes and their Flies* by Thomas Moffet (1599), edited with introduction and commentary by Victor Houliston, 1988.

SEVENTH SERIES

VOL. XIV. John Bale, *The Vocacyon of Johan Bale*, edited by Peter Happé and John N. King, 1989.

VOL. XV. *The Nondramatic Works of John Ford*, edited by L. E. Stock, Gilles D. Monsarrat, Judith M. Kennedy, and Dennis Danielson, with the assistance of Marta Straznicky, 1990.

SPECIAL PUBLICATION. *New Ways of Looking at Old Texts: Papers of the Renaissance English Text Society, 1985–1991*, edited by W. Speed Hill, 1993. (Sent gratis to all 1991 members.)

VOL. XVI. *George Herbert, The Temple: A Diplomatic Edition of the Bodleian Manuscript (Tanner 307)*, edited by Mario A. Di Cesare, 1991.

VOL. XVII. Lady Mary Wroth, *The First Part of the Countess of Montgomery's Urania*, edited by Josephine Roberts, 1992.

VOL. XVIII. Richard Beacon, *Solon His Follie*, edited by Clare Carroll and Vincent Carey, 1993.

VOL. XIX. An Collins, *Divine Songs and Meditacions*, edited by Sidney Gottlieb, 1994.

VOL. XX. *The Southwell-Sibthorpe Commonplace Book: Folger MS V.b.198*, edited by Sr. Jean Klene, 1995.

SPECIAL PUBLICATION. *New Ways of Looking at Old Texts II: Papers of the Renaissance English Text Society, 1992–1996*, edited by W. Speed Hill, 1998. (Sent gratis to all 1996 members.)

VOL. XXI. *The Collected Works of Anne Vaughan Lock*, edited by Susan M. Felch,1996.

VOL. XXII. Thomas May, *The Reigne of King Henry the Second Written in Seauen Books*, edited by Götz Schmitz, 1997.

VOL. XXIII. *The Poems of Sir Walter Ralegh: A Historical Edition*, edited by Michael Rudick, 1998.

VOL. XXIV. Lady Mary Wroth, *The Second Part of the Countess of Montgomery's Urania*, edited by Josephine Roberts; completed by Suzanne Gossett and Janel Mueller, 1999.

VOL. XXV. *The Verse Miscellany of Constance Aston Fowler: A Diplomatic Edition*, by Deborah Aldrich-Watson, 2000.

VOL. XXVI. *An Edition of Luke Shepherd's Satires*, by Janice Devereux, 2001.

VOL. XXVII. *Philip Stubbes: The Anatomie of Abuses*, edited by Margaret Jane Kidnie, 2002.

VOL. XXVIII. *Cousins in Love: The Letters of Lydia DuGard, 1665–1672, with a new edition of* The Marriages of Cousin Germans *by Samuel DuGard*, edited by Nancy Taylor, 2003.

VOL. XXIX. *The Commonplace Book of Sir John Strangways (1645–1666)*, edited by Thomas G. Olsen, 2004.

SPECIAL PUBLICATION. *New Ways of Looking at Old Texts, III: Papers of the Renaissance English Text Society, 1997–2001*, edited by W. Speed Hill, 2004. (Sent gratis to all 2001 members.)

VOL. XXX. *The Poems of Robert Parry*, edited by G. Blakemore Evans, 2005.

VOL. XXXI. *William Baspoole's 'The Pilgrime'*, edited by Kathryn Walls, 2006.

VOL. XXXII. *Richard Tottel's 'Songes and Sonettes': The Elizabethan Version*, edited by Paul A. Marquis, 2007.

VOL. XXXIII. *Cælivs Secvndus Curio: his historie of the warr of Malta: Translated by Thomas Mainwaringe (1579)*, edited by Helen Vella Bonavita, 2008.

SPECIAL PUBLICATION. *New Ways of Looking at Old Texts, IV: Papers of the Renaissance English Text Society, 2002–2006*, edited by Michael Denbo, 2008. (Sent gratis to all 2006 members.)